GUIDE TO
BIBLICAL COINS

FIFTH EDITION

10/5/10

To Paul
with appreciation
+ best wishes —

GUIDE TO BIBLICAL COINS

FIFTH EDITION

DAVID HENDIN

With values by

Herbert Kreindler

AMPHORA

New York
2010

Published by
AMPHORA
P.O. Box 805
Nyack, NY 10960
AmphoraCoins@aol.com

978-0-9654029-5-8

Library of Congress Catalog Number: 2010905599

1 2 3 4 5 6 7 8 9 0

Printed in the United States of America

For my father

AARON HENDIN, M.D.

who taught me the real value of the coins described herein

and for

JEANNIE, SARAH, BEN, ALEXANDER, MAX, AND CHARLIE

with much love
from generation to generation

TABLE OF CONTENTS

INTRODUCTION

Coins are among the most important historical documents that have survived from ancient times; coins often help historians define the cultures that produced them. Two of the principal benefits a nation derives from having its own system of coinage are proclaiming the establishment of sovereignty and controlling an economy. Since their invention in the seventh century BCE in Western Asia Minor, circulating coins have often been the ultimate preserved documents, indicating sovereignty and defining an independent nation. Because of overriding economic utility, the communication and political-propaganda values of circulating coins are often overlooked. This importance should not be underestimated, especially at a time when the coins were among the most advanced forms of mass communication. Although this may sound simplistic in a day of instant mass communications, when computers and smart phones are our constant companions, one calls to mind a time when the dissemination of news and information often took months, or even years. Unlike most artifacts, coins are often dated. They bear portraits, symbols, political and religious messages, and even titles and names that may be unknown from other sources.

The coins struck in the ancient land of Israel between the fourth century BCE and the second century CE represent a remarkable and readily available primary source of information about the history, heritage, and emerging culture of the Judeo-Christian tradition. Coins witnessed the return of Jews from the Babylonian captivity, the wars of the Hasmoneans with the Seleucids, the building and the destruction of the Second Temple in Jerusalem, the birth and ascent of Christianity, and the creation of Rabbinnic Judaism.

This fifth edition of *Guide to Biblical Coins* has been a work in progress for more than 40 years. I became fascinated with these coins when I lived in Israel during 1967 and 1968 as a volunteer of the Six Day War. Once I returned to the States to pursue my graduate degree in journalism, I repressed my interest for a while. But during classes in mass communications I recognized that the coins were an unheralded early stage of that precise field.

When I moved to New York in 1970 my horizons were opened to a new world of numismatic organizations and collectors who helped me expand my knowledge. And once I began to earn a living (as a journalist and author) I was able to begin to travel and return regularly to

Israel. Along the way I have been privileged to meet many exceptional people of unusual expertise and knowledge.

Over the years I have learned not to wax too eloquent about my interest in ancient coins, for even the eyes of one's closest friends and family can glaze over quickly. Some people just can't begin to understand the fascination ancient coins can hold.

To those who have requested that I move the catalog section to the back of the book and the history to the front, I respectfully refuse. The coins and the history are inseparable, and to be fully appreciated must be studied together.

This edition retains a great deal of the essential material from the previous one, but supplements it with new information from a new generation of scholars who have made progress in solving some of the mysteries. Space constraints have forced me to eliminate some material that is not related to the core topic of biblical coins, but there are other sources of information on those topics.

This book is intended as a collector's guide, but because of its use by students and scholars, I have added extensive endnotes to this edition. These are not only bibliographic references, but sometimes include related comments. They are not as extensive as one might find in a journal article, but they will help students target additional sources.

In the critical series of coins of Philistia and Samaria, I offer a small sample for their historic significance. Significant and complete volumes are readily available on these subjects, along with the important series of city coins, which I have omitted from this edition.

All of the additions and changes called for a new numbering system. Once again I have used numbers that do not duplicate previous editions and in this edition, a complete concordance is included.

INFORMATION AND ACKNOWLEDGEMENTS

Please note that in the catalog of the coins, the legends sometimes vary slightly between sketches, the photographs, and the descriptions. This may occur for several reasons. First, of course, there may be die variations on most of the coins. Many new drawings and composites have been added within the catalog to enhance understanding. Nevertheless, an illustrated coin may be the same *type* but not from the same *dies* as the drawn coins.

The sizes or weights are given for coins either in the author's collection, or from known references. They are offered as general guidelines, since both the size and weight of ancient coins can vary from coin to coin, the silver coins usually varying less than the bronze.

I'm sincerely sorry that some people have expressed dismay because I have chosen to designate dates using BCE (before the common era), equivalent to BC, and CE (of the common era), equivalent to AD. My thinking here was not along religious lines, but historical ones. The designations BC and AD do not do justice to history, counting from an arbitrary "year one," originally thought to be the birth year of Jesus. That was a confusing mathematical error made by a Russian monk named Dionysius Exiguus. Most historians believe that Jesus was born between 11 BCE and 4 BCE. So, to my way of thinking the BCE and CE designations are more logical, since Jesus was almost certainly not born in the year 1.

I am indebted to the many numismatists and historians who have written important works on Jewish numismatics and ancient history that I have drawn upon in compiling this volume. They are listed in the notes and bibliography. It should be noted that these scholars deserve much of the credit; while the amount of original research has increased in this edition, I have been trained as a journalist, and have done a journalist's job of sifting, merging, cutting, and clarifying the information, and supplemented it with lots of good stories.

I appreciate the help from scholars, collectors, dealers, and friends who have made both knowledge and resources available to me: Ken Abramowitz, John Aiello, Salem Alshdaifat. K. Baidun, Richard Beleson, Aaron Berk, Martin Brody, Ed Caine, Guy Clark, Curtis Clay, Selim Dere, Victor England, Ira Ettinger, Rob Freeman, Jay Galst, Steve Gerson, Ira Goldberg, Mark Hendin, Terry and Ron Hendin, Roy Hendin, Arthur Houghton, Kamal Imman, John Jencek, David Jesselsohn, Samir Kando, Jonathan Kern, Matthew Kreuzer, Doug Kroll, Simcha Kuritzky, Menashe Landesman, Tom Lee, Robert Maliner, Constantin Marinescu, Richard McAlee, Eric McFadden, Carol and Eric Meyers, David Michaels, Aba Neeman, Ali Novick, Yigal Ronen, Bill Rosenblum, Moshe Rotberg, Steve Rubinger, Arturo Russo, Shucri Sahuri, Wayne Sayles, Neil Schechter, Shanna Schmidt, Elliott Singer, Harry Sneh, Abraham Sofaer, Bill Stern, David Sundman, Sami Taha, Patrick Tan, Italo Vecchi, Ed Waddell, Alan Walker, Kerry Wetterstrom, Richard Witschonke, Daniel Wolf, J. Benjamin Yablok, J. Zadok, and others I have unintentionally omitted.

Special thanks to the American Numismatic Society and its librarians, the retired Frank Campbell and the current librarian Elizabeth Hahn who are always cheerful and helpful when I make impossible reference requests.

Photographs are provided courtesy of numerous private collections, author's collection, Classical Numismatic Group, Freeman & Sear, Gemini Numismatic Auctions, Harlan J. Berk Ltd., and Numismatica Ars Classica. The Israel Museum, the British Museum, and the American Numismatic Society also provided generous assistance.

I would like to mention several special friends no longer with us: Khalil Iskander Kando, G. Momjian, Meyer Rosenberger, Nasrallah Sahuri, Abu Ali al-Tawil, Fred Jacobs, Ed Janis, and Leo Mildenberg.

My teachers of some 30 years have died since the last edition. Ya'akov Meshorer was a dear friend who was most generous with his time and advice since we first met in 1976. Dan Barag also spent many of his valuable hours sharing insights and ideas with me, and was always ready to discuss and consult. If I had been studying at university with Meshorer or Barag I would not have acquired nearly as many hours of intensive study, friendship, and mentoring. I miss them both.

Rafi Brown and Shraga Qedar are also teachers and mentors who have taught me many valuable lessons.

Special thanks to Renee and Frank Kovacs for their intelligent, scholarly, and frequent assistance over our many years of friendship.

I proudly acknowledge with sincere appreciation the special contributions of scholars and friends who always find time to provide reliable advice and help in developing new insights: Donald T. Ariel, Gabriela Bijovsky, Robert Deutsch, J.P. Fontanille, Haim Gitler, Isadore Goldstein, Oliver Hoover, Alla Kushnir-Stein, Brooks Levy, Cathy Lorber, Andrew Meadows, Uriel Rappaport, Yigal Ronen, Ilan Schachar, Danny Syon, Oren Tal, David Vagi, Peter Van Alfen, and Ute Wartenberg.

My greatly appreciated and dedicated content editors for this edition are Danny Syon, Oliver Hoover, Harlan J. Berk, Herb Kreindler, and Eby Friedman; Kelly Zaug was the copyeditor.

Herb Kreindler has provided the price guide for this and previous editions as well as his encyclopedic knowledge, vast library, and friendship for nearly 40 years. Ronen Bachar is an Israeli numismatist I first met some 30 years ago, when he was only 14 years old; today he is among the most knowledgeable experts of the numismatics of the ancient Middle East, and I have learned and expanded my knowldge in our frequent conversations. Don Simon has been my closest friend through most of my adventures in antiquity, and his ideas, encouragement, and expertise have been critical to my work.

J.P. Fontanille has created and enhanced graphics for this edition. I have included his recreation of menorah coin dies on the dust jacket, which was designed by Jim Wasserman, of Studio 31. The special fonts were created by Cathy Lorber, and used with her kind permission.

Thanks to all of these people, who assisted me in reaching what I hope is a higher level in this fifth edition. But even with the help of all of those talented and dedicated friends and colleagues, and in spite of my best efforts, errors have no doubt crept into this book, and any factual or other errors are certainly the author's sole responsibility.

My wife Jeannie always encourages and enhances my studies with her level-headed good humor and essential wisdom. My children Sarah and Robert Cohen, Ben and Chrissy Hendin, and Alexander Hendin have lovingly tolerated and even sometimes shared my passion for these coins, their stories, and the land of Israel. Grandsons Max and Charlie Cohen help keep the twinkle in my eyes.

My father Aaron Hendin, M.D., first sparked my interest in ancient coins. He died in 1991 and I still miss him very much. Some background information for this book was taken from his manuscript *Jewish History as Portrayed on Coins*, which was partially published in *The Sheqel*. My mother Lillian Hendin, a long-time docent at the St. Louis Art Museum, encouraged the insanity of having two collectors in the family.

Dad ended his essay with these words: "To hold in one's hand a coin of the brave Maccabees or the hated Romans helps one transcend time and space and be more akin to our ancestors of old as well as our Israeli brethren of today."

Those words only begin to describe the fascination of the ancient coins of Biblical times. Each has been protected by the parched climate for some 2,000 years and then brought to light and given new life, not as a coin of the realm, but as a key to the mind. The doors this key can open will be limited only by your imagination.

David Hendin
June 2010
P.O. Box 805
Nyack, NY 10960
dhendin@aol.com

ABOUT THE CATALOG

Obverses and reverses. The classic numismatic definition of obverse is the side of the coin struck from the stationary or anvil die, while the reverse is struck by a hand-held or striking die. In the past when there has been uncertainty, the dated side or the side thought to be most important has been assigned as the obverse.

As a general rule there are many more reverse dies than obverse dies in almost every known case. This is probably because the striking die is not encased, and more heavily stressed than the anvil die.

I have taken advantage of all available information to define the obverses and reverses of the coin. For example with regard to the Bar Kokhba coins, Mildenberg is followed, since he has arranged the obverse and reverse dies according to the quantities.

Striking axis. The axis is the relationship between the obverse and the reverse dies. For example, a modern U.S. coin is struck at a 6 o'clock axis. This can be seen by holding the coin between thumb and forefinger, one placed at 6 o'clock and one at 12 o'clock, and swiveling the coin to view the reverse. In this case the reverse will point downward, so the axis is 6 o'clock. If this was done and the reverse pointed upwards, the axis would be 12 o'clock, and so on.

Weights provided are either averages for a particular group (when available, see Appendix B, p. 564), known ranges, or the known weight of a single specimen.

Diameters, when provided, are for known specimens. Photographs in the plates are as close to actual size as possible.

Drawings are sometimes enlarged to enhance viewing, check text or photograph for actual size. Occasionally there is a variance between a coin's photograph and drawing. This is mainly due to many die varieties for most coins. **Composites** created by J.P. Fontanille are images of multiple examples of actual coins, merged using computer graphics. **Photographs** are from public or private collections or used by permission of dealers or auction houses listed in acknowledgements.

Inscriptions given describe the illustrated and photographed coins. Occasionally the drawings will vary from the photographs by die, and there may be minor differences in inscriptions or letter placement.

Translations, in parenthesis, are generally given after the first use of a Hebrew, Aramaic, or Greek inscription.

The **location** of mints, **dates**, and **minting authorities** in general follow the most current available research.

Whenever possible the coins are listed according to mints and chronology, according to the most current research available.

Varieties. No attempt is made to list all varieties or dies of each coin type. Instead a few noteworthy variations, including irregulars are listed. Various error coins can occur in most coin types. They are shown here from time to time only as examples of production errors that are often seen in the Judaean series.

ABOUT THE VALUATIONS

The intent of the pricing guide is to give the collector relative dollar values of the principal coin types covered in this guide. The prices are based on the last five years of auction and private sales. Coins are valued in two different grades: bronze coins are priced for Fine and Very Fine conditions (F/VF) and gold and silver coins are priced for Very Fine and Extremely Fine (VF/EF) conditions. Coin grading is based on wear and not necessarily other categories such as boldness of strike, centering, or patina, thus the grades represent coins in average Fine, Very Fine, and Extremely Fine conditions.

The values represent the opinion of the cataloguers, and comparable coins may sell for more or less depending upon market conditions. Collectors who might be presented with obscure die varieties of small Judaean bronzes at extremely high prices, should approach with some caution due to actual importance and demand for such coins.

The best use of the values are as comparisons of relative rarity and desirability. Coins in better grades will bring significantly higher prices if they are well centered and well struck with full legends and devices. This is important to remember: a common coin of Agrippa I, No. 1244 for example, might sell for $20 in average Fine (F) condition. A specimen in average Very Fine (VF) condition might sell for $100, but the same type of coin in choice Very Fine (VF) or better condition, well centered and well struck on both sides, with a beautiful patina, could bring $500 or more.

These are NOT price evaluations for the coins shown in the photographs, which are among the best specimens seen during 40 years.

This book does not represent an offering of coins: it is merely a guide, to be used and supplemented as needed or desired by collectors or students.

The Ein Gedi Lamp Hoard of 139 *prutot* in a Herodian oil lamp was hidden in a plaster wall by a Jew in 60 CE (see p. 24). This amount equalled ½ *sheqel* plus the exchange fees, and was intended to bring good luck. (Photo: Israel Museum/Israel Antiquities Authority.)

CHAPTER ONE

COLLECTING BIBLICAL COINS

Biblical is an adjective referring to "the Bible," which can mean the sacred books of Judaism (Old Testament) or the sacred books of Christianity (Old Testament, New Testament). There are other related works such as the Apocrypha which are ancient, but not canonized by all religions or denominations. The Jewish Talmud is not part of the Bible, but is made up of commentary and explanations and was codified in ancient times.

The Jewish-Roman historian Josephus wrote several books recapping the wars and history of the Jewish people through the first century CE. Josephus gives us a good deal of information about places and times mentioned in the Bible.

Money is often mentioned in the Old Testament—we hear of *sheqels* and *darics* of both gold and silver.

Coins as we know them were invented late in the seventh century BCE. Most of the historical events presented in the Old Testament took place before that time, but the Old Testament was written down much later—at a time when these coins did exist and were in wide circulation. The people who codified the Old Testament may have assumed that the coins they were using had also been in circulation during earlier times. Thus the word *sheqel* in the context of the Old Testament must refer to weights of metal and not coins. The post-captivity references in Ezra (8:27) and Nehemiah (5:15, 7:70–72) might be references to actual coins in circulation at the time, since the stories in these books took place in the late sixth and fifth centuries BCE. However, archaeological evidence shows that *darics* or *sigloi* are almost never found in Israel, which suggests that these references may also be anachronistic.

Coins are frequently mentioned in the New Testament, but there are many differences in nomenclature, and it is often unclear which coins are discussed. In the King James translation, for example, we find the terms *farthing* and *penny*, among others, but these are references to coins that were in circulation at the time of the translation—in 1611—and thus add to confusion. (See pp. 472–476 for further discussion.)

Herod the Great, Herod Archelaus, Antipas, Philip, and Agrippa, Pontius Pilate, and other kings, prefects, and procurators are mentioned in the New Testament as well as in Josephus, and also in the Talmud. Even though their specific coins are not described, one must consider them to be "Biblical."

Frederick Madden, in his *History of Jewish Coinage*, published in 1864, refers specifically to "Jewish and Biblical Numismatics" as the subject of his work. Madden refers to earlier works in English by Ackerman, Evans, and Poole, that deal with "coins of the New Testament."[1]

The Rev. Edgar Rogers noted in 1914 in *Jewish Coins*, "Perhaps the disappointment of finding that there is so little [about coins] in the Old Testament and Apocrypha is in some degree compensated for by the large place which money occupies in the New Testament... Many a lesson of divine teaching is drawn from the fact of money: for example the parable of the talents or pounds; the women searching for the lost piece of silver... One miracle at least, the finding of the piece of silver in the fish's mouth; one Apostle, S. Matthew, the publican, whose profession was to raise money, whet the interest of numismatists."[2]

Florence Banks wrote in her 1955 book, *Coins of Bible Days*, "Not only the earnest student of the Bible but even the sophisticate who scoffs at biblical history cannot help feeling a genuine thrill when he discovers that he himself may actually see and feel the very bits of silver, bronze, and gold which served for the peoples of that distant day precisely the same purposes that our dimes and dollars serve for us."[3]

SURCHARGE OF THE MONEY CHANGERS

Around the time of Jesus, during the days of the Second Temple,

> ...*there were Jews living in Jerusalem, devout men, from every nation under heaven* (ACTS 2:5).

Jews from all over the ancient world traveled to the Holy Land. In addition to their traditions and languages they brought their own property—including money of their native lands, or that they picked up along the way.

Throughout the ancient Near East scores of types of money, weight standards, and currency systems came together and a network of independent money changers evolved. They provided a critical service, especially in Jerusalem, where visiting Jews needed to change their own money into silver coins from Tyre to pay the statutory annual half-*sheqel* dues to the Temple.

At one time the money changers were so ubiquitous and rowdy in conducting their business, that they brought unwanted attention onto themselves:

And Jesus entered the Temple and cast out all those who were buying and selling in the Temple, and overturned the tables of the money changers... (MATTHEW 21:12).

The Hebrew word for money changers, or exchange bankers, is *shulhani*. They changed foreign money into *sheqels* and half-*sheqels* of Tyre for use in the Temple. Since travelers carried money in the largest denominations possible for convenience, the money changers also traded these for the smaller denominations needed for everyday buying and selling.

Money changing in the ancient world was a business, just as it is today in cities worldwide where one can see the signs: EXCHANGE— CAMBIO. When one changes money from U.S. *dollars* to British *pounds* or *euros*, a fee is paid. The situation was similar 2,000 years ago. Money changers charged a small fee (*agio* in Greek), which in the Rabbinnic literature is called *kolbon*.

Three different terms are used for money changers in the New Testament. The word *kolbon* is apparently related to the usage in Matthew 21:12, where the word used is *kollybistes* from the Greek root *kollybos* (κόλλυβος, a small coin) referring to the function of changing foreign currency.

In John 2:14 ("And he found in the Temple those who were selling oxen and sheep and doves, and the money changers seated"), the word used is *kermatistes* (κερματιστής) from the Greek word *kerma* (κερμα) meaning "small bits" or, literally, small change. (This also sheds light on the use in ancient Judaea of coins that were hacked in half or quarters and used as small change.

In Matthew 25:27 ("Then you ought to have put my money in the bank, and on my arrival I would have received my money back with interest."), *trapezites* (τραπεζίτης) from the word *trapeza* (τράπεζα) or table, is used. This refers to the money changer as a banker who would receive money on deposit for investment or safe-keeping, and pay interest at a fixed rate. Even though this was specifically forbidden by Jewish law (DEUTERONOMY 23:20–21), there were various interpretations, and, as Daniel Sperber notes "The activity of the Jewish banker, *shulhani*, was of a closely defined nature, as his transactions had to be in accordance with the biblical prohibition against taking interest. The Talmud records much information relating to his activities. An additional and interesting feature of his business was the payment on request of sums deposited with him for that purpose."[4]

Thus there were three major functions of the money changers in the ancient Holy Land: foreign exchange, breaking large denominations into smaller ones, and banking.

There is special interest in the fees charged to change money into the Tyre *sheqels* and half-*sheqels* used for payment of dues to the Jerusalem Temple.

The Talmud interprets these in specific and interesting ways. I discussed this issue with a numismatist who is also a Talmudic scholar, Rabbi Benjamin Yablok. He observes that the Talmud specifies that if a man went to the Temple and wanted to pay his half-*sheqel*, but only had a full *sheqel* and needed change, a special situation existed. The man had to give to the Temple not only the Tyre *sheqel*, but an additional fee of "two *kolbonot*" (the plural of *kolbon*). He would then be credited with full payment and would receive half-a-*sheqel* as his change. In a footnote to his translation of the Mishnah, Herbert Danby explains that the surcharge was "compensation to the Temple's *sheqel*-collectors to reimburse them for any loss incurred in changing the *sheqels* or half-*sheqels* into or out of other money."[5] Thus a person should not be able to save by skipping the money changer, but instead that benefit should go to the Temple. This reflects the early Rabbinnic principal of *Yafeh Koach Hekdesh*, which means that the Temple must be the greatest beneficiary of any transaction

The money changer's fee to make change for one *sheqel* was one *kolbon*. Thus the Temple's financial experts considered such transactions as double ones, hence requiring two *kolbonot* as a fee. The Talmud goes a step further. If two men went to the Temple together and wanted to pay their half-*sheqels* together with one *sheqel* coin, they still had to pay the *kolbon* fee. If they each paid with correct change, a half-*sheqel* coin, there was no fee.

The Talmud mentions a unit called a *ma'ah*, equal to one twenty-fourth of a *selah* (*selah* is the Aramaic equivalent to *sheqel*). The *ma'ah* equaled about 4.2 percent of a *sheqel*. The amount of the *kolbon* fee is subject to dispute. Some Rabbis said it equaled one-half *ma'ah*, but Rabbi Meir posited that it equaled a complete *ma'ah*.

The *kolbon*, then, may have equaled either about 4.2% of a *sheqel* or 2.1% of a *sheqel*. Thus the *kolbon* was equal to either 11 or 5.5 *prutot*, based on the exchange standard during the Roman period (c. 6 to 70 CE), when the *sheqel* was worth 256 *prutot*, and the half-*sheqel* 128 *prutot*.

Rabbi Zev Goldstein explains that Rashi (the medieval commentator on the Talmud) believed that the *kolbon* was paid as an expense the Temple treasurers incurred when re-converting the half-*sheqels*. Rashi writes that the half-*sheqel* was a small and inconvenient coin, apt to get lost, and that they would want to change it into larger coins. Thus the Temple could not keep the full amount of a half-*sheqel* if they had to pay a fee for conversion. This fee was the *kolbon*, paid by the donor.[6]

The Talmud's Rabbi Meir stated his opinion in this way: even if a man went to the Temple with a silver half-*sheqel* of Tyre in his hand,

1.1. *Sheqel* plus surcharge: If a Jew in the early first century paid his annual Temple dues with a Tyre *sheqel*, he actually paid one *sheqel* plus a surcharge of two *kolbonot*, equaling 11 *prutot*. His change would be a half-*sheqel*. Shown here is one *sheqel* of Tyre plus 11 *prutot* of the Roman procurators of ancient Israel.

because the half-*sheqel* was made by humans, and therefore something less than perfect, the person still had to pay a bonus of one *kolbon* in order for the Temple to get full value.

There are several subtleties involved in this issue. Goldstein explains that the Talmudic commentaries say that silver coins cannot be made without a slight mixture of foreign material (*i.e.* alloys) and the weight of a half-*sheqel* had to be pure silver. Therefore, the *kolbon* was added in order for the Temple to receive the full half-*sheqel*.

Related archaeological evidence comes from the 1964 excavation at the ancient settlement of Ein Gedi on the shore of the Dead Sea, when a house from the first century CE was being explored.

In a plaster wall archaeologists discovered a Herodian-style oil lamp containing 139 *prutot*, from Agrippa I and the Roman governors who ruled Judaea after him until the beginning of the Jewish War. It was concluded that 139 small bronze coins could not constitute a hoard in the usual sense, because their value was so small. While showing me this oil lamp and group of coins at The Israel Museum many years ago, Ya'akov Meshorer reconstructed the story as follows:

"A Jew in the year 60 CE built his house, and, while finishing it, before its last plaster stage, decided to hide a sacred amount of money in the wall to protect against the evil eye."

The most sacred sum of money to the Jews at this time was the half-*sheqel* paid to the Temple annually. But, according to Meshorer, our first-century Jew did not want simply to put a single, silver half-*sheqel* into his wall for luck since "the large number of coins would make a better impression." The man also decided to put the money into a lamp—"a symbol of eternity."

But a half-*sheqel* was equal to only 128 *prutot* (during the Roman period). So why did the archaeologists find 139?

An exchange fee of two *kolbonot* on a half-*sheqel* equals about 11. Adding 128 plus 11—is 139 *prutot*. The owner of the house wanted to make sure that when it came to his good luck, every precaution was taken to insure accuracy!

COINS ARE WHERE YOU FIND THEM

On a cold, wet January in the mid-1970s, I sat on a stool outside a friend's shop near the Lion's Gate in Jerusalem's Old City.

The steady rainfall didn't get me down because it always rains in January in Jerusalem (except on the rare occasions when it snows). It is a cold rain that chills to the bone.

I was on vacation, so I sat and enjoyed friends, sometimes puffing on a water pipe, so as to blend in with the locals.

On that day I was staring into the cobblestone street, recently resurfaced with stones and fill from the Jerusalem area. I saw a small, round object being pelted by the rain. My friend Kamal saw it, too. He went to pick it up, but it was stuck fast between two cobblestones. I tossed him a pocketknife and he pried it loose. It was a small bronze coin of Alexander Jannaeus who reigned in Judaea from 104–76 BCE.

Ancient coins are found every day in Europe, Asia Minor, and the Middle East. Occasionally, one hears about the lucky tourist who finds a rare coin in the dirt. Most often, though, tourists will tell you of youngsters standing near excavation sites, offering handfuls of coins they swear are fresh from the ground.

When I lived in Israel in 1967, I bought a handful of dirty coins from a boy who suggested he had been digging around in Jerusalem. That afternoon, I saw the same boy replenishing his supply from the cheapest junk coins in the same shop I was patronizing. I felt so foolish that I pretended not to recognize him.

I have found a number of ancient coins over the last 40 years. Roman and Islamic coins in the dirt at Beit Shean; bronzes at Caesarea and Ashqelon; but my favorite find has the best story.

An Arab friend promised to take me coin hunting in the early 1970s. He picked me up at my Jerusalem hotel at midnight, and we drove to a farm outside of Hebron. He knocked at the door of the one-room farmhouse and spoke for a moment in Arabic to the inhabitants. Then he took his metal detector and two lanterns from the car and we went to a recently plowed field. We primed and pumped the kerosene lamps. We carried one and left the other one on the ground.

We systematically walked up and down the furrows, earphones in place. When I heard the telltale "ping" for the first time, my heart raced. It was a bronze coin, but a "junker." We found a few other ancient pieces of bronze, even a few more coins. My friend told me that this particular field had previously yielded some nice Athenian *tetradrachms.*

An hour later I was ready to give up with the worthless but interesting souvenirs of the expedition. As I walked back to break down the machine, I got a "ping" signal that was loud and clear. My friend and I bent over and sifted the soil underfoot in our hands. And, bingo, there it was: a lovely Athenian *tetradrachm*.

FINDERS KEEPERS?

Did you ever find a quarter and a friend asks: "Did it have Washington's face on it? I lost one and it must be mine." "Finders keepers, losers' weepers" is pretty accurate most of the time for generic objects.

But in ancient times, it did not necessarily work that way. The Talmud directly addresses the subject of lost coins, and offers some interesting twists.

In Talmud Baba Metziah, the question is posed: "If one found a *sela* coin in the market, and his friend encountered him and said to him: 'the coin is mine,' and the claimant went on to state one of the following features of the coin: 'it is new' or 'it is a Neronian,' or 'it is of king so-and-so,' he has said nothing of significance and the finder may keep the coin."[7]

So, it turns out that "finders' keepers" is an old concept, and the Talmud was already repeating wisdom from earlier times.

But what if a person's name was actually written on the coin? Ancient coins are often referenced with graffiti, the scratching or stamping of symbols, letters, and even names upon coins. Athenian and

1.2. Alexander III *tetradrachm* reverse (enlarged) struck at mint of Memphis, with Aramaic graffiti on reverse to left and right of head of Zeus.

Ptolemaic *tetradrachms*, and other ancient coins are often found with graffiti.

When interpreting this portion of the Talmud, one may assume it was discussed because it was a question that arose with some frequency.

As usual, the Talmud's discussion is wise: "But even if [the claimant's] name is written on [the coin], he has said nothing of significance because there is no valid identifying mark for a coin."[8]

One can scratch his name on a quarter, but, the rabbis recognized that, "For [the finder] can say: 'Perhaps [the claimant] spent [the coin] and it fell from another person."

Thus a name or graffiti proves only that the coin was once in your hands, not that you were the owner who lost it. As the commentary in the Art Scroll Talmud translation notes, "Since coins are commonly spent, we must consider the possibility that the claimant previously bought something with one of his inscribed coins, and it was the seller who subsequently lost it. Moreover, it is probable that the claimant wrote his name on more than one coin. Therefore, even if the claimant really lost a coin with his name on it, the coin that was found may not be his. So, a signature on a coin is never considered a *siman* (reliable sign or symbol)."

On the other hand, "if someone found a coin with a unique identifying mark, it would be treated as any other lost object, which must be announced and returned." (This argument, from the footnote, is referenced to the thirteenth century Spanish Rabbi known as Ramban.)[9]

Thus we have an ancient reference to graffiti on coins, but also a view of the way ancient rabbis discuss the contents of the Talmud.

Another interesting point in Talmud Bava Metzia is mention of the lost coin as a "Neronian." This identifies this coin as a "Neronian *sela*." These are the *tetradrachms* of Nero, struck at Antioch during Nero's

1.3. Neronian *sela* (*tetradrachm* of Nero) minted at Antioch in 63/64 CE. This type circulated widely in the ancient Holy land and was used in the Talmud to describe the size of a light-hole.

reign. Neronian *selas* represented an important part of the coinage of ancient Israel during the second part of the first century CE.

There is another specific reference to these coins in Talmud Bechoroth: "In a light-hole which was not made by the agency of man, the size required is as large as a big fist, such as the fist of Ben Battiah. Said R. Jose: And this [fist] is as large as a big head of a man. If [the light-hole], however, was made by the agency of man, [the Sages] fixed the size to be as large as a hole made with the large [carpenter's borer kept in the Temple cell], which is as large as an Italian *dupondium* or as large as a Neronian *sela*."

Buying Coins from Israel

Each country has its own laws regarding ancient coins. Israel is the only country in the Middle East that licenses dealers for ancient coins and artifacts, and allows them to sell them for export. This is based on Israel's antiquity law, which is a lengthy document. Israel is one of very few source nations that allow the export of ancient coins. Because so many people have questions about this, I offer a brief summary.

I asked Amir Ganor, director of the Israel Antiquity Authority's (IAA) Robbery Prevention Unit if he had advice to give to American collectors visiting Israel. He said, "We welcome collectors or dealers who visit Israel and wish to buy ancient coins. We ask you to obey the rules, which means to buy only from dealers who are licensed by the IAA to do this business, and request that the dealers obtain for you an export license."

Ganor explained that the IAA is now online and in computer communication with almost all of the licensed dealers in Israel. Whereas previously buyers might have to visit the IAA's offices at the Israel or Rockefeller Museums to obtain a license, this can now be done through the dealer and by computer. The IAA does not charge for an export license, and they maintain a full-time staff of three professional numismatists who are available to review material.

My advice: Do not forget that the IAA does not guarantee authenticity when licensing exports. Furthermore, prices can vary greatly from dealer to dealer. If you are not an expert, you should be extremely cautious when buying coins from a dealer with whom you do not have ongoing relations.

Whether you visit Israel or order by phone or internet, the rules are the same. All coins exported must have an official license from the IAA.

Just in case you are one of the lucky ones who picks up a coin at a beach or a site, the law specifically states that it must be reported to the IAA within 14 days. And, if you are really lucky, "there have been cases in which we let the finders be keepers," according to an IAA official.

For up-to-date information as well as an English version of the full Israel Antiquities Law, check the IAA website at:

http://www.antiquities.org.il/.

GHOSTS OF OLD JERUSALEM

I admit to a 40-year love affair with Jerusalem's Old City. There is something about the feeling I get when I step inside those walls, most recently rebuilt by Suleiman the Magnificent some 400 years ago. The sights, sounds, and smells of the place just seem to suit me.

Traditionally the Old City markets have been a good place to hunt for ancient coins. It was better when I first visited in 1967. Now, most of the Old City's active dealers of coins and antiquities are dead. Their shops are closed. I miss those many good friends: George Momjian (known as Abu Sala); Abu Ali al-Tawil, the man who found the Dead Sea Scrolls; Kando (called Abu Anton), the one-time shoemaker from Bethlehem who sold the Dead Sea Scrolls; Nasralluh Sahuri of Bethlehem; Meyer Rosenberger, a tailor who became a leading expert on city coinage of ancient Palestine; Kar'ein, whose shop always had an odd smoky smell, more pungent than tobacco; Baidun, previously Prof. Reifenberg's gardener, who kept finding coins around the shrubs and eventually became a leading dealer of ancient coins and antiquities.

Today one can count the legitimate antiquities dealers in Old Jerusalem on one hand; not as much variety or as much fun as the old days. At some shops I visit with the third generation of families I met in 1967.

I could dine out for weeks on the stories I've been told. One of the Arab dealers bought a handful of small Jewish bronzes from a peasant for a few dollars. In the group, he found one of the extremely rare menorah coins of Mattatayah Antigonus, at the time worth some $10,000. (Today it would be worth many times as much.) He sold the coin and used the money to buy himself a wife. A couple of years later he was fed up with the wife. So he went to the person to whom he'd sold the coin and asked if he would be willing to accept an exchange—the wife for the coin.

Once I looked at several coins in a small shop whose proprietor I did not know. He singled out one overpriced coin and told me, "David Hendin offered $600 for this one." I nodded and said, "I think you should sell it to him," and left. I have never returned to that particular shop, so he still has not yet had the pleasure of formally meeting David Hendin.

I am also struck by the number of times I've run into Americans I know while walking through the Old City. Once, walking along the Via Dolorosa, I ran into a woman I know who worked at a large Midwestern university.

"Oh, I'm so glad to see you," she said. "Just yesterday I bought some wonderful coins from a man who found them in the graveyard outside of the Golden Gate. I was going to send them to you back in the States."

She had them in her purse. So I said, "Let's see."

Proudly, she took out five silver coins and three bronze ones.

"How much did you pay for these?" I asked.

"What are they? How much are they worth?" she replied.

"Where did you say you bought these?" I asked.

"Well, we were walking around outside of the Golden Gate, in the cemetery. And we met an Arab man who was very nice. He was telling us stories about the place. He had a shovel; he had been digging there. He took these coins out of his pocket with a bunch of dirt. He'd just dug them up. Well, what are they?"

"I'll tell you what they are if you tell me how much you paid for them."

"Okay, it was just under $200. Now, what do I have?"

"Well," I said, "you have here five fake silver coins that were probably made last week down in the village of Silwan. And then there are these three bronze coins. They are genuine."

She breathed a sigh of relief. "How much are they worth?"

I replied: "In this condition, the three are worth at least a dollar each."

"Well," she said, "then I got my money's worth."

"How do you figure that?" I asked.

"He told us stories about Jerusalem for more than two hours."

Well, that's a generous hourly rate for story telling. I didn't bother to tell her my guess was that the stories had about as much truth to them as the silver coins.

The lessons: Don't buy what you don't know. Don't buy from whom you don't know. Don't ever expect to get something for nothing, because if you do, you will instead most probably get nothing for something.

DEAD SEA LEGENDS

A couple of my Jerusalem friends, both mentioned above, died in the mid-1990s. They were especially interesting because of the roles they played in the Dead Sea Scrolls drama.

Ironically, their deaths went largely unnoticed by the public, though publicity surrounding the scrolls—with best-selling books, museum exhibits, and lawsuits between scholars—reached a high level.

These two men brought the scrolls to light in the first place.

In 1946, a 13-year-old boy of the Ta'amira Bedouin tribe was hiking with an older friend in the cliffs on the western shore of the Dead Sea. Some say they were shepherds minding goats. Others observe that the Ta'amira Bedouins have dealt in antiquities for 150 years and they simply may have been combing those historically rich hills for artifacts to sell.

While throwing stones into a cave, the boys heard pottery break. They investigated and found several tall pottery jars containing leather and parchment scrolls. They took the scroll pieces to Jerusalem antiquities dealers, who chased the boys out of their shops. One exclaimed: "Those are old pieces of leather, not antiques. Sell them to a shoemaker."

The boys took his advice. A shoemaker in Bethlehem named Kando also dealt in antiquities. He recognized potential in the scroll fragments and bought them, although at that time the oldest known written manuscripts dated back only a few hundred years.

Eventually, Kando sold some of the scrolls to Samuel, the Syrian Metropolitan from the Monastery of St. Mark in Old Jerusalem. Samuel later advertised his scrolls in the *Wall Street Journal*.

Kando sold other scrolls to Professor E. L. Sukenik, chief archaeologist of Hebrew University. (Sukenik's son, Yigael Yadin, later also acquired the scrolls the Syrian Metropolitan had advertised in the *Journal* for the State of Israel.)

When the Bedouin boy who found the Dead Sea Scrolls grew up, he adopted a new name, in the Arab custom, after his first son was born. Abu Ali al-Tawil (father of Ali, the tall one—to differentiate him from a short Abu Ali with similar business interests) was well known by Israeli antiquities enthusiasts. Moshe Dayan wrote that he often bought antiquities from Abu Ali, who also once saved the famous general's life.

Here's how Gen. Dayan told the story: "I do not think anyone has ever succeeded in duping Abu Ali by trying to sell him a fake antique or a counterfeit coin. Whenever I bought anything from him, I could always be sure that it was authentic.

"One day I received a message from him telling me that he had a beautiful earthenware censer that he was sure would interest me. We arranged to meet in Jerusalem and there I saw it....I bought it and asked where it had been discovered. Abu Ali said it was found in a cave south of Bethlehem. I asked him to take me there. I wished to see what kind of cave it was, whether a burial cave, a dwelling, or one used for pagan rites.

"He promised to do so and we fixed a date. But shortly before we were due to meet, he informed me that he was very busy and asked for a postponement. He postponed the next meeting too on some pretext or other. I refrained from interrogating too closely one so much smarter

1.4. Abu Ali al-Tawil with the author
in Jerusalem's Old City around 1980.

than I, and I just went on waiting. The hoped-for day finally arrived and we set out for the cave.

"We passed Bethlehem, and about half way along the road to Hebron we turned off westward along a dirt track in the direction of the foothills.... [I saw what] had once been a burial cave. The remains of skeletons were still there. But in the course of time it had been used as a sheepfold and as shelter for shepherds in heavy rains.

"Now that my curiosity about the cave had been satisfied, I asked Abu Ali why he had kept postponing our visit. 'Oh, Wazir,' he replied, 'this cave was being used at the time by a band of PLO saboteurs. It was they who began digging in their spare time and they who unearthed the ancient vessels and put them on the market. How, then, could I bring you here, you who are Minister of Defense? I had to wait until they moved elsewhere. Imagine what would have happened if I had brought you while they were still here. Either they would have opened fire on you, in which case your soldiers would have shot me; or you would have shot them, in which case their comrades would have suspected me of betraying them and delivering them into your hands, and then they would have murdered me and my children.'"[10]

Abu Ali died in Bethlehem at age 60. He had been ill with cancer for some time. I had often met with Abu Ali over the previous 20 years. For a while he owned a little nut and sweet shop near Manger Square in Bethlehem. Over six-feet tall, with a strong, handsome face always framed by a white kafeyah, the traditional Bedouin headdress, Abu Ali cut a colorful figure. When I visited Abu Ali, he sometimes showed me coins or antiquities. Over the years, via friends as interpreters, he told me many stories, including the one of how he found and sold the Dead Sea Scrolls to Kando.[11]

It was only about three weeks before Abu Ali died that Khalil Iskander Kando, age 83, also of Bethlehem, also died. Unlike Abu Ali, Kando had been an officially licensed antiquities dealer for decades. Kando operated a small shop in East Jerusalem, in a room above his gift shop, adjoining the St. George Hotel.

Kando, called Abu Anton, wore a burgundy fez and traditional white robes each time I saw him. A tall man with larger-than-life features, he took delight in showing me coins and artifacts. He rarely discussed the scrolls. Yet in a nook off the stairway to his tiny, second-floor shop stood one of the very jars in which they were found.

Once in the 1970s, I sat across from Abu Anton, looking at ancient coins. He was cleaning one in a jar of dilute sulfuric acid he kept on his desk for that purpose. As we talked, he took a dental bridge out of his mouth and dipped it into the acid. Next he brushed it with the toothbrush he had been using to clean coins. Kando shook off the dental work and returned it to his mouth, resumed talking and never even puckered.

Abu Ali, a finder of the Dead Sea Scrolls, and Abu Anton, their first buyer, were both publicity shy. Both were tarnished during the 1950s when, reportedly, some scrolls were deliberately cut up and sold in pieces to extract higher prices from the market.

Yet the two men had honorable reputations. Ya'akov Meshorer, chief curator of archaeology at The Israel Museum, Jerusalem, told me that "From 1967, when we had dealings with him, Kando was always generous with the Museum."

When I telephoned my friend Samir Kando in Bethlehem to express condolences on his father's death, he said, "Aye, David, we are only guests in this life. But what we touch may live forever."

HOW ANCIENT COINS ARE DATED

Many have never given the dating of coins much thought, and are surprised to learn that the way we date coins today is relatively modern. The first coins using the current dating system were not struck until 1234 CE at the Roskilde mint, now in Denmark. By that time, coins had been minted for more than 1500 years. Many earlier coins had dates, but they were not dates as we know them. Ancient coins were dated by the regnal year of the ruler or by a local era. This would be the equivalent of dating 1977 coins of the United States "year one" corresponding to the first year of the rule of Jimmy Carter. Or perhaps those 1977 coins could be dated "201" corresponding to the 201st year of the republic of the United States.

The first dated Jewish coins were struck under Alexander Jannaeus (104–76 BCE). Not all of his coins were dated, but at least one type was. This is the small bronze that carries on its reverse an inverted (as we see it) anchor within a circle surrounded by the Greek legend "of King Alexander." The obverse shows a star of eight rays surrounded by dots and a crude Aramaic inscription, which translates to "King Alexander Year 25" (No. 1152).

Many specimens of this type have several dots at the points of the anchor. These are meant to spell out the letters L KE in a style almost identical to the lettering on Seleucid coins of the same period. These letters signify the date, year 25, referring to the twenty-fifth year of the reign of Jannaeus—80/79 BCE.

Some of Herod I's coins are dated LΓ, referring to the official third year after Herod was named tetrarch, or 40 BCE.

The coins of the Jewish War are dated from "year one" to "year five," which correspond to the five years the war spanned, 66–70 CE.

During the Bar Kokhba Revolt (132–135 CE) the coins were dated "year one" and "year two." A large number of the Bar Kokhba coins were not dated, but evidence from Mildenberg's study of die combinations, breaks, and wear shows that the undated coins were issued during the third and final year of the war, 134/135 CE.

ANCIENT COIN MANUFACTURE

The basics of striking coins have changed remarkably little since first-century Judaea. Of course there have been improvements in metallurgy and technology, but the basics of engraving and stamping remain.

The blanks, or flans, for the Judaean bronze coins were made by casting metal in molds consisting of shallow, round sockets connected by channels drilled into pieces of soft chalkstone. The drill bit had a point that began to cut the stone. This point left a small central hole on one side of the flan, and unstruck flans invariably show a nipple resulting from this. (See photos of unstruck flans on p. 47.) After pouring molten metal into the molds and letting it cool, strips of coin blanks connected by short metal ribbons were removed. These are called flan strips. An assistant would reheat each strip and then place the first blank flan in between two striking dies on a sturdy base, perhaps a tree trunk. The minter hit the top die with a hammer, thus striking the coin. Then, the assistant pulled the strip one coin further, and the process was repeated.

One misconception about the small Jewish bronzes is that the striking process causes the beveling of the flans, with the obverse being on the narrow side of the bevel and the reverse on the broader side. This is not correct. The form of the beveled-edge is purely a result of the casting of the flans, and any individual coin might be struck with the beveled edge narrowing toward either the obverse or reverse, it is simply a function of which way the flan strip was held between the dies.

This process was carried out fairly quickly, and the resultant coins were struck off center more often than not. After striking, the flan strip was chopped apart into coins and the remaining metal scraps were melted down.

Sometimes the man who chopped the coins apart did not do a very good job, resulting in coins with flat projections from one or both sides, such as the coin of the Jewish War shown as No. 1363a. Many of the other coins shown in the plates have obvious flat edges where they were chopped away from the flan strip. Photo 1.8 on page 38 shows three unstruck flans on a still-connected strip.

Occasionally the flan strip broke, one flan becoming stuck in the lower die (or vice versa) after striking. When the next flan was inserted and struck, it received the full strike from the top die, but instead of receiving the impression from the bottom die, it was struck by the face of a coin that had already been struck by the top die. This caused the design of the top die to be impressed in incuse on the reverse of the coin. The coin of Herod Archelaus shown as No. 1196b resulted from such an error. Its obverse shows the usual helmet, but the reverse shows the exact design struck in incuse, like a negative. This is called a brockage. Double striking, or striking a coin twice, is yet another minting error common in ancient times (No. 1360d).

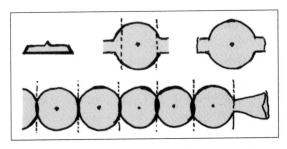

1.5. Drawings of (to row from left) side view of Judaean single-thick cast flan, top view with narrow cut, top view with wide cut; below is flan strip. (Drawings Y. Meshorer 1982.)
1.6. Below is reconstruction of struck flan strip of Agrippa I coins (No. 1244) notice chop marks where initial attempt failed to cut the strip. (Reconstruction by David Sundman.)

Sometimes the dies used for striking coins cracked or broke and one or more coins were struck with the damaged die before it was discovered and replaced.

All of these minting errors are interesting because of what they can reveal about the ancient methods of making coins. They are commonly encountered among ancient Jewish coins, and any collector with a sharp eye can find them.

Like the ebb and flow of the ocean's tides, theories regarding various aspects of ancient numismatics come and go. New ideas supplant old ideas. Old and discredited theories are dusted off and taken down from the shelves. Sometimes this happens over many decades, and sometimes the process is compressed into a shorter period of time.

1.7. Set of chalkstone molds discovered at Khirbet Rafi', in the area of Lachish. (Photo: Meshorer/Israel Antiquities Authority.)

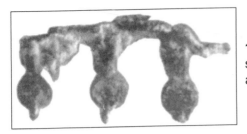

1.8. Portion of unstruck flan strip with three unstruck flans attached. (Photo: Meshorer.)

For example, it was long believed that the blanks, or flans, for the Judaean bronze coins were made by casting metal in molds consisting of shallow, round sockets connected by channels drilled into pieces of soft limestone. This sounded like a perfectly logical and sensible process, and was supported by various molds found in archaeological contexts.

However, several years ago an Israeli collector staged an experiment that seemed to disprove, or at least modify the theory. A. Levy created a mold from local Jerusalem area limestone. He carefully poured molten bronze into this mold, and it shattered. This was repeated more than once. The experiment was witnessed by a number of numismatic experts in Jerusalem, and was said to prove an alternate theory to the one posited above: the limestone molds were actually used to cast wax, which was, in turn used to create molds to cast the flan strips. According to Levy's experiment, creating flan strips through the lost-wax process was the only possibility. In fact, in the Hebrew edition of Ya'akov Meshorer's book *A Treasury of Jewish Coins*, he cites the Levy experiment as proof that the lost wax process was used.

However, the English edition of Meshorer's book (published two years later), cites another experiment. I received first-hand information on this from Donald Ariel, head numismatist with the Israel Antiquities Authority.

This experiment was conducted by Yehoshua Dray, a specialist in ancient technology. Dray described his work in a lecture to the Jerusalem branch of the Israel Numismatic Society. He explained that Levy had made an error in his experiment. His mistake was in believing that the ancient flan molds were made out of local soft limestone. In fact, Dray explained, the specific stone used to make the molds was not soft limestone, but a closely related stone—chalk.

Chalk has a higher degree of porosity. Thus the bubbles of air in the hot molten metal would be easily absorbed by the chalkstone molds, but these bubbles would cause the limestone to crack after coming into contact with the molten bronze.

Sure enough, when Dray created molds from chalk stone, and poured molten bronze into them they did not break. Ariel watched these experiments and reported that there was not even a "hint of tearing off of some parts of stone."[12]

IRREGULAR ISSUES, TYPES, AND DIES

Most modern and ancient coins are struck with numerous dies. Today dies are mass-produced after the first hand-engraved die, and it is a rarity to find die varieties in current coins. Early American coins were manufactured with hand-engraved dies with some help from technology. Ancient coins were manufactured with hand-engraved dies, and there are almost always at least minor but easily noticed differences from one die variety to the next. In most cases ancient dies are significantly different from each other. Thus a new coin type is not simply a variation in engraving a die, but it is a completely new design, new inscription, or different denomination.

Unpublished and "new" coin types are more common in certain extensive series, such as the Roman provincial coinage, since the references from the past have never been able to list every single type and certainly not every die variety. This is now changing, since more and more online references and supplements are becoming available. Mildenberg documented most of the Bar Kokhba dies in his pioneering book.[13] At the Menorah Coin Project, J.P. Fontanille has begun to systematically identify and illustrate die varieties of many of the Judaean coin types.[14]

Not a single ancient mint has yet been absolutely identified in ancient Judaea, Samaria, or the Galilee. However, flan molds for coins of Mattatayah Antigonus have been found in excavations in the Old City of Jerusalem. Similar molds for *prutah* and half-*prutah* size coins have also been found at locations as diverse as Khirbet Rafi' near Lachish and Sepphoris in the Galilee.

The mints in Judaea and the surrounding areas must have been relatively small, and there were probably only a few die engravers working on the same coin types. From analysis of the coins it seems probable that there were one or two master engravers—experts who took directions from a designer and cut the earliest dies for each coin type. Later, others with different levels of expertise, created coin dies and this accounts for the many die varieties in ancient Judaean coins (as well as other ancient coins).

When one discusses an ancient mint, it is easy to visualize a version of a modern mint—a production factory located within a single building or structure. That might have been the case, especially in sophisticated classical Greek mints such as Athens. However, characteristics and style of production in smaller mints such as Judaea lead to a possibly different concept, especially for the Judaean bronze coins. In the case of the Jewish War and the Bar Kokhba Revolt, there were almost certainly second mints, one possibly moving with troops, or manned by those hiding out in the Judaean Hills. A particularly crude issue of the famous *sheqel* of the Jewish War is known to have been struck in bronze as a local issue at Gamla (No. 1372). Die studies by Mildenberg, and later analysis by Barag,[15] clearly prove that crude Bar Kokhba coins were not struck in the same mint as the standard issues.

Instead of a factory, one might imagine that a mint in Judaea was more like an area in the government or Temple complex where a group of workshops manufactured coins. We know that in those days coins were not manufactured continuously, so the mint would not have been fully staffed at all times. The mint workshops were probably manned by highly skilled workers, who may have been brought in as contract workers, perhaps from skilled silversmiths in the area. When demand for minting coins was greater, less-skilled workers may have been brought in to copy the master-engraver's work, with varying degrees of success. Their designs are oddly shaped and strangely proportioned and inscriptions are incomplete, filled with errors, or retrograde (mirror-image engraving, often executed by poorly skilled die engravers). The output of each workshop may have been measured by a group supervisor who counted the coins and may have batched them together with the output of the other workshops. As discussed on pp. 43–46, there was little attention to the precise weight and appearance of bronze coins which have wide ranges in weight, centering, and style.

Thus when the mint was in operation, the first few workshops were operated by the most skilled engravers and manufacturers. Initial orders were made by these superior craftsmen. But as demand increased they could not keep up with it and the less-skilled metal workers were hired.

This conjectural scenario could explain a lot. For example, at the beginning of each day, a worker who was striking coins may have been issued a pair of dies—an obverse and a reverse—for the coin type they would be striking that day. Then he went to the work station, perhaps with an assistant, and began to produce coins. At the end of the day that worker would return the dies to storage. Workers were probably issued their own dies each morning, but there were probably more than one set for each workshop. This would explain why there are so many die combinations; why crude obverse and reverse dies are virtually always linked with each other; and even how an occasional error was made in issuing the dies and thus a small number of "mule" or hybrid coins were occasionally produced.

In the case of dies that were used to manufacture coins with dates, they were apparently destroyed each year or so. Also, dies frequently cracked and broke, and they were then discarded. On the other hand, some dies lasted for a very long time and may have been used to strike coins over a period of years, and even several different coin types.

Fontanille has made it his specialty to gather, classify, and organize various die types for the series of Biblical/Judaean coins. This work is important for continuing future studies, and it makes available a large number of photographs of examples of various coins.

At several points in this book the reader will see illustrations created by Fontanille that illustrate exact die types along with some of the various combinations that exist (see pp. 228, 316, 344).

In his book, Mildenberg focuses on the sequence of the striking of the coins of the Bar Kokhba Revolt. One of the main research tools that Mildenberg used was die combinations and comparisons of the dies, looking for progressive cracks and breaks. This allowed him to establish an actual sequential progression of when the coins were struck.

The possible mint scenario described above allows us a possible explanation for the crudely engraved and/or struck bronze coins in nearly every Judaean series. These have often been called "barbaric" or "barbarous" coins but this reference is anachronistic since it refers to the "barbarian" tribes that copied Roman and certain Greek coins. It is far more accurate to follow Mildenberg's lead and refer to all of these coins of the Judaean series as "irregular" issues.

While these crude, irregular issues were struck under the Hasmonean kings, they became more common during the reign of Herod I. These occur mainly in Herod's Jerusalem issues, but they are difficult to assess since all of Herod I's coins except for his dated series were so crudely engraved and manufactured in the first place. Under the prefects and procurators, however, the number and variations of irregular coins struck jumps greatly, especially beginning with the coins under

Tiberius. This may be attributed to the need for many more bronze coins in the increasingly-Romanized economy of Judaea. Crude coins were also issued during the Jewish War and the Bar Kokhba Revolt.

During the early first century there were many Jewish artisans, but few Jewish artists. The principal reason for this is the Jewish prohibition against graven images (see p. 172), so there was little demand for the fine arts of painting, sculpting, or engraving gems and dies. Consequently, for each coin type issued in Judaea there are several die types of fine, high-style work, more dies exhibiting average work, and additional dies exhibiting crude work, which also includes retrograde inscriptions, errors in inscription, and just weird-looking copies of the masterful designs. (Catharine Lorber comments that those in charge of the mints "should have been ashamed of some of the truly rotten stuff produced."[16])

Meshorer writes that, "Because of the unstable position of the Jewish administration, and the lack of a central mint, the mint masters were often changed. Occasionally unskilled people prepared the dies, and not only do the coins with the barbarous designs reveal bad style and obvious lack of skill, but also, they indicate work done under the pressures of the time limitations."[17]

Retrograde inscriptions occurred because the individual cutting the die was inexperienced and also probably illiterate. He did not understand the principle of die making that necessitates cutting the die in reverse. When the negative die strikes the metal flan, a true image is created. Die engravers, especially beginners, worked by copying. Thus, they probably cut their first dies by copying prototype coins, and not other dies or designs that may not have been available to them. When coins were stamped from those dies, the inscriptions appeared in retrograde.

Mildenberg writes that the irregular Bar Kokhba coins "seem to be drawn by the naive and hasty hands of children, and the inscriptions appear but mere hacks and lines, bordering on the completely illegible."[18]

NAMES OF THE SMALL BRONZE COINS

The actual names of the ancient Jewish bronze coin denominations are not known. For some 60 years it has been standard practice to refer to the most common denomination with the Hebrew word *prutah* (pl. *prutot*),[19] but this word is known to us only from later Rabbinnic literature.[20] The contemporaneous writer Josephus, for example, does not mention bronze coins or any terminology associated with them. However, since the Mishnah was codified early in the third century CE, and was based upon discussions among the Rabbinnical sages during the mid-first and second centuries CE, we can assume that the use of the word *prutah* was current during the time the small Jewish bronze coins were minted, c. 132 BCE–70 CE. The first *prutot* were the Jerusalem bronze lily/anchor coins issued under Antiochus VII/Hyrcanus I (No. 1131), probably equivalent to a Seleucid *chalkous*, and which aligned with the weight standard introduced by Alexander Balas (150–145 BCE).[21] During the first century, a *prutah* was the price of one pomegranate.[22]

Also, the Greek word *lepton* (pl. *lepta*) is used in the New Testament to describe the smallest bronze coin in circulation during the time the gospels were composed (c. first century CE), which was equal to half a Roman *quadrans*.[23] Kindler suggests that during the Hasmonean period Jewish bronze coinage consisted mainly of "the *dilepton*...commonly named *Perutah* (*sic.*)."[25] Hence a *lepton* was equal to a half-*prutah*, and the *prutah* equaled two *lepta*, as mentioned in Mark 12:42.

The late Ya'akov Meshorer told me that Israeli numismatists have used the word *perutah* (by Israelis who emigrated from Europe) or *prutah* (by native Israelis) since at least the late 1950s. Klimowsky explained the usage in a short essay in 1963.[25]

For our purposes, the terms *prutah* and *lepton* are used for the sake of consistency and comparison. As will be shown, however, neither the *prutah,* nor the *lepton,* nor half-*prutah* were absolute denominations vis-à-vis their weights, which varied greatly in individual issues.

OBSERVATIONS ON JUDAEAN BRONZE COINAGE

In 2009 I completed a metrological study of 10,312 Jewish bronze coins of 27 general types and various denominations.[26] The coins range in date from those of John Hyrcanus I (134–104 BCE) to those struck during the Jewish War.

The data from the study clearly show that Judaean bronze coins were manufactured based on the average weight of large groups of coins (*al marco*) and not the weights of single coins (*al pezzo*). As Meshorer observed: "[a]lthough it is likely that the mint masters knew the amount of coins to be produced from a specific amount of bronze, the exact quantity of the metal included in each coin would have been exceptionally difficult to control. It would not have been expedient to remove bronze from coins that were too heavy or to add bronze to the lighter issues." He also remarked that the range of weights of the Jewish bronzes was so great that "[i]t is difficult to assume that these light coins were given the same value in the market as the heavier *prutot.*"[27]

Results of this study, however, suggest that in Judaea, when coins were struck in the same metal, with the same or very similar designs, lacking indications on the coins to the contrary, they were intended to represent coins of the same denomination. Even with small bronzes, differences of 1 or 2 or even 3 grams would not have been of great concern between coins that shared types, since the relative weights of the coins were of little consequence in circulation. For example, Figure 1.9 shows three coins of the same type dated to year 5 of Nero, weighing (from left) 1.49, 2.43, and 3.67 g—the lightest of which weighs only 40 percent of the heaviest. The average weight of this type is 2.27 g. Yet it is almost impossible for a human weighing by hand to distinguish among the weights of these three coins. This group is only one of many examples of similar and even more drastic weight ranges within a single type. Despite the great variance in weight, these coins were undoubtedly the same denomination since *type, not weight, was the determinant.*[28] Similar extreme variances in weight were noted in every group of similar coin types we studied, wherein the heaviest coins weigh from 2x to 4x the weight of the lightest.

Although diameters were not measured, the range from narrowest to widest for any given type is within approximately 2–4 mm. The diameter of a particular coin is not necessarily a reflection of its weight. After handling thousands of coins, it was observed that the most sig-

1.9. Three *prutot* dated to the year 5 of Nero, weighing (from left) 1.49, 2.43, and 3.7 g.

nificant variable regarding the weight of a coin is most frequently *thickness*, not diameter. Thickness was determined by the depth molds were cut, from which the flans were cast.[29]

While the data gathered indicate that even though the weight of any coin type could vary dramatically, nevertheless the statistical analysis of the weights show trends in both denomination and standards among coins issued under specific political authorities.[30] (See table of results in Appendix B, p. 564.)

From the first Hasmonean bronze, struck under Hyrcanus I (beginning No. 1132), weighing an average 1.92 grams, the weight of the *prutah* under Jannaeus falls to a low of 1.20 grams for the coins of Jannaeus dated year 25 in both Greek and Aramaic (No. 1152).

The succeeding series (No. 1153) are those referred to by Hill as "wretched" imitations of the Jannaeus coins.[31] They may have been issued under Jannaeus, but due to the massive volume produced, it seems possible that they were issued through the reigns of his immediate successors.[32]

The weight of these "wretched" anchor/star coins (No. 1153) averages 0.81 grams, but the weight fluctuates dramatically from coins as light as 0.20 g to coins of 1.70 g (8.5x). These coins may well be degraded *prutot* and *not* half-*prutot* coins. Hyrcanus I (Nos. 1134, 1138) and Jannaeus (No. 1147) issued coins with different designs or inscriptions that were certainly intended to be smaller denominations, probably half-*prutot*.

The Talmud recognizes some coins, possibly the "wretched" imitations, as devalued *prutot* since it assigns the *prutah* a very small value indeed. The Talmud indicates that through the first century CE there were 768 *prutot* to the silver *sheqel* (BABA BATHRA 166b; 192 *prutot* equal one *zuz* or quarter-*sheqel*). The smallest possible version of the *prutah* is probably used in this calculation to insure that in any financial transactions that involved the Temple, which surely accounted for a large number of transactions in Judaea at the time, the value of the *prutah* was at the lowest rate possible vis-à-vis an actual silver equivalent in order not to deprive the Temple of its proper due. The Talmud reflects discussions of Jewish life around the first and second centuries CE, yet the devalued *prutot* were issued between around 76 BCE and 40 BCE. Bijovsky notes, however, that these poor, small coins were actually used in the area for hundreds of years, often up until at least the fifth century.[33]

Here is a summary of the probable value of the *prutah* during several periods:

- Hasmonean (Hellenistic) Period 140 BCE–134 BCE:
  1 *drachm* = 168 *prutot.*
- Herodian Period 40 BCE–6 CE:
  1 *denarius/drachm* = 96 *prutot.*
- Roman Period 6 CE–70 CE:
  1 *denarius/drachm* = 64 *prutot.*

FIDUCIARY COINAGE OF JUDAEA

During the Hellenistic and early Roman periods, Judaea was not a stranger to the use of small pieces of metal in trade (see Chapter 2).

The earliest Greek coins were struck from the purest possible metal. The reason was that they had specific value only within their issuing state, and if one wanted to undertake outside transactions, the metal needed to stand up to the test of weighing by balance scales. Eventually, however, the trading of metals ceased to be a commodity transaction and became a purchase; also at this time coins began to be counted, as opposed to pieces of metal being weighed, and the concept of fiduciary coinage began.[34]

The evolution from exchange of pieces of metal to coinage as we know it was not strictly economic. As Peter Van Alfen significantly notes, once coins are struck objects rather than chopped fragments, "the monetary instrument could now advance upon levels of political symbolism that were unattainable with anonymous bits."[35] This concept is even more applicable to Judaean coinage, since there were political and religious issues that needed to be considered in the creation of a Judaean royal coinage.[36]

While all manufactured coins were fiduciary, the bronze coinage "differed from that of coinages in the noble metals by the fact that the profit to the issuing authority was much greater, the bronze being used as a token coinage of very little intrinsic value,"according to Otto Mørkholm and Philip Grierson.[37] The profit motive for striking coins thus joins both market and political issues in driving the desire for local rulers to obtain the right to strike coins.[38] During the Hellenistic period in Judaea it was a royal prerogative to issue coins, and this grant was made to the Jews by Antiochus VII.[39]

Thus the ability to manufacture coins enriched the treasuries *and* underlined the political independence of the Hasmonean and Herodian rulers of ancient Judaea, even though they were permitted to issue only bronze coins. Silver coins were struck in ancient Judaea during the two revolts against Rome, 66–70 CE and 132–135 CE. Based on finds of coins in Judaea and the surrounding region, it is clear that the bronze coins were widely used in daily transactions; silver coins were far less common.

Dramatic weight variations among Judaean coin types can be explained by the low value of the small bronze coins. When the Talmud states that something is worth less than a *prutah* it means that it has no commercial value at all.[40]

The bronze coins were legal tender specifically within the territory controlled by the issuing authority. Outside of that territory their value was probably open to negotiation in the marketplace.[41]

In fact, the matter of fiduciary coinage, even for small bronze denominations, was significant enough to have been discussed in the Talmud, which asks whether copper coins are to be considered money or merchandise when traded against silver coins. The authors of the Talmud weighed both sides of the argument: pro-money, because in areas where the copper coins were the common form of currency, they were more readily accepted and exchanged than silver coins; pro-merchandise, because "copper coins are different, for where they circulate, they have greater currency."[42]

1.10. Unstruck coin flans from Judaea of various sizes, these are referred to in the Talmud as "uncoined metal which bears no imprint," and underline the fiduciary nature of bronze coinage in ancient Judaea.

More significantly, the Talmud refers to a specific small piece of bronze, coin-like, but not a coin. It is called a *protitot* and the Talmud says that this is "uncoined metal which bear[s] no imprint."[43] This seems to be a clear reference to unstruck coin flans, often found in Israel. The Talmud discusses whether they should be exchanged as barter or as a financial transaction. The conclusion was that while unstruck coins could be valid, they were to be strictly defined as "goods" and not as "money." Thus, there were two values to a small piece of bronze—the barter value or, if it was struck as a coin, the fiduciary value.

Since neither the Hasmoneans nor Herodians issued silver or gold coins, there was no built-in rate of exchange. It is possible that exchange rates for imported silver coins were established by decree, similar to a fourth century BCE decree in Olbia.[44] Bronze and silver coins were issued by the same authority in Judaea only during the Jewish War and the later Bar Kokhba Revolt. In Egypt, most surviving financial documents show that separate accounts were kept for amounts in silver and amounts in bronze. The same was true in third century BCE Egypt, when the bronze *drachm* was the official equivalent of the silver *drachm*, yet an exchange fee had to be paid if bronze was traded for silver.[45]

Along the same lines in ancient Judaea a system of money changers was required to exchange silver for bronze coins or vice-versa.[46] In the Greek world, Seaford notes, "even bronze coinage, which was probably sensed as having *some* intrinsic value, had a conventional value higher than this very low intrinsic value."[47]

In conclusion, we view Judaean coinage in its place, as Hellenistic issues already a few hundred years removed from the introduction of archaic or classical Greek coinage in electrum, gold, silver, or bronze. Ancient Judaea was an area in which many other issues of bronze and silver coinage circulated before and during the time that Jewish rulers and their Roman governors struck local bronze coinage. While the creation of Judaean bronze coinage certainly had economic elements, the need for Jews to establish and maintain an independent Jewish state at the time suggests this coinage had a political significance nearly as great as its economic significance.

Average weights calculated for the various issues fluctuate in an interesting, albeit relatively insignificant manner. They show little when they are contrasted to the *range* of weights for each particular coin type. These overlapping weight ranges essentially prove that the concept of fiduciary coinage at this time applied in ancient Judaea as it did in the rest of the world.

PRICES AND VALUES

Among the most frequent questions asked about ancient money deal with the relative value as well as the purchasing power of the coins.

Daniel Sperber has consolidated a most interesting series of price lists in ancient Israel during the first and second centuries CE. They are compiled from the Rabbinnical sources as well as the New Testament. A few interesting examples follow (note the equivalents between Biblical or Talmudic denominations and relative Roman denominations [in parentheses below] are those offered by Sperber; they may differ slightly from some other views; we offer Sperber's equivalents for consistency in his price list).[48]

Wages. In the early first century, Rabbi Hillel's daily wage was one *tarapik* (or one-half *denarius*); also the doorkeeper of the academy was given one-half *tarapik* (one-quarter *denarius*) as entrance fee. A vineyard worker's daily wages were one *denarius*, but the expenses for looking after a sick man were at least two *denarii*. The daily wages paid to a person for weaving a *tallit* (Jewish ritual shawl) were two *sela'im* or eight *denarii*.

A good scribe earned 12 *denarii* per week, or two *denarii* per day. He ate and drank for four *denarii* per week, and paid for his clothing with four *denarii* per week. Scribes were paid a few *prutot* per document.

Clothing. In the early first century the cost of the outfits of high priests was between 10,000 and 20,000 *denarii* in Jerusalem. However, clothing made of sacking which could last four or five years was only four *denarii*. The cost of a tallit, mentioned above, was in the range of 12 to 20 *denarii*.

Bread. In the first to second centuries, one loaf of bread cost one *pundion* (1/12 *denarius*), while a small loaf cost only one *issar* (1/24 *denarius*).

Wine. At the end of the third century, 100 ordinary bottles of wine cost 10 *aurei*, while 100 big bottles of wine cost 20 *aurei*.

Olive oil. Josephus reported that one amphora of olive oil from the Galilee cost one Tyrian *drachm*, the equivalent of one *denarius*.

Fruit. In the first to second centuries, a pomegranate cost between one *prutah* and eight *prutot*. A cluster of grapes or 10 figs cost one *issar* (eight *prutot*), and a cucumber (which must have been very desirable) cost a full *denarius*.

Livestock. In the first to second centuries, an ox cost 100 *denarii*, but a calf cost only 20 *denarii*. A newborn donkey foal cost two to four *denarii*. A ram cost eight *denarii* while a lamb cost only four *denarii*. In Jerusalem, two pigeons cost one *aureus*, which was later reduced to one *denarius*. Two sparrows cost one *as* (1/16 *denarius*) and five sparrows cost two *asses* (1/8 *denarius*).

Assorted foods. The cheapest meal for a bridegroom cost one *denarius*. A modest meal consisting of a small roll, a plate of lentils, two pieces of meat and two glasses of wine cost two *issars*.

Miscellanea. Several lamps and wicks cost one *prutah*. It cost up to 400 *aurei* to lease a ship. Rabbi Judah ben Ezekiel tells of Artabin, an examiner of *mezuzot* (Jewish ritual amulets) in the upper market of Sepphoris, and the quaestor, who once took 1,000 *denarii* from him as a tax. In another anecdote Rabbi Judah bar Nahman and Rabbi Levi appear as the equivalent of today's political advance men. Each of them used to receive eight *denarii* for convening the public to attend Rabbi Johanan's lectures.

Tooling, Smoothing, and Conservation

I was once referred to an internet posting for an eight-*prutah* coin of Herod I the Great (40–4 BCE). The photograph revealed that the coin had been heavily tooled and that at least half of the inscription and a good portion of the devices were re-engraved into a genuine coin.

Collectors want to know the difference between proper conservation of ancient coins and the type of cleaning that undermines a coin's integrity.

First, more than 99 percent of all ancient coins offered on the market—including the "uncleaned" coins—have been cleaned in one way or another. Why? Few would want to collect coins as they are found. After a couple of thousand years in the earth, only gold coins generally emerge unscathed except for a layer of earth and occasional minor encrustation. Silver and bronze both interact with the elements of the earth, and the patina that grows or attaches itself to the metal depends upon variables such as the acidity, moisture, and minerals that are present. Many ancient coins are barely recognizable when taken from the earth. Many of them are improperly treated. Others are conserved correctly and enter top collections.

In order understand this, here are some basics.

Mechanical cleaning is preferred. It involves using tiny wood or metal instruments under a powerful microscope. In this way an expert can remove surface encrustations without touching the surface of the metal. Sometimes certain chemicals can be used to soften encrustations in order to more efficiently remove them mechanically.

Smoothing is an aspect of mechanical cleaning that concentrates on scaling deposits or encrustations from the surface of a coin without cutting into the metal. Smoothing is sometimes wrongly taken to mean chasing, a nineteenth century and earlier technique of surface polishing in which layers of the metal surface are "shaved" off until pitting and other blemishes are removed. This practice is no longer acceptable in a modern numismatic context, and is more properly included in the category of tooling. Because of the confusion about the meaning of the word smoothing, I strongly recommend that it should not be used as a descriptive term for ancient coins.

Tooling is an illegitimate technique, done either by hand or precision power tools, in which metal is re-cut in order to either change a coin's identity such as restructuring the inscription, or to make it appear to be in better condition. Tooling can include heavy abrasion to the surfaces of a coin to make them appear smooth, cutting new details such as hair or a wreath into a coin, or to restore weak or missing letters of an inscription.

Sometimes a coin is improperly cleaned and gives the appearance of being tooled, but in fact only the encrustation has been affected.

1.11. Heavily tooled coin of Herod I (No. 1169) on top, compared with full composite image of coin struck from the same die set. Notice how details of both letters and designs have been changed by this illicit work. (Graphic: Fontanille.)

This can be resolved by mechanical cleaning or by chemically removing the encrustation and the offensive marks that remain.

Museum contrast, sometimes called 'desert patina,' is often applied to bronze coins in order to improve the contrast and enhance one's ability to see details. Professional conservators often use this technique because it is easier to display a coin conserved in this way. Few numismatists find this process offensive, and when done properly it is ph-neutral and can easily be removed from the coin. Such applications should be light and should never hide defects in the surface of a coin.

Gold coins often need only a rinsing with water since gold is the least subject to corrosion. Silver coins are almost always cleaned either chemically or electro-chemically. Bronze coins can also be cleaned in this way, but extreme care must be taken to use only chemical processes that work slowly and remove surface encrustation and mineralization, and without damaging the coin.

I once received a call from a collector who had attended a coin show and bought a "beautiful" bronze coin of Caligula with "great" surfaces and a "nice green patina." He paid a premium for the coin because it looked so nice. He drove home and left the coin in an envelope on the surface behind the back seat of his car, and forgot about it. It was summer time, and the car became quite hot. In a few days he remembered the coin, and retrieved it. Preparing to put it into his collection he was shocked to find an ugly bronze with green-brown sludge on both sides.

1.12. *Sheqel* of the year 1 of the Jewish War before and after conservation using electro-chemical and manual methods.

1.13. Large bronze of the year 1 of the Bar Kokhba Revolt before and after conservation using manual methods.

There was no way that the heat inside his car could damage any genuine patina, even one with proper conservation. This coin had been painted with a green-brown varnish or enamel to imitate a green patina. The heat in the car melted the paint and it shrank into globs.

The sludge was removed with solvent and the coin was chemically cleaned. It was then returned to its owner. It was now an "okay" coin instead of a "great" coin, but a lesson had been learned. There are few expert conservators of ancient coins. It is difficult and tedious work and may require the use of dangerous chemicals.

CLEANING ANCIENT COINS

Beginners can play with coins and try to learn to clean them with varying degrees of success. There are many internet sites and a few books. Of course they are filled with both good and terrible information, and even the good information is worthless without experience. In previous editions I have given some guidance in this field, however I am uncomfortable recommending the use of anything beyond standard household chemicals for cleaning coins unless one has the proper ventilation and safety equipment (gloves, goggles, laboratory jackets).

There is no simple method to clean coins beyond rinsing with water and gently using a soft brush, unfortunately, that does not usually accomplish much. Soaking a coins in olive oil for a long time is a commonly used system, and it can help a bit because olive oil is slightly acidic. However, if the olive oil is not completely removed from the coin with the proper solvents, the acidic oil continues to seep into the crevices of the coin and cause it to deteriorate from the inside out.

As mentioned earlier, thorough cleaning of silver coins normally involves chemicals. The downside of chemical cleaning is the depletion of some elements from the surface of the coin which interferes with accurate analysis of the alloy. Thus, an absolute rule of them is to always employ the least harsh chemicals that will do the job.

WARNING: even brushing a coin with distilled water can change it significantly, and it might be difficult to restore the original appearance.

THE COIN PLAGUE

This is a powdery form of oxidized copper chlorides that naturally occurs in some ancient coins, especially those exposed to chlorine when they were buried. This is not the same as hard green encrustation which is usually stable. The powdery "plague" can spread on a single coin. It is not caused by bacteria and is only contagious if other coins have similar problems with copper chlorides.

To prevent coin plague, make sure that your coins are kept in a clean, dry place. It is also critical to avoid the use of any solution that contains chlorine (including tap water) to clean coins. Some years ago the numismatic department of the Israel Antiquities Authority installed a powerful dehumidifier in the room where the country's national treasure coin collection is kept, and it has minimized the problem.

Here is Dr. Ya'akov Meshorer's method of treating coin plague. Beware that this or any treatment can change the appearance of a coin, and this is why expert conservation is preferred:

With a splinter of wood, a toothpick, or a bristle toothbrush, carefully scrape away as much of the powdery green material as possible. Soak the coin in a glass of distilled water. In serious cases you may add a drop or two of detergent to the water.

Change the water, rinsing the coin and the glass every two days. Keep repeating this process for at least three weeks, even if the plague seems to have disappeared sooner.

When the process is finished, dry the coin with a soft cloth, then place it in a warm oven for an hour or more until it becomes thoroughly dry. Brush the coin with a soft natural bristle brush 50 or 100 times on each side.

If all signs of the plague have disappeared, you may then apply Renaissance Wax, a commercial product, or spray the coin with a uniform, very thin coat of a flat-finish lacquer available from art supply stores.

If the plague returns to this coin, remove the lacquer with thinner and repeat the entire process. This method is effective only if coin plague affects mainly the surface of a coin. If the plague has penetrated to the core of the coin, it is unlikely that any home-treatment method will save it. If this has happened to a particularly valuable coin in your collection, I suggest you contact a conservation expert for advice.

IDENTIFYING FAKES AND FORGERIES

In medical terms, "differential diagnosis" is a systematic method of identifying a disorder (*e.g.* headache) that lacks unique symptoms or signs. A physician will examine the patient and then, based on findings, will make a likely diagnosis.

Being a numismatist is not the same as being a physician. But when a collector asks: "How do you know?" if a coin is not genuine, my answer is: "the same way your doctor knows how to diagnose an illness." In other words, experience and study. In Malcolm Gladwell's wonderful book *The Outliers*, he discusses the 10,000-hour rule which states that great mastery of complicated topics requires at least that much study and practice.

Over the past 40 years I have developed a system of "differential diagnosis" when examining ancient coins. It is not brain surgery, but here it is (this is adapted from my book *NOT KOSHER, Forgeries of Ancient Jewish and Biblical Coins*):

1. Study the general appearance with the naked eye and with a 3x to 7x magnifier. Do you have a question about any aspect of the coin? If yes, go to the next point. (If you know what you are looking for, a binocular microscope is invaluable.)

2. Weigh the coin. The weight of gold and silver coins is significant; compare the weight ranges with published weights in standard reference works. Note, however, that the weights of genuine ancient

silver coins can sometimes vary greatly, especially if the coins were found in the sea. In such instances, much of the alloy can leach out of the coins, leaving them 50 percent (or more) lighter than expected. The weights of bronze coins vary considerably, and in their case weight is not as critical, but can sometimes be significant. Unfortunately, most modern forgers are not so stupid that they get the weights wrong for the fakes they produce, though, sometimes, they make amazing errors.

3. Study the edge. Is there a seam around the edge? Has the edge been filed or hammered to hide the traces of casting? Keep in mind, however, that hammer marks are expected on the Jewish silver coins of the Jewish War, and that the silver coins of the Bar Kokhba Revolt were prepared for re-striking by hammering them in pan-like devices that caused the edge to become flat or slightly concave. Furthermore, all Bar Kokhba bronze and silver coins were overstruck upon coins that were already in circulation, and there are often file marks on the surfaces of the bronze coins, where the portraits and designs were filed down before re-striking. The filing, called adjustment marks, occurs on the surfaces and not usually the edges of the coins. If there are flan cracks, they should go completely through the coin and have ragged edges and not smooth edges. (Flan cracks can occur on some forgeries, especially when they are struck over genuine ancient bronze coins. However, flan cracks themselves are not absolute indicators of false coins.)

4. Examine the surfaces. The surfaces should be free of pits and pock marks unless the coin is clearly corroded and pitted from time, wear, or cleaning. Look for tiny holes resulting from casting air bubbles. Carefully look for places on the surfaces of the coin where a monogram, initials, or even the word "copy" might have been obliterated. Genuine crystallization of silver coins is a good sign, but one must learn to distinguish this from artificial corrosion made by acids, which are used to mimic natural aging. Flow lines (radial lines reflecting the flow of the coin's metal during the striking process), which are often apparent on struck gold and silver coins, are a good sign; but remember that any struck coin will have flow lines. Machine-struck coins will have extremely flat and even fields. Some forgers have been successful pressing coins on ancient flans, in which case genuine crystallization or patination may be present.

5. Examine the legend and the devices. Do letters rise sharply as with a struck coin, or does the coin have an overall fuzzy appearance? If it's fuzzy, this is a warning sign (although the lack of fuzziness is no

guarantee of authenticity and some fuzziness may appear on heavily worn or softly struck genuine coins).

6. Does the patina or oxidation appear to be genuine? An affirmative answer can be a valuable indicator, but remember that many ancient coins have been cleaned and darkened. This is true, even (or especially) for coins in old collections. Some collectors say that they refuse to buy coins that have been cleaned and re-toned. However, if you take this position you will not acquire many coins. There is a legend that forgers can create artificial patinas by feeding coins to goats, chickens, pigs, or cows and recovering them at the other end of the process! This is a technique used to "age" fake scarabs. People heard about this approach and assumed it could be done to coins—but it cannot! On the other hand, coins can be buried in chemically treated dumps for years or decades and later dug out with convincing patinas.

7. Do the dies match known specimens? Many groups of the Biblical/Judaean series of ancient coins have been studied and documented. If you can find a coin struck from the same dies as yours (note: struck and not cast!) it is a significant indication of authenticity. If, for

1.14. The left sides of the coins shown above are from a genuine *sheqel* of the Jewish War, the right side is a cast forgery. Note the lack of sharp details and lack of flow lines on right.

example, you have a Bar Kokhba coin and the dies do not match those published in Mildenberg's book (or its addenda) on the subject, there is a good chance it is a fake. Along these lines, however, one must also be aware of forgeries that are struck with dies created by using original coins, in which case the dies will, indeed, match. Note, however, that in some other groups of ancient coins, such as the Roman Provincial series, unique die varieties are relatively common.

8. Two or more completely identical examples of an ancient coin are proof of forgery.

9. Is the style accurate? This question is a matter of how the coin is designed and created, including the portrait, the legend, and the motifs. Sometimes a forger will misinterpret a detail and present it in a different way. How can one learn to judge style? See Gladwell's 10,000-hour rule above.

10. Die Axis. Compare the die axis of your coin to those of other known coins of the same type. Sometimes this comparison is not relevant because the axis varies greatly, but at other times it can be a critical diagnostic tool. (The axis of a coin is the relative position of the obverse as compared to the reverse as a result of the alignment of the dies when the coin is struck.)

11. Your reference library (and its use) is a helpful defense against allowing fakes into your collection. If you are buying "numbers" to fill holes in a collection, you are not likely to have much knowledge about the coins you are buying. Reading books, referring to photographs, and studying coins at museums, club meetings, and coin fairs will give you the experience you need to be a successful collector.

12. A reliable dealer sells genuine coins, and he or she will also usually consult with you on other coins you own to help you determine their authenticity. Be reasonable in your requests, however. A professional numismatist cannot spend unlimited time offering free advice on coins that a collector bought from someone's junk box. One reason junk box coins are so cheap is that most dealers do not want to spend time or effort to attribute them. Reputable dealers spend considerable time and energy to insure that the coins they sell are genuine and as described.

One of the many enjoyable aspects of collecting coins is the opportunity to find a coin that may be more valuable to the collector than to the person who owns it. Good fortune, however, usually results from lots of work and study. Film producer Samuel Goldwyn reportedly said, "The harder I work, the luckier I get." Another axiom still rings true: There is no such thing as a free lunch. Therefore, most collectors are wise to purchase ancient coins from reputable dealers who stand behind their sales. If you are not certain of a coin's authenticity, check it with other experts in the field. The extra time will be well spent, and will save you or your heirs from future disappointment.

IMPORTANCE OF CITY COINS

Even before the first Hasmonean coins were struck by the Jews in ancient Israel in the second century BCE, a few important cities in the area had issued their own coins. But the vast majority of city coins were issued after Augustus, when certain cities acquired the right to issue coins. Such powers were granted, probably by local authorities, to promote both loyalty to Rome and commerce in the area. City coins also developed as a means of local economic, political, and cultural expression.

Thirty-eight cities of ancient Israel and Transjordan issued coins. This is not a large number in comparison to more than 350 cities in Asia Minor and around 90 more in Greece and its islands.

Most city coins were issued between the late first century and middle third century CE. Although coins were minted in several cities of ancient Israel prior to the first century, these were either Ptolemaic, Seleucid, Macedonian, or autonomous issues, and not provincial coins. Thus, even if they were struck in specific cities, they are not usually referred to as city coins *per se*.

The city coins circulated in ancient Israel together with other coins of the area. City coinage came to an end during the reign of Gallienus, about 268 CE, when the economy changed so much that the value of the bronze was greater than the nominal value of the coins.

One particular group of cities is known as the Decapolis, a league of Syrian-Greek cities in Transjordan and the northern Jordan Valley during the Roman and Byzantine periods. Josephus, Pliny, and the New Testament all mention the Decapolis. Pliny lists the member cities as Damascus, Philadelphia, Raphaena, Scythopolis, Gadara, Hippos, Dium, Pella, Gerasa, and Canatha. This is not a definitive list, however, and Pliny explains there were as many as 14 to 18 other cities sometimes listed as Decapolis members. For example, in the early second century, Abila was also a member of the league. Most of the Decapolis cities date their eras from the time of Pompey's conquest of the area in 63 BCE. Some believe that the Decapolis was founded by Pompey himself when he freed the cities which had been conquered earlier by the Jewish king Alexander Jannaeus. It is known that large Jewish communities existed in the Decapolis cities and some of the Jewish population may have descended from people who had been converted by Jannaeus. Thousands of Jews were killed in the Decapolis cities at the outbreak of the Jewish War in 66 CE. Still, archaeological evidence indicates that Jews continued to live in the Decapolis cities for many generations.

Cities of the Decapolis were self-governing, and minted their own coins. The Decapolis was of special importance because its cities were located along the key trade routes between Syria and northern Arabia. Most city coins of ancient Israel carry Greek rather than Latin inscriptions, evidence that Greek was still spoken in the area at this time. Frequently, the city coins bear the portrait of the emperors under whom they were issued. However, the coins are not dated by regnal years, but mainly according to eras of each individual city.

The series of Roman provincial city coins of ancient Israel and nearby lands can be read as history books. Referring to the large number of coins struck by the cities of the Roman Empire, M. Rostovtzeff observes that they "supply us with first-class information on some important points in their political, religious, and economic life. These sources have revealed to us not only the external appearance of many ancient cities, but also the main features of every aspect of their life— their walls, streets, gates, public places, public and private buildings, on the one hand, and on the other their municipal organization, their income and expenditure, their wealth and their sources of wealth, both public and private, their religious beliefs, their amusements, and their intellectual interests."

City coins are omitted from this edition because they are an extensive series. One cannot do it justice by discussing only a few coins from each city. A major new work on the city coins will soon be published by the American Numismatic Society as *The Abraham D. Sofaer Collection at the American Numismatic Society*.

CHAPTER TWO

BALANCE WEIGHTS TO COINAGE

Abraham lived during a time of transition from nomadic life to settlement. In those days, pasture land, cattle, and sheep were among the basic means of measuring and exchanging wealth. Languages reflect this: the Latin word *pecunia* (money, coins) was derived from *pecus* the word for cattle, especially sheep; *rupee* is the name of money of India, it originates with the Sanskrit *rupa*, for pastures; the English *fee* shares its root with the German *Bieh*, which also refers to pastures. Counting head of cattle[1] (*capita*) evolved to the word *capital*, meaning wealth. This commodity was mentioned when Abraham asked Abimelech to witness his digging of a well at Beersheba:

And Abraham set seven ewe-lambs of the flock by themselves (GENESIS 21:28).

Barter also played a critical role when Joseph acquired all of the land of Egypt from the people on behalf of Pharaoh during the years of famine:

Buy us and our land for bread, and we and our land will be bondmen unto Pharaoh (GENESIS 47:19).

Elsewhere in Genesis, Abraham is described as having been

very rich in cattle, in silver, and in gold (GENESIS 13:2).

The time when man began to count remains a mystery. "Counting" time with marked bones and antlers could have taken place as early as

61

15,000 years ago.[2] Whenever this momentous event took place, counting was probably the first of four basic human inventions that changed society; measuring, weighing, and writing are the other three. Shraga Qedar points out, "It is generally assumed that the last three skills appeared in chronological proximity to one another; in other words, measuring and weighing were invented at the same time as writing and in the same region."[3]

Ancient systems of weights and measures in Mesopotamia and Egypt were used as early as 3500–3000 BCE, around the time of the Urban Revolution. Highly developed systems of weights and measures existed in Syria (*e.g.* at Ebla and Ugarit) beginning in the later part of the Early Bronze Age (3100–2000 BCE), during the Late Bronze Age (1550–1200 BCE) at Alalakh, around the same time as the Hittites, both in Anatolia, and in the ancient Holy Land. Archaeological evidence for various systems of weights and measures has been found in excavations throughout the Near East.

Our economic system did not grow either simply or universally. According to Powell, "The ancients themselves encountered great obstacles when they tried to define units of measure in the absence of standardized systems and the difficulty was especially great when diachronic or cross-cultural definitions were involved, making most ancient 'equivalences' only rough approximations."[4]

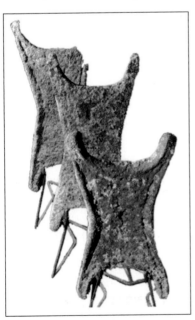

2.1. Three bronze *talent* or "load" ingots discovered in a shipwreck at Cape Gelidonia off the coast of Southern Turkey. (Photo: Institute Nautical Archaeology.)

An early Near Eastern weight unit, the *talent*, probably reflected the average "load" a man could carry. This is illustrated by ancient words with this translation such as *biltu* in Akkadian, *gun* in Sumerian, and *kikar* (round thing) in Hebrew. The word *talent* comes from the Latin derivation of the Greek word *talanton*, "a weight, something weighed" which may have been derived from the Akkadian word *biltu*.[5] By the Late Bronze Age the *talent* had become a basic trade weight, illustrated by a number of early copper ingots ranging in weight from about 28 to 30 kilograms.[6]

A number of systems used the *talent*; there is an Ashdodite *talent* (weighing 22 to 22.5 kilograms) and a Ugaritic *talent* (weighing 28 to 29.5 kilograms) as well as *talents* in other systems that could weigh either 34 or 38.5 to 39 kilograms.[7] These large pieces of metal were "not closely controlled equivalents of the *talent* mass but rather reflect some attempt to approximate the *talent* to facilitate reckoning."[8]

"The precise size of the load was bound to vary somewhat from locality to locality and when the transition from crude estimates of

2.2. Detail from a tomb at Thebes shows man carrying a "load" ingot. (After Davies in Metropolitan Museum of Art) (Bass 1967:63).

weight to genuine weighing with balances began, local tradition must have exerted a significant influence on the determination of the precise mass of the local *mina*."[9]

The Old Testament precisely defines a *talent*:

> *And the silver of them that were numbered of the congregation was a hundred talents, and a thousand seven hundred and three score and fifteen [1,775] sheqels, after the sheqel of the sanctuary: a beqa a head, that half a sheqel, after the sheqel of the sanctuary, for every one that passed over to them that are numbered, from twenty years old and upward, for six hundred thousand three thousand and five hundred and fifty [603,550] men* (EXODUS 38:25–26).

In other words, 603,550 men each gave half-a-*sheqel* to the congregation—301,775 *sheqels* in all. These 301,775 *sheqels* were equal to 100 *talents* plus 1,775 *sheqels*. Thus 100 talents of silver equaled 300,000 *sheqels*, and one *talent* of silver was equal to 3,000 *sheqels*. Another unit of weight mentioned in the Bible is the *mina*, which equaled either 50 or 60 *sheqels*. The Akkadian *mina* contained 60 *sheqels*, but the Canaanite-Israelite *mina* probably equaled 50 *sheqels* because in the Old Testament, sums of 50 *sheqels* and more are usually divisible by 50, but not by 60.[10]

The large "load" or *talent* ingots were just the right weight to be lifted and carried by a man, as shown in some Egyptian reliefs and paintings. Thus, for daily convenience, smaller bronze ingots were required. One small form of ingot is a wedge or tongue-shaped ingot. A hoard of these dating to the end of the third millenium BCE was found at the excavation at Har-Yeroham in the Negev.[11]

Other bronze ingots in the shape of rings or bracelets were illustrated in some Egyptian wall paintings. Similar pieces have been found at a number of sites, including in an eighth century BCE burial cave at Tel Halif in southern Israel.[12]

By the relatively simple process of cutting and smithing, bronze or copper ingots could be made into a variety of tools and weapons such as plows, spears, arrowheads, and knives. As commerce evolved, copper was replaced by the more precious silver and gold, of which smaller quantities provided equal value.

These economic transitions evolved toward a common basis for measuring quantity and quality. "Normative trading required the fixing of a standard that could be measured and that would have a recognized value. The standard would need to be a material that existed only in limited quantities and that could stand the test of time. Two precious metals, gold and silver, fulfilled these criteria because of their special qualities. Other metals, such as copper and lead, were also suitable because of the great effort required to produce them."[13]

The *mina* apparently went in and out of use. The typical *mina* "is attested at Ebla in the third millennium, but during the subsequent millennium it seems to mostly disappear as a unit west of the Euphrates."[14]

Thus the Old Testament treats the *sheqel* as a virtually exclusive primary weight, and this is so well understood in context, that sometimes the word "*sheqels*" is omitted altogether (*e.g.* GENESIS 20:16). Further, texts from both Alalakh and Ugarit contain sums of hundreds or thousands of *sheqels* but there are no references to the *mina* (another denomination in the Old Testament).[15]

For thousands of years the *sheqel* was the unit of weight throughout the ancient Near East in nearly every country, except for Egypt which used the *qedet* since the New Kingdom.

The earliest scale weights were made of stones. A round stone of a certain weight was found and weighed against a known example of a particular weight. Then the stone was rubbed against an abrasive surface until sufficient material was scraped away to make the weight true. Not incidentally, this process also gave weights a flat side, which prevented them from rolling around in the pan of scales. Later, round or elliptical stones were rubbed until the correct weight was achieved, and occasionally, if they were too light, they were drilled and filled with a dollop of lead.

The Hebrew word for weights used in the Old Testament is *even*, which means stone (LEVITICUS 19:36, DEUTERONOMY 25:13, 15; PROVERBS 11:1; 16:1). In Akkadian, the scale weights are called *abnu*, basically the same word. Such references reflect traditional use that goes back to the Early Bronze Age. The early *talent* denominations were large slabs of bronze, but silver and gold were much more portable and they are easily carried as jewelry.

And it came to pass, as the camels had done drinking, that the man took a golden earring of half a sheqel weight, and two bracelets for her hands of ten sheqels weight of gold... (GENESIS 24:22).

Thus gold bracelets and earrings became storehouses of wealth, worn by men and women alike. It was not uncommon for this wealth to be called upon when it was needed for commercial transactions or even for early fundraising, as when Aaron asked the Israelites to donate funds to make the golden calf.

Break off the golden earrings, which are in the ears of your wives, of your sons, and of your daughters, and bring them onto me (EXODUS 32:2).

Jewelry was also made of silver, which was commonly stored and exchanged in fragments or small ingots. Meshorer notes that the Biblical Hebrew text in Judges 5:19, *betsa kesef*, which is usually translated as "they took no gain of money," is more accurately translated from Hebrew as "they took no piece of silver."[16] Even many hundreds of years after coins were invented they were often referred to as "pieces of silver." Early Middle Eastern coin hoards from the fifth to fourth centuries BCE also contained cut coins, suggesting that their value was still based upon weight. Eventually people developed more confidence in stamped coins, and they no longer needed to be weighed in every transaction.[17]

"Economically inexact weighing instituted the use of silver as a medium of exchange for small commodities, and the facts themselves suggest that this barrier to commerce was not overcome until the minting of cheap coins became common."[18]

2.3. *Hacksilber* pieces of 7.4 to 21.3 mm, accompanied by fragments of a pottery jug c. 6th century BCE, purchased in Jericho, c. 1980.

The first mention of payment in the Old Testament occurs during the story of the covenant between God and Abraham:

He that is born in thy house, and he that is bought with thy silver, must needs be circumcised... (GENESIS 17:13).

The Hebrew word for money used here is *kesef*, which means silver, almost certainly referring to small ingots of silver similar to those found at Eshtemo'a, south of Hebron in the Judaean Hills. Archaeologists discovered a hoard of five jugs from the tenth century BCE filled with mostly chopped pieces of silver jewelry. Three of those jugs were inscribed "five" and this may have signified the measurement of five Mesopotamian *minas* in each jug.[19]

In a cooking pot discovered at Ein Gedi, hidden in a building that was destroyed early in the sixth century BCE, archaeologists discovered another type of ingot, made from silver that had been melted and poured into a shallow depression in the earth or sand. After cooling, the resultant mass was marked with lines in order to break or chop away some pieces, much like a modern chocolate bar.[20]

The common practice throughout the ancient Near East was to weigh these small silver ingots on balances against "stones" of known weight.

And Abraham weighed to Ephron the silver, which he had named in the audience of the sons of Heth, four hundred sheqels of silver, current money with the merchant (GENESIS 23:16).

These silver fragments, referred to as *hacksilber*, were the immediate precursors of coinage. *Hacksilber* hoards have been documented in the ancient land of Israel as early as around the twelfth century BCE, which of course suggests that there was also a system of weights available to use this silver in transactions.[21]

Early in his career, Israeli numismatic scholar Ya'akov Meshorer made a random surface find in Jerusalem of an archaic Attic *tetradrachm*.[22] Along with other late sixth and fifth century BCE silver coins of Athens, Acanthus, Aegina, Cannus, Chios, Corinth, Cyprus, Cyzicus, Kindya, Kos, Lampsacus, Lycia, Miletos, Paphos, Phocaea, Samos, Sinope, Stagira, and Thasos, these are the earliest coins found in Israel. From the fifth century BCE onward, coins became more common in the Holy Land, but even during the period of Persian rule, it is not clear whether coins were in wide circulation, or were limited to certain small groups such as merchants and officials. A clue lies in a fifth century BCE papyrus found at Wadi Daliyeh, which reports the sale of a slave named Nehemiah to a Samaritan named Yehonur for thirty 'pieces' of silver. Silver by weight is also mentioned in one of the Arad Ostraca (No. 41). Thus we learn that even in the fourth century BCE payments were sometimes made by units of weight instead of coins.[23]

"The same situation emerges even more clearly from a comparison with the Elephantine documents. As in Palestine, in Egypt too, Greek coins were in use, and were apparently very common as early as the end of the sixth century BCE. Nevertheless, a study of the papyri from Elephantine which deal with commerce reveals that throughout the fifth century BCE mercantile transactions in this city were carried out by weighed quantities of silver. The earliest document which mentions coins as a means of payment dates from the year 400 BCE. However, this document still employs the formula according to which coins are equated with the old weights, thus 'the sum of 2 *sheqels*, that is, the sum of 1 *stater*.' In another document from the year 402 BCE the *stater* is explicitly described as 'money of Greece.' These two statements (and they are by no means unique) thus confirm the fact that metal ingots were still being traded by weight as currency in business transactions in the fifth and fourth centuries, though coins were already in everyday use. It should also be noted that a number of coin hoards dating from this period which have been uncovered at various sites in the Near East contained both coins and metal ingots."[24]

Thus the use of weighed metal currency continued well into the time after coinage was invented. Even in much later periods, scale and balance weights were refined and continued to be used to weigh coins. These scales were used to weigh other precious commodities not limited to silver and gold, including gemstones and various herbs, spices, and medicinal items.

DUST ON THE SCALES

"Dust on the scales" is a phrase derived from some translations of Isaiah (40:12, 15–16) that refers to the inherent inaccuracies of the process of weighing with balance scales. Even today religious leaders may ask if congregants complain about the "dust on the scales" when the local grocer weighs out five pounds of potatoes. We do not, because although it exists, it is not significant to the transaction. Likewise, the Old Testament tells us that the weight of nations is equally small.

See, the nations are a drop in the pan [of the scales], like clouds on the scale are they reckoned. See, the coastlands lift it [the pan] like dust (ISAIAH 40:5–16).[25]

Early scales were crudely built and not always accurate. Depending on the scale, there was always an amount that could not be weighed. References from Mari in ancient Babylonia have given this quantity a name, *shiqu(m)*, and the Hebrew version of this word appears in Isaiah 40:15 as *shahak*.[26] This unweighable amount has often been referred to as "dust on the scales."

In general, ancient precision weights tolerated inaccuracies between about 3% and 5%. Dayton experimented with a simple scale used to weigh air mail letters to ½ ounce (14.15 grams). He found that 30 grains (1.94 grams) were needed to get the balance moving properly. From this experiment it follows that in the ancient world there must have been a similar quantity that simply could not be measured.[27]

In order to evaluate ancient weight systems, we must make educated guesses as to the standards and how they evolved. Today we recognize weight standards, the *pound* or the *kilogram*, which refer to original units of a measurable and reproducible weight or mass. For example, one *gram* was originally defined as the mass of 1 cubic *centimeter* of water at 4°C, but now is taken as the one-thousandth part of the standard *kilogram*, a mass preserved and maintained by the International Bureau of Weights and Measures. We don't know if such standards existed in the ancient world. There are Old Testament references to what may be official standards, such as "current money with the merchant" (GENESIS 23:16), "*sheqel* of the sanctuary" (EXODUS 30:13), and "the king's weight" (II SAMUEL 14: 26). Perhaps in some instances there were "master" units maintained in a Temple or other locale.

And Abraham weighed to Ephron…four hundred sheqels of silver current money with the merchant (GENESIS 23:16).

This they shall give, every one that passeth among them that are numbered, half a sheqel after the sheqel of the sanctuary (EXODUS 30: 13).

He weighed the hair of his head at two hundred sheqels, after the king's weight (II SAMUEL 14:26).

Similarly, in the Elephantine papyri, a "royal weight" is mentioned and there are other variations recorded in Akkadian and Sumerian texts that translate to "in the merchant's *mina*," "weight of the country," "weight of the city," "weight of the harbor," "true *mina*," "our weights," and "my weights."[28]

Today, when we talk about ancient weight standards, we cannot be very specific. In many cases, even inscribed weights from the same period vary in mass from one to the next. For some early examples, Dayton lists a group of known inscribed ancient Sumerian and Neo-Assyrian weights and their *sheqel* derivatives, which vary from 7.95 to 8.41 grams.[29]

Another source of variation in ancient weights results because each weight may not be directly copied from a "master." Instead, they were copies of copies, often several generations removed from the original.

Also, "a certain standard unit of mass may have regional and/or geographic variations that completely supplant its original value, or

2.4. Using a balance scale with bull-shaped weights and round ingots from a tomb in Thebes c. 1400 BCE.

it may become reserved for specialized applications such as taxation, tribute, or transactions involving specific commodities..."[30]

Thus, when we refer to the mass of ancient weights, we are referring to numeric averages that can only be calculated from existing weights or historic sources. Even though some sophisticated statistical techniques have been developed for a quantitative approach, these techniques are likely less accurate than one would hope due to the use of many standards in many areas at various times, a general lack of accuracy in ancient scale weights, as well as changes caused by encrustation or corrosion, wear, breaks or damages, unknown standards, and ancient fraud.

FRAUD WITH WEIGHTS AND SCALES

Proof of fraud can be found in the many ancient prohibitions against the use of false weights or scales.

"A balance could be falsified in the interest of the merchant by making the receiving arm shorter—even a minute degree shorter—than the paying out arm, but to judge from the Code of Hammurabi (1792–1750 BCE), which makes no mention of false balances but specifically legislates against the use of false weights, the latter crime was of far greater concern."[31]

The Code of Hammurabi (Section 94) refers specifically to weighing transactions by merchants (called *tamkaru* [*tamkarum*, singular] in Akkadian): "If the *tamkarum* tries to practice fraud with weights, he loses everything he has lent."[32]

There were plenty of scoundrels and thus we are also warned in the Old Testament:

> *Thou shalt not have in thy bag diverse weights, a great and a small. Thou shalt not have in thine house diverse measures, a great and a small. But thou shalt have a perfect and just weight; a perfect and just measure shalt thou have. . .* (DEUTERONOMY 25:13–15).

> *Just balances, just weights, a just ephah [measure of about 1.1 bushels], and a just hin [a measure of about 1.5 gallons] shall ye have* (LEVITICUS 19:36).

The Prophets had a dim view of the weighing associated with buying and selling. Amos condemns the people who cannot wait for the Sabbath to end so they can get back to making profits and who:

Make the ephah small, and the sheqel great, and falsifying the balances of deceit (AMOS 8:5).

Primary victims of such frauds were probably consumers. "I believe that ancient weight sets were highly personalized and valued tools that merchants were intimately familiar with. They would use these personal weights exclusively when weighing a certain quantity of merchandise for trade and weigh again, with their own sets, the amount of merchandise received in return. Similarly, the merchant with whom the trade took place would do the same with his own set of weights. Consequently, during such transactions involving two merchants, each equipped with their respective weight sets, whether conforming to the same standard or not, the deliberate use of fraudulent weights would not have been an issue. Merchandise or produce sold to consumers who could not check the quantity received, on the other hand, may have been another story."[33]

2.5. A bronze balance-beam scale with pans of early style, probably Persian or Hellenistic times. Original chains replaced with strings. Purchased in Israel. (Author's collection.)

The use of balances as a symbol of justice originated in ancient Egypt or earlier, and is reflected in a Biblical reference:

Let me be weighed in a just balance, that God may know mine integrity (JOB 31:6).

From Mesopotamia through the Levant some local temples and their officials may have been involved in the regulation of weight systems and trade. We do not yet have clear archaeological evidence of this, but "the temple and its agents frequently dealt in trade, lease, and purchase of land, loans of silver, and many other economically motivated activities. Bronze Age temple archives including those of Nippur, are often filled with documents and letters that clearly testify to the Temple's economic prowess."[34] Beginning in the Greek period, there existed a group of public officials known in Greek as *agoranomoi* (*agoranomos*, singular) who supervised the commercial aspects of the market (*agora*), including the assurance of the true nature of balance weights. Some of these officials are named specifically on weights from the Hellenistic to the Roman periods.

THE WEIGHT SYSTEM OF JUDAH

There were no coins in the ancient Land of Israel during the First Temple Period (1006–586 BCE), when a standard of specifically Judaean weight evolved. As might be expected for a later, derivative weight system, developed at a crossroads of civilization, the Judaean system appears to contain elements that link it to several other systems. The weights of Judah are also of special interest because the *sheqels* and some of its fractions are mentioned by name in the Bible:

This they shall give, every one that passeth among them that are numbered, half a sheqel after the sheqel of the sanctuary—the sheqel is twenty gerahs—half a sheqel for an offering to the Lord (EXODUS 30:13).

The weights of ancient Judah were used from the end of the eighth century up to 586 BCE, when the Babylonians destroyed Solomon's Temple. Almost all of these are polished, symmetric limestone domes with flat bases and often have engraved inscriptions referring to de-nomination. These weights were used to balance precious items.

Until 1998, only 211 of the inscribed Judaean weights had been found in archaeological excavations; more than half came from Jeru-salem and its surroundings (76), Lachish (25), and Arad (15).[35] Many non-inscribed weights have also been discovered and some of them show markings in ink or paint. Thus it is possible that most of the un-inscribed Judaean limestone weights were once labeled by this meth-od, both less expensive and less permanent than engraving upon the stone.

By any account, Judaean weights are rare. It was possible for a small village to do nicely with only one or two sets of weights that might have been set up at "stations" in the markets, although active merchants must have had their own sets of weights. When a commod-ity needed to be weighed, it was brought to the weight station where the transaction was completed, a small fee was charged and, perhaps, taxes may even have been assessed. Personal weights could also be standardized at such locations.

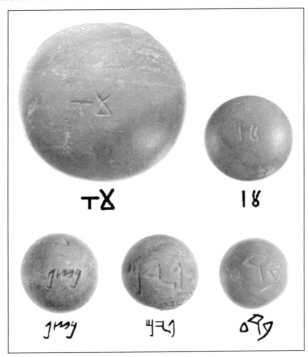

2.6. Limestone *sheqel* weights of (top row from l.) 8 *sheqels*, 1 *sheqel*; (bottom row from l.) *nezef*, *pym*, *beqa*.

The named fractions of the Judaean *sheqel* in the Old Testament are:

The *pym* or two-thirds of a *sheqel*, known to be the amount that was paid by the Jews to Philistine metal smiths for sharpening their tools and weapons:

And the price of the filing was a pym (I SAMUEL 13:21).

The *beqa*, or half-*sheqel*, became famous as the annual tribute to the Jerusalem Temple:

A beqa a head, that is, half a sheqel, after the sheqel of the sanctuary (EXODUS 38:26).

The third-*sheqel*, which is not known to have survived as an actual weight denomination, could either be a reference to the practice of an earlier or later time than the half *sheqel*, to a weight other than Judaean, or possibly even an editing error:

Also we made ordinances for us, to charge ourselves yearly with the third part of a sheqel for the service of the house of our God (NEHEMIAH 10:33).

The quarter *sheqel*, or *rebah*, was suggested as a gift from Saul to Samuel the prophet:

2.7. JUDAEAN WEIGHT TABLE

Denomination	Weight	Per *Talent*	Per *Mina*	Per *Sheqel*
Talent	34.2 kg	1		
Mina	570 kg	60	1	
Sheqel	11.40 g	3,000	50	1
Nezef	9.12 g	3,750	62.5	5/6
Pym	7.60 g	4,500	75	2/3
Beqa	5.70 g	6,000	100	2
Gerah (20)	0.57 g	60,000	1,000	20
Gerah (24)	0.48 g	71,250	1,187.50	24

*And the servant answered Saul again, and said: "Behold I have in my
hand the fourth part of a sheqel of silver, that I will give to the man of
God to tell us our way"* (I SAMUEL 9:8).

The smallest fraction of a *sheqel* mentioned in the Bible is the *gerah*
which is also the Akkadian word for a carob seed. The Bible tells us
that the Judaean *gerah* was one-twentieth of a *sheqel*:

...the sheqel is twenty gerahs... (EXODUS 30:13).

However, the number of *gerah* in a *sheqel* continues to be discussed.
Kletter believes that there are 24 *gerahs* (Hebrew plural *gerot*) to a *sheqel*
of Judah. He argues that the Bible's authors "who used the term 'holy
sheqel' wanted to distinguish it from another *sheqel*, which we shall call
...'ordinary *sheqel*.' For that reason they stressed time and again that
the holy *sheqel* was made of 20 *gerahs*. We can assume, therefore, that
an 'ordinary *sheqel*' had a different number of *gerahs* (since, otherwise,
why would the 20 *gerahs* in the holy *sheqel* be mentioned time and
again?)"[36]

Kletter suggests that the weights marked ٦ are of five *gerahs* and
the weights marked T are 10 *gerahs*, while their bigger brothers, also
marked with the ٦Ⴟ and TႽ, are equal to four and eight *sheqels* (and five
and ten *qedet*), respectively.

He further argues that the *beqa* is the actual half *sheqel* and the usually slightly lighter 10 *gerah* is worth 10/24 *sheqel*. Also, the flexible 24
is divisible by 2, 4, 6, 8, and 12 while 20 is divisible by the less helpful
2, 5, and 10.

In opposition to this argument, some scholars believe that the authors and editors of the Bible meant what was written: there are 20
gerahs to the *sheqel*, and the very fact that no other number is ever used
confirms this. This issue may never be resolved, although Kletter's pro-
posal of 24 *gerahs* seems likely. It is also a possibility that both circumstances existed, and at one point the number of *gerahs* per *sheqel* may
have changed from 20 to 24 during a re-valuation of the *sheqel*.

The various denominations—*nezef, pym, beqa,* and *gerah*—that make
up the Judaean weight system were previously thought to be parts of
a number of different weight systems. Meshorer, however, identified
them as a part of a single system of Judaean weights[37] and this concept
has since become generally accepted.[38]

The inscribed weights carry a series of symbols or Hebrew words. The symbols, once thought to have been specific royal Judaean symbols, have, in fact, been revealed as Egyptian hieratic signs. Even the Ɣ, once explained as a version of the winged sun disk found on the Judaean royal jar handles, or the *zror* (a sack in which currency was carried), has been explained more recently as "a sort of Hieratic shortening for the word *sheqel*."[39]

Sheqel weights ascend in multiples of eight—4, 8, 16, 24, and 40—and provide a convincing connection to the importance of international trade, especially with Egypt during the Iron Age II period. The system used in Judaea is directly linked to the Egyptian *qedet* system.[40] Four Judaean *sheqels* equal five Egyptian *qedet* (half a *deben*) and eight Judaean *sheqels* equal ten Egyptian *qedet* (one *deben*). Thus it is not surprising to learn: a) these are the most common sizes of Judaean weights that have been discovered and, b) that the symbols known to represent four and eight *sheqels* of Judah actually carry the hieratic numbers for five and ten. The *nezef* (5/6 *sheqel*), far from being the basis of its own weight metrology system as Sir Flinders Petrie and others previously suggested, is in fact the Judaean equivalent of one Egyptian *qedet*.

Other fractions of the *sheqel* correspond to other ancient weight systems (e.g., the *pym* of around 7.6 grams is related to the similar Late Bronze Age Ugaritic or Phoenician *sheqel*), but there was no link so close as between the systems of Judah and Egypt during this time. Kletter even remarks how surprising it is that there is such a "lack of direct correlation between the [limestone weights of Judah] and the Mesopotamian weight system [of roughly 8.4 grams]."[41]

2.8. JUDAEAN PARALLELS TO OTHER ANCIENT WEIGHT SYSTEMS

Weight	Judaean	Egyptian-Ugaritic	Phoenicia-Ashdod-Mesopot.
91.20 g	8 *sheqels*	1 *deben* (10 *qedet*)	12 *sheqels*
45.60 g	4 *sheqels*	1/2 *deben*	6 *sheqels*
11.4 g	1 *sheqels*	*	*
9.12 g	*nezef*	*qedet/sheqel*	*
7.60 g	*pym*	*	1 *sheqel*

*No known correlation

After the four- and eight-*sheqel* weights, the two-*sheqel*, *pym*, and *nezef* are the most common. Thus the one *sheqel* weight and its smaller fractions are rarer than the aforementioned weights. This scarcity is probably because the single *sheqel* and its fractions (other than the *nezef* and *pym*) were used mainly for local trade.

What then can we make of the various Biblical references to the "current money with the merchant" (Genesis 23:16), the "*sheqel* of the sanctuary" (Exodus 30:13), and *sheqels* of "the king's weight"? (II Samuel 14:26).

These are possibly simply references that are being used in this way to illustrate a number of differing weight standards simultaneously used in ancient Israel during the Biblical period.

With regard specifically to Judaean weights, Kletter has pointed out that they have been found "in 'secular' contexts, public or private. Furthermore, I doubt if the holy *sheqel* ever existed in Iron Age Judah. It probably reflects a utopian plan which did not exist (even during the times of the Priestly Code and Ezekiel)."[42]

The vast majority of the known weights of Judah during the Iron Age II period were limestone dome weights. Bronze weights of other shapes with similar Hebrew or Phoenician inscriptions that have been published are most probably contemporary with the Judaean weights but may have been made and used outside of Judah for trading purposes.

(This chapter is adapted from my book *Ancient Scale Weights and Pre-Coinage Currency*).[43]

CHAPTER THREE

PERSIAN PERIOD: PHILISTIA

In 1914 George Hill devoted a number of pages to coins he referred to as "Philisto-Arabian" and "Egypto-Arabian" in the *British Museum Catalogue on the Greek Coins of Palestine.* Even then Hill observed that these headings were "not very satisfactory"[1] for the earliest known coins struck in ancient Palestine. These coins have more accurately been referred to as "Philistian" by Haim Gitler, curator of numismatics at the Israel Museum, and Oren Tal, lecturer in Near Eastern Studies at Tel Aviv University. Philistia, they note, "is a geographical rather than an ethnic term. The fact that Gaza was the southernmost Palestinian minting authority bordering Arabian domination rather than being under Arabian rule, lends support to our understanding of these coins as Philistian."[2] Ancient Palestine is also a geographic term that is used in this book synonymously with the ancient land of Israel, Holy Land, or southern Levant.

Philistia is the portion of southwestern ancient Palestine that was occupied by the Philistines in the Old Testament period. The Philistine confederacy of five city-states included Ashqelon, Ashdod, Gaza, Gat (Gath), and Ekron. This area was influenced by Phoenicia and Egypt as well as some of the other Mediterranean metropolises. Leo Mildenberg observed that at that time, "Sidon and (Tyre) had developed their main coinages, the heavy denominations. Gaza is their counterpart, being the best of ports in the South. Her importance as the final destination of the desert routes and major junction of the coastal roads can hardly be overestimated."[3] Indeed Gaza was the central Philistian mint.

The ancient Near East is possibly the specific location "where metal economy was first initiated, which only later was modified into a proper monetary economy in Ionia and Greece."[4]

Before we discuss the coinage of the Persian Period, it is important to recall the portion of the ancient economy in which early coins were intermingled with small pieces of metal. Earlier I discussed the weighing of metal in the form of small silver ingots, hacked from larger dumped castings, called *hacksilber*, documented in Palestine as early as the Middle Bronze Age (2200–1550 BCE). Some of the *hacksilber* hoards also included bits of silver jewelry and chopped pieces of foreign silver coins. Use of *hacksilber* "as a unified form of payment" was prominent in the Iron Age II Period (1000–586 BCE) in the southern Levant. This use of metal may point to a "pre-coinage stage, an 'underground economy' in Iron Age Palestine, in which cut units of controlled standard weights constitute a metal economy which existed in the region prior to the traditional date of the 'invention' of coinage in the Greco-Lydian milieu of Western Asia Minor between 630 and 600 BCE,"[5] according to Gitler and Tal.

From multiple excavations in modern Israel and Palestine we have learned that hoards of *hacksilber* were often wrapped in cloth bags and sealed with one or more clay bullae, which would indicate who had guaranteed the purity and weight of the silver. These small bags are possibly the biblical *zror kesef* referred to in Genesis 42:35:

> ... *as they emptied their sacks, that, behold, every man's bundle of money was in his sack; and when they and their father saw their bundles of money, they were afraid.*

Quite a few archaic Greek silver coins of city-states from the sixth and early fifth centuries BCE have been found in the ancient land of Israel. These were the first coins to circulate in the area.

Many of those early coins were deliberately cut into rough halves, thirds, and quarters, or even smaller fractions. "We assume that they circulated as bullion. In some cases this widespread, intentional cutting may have accorded to a set of standards. This is also evident from their appearance in coin hoards together with jewelry dated mainly to the late sixth and fifth centuries BCE,"[6] write Gitler and Tal.

Even though archaic Greek coins made their appearance in areas of the Near East as early as the end of the sixth century BCE throughout the fifth century BCE, I have already noted that most or all commercial transactions continued to be carried out using weighed silver.

The transition from weighing silver to trading in struck coins was a lengthy one, and even the first coins were seen mainly as a source of bullion of a certain quality and weight. A next step would have been use of the coins themselves as more convenient than the little sacks filled with bits of *hacksilber*. This in turn led to the need for a local production of coins in the economic trading centers in and near Philistia. The local economic systems of ancient Palestine—Philistian, Samarian, Edomite, and Judaean—have quite small denominations as their most prevalent feature. These small silver coins may have reminded the people of the small pieces of *hacksilber* that continued to circulate alongside for many years.

The first issues of Philistian coins were struck just after 450 BCE. These coins tend to be patterned after their Athenian predecessors, but they expand into a number of fascinating oriental motifs such as the sphinx, local cult figures, flora, and fauna. The Philistian coins are among the most creatively conceived and executed of the entire ancient world.

A number of the Philistian coins contain so-called "elusive motifs." These are optical illusions that provide more than one way to look at a coin. Such designs are also known from a few coins of Lesbos and Samaria, but they are more prevalent in the Philistian coinage. For example, one tiny silver coin depicts a male head right wearing a cap; closer inspection reveals that the cap is really a dog's head facing in the opposite direction (No. 1024). Another pair of silver coins depicts what appears to be a helmeted, bearded oriental male bust to right. However, rotation of these coins by 90 degrees clockwise shows that they also depict a standing lion with his head turned back (Nos. 1021, 1022).

During the Persian Period in ancient Palestine there were several coin "series" in simultaneous circulation. Philistia, Judah, Samaria, and Edom each issued coinage that was mostly limited to use within specific and rather small regions. On the other hand, Phoenician cities such as Tyre, Sidon, Byblos, and Arados, issued a regional currency that circulated much more widely. It is no coincidence that this group of cities along the Mediterranean coast, where the earliest coins of the Levant were minted, lie along the ancient trade route known as the "Via Maris" or "Way of the Sea" (ISAIAH 8:23). In Israel today, this route is known as the Coastal Highway.

Philistian silver coins were probably autonomous local issues. Mildenberg notes, "The north of the satrapy was, obviously, a territory for the plentiful, long lasting coinage of the great cities at the sea: Arados, Byblos, Sidon, Tyros. The central area remained a large empty spot on the numismatic map until the finds of the thirties and early seventies appeared and suddenly unveiled an abundant provincial coinage of small silver struck by the Persian governors of Samaria and Judah. Not only do the names of these two provinces appear on these tiny coins, but also the names of governors, one with this title."[7]

Exactly which authority issued the early coins of Philistia is not known. Names of three cities appear on the coins—Gaza, Ashqelon, and Ashdod. Several coins also mention either the name Yehud or its first letter, *yod* (Nos. 1047, 1048). In general, the coins of Philistia are of similar fabric and design. Many of them copied Greek coin types, especially Athenian images, but there were other colorful and local images, such as the sphinx, local cult figures, flora, and fauna. "This kind of money could only come into being in that distant Southern area of transit under the astonishing rule of the late Persian Great Kings who had delegated power and guaranteed ethnic and religious freedom and local autonomy to their citizens," according to Mildenberg.[8]

DENOMINATIONS IN THE PERSIAN PERIOD

Studies by Oren Tal have expanded our discussion of denominations of the coins of the Persian Period. The silver coins of Philistia, Samaria, Edom, and Yehud have been catalogued for years as *tetradrachms*, *drachms*, and *obols* or simply fractions of them. Based on the earlier studies of Yigal Ronen, Tal concludes that *all* of the silver coins struck in these biblical lands were based upon *sheqel* standards, although the weight of the *sheqel* probably varied from place to place.[9]

As epigraphic evidence regarding the coins of Philistia, Tal points to a series of bronze weights in the shape of animals or truncated pyramids found in excavations at Ashqelon. Some of these weights carry Phoenician letters, which can be attributed to the Persian Period, although it is not certain whether these letters refer to the denominations of the weights or the specific standard, or perhaps other initials."[10] Based on the numismatic evidence, Tal suggests possible *sheqel* standards shown in table 3.1.

Today it seems strange for different monetary weight standards to exist in areas so near to each other, yet history bears this out. We know, for example, that Sidon and Tyre each had their own weight standards in ancient times. Even in modern times there are different monetary systems in neighboring lands. In Europe, for example, Great Britain and Switzerland use their own financial systems while their neighbors have converted to the system of Euros. The United States currency differs from the currency of Canada and Mexico. In the early twentieth century, the weight systems in Ottoman and British Palestine had different standards in the north, the south, and in Hebron, which had its own special standard. Y. Nevo observes that at that time "it was possible to weigh goods in Jaffa, for example, where the southern unit was customary, by means of northern weight units, provided that the nature of the units was clear to the parties involved in the transaction."[12]

Unfortunately, scant written evidence relates the *sheqel* to the Greek *stater*, but one reference in the fifth century BCE Elephantine papyri suggests there are two *sheqels* in one *stater*. This relationship must not refer to any of the *sheqel* standards discussed above, since the Attic *stater* weighed around 17.2 grams. However, there were numerous Babylonian and related *sheqel* weight standards from around 7.6 to 8.6 grams, and the reference may easily have been to these.

Ephraim Stern concludes "with a large measure of certainty that in the Persian Period, alongside the Babylonian-Persian system of weights...a local system existed in Palestine which preserved the ancient Hebrew names though it was based on a different standard..."[13]

The Samarian and Philistian weight standards are extremely close to each other, while the Edomite and Judaean standards differ significantly. Consistency is also affected because it is known that the smallest denominations of silver coins have the greatest range of weight in any particular series. The reason is because it was more difficult to regulate production of such tiny coins.

Discussion of these standards and denominations also relate closely to the annual tribute tax for the Jewish Temple. André Lemaire suggests that the annual Jewish Temple tax was one-third of a *sheqel* during the days of Nehemiah (10:33) and was later raised to a half *sheqel*, as referenced in the New Testament. Tal points out that the heavier

3.1. WEIGHT STANDARD AND CONTENT DIFFERENCES[11]

	Average Weight	Average AR Content	Amount of Silver
Edomite *Sheqel*	15.96 g	96.4%	15.38 g
Judaean *Sheqel*	11.33 g	97.0%	10.99 g
Samarian *Sheqel*	14.52 g	91.8%	13.32 g
Philistian *Sheqel*	14.32 g	94.3%	13.50 g

Edomite "quarter" was about equal to a "third" of a *sheqel* of Judah, and suggests that it would not be farfetched to suggest a Jewish religious duty by some Edomites, which accounts for this weight equivalent.[14]

Tal also suggests that some of the variations in silver standards during this early period had to do with the purity of the silver, with the coins of Judah having the highest silver content of 97 percent, since this level of purity was required for the Temple.

Overall there is a great deal to consider here, and good reason to carefully watch future excavation reports and translations of documents for further clues. In the meantime, I easily agree with Tal's conclusion that "the identification of a Greek (Attic) denominational system and weight standard in Palestinian coinages of the fourth century BCE is not likely. A local denominational system and weight standards based on the *sheqel* and its fractions should be preferred."[15]

ASHDOD

Modern Ashdod is the fifth largest city and largest port in Israel, with more than 200,000 inhabitants. It is on the Mediterranean coast not far from the archaeological ruins. Ancient Ashdod is mentioned in the Bible several times, notably as one of the five city-states of the Philistines:

> *And these are the golden emerods which the Philistines returned for a guilt offering unto the LORD: for Ashdod one, for Gaza one, for Askelon one, for Gath one, for Ekron one* (I SAMUEL 6:17).

Ashdod's history goes back to around the seventeenth century BCE, and people of Ashdod with north-west Semitic names are mentioned in Ugaritic texts dating to the fourteenth–thirteenth centuries BCE. Some of its citizens were known to be merchants of garments and purple wool.

During the Persian Period, Ashdod was conquered in 605 BCE by Nebuchadnezzar; in 539 BCE it was rebuilt by the Persians, and was later conquered by Alexander the Great. It was known as a prosperous trading center. Nehemiah reported that he saw:

...the Jews that had married women of Ashdod, of Ammon, and of Moab; and their children spoke half in the speech of Ashdod, and could not speak in the Jews' language, but according to the language of each people" (NEHEMIAH 13:23–34).

This means that the Ashdodites probably spoke a Philistine dialect of Aramaic and in addition to their language, many customs and social relationships were probably intertwined.

ASHQELON (ASCALON)

Thy beauty, O Israel, upon thy high places is slain! How are the mighty fallen. Tell it not in Gath, Publish it not in Ashqelon; Lest the daughters of the Philistines rejoice, Lest the daughters of the uncircumcised triumph (II SAMUEL 19–20).

Ashqelon is a coastal city just north of Gaza and around 36 miles south of Tel Aviv. It was another of the five Philistine cities listed in the book of Samuel.

Ashqelon is also the place where Delilah cut Samson's hair in order to drain his strength (JUDGES 14–16). Modern Ashqelon, just north of Tel Ashqelon, is a city of fewer than 100,000. During much of 1968, I lived and worked at an agricultural high school named Kfar Silver, on the outskirts of Ashqelon. On my days off I drove my Vespa to Ashqelon's beautiful beach, where remnants of Roman ruins jutted out from hillsides overlooking the Mediterranean. Pottery fragments and coins were easy to find scattered on the sand.

Ashqelon is one of the oldest cities in recorded history; it was first settled toward the end of the third millennium BCE. It is mentioned in some of the Amarna letters of the fourteenth century BCE and was conquered by the Philistines in the second half of the twelfth century BCE.

Beginning in 1985, Harvard's Lawrence Stager has led The Leon Levy Expedition, the most extensive excavations of ancient Ashqelon to date. The excavation has revealed a great deal of accumulated rubble from Canaanite, Philistine, Phoenician, Hellenistic, Roman, Byzantine, and Crusader occupation.

According to these excavations, the Persian Period occupation of Ashqelon extended from the sixth to the fourth centuries BCE and the city's population was mainly Phoenician.

A mysterious burial ground of the Persian Period was discovered containing the remains of several hundred dogs. Animal anthropologists identified all the dogs as greyhounds; each was placed in its own grave with its tail wrapped around the back of the body, tail pointing downward. At the time of the discovery, Stager was quoted in *The New York Times*: "You run across buried animals all over the Middle East. In Egypt, there are several pet cemeteries, where cats and other animals were mummified and buried. But this is not a pet cemetery. It's just for dogs, all the same breed, and a huge concentration of them."[16]

Phoenicians, at this time, revered dogs as sacred animals; they were connected to the cult of Ashtoret (Astarte) or possibly with a local version of Asklepios. Similar but much smaller dog burials have also been found in excavations from this period at Ashdod.

GAZA

And the border of the Canaanite was from Sidon...unto Gaza (GENESIS 10:19).

Gaza was the southernmost and largest of the Philistine city-states that issued coinage with its own name during the Persian Period. Thus the three coastal city-states struck coins, while the two inland city-states of Ekron and Gat did not. This is logical since currency for trade would be more important to a coastal trading city than to a land-locked area. Yehud and Samaria were also inland, but because they were both major religious centers they had specific financial needs.

Today Gaza is the largest city in the highly politicized Gaza Strip. When I lived in Israel during 1967–68, Gaza was only a short bus ride from my home in Ashqelon. My many walks through the Gaza markets revealed an abundance of local weights and coins for sale in the shops and stalls.

Although the city is certainly older, the first written mention of Gaza was during the fifteenth century BCE by Pharaoh Thutmose II (Eighteenth Dynasty). It is also mentioned later in the famous Amarna letters of correspondence between the administration of Egypt and its representatives in Canaan.

Gaza was an important stop on various trade routes, as well as the largest port in the area during the Persian Period. Thus, the people needed currency for local and international trade. Uriel Rappaport notes that, "The commercially dominant position of Gaza in Palestine is well attested by the numismatic data of the Persian Period. The coins of Gaza played a remarkable role in the currency of Palestine in that period. Many coins of Gaza, and many others attributed to its mint, are still extant. The importance of this coinage and its relation to international trade is evident from its resemblance to Athenian coins, which were then the regular international currency."[17]

Among the early coins of Gaza are silver *sheqels* (*tetradrachms*) and tiny silver 1/24 *sheqels* or *ma'in* (*obols*) resembling those of Athens, but carrying on their reverse the Phoenician letter ꤊ (*mem*), abbreviating the name of Marnas, chief god of Gaza, along with an owl and the AΘE ethnic of Athens. Other early coins of Gaza imitating Athenian types carry the Phoenician letters ο (*'ayin*) and ~ (*zion*) for *'Az*, abbreviating *'Aza*, the Hebrew (and Philistian/Phoenican) name for Gaza. Some coins carry only the *'ayin*.

The Persian satrap, Mazaeus (Mazday on coins, c. 361–334 BCE), was the governor of Cilicia as well as the land of *Eber Nahara* for some period of time. Mazaeus issued coins with the inscription "Mazday, who is over *Eber Nahara* and Cilicia." Mazaeus also had his name or initials placed on coins struck in Sidon and Samaria. It has been suggested that the early Gaza coins with the letter *mem* may actually refer to Mazaeus. However, since the *mem* mintmark was used on coins of Gaza continually from as early as the late fifth century BCE through the third century CE, an attribution to the local god Marnas rather than Mazaeus seems likely.

JUDAH

> *...I will give all Judah into the hand of the king of Babylon, and he shall carry them captive to Babylon...* (JEREMIAH 20: 4).

The name *Yehud* (Persian for Judah) was struck on at least two Philistian quarter-*sheqels* (Nos. 1045 and 1046) and the initial *yod*, its first letter, was struck on both quarter-*sheqels* and *ma'ah-obols* (Nos. 1047, 1048). These coins were manufactured on the Philistian weight standards, and in design and fabric resemble the Philistian coins and not the Yehud issues struck later and used in and around the Jerusalem area. One coin, No. 1049, possibly a quarter-*sheqel*, is of special interest because it relates to the Judaean weight standard, and it carries the name *yhwd* in four letters along with the ○ (*'ayin*), one of the traditional mintmarks of Gaza. This clue suggests that the earliest series of Yehud coins, all of which are either unique or extremely rare, may have been struck at Gaza for use in Judah, and later a mint was established in the Jerusalem area. Gitler and Tal have noted that both generic "Philistian" and specific coins of Gaza were minted at the same mint.[18] Gitler also confirms that there is now additional evidence for the increased probability of an initial central mint in Philistia.[19] These coins are discussed in the next chapter.

EDOM

> *And Jacob sent messengers before him to Esau his brother unto the land of Seir, the field of Edom* (GENESIS 32: 4).

The Edomites were a Semitic-speaking tribe that lived in the area of the Negev Desert and the Aravah Valley near the south of the Dead Sea and into the area of southern Jordan. Some believe the word Edom was derived from the area's extensive red sandstone features; *adom* is the Hebrew word for red.

Previously Edomite coins were not known, but the first possible Edomite coins were explained by Tal, Gitler, and Van Alfen. They discuss a previously unknown group of "peculiar Athenian-styled Palestinian coins" that were struck from dies that had very worn obverses which were recut, repolished, and reused to strike coins. The results depict an obverse that is not more than dome-shaped, with no traces of Athena's head visible. "The coins' distribution suggests that they circulated in the boundaries of what we define as Edom in the later part of the Persian Period and might well have been the silver money mentioned in several of the Edomite ostraca."[20]

Ostraca are pottery fragments that were used as note paper in ancient times. They contain various communications or records. Some, written in Aramaic, were discovered at Tel Arad, and they discuss monetary units of *ksp* or *kesef* in Hebrew or Aramaic, which refer both to silver and to money. The units of *kesef* in the Tel Arad ostraca are "s" (for *sheqel*), "r" (for *rebah*) or quarter, and "m" (for either *ma'ah* or *maneh*), probably a smaller denomination that seems to be parallel to the *gerah* (1/24 of a Judaean *sheqel*). Tal also points to a late fourth century BCE papyrus discovered near Jericho and additional Aramaic ostraca discovered at Tel Be'er Sheva; all of the references to *sheqel*, quarter, and *ma'ah* suggest "a vivid monetary economy in fourth-century BCE Edom in which the sheqel contained four quarters and each quarter contained six *ma'ahs*" (*ma'in* is the Hebrew plural).

"This denomination system is in fact similar to that of the Attic weight standard, even though the weights of the *sheqel* and Attic *tetradrachm* differ. In the Attic system it was the *tetradrachm* which formed the basic unit of weight, equal to four *drachms*, with the *drachm* corresponding to six *obols*."[21] The average weight of the possible Edomite coins suggests a *sheqel* standard of around 15.96 grams.

The local coinage of Philistia, Samaria, and Yehud is referred to by names that might have been used at the time they circulated. Hence the silver coins are referred to as *sheqels*, quarter-*sheqels*, and *ma'ah-obols*, while the tiny Persian Period coins of Yehud will be referred to as *gerahs* and the Macedonian and Ptolemaic Yehud coins are called *ma'ah-obols*.

TEST CUTS

Test cuts frequently appear on the quarter-*sheqels* (*drachms*) of Philistia, and less frequently on the *sheqels* and small denominations. Test cuts were made by a chisel in order to determine whether a coin was pure silver. Contrary to a general belief, the silver-plated, or fourrée, coins were not necessarily forgeries. Gitler and Tal observe that "Whether Philistian silver-plated coins were minted by the authorities in certain circumstances (*e.g.* shortage of silver bullion), or produced as fraudulent coins, is difficult to know. It is worth noting that the production of coin with bronze-, lead-, or copper-alloy cores should not be defined, *a priori*, as *falsa moneta*....[in some cases] counterfeits could have been tolerated by the authorities, if they contributed to the stability of economic conditions."[22]

There were also a large number of fourrée coins struck in Samaria during the same period and both silver coins and *fourrée* coins are known to have been struck from the same pair of dies.[23]

In Philistia, Gitler and Tal note, the earliest coins were struck over a span of some 110 years, yet there are only a small number known to exist. This suggests "that minting was carried out intermittently according to the needs of the local market in authorized metal workshops by metal smiths. It is therefore reasonable to assume that during this period there was no justification for the existence of a formal urban mint constantly engaged in the minting of royal or autonomous coins. Accordingly, after the coins were produced, the officials in charge would have sampled a certain number of pieces in order to test the purity of the metal."[24]

With a decentralized minting operation it is easy to see how, for example, a government official might bring a weight of silver to a workshop, for which he would expect a specific number of coins to be delivered. The smith might have decided to take a bit of extra payment for himself. He could do so by producing a small quantity of the fourrée coins and salting them into his delivery batch, hence netting additional profit.

Gitler and Tal also suggest that the test cuts are not random and usually appear at angles and locations, deliberately placed in order to minimize damage to central motifs on the coins.

ASHDOD

Philistian *sheqel* standard 14.32 g; see photos for correct size
Average quarter-*sheqel* 3.58 g
Average *ma'ah-obol* 0.65 g

1001   1002

1001.   AR quarter-*sheqel,* one published 3.67 g.
Obv: Hybrid head; male surmounted by forepart of a lion on the
    forehead (as headdress) facing l. and grotesque figure r., all within
    a twisted-rope circle.
Rev: ꓩꓩ∨⋆ *('Ashdod)* above double-protome bull bending forelegs,
    surrounded by twisted-rope (guilloche) border set in incuse
    square.   6,000/15,000

1002.   AR quarter-*sheqel,* one published 3.39 g.
Obv: Head r. wearing oriental headdress, hair arranged as a ponytail
    and knotted at bottom; ornamented ear with earring resembling
    ankh, within dotted circle.
Rev: ꓩꓩ∨⋆ *('Ashdod)* above ibex standing r., head turned back, lily
    (?) bent to right behind, surrounded by cable border in incuse
    square.   6,000/15,000

1003

1003.   AR *ma'ah-obol.*
Obv: Satyr head r. with oriental hair style.
Rev: ∨⋆ *('Ash[dod])* above bull walking r., concealed owl in bull's
    body.   2,000/5,000

ASHQELON

1004

1004.   AR *sheqel,* one published 16.86 g.
   Obv: Helmeted head of Athena r. The helmet is adorned with one erect olive-leaf and two *udjat* eyes appear between olive leaf and palmette.
   Rev: ꜥꜣ (*'A[sql]n*) in upper r. field, owl faces front, wings spread; upper l. field olive spray, all in incuse square.   RRR

1005.   AR quarter-*sheqel.*
   Obv: Helmeted head of Athena r.
   Rev: AΘE downward on r., ꜥ (*'A[sql]*) to l.; owl r., head facing, olive spray and crescent upper l., all within incuse square.
                                                        6,000/15,000

1006.   AR quarter-*sheqel,* one specimen published 3.80 grams.
   Obv: Janiform bearded male r. and female l., oriental hairstyle.
   Rev: ꜥ retrograde in upper r. field, ꜣ retrograde in lower r. field (*'A[sql]n*); owl r. head facing; two vertical recumbent lions, all in incuse square.   RRR

1007.   AR *ma'ah-obol.*
   Obv: Archaic oriental style female head r. within border of dots.
   Rev: ꜥꜣ (*'A[sql]n*) upper left; owl r., head facing, olive sprigs upper l.
                                                        2,000/5,000

GAZA

1008

1008. AR *sheqel*, 17.16 grams (Athenian standard, one specimen
published).
Obv: Helmeted head of Athena r.
Rev: ○ in lower r. field, ﹀ in lower l. field *('Az[a])*; owl facing front,
wings closed, in upper r. and l. fields olive sprays, all in incuse
square.   RRR

1009. AR *sheqel*, 16.79 grams (Athenian standard, one specimen
published).
Obv: Helmeted head of Athena r.
Rev: AΘE downward on r., two ካ flank it; owl r., head facing, olive
spray and crescent upper l., all within incuse square.   RRR

1010

1010. AR quarter-*sheqel*.
Obv: Janiform bearded male head, oriental hairstyle.
Rev: ﹀○ *('Az)* in upper field; antithetic gryphon-styled animals with
elongated necks, stylized as a wing with bovine's head; between
the heads female head with Hathor hairstyle faces front, all
in a guilloche-pattern border within incuse square.

3,000/8,000

1011.   AR quarter-*sheqel.*
   Obv: Head of Athena r. in crested helmet, ꜩ on cheek.
   Rev: AΘE downward on r.; owl.   2,500/6,000

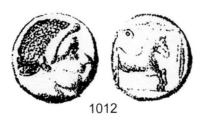

1012

1012.   AR quarter-*sheqel.*
   Obv: Bearded male head r., oriental headdress and hair bunched in
        back.
   Rev: ○~ (r. to l., '*Az*) above forepart of horse r.
                                                 2,000/5,000

1013.   AR *ma'ah-obol.*
   Obv: Janiform head, bearded male head l., female head r. Eyes are
        full, frontal, and hair is represented by granulated parallel lines.
   Rev: ○~ (r. to l., '*Az*) above forepart of horse r.   500/1,500

1014.   AR *ma'ah-obol.*
   Obv: Helmeted head of Athena r.
   Rev: AΘE downward on r. ꜩ, to its left; owl r., head facing, olive spray
        and crescent upper l., all within incuse square.   500/1,500

1015.   AR *ma'ah-obol.*
   Obv: Helmeted head of Athena r.
   Rev: AΘE downward on r.; owl r., head facing, olive spray upper l.
        and below it ○ ('*A[z]*), with, all within incuse square.
                                                 500/1,500

PHILISTIA

Philistian *sheqel* standard 14.32 g
Average quarter *sheqel* 3.58 g
Average *ma'ah-obol* 0.65 g

1016

1016.   *AR sheqel,* two published 17.05 g and 14.85 g.
  Obv: Helmeted head of Athena to r., the helmet adorned with three olive leaves and a palmette.
  Rev: Triple turreted city wall upon a rampart, two palm trees between the towers, a crouching lion in the forefield, all in incuse square.   RRR

1017

1017.   AR quarter-*sheqel.*
  Obv: Male head facing with female head right, with headdress. A more careful look will show that the headdress is a fierce, recumbent lion with head turned back, and between the two heads, facing right, an additional nose and mouth form a third additional profile to r.
  Rev: Helmeted head of Athena to right, with linear devices or monograms possibly appearing in some or all corners, all in incuse square.   3,000/8,000

1018   1020

1018. AR quarter-*sheqel.*
    Obv: Bearded male head l., with bunched hair represented by paral-
    lel granulations.
    Rev: ⅄ above r., ⅄ above l., ᵘ below l., and ᴴ below r.; paradise
    flower or Phoenician palmette.   3,000/8,000
    This coin was previously described (GBC 4: 435) as a Yehud coin, based
upon the discovery of a specimen that seemed to show clear letters ꟼꟼ⅄ (Yhd).
But upon examination of better preserved specimens, Gitler & Tal show this
type to clearly belong to the Philistian series. The legend is not yet understood.

1019. AR quarter-*sheqel, one specimen published 3.10 g.*
    Obv: Janiform bearded male r. and male l., oriental hairstyle.
    Rev: Bes stands facing, raised hands hold knife (?) in r. hand fights
    prancing lion in r. field; below and between the two figures hel-
    met or shield (?), within cable border and incuse square.   RRR

1020. AR quarter-*sheqel.*
    Obv: Antithetic standing horses frame two facing Bes heads; in up-
    per field ⅄ (bet); pearled guilloche border all in incuse square.
    Rev: Hybrid of male head to r. and bearded male facing, oriental
    hairstyle; pearled guilloche border all within incuse square.
                                        3,000/8,000

1021, 2 reverse orientations

1022, 2 reverse orientations   1024

1021. AR quarter-*sheqel*.
Obv: Male head r., oriental hair style, guilloche border.
Rev: Lion protome r. and hind part l., create the illusion of a full lion with head turned back. When turned 90 degrees counter clockwise, the type appears to be a bearded and helmeted male head r., border of dots all within incuse square.   3,000/8,000

1022. AR *ma'ah-obol*.
Obv: Male head r., oriental hairstyle, guilloche border.
Rev: Lion stands to l., head turned back. When the coin is turned 90 degrees counter clockwise, the main motif appears to be a bearded helmeted male r. with a helmet formed by the lion's body, within dotted border and incuse square.   1,000/3,000

1023. AR *ma'ah-obol*.
Obv: Helmeted head of Athena to r., helmet adorned with three leaves and palmette.
Rev: AΘE downward on r .; owl r. head facing, olive spray and crescent upper l., lily or possibly lotus between the Greek legend and the owl, all within incuse square.   750/2,000
Some suggest this type and similar larger and smaller denominations are products of the Jerusalem mint. While this is certainly possible, Gitler and Tal's identification of the flower as a lotus bud rather than the lily, closely associated with Jerusalem, coincides with the Egyptian theme in many of the coins of Philistia.[25]

1024. *AR ma'ah-obol*.
Obv: Head of bearded male right, his cap is a canine head left, probably showing open jaws, but could also be seen as closed-jaws.
Rev: AΘE downward on r.; owl r., head facing, olive spray and crescent upper l., lily or possibly lotus between the Greek legend and the owl, all within incuse square.   1,000/3,000

EDOM

Edomite *sheqel* standard 15.96 g
Average quarter-*sheqel* 3.99 g
Average *ma'ah-obol* 0.74 g

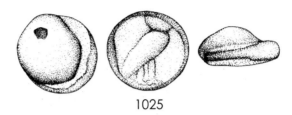

1025

1025. AR quarter-*sheqel*.
   Obv: Prominent dome shape rising sharply from coin's lowest flat
   plain.
   Rev: Owl r., head facing, olive spray and crescent upper l. are some-
   times visible, AΘE downward on r, all within incuse square.
   These coins were struck from worn, recut, and repolished dies.

   350/1,000

1026. AR *ma'ah-obol*.
   Obv: Dome shape rising sharply from coin's lowest flat plain.
   Rev: Owl r., head facing, olive spray and crescent upper l. are some-
   times visible, AΘE downward on r, all within incuse square.

   350/1,000

CHAPTER FOUR

PERSIAN PERIOD: SAMARIA & JUDAH

The coins of Samaria and Judah circulated mainly in their own territories, yet their history has so many connections that our initial discussion overlaps.

Both Judah (*Yehud*) and Samaria (*Shomron*) were provinces of the Fifth Satrapy of Persia, ruled from Tarsus in Cilicia. They were part of the vast territory known as *Eber Nahar*, "the land beyond the [Euphrates] river," today also referred to as Trans-Euphrates. Each of these provinces was ruled by a local governor or high priest; each had the same name as its capital city. With regard to Shomron, "The distinction between the city and the province...appears in one of the Wadi Daliyeh papyri from the time of Darius III, which mentions the place where it was signed: *Smryn* the capital city which is in *Smryn* the province [or country],"[1] according to Meshorer and Qedar. Both today are referred to as Samaria, although the city itself has been known as Sebaste since Roman times. Yehud was the Aramaic name for the Persian satrapy of Judah. The name Yehud was used as a local stamp on pottery jar handles until the second century BCE when it was replaced by Jerusalem.

While there were distinct religious and political similarities between Judah and Samaria during the Persian Period, there were also long-standing differences that began around 930 BCE when the United Kingdom of Israel was divided by conflicts after the death of King Solomon. Israel's twelve tribes split. Solomon's son Rehoboam led the tribes of Judah and Benjamin to the south, and this territory became the Southern Kingdom of Judah. The other 10 tribes, led by Jeroboam, one of Solomon's military advisors, settled in the Northern Kingdom called Israel, which was about the approximate territory today known as the Galilee and Samaria.

Samaria in Hebrew is *Shomron,* based on a root meaning "guard" or "watch." As capital of the Northern Kingdom of Israel, Samaria was literally a lookout point in the midst of the mountains along the west bank of the Jordan River and north of the Jerusalem hills. The ruins of the ancient city of Sebaste sit atop of a rocky hill, with the modern city spread out on its slopes.

The Old Testament tells a different story of how Samaria was named in the thirty-first year of Asa, king of Judah, when King Omri reigned over Israel for twelve years. For the first six years of his reign his capital was Tirzah. Then:

He bought the hill of Samaria of Shemer for two talents of silver; and he built on the hill and called the name of the city which he built, after the name of Shemer, the owner of the hill, Samaria (I KINGS 16: 24).

The hilly area around the city was known as the region of Samaria, which, in biblical times, stretched from the Jordan Valley to the Mediterranean Sea and included the Sharon plains. Before it was founded by Omri as his capital, around 879 BCE, Samaria was an agricultural center for producing wine and olive oil. Omri put it on the map, as witnessed by later Assyrian texts in which it is referred to as "Beth-khumri" or the "house of Omri."

Under Ahab and his queen, Jezebel, Samaria was built into a well-fortified, wealthy capital. Jezebel was a Phoenician princess, and she spurned the Israelite god and turned her husband away from Jewish worship and toward worship of the Phoenician Ba'al. Their full stories are told in 1 and 2 Kings.

In 723 BCE, the Assyrians conquered the Northern Kingdom, and brought the Kingdom of Israel to an end. In II Kings 17:24, we learn that most of Samaria's inhabitants after this time were resettled there by the Assyrians from remote places such as Babylonia, Syria, and Cuthah. Contrary to this, however, some scholars believe that a large number of the inhabitants of Samaria after 723 BCE were Israelites. Meshorer and Qedar suggest that, "There is some truth in both theories and it seems that due to the high percentage of Israelites in the area, the conglomerate of people who lived there had accepted the Hebrew Law."[2]

Assyrian ruins have been found in the excavations at Samaria, and one relief at Sargon's Palace at Khorsabad in Northern Iraq (Room

5) seems to depict the defeated Samarians.[3] The Assyrian rule ended in 612 BCE and briefly Judah and Egypt competed for hegemony over Samaria.

The governing family of Samaria had a long and tense relationship with Jerusalem which is reported in Ezra 4:10 and Nehemiah 2:1–8. After Alexander III defeated Darius III at the Battle of Issos in 333 BCE, Samaria became a Hellenistic town. By permission of Alexander the Great, and the Persian governor Sanballat II, the Samarians built a temple upon Mt. Gerizim dedicated to Yahweh, which competed directly with the Jerusalem Temple. This led to a final split between the Samaritan and Jewish religions. The Samaritan religion accepts the Torah (Five Books of Moses) and the Book of Joshua as its holy books, but disregards later Jewish theology. Up until today the Samaritans believe that Mt. Gerizim was the original Holy Place of the people of Israel and according to the Old Testament, this tradition goes back to the time when Moses ordered Joshua to take the Twelve Tribes of Israel to the mountains of Shechem and put half of the tribes on top of Mt. Gerizim—"the Mount of Blessing"—and the other half on Mt Ebal—"the Mount of the Curse." These historic mountains were used to symbolize the good and the bad with regard to those who followed the commandments.

The numismatic history of Samaria and Judah begin toward the end of the Persian period. Samaritan coins were minted fairly consistently between around 375 to 333 BCE while the Yehud coins were minted less frequently, between around 400 to 260 BCE.[4] Other than the coins, several references in Ezra, Nehemiah, and Chronicles, and a few manuscripts and ostraca, history knows little of these years. It is generally believed that around 400 BCE "the Samaritans were still considered Jewish, and as such were approached by the Jews of Elephantine [or Yeb, a small island in the Nile with an active Jewish population at this time]. The Samaritan high priests and governors in the fifth and fourth centuries bear Jewish names as recorded in the Elephantine documents and the Wadi Daliyeh papyri."[5]

The final separation between the Samaritans and the Jews probably evolved in the last years before Alexander the Great conquered the area. According to Josephus, it was Manasseh, a member of the high priest's family in Jerusalem, who left for Samaria, married Nikaso the daughter of Sanballat the governor of Samaria and became the high priest of the newly built temple on Mt. Gerizim. This temple was destroyed late in the second century BCE by Hyrcanus I, and the territory was later annexed by his son Alexander Jannaeus into lands ruled by the Hasmoneans under Greek hegemony.

Modern scientific methods add credibility to the written records regarding Samaria's occupants. A 2004 genetic study by Shedong Shen of Stanford University, who led a group that analyzed the genetic material of Samaritan families, concluded that the Samaritan "lineages present a subgroup of the original Jewish *Cohanim* priesthood that did not go into exile when the Assyrians conquered the northern kingdom of Israel in 723 BCE but married Assyrian and female exiles relocated from other conquered lands, which was a typical Assyrian policy to obliterate national identities. This is in line with biblical texts that emphasize a common heritage of Jews and Samaritans, but also record the negative attitude of Jews towards the Samaritans because of their association with people that were not Jewish."[6]

DIASPORA AND RETURN

There was no lack of political intrigue and religious contention between the people of Samaria and those of Judah. Earlier, in the sixth century BCE, Nebuchadnezzar (also known as Nebuchadrezzar II) moved to increase Babylonian influence in the provinces of Syria and Judah, which led to several rebellions. He captured Jerusalem under King Zedekiah, and in 586 BCE destroyed the city and its Temple. He also deported many Jews to lands of the east, including Babylon, which Cyrus the Great, king of Persia, conquered in 539 BCE.

Cyrus' historic declaration (c. 538 BCE) allowed the people he conquered, including (but not limited to) the Jews, to return to their homelands, rebuild, and worship in their own temples. Cyrus's words appear in cuneiform text on the Cyrus-cylinder discovered in 1879 in the ruins of the palace of Babylon which is now in the British Museum:

> *I am Cyrus, the king of the world.... Marduk, the great god, rejoices at my pious acts.... I gathered all their people and led them back to their abodes...and the gods...at the order of Marduk, the great lord; I had them installed in joy in their sanctuaries.... May all the gods whom I have led back to their cities [pray daily] for the length of my days.*[7]

Cecil Roth cites Ezra (2:64) where the number of returning Jews are said to have been 42,360, and those Jews who remained in Mesopotamia made financial contributions: "As the caravans successively entered the country, one may imagine that they dispersed, each family going to re-assert its claim on the plot of land which it previously owned. That autumn, however, they came together in Jerusalem in order to reinstitute Divine worship at the Temple. On the occasion of the solemnity at the beginning of the seventh month (subsequently known as the New Year), the debris was cleared away from the middle of the ruined courts, and a rough altar set up. From that date, for a period of three and a half centuries, the regular sequence of worship, morning and evening, was uninterrupted."[8]

Thus, Jews returned to the province called Yehud, and not surprisingly they had developed differences to their brethren, one of which was language. While the Jews who had remained in Judah continued using written and spoken Hebrew, the returning exiles now spoke Aramaic, which soon became the dominant language not only in Judah but throughout most of the ancient Levant. Hebrew was now used mainly on the coins of Yehud, as well as on some official seals and documents. This was a graphic show of nationalistic pride and religious tradition. (The Samarians by contrast, reflecting their own citizenry, used Aramaic inscriptions, with occasional Greek, on their coins.)

The written history of the Persian Period (c. 538–334 BCE) begins with the Old Testament books about the return and rebuilding of Jerusalem and its Temple by Ezra and Nehemiah, and ends at around the time the land was conquered by Alexander the Great in 334 BCE. As previously discussed, this land included the southern part of the huge Fifth Satrapy of Persia called the "land beyond the river." *Eber Nahara* included Syria, Phoenicia, Palestine, and Cyprus. Economic changes were significant in the life of this region whose basic financial system evolved from the exclusive use of weighed metal, to the use of foreign coins or fragments of them, and eventually to a local coinage.

Conflicts between the Jews and Samarians are illustrated in Ezra, in which it specifically notes, for example, that the Jews rebuffed offers of help to rebuild the Jewish Temple, which resulted in open animosity:

> ...the people of the land [Samarians] undermined the resolve of the people of Judah and made them afraid to build. They bribed ministers in order to thwart their plans all the years of King Cyrus of Persia and until the reign of King Darius of Persia (EZRA 4:4–5).

In fact the contemporary biblical books are filled with stories of bitter relations between the Jews and the Samaritans. In this context Dan Barag describes a conflict led by Tennes, king of Sidon, in which "the last six decades preceding the conquest of the East by Alexander the Great were marked by considerable unrest in the southwestern parts of the Persian Empire....and Phoenicia and Palestine had not recovered by the time of Alexander's invasion."[9]

We read about a current coin denomination:

> *...and they gave for the service of the house of God of gold five thousand talents and ten thousand darics, and of silver ten thousand talents, and of brass eighteen thousand talents, and of iron a hundred thousand talents (I CHRONICLES 29:7).*

There are other references to the *daric* in both Ezra 2:69; 8:27 and Nehemiah 7:70–72. Since these gold coins circulated during the fifth century BCE throughout the Persian Empire, one would think that a good number of them were carried back to ancient Palestine by the returning Jews, with whom they must have been current. However, until today only two gold double *darics* and one *daric* have been found in controlled archaeological excavations in Judaea, Philistia, Samaria, and Galilee.[10] No silver *sigloi* (singular *siglos*) have been found in archaeological excavations, and these common coins never appeared for sale in the markets of Israel until quite recently when they were imported from abroad for sale to tourists. Based on the large number of Jews who returned from Babylon, one might expect that more of these coins would have survived in the biblical lands. It therefore appears that while the post-captivity references in Ezra and Nehemiah might be references to actual coins in circulation at the time, the archaeological evidence so far suggests that even these references may be anachronistic, at least for the land of Judah.

4.1. Gold *daric*, c. 4th century BCE of the Great Kings of Persia, mentioned in Ezra and Nehemiah but almost never found in excavations in Israel.

COINS OF SAMARIA

The coins of Samaria were not known prior to the 1970s and they were first published during the early 1980s, when Meshorer wrote a few paragraphs about them and identified four coins in *Ancient Jewish Coinage I*.[11] By 1991 Meshorer, together with Shraga Qedar, published *The Coinage of Samaria in the Fourth Century BCE*. A second book, *Samarian Coinage* was published in 1999 and identified 224 coin types or subtypes. More types and varieties of the coins of Samaria continue to be discovered.[12] Even though the coins of Samaria have appeared in increasing numbers for some years, most individual types remain quite scarce, especially in choice condition. Considering the number now available, it is astonishing that these coins were virtually unknown as late as the mid-1970s. The earliest substantial discovery of Samarian coins came from two hoards, the "Nablus Hoard" of around 1,000 coins of which several hundred were Samaritan, and the "Samaria Hoard," which was found near Samaria (Sebaste) in the 1980s; of 334 coins, 182 were Samaritan, 43 from Sidon, 32 from Tyre, 11 from Arados, 66 Athenian prototypes, plus a number of pieces of jewelry including earrings, beads, and miscellaneous objects.[13] More recently, single coins and small hoards continue to be found in many locations north of Ramallah, in the ancient land of Samaria. (By contrast, the Yehud coins of Judah are found in many locations, but only south of Ramallah.)

Samaria issued silver coins to maintain parallel prestige with cities in other areas such as Judah, Phoenicia, and Philistia. The Samarian coins circulated locally, although rarely they have been found in both Judaea and further south. Samaria's small denomination silver coins filled needs for small payments in religious, military, and commercial transactions, alongside the continued use of other small pieces of silver in addition to coins.

Since coins of Samaria were apparently struck in about the forty-five years prior to Alexander's conquest in 330 BCE, they should be considered Jewish issues, according to Meshorer and Qedar.[14] A second interesting parallel is that the coins of Judah imitate mainly Athenian and Hellenistic Egyptian prototypes while the Samaritan coins parallel the coins of places to which Samaria was commercially connected such as Sidon, Tyre, and Cilicia. Samaria's geographic location—far to the north of Jerusalem—makes such commercial links logical. "Though only a few Cilician coins have been found in the Samaria area, the

Cilician prototypes are dominant and at least fifteen different coins have Cilician prototypes."[15]

Coins of both Samaria and Judah also carry personal names or their abbreviations, apparently the names of governors of the respective regions. Most of the names are Jewish; among those named on Samaritan coins are Jeroboam, Hiyam, Hananyah, Sanballat, and Delayah. Some coins also carry the name of the Persian satrap Mazaeus.

Meshorer and Qedar engage in thought-provoking speculation about some of the coins. One type, for example, a *ma'ah-obol* (No. 1040), has an obverse showing a bearded male figure seated on a throne, playing a five-stringed harp. The reverse design depicts a male figure on the right, stabbing a horse on the left with a spear. They observe that this type is not derived from any other coinage. Meshorer and Qedar speculate on the identity of the seated male figure, whose head is bare and thus represents neither king nor satrap. "One could suggest a possibility that this figure may represent some aspect of Samaritan religious practice. We know that in the fourth century BCE the Samaritans intended to build their own temple on Mt. Gerizim, a temple to rival the Temple in Jerusalem. The idea of building such a temple on Mt. Gerizim...meant that the Samaritans considered the Jerusalem Temple as a model. Moreover, Sanballat, the governor of Samaria, brought Manasseh, the brother of the high priest, from Jerusalem to Samaria, gave him his daughter in marriage and appointed him to serve as high priest in the new Temple. The ceremonies in the Jerusalem Temple were accompanied by music in praise of the Lord. This was the duty of the Levites who were musicians and played the harp and lyre. Can we perhaps associate the unusual figure on [this coin] with the sacred music of the Samaritan Yahvistic cult?"[16]

Many of the motifs of the Samaritan coins are unbelievably complicated, especially considering that they have diameters of 10 millimeters or less. One of the tiny *ma'ah-obols* (No. 1041), for example, depicts "two figures walking to the left, shouldering a bar from which an animal is suspended by its legs. Between them, another animal walks to the left with its head turned back."

"This motif," Meshorer and Qedar say, "seems to be a reminiscence of an ancient Syrian-Palestinian scene representing the offering of an animal killed in a hunt, either to the god or to the king. In a splendid early Syrian cylinder seal, there is a similar scene. Our coin shows that such scenes still existed in the fourth century BCE, though their meaning must have changed."[17] It is also possible that such scenes represent the slaughtered Paschal lamb, critical to the Samaritan religion

The scenes on many Samarian coins are syncretistic—representing a synthesis between elements of different cultures. A superb example of this is shown on the coin (No. 1028) that represents a standing frontal figure of the Egyptian god Bes. Images and figurines of Bes appear not only in Egyptian art, but throughout the ancient Near East from the second millennium BCE to the Roman period. Bes was sort of a household protector god, who represented good and opposed bad. With such a mandate, it's no wonder that this Egyptian deity was widely adopted in nearby Syria, Phoenicia, and ancient Palestine. Depictions of Bes had many variations, and there is evidence that in early times the attributes of Bes, among other non-Judeo-Samaritan deities, were associated and merged with local gods. In the case of this coin it seems possible that the physical attributes of Bes were merged with the iconography of the Samaritan god.[18]

Like the Philistian coins, a small percentage of Samaritan coins are fourrées (silver plated). It is not certain what role these coins played, yet since some were struck from the same dies as regular silver coins they must be mint products and not contemporary forgeries as once suspected (see pp. 116–117). A small group of Samaritan types have been listed here. Specialty references should be consulted for more complete information.

SAMARIAN COINS C. LATE 4TH CENTURY BCE

See photos for correct size of all coins.
Die axis varies, from loose dies to ↑↓.
Samaritan *sheqel* standard 14.52 g.
Average quarter-*sheqel* 3.63 g.
Average *ma'ah-obol* 0.61 g.

1027   1028

1027.   AR *ma'ah-obol.*
    Obv: Persian king on throne r. smells a flower in r. and holding scepter in l.
    Rev: ⲍⲩⲅⲅⲏⲩⲩ *(bdyhbl)* to l. of bearded male standing r., wearing kidaris, sniffing flower and holding another flower in l. hand.
                             750/2,000

    The name Bdyehibel appears on several coins, but is not yet fully understood or related to a person.[19]

1028.   AR *ma'ah-obol.*
    Obv: ⲍⲩⲅⲅⲏⲩⲩ, *(bdyhbl)* to l. of bearded and partly nude figure of Bes-like diety faces front, crouches slightly, hands rest on thighs, wears lionskin cape, tail and paw appear between legs.
    Rev: Persian king walks r., wearing jagged crown and kandys, holds bow in l. hand and arrows in r., three more arrows visible over king's shoulder, border of dots.　　　　1,000/2,000

1029.   AR quarter-*sheqel.*
    Obv: ⲏ, *(d)* above horse walking l., all in a dotted square border.
    Rev: ⲏ, *(d)* above winged sphinx with head of Persian king l., all in dotted square border.　　　　1,000/3,000

    The letter D could abbreviate the name Delayah, used in the Bible in the time frame of the sixth to fifth centuries BCE. It is also the name of one of Sanballat's sons mentioned in the Elephantine letters. He may have succeeded his father as governor early in the fourth century BCE. Meaning of the name is "healed by the Lord" as used in Psalms 30:2.[20]

1029 1030

1030. AR *ma'ah-obol.*
   Obv: Crude helmeted head of Athena r.
   Rev: AΘE on r., ⊓ᴍᴗꟻ *(hnny—Hannanyah, retrograde)* below it; owl
      standing r. head facing.   350/1,000
Hannanyah is named as a governor of Samaria in Wadi Daliyeh papyri,
(nos. 7 and 9). The Samaritan Chronicles also mention a high priest
named Hannanyah during the time of Queen Esther.[21]

1031 1032

1031. AR *ma'ah-obol.*
   Obv: Head of Athena r., wearing crested helmet.
   Rev: AΘE, the Θ has been moved outward to allow space for an Ar-
      amaic legend in the space between the A and the E, ᴗꓤ4ᴧ *(ydw')*
      to r. of owl standing to r., head facing; to r. between the owl and
      the inscription is an ear of barley, all within an incuse square.

                                                                         RRR
   Published by Spaer as a Yehud type, Meshorer and Qedar reclassified it as
a coin of Samaria.[22] *The name Yadua is known to have been used by the high*
priestly family in Jerusalem, but Meshorer and Qedar also suggest the possibil-
ity it is the name of a Samaritan governor.[23]

1032. AR *ma'ah-obol.*
   Obv: 4ᴗᴪꓬꓱꓬᴗ, *(yhrb'm—Jeroboam)* to l. of bearded male head l.
   Rev: Male figure rides bull, holds spear in upraised l. hand.

                                                                   350/1,000
   There is no certain information on the name Jeroboam on the fragmentary
list of governors of Samaria in the fourth century BCE.

1033   1034

1033.   AR *ma'ah-obol.*
   Obv: Crowned, bearded male head r.
   Rev: ꚗꚗꚗ, *(sn—Sanballat)* above lion seated l., all within square bor-
      der of dots.   350/1,000
   *Perhaps this is the Sanballat II referred to by Josephus as the one who "had
   been sent to Samaria as satrap by Darius the last king."[24]*

1034.   AR quarter-*sheqel.*
   Obv: ⳑⴸ *(s[h]l[emiyah]?)* above winged griffin with long curved horn
      r., letters on both sides of wing, another design, incense flower (?)
      in l. field, all in square border.
   Rev: ⳑⴸ, *(sl)* above l. of stag crouching r., head turned back, facing
      head of Bes between horns, in l. field, all in square border.
                                                   1,000/3,000
   *Shelemyah is named in one of the Elephantine letters from 408 BCE as a
   son of Sanballat, who may have struck them some 30 years later. Shelemyah
   was also a popular Hebrew name.[25]*

1035.   AR *ma'ah-obol.*
   Obv: Helmeted head of Athena to l.
   Rev: ꚗꚍꚙꚙⴸ *(shmryn—Shomron)* above lion attacking stag r.
                                                   350/1,000
   *As discussed above, it is not known whether Shomron (Samaria) represents
   the name of the city or the name of the province when used on these coins.*

1035   1036

1036.   AR *ma'ah-obol.*
   Obv: Facing female head, possibly Arethusa.
   Rev: ꚕꚍꙏꙏⴸ *(shmryn—Shomron, partly retrograde)* to l. of bearded male
      head in crested Athenian helmet l.   250/750

1037. AR *ma'ah-obol.*
Obv: Helmeted head of Athena r.
Rev: ᛋ∨ *(sn—Shomron)* flank owl standing front with wings spread.
                                                            250/750
This interesting little coin imitates the famous Athenian decadrachm.

1038. AR *ma'ah-obol.*
Obv: Helmeted head of Athena r.
Rev: ᛁᛋᛋ∨ *(shmrn—Shomron)* to r. of owl standing to r., head facing.
                                                            250/750

1039. AR *ma'ah-obol.*
Obv: ᛁᛞᛋᛋ∨ *(smryn—Shomron)* above galley l. with oars, rudder, row
    of shields, small figurehead, curved ornament over stern support-
    ing standard, double line of waves below.
Rev: ᛋᛞ *(mz—Mazday?)* between Persian king on l. standing r. wear-
    ing kidaris and kandys, fights lion standing on hind legs, l. hand
    on lion's head, r. holds dagger.   200/750

1040. AR *ma'ah-obol.*
Obv: Male figure (king?) sits r. on throne and plays harp, six pseudo-
    cuneiform signs of unknown significance above, below, and to r.
Rev: Male figure on r. stabs horse on l. with spear in his r. hand and
    dagger in his l. hand.   750/2,000

1041   1042

1041. AR *ma'ah-obol.*
   Obv: Persian king, bearded and wearing jagged crown and kandys,
      stands l., holds two lions by their hind legs.
   Rev: Two males walk l., carry pole over shoulders, animal hangs
      from it by its feet, another animal stands between men to left,
      head turned back.   350/1,000

1042. AR *ma'ah-obol.*
   Obv: Triple-faced male head, wearing cone-shaped crown, the eyes
      of the facing head also serve as eyes of the profile heads.
   Rev: Five Athenian coins, showing reverse owl motif.
                                                           500/1,500
   *This tiny coin is remarkable since it is engraved in such amazing detail that
one can identify the five* tetradrachms *it depicts.*

1043   1044

1043. AR half-*ma'ah.*
   Obv: Head of horned mythological animal to r.
   Rev: Forepart of bull r., traces of inscription on r.(?).
                                                           250/500

1044. AR *ma'ah-obol.*
   Obv: Crude helmeted head of Athena r.
   Rev: Crude owl stands to r, head facing, olive spray behind, some-
      times part of AΘE can be seen.   200/350

COINS OF YEHUD (JUDAH)

The unique Yehud quarter-*sheqel* in the British Museum (No. 1045) was first described in the early 1800s. The further types, chronologies, and standards of the Yehud coins have been under discussion since Sukenik's paper in 1934.[26] By 1966, Meshorer's *Jewish Coins of the Second Temple Period* listed only four different types of Yehud coins. After more discoveries in the 1960s and 70s, Mildenberg described 28 Yehud types in 1979.[27] New types of these coins continue to be discovered.

Mildenberg, in his comprehensive study, assigned the Yehud coins to three basic periods: under Persian rule, during Macedonian occupation, and during the Ptolemaic kingdom.[28]

In *A Treasury of Jewish Coins*, Meshorer essentially agreed with Mildenberg's classifications. The boom in discoveries of Yehud coins began after 1967 when good quality metal detectors became available in Israel and the Palestinian territories. At the time Meshorer observed that, "Most specimens were discovered within the borders of the ancient kingdom of Judah by peasants anxious to meet the increasing demands of the market for ancient coins."[29] Arnold Spaer, a noted Jerusalem attorney and authority on ancient Jewish coins, wrote that almost all of the tiny Yehud coins "seem to have come from the area south of Jerusalem, and more particularly from the Bethlehem district, both east and west of the main road from Jerusalem to Hebron."[30]

However, those are descriptions of the early days. More recently, the small silver Yehud coins have been found at many sites throughout the area of Persian and Hellenistic Judah, some have also been found to the south of this territory, but the Yehud coins are not found north of Ramallah, indicating their specific area of circulation. The discovery of more specimens of Yehud coins has allowed new studies that continue to suggest increasingly specific chronologies.

YEHUD TYPES

As already discussed, it seems likely that the earliest Yehud coins such as the rare quarter-*sheqels* of Philistian style (Nos. 1045, 1047, 1049) were actually struck at Gaza.[31] Later a mint was established in Judah to produce the local small silver denominations.

The first coin struck on the *sheqel-gerah* standard could have been the unusual quarter-*sheqel* (two examples known) that carry both the *'ayin* of Gaza and the name *yhwd* (No. 1049). This may also have been the final Yehud type struck at the mint of Gaza. It may have been followed by the small silver coins that imitate Athenian *tetradrachms*, but with the Yehud inscription instead of ΑΘΕ ethnic (No. 1050). These were followed by the coins that depict on one side the portrait of a Persian king (No. 1057) and share a reverse type with the Athenian copies. The obverse of coin No. 1057 has long been misunderstood. Meshorer believed that its obverse was simply a deteriorated die variety of a portrait of Athena.[32] Interestingly, he was closer to the currently accepted view in his 1967 book *Jewish Coins of the Second Temple Period*, in which he described this obverse as "Male head, oriental style, r."[33] While Meshorer came to believe that the three triangles atop the head were deteriorated leaves from Athena's helmet, the examination of more specimens allows us to see that this is actually the jagged crown that Mildenberg describes as a defining characteristic of the Persian king.[34] The overall confusion about this obverse motif was also partly due to the circular area under the head on many specimens, and this topic is also discussed below (pp. 125–126).

The next coins struck would logically be those with smaller busts of the Persian king wearing the jagged crown on obverse, and falcon with *Yhd* on reverse. The final coins in this early series comprise three types that are specifically and remarkably interlinked with Judaism of the period.

The lily (No. 1060) was widely seen as a symbol of Jerusalem and it makes its first appearance as such on a Yehud coin when it replaces the olive sprig behind the owl on the earlier types. Lilies decorated Solomon's Temple as well as architectural elements in excavations at Jerusalem, Samaria, Meggido, and Hazor.[35] We will also see that a similar lily is used on several Yehud coins of the Macedonian period as well as on coins minted by Antiochus VII and the Hasmonean kings.

Perhaps the most intriguing coins in this series carry the image of a human ear (No. 1061) and the shofar, or ram's horn (No. 1062). Both motifs probably relate to the Jewish concept of speaking to God and God hearing and understanding: in other words, graphic expressions of Jewish prayers. Meshorer identifies this relationship: "Can the ear and the shofar be regarded as the early manifestations of Jewish art and symbolism (together with the lily on the other Yehud coins), or are they a singular attempt at graphic expression of Jewish ritual? It is possible that the depictions of rituals and gods on the coins of other nations led the minters in Jerusalem to give the coins a Jewish expression differing from that of the pagans, one that would be understood by the Jewish inhabitants of Judah."[36]

...for ye have wept in the ears of the Lord (Numbers 11:18).

Incline Thine ear, O Lord, and answer me (Psalms 86:1).

Persian Period Weight Standards

During the Persian Period, the standard of Greek coins commonly struck in the coastal cities, especially Gaza, were based upon the Athenian *tetradrachm*, which had an average weight of around 17.2 g. An *obol* was $1/24$ of a *tetradrachm*, and thus Greek *obols* of this period weigh around 0.72 g. I previously discussed standards for Philistian, Edomite, and Samaritan coins.

Yehud coins are based on a different weight standard, as shown by Yigal Ronen, a professor of nuclear science at Ben Gurion University in Be'er Sheva, who has made a precise metrological study of them. He points out that "we can find coins minted with the same die which are different by a factor of two in their weight. With Persian Period techniques it was difficult to produce coins with the same weight. In particular, it was difficult to control the production process of the small silver coins in which the flans were hand-made. It is known that the weight of very small coins varies more greatly, by percentage, than the weight of larger coins. However, from a given amount of silver; mints were required to produce a given number of coins. Thus, the average weight of a large number of coins of the same type is a valid and correct measure for the weight of that type of coin."[37]

Ronen analyzed 64 "owl" coins and 82 "Persian king" coins—"quantities sufficient for reliable statistics." He learned that the average weight for the owl coins is 0.48 g and the average weight of the Persian king coins is 0.26 g.[38]

He concludes that Persian Period Yehud coins were not based upon the same standard as any other small silver of the period. There is simply too great a difference between average weights of 0.48 and 0.72 g or even the Philistian of 0.65 g. Ronen suggests a specific local standard in use during the Persian Period in Judah. Indeed, during the earlier Israelite Period (also known as the Iron Age, 1200–586 BCE), there was a unique weight system in Judah. Based upon scale weights from that period, we know that the *sheqel* at the end of the First Temple period weighed about 11.4 g. (A later Persic coin, the *siglos*, weighs around 5.5 g, quite close to a half-*sheqel*.)

It is a generally accepted concept that weight standards evolved slowly over a period of time, so it is logical to assume that this Judean *sheqel* standard would have had at least a transitional impact on the following periods in the lands where it was used.

Observes Ronen: "The *sheqel* was divided into 24 smaller denominations or *gerah*....thus the weight of the *gerah* was 0.475 g., which is nearly equal to the average weight (0.48 g) of the 'Owl' coins. It is our suggestion, therefore, that the *yhd* coins, during the late Persian rule, were in the denomination of a *gerah* ('Owl' coins) and half-*gerah* ('Persian king' coins). Taxpayers used these coins to pay the half-*sheqel* (12 *gerahs*) to the Temple in Jerusalem."[39]

In fact, the Bible states that there are 20 *gerahs* to the *sheqel* "… the *sheqel* is 20 *gerahs*…" (EXODUS 30:13). However, scholars of ancient weights of this period, including the leading expert Raz Kletter, formerly of the Israel Antiquities Authority, have concluded that there were more likely 24 *gerah* to the standard *sheqel*. Kletter suggests that the figure of 20 *gerah* may have been a scribe's error or perhaps a different, or perhaps later, *sheqel* standard, since several are mentioned in the Old Testament. One also may suggest anachronistic references such as those that exist elsewhere in various translations.[40]

Virtually all of the Yehud coins have been found within ancient Judah, but coins from the same period struck in Tyre, Sidon, and Arados have been found throughout the Middle East. Ronen suggests that "This situation might indicate that the Yehud coins were not used for international trade, as were the Phoenician coins. If the Yehud coins were only used locally, the use of a non-conventional weight system becomes more readily explicable," and indeed this is the case.

Ronen's final proof to his theory that these were the earliest local coins used as Temple payments is the fact that all of the Yehud coins discovered to date are true silver.[41]

Fourrée or "silver plated" coins with a base metal interior are especially common among the coins of the late Persian Period. Anyone who has handled even relatively small groups of coins from Gaza, Samaria, Sidon, Byblos, and Arados will notice that there are an unusually large number of *fourrée* coins among them. Once it was thought that the *fourrée* coins were simply ancient forgeries. However, this seems not to have been the case, as shown by Oliver Hoover:

"Although plated coins are frequently described as 'ancient forgeries,' it is difficult to be certain that criminal enterprise was responsible for all of the known plated specimens. Some series that are of especially high quality may possibly be official. Two examples in [Hoover's] catalog actually die link to apparently regular (un-plated) issues."[42] As already mentioned, similar die links occur in the Samaritan series between *fourrée* and silver coins.

Whatever the reason, why should the Yehud coinage be the only small silver coinage of the ancient Near East where there were no *fourrée* coins minted? Ronen suggests that the reason for this is that the Yehud coins were used for, among other things, payment of tribute to the Jerusalem Temple. "If the Yehud coins were indeed used for the biblical half-*sheqel* tribute to the Temple (MISHNAH SHEKALIM 2:4), the sheqel weight system is the appropriate standard. Moreover, pure silver was required for the Temple tribute, which explains the absence of silver-plated Yehud coins."[43] Surely no Jewish officials or even mint workers would have participated in a scheme that might perpetrate a fraud on the Jerusalem Temple.

So, what we have in these early Yehud coins are *gerah* and half-*gerah* denomination coins that were used to make up the annual silver half-*sheqel* to the Jerusalem Temple as well as other local commerce.

MACEDONIAN & PTOLEMAIC STANDARDS

Unlike their Persian Period predecessors, the Yehud coins of the Macedonian and Ptolemaic periods are based on the Athenian Greek standard. Ronen studied 72 coins of the Ptolemaic Period and found that the average weight of the Ptolemy and eagle coins (No. 1087) is 0.18 g. Gitler and Lorber weighed an additional 236 Ptolemaic Period coins and reached an identical average.[44] "This weight of the Ptolemaic coins clearly deviates from the Persian Period's weight of the 0.48 or 0.26 g of the *gerah* and half-*gerah*, respectively. However, the 0.18 is suitable to the *obol* system of weight. This coin clearly represents a quarter of an *obol* of 0.72 g. The shift from the *gerah* standard during the Persian Period to the *obol* standard during the Ptolemaic Period is unmistakable,"[45] Ronen explains.

This does not mean, however, that there is any reason to believe that the shift in standards precluded the continuous use of the earlier coinage. In fact there are documented hoards found in Israel that include coins of both the Persic and Attic weight standards.[46] This suggests that coins from both standards circulated simultaneously, and it is not known whether these tiny fractions were accepted equally or had different values.

Since the Macedonian and Ptolemaic Period weight standard changes from the Judean standard to the Greek-Attic standard, I follow Tal's suggestion and use a local weight terminology.[47] Hence, for the Yehuds of the Macedonian and Ptolemaic periods, struck according to the Attic standard, I will use the denominational term *ma'ah*, already introduced for *obol*-parallels of silver coins from Philistia, Edom, and Samaria.

The transition from the standards of the Persian Period to the Hellenistic Period seems to have begun with a late Persian issue (No. 1064) that depicts on its obverse the head of a lynx and on its reverse the head of a Persian king upon a winged lynx, with the inscription "Hezekiah" and struck prior to 332 BCE.[48] This type is followed by the related issues with bare male head to right or left and winged lynx with animal head facing left (Nos. 1065, 1066).

The first coin struck according to the Macedonian standard may have been the coin with a facing head and forepart of a horned and winged lynx to right (No. 1068). Fourteen examples of this coin have been registered, with an average weight of 0.19 g, extremely close to the average weight of a quarter-*obol* as shown by Ronen. The facing head obverse also makes a comfortable transition to the next probable group depicting the facing head and owl with the legend *Yehiziqiyah ha-pehah* (No. 1069). Similar coins carry inscriptions of *Yohanan ha-kohen* (No. 1071) and *Yehud Yehudah* (No. 1072); a recently discovered type shares the facing head and owl types but is inscribed with crude Greek letters instead of paleo-Hebrew or Aramaic (No. 1070).[49]

During the Macedonian period, the designs of the Yehud coins continue to focus around fantastic animal motifs, such as the winged lynx. The last coin in this series with the roaring lion or chimera head and duck (No. 1075) is worthy of discussion. Meshorer originally described the obverse as a horse's head. But the prickly mane, pointed nose, and the horn curving up from the head suggests a chimera and may be parallel to the mythological creature on the obverse and reverse of coin No.1064.

Gitler and Lorber suggest that this creature is a lion and observe that the die engraver attempted an optical illusion on this coin. Such illusions are common in the small silver coins of Philistia, but this is the only example in a Yehud type. With the illusion, the lower jaw of the creature could also be a neck; hence the horse head view (similar to a chess knight facing right).[50] Since this design could be viewed as either a horse or a feline, it suggests a chimera, a creature made of parts of several animals.

The reverse has previously been described as a dove, an eagle, or simply a bird with its head turned back. Some years ago J.P. Fontanille suggested to me that the bird on this coin could be a duck. But few coins of this type were known, and we did not have any examples struck well enough to make a firm observation. Eventually, however, I obtained a specimen that had a sharp depiction with the bird's beak particularly clear. I showed some photos to bird experts and asked their opinions.

Kevin McGowan, a behavioral ecologist who studies birds at the Cornell Ornithology Laboratory, told me "it is certainly not an eagle...identification of stylized bird images is problematic... artistic interpretation can be baffling," and suggested a duck was possible, but also a goose, or even a crane. John Faaborg, professor of biology and bird ecologist at the University of Missouri, Columbia, and the president of the American Ornithologists' Union, said: "it sure looks like a duck to me." Halbert Carmichael, emeritus professor of chemistry at NC State University, has been an amateur ornithologist and specialist in bird coins for more than 40 years.

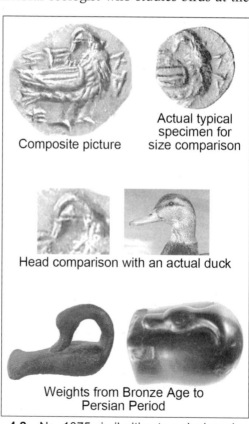

Composite picture

Actual typical specimen for size comparison

Head comparison with an actual duck

Weights from Bronze Age to Persian Period

4.2. No. 1075 similarities to a duck and to ancient duck-shaped weights. (Graphic: Fontanille.)

"There is no question that the bird is a duck. The bill is rendered beautifully and is distinctive. Beyond being a duck, I can't be much more specific except to say that it is of the family *Anatidae* which includes the common puddle ducks such as the mallard, widgeon, and teal," he said. The field guide *Birds of the Middle East*[51] lists several small-billed ducks native to the area of ancient Israel, including various types of teal and geese.

Why a duck on an early Jewish coin? There are no ducks or geese mentioned in the Old or New Testaments. On the other hand, stone or metal figures of ducks, geese, or swans, with head turned back, were commonly used as scale weights in the ancient Middle East. As I point out in *Ancient Scale Weights*, duck-shaped weights are found in Mesopotamia as well as Egypt and Syria/Palestine. Dates for the duck-shaped weights range from around the Middle Bronze Age (ending around 1550 BCE) to the Late Iron Age (mid-sixth century BCE) and may have extended into the Persian, Hellenistic, and Roman Periods.[52] Thus early coins from the Near East could carry an image similar to the form of some local, Babylonian, and Egyptian scale weights.

Chronology of the Ptolemaic coins has also been clarified by Gitler and Lorber. They studied more than 200 Yehud coins of the Ptolemaic period—types, legends, and die axes—to determine a chronology. Noteworthy is their comment that "the early Hellenistic period was a time when many mints adopted hinged or adjusted dies, resulting in a regular die position for their coinage, usually 12:00. In the overwhelming majority of cases, this was a permanent change in the mint's production practices."[53] Thus they suggest the chronology for these coins was strongly related to the coin type's tendency to a vertical die axis. This analysis is sound, and their method is followed in this catalog.

The Ptolemaic Yehud coins carry the general motifs of other Ptolemaic coins of the period, namely portraits of Ptolemy I and II and Berenike II and Arsinoë II. The young male heads on the earliest coins are not yet identified, although it is possible that these portraits could represent an idealized young head of Alexander III, or Ptolemy I. While the series of Ptolemaic Yehud coins was limited and short-lived, it was nevertheless a most unusual issue. Dan Barag explains that Judah "was the only area in which such a currency was issued under the Ptolemies (after 301 BCE) but for how long? Coin issues of that kind were contrary to the highly centralized monetary system of the Ptolemaic kingdom. Furthermore, the prolific issue of bronze coins by the state mints, some of which were quite heavy and of greater commercial value than the minute silver coins, as well as more practical for daily circulation in the marketplace, made Judaea's silver coinage redundant (the small silver coins were prone to break and were easily lost)."[54]

It is unusual that among all of the possessions of the early Ptolemaic empire, only the mint of Judah was allowed to issue coins with its own local paleo-Hebrew script and the name Yehud instead of the name of the Ptolemaic kings. Barag suggests that this could reveal a "political status beyond restricted local autonomy" even though the coins themselves "certainly display direct control from the center of government."[55] The rare examples of Aramaic script on the Yehud coins have not yet been adequately explained.

EXPRESSIONS OF THE COINS

Steve Gerson who is both a scholar of Persian Period coins as well as a Harvard psychiatrist, has analyzed the coins of Yehud and Samaria and concludes that they can indeed "project information about the characteristics of peoples that produced them, as well as the particular spirit" of an epoch. Even though the territories of Samaria and Judah had many parallels with each other, the coins themselves are quite different. There are around 10 times more specific types of Samaritan coins than Yehud coins.

"Focused analysis of the coins indicates a reality of many profound economic, cultural, and religious differences between these important provinces,"[56] Gerson says. Regarding the Persian Period Yehud coins, he observes that "Symbols can be the personification of important conscious (or unconscious) forces, spiritual beliefs, or values. They may represent, in a condensed form, very deep and complicated underpinnings. Thus, the choice of motif is not thought to be random. Given that coins are usually authorized by a source of administrative power or government authority, we generally assume that their images reflect important values of that specific leader, government, or populace."

In summary Gerson suggests that "the sensibility and vision of Judaea was more 'inward,' interior, and conservative while that of Samaria was to look 'outward' during this period. I am not attaching a value judgment to these differences, but am trying to characterize simply 'what was.' For example, the Judaean weight system, iconography, language, and circulation patterns can be described as idiosyncratic and inward, as compared to those of the Samaritans. The Samaritan weight system was more compatible with external trading partners as far away as Greece and as nearby as Phoenicia. The language on Samaritan coins was more congruent with the language of larger foreign entities that surround them." With regard to the Yehud coins, however, he also points to "relatively greater prominence of sacred 'Jewish' iconography....(the ear and the lily) suggest that the Judaean valuation of a more intense connection between the religious and the political; perhaps, too, the priests had more political power in Yehud."[57]

A great deal remains unknown about the ancient land of Israel during the Persian Period. Some scholars, for example, contend that the Yehud coins were issued by the Persian provincial authorities. Barag argues, however, that this explanation is not satisfactory. After all, he observes, "The Persian governors of Judaea were, in most cases, if not always, Jewish: Sheshbazzar (EZRA 1:8) and Zerubbabal (HAGGAI 1:1,14) in the late sixth century BCE, Nehemiah (NEHEMIAH 5:14; 12:26) in the second half of the fifth century. Epigraphic discoveries added the names of Elnathan in the late sixth century BCE, Yeho'ezer and Ahzai in the fifth century BCE, and Yehiziqiyah in the third quarter of the fourth century BCE. Whether Bagohi (Bagoas) known from the Elephantine papyri was Jewish is uncertain, but as all other known governors were Jewish, he may also be Jewish."[58]

Barag also discusses why these early Jewish rulers would have violated the commandment against placing graven images on coins at this time. "The liberal attitudes of the Achaemenid dynasty in religious matters and their favorable policy towards the cult of the God of Heaven are well known. It is thus inconceivable that Jewish governors in Judaea or the Persian authorities could have been insensitive in such matters and what is the likelihood that they would have issued currency which the majority of the population would have rejected as offensive? The coin of Yohanan (No. 1071) suggests that even the high priests saw it fit to issue coins with images. The norm in the fourth century BCE was thus entirely different from that of the Hasmoneans, King Herod, Herod Antipas, the mint of Agrippa I in Jerusalem, the Roman procurators of Judaea, and the Jewish authorities during the Jewish War and the Bar Kokhba War. The explanation may be sought in a different attitude towards the representations on coins. For Jews in the fourth century BCE, the two-dimensional representations on coins even if their subject matter was pagan did not constitute an offense against the command: 'Thou shalt not make thee any graven image...'

(DEUTERONOMY 5:8; cf. EXODUS 20:23; LEVITICUS 26:1, DEUTERONOMY 27:15). In the early Hellenistic period, culminating in the Maccabean Wars, attitudes in such matters changed drastically."

The matter of iconography, specifically on Hasmonean coins, is discussed broadly on pp. 172–176, but in general, it seems that when the Jewish population is secure, the use of graven images on everyday objects such as coins (as opposed to being used upon cult objects of worship) was not strongly resisted.

PRODUCTION OF THE YEHUD COINS

Because the Yehud coins, as well as the coins of Gaza and Samaria, are so tiny, they are often struck so none or only part of the design or inscription are visible. Very few are centered on both sides. Many of the Yehud coins discovered in the 1960s and 1970s were originally described as uniface, with blank obverses. In spite of their miniscule size, they were struck with dies and anvils just like other coins. During production, the hand-held top die (reverse) often was not aligned with the anvil-held bottom die (obverse), and uniface coins often resulted.

This occurred because the obverse dies were significantly larger than the flans being used. In some Yehud coins, Fontanille has shown that the obverse die can be 50 to 150 percent larger than the reverse die, quite an odd situation, which, strangely is repeated for some coins during both the Hasmonean and

4.3. Reconstruction of set of Yehud coin dies for No. 1057, notice large flat areas on obverse die. (Graphic: Fontanille.)

Herodian periods. Is it possible that these dies were originally made for larger denomination coins that were never made? Or was this possibly a matter of ease in production, since an obverse die as tiny as a Yehud coin would be difficult to engrave and use?

Fontanille has also observed that several of the Yehud obverse dies were used until they deteriorated beyond recognition, while the hand-held reverse dies suffered smaller cracks and breaks.[59] One may assume that this was a result of poor manufacturing complicated by a lack of quality control at this earliest known Judaean mint, probably in the Jerusalem area. The Yehud dies were especially prone to this deterioration because they were so small, and the majority of the dies had quite shallow relief work. The obverses did not break because they were set firmly into an anvil. But, during the striking process, small grains of silver and other waste fell into the dies and was pounded and hammered so hard and so often that it mutilated the dies. Anyone who has ever worked with silver understands this concept. This is a graphic explanation since the damage to the obverse die was not so much in the way of actual breakage or chips, but more pounding and filling. This

Original state	Progressive degradation on coins			
No. 1050				
No. 1057				
No. 1075				

4.4. After continuous use, the obverse dies for the tiny silver coins deteriorates beyond recognition. (Graphic: Fontanille.)

explains the resultant deterioration illustrations which show that the shallowest areas of the die filled quickly, while the deep areas ended up turning into the odd trapezoid and finally an egg-shaped object. It also explains how these strange designs could still be surrounded by a rather flat field (Nos. 1075b, c).

A related discovery solves a mystery regarding the early type with the large head of the Persian King with his chin resting over an enigmatic square structure and a circle within, and a reverse owl, head facing, with the Hebrew YHD (No. 1057). Originally believed to have been part of an unexplained motif, this actually resulted from a clashed die error. The square structure was the "incuse" design on the punch and the "circle" within it is the result of the reversed design of the owl. This occurred when, early in their life cycle, the obverse and reverse dies were "clashed" together without a flan between them. In this case, it resulted in permanent damage to this obverse die. Another clashed die error can be seen in at least one other Yehud coin and they occur in other related series as well.[60]

I once again note that the obverse die of this coin was significantly larger than any of the flans ever used, unlike the reverse punch dies, which seem to be about the correct size. The very fact that the obverse die was so large allows the clashed die to be so clear, especially on certain off-center strikes, and also easy to remedy, because depending on which portion of the die was used to strike the coin, it may not involve the king's head portion of the design.

Photographs and composite illustrations show

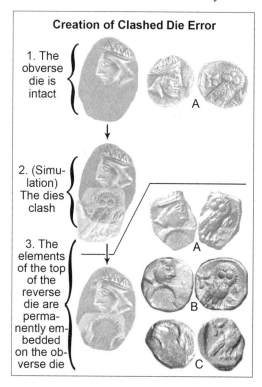

Creation of Clashed Die Error

1. The obverse die is intact

2. (Simulation) The dies clash

3. The elements of the top of the reverse die are permanently embedded on the obverse die

4.5. Illustration of the creation of a clashed die error for type 1057. (Graphic: Fontanille.)

that the obverse of this coin was re-engraved, struck from this same obverse die. In the first instance the Persian king's head appears plain. In the second instance, the Persian king's head appears with the addition of (a) what appears to be a jewel or an amulet of some sort draped from his forehead and (b) the top portion of the reversed owl outline appearing as an upside-down half crescent under the bust. Thus, when this die was re-engraved, at least the jewel (which certainly appears to be deliberate, but theoretically could also be a die crack) was added. Perhaps a mint official noticed that there was some clashing damage apparent in the die and ordered one of the celators to fix it. Therefore, the owl's face was also smoothed to minimize its visibility on subsequent coins.

YEHUD COINS, PERSIAN RULE

BEFORE 333 BCE

See photos for correct size of all coins.
Struck from loose dies.
Persian Period *sheqel* standard 11.4 g.
Theoretical quarter-*sheqel* 2.85 g.
Average *gerah* 0.48 g.
Average half-*gerah* 0.26 g.

1045

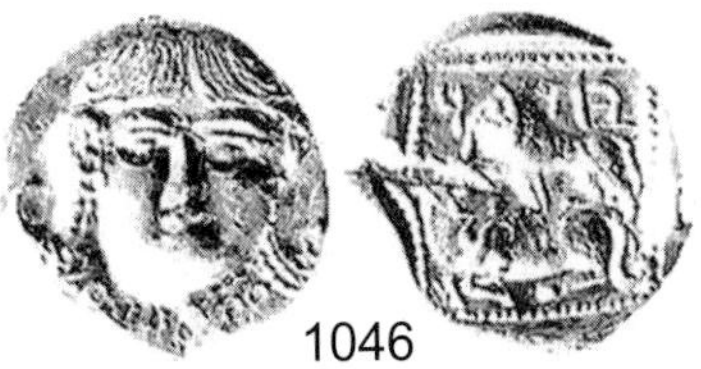
1046

1045. AR quarter-*sheqel*, 3.29 g (one specimen published).
Obv: Bearded oriental head (Bagoas ?) r. wearing Corinthian helmet, guilloche border.
Rev: 𐤉𐤄𐤃 *(yhd)* above bearded deity seated r. on winged wheel (chariot?), holding falcon in l. hand and r. hand resting on knee, small bearded mask below r.; within guilloche border and incuse square. UNIQUE

This was described by Hill and others as the first Jewish coin, with a reverse depiction of the Jewish deity upon a winged chariot as described in Ezekiel 10:16.

Barag identifies the obverse portrait as "Bagoas, a general of Artaxerxes III who was strategos and commander-in-chief of the Persian army invading

Egypt in 343 BCE [61] *... In choosing this representation with a helmet...he continued the precedent set during the preparations for the second war against Egypt in 378–374 BCE, namely that a Persian strategos may be represented wearing a Greek helmet." Barag also notices a parallel between the reverse of this coin "and the coins struck by Pharnabazos in 378–374 BCE showing the enthroned Ba'al Tarz (Ba'al of Tarsus)....One may thus conclude that the deity on the British Museum drachm is the God of Yehud, i.e. the God of Israel."* [62]

Gitler and Tal suggest that the coin was a product of the Philistian mint. They read the legend as YHW or YHR instead of YHD and believe that the production of this coin could have been carried out under Edomite Jews who disregarded the second commandment, or alternatively under gentiles who considered YHWH as yet another deity of their "cultic pantheon." [63] *It seems possible that this was among the earliest coins of the Yehud series, and without a local mint at this time, some coins were manufactured in Gaza, and only later in Judah. The two quarter-*sheqels *described below may also be members of this family. No. 1049 carries a clear legend of YHWD along with a symbol that appears to be the ○ mintmark of Gaza.*

1046.   AR quarter-*sheqel*, 3.54 g.
Obv: Facing Gorgoneion with curls in shape of snakes.
Rev: ꤤꢃꤥ *(yhd)* above lion facing l., on top of recumbent bovine, head turned, within guilloche border and incuse square.

UNIQUE

The lapidary Aramaic legend clearly reading יהד*, suggests that this* drachm *is a new coin-type of the Yehud series. The fact that there are only* three other recorded drachms *with the full Yehud legend (No. 1049 below) and those, however, are much lighter, and their Athenian style points to the importance of this new find.*

The fact that the iconography of this new type is completely different from that of the known late Persian Period coins of Judah and moreover that the reverse scene has a clear Philistian iconographical influence (see Gitler and Tal 2006: XIX. Oriental Head/Feline. 10D; XIX. Oriental Head/Feline. 11D and XXVIII. Animals. 6D) suggests that this is probably the earliest known coin of Judah. A similar scene appears on a Samaritan coin that depicts a lion holding a dagger in his right paw and standing above another animal (Meshorer and Qedar 1999: No. 204).

This issue is dated to the fourth century BCE based on the lapidary Aramaic legend and the late-style of the facing Gorgoneion. NOTE COURTESY HAIM GITLER, ISRAEL MUSEUM, JERUSALEM.

1047

1047. AR quarter-*sheqel*, Attic standard.

Obv: Head of Athena r., wearing crested helmet decorated with 3 olive leaves.

Rev: ΑΘ[Ε] and retrograde 𐤉 *(y)* to r of owl standing r., head facing, with olive leaves behind. 5,000/15,000

1048. AR *ma'ah-obol.*

Similar to 1047. 750/2,000

1049. AR quarter-*sheqel.*

Obv: Helmeted head of Athena r. decorated with olive wreath.

Rev: 𐤉𐤄𐤅𐤃 *(yhwd)* on r.; owl stands to r., head facing; in l. field olive spray; ○ between the owl and inscription. RRR

a. Similar with retrograde inscription and without ○.

Three known specimens of this type weigh 2.72, 2.70, and 2.22 g.

1050

1051

1050. AR *gerah.*

Obv: Helmeted head of Athena r., decorated with olive wreath.

Rev: 𐤉𐤄𐤃 *(yhd)* to r. of owl standing to r., head facing, small lily above l. 250/1,000

Several varieties of this coin exist, and some carry legends that are crude or retrograde.

1051. AR *gerah.*
Obv: Helmeted head of Athena r. decorated with olive wreath.
Rev: ꓱꓵꓭ *(yhd, retrograde)* to l. of owl standing to l., head facing; in r. field olive spray. 500/2,000
a. AR half-gerah (?), 0.26 g.
*Coin listed as 1051a is same type, but from a different die set. While worth noting, it is not clear that it is a half-*gerah. *Since the weights of these small coins vary dramatically, it is difficult to consider it a smaller denomination.*

1052. AR *gerah.*
Obv: Crude head of Athena r.
Rev: ꓵ on l. of ꓱꓭ *(yhd)* on r. of owl, standing to r., head facing. 250/1,000

1053. AR *gerah.*
Obv: Helmeted head of Athena r. decorated with olive wreath.
Rev: ꓱꓒꓭꓵ *(yhwd, retrograde)* around owl standing to r. head facing. 250/1,000

1054. AR *gerah.*
Obv: Helmeted head of Athena r., decorated with olive wreath.
Rev: ꓱꓭꓵ *(yhd)* crude and written horizontally to r. of owl standing to r. head facing. 250/1,000

1055. AR *gerah.*
Obv: Helmeted head of Athena r., decorated with olive wreath.
Rev: ꓸꓐꓵ *(yhd, retrograde Aramaic)* to r. of owl standing to r. head facing. 250/1,000

1056. AR *gerah.*
Obv: Bare male head r.
Rev: ꓱꓒꓭꓵ *(yhd)* to r. of owl standing to r. head facing, in l. field olive spray. RRR

1057   1059   1060

1057. AR *gerah*.
  Obv: Head of Persian king wearing jagged crown to r. On most examples, under the head, a circular motif due to a clashed die error.
  Rev: ꟼꟼꝛ *(yhd)* to r. of owl standing to r., head facing; in upper l. field lily flower.   250/1,000
      a. Same as 1057 but prior to the clashing of the dies

1058. AR *gerah*.
  Obv: Head of Persian king wearing jagged crown facing r.
  Rev: ꟼꟼꝛ *(yhd)* to r. of fat owl standing to r., head facing; in upper l. field lily flower.   350/1,250

1059. AR half-*gerah*.
  Obv: Head of Persian king wearing jagged crown facing r.
  Rev: ꟼꟼꝛ *(yhd)* to r. of falcon with wings spread, head r.
                                                    250/750
    a. Rev: Falcon, wings spread, head r.; on r. retrograde
       ꟼꟼꝛ *(yhd)*.
    b. Rev: Falcon, wings spread, head r.; on r. retrograde
       ꟼꟼꝛ *(yhwd)*.
    c. Rev: Falcon, wings spread, head l.; on l. ꟼꟼꝛ *(yhd)*.
    d. Rev: Same as c. but ꟼꟼꝛ *(yhd)* retrograde.
    e. Obv: Persian king's head faces l.

1060. AR half-*gerah*.
  Obv: Lily.
  Rev: ꟼꟼꝛ *(yhd)* above r. wing of falcon with wings spread, head r.
                                                    500/3,000
    a. Falcon with longer wings, legend on r.

1062   1063

1061

1061. AR *gerah*.
  Obv: Large ear, possibly representing the "Ear of God."
  Rev: ⟨yhd⟩ to r. of falcon with wings spread, head r.
                                                    2,000/5,000
  Gerson suggests that "the ear has to do with the Shema prayer, bedrock of Jewish liturgy and ethical monotheism: 'Hear O Israel, the Lord Our God, the Lord is one.'" This, then, is the "Shema coin."[64]
  When one side of the coin is shown significantly larger than the other in a composite, this means that one die was notably larger than the other.

1062. AR *gerah*.
  Obv: Horn or shofar.
  Rev: ⟨yhd⟩ to r. of crude falcon with wings spread, head r.
                                                    RRR

1063. AR *gerah*.
  Obv: Incense bowl (?) with flames and smoke.
  Rev: ⟨yhd⟩ to r. of falcon with wings spread, head r.
                                                    1,500/4,000
  Ronen suggests that the obverse description as a helmet is not consistent with the Jewish symbols in this sub-series (Nos. 1061–63).[65]

1064. AR half-*ma'ah-obol*.
  Obv: Lynx head with horns to l.
  Rev: ⟨yhzqyh—Hezekiah⟩ beneath forepart of winged animal with head of Persian king to l.   RRR

1065. AR half-*ma'ah-obol*.
  Obv: Young male head l.
  Rev: ⟨yhzqyh—Hezekiah⟩ beneath forepart of winged, horned lynx l.   1,000/5,000
  a. Brockage of reverse inscription on obverse to left of face.
  This is possibly the same Hezekiah mentioned by Josephus who, quoting Hecateus, tells us: "after the battle of Gaza, Ptolemy became master of Syria, and that many of the inhabitants, hearing of his kindliness and humanity,

*desired to accompany him to Egypt and to associate themselves with his realm,
'Among these (he says) was Ezechias [Hezekiah], a chief priest of the Jews, a
man of about 66 years of age, highly esteemed by his countrymen...'"* [66]

1065   1066

1066. AR half-*ma'ah-obol*.
   Obv: Young male head r.
   Rev: ﬠﬡﬢﬣﬤﬥ (*yhzqyh—Hezekiah*) beneath forepart of winged,
   horned lynx l.   1,000/4,000

MACEDONIAN PERIOD
C. 333 BCE – 302 BCE
Struck from loose dies.
Greek Attic *sheqel* (*tetradrachm*) standard 17.28 g.
Theoretical quarter-*sheqel* 4.32 g.
Theoretical *ma'ah-obol* 0.72 g.
Average half-*ma'ah-obol* 0.36 g.
Average quarter-*ma'ah-obol* 0.18 g.

1067. AR quarter-*ma'ah-obol*, one specimen 0.11 g.
   Obv: Blank.
   Rev: Winged and horned bull to right, no visible legend.   RRR
   a. Winged and horned bull to l.

1068. AR half-*ma'ah*.
   Obv: Small head facing front.
   Rev: Forepart of winged lynx as above, but turned to r.   RRR
   No inscription visible on known specimens.

1069. AR half-*ma'ah-obol*.
   Obv: Facing head in a circle of connected dots.
   Rev: ﬠﬡﬢﬣ (*hapecha—the governor*) to l., ﬠﬡﬢﬣﬤﬥ (*yhzqyh—Hezekiah*) to r. of owl standing r., head facing, the feathers of the head
   form a beaded circle. .   350/1,000
   a. Crude style and inscription.

1069

1070

1070.   AR half-*ma'ah-obol.*
Obv: Crude facing head.
Rev: Owl standing l., head facing, the feathers of the head form a beaded circle; on l. and r. pseudo Greek inscriptions which are not readily legible.   250/600

1071.   AR quarter-*ma'ah-obol,* one specimen 0.16 g.
Obv: Facing head in a circle of connected dots.
Rev: ᕼᕼᗷᏐᓚ *(ywhnn—Yohanan)* upwards on l., to r., ᕼᗄᏐᗄᏋ *(ha-kohen—the priest)* downwards to r. of owl standing r., head facing, the feathers of the head form a beaded circle.   RRR

1071

1072

1072.   AR quarter-*ma'ah-obol.*
Obv: Facing head in a circle of connected dots.
Rev: ᕼᗄᏐ *(yhd*-retrograde*)* to l., ᗄᕼᏐᗄᏐ *(yhwdh*-retrograde*)* to r. of crude owl standing r., head facing.   RRR

1073.   AR quarter-*ma'ah-obol*
Obv: Owl stands to r. head facing, possible remnants of paleo-Hebrew on r.
Rev: Lily.   RRR

1074.   AR half-*ma'ah-obol.*
Obv: Crude lily.
Rev: Duck stands to r., head turned back surrounded by ᗄᕼᏐᗄᏐ *(Yhwdh).*   RRR

1075

1075b

1075.   AR half-*ma'ah-obol.*
  Obv: Chimera head r.
  Rev: ⱻ٩ⴕⱻꒊ *(Yhwdh)* around duck standing to r., head turned
    back.   350/1,500
  a. Obv: Degraded Chimera head r.
  b. Obv: Unusual trapezoidal shape.
  c. Obv: Egg or pellet shape.

PTOLEMAIC PERIOD
c. 302 BCE – 260 BCE
Greek Attic *sheqel* (*tetradrachm*) standard 17.28 g.
Theoretical quarter-*sheqel* 4.13 g.
Unknown denomination around 1.7g (Nos. 1084, 1085).
Theoretical *ma'ah* 0.72 g.
Theoretical half-*ma'ah* 0.36 g.
Average quarter-*ma'ah* 0.18 g.

UNDER PTOLEMY I
c. 302/1 BCE TO 295/4 BCE
Loose dies.

1076.   AR quarter-*ma'ah-obol.*
  Obv: Stylized head facing forward, similar to 1069.
  Rev: ٩ⱻꒊ *(yhd)* to l. of eagle with wings spread standing l.   RRR

1077.   AR quarter-*ma'ah-obol.*
  Obv: Young male head r.
  Rev: ٩ⱻꒊ *(yhd)* to l. of eagle with wings spread standing l.
                                                            350/1,000

1078.   AR quarter-*ma'ah-obol.*
  Obv: Young male head l.
  Rev: ٩ⱻꒊ *(yhd)* to l. of eagle with wings spread standing l.
                                                            500/1,500
  a. Crude, narrow head l. on obverse.

After 295/4 bce
Tendency to vertical die axis.

1078   1079

1079. AR quarter-*ma'ah-obol.*
Obv: Diademed head of Ptolemy I r., fine style.
Rev: ꜰ⊐ꓱ⊥ *(yhwd)* to r. of eagle, wings closed, stands left.   RRR

1080. AR quarter-*ma'ah-obol.*
Obv: Diademed head of Ptolemy I l.
Rev: ꓱ⊐⊥ *(yhd)* to l. of eagle, wings spread, half turned l. and stand-
ing upon thunderbolt.   RRR

Under Ptolemy II
283/2 –after 270 bce
Tendency to vertical die axis.

1081. AR quarter-*ma'ah-obol.*
Obv: Diademed head of Ptolemy I r.
Rev: ꓱ⊐⊥ *(yhd)* downward to r. of head of Berenike I r.
                                   500/2,000

1081   1087

1082. AR quarter-*ma'ah-obol.*
Obv: Diademed head of Ptolemy I r.
Rev: ꓱ⊐⊥ *(yhd)* to l. of head of Berenike I l.   500/2,000
The inscription may be upward, downward, or retrograde.

AFTER 270 TO 261/60 BCE
Vertical die axis.

1083. AR quarter-*ma'ah-obol.*
Obv: Jugate heads Ptolemy I and Berenike I r.
Rev: ᔦᕂᕀ *(yhd)* to r. of jugate heads of Ptolemy II and Arsinöe II
r.   RRR

261/0 BCE OR EARLIER
Tendency to vertical die axis.

1084. AR unknown denomination, 1.71 g.
Obv: Diademed head Ptolemy I r.
Rev: ᕂᔦᕂᕀ *(yhdh)* to l. of eagle, wings spread, half turned left,
standing on thunderbolt, **BA** between inscription and eagle.
                                                                RRR

1085. AR unknown denomination, 1.66 g.
Obv: Diademed head of Ptolemy I r.
Rev: ᕂᔦᕂᕀ *(yhdh)* to l. of eagle, wings spread, half turned l. and
standing upon thunderbolt.   RRR

1086. AR *ma'ah-obol* (?), 0.80 g.
Obv: Diademed head of Ptolemy I to r.
Rev: ᕂᔦᕂᕀ *(yhdh)* to l. of eagle, wings spread, stands l. on thunder-
bolt.   350/1,000

1087. AR quarter-*ma'ah-obol.*
Obv: Diademed head of Ptolemy I r.
Rev: ᕂᔦᕂᕀ *(yhdh)* to l. of eagle, wings spread, half turned l. and
standing upon thunderbolt.   350/1,000
a. Double struck.
b. More finely detailed portrait style.

1088. AR quarter-*ma'ah-obol.*
Obv: Diademed head of Ptolemy I r.
Rev: Eagle as above, but inscription is crude, square letters, possibly
Aramaic.   350/1,500
a. Similar but the crude square letters are retrograde.

CHAPTER FIVE

MACEDONIAN, PTOLEMAIC, & SELEUCID COINS

ALEXANDER THE GREAT CONQUERS THE WORLD

As if to underline the local purpose of coins in Philistia, Samaria, and Yehud, the Macedonians, as well as the Seleucids and Ptolemies, established branch mints in several cities of ancient Israel. Coins of standard types in varying denominations were struck at these mints and circulated throughout their empires.

The influence of the Macedonians on the lands under Greek rule began with Philip II, King of Macedon, who was such an able statesman and skillful general that his son Alexander III (the Great) is said to have complained, "My father will get ahead of me in everything and will leave nothing great for me to do." In 338 BCE, Philip II brought all of Greece under his control, and planned his next step toward world conquest: the overthrow of the Persian Empire. This effort was interrupted by his assassination in 336 BCE, but Alexander (336–323 BCE) eventually completed the project.

Alexander was brought up in his father's court and tutored by no less a teacher than Aristotle. In his final decade, even though he lived only thirty-three years, Alexander's Macedonian army swept over every nation that lay before it. He crossed the Hellespont into Asia Minor in 333 BCE and defeated the Persians at Issos, effectively ending Persia's rule over the ancient land of Israel. His army then cut south along the coastline of the Levant, besieged Tyre, and occupied Egypt. In Egypt, he founded the city of Alexandria, which became one of the ancient world's greatest cultural and commercial centers. Alexander's army then reversed, heading to Mesopotamia, where he again crushed King Darius' army, this time in 331 BCE at Gaugamela, destroying the Persian Empire. Alexander marched across Babylon, Susa, and Persepolis, across Afghanistan, and on to India.

The Jews fared well under Alexander. He was tolerant of those who submitted to his rule. And, the good relations between Alexander and the Jews is reflected in a legend preserved in Josephus, who reports that when Alexander was besieging Tyre, Sanballat, the governor of Samaria, came to him with an army of 8,000 men.[1]

Alexander received him and granted his request to build a temple on Mount Gerizim, where Sanballat's son-in-law Manasseh would serve as high priest.

Josephus says Alexander demanded that the Jewish high priest Jaddua surrender Jerusalem and the Jewish people. Jaddua refused, and Alexander and his army marched on Jerusalem to punish them. Jaddua was able to keep the Jews calm by revealing his dream that no harm would befall the city or the Temple.[2]

The next day at Zofim, north of Jerusalem, Jaddua met Alexander with a procession of priests dressed in white, purple, scarlet, and gold. Alexander bowed down to them. His own generals thought he was insane for doing so, but Alexander appeased them by saying that he had seen Jaddua in a dream and he had foretold that Alexander would defeat the Persian king. Alexander then went to the Jerusalem Temple and offered a sacrifice to the Jewish God, granting special privileges to the Jews while he was there.[3]

The Talmud tells a similar story, albeit with different names for the high priest and the meeting place. It is clear that the Jewish people enjoyed good fortune under Alexander the Great.[4]

Many of Alexander's coins were struck upon the metal obtained from the melting of the stores of gold and silver in the Persian treasury. Alexander established a mint at Akko, a Phoenician city that today sits at the northern coast of Israel, (the only mint city of Israel to strike his coins), where both gold and silver coins were issued. Alexander's distinctive coinage based on gold *staters* and silver *drachms* and *tetradrachms* soon became common in ancient Israel. The *tetradrachms* carried on their obverse the head of Herakles wearing a lion skin, and on the reverse a half-naked Zeus seated on a throne holding both an eagle and a scepter. The coinage of Alexander the Great circulated widely in the ancient Holy Land, and the coinage in his name continued to be issued long after his premature death.

RULE OF THE PTOLEMIES

Upon Alexander's death in 323 BCE, the empire was divided by civil war between his generals and successors, called the diadochi. The Holy Land became a flashpoint because of its strategic location. This small strip of coast land was a crossroads to the entire Levant. It lay between Syria in the north, controlled by the Seleucids, and Egypt in the south, controlled by the Ptolemies. Between 320 to 301 BCE, the land of Israel changed rulers five times, each accompanied by all of the trauma and destruction of war. In 301 BCE, southern Syria, including the land of Israel, came under Ptolemaic rule, where it remained for 100 years. The Seleucids continued to control northern Syria, which allowed them vital access to the Mediterranean.

Josephus reports how Ptolemy I Soter (323–283 BCE) captured Jerusalem on a Sabbath when the Jews refused to fight in their own defense. Ptolemy entered the city on the pretense of making a sacrifice.

Under Ptolemy II Philadelphus (283–245 BCE), relations flourished between his capital at Alexandria and the center of the Jewish community at Jerusalem. Philadelphus freed many of the Jewish slaves who had been captured during his father's military campaigns.

But the best-remembered achievement of Ptolemy II was a literary one that made the Jewish Bible accessible to the entire Greek world. Ptolemy II had a large and splendid library, of which he was especially proud. One day, according to legend, the royal librarian told Ptolemy that he had gathered together 995 books of the best literature that all the nations of the world had to offer. However, the librarian added, the greatest books of all, the five books of Moses, were not included.

Ptolemy II sent envoys bearing gifts to the high priest in Jerusalem. The envoys were to ask not only for copies of the five books of Moses, but also for a group of scholars to translate them into Greek.

The high priest met the request and sent 72 scholars to Alexandria. It is said that each of them worked alone to complete the difficult and unprecedented task. When they were finished and the translations were compared, each of the 72 is said to have been identical. Thus, this Greek translation of the Bible was called the Septuagint or "the seventy." Now, the wisdom of the Jewish nation was available for the first time to others, including those Jews who had been born and raised outside their homeland, as in Alexandria, and had already lost fluency in the Hebrew language.[5]

Ptolemy II revitalized the major port city that had been called Akko since the earliest times, and renamed it Ptolemais. He established a mint there, as well as in Gaza, Ashqelon, and Jaffa. Additional coins were produced in nearby Egypt and Phoenicia, thus many Ptolemaic issues circulated in the ancient Levant. It is also worth noting once again that Ptolemy I and II allowed Judaea to issue Ptolemaic coins with the Yehud inscription upon them.[6]

Josephus writes that after Ptolemy III (Euergetes) (246–221 BCE) defeated the Seleucids in the third Syrian war (246–241 BCE), he offered a sacrifice of incense at the Jerusalem Temple.[7]

His son Ptolemy IV (Philopator) (221–203 BCE) was victorious over the Seleucid king Antiochus III in 217 BCE at Raphia. Josephus describes the Jews of this time as "in no way different from a storm-tossed ship which is beset on either side by heavy seas, finding them-selves crushed between the successes of Antiochus and the adverse turn of his fortunes." Josephus says that Philopator also visited Jerusa-lem with the idea of entering the Temple. But, the Jewish God stepped in and threw him to his knees. The Egyptian king was not pleased, and when he returned to Alexandria he ordered local Jews into the arena where they would be trampled by a herd of elephants. Instead, legend says, the elephants turned upon their keepers. This tale surely illus-trates how the Jews of the time felt about Ptolemy IV.[8]

In 205 BCE, Ptolemy IV died and was followed on the throne by his five-year-old son, Ptolemy V. This created a situation favorable to Ptolemy's enemies, and in 201 Antiochus III again invaded Palestine, this time conquering all of the country except Gaza.

Reference is also made to the Ptolemaic Yehud coins (Nos. 1076 to 1088). As already noted, Barag points out that Judaea "was the only area in which such a currency was issued under the Ptolemies (after 301 BCE) but for how long?" The striking of the Ptolemaic Yehud series for local circulation "certainly displays direct control from the center of government."[9]

SELEUCIDS AND THE GOD MADE MANIFEST

By the time Antiochus III defeated the boy king Ptolemy V, the Jews had become thoroughly fed up with the rule of the Ptolemies. They welcomed Antiochus III to Jerusalem. He rewarded the Jews by rescinding the taxes on Jerusalemites for three years, making large contributions to the Temple, and rebuilding portions of the city that had been destroyed. The Jews were not only left alone, but, according to Josephus, Antiochus III went so far as to pass a law forbidding anyone even to bring non-kosher animals to Jerusalem. He also granted Jews the right to live according to "their native laws."[10]

It was a dramatic turn of events when Antiochus III's son, Antiochus IV (175–164 BCE), succeeded his older brother, Seleucus IV, and pressed Greek culture and religion upon the Jews with such forcefulness that it represents a major turning point in Jewish history.

On his coins, Antiochus IV proclaims himself "Theos Epiphanes" or "God Made Manifest," but he was mocked by some contemporaries as Antiochus Epimanes, "the mad," who was bound and determined to force Greek culture and religion upon the Jews. Antiochus IV prohibited the worship of the Jewish God, burned the Torah, and defiled the Temple by sacrificing a sow upon the altar.

Pressured by Rome to remit huge sums of money following a war during his father's rule, Antiochus focused on Jerusalem as a key point in his kingdom. Not only did he loot and pillage, but he auctioned the high priesthood to the highest bidder. So High Priest Onias III was replaced in 173 BCE by his Hellenized brother Jason, who promised to pay 360 silver *talents* immediately and another 80 *talents* from future income.

"In addition," the Second Book of the Maccabees relates, "he undertook to pay another hundred and fifty *talents* for the authority to institute a sports-stadium, to arrange for the education of young men there, and to enroll in Jerusalem a group to be known as the 'Antiochenes.' The king agreed and as soon as he had seized the high-priesthood, Jason made the Jews conform to the Greek way of life."[11]

Soon Greek culture was flourishing among many of Jerusalem's citizens, and even the priests "placed no value on their hereditary dignities, but cared above everything for Hellenic honors."[12] Jason had built an athletic stadium of the Greek fashion in the Tyropoeon Valley, a stone's throw from the Temple. There was no law against Jewish youths participating in the games. However, all athletes participated in the games naked. This practice was abhorrent to the religious Jews, and the problems became more severe when a number of Jewish athletes had surgical operations that "removed their marks of circumcision" in order to save themselves embarrassment during competitions.[13]

Within a few years, even the corrupt were outdone. Menelaus, not of priestly birth, but loyal to the Seleucids, outbid Jason by 300 *talents* of silver, becoming the new high priest. Jason was forced to flee across the Jordan. Menelaus was "a wicked and impious man, who in order to have sole authority for himself had compelled his nation to violate their own laws."[14]

Antiochus continued to try to consolidate his rule, and in 168 BCE departed for his second expedition to Egypt. During this time, Jason returned to Jerusalem from Transjordan and unsuccessfully tried to re-establish his position as high priest. Many Jews were killed, but Jason retreated back across the Jordan. At about the same time as this civil turmoil, Antiochus returned in a fierce temper because he was convinced that the fighting represented a rebellion against him, and it may have been just so.

He stormed the city, looted the Temple, killed thousands of Jews and sold thousands more into slavery. He erected a citadel called the Akra in Jerusalem, and in every way transformed the city into a Greek city-state. "They shed the blood of the innocent round the temple; they defiled the holy place. The citizens of Jerusalem fled for fear of them; she became the abode of aliens, and alien herself to her offspring: her children deserted her. Her temple lay desolate as a wilderness; her feasts were turned to mourning, her Sabbaths to a reproach, her honor to contempt. The shame of her fall matched the greatness of her renown, and her pride was bowed low in grief."[15]

By the year 167 BCE, Antiochus had sent "an elderly Athenian to force the Jews to abandon their ancestral customs and no longer regulate their lives according to the laws of God. He was also commissioned to pollute the temple at Jerusalem and dedicate it to Olympian Zeus, and to dedicate the sanctuary on Mount Gerizim to Zeus, God of Hospitality, following the practice of the local inhabitants."[16]

Under the Seleucids, coins were minted in Akko, Ashqelon, Demetrias by the Sea, Gaza, Samaria, and one transitional bronze coin (No. 1131) in Jerusalem.

The coins listed in this chapter show representative examples; many types were struck in multiple years the dates and varieties can be found in specialized references.

MACEDONIAN COINS OF ANCIENT ISRAEL
ALEXANDER III, THE GREAT (336–323 BCE)

The gold and silver coins of Alexander struck in Akko (Ake) carry the mintmark of the Phoenician letters *ayin* and *kaph*. Some have dates. Martin Price suggests that the era of Ake began in 346/45 BCE. The undated issues are apparently the earliest, dating to the period 330 to 327 BCE. The first dated gold and silver issues carry the year "21," corresponding to 326/5 BCE and the latest date to 305/04 BCE.

MINT OF AKKO
AU *stater* c. 8.6 g.
AR *tetradrachm* c. 17 g.
Axis varies.

1089

1089.   AU *stater*.
   Obv: Athena head r. wearing Corinthian helmet decorated with griffin.
   Rev: ΑΛΕΞΑΝΔΡΟΥ *(of Alexander)*; winged Nike stands l., holding wreath and ship's mast, Phoenician mintmark and date in l. below wing (year 30). Struck 317/16 BCE.   1,750/3,000

1090

1090.   AR *tetradrachm*.
   Obv: Bust of Herakles r., wearing lion skin headdress.
   Rev: ΑΛΕΞΑΝΔΡΟΥ; Zeus seated l. on backless throne, holding eagle on r. hand, scepter in l., behind throne, Phoenician mintmark and date beneath eagle (year 32). Struck 315/14 BCE.
          200/750

1091. AR *drachm.*
Obv: Bust of Herakles r., possibly modeled after Alexander, wearing lion skin headdress.
Rev: Zeus seated l. as on 1090 (year 22). Struck 325/24 BCE.

50/200

1092. AR *obol.*
Obv: Bust of Herakles r., possibly modeled after Alexander, wearing lion skin headdress.
Rev: Zeus seated l. as on 1090 (no date). Struck 330–27 BCE.

75/300

PTOLEMAIC COINS OF ANCIENT ISRAEL

MINT OF AKKO-PTOLEMAIS

AU *octadrachm* c. 27.7 g.
AR *tetradrachms* c. 14 g.
Axis mostly ↑, some variations.

1093. Ptolemy II (284–47 BCE). AR *tetradrachm.*
Obv: Diademed head of Ptolemy I r. wearing aegis, border of dots.
Rev: ΠΤΟΛΕΜΑΙΟΥ ΒΑΣΙΛΕΩΣ *(of King Ptolemy)*; Eagle stands l. on thunderbolt; in l. field ∏ *(Ptolemais)* and control mark, on r. date ΛΑ and Θ (255/54 BCE), border of dots.   150/400

1094. Ptolemy III. AE *trihemiobol.* 30–31 mm.
Obv: Diademed head of Zeus Ammon r., border of dots.
Rev: ΠΤΟΛΕΜΑΙΟΥ ΒΑΣΙΛΕΩΣ, eagle stands l. on thunderbolt, ∏ in circle in l. field.   100/500

1095. Ptolemy III (246–221 BCE). AU *octadrachm.*
Obv: Diademed and veiled head of Arisinöe II r., border of dots.
Rev: ΑΡΣΙΝΟΗΣ ΦΙΛΑΔΕΛΦΟΥ *(of Arsinöe, brother-loving)*; double cornucopias, bound with fillet; to l. ς (year 6 = 242/41 BCE) below ∏ and Θ.

7,500/17,500

MINT OF DORA

1096. Ptolemy V (204–180 BCE). AR *tetradrachm*.
Obv: Bust of Ptolemy V r. wearing royal diadem, border of dots.
Rev: ΠΤΟΛΕΜΑΙΟΥ ΒΑΣΙΛΕΩΣ, eagle stands l. on thunderbolt; in
l. field ΔΩ, border of dots.   400/1,500

MINT OF GAZA

1097. Ptolemy II (285–246 BCE). AR *tetradrachm*.
Obv: Diademed head of Ptolemy I r. wearing aegis, border of dots..
Rev: ΠΤΟΛΕΜΑΙΟΥ ΣΩΤΗΡΟΣ *(of Ptolemy, savior)*; eagle stands
l. on thunderbolt; in l. field 𝕬 *(Gaza)*, in r. field ΚΓ (year 23 =
225/24 BCE) above control mark, border of dots.   350/1,250

MINT OF JOPPA

1098. Ptolemy II. AR *tetradrachm*.
Obv: Diademed head of Ptolemy I r. wearing aegis, border of dots.
Rev: ΠΤΟΛΕΜΑΙΟΥ ΣΩΤΗΡΟΣ, eagle stands l. on thunderbolt; in
l. field |ᴛ| *(Joppa)* above 𝕬 to l., and Θ in r. field, border of dots.
                                                               300/1,000

1099.   Ptolemy II. AR *tetradrachm*.
Obv: Diademed head of Ptolemy I r. wearing aegis, border of dots.
Rev: ΠΤΟΛΕΜΑΙΟΥ ΣΩΤΗΡΟΣ, eagle stands l. on thunderbolt; in
   l. field |Ͳ| *(Joppa)*, in r. field ΛΑ and Θ (year 31 = 255/54 BCE),
   border of dots.   300/1,000

1100

1100.   Ptolemy III (246–221 BCE). AV *octadrachm*.
Obv: Diademed and veiled head of Arsinoë II r., lotus-tipped scepter
   over shoulder, border of dots.
Rev: ΑΡΣΙΝΟΗΣ ΦΙΛΑΔΕΛΦΟΥ, double cornucopias, bound with
   fillet; ΛΓ (year 33 = 248/47 BCE) and |Ͳ| flank cornucopias, bor-
   der of dots.   10,000/20,000.

1101.   Ptolemy III. AE 20–22 mm.
Obv: Bearded head of Zeus Ammon r.
Rev: ΠΤΟΛΕΜΑΙΟΥ ΒΑΣΙΛΕΩΣ, eagle stands l. on thunderbolt,
   harpe in l. field, border of dots.   150/600

1102.   Ptolemy V (204–180 BCE). AR *tetradrachm*.
Obv: Bust of Ptolemy V r. wearing royal diadem, border of dots.
Rev: ΠΤΟΛΕΜΑΙΟΥ ΒΑΣΙΛΕΩΣ, eagle stands l. on thunderbolt; in
   l. field |Ͳ| monogram, border of dots.   400/1,250

SELEUCID COINS OF ANCIENT ISRAEL

MINT OF AKKO-PTOLEMAIS
Axis mostly ↑, some variations.

1103. Antiochus III (223–187 BCE). AE 10–12 mm.
Obv: Laureate head of Apollo r.
Rev: Apollo stands l., testing arrow and resting hand on bow, blundered legend. 50/300

1104. Antiochus IV (175–164 BCE). AR *tetradrachm*,
Attic standard.
Obv: Diademed head of Antiochus IV r., fillet border, ⚹ monogram behind head.
Rev: ΒΑΣΙΛΕΩΣ ΑΝΤΙΟΧΟΥ ΘΕΟΥ ΕΠΙΦΑΝΟΥΣ ΝΙΚΗΦΟΡΟΥ
(of King Antiochus, god made manifest, bringer of victory); Zeus seated l. on throne, holds Nike and scepter, palm branch to far left, various control marks in exergue or on left. 400/1,250

1105. Antiochus IV. AE 19–20 mm.
Obv: Diademed, radiate head of Antiochus IV r., border of dots.
Rev: ΒΑΣΙΛΕΩΣ ΑΝΤΙΟΧΟΥ, Nike in biga gallops l., monogram between horse's legs, border of dots. 100/400

1106. Antiochus IV. AE 12–15 mm, serrated.
Obv: Laureate head of Apollo r., ⚹ monogram behind head, border of dots.
Rev: ΒΑΣΙΛΕΩΣ ΑΝΤΙΟΧΟΥ, nude Apollo seated l. on omphalos, holds bow and arrow, aphlaston to far l., various control marks in exergue, border of dots. 50/300

1107. Antiochus IV. AE 13–16 mm, serrated.
Obv: Diademed, radiate head of Antiochus r. ⚹ monogram behind head, border of dots.
Rev: ΒΑΣΙΛΕΩΣ ΑΝΤΙΟΧΟΥ, (often blundered or abbreviated) veiled and draped goddess stands facing front holding long scepter, border of dots. 50/300

1108.   Antiochus V (164–162 BCE). AR *tetradrachm*,
        Attic standard.
   Obv: Diademed head of Antiochus V r., control mark to left, fillet
      border.
   Rev: ΒΑΣΙΛΕΩΣ ΑΝΤΙΟΧΟΥ, nude Apollo sits l. on omphalos,
      holds arrow in r. hand and rests l. on bow, control marks in fields,
      border of dots.   1,000/3,000

1109.   Demetrius I (162–150 BCE). AR *tetradrachm*,
        Attic standard.
   Obv: Diademed head of Demetrius I r., laurel wreath border.
   Rev: Tyche, nude to hips, sits l. on throne with winged triton sup-
      port, holds scepter and cornucopia. ΒΑΣΙΛΕΩΣ ΔΗΜΗΤΡΙΟΥ
      (of King Demetrius).   500/1,500

1110.   Demetrius I. AE 13–16 mm, serrated.
   Obv: Diademed head of Demetrius r., border of dots.
   Rev: ΒΑΣΙΛΕΩΣ ΔΗΜΗΤΡΙΟΥ, veiled and draped goddess stands
      facing front holding long scepter, border of dots.   50/300

1111. Tryphon (142–138 BCE). AR *tetradrachm*,
Phoenician standard.

Obv: Diademed head of Tryphon r., border of dots.

Rev: ΒΑΣΙΛΕΩΣ ΤΡΥΦΩΝΟΣ ΑΥΤΟΚΡΑΤΟΡΟΣ, *(of King Tryphon, the self-empowered)* eagle, wings closed, stands l. on thunderbolt, date ΛΔ (138 BCE), control marks in fields.

3,500/8,500

1112. Antiochus VII (138–129 BCE). AR *tetradrachm*,
Phoenician standard.

Obv: Diademed, draped bust Antiochus VII.

Rev: Eagle, wings closed, stands l. on thunderbolt, IOP r. field (136/5 BCE) Ⱥ monogram to l., border of dots, ΑΝΤΙΟΧΟΥ ΒΑΣΙΛΕΩΣ.

300/850

1113. Cleopatra Thea and Antiochus VIII (125–121 BCE).
AR *tetradrachm*, Attic standard.

Obv: Jugate busts of Cleopatra, diademed, with stephane and veil, and Antiochus diademed, r., fillet border.

Rev: ΒΑΣΙΛΙΣΣΗΣ ΚΛΕΟΠΑΤΡΑΣ ΘΕΑΣ ΚΑΙ ΒΑΣΙΛΕΩΣ ΑΝΤΙΟΧΟΥ *(of Queen Cleopatra, the goddess, and King Antiochus)*; Zeus sits l. on throne, holds Nike in outstretched r. hand and scepter in l., control mark in l. field.

650/2000

1114.   Antiochus VIII (121–96 BCE). AR *tetradrachm*,
        Attic standard.
   Obv: Diademed head of Antiochus r., fillet border.
   Rev: ΒΑΣΙΛΕΩΣ ΑΝΤΙΟΧΟΥ ΕΠΙΦΑΝΟΥΣ *(of King Antiochus, the
        illustrious)*; Zeus Uranius stands l., crescent above head, holding
        star and scepter, control mark in l. field, laurel wreath border.
                                                                    300/850

1115.   Antiochus IX (113–95 BCE). AR *tetradrachm*,
        Attic standard.
   Obv: Diademed, bearded head of Antiochus r., dotted border.
   Rev: ΒΑΣΙΛΕΩΣ ΑΝΤΙΟΧΟΥ ΦΙΛΟΠΑΤΟΡΟΣ *(of King Antiochus,
        the father-loving)*; Athena stands l., holds Nike in r. hand and spear
        in l. arm resting l. hand on shield. control mark in l. field, laurel
        wreath border.   500/1,000

1116.   Civic issue under the Seleucids. AE 15–17 mm.
   Obv: Jugate busts of the Dioscuri r., wearing laurel wreaths and sur-
        mounted by stars. border of dots.
   Rev: ΑΝΤΙΟΧΕΩΝ ΤΩΝ ΕΝ ΠΤΟΛΕΜΑΙΔΙ ΙΕΡΑΣ ΑΣΥΛΟΥ *(of the
        Antiochenes who are in Ptolemais, the sacred [and] inviolable)*; cornuco-
        pia. dates, monogram.   100/400
   *These are civic issues struck under Seleucid control. They do not identify a
   king, but name the city as Antioch in Ptolemais. Confusion stems from Newell's identification. Various dates and monograms, often hard to distinguish,
   legend often abbreviated or blundered.*

MINT OF ASHQELON

1117.   Antiochus IV (175–164 BCE). AE 13–15 mm.
   Obv: Diademed, radiate head of Antiochus r.; border of dots.
   Rev: Dove stands l., BA above, monogram below, border of dots.
                                                                    350/750

1118.   Antiochus VI (144–142 BCE). AR *tetradrachm*,
        Phoenician standard.
   Obv: Diademed bust Antiochus r., border of dots.
   Rev: ΒΑΣΙΛΕΩΣ ΑΝΤΙΟΧΟΥ, eagle stands l. on thunderbolt,
        on l. dove to l., ΑΣ below dove, date LAOP (142/41 BCE).
                                                                    500/2,000

1119.   Tryphon (142–138 BCE). AE 21–23 mm.
Obv: Diademed bust Tryphon r., border of dots.
Rev: ΒΑΣΙΛΕΩΣ ΤΡΥΦΩΝΟΣ ΑΥΤΟΚΡΑΤΟΡΟΣ, Zeus stands front, head l., holds wreath in raised hand, date and ΑΣΚΑ in outer l. field, border of dots.   4,000/10,000

1120.   Antiochus VII (138–129 BCE). AE 12–14 mm.
Obv: Crested helmet with cheek pieces r., border of dots.
Rev: ΒΑΣΙΛΕΩΣ ΑΝΤΙΟΧΟΥ, aphlaston (aplustre), border of dots.
                                                                   350/1,000

1121.   Cleopatra Thea and Antiochus VIII (125–121 BCE).
AR *tetradrachm*, Phoenician standard.
Obv: Jugate busts of Cleopatra, diademed, with stephane and veil, and Antiochus diademed, r.
Rev: ΒΑΣΙΛΙΣΣΗΣ ΚΛΕΟΠΑΤΡΑΣ ΒΑΣΙΛΕΩΣ ΑΝΤΙΟΧΟΥ *(of queen Cleopatra [and] King Antiochus)*; eagle stands l. on thunderbolt, palm branch under far wing, ΑΣ above dove in l. field, control mark between legs, and date ΑϞ Ρ (SE 191 = 122/21 BCE).
                                                                   1,000/3,500

1122

1122.   Antiochus VIII (121–96 BCE). AR *tetradrachm*, Phoenician standard.
Obv: Diademed bust of Antiochus r., border of dots.
Rev: ΒΑΣΙΛΕΩΣ ΑΝΤΙΟΧΟΥ; eagle stands l. on thunderbolt, palm branch behind r. shoulder, to l. ΑΣ above dove, date to r. ϚϞ Ρ (SE 196 = 117/16 BCE), border of dots.
                                                                   750/2,000

Didrachms *exist in this series, but are quite rare.*

1123.   Antiochus IX (113–95 BCE). AR *tetradrachm*,
        Phoenician standard.
   Obv: Diademed and draped bust of Antiochus r., border of dots.
   Rev: ΒΑΣΙΛΕΩΣ ΑΝΤΙΟΧΟΥ ΦΙΛΟΠΑΤΟΡΟΣ (*of King Antiochus,
   the father-loving*); eagle stands l. on thunderbolt, palm branch be-
   hind r. shoulder, to l. ΑΣ above control mark beneath dove, to r.
   ΘϞ P (SE 199 = 114/13 BCE), border of dots.   400/1,250

MINT OF DEMETRIAS BY THE SEA

1124.   Demetrius II, First Reign (145–140/39 BCE).
        AR drachm, Attic standard.
   Obv: Diademed head of Demetrius II r.
   Rev: Cornucopia to l. flanked by ΒΑΣΙΛΕΩΣ ΔΗΜΗΤΡΙΟΥ on r.,
   ΦΙΛΑΔΕΛΦΟΥ ΝΙΚΑΤΟΡΟΣ (*of King Demetrius, the father-loving
   victor*); on l., monogram of ΔΗ in inner r. field and ΔΟΡ (SE 174 =
   139/38 BCE).   250/1,000
   *This mint was a predecessor to Caesarea Maritima, also possibly known
   as Strato's Tower, and it also issued a series of autonomous bronze coins dated
   between 63/62 and 42/41 BCE.*[17]

MINT OF GAZA

1125.   Alexander I Balas (150–145 BCE). AE 15–17 mm.
   Obv: Diademed head of Alexander to r., border of dots.
   Rev: ΒΑΣΙΛΕΩΣ ΑΛΕΞΑΝΔΡΟΥ (*of King Alexander)*; nude Apollo
   stands l. holds arrow in r. hand with l. hand on small bow at side,
   in outer l. field ΓΑΙ.   50/150

1126.   Demetrius II, First Reign (144–140 BCE). AE 15–18 mm.
   Obv: Diademed bust of Demetrius to r., border of dots.
   Rev: ΒΑΣΙΛΕΩΣ ΔΗΜΗΤΡΙΟΥ; tripod, ΓΑ and ↳ in fields and ΑΟΡ
   (year 171 = 142/41 BCE).   50/150

1127.   Antiochus VI (145–142 BCE). AE 14–17 mm.
   Obv: Laureate head Apollo r., border of dots.
   Rev: ΒΑΣΙΛΕΩΣ ΑΝΤΙΟΧΟΥ; draped Tyche stands r., holds object
   in r. hand and cornucopia with l., control marks, border of dots.
                        50/150

1128.   Antiochus VII (138–129 BCE). AE 18–21 mm.
Obv: Diademed head of Antiochus r.; border of dots.
Rev: ΒΑΣΙΛΕΩΣ ΑΝΤΙΟΧΟΥ (usually abbreviated); double cornucopias facing r., border of dots.

50/150

MINT OF SAMARIA

1129. Antiochus IV (175–164 BCE). AE 13–15 mm.
Obv: Radiate head of Antiochus IV, r; in field behind a monogram, astragal border.
Rev: ΒΑΣΙΛΕΩΣ ΑΝΤΙΟΧΟΥ; female deity seated l. on throne with high poles on back, seen in frontal view, her r. hand outstretched holds small winged Nike, l. holding wreath, bird l. at feet of diety, border of dots.   250/750
Published by Barag as a coin struck at Jerusalem,[18] more recent evidence suggests that this coin was struck in Samaria.[19]

1130. Antiochus IX (113–95 BCE). AR *obol.*
Obv: Diademed head of Antiochus IX r., with short, curly beard, both diadem ends fall straight behind, border of dots.
Rev: ΒΑΣΙ downward on r., ΑΝ ΦΙ upward on l., Athena stands l., holds Nike and rests hand on shield, spear behind.

500/1,500

MINT OF JERUSALEM

See coin 1131, p. 185.

HASMONEAN FAMILY TREE (Partial)

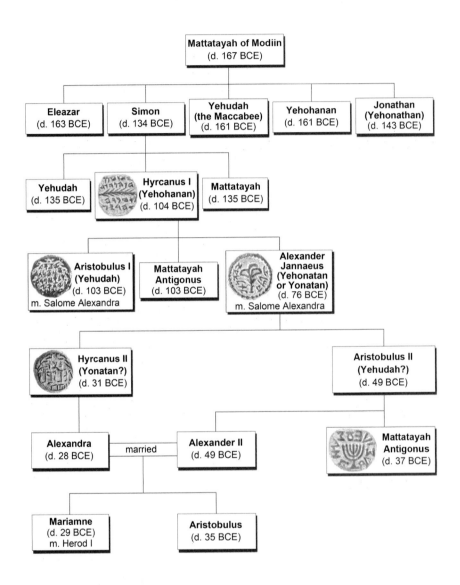

CHAPTER SIX

HASMONEAN DYNASTY

REVOLT OF THE MACCABEES

Certainly there were a number of Jews who willingly adopted the Hellenistic life.[1] Yet the nation would not betray itself and revolution fomented. Many Jews "...died for their beliefs" (I MACCABEES 1:63). There were others who would not die, but neither would they live with the profanities the Seleucids wanted to force upon them. The leader of those keepers of the faith (called Hasidim) was an old man, Mattathias [Mattatayah] the Hasmonean,[2] from the village of Modiin, around 19 miles west of Jerusalem. When Mattathias and his five sons saw the desecration in the land, they "tore their garments, put on sackcloth, and mourned bitterly" (I MACCABEES 2:14).

When the soldiers of Antiochus came to Modiin to force the local Jews to sacrifice to the heathen gods and forsake their laws, Mattatayah and his sons refused to obey. Others were not as strong.

As soon as he had finished, a Jew stepped forward in full view of all to offer sacrifice on the pagan altar at Modiin, in obedience to the royal command. The sight stirred Mattathias to indignation; he shook with passion and in a fury of righteous anger rushed forward and slaughtered the traitor on the very altar. At the same time he killed the officer sent by the king to enforce sacrifice, and pulled the pagan altar down. Thus Mattathias showed his fervent zeal for the law.... He and his sons took to the hills, leaving all their belongings behind in the town (I MACCABEES 2:23–28).

Thus the Hasmonean Revolt began. Mattatayah, his sons, and their band of men waged a successful guerilla war against the oppressive Seleucids. When Mattatayah died, he directed his son Judah (called the Maccabee) to become the military leader and his son Simon to become the political leader. The name Maccabee, according to legend, is an acronym for the initial Hebrew letters of each word (מכבי) in a verse from Exodus (15:11) that was Judah's battle cry: "Who is like unto Thee, O Lord, among the mighty?" (מי כמכה באלם יי?) Another legend suggest the name Maccabee derives from the Aramaic *maqqaba*, "the hammer," recalling Judah's hit-and-run guerilla warfare.

At the time of the first Hasmoneans, the traditional title of the principal leader of the Jews was high priest. The priests, led by the high priest, presided over the Jerusalem Temple. They were also the supreme political authorities of their people. However, even though Mattatayah of Modiin was from a priestly family, the Hasmoneans do not seem to have been related to any previous high priests. Thus, the Hasmoneans established their own dynasty.[3]

During these perilous times, the Jews shunned idolatry, or even the appearance of idolatry. The story of Hannah and her seven sons, one of the most frequently told Jewish folk tales,[4] is a good example. At the time of Mattatayah, Hannah and her seven sons were brought before the Syrian king. Each son, beginning with the eldest, was commanded to bow before an idol. Each of the older six refused and was executed. When the ruler finally came to the seventh son he made the same demand and the boy refused. Even the brutal king felt some pity for the mother and said to the boy, "Look, your brothers are all slain. I shall throw my signet ring in front of the idol. All you need to do is bend down and pick it up. People will then say that you finally submitted to the authority of the king." The boy replied, "Alas for you, O king, if you are so zealous for your honor, how much more so ought we be for God's honor." He refused even the appearance of bowing. The boy was killed and his mother, Hannah, went to the roof and jumped to her death.

This story illustrates how Mattatayah and his followers aggressively rejected all forms of Hellenism. Idolatry was a touchstone issue to the Hasmoneans, who believed, "that no reconciliation whatsoever between Greek polytheism and Jewish monotheism was possible; they succeeded in their revolt against the spread of Hellenism in Judaea and in this way they preserved monotheism for Judaism and the world," Reifenberg writes.[5]

Early in the struggle, Judah defeated a small Seleucid force and killed its commander Apollonius, whose sword Judah took and used for the rest of his life as a symbol of vengeance. After successfully capturing cities such as Beit-Horon, Emmaus, and Beit-Zur, Judah and his men liberated Jerusalem in 164 BCE. They re-entered the Temple, cleaned and re-purified it:

> *They celebrated the rededication of the altar for eight days; there was great rejoicing as they brought burnt-offerings and sacrificed peace-offerings and thank-offerings.... There was great merry-making among the people, and the disgrace brought on them by the Gentiles was removed. Then Judah, his brothers, and the whole congregation of Israel decreed that the rededication of the altar should be observed with joy and gladness at the same season each year, for eight days...* (I MACCABEES 4:56–59).

Thus, the Jews proclaimed a festival beginning on the twenty-fifth day of Kislev of the year 148 of the Seleucid Era (SE), or 164 BCE. This is the origin of the Jewish holiday Chanukah, which has been celebrated by Jews worldwide for eight days every year since that time.

The victory of Judah Maccabee ended the Seleucid persecution of the Jews—but not the Seleucid rule over them. Perhaps Judah initiated a treaty with the Romans in 161 BCE in order to warn the Seleucids against any further incursions, and the Romans were only too happy to find another possible way to weaken the power of the Seleucid Empire.

Judah was not content with his liberation of Jerusalem and continued his exploits in Galilee, Transjordan, and elsewhere in the area. His success forced the young Antiochus V Eupator (son of Antiochus IV) and his viceroy Lysias once again to bring an army against the Maccabees. This time, at a battle near Beit-Zachariah (today known as Kfar Etzion), the Maccabean army was defeated by a large Seleucid force, which included 32 armored elephants. During this battle, Judah's brother Eleazar was crushed and killed when he crawled under an elephant he mistakenly believed was carrying the king and stabbed it in the belly. Judah and his men withdrew to the mountains of Gophna, which they used as an operating base for the next few years.

After his victory, Lysias moved on to Jerusalem and besieged Judah's forces on Mt. Zion. But, at this time Lysias also learned that a rival faction of the Seleucid army was going to enter Antioch and seize power. This news prompted Lysias to go there quickly. First, he proposed favorable terms for a peaceful settlement with the Jews—better a strong ally than a vanquished foe. Thus, the son rescinded the hated decrees of the father. Freedom of worship was once again guaranteed, and Jerusalem was recognized as the religious capital of the Jewish nation.

In 162 BCE, Demetrius I took the throne. He installed Eliakim (Alcimus) as the new high priest in Jerusalem. Eliakim was from a priestly line, so many of the Hasidim recognized him. In effect, this constituted a *de facto* decision that religious freedom was sufficient for the Jews and that they did not also need political liberty from the Seleucids. Now, the Hellenizers again wielded power in Jerusalem and the Seleucid king kept armed forces near the Temple Mount.

Judah was killed in battle and succeeded by his brother Jonathan, who continued to enlist support from his outpost in the hills north of Jerusalem. In 153 BCE, Alexander Balas, a young man of undistinguished birth, tried to pass himself off as a son of Antiochus IV. The Roman Senate—although it knew the truth about him—acknowledged Balas' supposed royal origin in a move to further confuse the Seleucids.

Anticipating internal struggle with Demetrius I, Balas appointed Jonathan as high priest and ethnarch, sending him a purple robe and a gold wreath. The ploy worked and gained Jonathan's support. In 150 BCE, Demetrius I was defeated and Balas became king of Syria. His ally Jonathan, brother of Judah Maccabee, had essentially become an autonomous ruler in Judaea, with only a token Seleucid force remaining near the Temple Mount. But Balas was an unpopular ruler, and in 147 BCE Demetrius II claimed rights to his father's throne. Jonathan remained loyal to Balas, but in 145 BCE Demetrius II Nikator (the Victorious) became king of the Seleucids.

In short order, however, Balas' former general, Diodotus Tryphon, appeared with Balas' young son, Antiochus VI, and in 143 BCE Tryphon proclaimed the boy king in place of Demetrius II. Tryphon hoped eventually to do away with the boy (who may not have even been of royal blood) and assume the throne himself. Rebellion broke out against Demetrius II, and Jonathan took the opportunity to demand removal of the Syrian troops from the Akra fortress in exchange for sending 3,000 Jewish troops to Antioch to help Demetrius. They succeeded, and Demetrius was saved. This twist was ironic, since it had been only some 30 years earlier that Antiochus IV Epiphanes had brought his army to Jerusalem to crush the revolt of the Jews against his crusade of Hellenism.

Once out of danger, however, Demetrius reneged on his promise to clear the Syrian troops from the Akra. Meanwhile, many of his soldiers, who had not been paid, deserted him for Tryphon, who soon conquered Antioch and in the name of young Antiochus VI confirmed all of Demetrius' earlier promises to Jonathan.

Jonathan and his brother Simon allied themselves with Tryphon, who was in fact only the regent for the young Antiochus VI. In his name, Jonathan and Simon captured Ashqelon, Gaza, and other areas. As Jonathan's power increased, Tryphon became frightened of him, especially since Jonathan had remained loyal to the memory of Alexander Balas and thus was devoted to his son, the young Antiochus VI.

Tryphon felt he had to get rid of Jonathan before he could do away with the young king. So, Tryphon marched to Beit-Shean at the head of a large army. But, Jonathan's force of 40,000 men was just as strong. Fearing defeat, Tryphon resorted to trickery. He received Jonathan with great pomp and told him he had not come to fight, but to bestow honor on him.

Always ready to be flattered, Jonathan fell for the ploy and sent most of his men home. With a force of only 1,000, he accompanied Tryphon and his army to Akko. Suddenly, Tryphon's army turned on the Jews and killed them all save Jonathan.

With Jonathan imprisoned, Tryphon moved toward Judaea, hoping to defeat the leaderless Jews. Hearing of his brother's capture, Simon had already rushed to Jerusalem where he was accepted "in place of Judah and your brother Jonathan" (I MACCABEES 13:8).

Simon swiftly began a campaign to Judaize other cities, beginning with Gezer and the port of Jaffa, from which he began to establish trade with foreign lands. Simon's success infuriated Tryphon so much that he had Jonathan and two of his sons killed. Shortly thereafter, in 142 BCE, Tryphon also disposed of Antiochus VI. This act gave Simon more reason to hate Tryphon, so Simon set about making a deal with Demetrius II, who by this time was penniless. In exchange for gold to pay his mercenaries, Demetrius gave Simon in writing the complete independence of Judaea, even dismissing the Jews from paying annual tribute:

In the year 170 [142 BCE] Israel was released from the gentile yoke. The people began to write on their contracts and agreements, 'In the first year of Simon, the great high priest, general and leader of the Jews' (I MACCABEES 13:41–2).

Simon was the first Hasmonean who was not encumbered by oppressive military obligations, and the Jews flourished during his dominion.

Old men sat in the streets, talking together of their blessings; and the young men dressed themselves in splendid military style.... He restored peace to the land, and there were great rejoicings throughout Israel. Each man sat under his own vine and fig-tree, and they had no one to fear. Those were days when every enemy vanished from the land and every hostile king was crushed (I MACCABEES 14:9–13).

Simon placed his son, John Hyrcanus I, at the head of the Jewish army, which rebuffed continued attempts by Tryphon to invade their land. Antiochus VII Sidetes (138–129 BCE) continued the fight his brother had waged against Tryphon. It was so important for the latest Antiochus to keep Simon and the Jews on his side in the battle for the Syrian throne, that he granted them even more privileges in 139 BCE. These included permission to "mint your own coinage as currency for your country. Jerusalem and the Temple shall be free..." (I MACCABEES 15:6).

However, Simon did not issue any coins before Antiochus VII reneged on his promise while he was besieging the city of Dora, a stronghold for Tryphon. Antiochus hoped to finally defeat Tryphon and destroy him.

Simon sent along a tribute payment of 2,000 men, gold, silver, and armor, but Antiochus, now feeling infallible, "repudiated all his previous agreements with Simon and broke off relations" (I MACCABEES 15:27).

Oddly, Simon's end did not come through a foreign enemy, but by the hand of his own son-in-law Ptolemy (son of Abubus) who wanted to be leader of Judaea. Simon and his sons Judah and Mattatayah were killed in 134 BCE. Ptolemy also sent his killers after John Hyrcanus I, but he escaped to Jerusalem where he was welcomed by the people as the only heir to Simon the Hasmonean. Thus, John Hyrcanus I assumed the position of high priest.

CHRONOLOGY OF THE EARLY COINS

Simon's son and successor, John Hyrcanus I, reigned from 135 to 104 BCE. His first coins were probably issued at the Jerusalem mint in the name of Antiochus (No. 1131). These small coins depicted on the obverse the lily of Jerusalem which "usurped the traditional place of the Seleucid king on the coinage." On the reverse, "the presence of the Seleucid anchor and the inscription naming Antiochus seemed to respectfully acknowledge the source of the privilege" of minting independent coinage, Oliver Hoover explains.[6] These coins are found primarily in Judaea, and it is widely assumed that they were issued in Jerusalem.[7] These anchor/lily coins are dated to the years SE 181 and 182 (132/1 and 131/0 BCE, respectively). The last issue was struck less than a year before Antiochus VII died in battle against the Parthians.[8] There is no evidence that other Seleucid coins were issued in Jerusalem, especially with portraits of the Seleucid kings such as those which were issued in Gaza, Ashqelon, Akko, and other cities in the area.[9]

The lily of Jerusalem appears on several other Hasmonean coins (Nos. 1134, 1138, 1147, 1148), and continues as a symbol of Jerusalem for some time. Most significant, however, is that the anchor makes its debut here as a Jewish image. "The anchor symbolism continued to be present in Judaea after the fall of the Hasmoneans, reappearing on several series of bronze coins struck at Jerusalem under Herod the Great. Even after Herod's death in 4 BCE, the anchor emblem lived on, apparently now as a Herodian symbol...the purpose seems to have been to express continuity and legitimacy."[10]

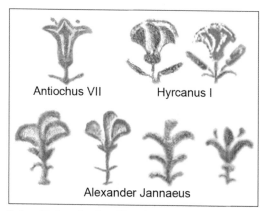

6.1. Styles for the lily of Jerusalem on Hasmonean coins. (Graphic: Fontanille.)

Early scholars in this field studied the first Jewish coins with paleo-Hebrew legends and attempted to identify who issued them. It had been believed that Simon the Maccabee (142–135 BCE), Judah's brother and the first Maccabee to actually achieve the high priestly title, struck the first Jewish coins in the mid-130's BCE.[11] Later, in light of evidence established by archaeological excavations at Beit Zur and elsewhere, all of the coins once attributed to Simon were re-attributed to the Jewish War (66–70 CE).[12] Next, Simon's son, John Hyrcanus I, was identified as the leader likely to have issued the first Jewish coins.[13] In 1967, however, Meshorer suggested that it was Hyrcanus I's son, Alexander Jannaeus, who struck the first Jewish coins. This was widely debated for years. Today, while all chronological problems of the Hasmonean coins have not been fully resolved, there is a consensus that the first coins were struck by John Hyrcanus I (135–104 BCE), the son of Simon and nephew of the legendary Judah Maccabee, hero of the Chanukah story, using his Hebrew name "Yehohanan."[14] This scenario was firmly established by the discovery of a hoard of coins in Nablus (ancient Shechem) in Samaria.

Professor Dan Barag of the Hebrew University Institute of Archaeology in Jerusalem narrated his eureka moment in resolving the mystery:

"In January of 1988, an Arab antiquities dealer in Jerusalem showed me a hoard of coins covered with the same type of earth. It was evident that it was a part of a hoard. No doubt it was the most important Hasmonean hoard ever discovered. The coins were so encrusted that I could not read their inscriptions. Thus there could not have been a previous classification or sorting of the group.

"On cleaning and sorting through the first group of about 180 coins, it became evident that it contained all types of coins referring to 'Yehohanan the High Priest' along with Seleucid issues of the second century BCE and a very early issue Nabataean coin.

"Within a few weeks after seeing the first group, I was able to trace almost 700 pieces from the same find. There was not a single coin of Alexander Jannaeus, but the hoard contained all types of coins with the Hebrew name Yehohanan. This, then, confirmed what I and others claimed on stylistic and circumstantial evidence before, that is, all of the coins of Yehohanan belong to the same ruler. It also proved, in the absence of the later coins of Jannaeus, that this ruler must be Hyrcanus I. It also raised the question of whether the name of Hyrcanus II was actually Yehohanan, as some theorized."[15]

After reviewing the coins gathered by Barag, Jerusalem numismatist Shraga Qedar agreed that this was the "empirical proof" that had long been sought.[16] In 1980 Barag and Qedar published a study analyzing the style of the cornucopias and other graphic elements of the Maccabean coins. They concluded that all of the Yehohanan coins were struck by Hyrcanus I.[17] This discovery proved their theory was correct.

The evidence of Barag's hoard, along with data on the results of excavations on Mt. Gerizim in Nablus by Y. Magen,[18] caused Meshorer to promptly state: "I am now convinced that all of the coins with the Hebrew name Yehohanan were struck by Hyrcanus I."[19]

Even with the new evidence, however, there remain many areas for discussion about the Maccabean coin series. These coins are complicated because contemporaneous historians refer mainly to Greek names of rulers (Hyrcanus, Jannaeus, Aristobulus, Antigonus) while three of the five classes of Maccabean coins refer only to Hebrew names—Yehohanan, Yehonatan, Yonatan, Yehudah, and Mattatayah. Coins of Jannaeus (Yehonatan and at least some Yonatan) and Antigonus (Mattatayah) are bilingual and have definite name linkage, and thus definite attribution. The other three names, however, cannot be directly linked with Greek equivalents.

This situation has allowed room for interpretation. A portion of Meshorer's early theory (that it was Jannaeus who struck the first coins, followed by Aristobulus II and Hyrcanus II), for example, suggested that Hyrcanus II, like Hyrcanus I, was also named Yehohanan. He suggested that both Aristobulus I and II were named Yehudah, thus raising other possibilities.

I will not rehash all of the previous theories of Maccabean coinage in detail. Suffice it to say that major experts had each developed theories of their own and, as Alexandre Adler wrote in 1976, "Everyone has stuck to his own position." In 1981, Meshorer himself predicted the outcome, "I have no doubt that future archaeological evidence will finally lay these discussions to rest."[20]

Now that the archaeological evidence has spoken, and there is agreement over the first Jewish ruler to issue coins—Hyrcanus I—questions remain about his successors, and some interesting material has come to light.

THE MONOGRAMS

What was the purpose of the obverse A monograms and the assorted reverse Greek letter monograms on the Yehohanan coins? In Meshorer's theory that Hyrcanus II minted these coins, he posited that the monograms referred to Antipater who was Herod I's father, Hyrcanus II's father-in-law, and the power behind the throne. Arie Kindler, among others, suggested that the obverse A monogram referred to Hyrcanus II's mother, Queen Salome Alexandra. Harry J. Stein's 1943 theory, suggested that the A monogram on the obverse refers to Hyrcanus I's son and successor Aristobulus I, and that the other reverse monograms refer to magistrates who may remain forever anonymous.[21]

Most promising, however, is the idea that both the letter A on No. 1132 and the various A and AΠ monograms suggest a continuing numismatic relationship between Hyrcanus I and the Seleucid kings— first Antiochus VII and on these coins his successor Alexander Zebina (128–123 BCE). This relationship was suggested as early as 1864 by Madden, who said, "if the coins with the two cornucopiae originated with Alexander II Zebina, then John Hyrcanus made this type the sign of his alliance with Zebina, and it helps to prove that the Greek letter A on some of his coins refers to this king...."[22] More recently Barag and Qedar[23] and Hoover[24] have agreed. It seems likely that these monograms were discontinued when Hyrcanus "severed his last ties with the Seleucids."[25] Josephus' reports support the Zebina connection. He observes that Hyrcanus I "flourished greatly during the reign of Alexander Zebina..." and was a friend of the king.[26]

Hoover follows Gardner and suggests that Hyrcanus I's cornucopia motif was copied directly from a coin of Zebina. "The peculiar U-shaped arrangement of the cornucopia and the hanging ribbons strongly suggest a link between the Zebina coin and the *prutot* of Hyrcanus."[27] He further points out that the A or AΠ may simply be derivative of the copied types, with no actual meaning except deference to Zebina.

6.2. Bronze coin of Alexander Zebina, 128–122 BCE, with intertwined cornucopias on reverse. SC II 2235.

Another question now arises from the title "rosh," or "head," inserted in the inscription on some of the Yehohanan coins (Nos. 1136, 1137). Why did Hyrcanus I issue some coins referring to himself as "Head of the Council of the Jews," and others mentioning only the authority of "The Council of the Jews," omitting the title "head"? ("The Council of the Jews" was probably a governing body that later emerged as the Sanhedrin.) It seems possible that the coins using the word "head" came later and may have represented a "move toward the crown, but before the title 'king' was actually claimed."[28]

It's now a general consensus that Hyrcanus I's son, Aristobulus I (104 BCE), issued coins under his Hebrew name Yehudah during his brief reign, and our epigraphic typology supports this (see comments on p. 171).

Most coins attributed to Jannaeus (104–76 BCE) are relatively straightforward, since more than one type carry both the names Yehonatan in Hebrew, and Alexander in Greek. Thus, there is little doubt under which ruler they were issued. Yet, there remains the matter of the similar name Yonatan. It had long been thought that the name Yonatan, appearing on a parallel series of coins, was simply another version of Yehonatan that omitted several letters. As if to underline the issue, in 1992 a new translation of Dead Sea Scroll fragment 4Q448 by Eshel, Eshel, and Yardeni further complicated the matter.

They translated the four-by-six-inch fragment as follows: "Holy city, for King Yonatan and all the congregation of your people Israel who are in the four winds of Heaven."[29] This translation was the first reference ever found in the Dead Sea Scrolls to a Jewish historical figure. We know that it refers to Jannaeus since he was the only one at about the time this scroll was written who had a name like this and the title king. There was another Yonatan, the brother of Judah Maccabee, one of the immediate family members who liberated Jerusalem from the Greeks. But that Yonatan ruled Judaea between 157–142 BCE and held only the title high priest, never the title king. (There is no possibility that this Yonatan issued the coins with that name, since the Jewish rulers did not mint their own coins until the later reign of Antiochus VII, 138–129 BCE.) Thus, since scroll fragment 4Q448 refers to Jannaeus with the name Yonatan, it hints that both the Yehonatan and the Yonatan coins may have been struck by Jannaeus.

It is also possible that the name Yonatan was no more than a space-saving abbreviated form of Yehonatan, Jannaeus' Hebrew name.[30] There are a few examples of No. 1150 where the form of the name between the rays of the star is Yonatan rather than Yehonatan. Further, there are two ancient seal impressions, apparently belonging to the same person, which are engraved "Yonatan the King" and "Yehonatan the High Priest."[31]

EXPLORING THE OVERSTRIKES

The overstruck issues (No. 1149) are especially important. In previous editions of this book I explained both theories regarding the overstruck coins. When, why, and by whom they were overstruck has long been a question. Since the second coin struck on every example carries the name Yonatan, it is significant. In 2007, while sorting through a group of Hasmonean coins, I found a remarkable coin which constitutes nothing less than a "smoking gun." The coin (No. 1150f) is in effect a triple strike—that is a typical Yonatan coin overstruck upon the lily anchor coin (No. 1148) but on this coin I noticed that the anchor/wheel coin (No. 1150) had been overstruck upon the overstrike. This coin is like a miniature archaeological excavation since the first strike referred to "Yehonatan," the second strike referred to "Yonatan" and the third and final strike once again referred to "Yehonatan." Since both the first and third coins are clearly assigned to Jannaeus, the coin sandwiched between the two Jannaeus strikes must by definition have also been struck under the same ruler. This meant (*eureka!*) that the massive issue of overstrikes must have been struck by Jannaeus and not a successor.[32]

The types of coins involved are partial, but absolutely clear on this example. Hence this established for the first time a positive internal chronology for these coins, and proves that the overstrike of the Yehonatan coins by the Yonatan coins was undertaken by Jannaeus. I published this coin together with Israeli archaeologist and numismatist Ilan Shachar, who had previously argued in favor of this chronology.[33]

Even with this knowledge, the reason for the massive overstrike is not known. Shachar and I noted:

"Various attempts have been made to explain why Jannaeus' mint chose (or was directed) to overstrike Jannaeus' anchor/flower type bearing the title 'king' with a cornucopias/inscription type bearing the title 'high priest.' According to Josephus, Jannaeus provoked a civil insurrection in the course of which thousands were killed. At one point he tried to appease his enemies. One theory is that Jannaeus' adoption of the royal title was offensive to many, especially the Pharisees, and a way to appease them might have been to overstrike stocks of his flower/anchor coin with a new version of his cornucopias/inscription coin, thus abandoning the Greek inscription and royal title on the flower/anchor coin and promoting his status as 'high priest.' Attempts at appeasement did not succeed, and rival forces asked the Seleucid ruler, Demetrius III, for military assistance. Demetrius ruled from 96–88 BCE and died shortly after his campaign against Jannaeus. If the appeasement theory is correct this would give a time frame of the latter part of Demetrius' reign for the overstriking phenomenon. Later issues of Jannaeus coins, which once again give the title 'king,' could reflect his improved self-confidence after military victories abroad and an end to the civil war."

Absent the discovery of some lost work by a contemporaneous writer, it is unlikely that we will ever know for sure why this massive overstriking took place.

With the discovery of this double overstrike, one attribution argument is resolved. However, other uncertainties remain. Shachar and I also pointed out that having established this chronology, "it might be tempting to assume that the non-overstruck struck Yonatan coins (No. 1159) should also be attributed to Jannaeus. However, the very distinct and highly stylized paleography of [this coin] leaves open the possibility that these belong to a different high priest."[34] Metallurgical studies by Michael Krupp conclude that the stylized Yonatan coins are, according to their metal content, most likely issued by successors to Jannaeus.[35] I suggest that since this is the case, those coins were possibly issued by Jannaeus's widow, Queen Salome Alexandra, in the name of her son Hyrcanus II, the high priest. But, as Kindler suggested, one should not rule out Aristobulus II,[36] since his Hebrew name is uncertain and he may have been involved in the continued use of the anchor/star types after Jannaeus's death.

It is also possible that Salome Alexandra continued to mint coins and, as a follower of the Pharisees, she used the non-offensive name Yonatan. This scenario also fits the theory that during that time and culture it would have been presumptuous for her to issue coins in her own name.

Evolving scholarship unsettles collectors since they tend to be orderly personalities who are not pleased by coins that cannot be labeled with certainty. I once posed this issue to Ya'akov Meshorer, who responded, "First of all, the coin is the coin and any particular coin may defy exact attribution forever. In scholarly endeavors we often deal with theories that change from time to time because of new information. In the case of the chronology of the Hasmonean coins, we actually solved one important problem, but while doing so several others were created."[37]

It might take another find or series of finds from controlled archaeological excavations to sort all this out. And then again, the chronology of the Hasmonean coins may be one of those numismatic problems that will defy resolution forever. In the meantime, I shall continue to list the Yonatan/cornucopia coins (No. 1159) tentatively to a succesor of Jannaeus.

This decision leads to another long-standing topic of interest regarding the massive number of poorly manufactured, light-weight anchor/star coins often called "mites" or "leptons" and most frequently attributed to Jannaeus. Earlier numismatists suggested that these might have been later copies of the reduced *prutah* (No. 1152) with dates in both Greek and Aramaic, perhaps struck late during the reign of Jannaeus as well as under Aristobulus II or Hyrcanus II or both. After considerable study and metrological research (see pp. 43–46), this idea may have merit. The essence of this theory solves several problems:

Since these coins are crude copies of No. 1152, which was struck quite late in Jannaeus's reign (80/79 BCE), they could all have been struck during his lifetime, but the large quantity suggests they may have been struck over a longer period.

Jannaeus was succeeded by his powerful wife Salome Alexandra (76–67 BCE) as queen and his son Hyrcanus II as high priest. Aristobulus II ruled for an interval between 67 and 63 BCE. It seems unlikely that no coins at all would have been issued between the death of Jannaeus in 76 BCE and the reign of Mattatayah Antigonus, which began in 40 BCE.

The "mite" coins reflect a deterioration in both weight standard and style that probably reflected inflation and devaluation during this period. Finally, we have evidence that the production types and style of these coins may have carried over to some of the early coins minted by Herod I (see p. 236). This theory suggests that the "mites" could have been issued at a date closer to the Jerusalem issues of Herod I.

EPIGRAPHY ON THE HASMONEAN COINS

There has been a great deal of misunderstanding about the epigraphy on the Hasmonean coins. The paleo-Hebrew inscriptions are remarkable not only for their content but for their form. The ancient Hebrew script was mainly discontinued several hundred years earlier and "saw only very limited use in the Maccabean age."[38] During this period, Aramaic was the principal language and script of the Jewish people. According to Naveh, "Texts written in the Hebrew script in the Second Temple period are rare.... These texts are official in nature and seem to indicate that the use of the Hebrew script in this period had nationalistic connotations."[39] The texts to which Naveh refers are seals, scrolls, and coins. The use of this archaic Hebrew script "represented the former glory of the Davidic kingdom which the Hasmonean rulers attempted to regain and restore."[40] Among all of the Hasmonean coins, almost all types are inscribed with the paleo-Hebrew script. Thus, even the script selection was part of the effort of the Jewish monarchs to make a statement about themselves and their kingdom.

Instead of paleo-Hebrew, evidence shows that during the first century BCE, "the Aramaic script, also known as the 'square script' or 'Syrian script,' was the leading one. It was used for writing both in Hebrew and in Aramaic, and it seems that the early paleo-Hebrew script was almost completely forgotten and only few were able to read it," Meshorer explains.[41]

Among the Dead Sea Scrolls, the only paleo-Hebrew manuscripts, except for Job, are from the Pentateuch.[42] In some other scrolls written in Aramaic script, only the Tetragrammaton, or name of the Lord, is written in paleo-Hebrew, "thus indicating that the scribes who preserved this script knew that it was the original Hebrew one and its archaic flavor made it suitable for writing the name of the Lord."[43]

Limited use of paleo-Hebrew script was meant to revive thoughts of the glorious days of the Israelite period around the time of King David and as Meshorer notes, even "the desire to create a link between the earlier kingdoms of Judah and Israel and that of the Hasmonean dynasty....These were, however, not living letters to which the principles of development and evolution could apply...."[44]

One of the earliest known inscriptions using paleo-Hebrew was the Gezer Calendar, which is dated to the late tenth century BCE. It is closely related to Phoenician inscriptions from the same period. The paleo-Hebrew script was used on jar handles dating from the late eighth century BCE and to stone scale weights of Judah dating to eighth to sixth centuries BCE, as well as hundreds of stone and bone seals dating from the eighth to sixth centuries BCE. The earliest known fragments of a biblical text are written in paleo-Hebrew script and make up the Priestly Benediction in Numbers 6:24–26: "The Lord bless you and protect you. The Lord makes his face to shine upon you and be gracious to you. The Lord lift up his countenance to you and give you peace." It is inscribed on a small silver scroll found in a burial cave at Ketef Hinnom and dated to the late seventh century BCE.[45]

After the Babylonian capture of Judah and the exile of many Jews, including most of the nobles, in 586 BCE, those who remained behind continued to use the paleo-Hebrew script. Two generations later, when many Jews returned from exile, their language had become Aramaic and only those Jews who stayed behind continued to use the paleo-Hebrew script. Soon both the Aramaic language and the "square" Hebrew script became the official means of communication in ancient Judaea.

In summary, then, it is impossible to undertake a meaningful epigraphic study of the paleo-Hebrew script used on the coins of the Maccabees, the Jewish War, or the Bar Kokhba Revolt, because it was an alphabet no longer in regular use.

Instead of evolving as a living alphabet, variations in script forms resulted from the way individual master engravers and their assistants or apprentices cut these scripts into the coin dies. Since the paleo-Hebrew was no longer used, and it is not likely that artisans such as die cutters were literate, one may assume that each workshop was supplied with a written version of the legends to be used. Meshorer notes that these may have been copied from "the letters from ancient manuscripts which were no doubt kept in the library of the Temple at Jerusalem."[46] Further script variations could have been introduced when the coin legend was copied for the various die cutters. More style differences were surely introduced by the illiterate die cutters who used chisels and other tools to make die cuts, often smaller than an eyelash, and also to engrave the inscriptions in confusing mirror-writing in the dies.

Thus each die cutter transferred his version of the designated legend to a die for striking coins—the more skilled and artistic the engraver, the better the style. Hence, we can see various script styles on the Hasmonean coins. Other than a few instances where we can suggest that the same die cutter worked during transitions between rulers, there is little to be learned about the chronology of the coins from the style of the paleo-Hebrew scripts.

The best example of this is the coins struck during the brief reign of Yehudah (Judah) Aristobulus I in 104 BCE. The very rare type (No. 1142), uses wedge-like characters that probably came from the same workshop as the Hyrcanus I coins with the same style (Nos. 1135, 1137). However, the more common Aristobulus coins (No. 1143) are inscribed in a "block-style" script almost identical in style to a group of coins of his successor, Alexander Jannaeus (No. 1144), and probably came from the same workshop, if not the same engraver. This connection between the workshops of Aristobulus' predecessor and successor allow us to establish a chronology for his coins. (Not incidentally, the style of the cornucopias on the reverse of these coin types can also be accurately connected.)

In order to understand the very crude versions of inscriptions, or those with many errors and omissions, we suggest that these dies were engraved at second-rate workshops or by assistants, sometimes unskilled beginners. We also note that the characters were cut into the dies with very tiny tools, and a slip of the hand was inevitable. In an ideal world, these dies would have been written off and not used. But at a time when there were few artisans among the Jews capable of this work and a great need for bronze coinage, it seems that all dies created that were capable of striking coins were, in fact, used to strike coins. The phenomenon of crude, irregular coins issues continues throughout all of the Jewish coinage until the Bar Kokhba war. (See pp. 39–42 for further discussions of these "irregular issues.")

Late in Jannaeus' reign, he implemented the use of Aramaic (square Hebrew) script on coins while, at the same time, eliminating use of the high priest title (No. 1152).

As with the overstruck issues, this change was probably prompted by the conflicts between the Pharisees and the Sadducees. Notes Meshorer: "Broad public circles, and certainly the Pharisees, undoubtedly had disapproved of his adoption of the title 'king' in addition to that of high priest,"[47] as were used on some of his early coins.

The Babylonian Talmud reflected this: "Said he [Judah son of Gedidiah] to King Yannai: 'O King Yannai! Let the royal crown suffice thee, and leave the priestly crown to the seed of Aaron.'"[48]

This group of Aramaic-inscribed coins, dated to the year 25 of Jannaeus (80/79 BCE), were struck near the end of his reign in 76 BCE. There is no suggestion that he gave up his title of high priest, but he simply stopped flaunting it, not only by eliminating the reference on his coins, but by changing to the current *lingua franca* of Aramaic.

Jannaeus was succeeded by his wife, Queen Salome Alexandra, who, according to Josephus, "permitted the Pharisees to do as they liked in all matters, and also commanded the people to obey them; and whatever regulations, introduced by the Pharisees in accordance with the tradition of their fathers, had been abolished by her father-in-law Hyrcanus, these she again restored...."[49]

Only in the waning years of the Hasmonean dynasty, facing off against Herod I, already named King of the Jews by the powers in Rome, did Mattatayah Antigonus reclaim both titles of king and high priest, as reflected on his coins.

PENTATEUCHAL CODE AND GRAVEN IMAGES

From the third to the first centuries BCE, coins were struck in the Greek world by the authority of the great kings who succeeded Alexander III (the Great) of Macedon, as well as minor dynasts and potentates of out-of-the-way cultures. A common feature of this coinage of gold, silver, and bronze was its use to aggrandize the rulers under whom the coins were struck, by, among other things, showing their faces to the masses. Thus, today we can look at numismatic portraits of the dynastic kings of Macedon, Seleucid Syria, and Ptolemaic Egypt, as well as the rulers of Bithynia, Pontus, Cappadocia, Armenia, Bactria, India, Parthia, Commagene, Nabataea, and even Numidia and Mauretania.[50]

Yet the Hasmonean rulers of the Jewish nation following its revolt against Antiochus IV did not advertise their faces on coins. The Jewish rulers were no less vain and no less in need of consolidating power, but they deliberately refrained from putting their portraits on coins, even though it was the style in the rest of the Hellenistic world.

This was true even though many of these Jewish rulers and their aristocratic friends adopted some of the ways of their former hellenistic overlords. Even the Hellenized Jews refused to cross some lines. Whether or not the Jews organized their army in the Greek style, raised Greek mercenaries, dressed like Greeks, and participated in athletic events in local gymnasia, there must be no misunderstanding about one crucial point: the Jews worshipped one God.

The significant question posed regards the motivation for the Jewish decision not to use human portraits, as well as the designs used in their stead, especially as they relate to the political and religious environment under the Hasmonean dynasty.

Writers including Madden, Reifenberg, Romanoff, Kindler, Kanael, Barag, Qedar and Meshorer have made major contributions to the discussion of the iconography and epigraphy of the first coins issued by Jewish sovereigns.[51] A study of their work shows an understanding of the absence of graven images on early Jewish coin designs, but only brief discussion of the reason for this.

Kindler, for example, states only that "strict adherence to the Second Commandment precluded the use of a ruler's portrait on Hasmonean coins."[52] Meshorer notes: "Because of religious injunctions, Jewish kings could not, at the time of Jannaeus, depict their own portraits on coinage."[53] Romanoff writes: "No human portraits nor animal sacrifices nor pouring of blood upon the altar are to be found among the emblems"[54] on the coins of the Hasmoneans. In his seminal article, Kanael mentions that the Hasmonean coins "have a rather dull appearance."[55]

While these numismatists were preoccupied with the critical matter of the chronology of the Hasmonean coins, the paucity of discussion of the biblical ban on "graven images" seems to be an oversight. The issue of the Second Commandment is not so clear in either ancient or modern Judaism that it can be taken for granted. If it were, we might more easily explain why at certain times in their history Jews and Samaritans abided by this ban, and at other times they simply did not. For example, the Persian and Samarian coins struck in the fourth century BCE by local authorities in ancient Judaea and Samaria virtually all portray graven images.[56]

What were the conditions during the Hasmonean period that compelled the Jews to follow this ban, and what iconographic conventions did they devise to obviate the need for the otherwise universal approach to coins?

Between the second century BCE and the first century CE, the Jews in their land, with few known exceptions, strictly obeyed the biblical admonition against graven images:

Thou shalt not make unto thee a graven image, nor any manner of likeness, of any thing that is in heaven above, or that is in the earth beneath, or that is in the water under the earth" (EXODUS 20:4).

This Pentateuchal code sternly prohibits making any graven image of man or beast, and is repeated (DEUTERONOMY 5:8) and expanded upon:

> ...lest ye deal corruptly, and make you a graven image, even the form of any figure, the likeness of male or female, the likeness of any beast that is on the earth, the likeness of any winged fowl that flieth in the heaven, the likeness of anything that creepeth on the ground, the likeness of any fish that is in the water under the earth (DEUTERONOMY 4:16–18).

The prohibition is presumably aimed directly at the manufacture of such images for the purpose of worship. While that reservation is hinted at (see DEUTERONOMY 4:19 and EXODUS 20:19–21), it is not spelled out in the biblical text. This ambiguity allowed Jewish culture to run the gamut from outright prohibition of figurative art of any kind to complete disregard of the prohibitions.

In biblical Judaism, the *cherubim* in the Tabernacle and in Solomon's Temple were certainly graven images. The Rev. Chris Connel called to my attention the irony that the text of Exodus 25:18–22 calls for "graven images" of cherubs to appear on the very Ark of the Covenant that contained the commandment against making graven images. As discussed in Chapter 4, the Yehud and Samarian coins of the fourth century BCE from ancient Palestine consistently depict a variety of graven images. Rabbi Gamaliel in the second century CE was said to have had a human head engraved on his personal seal. Humans as well as animals are forthrightly depicted in mosaics at the ancient synagogues at Chorazin and Beit Alfa, among others, not to mention the fabulous paintings of Old Testament vignettes in the synagogue at Dura Europos.

Expanding on this thesis, Cecil Roth specifically refers to the time period under examination: "The meticulous obedience or relative neglect of the apparent biblical prohibition of representational art seems in fact to have been conditioned by external circumstances, and in two directions—revulsion, or attraction. In the later biblical period and throughout classical antiquity, in an environment in which the worship of images by their neighbors played a great part, the Jews reacted strongly against this practice and up to a point representational art was sternly suppressed....On the other hand, when the Jews were to some extent culturally assimilated, they began to share in the artistic outlook of their neighbors and the prejudice against representational art dwindled, and in the end almost disappeared. To this generalization, however, other factors must be added. Sometimes the religious reaction of the Jews was influenced by political consideration. The almost frenzied Jewish opposition to images of any sort toward the close of the Second Temple period seems to have been prompted by the extreme nationalist elements, happy to find a point in which their political opposition could be based on a clear-cut religious issue."[57]

Thus, with respect to the iconography of graven images, the evolution of the first Jewish royal coinage closely reflects the evolution of Jewish independence, interdependence, and assimilation with the Greeks and Romans. There is little doubt that the time of the Hasmonean dynasty was extremely nationalistic and that the question of graven images moved to the fore as a result.

The money in circulation in ancient Israel at this time consisted mainly of Tyrian, Seleucid, and Ptolemaic silver coins. Other bronze and silver coinage also showed up in the area as a result of travelers or trade. Virtually all of these coins carried graven images of kings or gods.[58]

Hyrcanus I's challenge was to issue coinage that not only would improve his nation's economy,[59] but also make a bold statement regarding its sovereignty while maintaining the then current understanding of Jewish religious law. As a result, Hyrcanus' small bronze coins were unlike most other coins in use at the time. They had sufficient impact to become the prototype for the principal coin type of all four successive Hasmonean rulers over a period of some 90 years. On the obverse, instead of the image of a dynast or a god, the coins carried an inscription in a laurel or olive wreath. The wreath itself had long been associated with leadership and royalty in both the Hellenistic and Roman worlds.[60] Meshorer also observes that the wreath was a popular metaphor in Rabbinnic sources, and that in the Jerusalem Temple, wreaths adorned the altar, the Holy Ark, and the showbread table.[61]

Hyrcanus I's coin inscription, which became a formulaic for his descendants, was also remarkable: "Yehohanan the High Priest and the Council of the Jews" inside a wreath. This clearly stated that it was not the high priest alone who ruled the Jews, but that he shared governance with his council. "Judaea was not a monarchy but a diarchy," explained Kanael.[62] He believed that the "Council of the Jews," was simply a "continuation of the Great Assembly, which dated from the Persian Period. Later on, with changed and curtailed powers, it became the famous Sanhedrin."[63]

To adorn the reverse of his coins, Hyrcanus I chose the cornucopia, borrowed and adapted from contemporary Hellenistic art, specifically both Ptolemaic and Seleucid coins.

The Hasmoneans had prevailed in their grave confrontation with Hellenism, only to give way later to Rome. At least part of the Hasmonean legacy to Herod I, who also claimed the title "King of the Jews," was a numismatic one. Throughout his 33-year reign, Herod never once put a human graven image on his coins. Herod's successors, however, are a more complicated matter to be discussed later.

CORNUCOPIA AS A JEWISH SYMBOL

The cornucopia[64] was one of the most popular religious symbols of the ancient world. It came into use on the coins of the Hasmonean kings and later on the coins of Herod the Great and his son, Herod Archelaus, via hellenistic influence. As previously noted, it may have been copied from a coin of Alexander Zebina.

Meshorer explained, "During the Hellenistic period, and in particular during the third to the first centuries BCE, Greek culture spread all over the ancient world. Its influence resulted in the hellenization of the oriental countries and nations. We can confidently say that, during this period, all cultures of the Near East were influenced by the Greek culture. This does not mean that these peoples changed their religions or customs entirely. They simply adopted some of the new elements and produced a combination of eastern and western religions; this phenomenon is known as syncretism. Sometimes an oriental cult kept its entire meaning and content, and changed only its name or shape of god. The same process occurred with respect to certain symbols which, although adopted from the Greeks by an oriental religion, retained an independent oriental significance."[65]

The cornucopia, a hollow animal horn, was used as a container for many purposes. As the overflowing "horn of plenty," it contained

6.3. Bronze ring inlay with cornucopia and branches, c. 1st century CE. (Author's collection.).

agricultural fertility symbols such as ears of grain, bunches of grapes, and pomegranates. On Hellenistic coins, the cornucopia is often associated with Tyche, the city goddess, or Demeter, goddess of the earth. According to Barag and Qedar, the cornucopia was also "re-interpreted and given some Jewish meaning, perhaps connected with the fertility of the Land of Israel."[66] Romanoff writes that, "The cornucopias appearing alone, without the goddesses...were abstract symbols. In this respect the horns of plenty were akin to the Jewish symbols."[67]

Meshorer adds, "It is logical to assume that the symbol filtered into Judaism as an object related to fertility, and then acquired additional Jewish connotations.... In Jewish life animal horns were used for a number of purposes, including as an oil container, an object to anoint kings, or as 'shofars'—musical instruments of the Temple service."[68]

The use of the animal horn as a holder for oil is referred to during the coronation of King David:

Then Samuel took the horn of oil and anointed him in the midst of his brethren (I SAMUEL 16: 13).

Possibly, the horn of plenty became a symbol for the ancient Jews because of the legendary richness of the ancient Holy Land itself—the land of milk and honey. We know, for example, that cornucopias were used by the Jews in the Holy Land in the first few centuries BCE/CE not only on coins, but on other small objects such as seals, rings, amulets, and also in larger architectural contexts. A relief of a double cornucopia with a pomegranate between was found in the excavations of the Jewish Quarter of the Old City of Jerusalem and can be seen in the Israel Museum. It dates from the first century BCE to the first century CE.

The Hasmonean cornucopia design was formed with two symmetric horns of plenty joined at their narrow bottoms within a flower petal.[69] On coins struck from the best-style dies, a ribbon with a bow is tied around each cornucopia; each horn containing an ear of grain and a bunch of grapes. The ultimate Jewish addition in this design seems to be a pomegranate standing between the horns on a long, thin stalk.

Mattatayah Antigonus (Mattathias), the last Hasmonean king (40–37 BCE), struck larger denomination coins with a double cornucopia and no design element between, coins with a single cornucopia, and also coins with double cornucopias and an ear of grain (often referred to as an "ear of corn" by folks who wrote in "British English," meaning, "ear of grain") between the horns. A variation of this design that appears on many small objects, but not on coins, shows a lily between the horns. This combination seems to appear only in Jewish art.

During the period of Herod the Great, according to Meshorer, the cornucopia "seems to lose its Jewish nature; it was used in a different fashion by Herod the Great and his son Herod Archelaus, who replaced the pomegranates and ears of barley by a caduceus, a clearly pagan symbol."[70]

Herod seems to have taken great care that the symbols on his coins would not appear either too Jewish or too pagan, reflecting his attempts to bridge the two cultures with his own reign. Remember that Herod was a client of Rome and had taken over from the popular Hasmonean dynasty by force.

After Herod I and his son Archelaus, cornucopias show up only a few times as symbols clearly intended to acknowledge local Jewish populations. Two issues of the prefects and procurators of Judaea, a Roman administration coin from the pre-royal period of Agrippa II struck at Sepphoris with Vespasian's name (No. 1276), and city coins of Tiberias (under Trajan) and Neapolis (under Domitian) depict cornucopias as significant reverse motifs.

POMEGRANATE AS A JEWISH SYMBOL

The pomegranate as a symbol on ancient Jewish coins has been given surprisingly little attention considering its frequency. It appears on the coins of John Hyrcanus, Alexander Jannaeus, and Judah Aristobulus. Pomegranates are also a major feature on the silver *sheqels* and half *sheqels* of the Jewish War.

Many early writers misidentified the pomegranate between the cornucopias as the seed head of a poppy flower. However, Romanoff notes that "the small fruit which resembles a poppy appears on the Jewish coins between the cornucopias. This fruit which has been taken for a poppy is obviously a pomegranate, the circle representing the fruit itself and the horizontal line over it — the pitma or top-piece."[71]

Three pomegranate buds on a staff also adorn the reverse of the Jewish war *sheqels* and half-*sheqels*. Conventionally, these coins are viewed with the central pomegranate upright. But, anyone who has seen near-ripe pomegranates hanging on a tree will notice the similarity to the *sheqel* design when viewed with the central pomegranate downward. The argument for viewing the pomegranates upright is based on the paleo-Hebrew legend beginning on the lower right rather than the upper left. This is convincing, but not absolute, and this discussion is without conclusion. One can observe, however, that placing a three-dimensional object, such as a coin, into two-dimensions, is a necessity of modern technology, mainly the photograph or drawing. Prior to these innovations, there was no reason to view a coin as anything but a three-dimensional object. Thus, one could even suggest that a design such as the one we are discussing was meant to be viewed as a tray with a sprig of pomegranates on top of it![72]

Prominent appearances of this fruit on the coins of the ancient Jews are far from coincidental. The pomegranate is one of the seven celebrated plant species of ancient Palestine.[73] It is just as visible today in Israel and Palestine when it is in season.

I remember one day in the late 1970s when visiting the home of my late friend Nasrallah Sahuri in Bethlehem; we had come in out of the sweltering heat and sat in the relative cool of his traditionally decorated living room. Shortly, his wife Angel appeared with a pitcher and cups. The pitcher contained a ruby-red liquid. When I tasted it, I felt I had finally found genuine ambrosia: it was pomegranate juice. It had never occurred to me that such a lovely juice could be made from the interesting fruit with so many seeds.

6.4. Gold pomegranate decoration from Judaea c. 8–6 centuries BCE.

During the holiday of Succot (the Feast of Tabernacles), pomegranates are among the chief decorations hung in the *sukkah* (the hut covered by branches). Many Jewish families also use the pomegranate as part of the celebration of Rosh Hashanah, the Jewish New Year. "The pomegranate," explains physician and numismatist Dr. Martin Brody, "is eaten with the hope that our merits will increase as the seeds of the fruit. The Torah has 613 commandments, and some say that is the number of seeds in a pomegranate."[74] Certainly this ruby red fruit also represented some aspects of fertility from very early times. The pomegranate, for example, was among the fruits given to mankind by the goddess Hathor. In ancient Greece, the pomegranate was often worn as a fertility amulet.

In ancient times it was one of the symbolic plants that was used to decorate the Jerusalem Temple."[75]

A famous ivory pomegranate from a priestly scepter, dating to the Israelite Period (Iron Age II), is on prominent display in the Israel Museum. This object, with an ancient Hebrew inscription referring to the priests of the Temple, is thought to be among the few remaining artifacts from King Solomon's Temple.[76] Josephus reports that pomegranates adorned the golden menorah in the Temple, accompanied by lilies and bowls. The robes of the high priest was also decorated with pomegranates (EXODUS: 25–26).

"It seems likely," Klimowsky wrote, "that those emblems were being given a transcendental meaning whose exact contents, however, we can but guess, *viz.* that the pomegranates should point to the everlasting life of the Jewish people."[77]

LILY, ANCHOR, AND STAR SYMBOLS

Three more common symbols on the early coins of the Jews, including those in circulation during the period covered by the New Testament, are the lily, anchor, and star.

The lily, or *shoshan* in Hebrew, was considered a standout among flowers. Its fragile beauty, combined with the fact that it bloomed rapidly—thus linking it to fertility—enhanced its position.[78]

Romanoff notes that, "Strange as it may seem, the lily on the Jewish coins resembles the Rhodos flower—the rose. This seeming inaccuracy is explained by the generic term *shoshan* which might have included such flowers as the lotus and even the rose."[79] Rabbinic sources refer to a "lily-rose," which is a symbol of Israel, as well as a "soft lily" and the "lily of the valley."

The lily first appears on the Jewish coinage of Hyrcanus I, struck in Jerusalem with the name of Antiochus VII. This coin was a transitional issue from Seleucid domination to Jewish control. The selection of the lily seems to be based on its ornamental use in the Jerusalem Temple. The lily, along with two hundred pomegranates, graced the capitals of the two main pillars, Yachin and Boaz, at the entrance. Lilies also graced other ornamental and ritual objects, and many objects of everyday life. The lily was a symbol of Jerusalem itself and, as already noted, Hoover suggests it replaces the obverse portrait of the Seleucid king in order to satisfy Jewish needs to avoid the use of graven images.[80]

On the small half-*prutah* coin of Hyrcanus I, the lily appears between two ears of grain (No. 1134, 1138), which provide additional symbolism relating to agriculture and fertility.

While the lily had been used as a Jewish symbol for hundreds of years, the anchor was a Seleucid symbol officially introduced in Judaea on the early coin of Hyrcanus I/Antiochus VII. The anchor referred to a symbol said to have appeared on the ring of Seleucus I, and may refer to naval strength. It frequently appears as both a symbol and countermark in the Seleucid series. As discussed earlier in this chapter, the Seleucid image was transformed into a Jewish one. The anchor is depicted upside down on both the early Seleucid and Hasmonean issues, as determined by the correct placement of the coins relative to their inscriptions. This was a puzzle to me until a seafaring friend observed that anchors are invariably stored upside down, in ready position to be pushed overboard.

Alexander Jannaeus' first use of the anchor was on his own lily/anchor issue, copied directly from the early coin of Hyrcanus I.

6.5. Bronze pilgrim's rings with lily and double cornucopia designs circa 2nd-1st centuries BCE from Jerusalem. (Author's collection.)

Jannaeus later used the anchor on his dated series of light *prutot*, as well as the related undated issues, perhaps also issued by his successors, and his lead tokens. The use of the anchor on his largest single coin series, struck late in his reign, may have been related to his conquest of a number of the coastal cities, which greatly strengthened his empire.

Since Herod I was paranoid about his heritage, and sought every opportunity to underline his role as successor to the Hasmonean kings, he probably used the anchor as a matter of familiarity. He also may have felt that its use, along with the double cornucopia also common on Hasmonean coins, underlined ties with the Hasmoneans which he gained by his marriage to Mariamne (whom he later murdered). His son Herod Archelaus also frequently used the anchor on coins. Herod's special interest in the coastal cities, specifically Caesarea Maritima, must also be mentioned as a factor in this symbolism.

The star in various forms was a common element in ancient coins long before its first use by Jannaeus. Because of its link to the heavens, the star was used as a symbol in virtually every ancient civilization. It may seem like a pagan image, but it was adopted by the Jews, as were other astrological signs and symbols. Meshorer cites a Talmudic quotation—"Stars and planets pray for me"—to underline this connection. He further notes that, "Despite the biblical injunction against astrology (DEUTERONOMY 4:19), the stars were inevitably used by the Jews to calculate weeks, months, festivals, and other important dates. Such astronomical observations also included some emphasis on astrological concerns."[81]

On the *prutah* coins of Jannaeus, the star is surrounded by a diadem, although it has also been described as a circle or a wheel. This combination of the star and the diadem originated under Jannaeus, and his name and title "King Alexander" are incorporated into the motif. According to Kanael, the diadem was the Hellenistic symbol of royalty and the star was the Jewish symbol for monarchy, derived from the phrase in Numbers 24:17, "There shall come a star out of Jacob and a scepter shall rise out of Israel."

Since, at the time of Jannaeus, Jewish kings were prohibited from using their own portraits on coinage, the star with diadem seems an interesting and apt replacement.

JOHN HYRCANUS I (YEHOHANAN), 135–104 BCE

John Hyrcanus I ruled from 135 BCE until his death in 104 BCE. He was the son of Simon and nephew of the folk hero Judah the Maccabee. According to Josephus, Hyrcanus was endowed with three godly gifts—temporal power, the dignity of a high priest, and the gift of prophecy. The young Jewish kingdom lost a great deal of prestige when he died after a 30-year reign.

Indeed, according to Graetz, "The reign of Hyrcanus is at once the pinnacle and the turning-point of this period. He not only carried on his father's work, but completed it. Under his predecessors Judaea was confined to a narrow space, and even within these bounds there were territories in the possession of foreign foes. Hyrcanus enlarged the boundaries to the north and to the south, and thus released the State from the external pressure that had been restricting its growth. His genius for war was aided by fortunate circumstances in bringing about these happy results."[82]

Hyrcanus' Hebrew name, Yehohanan, appears on all of his coins. It is generally believed that the governing council, referred to on coins as *Hever ha-Yehudim*, became known as the Sanhedrin during his reign or shortly after it. Apparently satisfied with the title high priest for all of his life, he never assumed the title of king, although at one point he styled himself on his coins as "head" of the *Hever ha-Yehudim* (Nos. 1136–1138).

While his reign was successful by all accounts, it began and ended during difficult times. When he ascended, he was unable to avenge his father. Simon was murdered by Ptolemy (Hyrcanus' brother-in-law), and Hyrcanus confined him in the fort of Dagon. But every time Hyrcanus attempted an attack, Ptolemy subjected Hyrcanus' mother to cruel tortures on the walls of the fort. Even though his mother was said to have borne the torture heroically, encouraging her son to punish the murderer, Hyrcanus nevertheless was forced to lift his siege after several months. Ptolemy killed his mother-in-law anyway, and also another of Hyrcanus' brothers, and fled to Rabbath Ammon in 135 BCE.[83]

Not long after Hyrcanus' reign began, Antiochus VII Sidetes and a large army marched on Jerusalem and besieged it. The Jews suffered from a lack of provisions, but the Syrians were short of water. After a full summer, facing the dangerous Parthians to his east, Antiochus entered into peace negotiations with Hyrcanus, who had bolstered his army with mercenaries, mainly Pisidians and Cilicians. (Hyrcanus was the first Hasmonean ruler to imitate the Syrians by hiring mercenaries to supplement the Jewish army.)

Antiochus first agreed to a seven-day armistice which took place during the Feast of Tabernacles. He even sent bulls with gilded horns for sacrifice and spices for the Temple incense.

In the ensuing treaty, Hyrcanus gave up weapons and paid tribute for a number of towns that were formerly Syrian. Antiochus in turn agreed not to suppress the Jewish religion and not to occupy Jerusalem. Hyrcanus also gave Antiochus hostages—including his own brother—and paid Antiochus 500 *talents* of silver. Josephus reports that Hyrcanus took the initial portion of the payment, 300 *talents*, from the treasure in King David's sepulcher.

Thus a vassal to the Syrian king, Hyrcanus marched on his behalf against the Parthians in 130 BCE. Antiochus Sidetes died in this battle, and his brother Demetrius II ascended to the Syrian throne for the second time, although he retained it for only a short period.

Hyrcanus took advantage of this weakness to expand his territories and to send an emissary to Rome. He captured Medaba in Transjordan. He also conquered the Samarians who lived in Shechem and destroyed their temple on Mt. Gerizim.

Before finishing off the Samarians, Hyrcanus marched against Idumaea, conquering the cities of Adora (near Hebron) and Marissa (near Beit Guvrin). He gave the Idumaeans (also called the Edomites, see p. 88) the choice of leaving the land or converting to Judaism. Most of them chose the latter, and thus became Jews in every respect.

This episode is said to have been the first example of forced conversion in Jewish history. Ironically, it later led to the downfall of the Hasmonean dynasty. The Herodian family was among the Idumaeans forcibly converted to Judaism, and it was their descendant, Herod I (the Great) who took the throne from Hyrcanus' descendant Antigonus Mattatayah in 37 BCE.

The Samarians still held their fortified town of Samaria, and they remained hostile to the Jews. Hyrcanus once again turned his armies against the Samarians, sending his sons Antigonus and Aristobulus to attack and besiege them. The Samarians got some help from Antiochus IX, but Hyrcanus' eldest son Aristobulus routed him and chased him to Beit Shean (Nysa-Scythopolis). Next, Ptolemy Lathyrus, the governor of Cyprus, was called to assist the Samarians. In spite of the Syrian reinforcements, the two sons of Hyrcanus successfully conquered Samaria and all of the Jezreel plain, as well as the town of Beit-Shean.

Meanwhile Hyrcanus remained in Jerusalem, refortifying the walls and attempting to raise his kingdom to a higher level in the eyes of Rome. His embassy to Rome requested the Senate to "send envoys to bring about the restitution of the places taken from the Jews by Antiochus and to estimate the value of the territory ruined during the war." The Senate granted this and issued a decree that "the alliance of friendship be renewed with the worthy men who have been sent by a worthy and friendly people." The Jews were then given "money from the public treasury and a decree of the Senate to those who were to conduct them on their way and furnish them a safe return home."[84]

During Hyrcanus' reign, the sects of the Pharisees, Sadducees, and Essenes became well established. Hyrcanus was a faithful student of the Pharisees, but broke with them late in his life and enacted the Sadducee beliefs as the basis of law.

Hyrcanus died at age 60 after governing his land for 31 years. Reviews of his reign were excellent. Josephus wrote: "He was the only man to unite in his person three of the highest privileges: the supreme command of his nation, the high priesthood, and the gift of prophecy. For so closely was he in touch with the Deity that he was never ignorant of the future; thus he foresaw and predicted that his two elder sons would not remain at the head of affairs...."[85]

JOHN HYRCANUS I WITH ANTIOCHUS VII
Average weight prutah: 2.47 g.

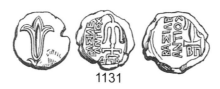

1131

1131. AE 14–15mm. Antiochus VII (Sidetes).
   Obv: ΒΑΣΙΛΕΩΣ ΑΝΤΙΟΧΟΥ ΕΥΕΡΓΕΤΟΥ *(of King Antiochus, benefactor)*; inverted anchor, below anchor ΑΠΡ (SE 182 = 132/131 BCE).
   Rev: Lily. Struck 132/131. BCE.   35/150
   a. ΑΠΡ is along left side of anchor.
   b. ΒΠΡ (Year 181), struck 131/130 BCE.
   c. ΒΠΡ is along left side of anchor.

JOHN HYRCANUS I (YEHOHANAN)
Average weight *prutah*, 1.92 g.
Mostly vertical axis.

1132

יהוחנן
הכהן הגד
ל וחבר הי
הודים

1132.   AE *prutah*.
Obv: Paleo-Hebrew יהוחנן הכהן הגדל וחבר היהודים *(Yehohanan the High Priest and the Council of the Jews) within wreath, Greek A above inscription.*
Rev: Double cornucopia adorned with ribbons, pomegranate be-
tween horns, border of dots.   35/150
a. Double struck reverse.

On each of the types of Hasmonean prutot with paleo-Hebrew, the inscrip-tions appear in many formats which may vary in number of lines, arrange-ments of letters, and occasional misspellings or abbreviations. In this guide we list general types; varieties are often shown in the photographic plates.

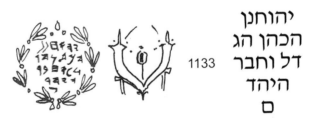

1133

יהוחנן
הכהן הג
דל וחבר
היהד
ם

1133.   AE *prutah*.
Obv: Paleo-Hebrew *(Yehohanan the High Priest and the Council of the Jews) within wreath.*
Rev: Double cornucopia adorned with ribbons, pomegranate be-
tween horns; no monogram.   25/100
a. Monogram AΠ below r.
b. Monogram AΠ below l.
c. Monogram A high left near top of cornucopia.
d. Reverse brockage with monogram A below r.

A number of interesting monogram varieties appear on these coins see il-lustration 6.7 on p. 189.

יהוחנוה
כהן הגדל
וחבר הי
הדים

1134. AE half-*prutah*.
Obv: Paleo-Hebrew *(Yehohanan the High Priest and the Council of the Jews)*; two lines above and below palm branch.
Rev: Lily, monogram A on l. below flower between two ears of grain, border of dots.   250/1,000
a. Similar coin, but without monogram.

יהו
חנן הכהן
הגדול
חבר ה
יד

1135. AE *prutah*.
Obv: Paleo-Hebrew in wedge style characters *(Yehohanan the High Priest and the Council of the Jews)* within wreath.
Rev: Double cornucopia adorned with ribbons, pomegranate between horns; monogram as noted on pp. 188–189.   25/100

1136. AE double *prutah*.
Obv: Paleo-Hebrew יהוחנן הכהן הגדל ראש חבר היהודים *(Yehohanan the High Priest and Head of the Council of the Jews)*; double cornucopia, horns face in same direction, adorned with ribbons.
Rev: Helmet with decorative crest facing r., border of dots.
3,500/15,000

This rare coin is the only Hasmonean type that was not struck with beveled edges and for this reason it is suggested that it was not struck at the Jerusalem mint, Samaria is often mentioned as a possibility.

The reason for the addition of the designation "head" in the inscription is significant, but the reason for this change in title is not fully understood (see p. 183).

יהו
חנן הכהן
הגדל רא
ש חבר ה
יהדם

1137

1137.   AE *prutah.*
   Obv: Paleo-Hebrew *(Yehohanan the High Priest and Head of the Council of the Jews)* in wedge-style characters within wreath.
   Rev: Double cornucopia adorned with ribbons, pomegranate between horns; monogram A below r., or as noted below, border of dots.   35/150
   a. Reverse is obverse brockage.
   Although most specimens are not well centered, Meshorer suggested that they all probably carry monograms; for their likely locations see below.

1138.   AE half-*prutah.*
   Obv: Paleo-Hebrew *(Yehohanan the High Priest and the Head of the Council of the Jews)*; two lines above and below palm branch.
   Rev: Lily between two ears of grain, border of dots.   350/1,250

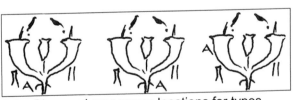

6.6. Observed monogram locations for types 1133, 1135, 1137.

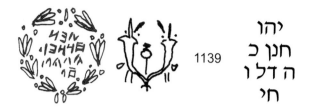

1139. AE *prutah*.
Obv: Paleo-Hebrew *(Yehohanan the High Priest...)* within wreath.
Rev: Double cornucopia adorned with ribbons, pomegranate between horns, border of dots.   25/100
Crude, angular letters, many errors, the letter ה appears as ⅃.

1140. AE *prutah*.
Obv: Paleo-Hebrew inscription *(Yehohanan the High Priest...)* within wreath.
Rev: Double cornucopia adorned with ribbons, pomegranate between horns, border of dots.   25/100
Crude, angular letters, many errors, to distinguish from 1139, note that the letter ה appears as ⅂.

1141. AE *prutah*.
Obv: Paleo-Hebrew inscription *(Yehohanan the High Priest...)* within wreath.
Rev: Double cornucopia adorned with ribbons, pomegranate between horns, border of dots.   20/75
This group consists of coins with unusual epigraphy, often crude, incomplete, and sometimes illegible.

6.7. Monograms noted and drawn by Meshorer which occur on types 1132, 1133, 1135, 1137.

JUDAH ARISTOBULUS I (YEHUDAH), 104–103 BCE

After the death of Hyrcanus, Aristobulus, the eldest of his sons, trans-
formed the government into a monarchy, and was the first to assume
the diadem… (JOSEPHUS, BJ I: 70).

Judah Aristobulus I, oldest son of Hyrcanus I, struck the Hasmonean coins with the name Yehudah. Josephus reports that Aristobulus was the first Hasmonean who officially adopted the title "king." But, it was probably well into his brief reign (104 BCE), because none of his coins carry that title. In fact, the coins of Aristobulus are almost identical to those of his father.

Hyrcanus I had proclaimed that upon his death his wife would become queen and Judah, his oldest son, would become high priest. His Greek name, Aristobulus, means "best counselor," and according to Heinrich Graetz, His Greek name alone was enough to give "such offense to the people that they were ready to ascribe to him the au-thorship of any evil deed that might occur in the kingdom. Whilst the Greeks called him fair-minded and modest, the Judaeans accused him of heartlessness and cruelty."[86]

After his father's death, Judah quickly imprisoned his mother along with three of his brothers. His favorite brother, Antigonus, not only remained free, but played an important part in his government. The mother died in prison. Charitable accounts list the cause as simply old age, while the gossips whispered that she was starved to death.

Aristobulus battled against both the Samarians and Syrians, and he acquired new land for his nation. But a severe illness caused him to abandon the campaign and return to Jerusalem. Antigonus fought on-ward on his brother's behalf, but returned to Jerusalem for the festivals. His opponents used the occasion of his triumphal return to prod the fatally-ill king into a jealous fit.

Josephus completes this gruesome, melodramatic story: "To Anti-gonus himself he sent instructions to come unarmed. To meet the occa-sion the queen [Aristobulus' wife, Salome Alexandra, or Shlomozion in Hebrew, later followed the Jewish custom by marrying her brother-in-law, Alexander Jannaeus, after her husband's death] concerted with the conspirators a very crafty plot. They induced the messengers to keep the king's orders to themselves, and instead to tell Antigonus that his brother had heard that he had procured for himself some very fine armor and military decorations in Galilee; that illness prevented him from paying a visit of inspection; 'but now that you are on the point of departure, I shall be very glad to see you in your armor.'

"On hearing this, as there was nothing in his brother's disposition to arouse his suspicions, Antigonus went off in his armor as for a parade. On reaching the dark passage, called Strato's Tower, he was slain by the bodyguard; affording a sure proof that calumny severs all ties of affection and of nature and that of our better feelings none is strong enough to hold out interminably against envy....

"Remorse for his foul deed had the instant effect of aggravating the malady of Aristobulus. His mind ever distracted with thoughts of the murder, he fell into a decline; until sheer grief rendering his entrails, he threw up a quantity of blood. While removing this, one of the pages in attendance slipped, so divine providence willed, on the very spot where Antigonus had been assassinated, and spilt on the yet visible stains of the murder the blood of the murderer. An instantaneous cry broke from the spectators, believing that the lad had intentionally poured the bloody libation on that spot.

"The king, hearing the cry, inquired what was its cause, and, when no one ventured to tell him, became more insistent in his desire to be informed. At length, under pressure of threats, they told him the truth. With tears filling his eyes and a groan such as his remaining strength permitted, he said: 'My lawless deeds, then, were not destined to escape God's mighty eye; swift retribution pursues me for my kinsman's blood. How long, most shameless body, wilt thou detain the soul that is sentenced to a brother's and a mother's vengeance? How long shall I make them these drop by drop libations of my blood? Let them take it all at once, and let heaven cease to mock them with these dribbling offerings from my entrails.' With these words on his lips he expired, after a reign of no more than a year."[87]

JUDAH ARISTOBULUS I (YEHUDAH), 104 BCE

יהו
דה הכה
ן הגדו
וחבר ה
יהד

1142. AE *prutah*.
Obv: Paleo-Hebrew יהודה כהן גדל וחבר היהודים *(Yehudah the High Priest and the Council of the Jews)* in wedge-style characters within wreath.
Rev: Double cornucopia adorned with ribbons, pomegranate between horns, border of dots.   300/750

The dies for this coin were either made by the same die cutter, or at least the same workshop of Hyrcanus I Nos. 1135, 1137, which suggests that this was the earlier of the Aristobulus types, and puts the coin immediately after the coins of Hyrcanus I. [87a]

יהוד
הכהוגד
ולוחברה
יהוד
ים

1143. AE *prutah*.
Obv: Hebrew inscription in block style characters *(Yehudah the High Priest and the Council of the Jews)* within wreath.
Rev: Double cornucopia adorned with ribbons, pomegranate between horns, border of dots.   75/300

a. Same style but the letter ד is on second line.
b. Reverse is double struck with obverse die.

The dies for this coin were either made by the same die cutter, or at least the same workshop of Jannaeus coin No. 1144, which suggests that this was the later of the Aristobulus types, and puts the coin immediately before the coins of Jannaeus. [87b]

ALEXANDER JANNAEUS (YEHONATAN, YONATAN) 104–76 BCE

And now the king's wife loosed the king's brethren, and made Alexander king, who appeared both elder in age, and more moderate in his temper than the rest (JOSEPHUS, BJ, I, IV:1).

Alexander Jannaeus, great-nephew of Simon and Judah Maccabee, became ruler of the Jews in 104 BCE upon the death of his brother, Judah Aristobulus I. Not only did he become high priest, he assumed the title "king," and for the first time the ruler of the Jews had equal rank with rulers of the Hellenistic world.

The young king was an ambitious warrior, hungry for conquest, and his reign was prosperous, if bloody. Early in his rule he managed to gain control of the entire coast of Palestine, from Mount Carmel in the north to Egypt in the south, with the exception of Ashqelon (Ascalon), which escaped his army because of the city's strong ties with Ptolemaic Egypt. Jannaeus' kingdom was roughly the same size as that ruled by King David.

The second decade of Jannaeus' reign was fraught with internal strife in Judaea. Jannaeus had surrounded himself with opulence and grandeur. His Hellenization and militarism deeply disturbed many of his countrymen, particularly the Pharisees, who devoutly believed the laws of the Torah must be carefully obeyed and thought Jannaeus was neglecting his sacred duties. In short, they didn't want a Hellenized warrior—and one who obviously enjoyed this role—as high priest.

On one occasion his enemies embarrassed Jannaeus by pelting him with fruit while he officiated over the Feast of Tabernacles in the Temple. The king retaliated by having several hundred of the rebels killed. Civil war raged in Judaea for six years beginning about 95 BCE; 50,000 Jews perished, according to some accounts.

The opposition among the king's followers encouraged his enemies. In 89 BCE, Demetrius III of Syria attempted an invasion of Judaea and defeated Jannaeus near Shechem (Nablus). This setback, however, reunited the Jews somewhat, and the renewed unity gave them the power to drive Demetrius out of Palestine.

Toward the end of his reign, Josephus reports, Jannaeus became ill from heavy drinking, which ultimately led to his death. But before the king died he was probably involved in a partial reconciliation with the Pharisees.

Jannaeus expanded on the coin types of his father and brother. He found the Jewish numismatic tradition strong enough in the context of his subjects' nationalistic religious feelings to continue to shun graven images. He initially copied the inscription/cornucopia coins pioneered by his father replacing his father's name with his own Hebrew name, "Yehonatan" or a shorter version "Yonatan." But after these issues, a change occurred. First, a half-*prutah* with a palm branch on one side and lily on the other bore a new paleo-Hebrew inscription: "Yehonatan the King" (No. 1147). Thus Jannaeus' title was changed from "high priest" to king, and mention of the Council of the Jews was discontinued. The significance of this body appears to have been dramatically reduced.

In another innovation, Jannaeus issued a series of bilingual coins with a Greek legend stating, "of King Alexander" (ΒΑΣΙΛΕΩΣ ΑΛΕΞΑΝΔΡΟΥ) and the paleo-Hebrew "Yehonatan the King." These bilingual issues feature the anchor design, perhaps resurrected from the Jerusalem coins struck earlier in a joint arrangement between Hyrcanus I and Antiochus VII. Jannaeus' use of this symbol underlines his conquest of a number of the Mediterranean coastal cities, greatly strengthening his kimgdom. Jannaeus' first anchor coins once again depict a lily on their reverse (No. 1148).

The other coin in this series is of more interest because of its symbolism. At first glance the design appears to be a wheel with spokes. Madden described this design as a "star with eight rays"[88] and Reifenberg as a "sun-wheel."[89] It was, however, Kanael who made the correct identification: a star encircled by a diadem, with the inscription in ancient Hebrew "Yehonatan the King" within the star.[90]

Diadems adorned the heads of kings and princes throughout the ancient world. Kanael further suggested that this design "reflects the ideology of the Maccabean monarchy; the star is the Jewish symbol of monarchy, derived from the song of Balaam: "There shall come a star out of Jacob, and a scepter shall rise out of Israel" (NUMBERS 24:17), while the diadem presents the Hellenistic symbol of kingship."[91]

Civil war raged in Judaea for six years beginning about 95 BCE. Kanael suggests that the Pharisee-controlled government struck the large issue of crude imitations of the anchor/star coins during their uprising against the Sadducee king[92] and continued to strike them after his death through the reign of his Queen Salome Alexandra and possibly their sons Aristobulus II and Hyrcanus II (Nos. 1159–1161).

Among the numismatic aftermaths of this civil war may have been the issue of two coin types of Jannaeus in which the inscription for the first (and only) time is altered from the paleo-Hebrew script to the contemporary Aramaic, the language of the people. One of these is dated to 80/79 BCE and follows the anchor/star style. But instead of paleo-Hebrew between the rays, around the star is the Aramaic inscription, "King Alexander Year 25." (This is the *only* dated Hasmonean coin type.) The second coin, possibly a token, with an Aramaic inscription is struck from lead instead of bronze.

THE LEAD PIECES

The lead coins or tokens of Jannaeus create an enigma. They were mentioned in 1871 by deSaulcy in one of the earliest known scholarly works on the coins of the Jews.[93] In 1967, Meshorer wrote that he knew of only about 20 examples of the lead issue.[94] In 1974, Arie Kindler observed that the Jannaeus lead coins "seem to have been issued for only a short period during some temporary economic crisis."[95] Here are a few points regarding the Jannaeus lead pieces deduced from knowledge acquired more recently:

1. Although they remain far more scarce than bronze coins of Jannaeus, the lead issues are no longer as rare as once believed. Several small hoards have been found, and I have examined more than 400 specimens.

2. It seems clear that none of the lead issues was actually uniface, all were intended to carry reverse inscriptions in Aramaic, but they are weakly struck or worn due to the softness of lead.

3. A number of die varieties of the lead pieces exist, which indicates that this was probably a larger issue than originally believed.

The questions raised are two-fold: first, when were the lead pieces issued and second, why?

The answer to the first question can be traced to J. Naveh's 1968 article, in which he deciphered the reverse inscriptions of the dated coins of Jannaeus. These are the light *prutahs* (No. 1152) with anchor obverse and star reverse. Naveh showed that the reverse inscription was in Aramaic, translates as: "of King Alexander, Year 25."[96] This twenty-fifth year of Jannaeus' reign corresponds with 80/79 BCE and is relevant to our study of the lead pieces because they, too, carry a similar Aramaic inscription on their reverse: "of King Alexander."

Epigraphically, the legends on the lead and dated bronze issues are similar. Since these are the only two types of Jannaeus with Aramaic inscriptions, one can conclude they were struck around the same time.

To find clues to the motivation for these lead pieces, one looks at what was happening in about 80/79 BCE. Not many years before (circa 95 BCE), a bloody civil war raged in Judaea. It stemmed from rivalry between the Sadducees, the party supporting the king and his Hellenized ways, and the more traditional Pharisees. Ill will between the factions did not end with the war, but continued for several years thereafter.

Jannaeus died in 76 BCE, but it is believed that for several years before his death he adopted a more benevolent policy toward the rival Pharisees, encouraged by his wife Salome Alexandra. One method for a ruler to ingratiate himself was to offer gifts to be redeemed for food or other commodities; this largess was called *congiarium*. The Roman emperors issued special tokens of bronze or even precious metals, but in the poor province of Judaea where only bronze coins were struck, lead may have sufficed. Since the language of the masses during Jannaeus' time was Aramaic, it is not far-fetched to conclude that the lead issues in question were tokens issued by the Jewish king to the masses to be redeemed for gifts. This possibility may also explain the several true hoards made up exclusively of these lead pieces.[97]

This lead issue by Jannaeus in about 79/78 BCE may represent the first Jewish tokens. They remind us of a time when the Jewish nation was ruled by royalty, but even to a powerful monarch, the will of his people was important enough to warrant significant consideration.

A second lead issue (No. 1156) was likely also struck under Jannaeus. Its obverse has a star with six rays alternating with dots around a central dot, no inscription is visible and all known examples are blank on the other side. The similarity between this and the star-within-diadem on the coins of Jannaeus is noticeable, particularly to the style of No. 1151. I first discovered this type while examining an accumulation of several thousand Jewish coins acquired in the Jerusalem marketplace in the 1980s. Possibly this is a trial-strike or prototype coin.[98]

It is also probable that after their value as tokens expired, both lead types entered circulation at a specified value. This conclusion is based on the fact that many of the lead pieces of both types are found scattered among other Jewish coins of the time in surface or near-surface finds. In other cases they are found in hoards of only lead pieces.

When Jannaeus was succeeded by his queen, Salome Alexandra, power was concentrated in the hands of the Pharisees.

ALEXANDER JANNAEUS (YEHONATAN)

Average weight *prutah,* 2.15 g unless noted.

1144

יהונ
תנהכהן
הגדולחב
רהיהו
דים

1144. AE *prutah.*

Obv: Paleo-Hebrew יהונתן הכהן הגדל חבר היהודים *(Yehonatan the High Priest and the Council of the Jews)* in block-style characters within wreath.

Rev: Double cornucopia adorned with ribbons, pomegranate between horns, border of dots. 25/100

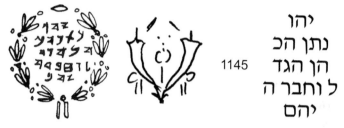

1145

יהו
נתן הכ
הן הגד
ל וחבר ה
יהם

1145. AE *prutah.*

Obv: Paleo-Hebrew *(Yehonatan the High Priest and the Council of the Jews)* within by wreath.

Rev: Double cornucopia adorned with ribbons, pomegranate between horns, border of dots. 25/100

1146

יהונת
ן הכן גדל
וחבר ו
יהודי
ם

1146. AE *prutah.*

Obv: Paleo-Hebrew inscription in cursive style characters *(Yehonatan the High Priest and the Council of the Jews)* within wreath.

Rev: Double cornucopia adorned with ribbons, pomegranate between horns, border of dots. 25/100

המלך
יהונתן
1147

1147.   AE half-*prutah*.
   Obv: Upright palm branch flanked by paleo-Hebrew; המלך יהונתן
   (Yehonatan the King), border of dots.
   Rev: Lily, border of dots.   1,000/4,000

 1148   המלך
יהונתן

1148.   AE *prutah* average weight 1.71 g.
   Obv: Lily flanked by paleo-Hebrew *(Yehonatan the King)*, border of
   dots.
   Rev: ΒΑΣΙΛΕΩΣ ΑΛΕΞΑΝΔΡΟΥ *(of King Alexander)*; inverted anchor within circle.   75/200

 1149   ינתן
הכהן ה
גדל וחבר
היהד

1149.   AE prutah, average weight 1.71 g.
   Obv: Paleo-Hebrew *(Yonatan the High Priest and the Council of the Jews)*
   within wreath.
   Rev: Double cornucopia adorned with ribbons, pomegranate between horns. Overstrike obliterates nearly all signs of previous
   coin.   50/250
   a. Hebrew over anchor, cornucopias over lily.
   b. Hebrew over lily, cornucopias over anchor.
   c. Similar but the overstrike is cursive type No. 1146.[98a]

Since there are so many of these overstrikes and the original lily/anchor type is far more scarce than the overstrikes, it may be surmised that almost all of these coins were restruck before they left the mint rather than upon recall from circulation, which would have led to a far less consistent output.

1150

יהונתן
המלך

1150.   AE prutah. average weight 1.71 g.

Obv: Paleo-Hebrew *(Yehonatan the King)* between the rays of star with eight rays within diadem.

Rev: ΒΑΣΙΛΕΩΣ ΑΛΕΞΑΝΔΡΟΥ *(of King Alexander)* around inverted anchor.   25/100

a. Extremely heavy example, 6.33 g.
b. Irregular issue.
c. No visible Hebrew legend.
d. Obverse brockage.
e. Reverse brockage.

1150f.

Obv: Paleo-Hebrew *(Yehonatan the King)* between rays of star of eight rays within diadem, several letters visible *(yh)wntn*. Part of a border of dots, visible from 1 to 4 o'clock, represents a trace of a previous striking.

Rev: ΒΑΣΙΛΕ(ΩΣ ΑΛΕΞΑΝΔΡΟΥ), around inverted anchor within border of dots; the most prominent trace of a previous striking is a clearly identifiable portion of the inscription from No. 1149 (cornucopias/inscription overstruck on anchor/flower).

UNIQUE

See No. 1149c for yet another variation overstruck on an earlier coin of Jannaeus.

1151.   AE *prutah* usually less than 1 g.

  Obv: Paleo-Hebrew *(Priest the King)* between dots of star with eight (instead of rays) within diadem; a Π-like monogram included.

  Rev: ΒΑΣΙΛΕΩΣ ΑΛΕΞΑΝΔΡΟΥ; finely engraved letters around round finely engraved anchor.   25/100

  a. Obverse brockage, unusual since full legend is clear in both impressions.

It is difficult to understand this coin. At first glance it appears to be simply a reduced weight version, and inscription error of No. 1150. Yet, Meshorer suggests that if the monogram "has some symbolic significance it can be suggested that the inscription too is not incidental."[99] Barag adds that it can hardly "be a mistake or initiative of the die engraver. It seems, rather, that at some point the royal mint issued for political reasons these double-titled coins and after a very short time refrained from further issues of that kind." Barag says Josephus and Rabbinnic sources "leave no doubt that the Pharisees demanded that Hyrcanus I should give up the position of high priest and be content with his secular power. During the reign of Alexander Jannaeus their attitude reached an extreme point—the Hasmoneans were priests and therefore not from David's line and thus usurpers of the crown.... The coins described above seem to be related to that division between the Pharisees and Hasmoneans by presenting the legend 'Priest the King.' The impact of this coin issue was, apparently, thought to be ineffective for the sake of dynastic propaganda and stopped soon after its introduction."[100]

1152

1152a

1152.   AE *prutah*, average weight 1.20 g.

  Obv: Aramaic מלכא אלכסנדרוס שנת כה *(King Alexander, year 25)* around star of eight rays and border of dots.

  Rev: ΒΑΣΙΛΕΩΣ ΑΛΕΞΑΝΔΡΟΥ around inverted anchor within circle; L KE *(year 25 = 80/79 BCE)*, made of dots often connected by fine lines.   25/100

  a. No Greek date at points of anchor.

L KE, stylistically similar to Seleucid coins, refers to Year 25 of Jannaeus, corresponding to 80/79 BCE. Increasingly crude and lighter versions of this coin continue to be manufactured, See Nos. 1153, 1154.

1153.   AE *prutah*. average weight 0.81 g.

Obv: Aramaic inscription, crude and stylized, mostly illegible, around star within border of dots.

Rev: Incomplete and stylized Greek inscription around inverted anchor within circle.   25/75

a. Same but struck in lead.   No Aramaic or Greek.

b. Reverse is obverse brockage.

This coin, copying No. 1152, is found in innumerable varieties, some of which seem to carry crude linear designs instead of stars on obverse (p. 474).

1154.   AE *prutah*.

Obv: *(Yeho...)* paleo-Hebrew (instead of Aramaic) inscription, partial and crude, around star within border of dots.

Rev: Stylized and incomplete Greek inscription around inverted anchor within circle.   25/75

1155

מלכא
אלכסנ
דרוס

1155.   Lead *prutah* (or token), average weight 4.10 g.

Obv: Aramaic *(King Alexander)* usually in three lines within border of dots.

Rev: ΒΑΣΙΛΕΩΣ ΑΛΕΞΑΝΔΡΟΥ around inverted anchor in circle.
    25/200

a. Similar but with stylized legends and design.

b. Blank lead flan.

1156.   Lead *prutah* (or token).

Obv: Star with eight pellets instead of rays within diadem.

Rev: Blank.   100/300

The obverse is nearly identical to that of coin No. 1151, but without any letters. The reverse of all known examples to date is blank. Similar types, larger or smaller and with similar or rosette motifs, often with loops on one or both ends, are definitely from the medieval period. Recent evidence suggests that this type is cast and not struck. This indicates they might also be from a later period, and only evidence from a controlled archaeological excavation will eventually prove the nature of this enigmatic coin or token.

ANONYMOUS HASMONEAN ISSUES

1157. Lead *prutah* (or token).
  Obv: Double cornucopia, upright rod between, border of dots.
  Rev: Stylized palm tree that appears to be set between two blooming
    lily flowers.   RRR

1158. Lead *prutah* (or token).
  Obv: Paleo-Hebrew ‛ above double cornucopia, palm tree between
    horns, within solid circle.
  Rev: Lily flower between 2 grain ears, tied at bottom, small leaves
    on both sides of central stalk.   RRR
    *Bijovsky, who is studying coins from excavations at Mt. Gerizim for pub-
    lication, attributes these coins to the Hasmonean period based on iconography
    and archaeological context of second century BCE. "Due to their presence at Mt.
    Gerizim, they were probably produced in Samaria."* [101]

SALOME ALEXANDRA (76–67 BCE), HYRCANUS II (YONATAN) (67 AND 63–40 BCE), ARISTOBULUS II (67–63 BCE) (?)

*Alexander bequeathed the kingdom to his wife Alexandra, being con-
vinced that the Jews would bow to her authority as they would to no
other, because by her utter lack of his brutality and by her opposition
to his crimes she had won the affections of the populace* (JOSEPHUS BJ
I: 107).

*Hyrcanus, to whom even in her lifetime his mother had entrusted the
kingdom, was sole heir to the throne, but in capacity and courage,
was surpassed by Aristobulus. A battle for the crown took place near
Jericho...* (JOSEPHUS BJ I: 120).

After the death of Alexander Jannaeus, rule of the ancient Land of
Israel was inherited by his queen, Salome Alexandra (Shlomozion).
She apparently issued no coins bearing her name. During her reign,
Hyrcanus II, her oldest son, was appointed high priest and thus was
regarded as heir to the throne.

Hyrcanus, unlike his grandfather and namesake, was weak, and not as politically sophisticated as his younger brother Aristobulus II. He became involved in a bitter struggle when his mother died. Aristobulus was just the opposite of his brother and had inherited his father's bellicose nature. During a skirmish between the two near Jericho, most of Hyrcanus' men went over to Aristobulus.

With Aristobulus II now king and high priest (from around 67 to 63 BCE), Hyrcanus received an honorary title, but no power, which he dearly wanted. His ambitions were encouraged by his advisor, Antipater, an Idumaean whose family had been converted to Judaism 50 years earlier by Hyrcanus I. Antipater was a rich chieftain and had a good deal of power on his own. But he wanted more for himself and his sons. He thought he might get it through the weak Hyrcanus, so he started to agitate for him to fight his younger brother and again seize the power he thought was rightfully his.

Hyrcanus, on Antipater's advice, fled Jerusalem to the Nabataean king Aretas III. By making territorial concessions to the Nabataean, Hyrcanus induced him to join forces against Aristobulus II. Their armies besieged Aristobulus II in Jerusalem in 65 BCE.

At about this time, Pompey's armies, led by the general Marcus Scaurus, marched into the East. Initially, Scaurus favored Aristobulus II (probably due to bribes). But, when Pompey arrived in Syria in 63 BCE, the two brothers laid their claims before him. Antipater went along to support Hyrcanus.

Pompey, feeling that Hyrcanus was the weaker of the brothers and hence less likely to cause trouble later, ruled that he was the rightful king. Now, Aristobulus II and his followers fled to Jerusalem where they fortified themselves. But the great Pompey, terror of pirates and kings, followed. Aristobulus II foolishly tricked and teased Pompey, pretending that he was going to surrender, but fleeing instead to safety in Jerusalem. When Pompey's men burst into the city after a three-month siege, they inflicted heavy casualties on the Jews. Pompey himself entered the Temple's Holy of Holies, the inner sanctuary, thus defiling it. For all practical purposes this act ended the great Hasmonean dynasty. It would never recover even a fraction of its previous strength.

Aristobulus II was captured and sent with his children to Rome, where he was ridiculed and paraded through the streets. Later he would escape and again try, unsuccessfully, to regain control of Judaea. (See No. 1443 for a Roman Republican issue related to the defeat of Aristobulus.)

Hyrcanus II, now virtually a puppet of Rome, was reappointed high priest. In 47 BCE, he was named "ethnarch," which meant "ruler of the people," but was clearly something less than king.

With the weak Hyrcanus ruling Judaea, Pompey easily cut its size by granting autonomy to several cities, including Gaza, Gadara, and Marisa. Furthermore, Pompey's general Gabinius was left as the governor of Syria, also charged with looking after Judaea. He divided the Land of Israel into five districts, mainly for taxation purposes.

Throughout the remainder of Hyrcanus II's rule, Antipater, closely allied with Rome, became his prime minister and played a major role in governing. This is best shown by the eventual succession of Antipater's son Herod to the throne.

Unfortunately, Hyrcanus II's Hebrew name is not known. As discussed earlier, it is theorized that the non-overstruck coins with the name Yonatan *may* belong to him, along with the smallest versions of the anchor/star coins issued first under Jannaeus. It seems to be a long gap without new coins between the death of Jannaeus in 76 BCE until the reign of Mattatayah Antigonus beginning in 40 BCE. There is some logic to the striking of coins by Queen Salome Alexandra as the head of state on behalf of her son Hyrcanus II the high priest and it's *possible* that they continued being struck for years, even under Aristobulus II. The huge number of these coins, especially the reduced light prutah anchor/star type suggests that they may have been manufactured over a long period of time. Not coincidentally these coins helped fill a need for small bronze coinage as long as a few hundred years after they were struck. It could be argued that the Yonatan coins with an unusual epigraphic style (No. 1159) were not the product of the more sophisticated engravers who worked under Jannaeus, but were produced later in the reign of his successors.

It is far from certain that the successors of Alexander Jannaeus issued coins. In fact, one coin listed here for the first time suggests that all of the coins in this section could possibly be attributed to Jannaeus. However, we include them in this location to complete the historical perspective of the Hasmoneans and with the hope that in the future this enigma will be clarified by numismatic evidence or evidence from controlled archaeological excavations.

SALOME ALEXANDRA AS REGENT FOR
JOHN HYRCANUS II OR ARISTOBULUS II (?)

ינתן
הכהן ג
דל וחב
ר יהדי
ם

1159. AE *prutah*, average weight 1.81 g.

Obv: Paleo-Hebrew ינתן הכהן גדל חבר יהדם *(Yonatan the High Priest and the Council of the Jews)* highly stylized, within wreath. Many letters are illegible.

Rev: Double cornucopia adorned with ribbons, pomegranate between horns.   25/100

a. More stylized legend.

b. Overstruck on Jannaeus type 1148.

Coin 1159b is a recent discovery. Could it be a coincidental overstrike on this Jannaeus coin or does it suggest that this is a Jannaeus coin that was overstruck on another Jannaeus coin as 1149?

These appear in many varieties. The highly stylized letters are surprisingly readable, but there are often errors. Note the abbreviated spelling of the king's name as on the overstruck issue of Jannaeus, No. 1149.

1160. AE *prutah*.

Obv: Crude paleo-Hebrew חבר יהדם *(Council of the Jews)* in crude script, within crude wreath.

Rev: Double cornucopia adorned with ribbons, pomegranate between horns.   25/100

It has been argued that there is special significance to this group of coins, omitting the king's name and mentioning only the "Hever ha Yehudim" (Council of the Jews). Based on the messy script, however, it seems more logical to assume that this type is simply a variation of the previous and succeeding types.

1161. AE *prutah*.

Obv: Complete imitation of Hebrew inscription within highly stylized wreath. Inscription is totally illegible.

Rev: Crude double cornucopia, pomegranate between horns.

35/125

MATTATAYAH ANTIGONUS, 40–37 BCE

Hatred of Herod had led to his [Orodes II] taking part in bringing back the exiled Antigonus, a son of Aristobulus... (JOSEPHUS, BJ: 239).

By 40 BCE, Judaea was almost completely dominated by Rome. Antipater the Idumaean had been prime minister behind Hyrcanus II for some time, and his sons Phasael and Herod were made governors of Jerusalem and Galilee, respectively. Herod, meanwhile, was gaining considerable power through political alliances, especially with Rome.

In the year 40, Mattatayah (Mattathias) Antigonus, youngest son of Aristobulus II and four generations removed from Judah Maccabee, bribed the Parthians (Rome's greatest foe in the area) under Orodes II to invade Jerusalem and help him win the crown and position of high priest, still held by his uncle, Hyrcanus II. (It is reported by Josephus that the bribe to Orodes included some 500 Jewish women.)

When the Parthians and Antigonus' men marched into Jerusalem and occupied the Temple Mount, Hyrcanus II and Herod and his troops retreated to the royal palace. Josephus reports that the Parthians "let loose on the whole country the horrors of implacable war...and, not content with raising Antigonus to the throne, delivered up to him Phasael and Hyrcanus, in chains, for torture. Hyrcanus threw himself at the feet of Antigonus, who with his own teeth lacerated his suppliant's ears, in order to disqualify him forever, under any change of circumstances, from resuming the high priesthood; since freedom from physical defect is essential to the holder of that office."[102]

Herod's brother Phasael, hands bound, "courageously forestalled the king's malice by dashing his head upon a rock...he died a hero's death. According to another account, Phasael recovered from his self-inflicted blow, and a physician sent by Antigonus, ostensibly to attend him, injected noxious drugs into the wound and so killed him.... It is said, moreover, that before he expired, being informed by a woman of Herod's escape, he exclaimed, 'Now I shall depart happy, since I leave one behind me who will have vengeance on my foes.'"[103]

Indeed, Herod escaped Jerusalem and soon made his way to Rome, where he was officially designated King of Judaea in 40 BCE.

Antigonus' effort went for naught. When Herod returned to Judaea to resume hostilities, he fought Antigonus's army for more than two years, albeit without substantial support from Ventidius, Mark

Antony's legate and eventual victor in the Parthian war. In 37 BCE, after a siege of several months, Herod, with the Roman troops of Gaius Sosius, took Jerusalem and captured Antigonus, who was later executed at Antioch, thus ending five generations of Hasmonean rule (see No. 1444, C. Sosius).

During his war against Herod, Antigonus used coins as important propaganda tools. He rushed out an emergency series that was inferior in both metal content and workmanship. But, for the first time, a Hasmonean ruler minted large denomination coins—eight and four *prutot*—along with a one-*prutah* type. The flans for these coins were created when molten metal was poured into a double mold. (Just such a double mold, with openings the diameter of the second-denomination coin of Mattatayah, were found in excavations near Jerusalem's Jaffa Gate, suggesting this was the location of Antigonus' mint.

Flans cast in this way appear to be two coins stuck together. Sometimes the two sections of the mold did not fit properly and so-called stepped flans were produced. Antigonus struck all three denominations of his coins on these double-thick flans. However, rare coins bearing his name were also struck on normal Hasmonean flans—one type was the extremely rare menorah/showbread table coin and the other was a basic imitation of the coins of his predecessors—on their obverse a double cornucopia with the paleo-Hebrew inscription "Mattatayah" or "Mattatayah the Priest." The coins of Mattatayah Antigonus are also struck from a far less pure copper alloy than the earlier Hasmonean coins.[104] One can assume that this was due to dire circumstances during the reign of the last Hasmonean king.

The reverse of the larger denominations carries a Greek inscription reading "of King Antigonus," either outside a wreath (8 *prutot*—No. 1162) or inside one (4 *prutot*—No. 1163). Antigonus also issued small coins following the Hasmonean prototype, some with minor variations. Instead of the typical Hasmonean formulaic inscription, only the name, "Mattatayah," or "Mattatayah the Priest" appears.[105]

Antigonus' rule overlapped the first three years of the rule of Herod, who also claimed to begin rule in 40 BCE.

6.8. Side view of normal flan (left) and double-thick flan from mint of Mattathias Antigonus.

THE MENORAH COINS

The last coin issued by Mattatayah Antigonus is unique in its images. It is a clear propaganda tool, and must have been designed out of desperation, to show the people why Antigonus was fighting. The coin depicts the two most important cult objects of the Jewish Temple: the showbread table on one side and the menorah on the other. The inscriptions are in Greek and paleo-Hebrew, but they are not complete on any known examples.[106] The objects were critical symbols of the Jerusalem Temple.

In the view of some of the people, Antigonus may have violated at least the spirit, if not the letter, of basic Jewish law by depicting these symbols of Jewish Temple worship on a coin for ordinary circulation. The Babylonian Talmud forbids making "a table after the design of the table [in the Temple] or a candelabrum after the design of the

6.9. Graffiti of seven-branched menorah and show-bread table, below r., from Old City of Jerusalem dating to the first century CE. Courtesy D.Barag.

candelabrum".[107] This could be interpreted as actually manufacturing copies of these objects. Whether it relates to depicting them in art remains controversial.[108]

This Talmudic reference singles out both the menorah and the showbread table from all of the objects in the Temple and forbids their reproduction, although it is not clear if the ban covers only actual reproduction of the objects or also their images. One also may wonder if the Talmud mentions these two objects in the same category as a reference to this very coin. It wasn't until around 200 years later that the menorah became the most important Jewish symbol. It is more than likely that at the time the coin was issued, the showbread table was as important as the menorah as a symbol of Judaism. This equivalence was perhaps underlined since the table is depicted on the side of the coin with the paleo-Hebrew legend, while the menorah is depicted on the side with the Greek legend.

"Thus the depiction of the image[s] on a coin minted as early as the reign of Antigonus is a remarkable and daring phenomenon, which must be seen in the context of the contemporary historical circumstances. Antigonus may have depicted the candelabrum and the table on his coins both to encourage his supporters and to remind the people of their duty to preserve the sanctity of the Temple (and its high priest) from the 'foreigners,'" Meshorer explains.[109]

While it is often stated that this coin of Antigonus carries the first appearance in figurative art of either the showbread table or the menorah, this is not accurate. Both of them appear, together, in first-century graffiti scratched onto a plaster wall found in excavations of the Old City of Jerusalem. Graffiti drawings of five seven-branched menorahs were also scratched into a plaster wall in Jason's Tomb in Jerusalem, and they date no later than 30/31 CE.[110] Crude menorah designs are also scratched into a few ossuaries dating from the mid first century BCE to the mid first century CE found in the area of ancient Judaea.

These represent the few menorah or showbread table images prior to Mattatayah Antigonus's coin.

The next appearance of the menorah in Jewish art occurs in remains ranging from the period of Herod I to the Jewish War, and these symbols are also used in Jerusalem graffiti.

According to Prof. Barag, it is important to keep in mind that at this time these "are not symbols of Judaism but symbols of the Temple. The idea of a symbol of Judaism is very late, and much later than the cross as a symbol of Christianity. Some time after the Jerusalem

Temple was destroyed in 70 CE, the menorah became a symbol of messianic hopes for rebuilding it."[111] A menorah is also featured as part of the Temple booty on the Arch of Titus in Rome, completed in 81 CE, and also on oil lamps beginning at the time of manufacture of the "darom" oil lamps in the late first and second centuries CE. But it was not until the third century CE that the menorah begins to appear more commonly as a symbol of Judaism. This is quite interesting, since it suggests that when we look at the menorah on an ancient coin today, we probably ascribe an anachronistic meaning to it.

There are two varieties of the showbread table on the coins of Antigonus. One of them (No. 1168) is a plain table, while the other variation (No. 1168a) has two stacks of bread loaves upon it. Bread itself was an early symbol of prosperity. Some catalogers have suggested that the showbread table is not venerated in modern Judaism "because of the importance of bread and the Lord's Table in Christian services."[112] Professor Barag, one of the leading experts of the use of these symbols in ancient times, however, suggests that this connection is extremely *unlikely*. "I have often been asked this question about the bread and the Church. The meaning of wine and bread in the Christian Church is

6.10. From left, bronze box hardware with menorah flanked by etrogs, c. 1st century CE; top center, bronze medallion with menorah, shofar and lulav, c. 3rd–4th centuries CE; below center, fragment of bronze bracelet with gilded menorah, c. 4th–6th centuries CE; terra cotta oil lamp with menorah flanked by incense shovels, above the central hole, c. 3rd–5th centuries CE. Author's collection.

entirely different and has nothing to do with the Temple and the hopes of salvation and rebuilding the Temple."[113]

It is far more likely, he explains, that the menorah continued as a symbol of Judaism because it was more of a useful device; and heavily publicized by the Romans as important booty removed from the Temple. After the destruction of the Temple, menorahs could be built and used functionally in synagogues or in homes, or graphically used to adorn various objects and architecture.[114]

The menorah coins of Mattathias Antigonus are among the most sought-after coins of ancient Israel. Because of their great value they are often copied, sometimes with the intent to deceive unwitting collectors. They were also copied in ancient times, and a famous Islamic "menorah" coin (of either five or, rarely, seven branches) dates to the Umayyad post-reform period after 696 CE.

The Islamic coins, several modern forgeries, and an error in a 125-year-old (but widely-used) book on Jewish numismatics have caused significant confusion. Much of it is clarified by Dan Barag.[115]

In 1864, Madden accepted the 1860 view of Count Melchior de Vogue, who attributed the coins with a 7-branched menorah and "a row of four parallel trees" to Abd al-Malik, Islamic ruler of the mid-seventh century. It was only in 1871 that deSaulcy showed that this coin was actually a coin of Mattatayah Antigonus. He also realized that the reverse design was really the showbread table and not a row of trees.[116]

Madden corrected the error he picked up from Count Melchior in his 1881 edition. But his 1864 book is the one that is most widely reprinted (probably because of the smaller format) and this is especially confusing to modern collectors because the coin with a seven-branched menorah and showbread table was shown in a line drawing. That line drawing is strikingly similar to contemporary forgeries of the Antigonus showbread table/menorah coin.

Until 1967 when Meshorer's *Jewish Coins of the Second Temple Period* was published, few other references were widely available. Thus, both the Jewish and the Islamic menorah coins were known mostly from drawings and not from photographs.

Many collectors who purchased realistic forgeries of these coins could therefore compare them only with drawings—to which they compared favorably—and not with good quality photographs. Further confusion is added by the extreme rarity of these coins.

In 1967, I purchased a forgery of the Mattathias Antigonus coin in Jerusalem. I was told it was a forgery, but I doubted if I'd ever be able to afford the real thing, so what the heck. I later learned that this was an especially tricky forgery, since it was struck upon an ancient bronze coin of approximately the correct size. Also in 1967, I purchased a bronze cast of this type which was not made to deceive collectors, but as part of a legitimate set of museum replicas.

Some months after I bought that set, a rather shady dealer of antiquities called me into the far-back room of his shop in Jerusalem's Old City, opened a huge safe, and took out a nicely patinated coin of Mattatayah Antigonus. He explained that I could get a "great bargain" on this coin because of the circumstances under which he had acquired it. I was naïve, but not stupid. When I first saw the coin, I assumed it was genuine. I also believed this fellow was my friend and was really trying to give me a good deal—lucky for me I couldn't afford it. But something about the coin rang a bell, and when I returned home that evening, I looked at my cast replica. Sure enough, it was exactly the same shape, same centering, and same strike. It was only missing the patina. I never saw that coin again (or bought from that dealer again!), but I assume that in a better light the telltale traces of casting—pinholes and file marks on the edge—would have been more easily noticed.

The Islamic menorah coins are easy to distinguish from those issued by Antigonus. First, the style of the menorah is totally different. Most menorahs on these coins have five branches, but there is a rare variety, possibly struck early in the series, with seven branches. Second, the Islamic coins carry an inscription in Arabic ("Mohammed is Allah's messenger") instead of the showbread table.

The Islamic coins are nevertheless of genuine interest to collectors of Biblical coins. Barag explains that, "It is of course undeniable that by choosing the candlestick, and at first a seven-branched candlestick, the mint authorities adopted the ancient Jewish menorah, albeit changing it slightly (*e.g.* the flat base). There is no way of determining how this influence was effected and whether Jewish die-makers or mint-masters were involved in the production of these coins.... Does the preference of a five-branched candlestick demonstrate more than the mere wish to move away from the Jewish prototype? The introduction of (a variety with) the two-leaved stem may indicate the acceptance of Christian traditions concerning the Menorah."

Barag also suggests the intriguing possibility that "the inception of this series was connected to a particular event. The construction of the Dome of the Rock was finished in 691/2 CE, a date too early by far for the series. The construction of the second Aqsa Mosque around 715/16 CE could have prompted the striking of such coins, but there is no positive indication that this was the case.[117]

"After a while," Barag notes, "the Muslim authorities of Jerusalem abandoned this unusual experiment, leaving to posterity a series of coins which testify in their own modest way of the struggle for Jerusalem."[118]

These tips can help determine the authenticity of a menorah coin:

A menorah coin of Mattathias Antigonus is struck on the typical Maccabean coin flan with beveled rim. It should have clear signs of being cut from a strip of flans.

Forgeries of this coin are of three basic types:

1. Cast copy, which is cast from a genuine coin. Upon close inspection you will find "pinholes" from the casting process as well as a telltale rim on the edge, or file marks where someone tried to obliterate it.

2. Struck copy, often struck upon an ancient bronze coin. I have heard of at least one example struck upon a Late Roman bronze coin which could still be identified! If the coin does not have a tapered rim and has a series of uniform hair-like cracks directed inward from the edge, you should be suspicious, but this is not an absolute diagnostic.

3. A third type of forgery is actually engraved on an authentic Maccabean *prutah*. At first it really appears to be a menorah coin, but at second glance one sees that the design is in incuse rather than in relief.

6.11. Forgeries of showbread table / menorah *prutah* of Mattatayah Antigonus. The coin on far left is cast, the others are struck upon old bronze coins. Hendin Collection at the Israel Museum.

MATTATAYAH ANTIGONUS

1162

1162.   AE 8-*prutah*, average weight 14 g.

Obv: Paleo-Hebrew; מתתי הכהן הגדל חבר יד *(Mattatayah the High Priest and Council of the Jews)*, around and between double cornu-copia, some specimens have the letters נא, apparently retrograde for An[tigonus].

Rev: BACIΛEΩC ANTIΓONOY *(of King Antigonus)* around ivy wreath tied with ribbons   150/500

a. Irregular with retrograde reverse legend.

b. Double struck.

On this and the following coin, the paleo-Hebrew inscriptions appear in many versions struck from many die sets not yet studied.

   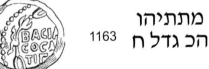
1163

1163.   AE 4-*prutah*, average weight 7.19 g.

Obv: Paleo-Hebrew; מתתיה הכהן גדל *(Mattatayah the High Priest)* around cornucopia tied with ribbons, decorated with vine leaf and grapes.

Rev: BACIΛEΩC ANTIΓONOY in 2, 3, or 4 lines, often abbreviated, within wreath and border of dots.   100/300

a. Mule type with reverse of No. 1162.

b. Irregular with retrograde reverse legend.

c. Blank flan.

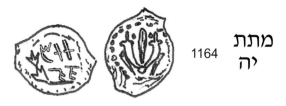

מתת
יה   1164

1164. AE *prutah*, average weight 1.68 g.
  Obv: Paleo-Hebrew, retrograde, מתתיה, *(Mattatayah)* within wreath
    and border of dots.
  Rev: Double cornucopia adorned with ribbons, ear of barley be-
    tween horns, border of dots.   75/200
  a. Struck upon a single thickness flan.

1165. AE *prutah*.
  Obv: Paleo-Hebrew מתתיה *(Mattatayah)* within wreath and border
    of dots.
  Rev: Double cornucopia adorned with ribbons, ear of barley be-
    tween horns, border of dots.   RRR
  This is often described as a "mule" with the inscription of 1166 and the
cornucopias of 1164. This is not true, since the obverse die was made in the
style of 1164. Also, this type is struck only on double-thick flans as is 1162, but
1166–67 are always struck on flans of single thickness.

מתתי   מתתיה
ההכהן   הכהן
1166   1166a

1166. AE *prutah*.
  Obv: Paleo-Hebrew; מתתיה הכהן *(Mattatayah the High Priest)* with-
    in wreath.
  Rev: Double cornucopia adorned with ribbons, pomegranate be-
    tween horns.   300/1,000
  a. Inscription reads *"Mattatayah the High Priest."*

1167   מתת
 יה

1167.   AE *prutah.*
   Obv: Paleo-Hebrew מתתיה (*Mattatayah*) within wreath.
   Rev: Double cornucopia adorned with ribbons, pomegranate be-
      tween horns.   300/1,000
   a. Double-thick flan.

1168   מתתיה
כהן גדול

1168.   AE *prutah.*
   Obv: Traces of paleo-Hebrew (*Mattatayah the High Priest*) around
      showbread table.
   Rev: ΒΑΣΙΛΕΩΣ ΑΝΤΙΓΟΝΟΥ; seven-branched menorah.
                                                  35,000/75,000
   a. Variation of same coin but clearly depicting two stacks of the
      "showbread" on the table.
   *The inscriptions are never complete because the dies were cut to strike coins
on flans larger than actually used, and the obverse die with the showbread table
was considerably larger than the reverse die, as shown in the composite. This is
the only ancient Jewish coin depicting the seven-branched menorah. Meshorer
speculated that this coin was issued mainly for its propaganda value in the dying days of the reign of the last of the Hasmonean rulers.*

6.12. More objects depicting menorahs: top left, menorah flanked by shofar and palm branch on bronze hanging ornament, c. 3–4 centuries CE; beneath it on l. menorah on bronze ring fragment, c. 2–4 centuries CE; on r. menorah on carnelian ringstone fragment c. 2–4 centuries CE; bottom row three menorah details from terra cotta oil lamps c. 3–5 centuries CE; on right amulet with magic symbols words taken from Old Testament quotations, in lower right area is an angular menorah and below it a bread loaf, c. 3–4 centuries CE. (Author's collection.)

HERODIAN FAMILY TREE (Partial)

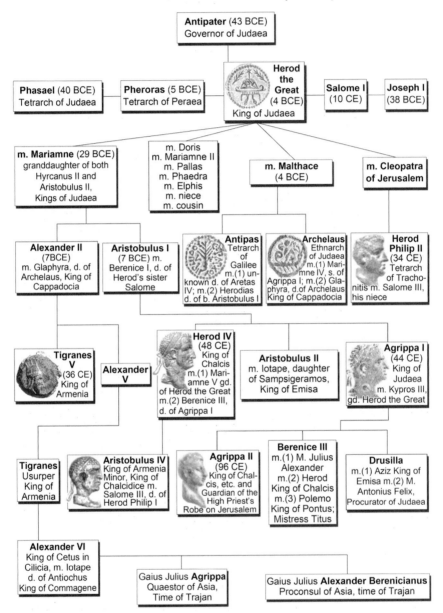

Antipater (43 BCE)
Governor of Judaea

Phasael (40 BCE)
Tetrarch of Judaea

Pheroras (5 BCE)
Tetrarch of Peraea

Herod the Great (4 BCE)
King of Judaea

Salome I (10 CE)

Joseph I (38 BCE)

m. Mariamne (29 BCE)
granddaughter of both
Hyrcanus II and
Aristobulus II,
Kings of Judaea

m. Doris
m. Mariamne II
m. Pallas
m. Phaedra
m. Elphis
m. niece
m. cousin

m. Malthace (4 BCE)

m. Cleopatra of Jerusalem

Alexander II (7BCE)
m. Glaphyra, d. of
Archelaus, King of
Cappadocia

Aristobulus I (7 BCE) m.
Berenice I, d. of
Herod's sister
Salome

Antipas Tetrarch
of Galilee
m.(1) un-
known d. of Aretas
IV; m.(2) Herodias
d. of b. Aristobulus I

Archelaus Ethnarch
of Judaea
m.(1) Mari-
mne IV, s. of
Agrippa I; m.(2) Gla-
phyra, d.of Archelaus
King of Cappadocia

Herod Philip II (34 CE)
Tetrarch
of Tracho-
nitis m. Salome III,
his niece

Tigranes V (36 CE)
King of
Armenia

Alexander V

Herod IV (48 CE)
King of
Chalcis
m.(1) Mari-
amne V gd.
of Herod the Great
m.(2) Berenice III,
d. of Agrippa I

Aristobulus II
m. Iotape, daughter
of Sampsigeramos,
King of Emisa

Agrippa I (44 CE)
King of
Judaea
m. Kypros III,
gd. Herod the Great

Tigranes Usurper
King of
Armenia

Aristobulus IV
King of Armenia
Minor, King of
Chalcidice m.
Salome III, d. of
Herod Philip I

Agrippa II (96 CE)
King of Chal-
cis, etc. and
Guardian of the
High Priest's
Robe on Jerusalem

Berenice III
m.(1) M. Julius
Alexander
m.(2) Herod
King of Chalcis
m.(3) Polemo
King of Pontus;
Mistress Titus

Drusilla
m.(1) Aziz King of
Emisa m.(2) M.
Antonius Felix,
Procurator of Judaea

Alexander VI
King of Cetus in
Cilicia, m. Iotape
d. of Antiochus
King of Commagene

Gaius Julius Agrippa
Quaestor of Asia,
Time of Trajan

Gaius Julius Alexander Berenicianus
Proconsul of Asia, time of Trajan

KEY: CAPS=Rulers or governor; ( )=dates of death; m.=married; d.=daughter; s.=sister; b.=brother;
gd.=granddaughter; ()=spouse number Copyright 2010 by David Hendin

CHAPTER SEVEN

HERODIAN DYNASTY

HEROD I (THE GREAT), 40–4 BCE

Now when Jesus was born in Bethlehem of Judaea in the days of Herod the king… (MATTHEW 2:1. See also MATTHEW 2:1–13 and 16–18)

HEROD'S EARLY CAREER

Herod I was born in 73 BCE into an assimilated Jewish Idumaean family. His grandfather, Antipas, and his father, Antipater, were both important advisors to the Hasmonean rulers. Members of the dynasty Herod founded became official and unofficial spokesmen for the Jewish people not only in their kingdom, but throughout the ancient world. The influence of Herod and his descendants continued to affect decisions by the imperial court in Rome for more than a century.

Herod is often portrayed as a converted or an unwilling Jew. This is not the case. The Jews under John Hyrcanus I (135–104 BCE) conquered the Idumaeans (Edomites), who occupied the south of Judaea. Some sources refer to a forced conversion to Judaism. Strabo noted, however, that "The Idumaeans are Nabataeans, but owing to sedition they were banished from there, joined the Judaeans, and shared in the same customs with them."[1]

Thus, according to Peter Richardson, "The reassessment of Idumaean conversion means that Herod's attachment to Judaism resulted from his grandfather's voluntary adherence and willing 'full' conversion to the Temple cult in Jerusalem and not from a forced submission to a bare bones form of Judaism."[2]

After Hyrcanus I annexed Idumaea, "no Idumaean delegation begged Pompey for separate status and a revival of the Idumaean cult." The Talmud says there were Idumaean disciples in the House of Shammai, who were "learned in Torah and punctilious in their observance."[3]

Moreover, Hyrcanus II, a Hasmonean, married an Idumaean, and Herod, an Idumaean, married a Hasmonean. Most important, says Richardson, is that just a short time later, Hyrcanus I's son Alexander Jannaeus (104–76 BCE) appointed Herod's grandfather, Antipas, as the *strategos* (or governor) of Idumaea. Richardson notes that this would be "an unusual degree of trust had Antipas only recently accepted Judaism unwillingly."[4]

In the next generation Herod's father Antipater was married to a Nabataean woman, Cypros. Two of their five children received Hebrew names—Joseph and Salome. Antipater became the closest advisor of Hyrcanus II (67 and 63–40 BCE), linking him inextricably to Rome as Hyrcanus II struggled against his brother Aristobulus II for the throne of Judaea and the high priesthood.

Hyrcanus II and Antipater were victorious, and their alliance with Caesar had been most helpful. Josephus says that Antipater recognized that Hyrcanus "was ignoble and unmanly to those who observed him,"[5] and made his son Phasael the governor of Jerusalem and the vicinity, "and entrusted Galilee to his second son Herod, who was still quite young; he was, in fact, only 15 years old."[6]

Thus, Herod became governor of Galilee, and a junior partner to his elder brother, the governor of Jerusalem and environs. Young Herod did not rest on his laurels and quickly turned the tables. Josephus recounts how this "youth of high spirit" found and executed a man named Hezekias, captain of a band of robbers who had been terrorizing the towns and cities of the north. Now "they sang his praises for this deed throughout their villages and cities...and through this action he became known to Sextus Caesar...who was Governor of Syria."[7]

Josephus says Phasael, Herod's brother, "was moved by the thought of the reputation Herod had won, he was ambitious not to be behind him in achieving like fame...."[8]

However, in a complicated twist, some of the aristocrats in Jerusalem tried to create a rift between Hyrcanus and Antipater. To drive a wedge, they accused Herod of murdering Hezekias, and he was ordered to Jerusalem to be tried by the Sanhedrin. Meanwhile, Sextus Caesar demanded that Hyrcanus clear Herod of the charges.

Herod, flanked by his troops, appeared before the Sanhedrin. A respected elder, Samaias, stood and declared that Herod's demeanor was not proper. He said that when a person appears before the Sanhedrin, he should show "himself humble and has assumed the manner of one who is fearful and seeks mercy from you by letting his hair grow long and wearing a black garment." On the other hand, Herod, this "fine fellow" accused of murder "stands here clothed in purple, with the hair of his head carefully arranged, and with his soldiers around him, in order to kill us if we condemn him as the law prescribes, and to save himself by outraging justice."[9]

Now the story becomes more complicated and to get the full tale, one must read Josephus (which I heartily recommend). In quick summary, however, Josephus reports that Herod is acquitted because he was loved by Hyrcanus. But in *Antiquities,* Josephus writes that Hyrcanus advises Herod to flee to Damascus and join Sextus Caesar, where he received a subordinate military command. Herod later used his troops to perform a show of strength before Hyrcanus, and set the stage for the future.

Not too many years later, Mark Antony visited Syria. During this visit a contingent of some 100 Jewish leaders came to him and complained against Herod. Antony patiently listened and then asked Hyrcanus, also in attendance, who he thought was the fittest to govern. He replied that Herod and his friends were the most competent. "Antony was delighted, because he had formerly been their father's guest and had been hospitably entertained by Antipater when he accompanied Gabinius on his Judaean campaign. He, accordingly, created the brothers [Herod and Phasael] tetrarchs, entrusting to them the whole of Judaea."[10] This promotion for Herod and Phasael took place in 42 BCE.

Along with Hyrcanus II, Phasael was later captured by the Parthians. Phasael did not want to die at the hands of his enemies, and so, while in captivity, he chose what he considered a hero's death by "dashing his head upon a rock, being denied the use of hands or steel."[11]

"According to another account, Phasael recovered from his self-inflicted blow, and a physician sent by Antigonus, ostensibly to attend to him, injected noxious drugs into the wound and so killed him. But whichever account be true, the initial act redounds to his glorious credit. It is said, moreover, that before he expired, being informed by a woman of Herod's escape, he exclaimed, 'Now I shall depart happy, since I leave one behind me who will have vengeance on my foes.'"[12]

HEROD KING OF THE JEWS

Herod was made king in 40 BCE by a declaration of the Roman Senate and approval of the triumvirate, marshaled by Mark Antony. His power was reaffirmed by Augustus, the first emperor. Initially Herod was a king without a kingdom since Mattatayah Antigonus was king of Judaea and remained so for more than two more years. The decision of the Senate and the leaders of Rome to elevate Herod in 40 BCE may have been related to the alliance between Antigonus and the Parthians, arch enemies of Rome. There is little doubt that Herod's rule was contrary to the desires of the majority of the Jewish people, whose sympathies lay with Antigonus of the storied Hasmonean family.

In 37 BCE with help from the Roman general C. Sosius, Herod besieged Jerusalem and captured it, along with Antigonus and his Parthian sponsors. One of Herod's first official acts as king was to order death for forty-five members of the Sanhedrin who had supported the Hasmoneans. This effectively reduced the power of the Sanhedrin to little more than a religious court.

Herod ruled Judaea by the grace of Rome. His administration was Hellenistic in character. One of Herod's continuing policy goals seemed to be to strengthen the foreign element in ancient Israel and to bring the kingdom completely into line as a strong link in the Roman Empire.

Antigonus claimed the title king, but Alexander Jannaeus was the last internationally recognized King of Judaea. Thus the Romans resurrected this title for Herod, who was not of priestly family and therefore could not occupy the office of high priest, yet had to be given a title equal or better in prestige. Furthermore, Antigonus had styled himself "king" on his coins, thus nothing less would do for Herod.

Herod recognized that being from a non-priestly family, that was, furthermore, converted to Judaism a few generations earlier, meant potential problems with the Jewish people. So, to strengthen his ties with the royal Hasmonean family, he married Mariamne, a granddaughter of Hyrcanus II. By all accounts, she was the love of Herod's life, but he was paranoid about threats to his power and this last remaining Hasmonean princess was a threat, whether real or imagined.

When Herod took the throne, he ignored the legal heir to the office of high priest even though he was Aristobulus III, his wife's brother. Instead, he appointed Hananel, whom he brought back to Jerusalem from the Egyptian diaspora. This act caused Herod's mother-in-law to complain to Cleopatra VII, Queen of Egypt, whose Roman ties enabled her to wield power over Herod. Cleopatra compelled Herod to dismiss Hananel and appoint Aristobulus. But the young Hasmonean's popularity with the people grew and Herod decided to have him killed, a fate he also arranged for the former king Hyrcanus II. These family murders caused severe tension between Herod and his beloved wife Mariamne, and in 30/29 BCE Herod ordered her executed.

Some years later Herod also sentenced his two sons by Mariamne, Antipater and Aristobulus (father of the child Agrippa, later to become Agrippa I), to death. When Augustus heard about the sentences, he reportedly said, "It is better to be Herod's pig than his son."[13] These executions eliminated every member of the Hasmonean family who might threaten Herod's throne in the immediate future.

To advance his pro-Hellenistic policies, Herod embarked on many construction and cultural projects. Ehud Netzer the archaeologist-architect who excavated many Herodian ruins and who recently discovered what is believed to be Herod's tomb at Herodium, explains that, "The scope and vibrancy of Herod's building enterprise in general lead us to the inevitable conclusion that planning and erecting buildings was an integral part of his ongoing operations."[14] Netzer further observed that while Herod was almost certainly not an architect, he was intensively involved in the conception and planning of his various building activities.[15]

Broshi identifies four of Herod's many building projects as being the finest or the largest in the world at the time:

- Largest temenos—the structural enlargement of the Temple Mount;
- Largest palace—Herodium, eventually surpassed in size by Nero's palace in Rome;
- Longest building—the splendid stoa on the Temple Mount;
- Best port—Caesarea Maritima.[16]

It has been noted that Herod could build only one Temple in Judaea, but he could build many palaces and fortresses. Hence, he also built the gleaming white city of Sebaste (Greek for Augustua) on the ruins of ancient Shomron-Samaria. Well-acquainted with the politics of Rome, he also named his new port city Caesarea after Augustus (Sebastos). Herod sponsored athletic contests and sat in a royal court that reflected at least a partial cultural alienation from Judaism. On a visit to Rome in either 18 or 12 BCE, Herod was made president of the Olympic Games.[17] And while Herod was earlier praised for his help to the Jewish population, Josephus now complains that Herod was sucking the blood of the Jewish people in order to curry favor among the non-Jews.

Herod's pathological suspicions led him to construct a string of splendid mountain fortresses leading toward Nabataea, which doubled as palatial resort homes for himself and his entourage. These fortresses were to serve Herod if he had to make a hasty retreat in case of insurrection, and included Herodium in Judaea, Masada on the Dead Sea, and Machaerus in Transjordan.

Herod was generous to an extreme with building projects inside and outside his immediate territory. Above Jericho he built a fortress and named it Cypros after his mother. In Jerusalem he built three towers and named them after his murdered wife Mariamne, his friend Hippicus, and his brother Phasael. He built and named Herodium after himself. Then he built gymnasia for Tripolis, Damascus, and Ptolemais; a wall for Byblos; temples and marketplaces for Berytus and Tyre; theaters for Sidon and Damascus; an aqueduct for Laodicea ad Mare; and baths, fountains, and colonnades for Ashqelon. That was the beginning. He donated to the Olympic games and to Lycia, Samos, and every district of Ionia. "And that broad street in Syrian Antioch, once shunned on account of the mud, was it not he who paved its twenty furlongs with polished marble, and, as a protection from the rain, adorned it with a colonnade of equal length?"[18]

Herod hoped to improve his status with the Jewish people by restoring the Temple. He did it in a magnificent way: it took 10,000 commoners and 1,000 priests at least nine years to complete the project. They erected magnificent walls of majestic stones—many of which can still be seen in Jerusalem today—doubled the Temple's size, and encircled it with beautiful columns, gates, and courtyards. Herod also enlarged and strengthened the fortress adjoining the Temple Mount and renamed it Antonia, after Mark Antony.

With these construction expenses and other costs of a lavish court, gifts and bribes to relatives and Roman allies, and heavy taxes to Rome, Herod amassed a huge debt. To pay it, he taxed his people heavily. Josephus reports that "the numeration of the debts and taxes discharged by himself would be endless."[19]

Herod is today referred to as Herod the Great. But during his life and the generations after it, the words "the Great" were almost certainly not associated with his name. The first clue we have to this is in Josephus, where Herod is referred to as "King" but never as "the Great." Only once is the description "the Great" used for a Herodian king, and that refers to Herod's grandson, Agrippa I. Even this may not be meant to comment on the man's greatness, but to distinguish him from his son, Agrippa II. Thus "the Great" may have been synonymous with "the elder." Interestingly, Agrippa I is also referred to by the adjective "the Great" on his coins (Nos. 1245, 1246). Herod I himself, however, is cited only as king on his coins, never as "the Great."

While Herod was undeniably Jewish, he was less popular with Jews than with the Romans. Inside his own nation, Herod was considered cruel, vengeful, and power hungry. "Among his own people if anyone was not deferential to him...or was thought to be raising questions about his rule. Herod was unable to control himself and prosecuted his kin and his friends alike, and punished them as severely as enemies."[20] But as Richardson notes, "He was regarded externally as an important patron, a man of kindness, generosity, good will, and piety, a friend of Romans and of the Emperor."[21]

Herod's publicity over the past 2,000 years has not been good; but he was not completely insane to his subjects. It is clear that at certain times of crisis Herod assisted his people. For example, when his kingdom suffered a severe drought in 27 BCE, he took steps to alleviate not only the needs of his people, but in some neighboring lands as well.[22]

Herod's achievements must be viewed alongside his domestic woes. Stories of his cruelty continued well into the first century and appeared in the Gospels. Josephus, in his *Antiquities of the Jews*, was quite negative about Herod, and especially criticized Herod's disregard for Jewish religious law and customs.

On the other hand Herod clearly identified himself as a Jew and presented himself as a protector of Jews in the Diaspora. This was apparent when he interceded before Marcus Vipsanius Agrippa, representative of Augustus, on behalf of the Ionian Jews around 14 BCE.[23] Herod later bragged to the people of Jerusalem that thanks to him, the Jews of Asia "would be unmolested in the future."[24] The fact that Herod did not eat pork was well known to Augustus, and the Roman poet Persius later referred to the Jewish Sabbath as "Herod's Day."[25]

The great offense of which Herod has been accused through the ages is the "slaughter of the innocents," in which he allegedly ordered the killing of all male babies in the area of Bethlehem because he heard that a future "king of the Jews" (Jesus) had been born. However, there is much disagreement about this account. Grant explains, "Matthew's story of the Massacre of the Innocents by Herod the Great, because he was afraid of a child born at Bethlehem 'to be King of the Jews,' is a myth allegedly fulfilling a prophecy by Jeremiah and mirroring history's judgment of the great but evil potentate Herod, arising from many savage acts during the last years before his death in 4 BCE"[26]

Tabor also refutes the story: "It is inconceivable that such a 'slaughter' of infants would go unrecorded by the Jewish historian Josephus or other contemporary Roman historians. Matthew's account is clearly theological, written to justify later views of Jesus' exalted status."[27]

Herod did not offend his fellow Jews by bringing statues or other physical effigies into Jerusalem until late in his reign, when he affixed a golden eagle to the Temple gate.[28] This eagle was no doubt a sign of Herod's fealty to Imperial Rome. The people of Jerusalem, especially the Pharisees, were agitated by it. In spite of intense opposition, no action could be taken as long as Herod lived. At around this time, rumors circulated that the ailing Herod had died at his palace in Jericho. Immediately upon hearing this, a group cut down the eagle and hacked it to pieces. Herod, however, was alive and ordered some 40 of the culprits captured and brought to him. Herod was carried in on a sick-bed and harangued the group bitterly for not honoring him after he built the glorious Temple. He finished the session by ordering the few who actually cut down the eagle to be burnt alive, and the rest of the group summarily executed.

This was only one of many reasons that Herod felt the Jewish people would not mourn him. Thus, in anticipation of his death, Herod ordered that upon his demise a group of "the distinguished men from every village from one end of Judaea to the other" should be rounded up in the hippodrome of Jericho. He told his sister Salome that "the moment I expire have them surrounded by the soldiers and massacred; so shall all Judaea and every household weep for me, whether they will or no."[29] The round-up took place, but once Herod died, his heirs released the captives. Nevertheless, Herod's intentions for his final act illustrate the relationship between Herod and his fellow Jews.

As we learn in Matthew, Jesus was surely born during Herod's tenure.[30] Grant explains that, "About the date of Jesus' birth there are...

perplexing problems. The belief that he was born in 1 CE only came into existence in the sixth century CE when a monk from South Russia living in Italy, Dionysius Exiguus, made a mathematical miscalculation. His birth date should be reassigned to 6 or 5 or 4 BCE, though some prefer 11 or 7."[31]

HEROD'S COINAGE

During Herod's 33-year reign his kingdom was relatively tranquil. This relative peace allowed him to develop building projects as well as fostering improvements in agriculture and commerce. To finance his works he taxed his subjects heavily.

Even as late as Herod's time, the economy in Judaea was not fully monetized; the barter system remained. Local coinage in Herod's realm continued to be struck only of bronze, although there is some evidence that Herod may have ordered groups of Tyre *sheqels* struck specifically for purchase and use in his territories.[32] Greek and Roman coinage circulated only infrequently in Herod's lands, and other bronze coins, including some from his Hasmonean predecessors continued to circulate. Gold and silver, however, were the coins of big cities and big commerce. The villagers almost exclusively used bronze coins.

Herod issued his own coins to broadcast his power of governance; to generate a profit, since the coins minted were more valuable than the metal they contained (see pp. 43-46). Finally, to facilitate payments his government had to coin money to provide for either military payrolls or civil construction projects.

Ariel suggests that Herod did not mint coins regularly during his reign. This was true during the reigns of the later Herodians and the prefects and procurators of Judaea, whose coins each carried dates. They were probably minted at the same Jerusalem mint as Herod's undated coins, beginning ten years after Herod's death, still under his patron Augustus. The prefect and procurator coins have gaps of 3, 4, 5, 6, and 13 years between issues. Meshorer points out that if one of the governors had minted a sufficient number of coins to satisfy the needs of the marketplace, it might supplant the need for further minting for some time.[33]

Ariel explores some of the reasons Herod issued coins. Stocking the marketplace with coins of appropriate size was important, as was the requirement for small change so soldiers, construction workers, or other employees could be paid in exact amounts, thus not overpaid. "Without his own mint, when Herod had to purchase something worth less than a drachm or denar, he would only be able to pay with the available coins in circulation. This could entail a loss for him," writes Ariel.[34] Harl more practically notes that paymasters needed to provide some of a soldier's pay in bronze, since small denominations were always needed "for dice and drink."[35]

At certain times the Roman emperors issued a form of largess known as a *congiarium*. Ariel believes that some of Herod's coins may have been issued and used as these handouts. They might have celebrated the entertainment structures and Herod's founding and hosting of the quadrennial games in Jerusalem[36] and especially in Caesarea,[37]

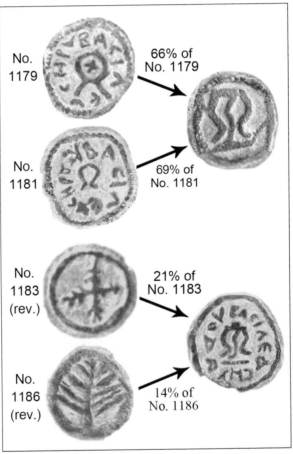

7.1. Illustration of how obverse and reverse dies were often used in different combinations. (Graphic: Fontanille.)

where games were instituted in 12 BCE at Herod's dedication festival for the city and its port. "Games were the type of event in which civilian handouts were common. It would be unreasonable to think Herod initiated all of those events, and did not include some form of distribution of gifts," writes Ariel.[38] Herod also proclaimed an annual festival on the day he ascended as king,[39] a logical time to distribute gifts.

Another form of gift-giving by rulers was the *donativum*—a gift of money to soldiers in the legions. Ariel points to such a probability, just after Herod's troops conquered Jerusalem in 37 BCE, when the Romans began to plunder the city. Their commander Sosius was not inclined to be firm with them. In order to stop the plundering, Herod agreed to "distribute rewards to each of them out of his own purse."[40]

Once issued, these coins of *congiarium* and *donativum* could possibly be kept as souvenirs, but more likely would enter and remain in circulation, eventually being supplemented in greater numbers by the government.

Thus Ariel suggests "there is cogency in viewing at least some of his coins as commemorative issues related to his (building or other) activity."[41]

Ariel, assisted by Fontanille's die studies,[42] gathered archaeological, typological, epigraphic, and other evidence and presented it coherently to shed fresh light on the internal chronology of the Herodian coins. Ariel's research is extensive, and his conclusions will be the basis of scholarly discussions in the future.[43]

THE HELMET ON HEROD'S LARGE COINS

There have been several theories about the object on the obverse of the largest coin (No. 1169) struck by Herod I in 37 BCE.

Madden, in 1864, called this item a "vessel." Later, Kindler and others refer to it as a thymiaterion, a kind of incense burner. Meshorer and others referred to it as a helmet. In general, however, these descriptions have been without conviction.

Around 1990, I purchased an example of this large coin of Herod in Jerusalem. After careful cleaning it turned out to be unusually well preserved, and, in fact, solved this mystery. The results were eventually published in the *Israel Numismatic Journal*. This coin revealed a wreath around the hemispherical portion of the object. The wreath features one large leaf as a central device. Thus, the object can be identified as a soldier's helmet, facing forward. Cheek pieces and straps for securing it behind the head can now be clearly identified. The star surmounting the helmet parallels similar designs commonly found on coins depicting the caps of the Dioscuri.[44]

Wreaths were commonly used as design motifs on helmets of this period. For example, a silver cavalry helmet in the Rheinisches Landesmuseum features a gold wreath terminating in the front center with the medallion of a human face. Since Herod I did not depict human images on any of his coins, it was logical to substitute an acceptable decorative symbol—in this case, a large leaf.

A similar helmet also appears not only on the second denomination bronze of Herod I, but earlier on a coin of Hyrcanus I (No. 1136), and later on a coin of Herod's son, Archelaus (No. 1196). Since the helmet is a military item, one assumes that in all cases the reference is to the military powers of the regime.

It is possible that not all dies for Herod's large bronze coins were actually engraved with the leaf and wreath motif. We have examined several hundred specimens and the hemispherical area of the helmet is often flat.

TABLE, CROSS, AND DIADEM

The undated double-*prutah* coin of Herod with a three-legged table reverse and a diadem with a cross in the center on its obverse is of special interest (No. 1178). Similar motifs also appear on both *prutah* and half-*prutah* coins in this series.

The table is not the pagan tripod as had been widely believed.[45] Instead, it is a short, wide table on three legs. Tables almost identical to these have been found in the excavations of Jerusalem from the Herodian period.[46] (They can be seen at both the Israel Museum and the Jewish Quarter Archaeological Museum.) These tripod tables were part of the furniture of the

7.2. Stone table, legs reconstructed, from excavations in Jewish Quarter, Jerusalem.

Jerusalem Temple. In the Talmud it is written: "There were thirteen tables in the Temple, eight of marble, in the slaughterhouse upon which they rinsed the innards, and two to the west of the slope, one of marble and the other of silver, upon the marble one they laid the parts of the offerings, and upon the silver one the service vessels."[47]

Meshorer suggests that the table shown on Herod's coins must have been quite important, since it was shown on three denominations—the only device depicted so widely. In the largest denomination, there appears to be some sort of a flat, round vessel upon the table. It might be a basin or similar object, thus it's possible that this is a depiction of the Temple's silver table for "service vessels."

In Herod's day it was forbidden to depict Temple implements, including the menorah and the sacred tables, outside of the Temple. However, Herod's predecessor and nemesis Mattatayah Antigonus had depicted both the showbread table and menorah on a coin issued late in his reign. It seems possible, then, that at the appropriate time Herod issued this series of coins with the Temple table to commemorate, or call attention to, his own major rebuilding of the Jerusalem Temple.

Further indication of his intention is that on the largest coin depicting this table, it is flanked by two palm branches, which were "used in religious processions, and also symbolized dignity, royal honor, jubilation, and victory," according to Romanoff.[48]

The reverse of this coin is also of special interest. Some have described the X inside the diadem as a cross, and relate it to the birth of Jesus. This is impossible since Jesus was born near the end of Herod's reign and these coins were struck much earlier. Further, the cross as a symbol does not become associated with Christianity until some 350 years after the death of Jesus, who likely had not even been born when this coin was struck.

Meshorer points to the Babylonian Talmud: "Our rabbis have taught: 'In anointing kings one draws the figure of a crown [diadem, or in Hebrew *nezer*] and with the priest in the shape of the letter *chi*, R. Menashiah said: like a Greek *chi*."[49]

It's remarkable that this sentence from the Talmud zeros in on both designs depicted on this coin type—the X or Greek *chi* and the diadem—the gold band or ribbon worn symbolically by kings to signify their position.

But why would Herod display the symbols of both the king and the high priest together? Unlike his Hasmonean predecessors, Alexander Jannaeus and Mattatayah Antigonus, who proclaimed themselves both

king and high priest on their coins, Herod held only the title king, since
he was not from a priestly family. This may suggest that Herod was
making a statement that he was the king and that he also controlled the
Temple through his appointment of the high priest. As already mentioned, Herod imported a priest named Hananel from the diaspora.
This move was intended to prevent any Hasmonean descendant or loy-
alist from making claim to the post.

Hananel was clearly "Herod's high priest." Possibly, to reinforce
this duality of kingship and control of the Temple, Herod depicted the
two symbols—the *chi* within the diadem—on these coins to reinforce
this message.[50]

CHRONOLOGY AND DENOMINATIONS

It is generally believed that the dated series of Herod's coins were
the first struck during his rule (Nos. 1169–72). These are dated "year
three," yet their actual date of issue has been a matter of much discussion. Some have argued that they must have been struck in 37 BCE,
which was the "third year" of Herod's kingship—he was proclaimed
"King of Judaea" by a declaration of the Roman Senate and the approval of Octavian. Meshorer, however, argued that they were struck
in 40 BCE. He explains that Mark Antony appointed Herod as Tetrarch
of Samaria in 42 BCE. Meshorer suggests that the Ͳ (TP) monogram
on this series has a parallel in some of the Ituraean coins of Chalcis,
and that it stands for the title "tetrarch." Therefore, he concludes that
these coins were first struck in 40/39 BCE, the third year of Herod's
tetrarchy and possibly issued for several years.

Kanael suggests that the Ͳ monogram on Herod's early coins probably represents a combination of the Greek letters TP—a contraction
for *trito*, or "third year." Kanael says, "It is likely that Herod wanted to
accentuate the fact that 37 BCE, which was in fact his first year as king,
should be regarded as his third year, and reckoned from 40 BCE when
Rome had appointed him."[51]

Some denominations of this series appear without both date and
monogram. One might suggest that this was an inadvertent omission.
However, Fontanille's die studies have shown that none of the dies
without dates and monograms has been re-engraved to add them and,
in fact, in at least one die there is evidence that the date and monogram
were filed or obliterated so they would not appear on the coins.[52]

Possibly these were later issues and their notations to the "third year" were deliberately omitted.

Herod's dated coins were struck in four denominations, usually described as 8, 4, 2 and 1 *prutot*. However, our metrological studies indicate that Herod's coins, struck almost simultaneously with the coins of Mattatayah Antigonus, are almost exactly half the weight of the Antigonus coins of comparable diameters.

In spite of this, it is not likely that these changes of weight represented any devaluation since bronze coinage was fiduciary in nature (pp. 46-49). Price discusses this concept with regard to the coinage of early Athens and elsewhere.[53] Once people were willing to accept overvalued pieces of small bronze, size and weight simply became symbols of their value. In Herod's fledgling kingdom, he may have been attempting to create more coinage with fewer raw materials and thus increase his profits from the creation of coinage.[54]

Meshorer suggested that the denominations of the Herodian series were 8/4/2/1 *prutot*, which in spite of lighter weight still seems likely.[55] It does not, however, seem likely that both Herod and Mattatayah Antigonus would be striking similar diameter coins with drastically

7.3. Recreation of Herodian dies show disproportionate size difference between obverse and reverse dies. (Graphic: Fontanille.)

different weights at the same mint city at about the same time. Thus, Meshorer's suggestion that Herod's dated coins were struck at a mint in Samaria, rather than Jerusalem, seems more credible. Samaria was the capital of Herod's tetrarchy, "and it was natural for him to have minted his coins there."[56] Further evidence can be found in the excavations in Jerusalem where hundreds of Herodian coins were found, but only around one percent were dated. At Masada where 393 Herodian coins were found, only one of them was a dated coin. Yet, Meshorer cites excavations in Sebaste/Samaria where 20 percent and more of the coins of Herod I come from the dated group. "From experience we learn that bronze coins become rarer as the distance between the excavation site and their mint increases. The discovery of so many dated coins in Samaria is firm evidence that they were minted there."[57]

All other coins of Herod I were probably struck at Jerusalem. The coins are cruder in design, execution, and manufacture than those struck at Samaria. Another interesting phenomenon that occurs on many of the Herodian coins is that the obverse dies were cut for a coin far larger than the reverse dies. This results in coins that are never fully centered on one side because the flan is not sufficiently large. The

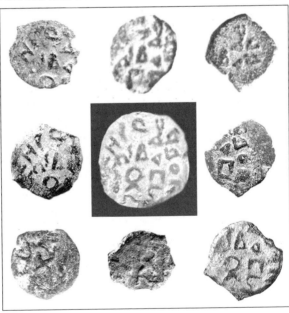

7.4. Composite of complete Herodian obverse die (No. 1183) with eight coins struck from this die. Note the completely different appearance of the coins. (Graphic: Fontanille.}

reason for this anomaly is not known, but it also existed previously in some later Hasmonean coin types (Nos. 1152, 1153, 1168) in which both obverse and reverse dies were much larger than the flans upon which they were struck.

Ariel proposes an internal chronology for Herod's undated coins. He suggests, for example, that the final series of coins struck by Herod included the common *prutot* with the anchor/double cornucopia motif. "As a type, Herod's coin bearing the anchor on the obverse and double cornucopia with caduceus in between the horns on the reverse (No. 1188) is copied exactly by his son Archelaus on his coinage (No. 1192). In fact, for the most part, one may differentiate between the poorly preserved of such coins of Herod and those of his son only from the inscriptions."[58]

"On the other hand," Ariel writes, "the anchor of Herod's inscription/anchor type (No. 1174–77) which also appears both in the pre-Herod and post-Herod series, should be aligned closer to Jannaeus' reign. This is because the depictions of Jannaeus and Herod's anchors are so similar...and so dissimilar from the anchor on Archelaus' coins."[59] It actually appears that the obverse of these coins were copied from the poor, late Hasmonean issues, to the extent that the lily-like designs, also described as Y-like, V-like, or just lines, are intended to copy the crude imitation Greek legends on some of the Hasmonean issues.

From the archaeological evidence, Ariel notes the "near absence of the anchor/double cornucopia type from Area E in the Jewish Quarter, and over-representation there of the inscription/anchor and single cornucopia/eagle types."[60]

He adds that "One may create a relative chronology of Herod's undated coin types based upon the coin's typological continuity/discontinuity with his predecessors and successors at the Jerusalem mint. The validity of such an approach is supported by the overall impression of continuity in other features of the Jerusalem mint throughout the first century BCE."[61]

Ariel also places Herod's diadem and table coins early in the series. "The coins bearing the diadem symbol are the closest that Herod's undated coins come to being a denominational series. The diadem appears on all three denominations in Herod's undated coins and is certainly an important symbol in his coins.

"The diadem was a symbol of kingship or the high priesthood and...symbolic of Herod's claim to legitimacy. The series could have been the first of Herod's undated coins."[62]

In spite of his continuing adverse relationship with his own people, Herod did not mint coins overtly offensive to the Jews. He used no graven images except for the late small bronze with the golden eagle Herod had affixed to the Temple gate. Herod was the first Jewish ruler to use exclusively Greek inscriptions on his coins.

Ariel also makes the interesting observation that "After the diadem 'denominational series' the Jerusalem mint did not mint in such clearly arranged denominations until perhaps a century later, during the Jewish war. This fact also may support the series' placement at the beginning of Herod's undated coins, soon after Antigonus' denominational series."[63]

Ariel's "conjectural" internal chronology[64] of Herod's undated coins suggests that the Temple table series (Nos. 1178–1187) are earliest (c. 30–20 BCE), with the anchor/legend series (Nos. 1174–1177) overlapping and slightly later (25–15 BCE), and finally, the double cornucopia/anchor series (c. 15–5 BCE) and other issues, which commemorates the dedication of Caesarea (Nos. 1188–1191).

I suggest placing the anchor/legend series as the earliest group of coins struck at Herod's Jerusalem mint, due to the great similarity in both style and manufacture to the Jannaeus (and possibly successor) coins from which they may have been copied (No. 1153).

7.5. Similarities between Hasmonean small *prutot*, above (No. 1153), and Herodian small *prutot*, below (Nos. 1173–1177). (Author's collection.)

COINS OF HEROD I THE GREAT
MINT OF SAMARIA, DATED SERIES, YEAR 3 = 40 BCE.
Border of dots both sides unless noted.
Axis is usually vertical.

1169.   AE 8-*prutot*, 6.43 g average.
Obv: Military helmet, frontal view, wreath featuring acanthus leaf
around, cheek pieces and straps, star above flanked by palm
branches.
Rev: ΗΡΩΔΟΥ ΒΑΣΙΛΕΩΣ *(of King Herod)*; tripod, ceremonial bowl
(lebes) above, flanked by date ΛΓ *(year 3)* and monogram Ⴔ.

250/600

To date, 31 obverse, 122 reverse dies noted (MCP).

1170.   AE 4-*prutot*, 4.45 g average.
Obv: Shield with decorated rim.
Rev: ΗΡΩΔΟΥ ΒΑΣΙΛΕΩΣ; crested helmet flanked by date ΛΓ *(year
3)* and monogram Ⴔ.   150/500
To date, 3 obverse, 6 reverse dies noted (MCP).

1171.   AE 2-*prutot*, 3.12 g average.
Obv: Poppy on stalk.
Rev: ΗΡΩΔΟΥ ΒΑΣΙΛΕΩΣ; winged caduceus flanked by date ΛΓ
(year 3) and monogram Ⴔ.   200/550
a. Variety without date or monogram.
To date, 3 obverse, 3 reverse dies listed (MCP).

1172. AE *prutah*, 2.50 g average.
  Obv: Palm branch with objects (leaves?) on either side.
  Rev: ΗΡΩΔΟΥ ΒΑΣΙΛΕΩΣ; aphlaston flanked by date LΓ *(year 3)*
    and monogram ꝑ.   200/500
  a. Variety without date or monogram.
  To date, 1 obverse, 3 reverse dies listed (MCP).

Mint of Jerusalem, Undated Series, 40-4 bce.

1173. AE *prutah*, 0.08 – 1.5 g range for 1173–1177.
  Obv: ΒΑCΙΛ ΕVC ΗΡ ΩΔΗC *(King Herod)*.
  Rev: Anchor within laurel wreath.   150/400
  To date, 3 obverse, 2 reverse dies listed (MCP).

1174. AE *prutah*.
  Obv: ΒΑCΙΛΕΩC ΗΡΩ ΔΟΥ in uneven lines.
  Rev: Anchor within circle decorated with stylized lily flowers.
                                                          50/100
  a. Anchor within circle and zigzag line.
  b-d. Inscription variations.

1175. AE *prutah*.
  Obv: ΒΑCΙΛΕΩC ΗΡΩΔΟΥ in concentric circles; .
  Rev: Anchor within a circle decorated with fine vertical strokes or
    rays.   150/400
  a. Circle around anchor with stylized lily flowers as 1174.

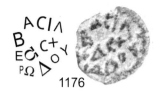

1176

1177

1176. AE *prutah*.
Obv: Similar to 1175, but crude and H is reduced to + or similar.
Rev: Anchor within circle similar to 1174.   100/300

1177. AE *prutah*.
Obv: Similar to 1174, but retrograde.
Rev: Anchor within circle similar to 1174.   150/350

1178

1178a

1178. AE 2-*prutot*, 2.94 g average.
Obv: HPΩΔOY BACIΛEΩC; cross within closed diadem.
Rev: Tripod table, flat object (vessel?) upon it, flanked by palm
    branches.   100/350
a. Diadem is open.

1179. AE *prutah*, 1.48 g average for 1179-1184.
Obv: HPΩΔOY BACIΛEΩC; cross within open diadem, inscription
    often incomplete.
Rev: Tripod table in circle.   75/250
  *Obverse dies are much larger than reverse dies for types 1179–1187 and
1191; this results in their especially crude and incomplete appearance.*

1180. AE *prutah*.
Obv: HPΩΔOY BACIΛEΩC; cross within closed diadem, inscrip-
    tion often incomplete.
Rev: Tripod table in circle.   75/250

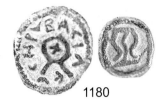

1180

1181

1181. AE *prutah.*
  Obv: ΗΡΩΔΟΥ ΒΑCΙΛΕΩC; cross outside of diadem, inscription
  often incomplete.
  Rev: Tripod table in circle.   75/250

1182. AE *prutah.*
  Obv: ΗΡΩΔΟΥ ΒΑCΙΛΕΩC; open diadem with no cross, inscrip-
  tion often incomplete.
  Rev: Tripod table in circle.   65/200

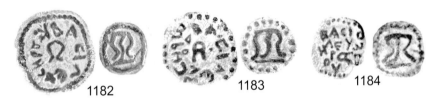

1182

1183

1184

1183. AE *prutah.*
  Obv: ΗΡΩΔΟΥ ΒΑCΙΛΕΩC; small closed diadem, inscription often
  incomplete.
  Rev: Tripod table.   65/200

1184. AE *prutah.*
  Obv: ΗΡΩΔΟΥ ΒΑCΙΛΕΩC in irregular lines; diadem resembles Ω.
  Rev: Tripod table in circle.   65/200

1185. AE half-*prutah.*
  Obv: ΗΡΩΔΟΥ ΒΑCΙΛΕΩΣ; tripod table with object upon it.
  Rev: Two crossed palm branches in circle.   100/300

1186. AE half-*prutah.*
  Obv: ΗΡΩΔΟΥ ΒΑCΙΛΕΩC; tripod table.
  Rev: Palm branch upright within circle.   150/450
  a. Obverse with small closed diadem and ΗΡΩΔΟΥ ΒΑCΙΛΕΩC.

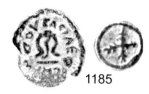

1185

1186

1187. AE half-*prutah*.
Obv: HPΩΔOY BACIΛEΩC; tripod table.
Rev: Bunch of grapes with vine branch.   RRR
a. Irregular crude variety.

Grapes and vine are clear on at least one recently discovered specimen, thus this is the first Jewish coin to feature grapes, which are repeated on a coin of Archelaus and coins of the the Bar Kokhba Revolt.

1187

1188

1188. AE *prutah*, 1.42 g average.
Obv: HPW BACIΛ; anchor.
Rev: Double cornucopia with caduceus between, dots above.

65/200

a. Greek reads outward.
b. Irregular issue, Greek is retrograde.
c. Irregular issue, extremely crude.

Many varieties of this coin exist with various inscription combinations, all based on HPWΔOY BACIΛEWC, *including many errors.*

Nos. 1188–91 may be related to the founding of Herod's magnificent port at Caesarea Maritima, 22–10/9 BCE.

1189. AE *prutah*.
Obv: Anchor, no legend.
Rev: Double cornucopia, caduceus between, dots above.   75/200
a. Irregular, crude anchor.
b. Both sides quite crude.

This type resembles No. 1188 of Herod I, but Bijovsky suggests it may be a coin of Herod Archelaus, since there is no inscription and the shape of the anchor quite resembles No. 1193.[65]

1190. AE half-*prutah*, 0.86 g average.
Obv: BACIΛ HPWΔ; cornucopia with inscription above and below.
Rev: Eagle standing r.   75/250
a. Crude variety.
b. Eagle faces left.

    The first coin issued by a Jewish ruler with a graven image. The eagle may represent the golden bird King Herod placed above the entrance to the Jerusalem Temple.

1191. AE half-*prutah*.
Obv: HPWΔOY BACIΛEOC; anchor.
Rev: War galley with oars, ram, and aphlaston, sails l.
                                           100/300

HEROD ARCHELAUS, 4 BCE TO 6 CE

    But when he heard that Archelaus did reign in Judaea in the room of his father Herod, he was afraid to go thither... (MATTHEW 2:22)

Archelaus was the oldest son of Herod by his Samaritan wife Malthace. In Herod's final will, he designated Archelaus as future king of Judaea and Samaria. But since Herod's title was not hereditary, Archelaus needed confirmation by Augustus. After the mourning period for his father, Archelaus prepared to travel to Rome. Before he departed, however, he met with spokesmen for various groups in the Temple area. A crowd gathered and began to test Archelaus' sincerity and good will by making demands. They wanted him, for example, to drastically reduce taxes. Members of the crowd also began to protest the death of the group of scholars who Herod had executed for removing the golden eagle from the Temple gates. This interaction led to riots against Archelaus' troops, intensified by the huge influx of pilgrims into Jerusalem for the Passover festival. Archelaus soon lost his patience and sent his soldiers against the crowd, killing some 3,000 Jews.[66]

In Rome, where Archelaus hoped to argue his case before the emperor, there was a bitter power struggle between him and Antipas.[67] After hearing arguments, Augustus altered the terms of Herod's will and named Archelaus ethnarch of Judaea, Samaria, and Idumaea. Philip (4 BCE–34 CE) received the title tetrarch of Batanaea, Trachonitis, Auranitis, and some other minor lands. Antipas (4 BCE–39 CE) was named tetrarch of Peraea and Galilee.[68] This decision abolished the Judaean monarchy, but the emperor promised that the title "king" would be forthcoming if Archelaus governed well.

Archelaus, however, "on taking charge of his ethnarchy did not forget old feuds, but treated not only the Jews but even the Samaritans with great brutality. Both parties sent deputies to Caesar to denounce him, and in the ninth year of his rule he was banished to Vienna, a town in Gaul, and his property transferred to the imperial treasury."[69]

Thus Archelaus' territories were annexed to the province of Syria and placed under direct rule of the prefect Coponius.

The Parable of the Pounds mentions a hated ruler, believed to have been Archelaus: "But his citizens hated him, and sent a message after him, saying, we will not have this man to reign over us" (LUKE 19:14).

Based upon his inability to reasonably govern his subjects, one may conclude that Archelaus can be blamed for the areas he governed falling into Roman hands.

Archelaus' coins continued to be manufactured at Herod's Jerusalem mint. His earliest issue was probably a *prutah* nearly identical to one of Herod's latest issues, with the addition of the abbreviation of ethnarch on the reverse (No. 1192).

The style and method of manufacturing coins at the Jerusalem mint continued and Archelaus issued a two-*prutot* coin (No. 1194) comparable in size to Herod's two-*prutot* coin (No. 1178) as well as *prutah* coins. Archelaus' coins generally copied the designs of his father with minor variations—anchors, cornucopias, wreaths, galleys, grapes, and helmet. All of the inscriptions on the coins of Archelaus are in Greek.

Archelaus' coins carry the word (or abbreviation) *ethnarch* and his name, meant to be read as "of Herod the Ethnarch." Archelaus did not use graven images or other symbols offensive to the Jews on his coins, nor do any of them carry dates.

COINS OF HEROD ARCHELAUS
Border of dots on both sides unless noted.

1192 1193

1192. AE *prutah*, 1.16 g average.
Obv: HPWΔOY *(of Herod)*; anchor.
Rev: EΘ on r., N above *(Ethnarch)*; double cornucopias adorned with ribbons, caduceus between horns, dots above.   100/300
There are many varieties for inscription and placement of letters.

1193. AE *prutah*, 1.28 g average.
Obv: HPWΔOY; anchor with long, slender arms.
Rev: EΘ / AN within by wreath.   50/150
Reverse varieties with four to eight letters exist, including EΘ PAN XOY, some letters may be retrograde.

1194

1194. AE 2-*prutot*.
Obv: HPWΔHC *(Herod)*; double cornucopias, adorned with grapes, horns parallel, turned to the l.
Rev: EΘN PXA CH *(Ethnarch)*; war galley facing left with aphlaston, oars, cabin, ram.   150/400
  a. Cornucopias turned to right.

1195. AE *prutah*.
Obv: HPW; double cornucopias, adorned with grapes, horns parallel, turned to the l.
Rev: EΘN / PA / HX *(Ethnarch)*; war galley facing left with aphlaston, oars, ram.   100/250
  a. Cornucopias turned to right.

1196

1197

1196.   AE *prutah.*, 2.06 g average.
Obv: EΘNAPXOY *(of the Ethnarch)*; crested helmet with cheek straps, viewed from front, caduceus below l.
Rev: HPWΔOY *(of Herod)*; bunch of grapes on vine with small leaf on left.   50/150
a. Inscriptions are juxtaposed obverse to reverse.
b. Obverse carries incuse of helmet motif on reverse.
c. Irregular issue.

1197.   AE half-*prutah*, 1.19 g average.
Obv: HPW; prow of galley facing l.
Rev: EΘN within wreath.   50/150
a. Prow facing r.
b. Reverse inscription NEΘ.

HEROD ANTIPAS, 4 BCE TO 39 CE.

And when the daughter of the said Herodias came in and danced, and pleased Herod...the king said unto the damsel, ask me whatsoever thou wilt... And she came in...and asked saying, I will that thou give me by and by in a charger the head of John the Baptist. (MARK 6:22–25)

Antipas was full brother to Archelaus. With their half-brother, Philip, they had been educated in Rome. Herod willed to Antipas the tetrarchy of Galilee and Peraea and the Jewish portion of Transjordan. Augustus confirmed this territory and title.

Antipas' established his first capital at Sepphoris, the capital of Galilee, which had fallen on hard times after previous rebellions. Antipas expanded and rebuilt Sepphoris into "the ornament of all Galilee and called it Autocratoris [the equivalent to *Imperator* in Latin or Emperor in English]."[70]

Later Antipas began building the town of Tiberias on the Sea of Galilee, and he moved his capital there, probably around 20 CE. It was built after the death of Augustus and named after his successor in order to garner favor.

Not only did Antipas share his father's interest and talent for building great cities, he seems to have been "the most talented ruler and politician among all of Herod's sons," according to M. Stern.[71] Antipas' tetrarchy had a clear Jewish majority, including the often rebellious population of the Galilee. Yet Antipas ruled for 43 years without any armed rebellions in either Galilee or Peraea.

Called "that fox" by Jesus, Antipas is usually the "Herod" mentioned in the New Testament. John the Baptist lived and preached in the Galilee, and loudly protested the marriage of Antipas to his own niece Herodias. John was arrested for his activities. Antipas ordered his execution at the behest of Herodias after her daughter by an earlier marriage, Salome, had pleased Antipas with a dance. He offered Salome a wish and she requested John's head on a platter.[72]

Pontius Pilate sent Jesus to Antipas when he learned the man was a Galilean:

> As soon as he knew that he belonged unto Herod's jurisdiction he sent him to Herod who himself was also in Jerusalem at the time. Then he questioned with him in many words; but he answered him nothing.... And Herod with his men of war set him at nought, and mocked him, and arrayed him in a gorgeous robe, and sent him again to Pilate. (Luke 23:7–15)

When Caligula became emperor in 37 CE, Antipas tried to get into his good graces, but Caligula's good friend (and Antipas' nephew and brother-in-law) Agrippa I, grandson of Herod I, had already been granted the title of king in Herod Philip's previous territory. It troubled the ambitious Antipas that he remained only a tetrarch; it was not difficult for Herodias to persuade him to appeal to Caligula for equal recognition. Antipas and Herodias sailed to Rome to press his case. Part of this campaign consisted of striking the coins dated year 43 (Nos. 1215–1218), naming Caligula, the only coins of Antipas naming a Roman emperor. Agrippa used his powerful position at court to accuse his uncle of allying himself with the Parthians and building an arms cache to battle Rome. Caligula banished Antipas to Lugdunum in Gaul and confiscated his property, adding it to Agrippa's kingdom.[73]

PRUTAH OF SEPPHORIS

One might reasonably suppose that an ethnarch and the tetrarchs would use every possible means to assure superiority, even though Archelaus ended up with the more important title and larger territory than his brother Antipas.

Archelaus assumed the reins of his father's government and the royal mint in Jerusalem that was part of it.[74] Antipas, on the other hand, inherited a territory without much infrastructure; indeed, his new capital was Sepphoris, probably the only real town in his territory at the time.

Eventually Antipas began to devote his attention to the creation of a new city, Tiberias. He moved his capital there, and apparently founded the city between 17/18 and 20/1 CE. Avi Yonah explains that the actual event most probably took place in the year 18, which was not only the sixtieth birthday of Tiberius, but also the twentieth anniversary of his holding the *Tribunicia Potestas*.[75] The year 18/19 CE was also the twenty-second year of the reign of Antipas as tetrarch.

Previously, the first coins known to be struck by Antipas were dated "Year 24" (of Antipas' reign) and thought to be struck at Tiberias in 20/1 CE.[76]

Meshorer suggests the delay in Antipas' first coinage occurred because he was "forced to establish an original basis for his administration; no previous governing system existed for his tetrarchy."[77] Antipas started with no government, little infrastructure, and, ergo, no mint.

But a new coin discovered by the author sheds a different light on the situation and seems to prove that Antipas did not wait 24 years to issue his first coin.[78] This unique coin is dated to the fourth year of Antipas's reign and indicates that he probably struck at least a trial coinage at his first capital Sepphoris (No. 1198).[79]

Method and style of production was typical of Herodian and procuratorial *prutot* of the period. The weight (1.58 g) is consistent with *prutot* from the period of Herod Archelaus; the edges are beveled, it was clearly struck on a strip of cast flans, chopped away from coins on either side in the style standard at Jerusalem.[80]

The palm tree motif is not remarkable for Jewish coins, however, this coin marks its first appearance. In 6/7 CE, only six years after its appearance on this Antipas coin, the palm tree reappears on a coin of Coponius; later it is seen on coins of the Jewish War, Bar Kokhba Revolt, and in the Judaea Capta series, among others.

Depiction of a barley or wheat grain is also not a surprising design for an ancient Jewish coin, although this coin is unique in its presentation of a single grain. Ears of grain appear on coins of Mattatayah Antigonus, Herod Philip, Agrippa I, Agrippa II, and procuratorial issues.[81]

The reverse legend is clear. It corresponds with abbreviations of the name Herod used on both coins of Herod I and Herod Archelaus.

Most of the obverse legend is clear. By inserting two letters where there appear to be spaces, we can reconstruct it as follows: TETPA[PX] HC Δ.

On all of the dated coins of Herod I as well as the other known coins of Antipas, the date is preceded by the letter L, which signifies that the letters following it represent numerals, or a date. No letter L can be seen on this coin, nor is there a space for it. This is not an alarming omission, however, since most of the bronze and the silver coins of Tyre struck from the first century BCE well into the first century CE do not carry either the letter L or the notation ETOY, which also stands for "year."[82]

Most of the other coins of Antipas carry his title in the genitive form HPWΔOY TETPAPXOY ([money] of Herod the Tetrarch). However, this coin states the name and title in the nominative form, HPW TETPAPXHC (Herod the Tetrarch).[83]

The reason for the use of the nominative form of the name may simply be a result of copying the inscription style of the coins of Antipas' brother, and rival, Archelaus, who had a "running start" since he was able to immediately begin issuing coins from his father's Jerusalem mint.[84]

On his coins, Archelaus, at least initially, uses either abbreviations or the nominative form. The other coins that carry his name and title in the genitive form were probably issued toward the end of his reign.[85]

This coin can thus be dated to the fourth year of the Tetrarchy of Herod. This corresponds to the year 1 BCE/1 CE—the exact year we change our reckoning from BCE to CE!

Some have attempted to argue that the use of the so-called dynastic name "Herod" was not used by Antipas, as the junior ruler, until Archelaus was banished to Gaul in 6 CE.[86] However, this coin, as well as other information,[87] allows us to firmly refute the idea.

With regard to the date on this coin, it is worth noting that the third brother, Philip, issued his first dated coins only one year later, in 1/2 CE at the mint of Caesarea Paneas.[88]

Because Antipas' original capital was known to be Sepphoris, there can be little doubt that the mint of this new coin type was indeed Sepphoris. Until now there were no known Judaean *prutot* or half-*prutot* coins with beveled edges known to have been struck at Sepphoris.[89] But there is other evidence that such coins were struck there. In a remarkable coincidence, a fragment of a typical Judaean chalk flan mold was found in excavations at Sepphoris in 1985, the very year that the author was the numismatist for the excavation.[90, 91]

While Sepphoris was clearly not much of a town before Antipas rebuilt it, a number of public structures existed there for some time and were probably still in use when Antipas became tetrarch. Eric Meyers reported a fortified structure in Sepphoris, which "appears to have been in use by ca. 100 BCE judging by the coins, pottery, and other late Hellenistic finds. Several *mikvaot* (ritual baths) also date back to this period and their large size suggests some form of public usage."[92]

The *prutah* from Sepphoris is alone in this denomination and style among the coins of Antipas.[93] None of his subsequent coins were struck on flans with beveled edges, but resembled Roman provincial coins. Since he ruled a territory with a significant Jewish majority, Antipas was careful not to use portraits or graven images. The designs are reeds, palm branches, or palm trees, save one late issue that depicts a bunch of dates, and inscriptions within wreaths. Except for the last coins of Antipas, all carry the name of the city in which they were struck, Tiberias. This issue was the first Jewish ruler's coins to carry the name of a Roman Emperor, Caligula, and no doubt honored him in anticipation of the previously discussed voyage to Rome prior to Antipas' banishment.

The Antipas coins of Tiberias were struck in four denominations for each date of issue. Meshorer equates these coins with the Roman *dupondius, as, semis* and *quadrans*, and points out that in Jewish sources they have the corresponding names of *pundion, issar, musmis,* and *kuntrunk*. Meshorer cites Rabbinnic sources that suggest the largest denomination is equivalent to 1/12 *denarius*; the half 1/24 *denarius*; the quarter 1/48 *denarius*, and the eighth 1/96 *denarius*; although the standard Roman relationship to the silver *denarius* would have been 1/8: 1/16: 1/32: 1/64.[94]

Antipas was the first Jewish ruler who had a date struck on each coin issued. The dates were not consecutive. Coins were struck in his regnal years 4 (1 BCE/1 CE), 24 (19/20 CE), 33 (28/9 CE), 34 (29/30 CE), 37 (32/3 CE), and 43 (38/9 CE). Since the coins are all quite scarce, one may assume that they were struck only during the date years, and not continued during the intervening years. What possible events might have prompted a coin-issuing year is not known.

The coins of Antipas are usually found in poor condition, quite corroded. This is due to the poor alloy of the coins as well as moisture and other environmental conditions in the northern territories Antipas ruled, and where the coins circulated. They also circulated in the Jordan Valley, and the coins found in that drier area are generally much better preserved.

Herod Antipas is consistently referred to as "Herod" in the Gospels. In Matthew 14:1 and Luke 9:7 he is correctly called "Herod the tetrarch." But in Mark 6:14 he is incorrectly called "King Herod." Antipas is also mentioned in the following New Testament verses: Matthew 14:3, 14:6, 14:9; Mark 6:14–27; Luke 3:1, 3:19, 9:9, 23:7–15; Acts 5:27, 13:1.

COINS OF HEROD ANTIPAS
MINT OF SEPPHORIS, YEAR *4*, *1* BCE/CE
Border of dots on both sides unless noted.
Axis of Antipas coins is ↑.

1198

1198.   AE *prutah*, 14.1 mm, 1.58 g.
   Obv: Grain of barley or wheat; TETPA[PX]HC Δ *(Tetrarch [year] 4)*.
   Rev: Palm tree with seven branches and club-like trunk; below and
      to right, reading outwardly, HPW *(Herod)*.

UNIQUE

Only one specimen recorded to date.

MINT OF TIBERIAS
YEAR 24, 20/21 CE

1199

1200

1199. AE full denomination.
Obv: TIBE PIAC *(Tiberias)* within wreath.
Rev: HPWΔOY TETPAPXOY *(of Herod the Tetrarch)*; L KΔ *(year 24)*
in fields; reed upright.   350/900
To date, 3 obverse, 7 reverse dies noted (MCP).

1200. AE half-denomination.
Obv: TIBE PIAC within wreath.
Rev: HPWΔOY TETPAPXOY; L KΔ in fields; reed upright.
                                                                  250/750
To date, 5 obverse, 10 reverse dies noted (MCP).

1201

1202

1201. AE quarter-denomination.
Obv: TIBE PIAC within wreath.
Rev: HPWΔOY TETPAPXOY; L KΔ in fields; reed upright.
                                                                  250/600
To date, 7 obverse, 18 reverse dies noted (MCP).

1202. AE eighth-denomination.
Obv: TI BE within wreath.
Rev: HPWΔ TETPAP *(Herod the Tetrarch)* LKΔ; in fields; reed up-
right.   300/900
To date, 6 obverse, 8 reverse dies noted (MCP).

YEAR 33, 29/30 CE

1203. AE full denomination,
 Obv: TIBE PIAC *(Tiberias)* within wreath.
 Rev: HPWΔOY TETPAPXOY *(of Herod the Tetrarch)*; L ΛΓ in fields;
   palm branch upright.   350/900
   To date, 7 obverse, 23 reverse dies noted (MCP).

1204. AE half-denomination.
 Obv: TIBE PIAC within wreath.
 Rev: HPWΔOY TETPAPXOY; L ΛΓ in fields; palm branch upright.
                                                           250/700

   To date, 3 obverse, 25 reverse dies noted (MCP).

1205. AE quarter-denomination.
 Obv: TIBE PIAC within wreath.
 Rev: HPWΔOY TETPAPXOY; L ΛΓ in fields; palm branch upright.
                                                           250/600

   To date, 6 obverse, 8 reverse dies noted (MCP).

1206. AE eighth-denomination.
 Obv: T C *(T[iberia]s)* within wreath.
 Rev: HPWΔOY *(of Herod)*; L ΛΓ; palm branch upright.
                                                           250/750

   To date, 1 obverse, 2 reverse dies noted (MCP).

YEAR 34, 30/1 CE

1207. AE full denomination.
Obv: TIBE PIAC within wreath.
Rev: HPWΔOY TETPAPXOY; L ΛΔ *(year 34)* in fields; palm branch
upright.   350/900
To date, 2 obverse, 14 reverse dies noted (MCP).

1208. AE half-denomination.
Obv: TIBE PIAC within wreath.
Rev: HPWΔOY TETPAPXOY; L ΛΔ in fields; palm branch up-
right.   250/700
To date, 1 obverse, 12 reverse dies noted (MCP).

1209. AE quarter-denomination.
Obv: TIBE PIAC within wreath.
Rev: HPWΔOY TETPAPXOY; L ΛΔ in fields; palm branch up-
right.   250/600
To date, 2 obverse, 3 reverse dies noted (MCP).

1210. AE eighth-denomination.
Obv: T C *(T[iberia]s)* within wreath.
Rev: HPWΔOY *(of Herod)*; L ΛΔ in fields; palm branch upright.
                                                                 250/750
To date, 1 obverse, 2 reverse dies noted (MCP).

YEAR 37, 33/4 CE

1211. AE full denomination.
Obv: TIBE PIAC within wreath.
Rev: HPWΔOY TETPAPXOY; L ΛZ *(year 37)* in fields; palm branch
upright.   300/900
To date, 3 obverse, 6 reverse dies noted (MCP).

1212.   AE half-denomination.
Obv: TIBE PIAC within wreath.
Rev: HPWΔOY TETPAPXOY; L ΛZ in fields; palm branch upright.
250/700

To date, 6 obverse, 30 reverse dies noted (MCP).

1213

1214

1213.   AE quarter-denomination.
Obv: TIBE PIAC within wreath.
Rev: HPWΔOY TETPAPXOY; L ΛZ in fields; palm branch upright.
250/600

To date, 1 obverse, 3 reverse dies noted (MCP).

1214.   AE eighth-denomination.
Obv: T C *(T[iberia]s)* within wreath.
Rev: HPWΔOY; L ΛZ in fields; palm branch upright
250/700

To date, 1 obverse, 1 reverse die noted (MCP).

YEAR *43, 39/40* CE

1215

1216

1215.   AE full denomination.
Obv: ΓAIΩ KAICAP ΓEPMA NIKΩ *(for Gaius Caesar Germanicus)* within wreath.
Rev: HPWΔHC TETPAPXHC *(Herod the Tetrarch)*; ETO CMΓ *(year 43)* in fields; seven-branched palm tree with two date clusters.
650/2,000

To date, 9 obverse, 10 reverse dies noted (MCP).

1216. AE half-denomination.
Obv: ΓΑΙΩ ΚΑΙCΑΡ ΓΕΡΜΑ ΝΙΚΩ within wreath.
Rev: ΗΡΩΔΗC ΤΕΤΡΑΡΧΗC; L ΜΓ in fields; palm branch upright.   500/1,250
To date, 5 obverse, 19 reverse dies noted (MCP).

1217   1218

1217. AE quarter-denomination.
Obv: ΓΑΙΩ ΚΑΙ CΑΡ *(for Gaius Caesar)* within wreath.
Rev: ΗΡΩΔΗC ΤΕΤΡΑΡΧΗC; L ΜΓ in fields; bunch of dates.
                                                          550/1,350
To date, 3 obverse, 4 reverse dies noted (MCP).

1218. AE eighth-denomination.
Obv: ΓΑ ΙΩ *(for Gai[us])* within wreath.
Rev: ΗΡΩΔΗC ΤΕΤΡΑΡΧΗC; L ΜΓ in fields; palm branch upright.   450/900
To date, 1 obverse, 2 reverse dies noted (MCP).

HEROD PHILIP, 4 BCE TO 34 CE

Now in the 15th year of the reign of Tiberius Caesar, Pontius Pilate being governor of Judaea and Herod being tetrarch of Galilee, and his brother Philip tetrarch of Ituraea and of the region of Trachonitis...
(LUKE 3:1)

Son of Herod I and Cleopatra of Jerusalem, Philip was educated with his older half-brothers, Archelaus and Antipas, in Rome. He received the final portion of his father's kingdom—the northeastern section—as well as the title tetrarch, parallel to his brother Antipas.

Like his father and brother Antipas, Philip also enjoyed building cities. The most important was Paneas at the spring that creates a main tributary of the Jordan River, which was named (of course) Caesarea after the emperor. It became known as Caesarea Philippi to avoid confusion with his father's city of Caesarea Maritima, and was Philip's capital:

When Jesus came into the coasts of Caesarea Philippi, he asked his disciples... (MATTHEW 16:13)

Philip became a ruler at the whim of the emperor. In Herod's original will, he designated Antipas to succeed him. In a second will, however, he gave the nod to son number two, Archelaus. Herod I should have known that only the emperor was powerful enough to decide who would succeed him. Thus, when Herod died, Augustus modified Herod's second will. He did not name any one of the three sons to be "king" to succeed his father. Instead, Augustus named Archelaus "ethnarch" and entitled him to 500 *talents* income each year from his domain, and named Antipas and Philip as "tetrarchs," giving them 200 and 100 *talents* annual income, respectively.

While Archelaus and Antipas battled it out for the favor of Augustus, each vying for the kingship, Philip seems to have been quite satisfied with the small domain assigned to him. Stern calls Philip "least colorful" of Herod's sons.[95] He was also the least violent and achieved the historic status of being a peace-loving man and a good administrator. Josephus tells how Philip traveled through his kingdom

7.6. Herod Philip's image recreated from his coins. (Graphic: Fontanille.)

and set up tribunals in a stately manner to settle the problems of his constituents.[96]

Herod Philip was the first husband of the notorious Berenice, his own niece and sister of Agrippa II. Upon his death, in 34 CE, she married another member of the Herodian family, Aristobulus, king of Chalcis. At that time Philip's land was annexed to the Roman province of Syria, but in 37 CE it was given to Herod I's grandson, Agrippa I. Philip was buried at Bethsaida, which he had rebuilt and renamed Julias in honor of Julia, the daughter of his original patron Augustus.[97]

As the least well-known of Herod's three sons, it's ironic that Philip is the only one, and the first Jewish ruler, whose face we are able to see. His jutting nose was almost comically large for the rest of his face. He had curly, short hair and a sharp jaw line with a prominent chin.

There are no photographs of Herod Philip, but he was the first Jewish ruler to place his own portrait, as well as the portraits of Augustus and Tiberius upon coins, thus rendering his image eternal. Philip was able to immortalize his face on his coins largely because so few Jews lived in the territories over which he ruled. Jews would have taken this act as an insult and violation of the Mosaic Law against "graven images." Philip was also the first Jewish ruler to put Roman imperial portraits on his coins. Augustus, Tiberius, and Livia were so honored.

Herod I had built a splendid Roman temple at Caesarea Philippi, the Augusteum of Paneas, which Philip depicted on most of his coins with a façade of four columns and a staircase. His coins were issued in three denominations.

Herod Philip is also mentioned in the following New Testament verses: Matthew 14:3; Mark 6:17–29; Luke 3:19.

COINS OF HEROD PHILIP
MINT OF CAESAREA PHILIPPI (PANEAS)
YEAR 5, 1/2 CE, UNDER AUGUSTUS,
Border of dots on both sides unless noted.
Many coins have blundered legends, Greek Σ may also appear as C.

1219

1220

1219.   AE 24 mm.
   Obv: KAICAP CEBACTOY *(of Caesar Augustus)*; bare head of Augustus to r.
   Rev: ΦΙΛΙΠΠΟΥ ΤΕΤΡΑΡΧΟΥ *(of Philip the Tetrarch)*; LE *(year 5)* in fields; bare head of Herod Philip r.   3,750/10,000

1220.   AE 18 mm.
   Obv: ΦΙΛΙΠΠΟΥ ΤΕΤΡΑΡΧΟΥ *(of Philip the Tetrarch)*; LE in fields; bare head of Herod Philip to r.
   Rev: CEBAC KAICAP *(Augustus Caesar)*; the Augusteum of Paneas (shown as a tetrastyle temple) on high platform, lily in pediment.   1,750/7,500

1221

1221a

YEAR 12, 8/9 CE.
1221.   AE 20 mm.
   Obv: KAICAPI CEBACTΩ *(for Caesar Augustus)*; laureate head of Augustus to r.
   Rev: ΦΙΛΙΠΠΟΥ ΤΕΤΡΑΡΧΟΥ; LIB *(year 12)* between columns of the Augusteum of Paneas with stairs leading to it, dot in pediment.   500/1,250

a. Retrograde reverse.
b. Star countermark on obverse.

1222. AE 20 mm.
   Obv: KAICAPI CEBACTΩ *(for Caesar Augustus)*; laureate head of
     Augustus to l.
   Rev: ΦΙΛΙΠΠΟΥ ΤΕΤΡ *(of Philip the Tetrarch)*; LIB between columns
     of the Augusteum of Paneas, floral design in pediment.
                                       500/1,250

a. Reverse is retrograde.

1223   1224a

YEAR 16, 12/13 CE

1223. AE 20 mm.
   Obv: KAICAPI CEBACTΩ; laureate head of Augustus to r.
   Rev: ΦΙΛΙΠΠΟΥ ΤΕΤΡΑΡΧΟΥ; L Iς *(year 16)* between columns of
     the Augusteum of Paneas with stairs leading to it, dot in pedi-
     ment.   500/1,250
a. Φ countermark on obverse.
b. Star countermark on obverse.

YEAR 19, 15/16 CE

1224. AE 19 mm.
   Obv: TIB KAICAPI ΣΕΒΑΣ *(for Tib[erius] Caesar Augustus)*; laureate
     head of Tiberius to r.
   Rev: ΦΙΛΙΠΟΥ ΤΕΤΡΑΧΟΥ; L ΙΘ *(year 19)* between columns of the
     Augusteum of Paneas, no podium, staircase below, dot in pedi-
     ment.   500/1,250
a. Φ countermark on obverse.
b. Star countermark obverse.

YEAR 30, 26/7 CE

1225.   AE 19 mm.
Obv: ΤΙΒΕΡΙΟΣ ΣΕΒΑΣΤΟΣ ΚΑΙΣΑΡ *(Tiberius Augustus Caesar)*;
laureate head of Tiberius to r., laurel branch in r. field.
Rev: ΕΠΙ ΦΙΛΙΠΠΟΥ ΤΕΤΡΑΡΧΟΥ *(in the time of Philip the tetrarch)*;
LΛ *(year 30)* between columns of the Augusteum of Paneas on
low platform, dot in pediment.   500/1,250

1226.   AE 17 mm.
Obv: Laureate head of Tiberius to r., no inscription.
Rev: Augusteum of Paneas as 1225.   1,000/2,500

1227.   AE 14 mm.
Obv: ΙΟΥΛΙΑ ΣΕΒΑΣΤΗ *(Augusta Julia)*; draped bust of Livia to r.
Rev: ΚΑΡΠΟΦΟΡΟΣ *(fruit-bearing)*; L Λ in fields; hand holds three
ears of grain.   500/1,500

YEAR 33, 29/30 CE

1228.   AE 18 mm.
Obv: ΚΑΙΣΑΡΟΣ ΣΕΒΑCΤΟΥ. laureate head of Tiberius to r.
Rev: ΦΙΛΙΠΠΟΥ ΤΕΤΡΑΡΧΟΥ; L ΛΓ *(year 33)* between columns of
the Augusteum of Paneas on low platform, dot in pediment.
                                                         500/1,250
a. Obv: ΤΙΒΕΡΙΟΣ ΣΕΒΑΣΤΟΣ ΚΑΙΣΑΡ.
Rev: ΕΠΙ ΦΙΛΙΠΠΟΥ ΤΕΤΡΑΡΧΟΥ.

YEAR *34, 30/1* CE

1229.   AE 24 mm.
Obv: ΣΕΒΑΣΤΩИ *(of the Augusti)*; jugate heads of Tiberius and Livia to r.
Rev: ΕΠΙ ΦΙΛΙΠΠΟΥ ΤΕΤΡΑΡΧΟΥ *(in the time of Herod the Tetrarch)*; the Augusteum of Paneas on high platform with round design in center.   750/2,000
a. Star countermark obverse, X countermark reverse.

This issue is not dated, but as noted in the previous edition, Shraga Qedar believes this coin belongs to the series of the year 34, based on style and historical circumstance. Strickert has agreed with this conclusion.[98]

1230.   AE 19 mm.
Obv: ΤΙΒΕΡΙΟΥ ΣΕΒΑΣΤΟΣ ΚΑΙΣΑΡ; laureate head of Tiberius to r., laurel branch in r. field.
Rev: ΦΙΛΙΠΠΟΥ ΤΕΤΡΑΡΧΟΥ ΚΤΙΣ *(of the founder, Philip the tetrarch)*; L Λ Δ *(year 34)* between columns of the Augusteum of Paneas, small inverted triangle on pediment.   500/1,200

1231   1232   1233

1231.   AE 14 mm.
Obv: ΙΟΥΛΙΑ ΣΕΒΑΣΤΗ; draped bust of Livia to r.
Rev: ΚΑΡΠΟΦΟΡΟΣ; L ΛΔ in fields; hand holds three ears of grain.   500/1,500

1232.   AE 11 mm.
Obv: ΦΙΛΙΠΠΟΥ *(of Philip)*; bare head of Herod Philip to r.
Rev: L Λ Δ within wreath.   1,000/6,500

YEAR 37, 33/34 CE

1233. AE 18 mm.
Obv: ΤΙΒΕΡΙΟC CΕΒΑCΤΟC ΚΑΙCΑΡ., laureate head of Tiberius
to r., laurel branch in r. field.
Rev: ΕΠΙ ΦΙΛΙΠΠΟΥ ΤΕΤΡΑΡΧΟΥ; L Λ Z (year 37) between columns of the Augusteum of Paneas on low platform, small inverted triangle in pediment.   500/1,750

1234. AE 14 mm.
Obv: ΙΟΥΛΙΑ CΕΒΑCΤΗ; draped bust of Livia to r.
Rev: ΚΑΡΠΟΦΟΡΟC; L ΛZ in fields; hand holds three ears of
grain.   500/1,500

1235. AE 11 mm.
Obv: ΦΙΛΙΠΠΟΥ; bare head of Herod Philip to r.
Rev: L Λ Z within wreath.   1,000/6,500

AGRIPPA I, 37 TO 44 CE

*Now about that time Herod [Agrippa] the king stretched forth his
hands to vex certain of the church. And he killed James the brother of
John with the sword* (ACTS 12:1–2).

Grandson of Herod I and Mariamne the Hasmonean, Marcus Julius
Agrippa was born in 11/10 BCE. His parents were Aristobulus, son
of Herod I and Mariamne, and Berenice, daughter of Costobar and
Herod's sister Salome; his parents were first cousins, rather common
in royal families at the time.

Agrippa's family was devastated by his own grandfather Herod
I, who executed Mariamne and Costobar before Agrippa was born.
When he was 3, his father and uncle Alexander were also murdered
by Herod.

Agrippa was named after Mark (Marcus) Antony, who was responsible for Herod's kingship, Julius Caesar, who granted citizenship
to Herod's father Antipater, and Marcus Vipsanius Agrippa, son-in-
law and friend of Augustus.[99]

Josephus reports that Herod raised Aristobulus' children after he killed their father, "taking care of the orphans and showing his remorse for the murder of his sons by his compassion for their offspring."[100]

Agrippa was educated in Rome, where he was taken, at around age 5, by his mother, who may have been protecting him against his grandfather's paranoid whims that had already resulted in so many family murders. The young Agrippa was especially friendly with Claudius and Gaius (later Caligula).

Once when Agrippa and Caligula were driving together in the former's chariot, Agrippa commented that he hoped that Caligula would succeed the elderly Tiberius as emperor and become "lord of the world." Agrippa's coachman, Eutychus, overheard this and later, when he was in trouble on another matter, bargained and declared that he had an important secret to tell the emperor.

When Tiberius heard about what Agrippa had said, he had him fettered and taken to prison. While leaning against a tree, still wearing his royal purple, waiting to be taken to his cell, an owl landed on a branch above his head. Another prisoner saw this and asked a soldier for Agrippa's identity. Then he asked to talk to him, and told him that he was skilled in fortune-telling by way of birds, and the owl was a good omen sent by Agrippa's god, and it meant he would soon be released and restored to his former positions. He warned Agrippa, however, that when he saw that owl again he would die within only five days.

Agrippa was imprisoned for about six months, until Tiberius died on March 16, 37 CE. Caligula indeed ascended to the throne and quickly

7.7. Agrippa I's bust recreated from his coins by artists at The Israel Museum, Jerusalem. (Courtesy Israel Museum.)

proved his friendship to Agrippa by setting him free and crowning him king of his uncle Philip's former tetrarchy. The Roman Senate then conferred the rank of praetor on Agrippa, and Caligula presented him with a golden chain equal in weight to the iron chain he had worn in prison.

Two years later, Agrippa's uncle Antipas, egged on by his wife Herodias, visited Caligula and asked for more power. But Caligula became annoyed and instead banished Antipas to Gaul, adding his territories to Agrippa's.

We have several primary sources for information on Agrippa I's life, career, and death: *The New Testament* (ACTS 12), Josephus, Philo, and Cassius Dio. He is also mentioned many times in the Rabbinnic literature, but Daniel Schwartz notes that "those rabbis who looked back upon him after a few generations, and especially in light of the destruction of the Second Temple, seem to have viewed his reign as a transient and insignificant episode. And, in fact, there is something to say for this view of the monarch, a man whose burial place no one even cared to record."[101]

Overall, though, the sources leave little doubt that Agrippa was a benevolent king for the Jewish people. He carefully followed Pharisaic tradition in Jerusalem and was quite popular. Both Josephus and the Talmud praise him. His initial unquestioning loyalty to Rome eventually gave way to deep religious and nationalistic feelings, and Agrippa soon set about surrounding Jerusalem with "a wall on such a scale as, had it been completed would have rendered ineffectual all the efforts of the Romans in the subsequent siege. But before the work had reached the projected height, he died...."[102]

Agrippa was also a consummate politician. When he traveled out of his Jewish territories, he was a liberal patron of Greek culture. He also had "a gentle disposition and he was a benefactor to all alike... but to his compatriots he was proportionally more generous and more compassionate...he scrupulously observed the traditions of his people. He neglected no rite of purification and no day passed for him without the prescribed sacrifice."[103]

The Talmud tells of Agrippa's attendance at the Feast of Tabernacles in 41 CE According to tradition, Agrippa read from the Book of Deuteronomy, and when he got to the passage, "Thou mayest not set a stranger over thee that is not thy brother,"[104] he burst out in tears because he felt this passage referred to his own rule. But the Talmud says that when the people observed the king's emotions, they cried out to him: "Fear not, Agrippa! Thou art our brother! Thou art our brother!"[105] Much of his popularity among the Jews was because he went out of his way to reach an understanding with the leaders of the Pharisees.

Since Agrippa was king of Judaea during the decade after the death of Jesus, he was faced with many issues related to the spread of Christianity and in these matters he sided more with the stern views of the Sadducees. Agrippa ordered the execution of the apostle James, son of Zebedee, and also imprisoned the apostle Peter with the intention of killing him, although Peter escaped.[106]

Agrippa was present in Rome when his patron Caligula was murdered, and Josephus tells us he contributed significantly to insuring the succession of Claudius, another of his close childhood friends. In return, Claudius not only confirmed Agrippa's position, but handed over the territories of Judaea and Samaria, plus consular rank. Agrippa I now had united under his rule the entire territory governed by his grandfather.

Agrippa was an enthusiastic client king of Rome. Josephus tells of a royal meeting Agrippa convened in Tiberias. The prelude to this meeting took place shortly after Agrippa built a "sumptuous and elegant" theater in Berytus and when it was finished he staged a giant gala/execution in which 1,400 'malefactors' were punished by being pitted against each other, 700 versus 700, as gladiators, "In this way he brought about the utter annihilation of these men."[107]

When Agrippa finished his massacre of criminals at Berytus, he proceeded to Tiberias, where he convened a meeting of other Roman client kings from eastern territories. He was visited by Antiochus IV king of Commagene, Sampsigeramus king of Emisa, and Cotys IX king of Armenia Minor, as well as by Polemo II, king of Pontus, as well as Agrippa's brother Herod, king of Chalcis.

7.8. Meeting of the kngs: from left, Agrippa I; his brother, Herod of Chalcis; Polemo II, king of Pontus; and Antiochus IV of Commagene.

"His converse with all of them when he entertained and showed them courtesies was such as to demonstrate an elevation of sentiment that justified the honour done him by a visit of royalty."[108]

The meeting had a rather disastrous end, however, because at the same time, "[Vibius] Marsus, the governor of Syria arrived. The king therefore, to do honor to the Romans, advanced seven furlongs outside the city to meet him. Now this action, as events proved, was destined to be the beginning of a quarrel with Marsus; for Agrippa brought the other kings along with him and sat with them in his carriage. But Marsus was suspicious of such concord and intimate friendship among them. He took it for granted that a meeting of the minds among so many chiefs of state was prejudicial to Roman interests. He therefore at once sent some of his associates with an order to each of the kings bidding him set off without delay to his own territory. Agrippa felt very much hurt by this and henceforth was at odds with Marsus."[109]

Agrippa's meeting of the kings gives us an interesting look at the potential alliances between the men who ruled at the pleasure of Rome during the first century, not to mention how nervous those alliances could make the local Roman representatives.

We can see some of these rulers via portraits on their coins, specifically Agrippa himself, Antiochus IV of Commagene, Agrippa's brother, Herod of Chalcis (who became the second husband of Agrippa's daughter Berenice), and Polemo king of Pontus (who became the third husband of the same Berenice).

Josephus' account of this meeting is contained in the same chapter that describes Agrippa's death, so it probably occurred quite late in his life, around 42 CE.

Schwartz summarizes an historic view of Agrippa's reign as related to Judaea and Rome: "On the one hand, under Agrippa all of Palestine was reunited under a Jewish monarch—only to allow all of it, rather than a third as formerly, to return to direct Roman rule after his death. In other words, while it briefly appeared that through Agrippa Judaea could avert the steamroller of Roman history, it turned out that he helped smooth its path. And, on the other hand, a man who knew better than anyone that the fate of Judaea, and of the Jews of the Mediterranean world, was dependent upon Rome, was stubbornly viewed by too many people as a harbinger of the type of anti-Roman Jewish nationalism embodied by some of his ancestors. The hopes which were raised by his enthronement, and which refused to die with him, contributed to the faith which led to the great rebellion of 66–73 CE, and to catastrophe."[110]

In 44 CE, Agrippa attended games and celebrations in honor of the emperor at Caesarea Maritima. On the second day of the festivities, Agrippa wore a robe of woven silver to the amphitheater. Flatterers who saw his robe sparkling in the sun called out that he was a god and begged him to take mercy on them. Josephus says that Agrippa received the flattery a bit too seriously, and began to think of himself a god. Shortly thereafter, he saw an owl sitting on a rope. The owl harkened back the day he was imprisoned in Rome by Tiberius, and Agrippa recognized it as a warning of his impending death. Soon he developed severe pains in his bowels, and he had to be carried away. In five days, Agrippa died.[111] A much more likely scenario is that he was poisoned by enemies.

In the Acts of the Apostles, we have a similar telling: "And he went down from Judaea to Caesarea and was spending time there. Now he was very angry with the people of Tyre and Sidon and with one accord they came to him, and having won over Blastus the king's chamberlain, they were asking for peace, because their country was fed by the king's country. And on the appointed day Herod, having put on his royal apparel, took his seat on the rostrum and began delivering an address to them. And the people kept crying out 'The voice of a god and not of a man!' And immediately an angel of the Lord struck him because he did not give God the glory, and he was eaten by worms and died."[112]

Agrippa I died in 44 CE at age 54. His reign of seven years was a brief golden age in the period of Roman rule over Judaea, especially for the three years that he reigned over Judaea itself, and a kingdom as large as that of his grandfather's. It's somewhat fitting that Agrippa I, an heir to both the Hasmonean and Herodian bloodlines was the last Jewish king to reign over Judaea.

The coins struck under Agrippa I are rare, with the exception of the single coin that was minted in large numbers in Jerusalem for use by the people of Judaea, Samaria, and Galilee. This common type stands alone among Agrippa's coins because it carries no graven image—on one side it depicts three ears of grain and on the other an umbrella-like canopy that was a symbol of power (No. 1244). Aside from this typical Judaean *prutah*, however, the denomination and value of Agrippa's other coins are not clear. Agrippa's other coins were struck at Caesarea Paneas and dated years 2 (38/9 CE) and 5 (40/1 CE), and at Caesarea Maritima and dated years 7 (42/3 CE) and 8 (43/4 CE).

Coins minted at Caesarea Paneas and Caesarea Maritima for use in non-Jewish areas of his territory reflect on Agrippa's early life and friendships at the Roman Court, as recalled by Josephus. Thus his coins depict Caligula, his wife Caesonia, his sisters, Julia, Drusilla and Agrippina, and his daughter Drusilla.

A remarkable coin (No. 1248) depicts on one side a scene in which Agrippa I and his brother Herod of Chalcis crown Claudius with a wreath. On the other side, two clasped hands appear within a wreath and two concentric circles of Greek, which translate as "A vow and treaty of friendship and alliance between the Great King Agrippa and Augustus Caesar [Claudius], the Senate and the People of Rome."

Other rare coins of Agrippa I depict his portrait, as well as the name and image of his wife, Cypros. Because of the prohibition against graven images, there are no known busts of the ancient Jewish kings. This, of course, has led to a lot of curiosity, and some years ago, Ya'akov Meshorer, then numismatic curator at the Israel Museum, commissioned a sculptor to create a bust of Agrippa based on his interpretation of Agrippa's images on various coins (p. 263).

Agrippa I is the "Herod" who is mentioned throughout verses 1 to 23 of the Book of Acts.

COINS OF AGRIPPA I
Border of dots on both sides unless noted.
Axis is ↑.

MINT OF CAESAREA PANEAS, YEAR 2, 37/8 CE

1236. AE 24 mm.
  Obv: ΓΑΙΩ... *(for Gaius...)*; LB *(year 2)* in l. field; head of Caligula to l.
  Rev: ΙΟΥΛΙΑ ΔΡΟΥΣΙΛΛΑ ΑΓΡΙΠΠΙΝΑ *(Julia, Drusilla, Agrippina)*; Julia, Drusilla, and Agrippina (from l., the sisters of Caligula), Julia leans on column, the other two hold cornucopias.
  1,750/7,500

1237. AE 20 mm.
Obv: ΒΑCΙΛΕΩC ΑΓΡΙΠΠΑC *(of King Agrippa)*; diademed head Agrippa I to r.
Rev: ΑΓΡΙΠΠΑ ΥΙΟΥ ΒΑCΙΛΕΩC *(Agrippa, son of the king)*; Agrippa II rides horse r., LB beneath horse. 1,500/6,500

1238. AE 16 mm.
Obv: ΚΥΠΡΟC *(Cypros)*; head of Cypros (wife of Agrippa) to r.
Rev: ΓΑΙΩ ΚΑΙCΑΡΙ *(for Gaius Caesar)*; LB in r. field; hand holding ears of grain and vine. RRR

1239. AE 14 mm.
Obv: ΓΑ / ΒΑΣ *(King Gaius)* within wreath.
Rev: Tetrastyle temple, LB *(year 2)* in field. RRR

Struck Year 5, 40/1 CE

1240. AE 24 mm.
Obv: ΓΑΙΩ ΚΑΙΣΑΡΙ ΣΕΒΑΣΤΩ ΓΕΡΜΑΝΙΚΩ *(for Gaius Caesar Augustus Germanicus)*; laureate head of Caligula to l.
Rev: ΝΟΜΙΣΜΑ ΒΑΣΙΛΕΩΣ ΑΓΡΙΠΠΑ *(money of King Agrippa)*, LE *(year 5)* in exergue; Germanicus stands in triumphal quadriga r. 2,000/7,500

1241. AE 19 mm.
Obv: ΚΑΙΣΩΝΙΑ ΓΥΝΗ ΣΕΒΑΣΤΟΥ *(Caesonia, wife of Augustus)*; head of Caesonia to l.
Rev: ΔΡΟΥΣΙΛΛΗ ΘΥΓΑΤΡΙ ΣΕΒΑΣΤΟΥ *(for Drusilla the daughter of Augustus)*; LE in l. field; Drusilla (daughter of Caligula) stands l. with a branch over her shoulder, holding a small Victory. 2,000/7,500

1242.   AE 17 mm.
Obv: ΒΑΣΙΛΕΥΣ ΑΓΡΙΠΠΑ, diademed, draped bust of Agrippa to r.
Rev: ΒΑΣΙΛΙΣΣΗΣ ΚΥΠΡΟΣ *(of Queen Cypros)*; LE in l. field; veiled Cypros (wife of Agrippa) stands front, holding long scepter in her l. hand and object in her raised r. hand.   2,500/8,500

1243.   AE 15 mm.
Obv: ΑΓΡΙΠΠΑ ΥΙΟΥ ΒΑΣΙΛΕΩΣ ΑΓΡΙΠΠΑ *(Agrippa, son of King Agrippa)*; LE in field l.; bare bust of young Agrippa II to l.
Rev: ΒΑΣ ΑΓΡΙΠΠΑ ΦΙΛΟΚΑΙΣΑΡ *(King Agrippa, friend of Caesar)*; double cornucopias crossed at bases.   1,750/5,000

MINT OF JERUSALEM
YEAR 6, 41/2 CE

1244

1244.   AE *prutah*, 2.33 g average.
Obv: ΒΑCΙΛΕWC ΑΓΡΙΠΑ *(of King Agrippa)*; umbrella-like canopy with fringes.
Rev: Lϛ *(year 6)* flanks three ears of barley and leaves.   35/100
a. Retrograde inscription.
b. Brockage of obverse on reverse.

This was Agrippa I's coin struck in large numbers for his territories largely populated by Jews. We cannot agree with Lönnqvist, who suggests it may be a coin of Agrippa II. It is commonly found amidst coins of the procurators,[113] and is of the same general weight , which places it among the coins of Agrippa I.[114] Recent study using X-ray fluorescence and lead isotope ratio analyses of this coin type confirms attribution to Agrippa I.[115]

MINT OF CAESAREA MARITIMA
YEAR 7, 42/3 CE

1245. AE 25 mm.
Obv: ΤΙΒΕΡΙΟΣ ΚΑΙΣΑΡ ΣΕΒΑΣΤΟΣ ΓΕΡΜ *(Tiberius Caesar Augustus Germanicus)*; laureate bust of Caligula to r.
Rev: ΒΑΣΙΛΕΥΣ ΜΕΓΑΣ ΑΓΡΙΠΠΑΣ ΦΙΛΟΚΑΙΣΑΡ *(the Great King Agrippa, friend of Caesar)*; distyle temple, LZ *(year 7)* in pediment, within temple, two figures stand facing each other and hold circular objects (pateras?), below, figure kneels l., in center, torso holds another object. 2,750/8,500

1246. AE 20 mm.
Obv: ΒΑΣΙΛΕΥΣ ΜΕΓΑΣ ΑΓΡΙΠΠΑΣ ΦΙΛΟΚΑΙΣΑΡ; diademed, draped bust of Agrippa I to r.
Rev: ΚΑΙΣΑΡΙΑ Η ΠΡΟΣ ΤΩ ΣΕΒΑΣΤΩ ΛΙΜΗΝΙ *(Caesarea, which is by the port of Sebastos)*; LZ in r. field; Tyche stands l., her r. hand on rudder and her l. holds palm branch. 2,500/6,000

1247. AE 16 mm.
Obv: ΑΓΡΙΠΠΟΥ ΥΙΟΥ ΒΑΣΙΛΕΩΣ *(of Agrippa, son of the King)*; bust of young Agrippa II to l.
Rev: Inverted anchor, LZ in fields. 3,000/8,500

YEAR 8, 43/4 CE

1248

1248.   AE 24 mm.

Obv: ΒΑΣ ΑΓΡΙΠΠΑΣ ΣΕΒ ΚΑΙΣΑΡ ΒΑΣ ΗΡΩΔΗΣ (*King Agrippa, Augustus [Claudius] Caesar, King Herod*), date LH (*year 8*) in exergue; Agrippa I (on l.), and his brother Herod of Chalcis r., crown Claudius with a wreath while he sacrifices with patera over altar.

Rev: ΟΡΚΙΑ ΒΑΣ ΜΕ ΑΓΡΙΠΠΑ ΠΡ ΣΕΒ ΚΑΙΣΑΡ ΑΚ ΣΥΝΚΛΗΤΟΝ Κ ΔΗΜΟ ΡΟΜ ΦΙΛΙ Κ ΣΥΝΜΑΧΙ ΑΥΤ *(A vow and treaty of friendship and alliance between the great King Agrippa and Augustus Caesar, the Senate and the People of Rome)*; two clasped hands within wreath in two concentric circles.   3,500/15,000

This historic coin is invariably in poor condition. This is Meshorer's restoration of the inscription. Many specimens, including the drawing, contain an oval countermark of a male head l.

1249.   AE 25 mm.

Obv: ΤΙΒΕΡΙΟΣ ΚΑΙΣΑΡ ΣΕΒΑΣΤΟΣ ΓΕΡΜ *(Tiberius Caesar Augustus Germanicus)*; laureate bust of Caligula to r.

Rev: ΒΑΣΙΛΕΥΣ ΜΕΓΑΣ ΑΓΡΙΠΠΑΣ ΦΙΛΟΚΑΙΣΑΡ *(the Great King Agrippa, friend of Caesar)*; distyle temple, LH (*year 8*) in pediment, within temple, two figures stand facing each other and hold circular objects (pateras?), below, figure kneels l., in center, torso holds another object.   3,000/10,000

a.   Oval countermark with head on obverse.

1250.   AE 20 mm.

Obv: ΒΑΣΙΛΕΥΣ ΜΕΓΑΣ ΑΓΡΙΠΠΑΣ ΦΙΛΟΚΑΙΣΑΡ; diademed, draped bust of Agrippa I to r.

Rev: ΚΑΙΣΑΡΙΑ Η ΠΡΟΣ ΤΩ ΣΕΒΑΣΤΩ ΛΙΜΗΝΙ; LH in r. field; Tyche stands l., her r. hand on rudder and her l. holds palm branch.   2,500/7,500

HEROD OF CHALCIS, 41 TO 48 CE
ARISTOBULUS OF CHALCIS, 57 TO 92 CE

Salute Apelles approved in Christ. Salute them which are of Aristobulus' household (ROMANS 16:10).

The descendants of Herod I remained loyal to Rome, and thus received both rank and privilege. Herod of Chalcis (sometimes called Herod III) was the brother of Agrippa I. The traditional Herodian relationship with Rome led not only to the descendants of Herod the Great ruling Jewish districts, but also large areas in the Near East that had little or no connection with the Jews.

At Agrippa I's request, Claudius granted his older brother Herod the kingdom of Chalcis in Coele-Syria, a land neither considered part of the Jewish territory nor inhabited by Jews. Among Herod the Great's other descendants were a grandson Tigranes V (6–12 CE) and another descendant (possibly a great-grandson) Tigranes VI (60–62 CE) who became Herodian Kings of Armenia[116] but showed no interest in the Jewish people or their religion.

Herod of Chalcis, however, was keenly interested in his Jewish brethren. Josephus reports that he "…asked Claudius to give him authority over the Temple and the holy vessels and the selection of the high priests—all of which requests he obtained. This authority, derived from him, passed to his descendants alone until the end of the war."[117]

7.9. Portrait coins of Tigranes V (top row) and Tigranes VI, scions of the Herodian Dynasty. (Photos: Kovacs.)

Upon Herod of Chalcis' death in 48/9 CE, his throne was assigned by Claudius to Agrippa II, Herod of Chalcis' nephew and brother-in-law, who shortly gave up that throne to rule his great uncle Herod Philip's former kingdom, more directly connected with his ancestral fortunes. The repetition of names and the assorted inter-marriages amongst the Hasmoneans and Herodians can be confusing. But here is one clarification—Agrippa II was Herod of Chalcis's brother-in-law due to the fact that upon the death of his first wife (and cousin) Mariamne, Herod of Chalcis married Berenice, sister of Agrippa II and his own (much younger) niece!

Herod of Chalcis' son was Aristobulus, the great grandson of Herod I. Aristobulus was married to the infamous Salome, who earlier had danced before Herod Antipas and demanded (at her mother's insistence) the head of John the Baptist. (Aristobulus struck coins with his own portrait on the obverse and Salome's portrait on the reverse, Nos. 1255, 1257a.) As previously mentioned, Salome's first husband was her uncle, Herod Philip, a son of Herod I.

Aristobulus did not succeed to any throne upon his father's death. He had to wait until Claudius died to achieve royalty in his own right. Josephus reports: "In the first year of Nero's reign [54 CE]...the government of Armenia Minor was placed by Nero in the hands of Aristobulus, son of Herod, King of Chalcis."[118] Josephus later mentions "Aristobulus of the region named Chalcidice."[119] Aside from these two

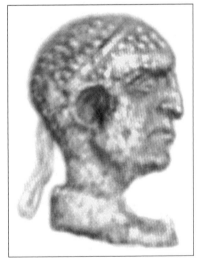

7.10. Images of Herod of Chalcis, left, and Aristobulus of Chalcis recreated from their coins. (Graphic: Fontanille.)

references, we have no additional information from the literary sources even though he ruled for 38 years, until 92 CE.

The final coin struck in Chalcis was dated to 70/1 CE. Aristobulus' coins were issued irregularly. The final year of his reign is deduced from the other coins of Chalcis. The first Roman provincial coins were minted there in 92 CE, and this year seems to have marked the end of the Herodian leader's rule.

Reifenberg also suggests that the last issue of the Aristobulus coins may have been minted by another Aristobulus, the son of this Aristobulus, but "it remains an open question whether he ruled over Chalcis, his grandfather's realm, or whether he was King of the region of Chalcidene." Chalcidene included Armenia Minor and parts of Armenia Major. Reifenberg bases his assignment of dates for Aristobulus upon the fact that the coin in question (No. 1258) mentions Titus instead of Vespasian.

As the history is told by Josephus, however, the revision of the initial date of Aristobulus's reign would render Reifenberg's argument incorrect. Meshorer believes the coin was struck in the year 71 CE. "Although Vespasian, not his son, was the emperor in this year, the appearance of the name of Titus on the coinage is not surprising. This Roman leader was renowned for his victory over the Jewish forces in the war which had just ended."[119]

Recently, Frank Kovacs discovered a coin with portraits of Aristobulus and Salome that is clearly dated to the year 13 (No. 1257a). Kovacs is a long-time student of this series and based on the facts that these coins are extremely rare, generally in poor condition, and the dates consist of similar angular letters, he observed that "the only years that I have found to be clear enough to confirm are 13 and 17. Those reported (with reservations) for years 3 (Γ) and 8 (H) seem most likely to be misreadings of year 13 (IΓ). Since year 13 corresponds to 66/67 CE, the first year of the Jewish War, Aristobulus' coinage makes perfect sense as a show of loyalty to Rome and his patron Nero. The propaganda value of a pro-Roman coinage by a Herodian client king is self-evident in this context. The same applies to Aristobulus' issue in year 17 which corresponds to 70/71 CE, recognizing the new emperor Vespasian and the destruction of the Jerusalem Temple. Thus the issues of Aristobulus appear to have been struck in the context of the Jewish War for propagandistic and political purposes."[119a]

COINS OF HEROD OF CHALCIS
YEAR 3 = 43/4 CE
Border of dots on both sides unless noted.
Axis is ↑.

1251. AE 26 mm.
Obv: ΒΑΣΙΛ. ΗΡΩΔΗΣ. ΒΑΣΙΛ. ΑΓΡΙΠΠΑΣ *(King Herod, King Agrippa)*; in exergue ΚΛΑΥΔΙΟΣ ΚΑΙΣΑΡ ΣΕΒΑΣΤΟΣ *(Claudius Augustus Caesar)*; Claudius stands l. with toga over his head between Agrippa I and his brother Herod of Chalcis, who crown the emperor with a wreath;
Rev: ΚΛΑΥΔΙ ΩΚΑΙΣΑ ΡΙ ΣΕΒΑΣ ΤΩ ΕΤΓ *(for Claudius Caesar Augustus, year 3)*; within a circle and wreath.   5,000/15,000

1252. AE 25 mm.
Obv: ΒΑΣΙΛΕΥΣ ΗΡΩΔΗΣ ΦΙΛΟΚΛΑΥΔΙΟΣ *(King Herod, friend of Claudius)*; diademed bust of Herod of Chalcis to r.
Rev: Same as 1251.   3,000/10,000

1253. AE 20 mm, half-denomination.
Obv: Bust of Herod of Chalcis as 1252.
Rev: Same as 1251.   2,500/8,500

1254. AE 16 mm, quarter-denomination.
Obv: ΒΑΣΙΛΕΥΣ ΗΡΩΔΗC *(King Herod)*; diademed bust of Herod of Chalcis to r.
Rev: ΚΛΑΥ ΔΙΩ ΚΑ ΙΣΑΡΙ *(for Claudius Caesar)* within a wreath.   2,500/8,500

ARISTOBULUS KING OF LESSER ARMENIA
YEAR 3 = 56/7 CE

1255. AE 20 mm.
Obv: BACIΛEΩC APICTOBOYΛOY ET Γ *(of King Aristobulus, year 3)*; diademed bust of Aristobulus to l.
Rev: BACIΛICCHC CAΛΩMHC *(of Queen Salome)*; bust of Salome to l. 7,500/20,000
Aristobulus received his title and kingdom from Nero in 54 CE.

YEAR 8 = 61/2 CE

1256. AE 25 mm.
Obv: BACIΛEΩC APICTOBOYΛOY ET H *(of King Aristobulus, year 8)*; diademed bust of Aristobulus to l.
Rev: NEPΩNIKΛAY ΔIΩKAICA PI CEBACTΩ ΓEPMANIKΩ *(for Nero Claudius Caesar Augustus Germanicus)* within a wreath.
5,000/12,500

YEAR 13 = 66/7 CE

1257. AE 24 mm.
Obv: Same as 1256, but date is ET IΓ *(year 13)*.
Rev: NEPΩ NI KΛAY ΔIΩ KAICA PI CEBAC TΩ ΓEPMANIKΩ *(for Nero Claudius Caesar Augustus Germanicus)* within a wreath. RRR

1257a. AE 21 mm.
Obv: Diademed bust Aristobulus to r. as 1255 but date is ET IΓ.
Rev: Salome bust to l as 1255. RRR

YEAR 17 = 70/1 CE

1258. AE 23 mm.
Obv: Diademed bust of Aristobulus as 1256, date is ET IZ *(year 17)*.
Rev: TITΩ OYECΠA CIANΩ AY TOKPATΩP CEBACT Ω *(for Titus Vespasian Emperor Augustus)* within a wreath. 5,000/12,500

AGRIPPA II, 49/50 TO 94/95 CE

King Agrippa, do you believe in prophets? I know that you do. And Agrippa replied to Paul, In a short time you will persuade me to become a Christian. (ACTS 26:27, 28)

Agrippa II issued the most extensive series of coins struck by a Jewish ruler in Ancient Israel. The coins were struck in five bronze denominations, over more than half a century, at various mints, and based on two major eras and one secondary era. Agrippa II's extensive coinage still holds much to learn and more to be understood.

There is little doubt that Agrippa II, whose full name was Marcus Julius Agrippa, was a full client of Rome and even supported the Romans in battle during the Jewish War. At the time there were three camps among the Jews: the Zealots, the moderates, and the pro-Romans. Besides Agrippa II and his family, one of the most prominent of the moderate party was Rabbi Yochanan Ben Zakkai. Ben Zakkai had his followers smuggle him out of the besieged Jerusalem in a coffin. The famed teacher then received approval from either Vespasian or Titus to open an academy for Jewish learning in Yavne (Jamnia), to the northeast.[121] In Yavne, he formulated the changes in Judaism

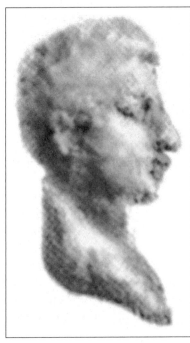

7.11. Young Agrippa II's image recreated from his coins. Graphic: Fontanille.

that enabled it to survive the destruction of the Jerusalem Temple and move forward to become one of the few world religions to flourish for thousands of years.

(It is ironic that if the Jews had won the war against Rome, Ben Zakkai would have never led the movement for Judaism to develop the way it did. Arguably, Judaism would have continued to exist as a Temple cult, based on pilgrimage and animal sacrifice, and would never have evolved into a religion that substituted prayer for sacrifice and the "heavenly" Jerusalem for the "earthly" Jerusalem. One key reason the Jews did not win the war against Rome was that civil war was raging among the Jews themselves. Perhaps if the Jews had won, the civil war coupled with the Jerusalem Temple cult might have prevented Judaism from surviving and thriving, meanwhile other religions and civilizations from that time have become extinct.)

I mention Rabbi Ben Zakkai's story here to underline that Agrippa was not alone in his support of making accommodations with Rome. In effect, the pro-Roman party believed that Roman rule would continue to allow Jewish institutions and teachings to flourish. But, the Zealots (as exemplified by those of Masada) preferred death to being subjugated to Roman rule.

Both sides had defensible viewpoints. In taking the Roman side, one can argue, both Ben Zakkai, who was pro-negotiation, and Agrippa II, who was pro-capitulation, tried to achieve a solution allowing survival of the Jewish people.

When his father Agrippa I died, Agrippa II was about 16 years old. Toward the end of his reign, Agrippa I was involved in some activities that antagonized Rome. Still, he was a favorite of Claudius. Josephus says the emperor was inclined to pass along the kingdom directly to Agrippa II. But, he was persuaded not to delegate the kingship "to one who was quite young and had not even passed out of boyhood, and who would find it impossible to sustain the cares of administration."[122]

The young man was, however, immediately given key responsibilities. For example, Claudius assigned him guardianship of the high priest's robes in Jerusalem.[123] Meanwhile, Claudius again brought the Jewish kingdom under direct Roman rule and sent the procurator Cuspius Fadus to govern in 44 CE. But when Agrippa II's uncle, Herod, King of Chalcis, died in 48 CE, Claudius gave his throne to Agrippa II. In 53 CE, not long before Claudius died, he transferred Agrippa II to a larger kingdom including his great-uncle Philip's former tetrarchy as well as some other areas. The young Agrippa II continued to acquire power in 54 CE, when Nero assigned to him a portion of the Galilee including Tiberias, Tarichaeae, Abila and Livias-Julias.

By that time Agrippa II was around 28 years old, and seemed to have full control over his domain. This phase is marked by the first era mentioned on his coinage, discussed below.

Agrippa II issued more denominations, dated to more years, over a longer period of time than any other Jewish ruler of the Second Temple period. This might lead one to assume that the coins have been more carefully studied and better understood than any other group. Quite the contrary is true. More questions exist surrounding the coins of Agrippa II than any other section of the ancient Judaean series; for example, we are not certain of the mints, the dating eras, and, like all ancient Judaean coins we are not even certain of the denominations.

These subjects have been discussed since Madden's 1864 work,[124] with various views prevailing at different times. Interestingly, Kanael's seminal article of 1963 dismissed the coins of Agrippa II in a sweeping paragraph:

"Agrippa's son, Agrippa II, ruled for some fifty tedious years, surviving by some thirty years the destruction of the Temple in Jerusalem. As a client king of the Romans, he took part in the war against his own nation. His coins are undistinguished…. His coins under the Flavians usually feature a tedious repetition of the Emperor's head on the obverse, and a heathen goddess, Tyche (Fortuna) or Nike (Victory) on the reverse."[125] Barag also contributed to this discussion.[126]

Meshorer focused on various eras, types, denominations, and mints, but was not successful in solving all of the problems.[127] The leading expert on Agrippa II's coins is Alla Kushnir-Stein. She has devoted years to the solution of the numismatic/historical problems in the Agrippa II series.[128] In this section we will review the most relevant information, but will not include detailed arguments from every point of view.

AGRIPPA'S PRE-ROYAL COINAGE

During the years before his first royal coin was struck—49 to 60/1 CE—Agrippa II became the most important and influential Jewish personality in the Roman world.

From around 48/9 CE (when he took control of Chalcis) until around 67/8 CE (when he issued the first dated coin with his own royal title) a series of provincial bronze coins were struck at Tiberias and at mints believed to be Caesarea Paneas and Caesarea Maritima. These coins continue the tradition of Agrippa I and each depicts one or more members of Agrippa's friends and allies in the imperial family of Rome, with the exception of the coins struck at Tiberias. These coins resemble the coins of Antipas and carry both the date and name of mint (Nos. 1266–68). Although none of these coins refer to Agrippa II by name, we know that he had clear and growing responsibilities over at least some of these areas. It is logical to suggest that these were early coins under his authority. Kushnir-Stein argues that these may have been issued by the Roman procurators or perhaps that they were city coins.[129] Meshorer, on the other hand, suggests attribution of this group to the Roman administration under Agrippa II. His suggestion is based "on numismatic and historical data, after an increase in the number of Land of Israel coins in the possession of scholars within a specified area of distribution." This, then, may well be the series that led up to Agrippa II's first royal coinage.

During the years these coins were struck, the former territories of Agrippa I were governed by Roman procurators or legates of Syria. While Agrippa II was gaining an increasingly powerful position in these territories, it is possible that he controlled mints outside of Jerusalem, although he was not yet in a position to issue coins with his own name on them. The coins minted at Tiberias resemble those of Agrippa II's great uncle Antipas, while the others are similar to Roman provincial coins, except that some use Latin rather than Greek legends. None of these coins bear any similarities to the coins of the Roman procurators of Judaea and it seems likely that Agrippa II had a hand in these coins, which we attribute to the Roman Administration of the territories during Agrippa II's pre-royal period.

Daniel Schwartz notes that when Agrippa I returned to Judaea in the late 20s CE, one of his early positions was as *agoranomos* of Tiberias, his uncle Herod Antipas' capital, where young Agrippa supervised the markets, weight standards, and related matters.[130] Qedar published several lead market weights used by first century *agoranomoi* in Tiberias, several of them specifically referring to Herodian family members.[131] Thus it is also possible that Agrippa II filled a similar position as a young man, and could have been responsible for this nonspecific Roman provincial coinage.

ERAS OF AGRIPPA II

Among the great enigmas of Jewish numismatics have been the eras of the coins of Agrippa II. Even though the vast majority of his coins carry dates, it has not been easy for scholars to understand the relative dating of these eras. Two basic problems exist. First, two coins of Agrippa II are dated according to two distinct systems (Nos. 1278, 1279) on the same coins. If those two dating eras are applied to all of Agrippa II's coins as the principal eras, however, an illogical picture emerges.

Scholars, therefore, have long attempted to understand the dating of Agrippa II's coins, and there has been a general conclusion that multiple eras exist. In an attempt to solve this, Madden, in 1864, suggested four different dating eras that applied to Agrippa II's coins. Meshorer suggested two eras, beginning in 55 and 60 CE. Kushnir-Stein's monumental work on this subject brings us to the conclusion that multiple eras are indeed appropriate for the coins of Agrippa II, and she has quantified them. She also concludes that "Coins dated by two different eras could have hardly been produced in the same place simultaneously,"[132] which means that different mints operated and produced similar coins at the same time, but they were dated according to different regnal eras.

Kushnir-Stein believes that Agrippa II's most logical era began in the year 49, "mentioned by Josephus in *BJ* 2.284. Josephus says that the Jewish revolt began in the twelfth year of Nero and the seventeenth year of Agrippa, in the month of Artemisos. This means the spring of 66. Seyrig has [also] shown that the starting point of Agrippa's era is the autumn of 49." She adds that "Since one of the anachronistic coins features Pan, the tutelary deity of Caesarea Paneas, the era of 49 must belong to this city."[133]

This leads us back to Agrippa II's two rare double-dated coins, which belong to this series. They both carry reverse inscriptions proclaiming "year 11 which is also year 6." One coin was apparently struck in 60 CE, and thus corresponds to the era of 49 combined with a secondary local era of 54 CE. Kushnir-Stein explains: "When Agrippa was appointed king over Chalcis, there must have been a counting by his regnal years which started in 49/50. Josephus reports that, several years later, Claudius took Chalcis away from Agrippa, but gave him instead the former territories of Philip, Lysanias and Varus. When he moved into these new territories Agrippa may well have retained his earlier era, with an additional era, marking the beginning of his actual rule in these territories, being introduced as well." It seems, then, that the small double-dated issues were the earliest coins bearing Agrippa II's royal title, and the only coins referring to both the eras beginning in 49 CE and 54 CE with the possible exception of No. 1280 which also seems to have been dated according to the era of 54 CE.

Kushnir-Stein further concludes that Agrippa II's second major era began in 60/1, but "We do not know what exactly happened in the year 60/1," although she suggests it might have been "a further enlargement of Agrippa's kingdom by Nero."[134] If that was the case, "the coins of Agrippa dated by the era of 60 CE could thus have been struck in a place which came under his control in 60/1 CE.... Agrippa's father struck coins in Caesarea Paneas, Jerusalem, and Caesarea Maritima."[135]

AGRIPPA II'S FLAVIAN COINAGE ACCORDING TO THE ERAS OF 49 AND 60 CE

ERA OF 49 CE	TYCHE	NIKE WREATH	NIKE SHIELD	OTHER	JULIAN YEAR	TYCHE	NIKE WREATH	NIKE SHIELD	OTHER	ERA OF 60 CE
6/11					60/1					
--					73/4	V	T	D		14
26	V	T	D	T/D MED.	74/5	V		D		15
27	V	T	D	T/D MED V MED 2 CORNUC.	75/6					--
29	V	T	D		77/8	V	T	D		18
30	T				78/9	T		D	SHIP, JULIA	19
34				TYCHE/ CORNUC.	83/4					--
35				WREATH	84/5		D(G)	D(G)	WREATH	24
					85/6			D(G)	COS X	25
					86/7		D(G)		COS XII	26
					93/4	D(G)				29

7.11. V=Vespasian; T=Titus; D=Domitian without titles; D(G)=Domitian with Germanicus title; Med. = Medallion. Coins dated year 35 could have been struck according to the era of 60. Table modified after Kushnir-Stein (2002).

Agrippa II's first mint has been established to be Caesarea Paneas based upon use of the Pan motif on early coins of the Flavian series from the era of 49 CE; he never controlled Jerusalem. It seems likely, but unproven, that Caesarea Maritima was the mint that struck coins according to the era of 60 CE.

Agrippa II's coins follow clear patterns. He struck coins in four basic denominations—the full unit, half-unit, quarter-unit, and eighth-unit. There are also two types of commemorative medallions (Nos. 1281, 1287) which are larger than the full units and carry different reverse motifs. One type depicts Pan with dual obverse portraits of Titus and Domitian and the second depicts a portrait of Vespasian with a reverse showing Tyche-Fortuna holding a rudder on a globe. The globe on ancient coins generally represents the sphere of the heavens.

We also note that Agrippa II's coins with Latin legends have other traits that make them stand out, including the axis which is 6 o'clock, similar to the Roman Imperial coins, as opposed to 12 o'clock, characteristic of provincial coins, on the other Flavian issues. It has been suggested that the Latin series may have been struck in Rome,[136] but it is also possible that the dies were made in Rome and sent to Judaea for final manufacture, which used locked die equipment set in the Roman style regarding the axis.

Agrippa II's Flavian coins for the most part also follow a specific pattern of obverse-reverse combinations. The largest coins generally carry Vespasian's portrait and a Tyche reverse; the second denomination carries Titus' portrait and a Nike (Victory) carrying a wreath reverse; the third denomination portrays Domitian and a reverse with Nike supporting a shield on her knee, and the fourth denomination carries portraits of Domitian or Tyche with legend or cornucopia reverses.

The necessity of assigning multiple eras to the coins of Agrippa II can be seen when one compares, for example, the series dated year 18 (Nos. 1307–09) and the series dated year 29 (Nos. 1292–94). The coins with these dates follow the pattern of types discussed above. Furthermore, obverse inscriptions naming the rulers are the same. One must, therefore, wonder how these coins could both be struck according to the same era considering these scenarios: If, for example, they were struck according to the era of 49 CE, when Agrippa II assumed his first royal position, the year 18 coins would have been struck in 66/7 CE and the year 29 coins would have been struck in 77/8 CE. Since Vespasian only became emperor in 69, however, this era would be impossible. On the other hand, if Agrippa II's dating era began in 60 CE, the year 18 coins would have been struck in 77/8 CE and the year 29 coins would have been struck in 88/9 CE. It is unlikely that Vespasian would have been portrayed as emperor some ten years after his death, but with the same legend as when he was alive.

The recognition of these two major eras and one secondary era solve a number of problems in the dating of coins of Agrippa, although they still may not fit perfectly. This is an area for further study and discussion, and one hopes that evidence from controlled archaeological excavations might shed additional light.

AGRIPPA II UNDER NERO

Meshorer believes that Agrippa II's next series consisted of the two coins issued at Sepphoris that "impressively reflect the political situation at that time. His name does not appear on the two coin types, and only the name of Sepphoris is mentioned on them. However, it is absolutely clear that he was behind the minting..."[137] Josephus explained that at this time "Sepphoris, by submission to Rome, had forthwith become the capital of Galilee, and the seat of the royal bank and the archives."[138] This was then a movement of the main bank, and we can assume mint, from a city of rebels to a place that received the Romans happily. In fact, the reverse legend on these coins (Nos. 1276, 1277) reads, "in the days of Vespasian in Neronias-Sepphoris city of peace."

A second group of coins was struck by Agrippa II referring to Nero, this time with his portrait. All three denominations of this type (Nos. 1273–75) carry the inscription "Caesarea which is also Neronias." Also, one double dated coin (No. 1278) carries an inscription "Caesarea which is also Neronias." It was Agrippa II's great-uncle Herod Philip who gave Paneas the name "Caesarea" and then Agrippa II added "Neronias" to it.[139]

Neronias, as a city name, did not last, "since immediately after Nero's murder the Roman Senate ruled on *damnatio memoriae*, an act intended to blot out his name and memory. All the acts of commemoration carried out in his honor during his lifetime were annulled including the naming of places after him. The name Neronias, which was added to Paneas and Sepphoris, thus vanished soon after its appearance."[140]

The Sepphoris coins, and quite possibly the Nero portrait coins, were both minted in 66/7 CE, the first year of the Jewish War and when Agrippa II took the Roman side during the Jewish war, and gained their full support. Other mints at cities that also welcomed the Romans struck coins for the same political reasons. They include Caesarea Maritima, Beit Shean (Nysa-Scythopolis), Gerasa, Dora, and Hippos.[141]

JUDAEA CAPTA ISSUES OF AGRIPPA II

After the double-dated coins, there were no additional issues for almost seven years. This gap can probably be attributed to the Jewish War. Indeed, the year minting resumed, 73/4 CE, was the year following the fall of Masada in 73 CE.

Not only did Agrippa support the Roman position during the Jewish War, but he actively assisted the Romans. When some of Agrippa's Jewish subjects joined in the revolt, he sent forces to besiege Gamla, where his troops were not succesful. When Vespasian's army arrived, Agrippa's forces continued to support the Romans in controlling Tiberias and again besieging Gamla, during which Agrippa himself was slightly wounded.[142]

Meshorer notes, "Only following the end of the conflict, when life under the new political situation achieved some stability, did the Jewish king mint coins honoring the three Flavians."[143]

Among the most interesting aspects of Agrippa II's coinage, which seems to have been largely overlooked, is that from the first year of this series, the coins commemorate not only the Emperor Vespasian, but both his sons Titus and Domitian. This characteristic is noteworthy because of the lengths to which some researchers have gone to underscore their beliefs that Domitian did not participate in the Jewish War, and thus never referenced it on his coinage.[144]

Historic evidence indeed shows that Domitian did not visit Judaea, as did Titus. Nevertheless, Domitian was Vespasian's second son, and as such he lent political and other support back in Rome. Josephus tells us that Domitian rode a white horse during the famous victory procession, commemorated on the Arch of Titus, which was built by Domitian.

So if Domitian was so far removed, why was he commemorated on coins by Agrippa II long before it was even known that he would become emperor? The only answer may be that he really was sufficiently politically involved to warrant it. This position has significant bearing on the series of coins struck in Palestine under Domitian, and this is discussed further in Chapter 11.

Consider the coins that depict Nike walking to the right and holding both a wreath and a palm branch. Nike corresponds to Victory, and this seems to refer to Rome's defeat of Agrippa II's own Jewish people. Meshorer suggests that, "Agrippa II was both a devout Jew and a loyal vassal of Rome. He would not have desired to arouse the antagonism of either side. Consequently, it is probable that the depiction of Nike on his coinage denotes no particular historical event."[145]

However, this argument can be disputed in light of the fact that most of the quarter-unit coins depict Nike once again. This time, Nike is writing on a shield and the type bears a striking resemblance to local Judaea Capta issues struck under Vespasian and Titus (Nos. 1445–47). In fact one locally issued Judaea Capta coin of Titus (No. 1448) depicts Nike with shield on knee, without a palm tree, virtually identical to the Agrippa II issues. Israeli numismatist Dan Barag agrees that this image relates to the Judaea Capta series.[146] Meshorer rules that out because all of Agrippa II's coins with this reverse depict obverse portraits of Domitian.

It seems improbable that the people who handled these coins daily could have to applied any other meaning to the use of Nike/Victory on Agrippa II's coins than a reference to Rome's recent victory. After all, it was the victory of Rome over the Jews that allowed Agrippa II to retain his kingship. The fact that he was a vassal of Rome does not mitigate some loyalty to the Jewish tradition. At the end of Agrippa's speech to the Jewish people, pleading with them to avoid war, he wept when he said: "Take pity, then, if not on your children and your wives, at least on your mother city and its sacred precincts. Spare the Temple and preserve...the sanctuary with its holy places.... I call your sanctuary and God's holy angels and our common country to witness, that I have kept back nothing which could conduce to your preservation..."[147]

Further proof that Agrippa II did not hesitate to commemorate the Roman victory over the Jews on his coins can be found in a coin explained by Shraga Qedar (No. 1280). This bronze coin was struck in 69/70 CE in Tiberias. On the obverse, around a palm branch, it carries the legend NIK[H] CEB[ACTOY]. This is the Greek translation of VICTORIA AVGVSTI and was certainly a tribute to the Roman victory over the Jews. This coin was no doubt Agrippa II's official proclamation of the victory of Rome in the Jewish War.[148]

The eighth-unit coins and the sixteenth-unit coins of Agrippa II depict various motifs, including palm tree, cornucopia, anchor, and simple inscriptions within a wreath.

AGRIPPA, BERENICE, AND TITUS

Agrippa II had two sisters. The first, Drusilla, married Aziz, king of Emisa, and later married Antonius Felix, procurator of Judaea. His other sister, Berenice III, was perhaps one of the most fascinating personalities in Judaea during the first century. Although she is not well known outside of scholarly circles, Berenice had three notable husbands, almost became Empress of Rome, and reigned as queen alongside her brother Agrippa, as confirmed in a first century Latin inscription from Beirut. The inscription commemorates the restoration of a building by "Queen Berenice" and "King Agrippa II." [149] Another inscription from this period in Athens honors her as "great" queen.[150]

Berenice was born in about 28 CE, one of the five children of Agrippa I and Cypros (the first cousin he married). Berenice was a great-granddaughter of Herod I. When she was about 15 years old, she married Marcus Julius Alexander, nephew of the Alexandrian Jewish philosopher, Philo, and the son of Alexander, alabarch of Egypt. Her brother-in-law through this marriage was the apostate Jew Tiberius Julius Alexander, who became procurator of Judaea, prefect of Egypt, and one of Titus's staff generals during the siege of Jerusalem.

When Marcus died, Berenice married her uncle, Herod, king of Chalcis. When he died around 48 CE, Berenice was once again a widow, now with two small sons. She went to stay with her brother, who already succeeded her husband as king in the northern territories.

Brother and sister lived under the same roof and Berenice presided over the royal court. The situation gave rise to speculation that they were engaged in an incestuous relationship. Emil Schürer relates that Berenice "soon had the weak man completely caught in the meshes of her net, so that regarding her, the mother of two children, the vilest stories became current. When the scandal became public, Berenice, in order to cut away occasion for all evil reports, resolved to marry Polemo of Cilicia, who, for this purpose, was obliged to submit to be circumcised. She did not, however, continue long with him, but came back again to her brother, and seems to have resumed her old relations with him. At least this somewhat later came to be the common talk of Rome."[151]

Berenice is mentioned by name in the book of Acts (25:13–26:32), where she is with Agrippa, although not identified as his sister, it is clearly the same person. In this narrative, taking place around 60 CE, Agrippa and Berenice hear Paul's defense in front of the procurator Antonius Felix, and pronounce him blameless.

"And the king arose and the governor and Berenice, and those who were sitting with them, and when they had drawn aside they began talking to one another, saying, 'This man is not doing anything worthy of death or imprisonment.'"[152]

When the Jewish War against Rome began in 66, Berenice was in Jerusalem fulfilling a Nazarite vow she made when she had been ill. The procurator Gessius Florus had become enraged because a group of Jews had mocked him by begging on street corners, pretending to raise money for the "poor Florus." His troops began a wanton killing spree, plundering Jerusalem's markets. Berenice became a popular heroine when she risked her life to intercede against Florus's violence. Josephus relates: "... Berenice...who was at Jerusalem, witnessed with the liveliest emotion the outrages of the soldiers, and constantly sent her cavalry-commanders and bodyguards to Florus to implore him to put a stop to the carnage. But he, regarding neither the number of the slain nor the exalted rank of his suppliant, but only the profit accruing from the plunder, turned a deaf ear to her prayers. The mad rage of the soldiers even vented itself upon the queen. Not only did they torture and put their captives to death under her eyes, but they would have killed her also, had she not hastened to seek refuge in the palace, where she passed the night surrounded by guards, dreading an attack of the troops. She was visiting Jerusalem to discharge a vow to God; for it is customary for those suffering from illness or other affliction to make a vow to abstain from wine and to shave their heads during the thirty days preceding that on which they must offer sacrifices. These rites Berenice was then undergoing, and she would come barefoot before the tribunal and make supplication to Florus, without any respect being shown to her, and even at the peril of her life."[153]

As a result of the violence, Florus, Berenice, and the Sanhedrin sent reports to the governor Cestius Gallus about what was going on in Jerusalem. Gallus sent one of his officers to Judaea to determine which stories were accurate. Gallus' tribune, Neapolitanus, was a good diplomat and "satisfied himself as to the amenable temper" of the Jews.

Then he went up to the Temple and "called the multitude together, highly commended them for their loyalty to the Romans and earnestly exhorted them to keep the peace; then, after paying his devotions to the sanctuary of God from the permitted area, he returned to Cestius."[154]

Shortly after this, Berenice stood at her brother's side when he made an eloquent speech pleading with his fellow Jews to avoid battle with Rome. But, when Cestius Gallus and his army marched on Jerusalem, she went to his camp along with her brother Agrippa.

According to Mary Smallwood, Titus and Berenice probably "first met in the summer of 67, when Vespasian and his son visited Agrippa's court at Caesarea Philippi for a brief rest after the siege of Jotapata."[155] Berenice, now 39, was said to be more beautiful than ever. The Roman historian Tacitus said "It is quite true that she attracted the young man [Titus], but practical efficiency never suffered from this."[156]

This initial relationship was short-lived, since Titus was recalled to Rome to support his father, now emperor. Berenice took the opportunity to make a generous gift to Vespasian. Tacitus reports that "she was in her best years and at the height of her beauty, while even the elderly Vespasian appreciated her generosity."[157]

Titus and Berenice may not have seen each other again until Agrippa and Berenice made a state visit to Rome in 75. At this time, Agrippa "was given the rank of praetor, while she dwelt in the palace, cohabiting with Titus. She expected to marry him and was already behaving in every respect as if she were his wife."[158] Suetonius even talks of a promise by Titus to marry Berenice. But, as Smallwood notes, "Whether Titus with his knowledge of Roman prejudices took the same view of the situation is another matter. An oriental mistress might be tolerated where an oriental wife, and a Jewess at that, would not...."[159] Whatever the specifics, the politics of Rome clearly opposed this relationship and Titus, caved to the public pressure, and sent her back to Judaea.

However, after Vespasian's death, in 79 CE, Agrippa and Berenice sailed back to Rome where they hoped, now that Titus was emperor, he would be allowed to choose his own wife. This journey was commemorated on two coins of Agrippa II struck in 79 and portraying galleys on their reverses (Nos. 1311, 1312).

Coin 1314 depicts a veiled female portrait on its obverse. This portrait is sometimes suggested to be Livia, but Jacob Maltiel-Gerstenfeld suggests that this is actually a portrait of Berenice, and was struck "in anticipation of the forthcoming marriage and elevation of Berenice to the status of **CEBACTH** (Augusta). One may further conjecture that the anchor on the reverse hints at Berenice's voyage by sea to Rome."[160] While some have argued against this identification of the portrait as Berenice, no evidence points to a more likely candidate, and this coin is dated to the same year as the galley issues. The brother-and-sister voyage ended in disappointment. Smallwood observes, "Popularity was now all-important to Titus, and private feelings had to take second place. He had to dismiss her again immediately."[161] In the words of Suetonius, "He sent Queen Berenice away from Rome, which was painful for both of them."[162]

MINTS OF AGRIPPA II

Agrippa II ordered coins to be struck in at least four different mints throughout his territories. Some of these mints operated while Agrippa II was in various positions of power, but before he received the royal title, his precise involvement is not certain. Others operated after he became king. Some mints produced coins during both periods.

The use of a number of coin mints throughout his territories was a necessary step for Agrippa II. As far as we know, the Hasmonean kings minted mainly in or around Jerusalem. Remains of what was apparently a Hasmonean mint were uncovered in excavations at the Citadel in Jerusalem.[163] Herod I also probably minted in or near Jerusalem, although large numbers of his coins are also found near Sebaste as well as Jericho. This suggests that more than one mint may have existed.

With the sons of Herod I, we can trace new mints in the ancient land of Israel. Archelaus, ethnarch of Judaea and Samaria, probably minted coins just where his father did, since the fabric and types of the coins are similar.

Antipas's first capital was Sepphoris, where he minted small coins which may have only been prototypes.[164] Later, he established a mint at Tiberias, his second capital, built on the Sea of Galilee after the death of Augustus.

Philip, Herod's third son, ruled over territories farther to the north and minted coins at his capital of Paneas, also called Caesarea Philippi.

Herod's grandson, Agrippa I, struck coins at Paneas, Tiberias and Jerusalem. He also struck coins at Caesarea, which had already become the seat of power for the Roman governors of the area, also known as the Roman governors (prefects and procurators).

PRE-ROYAL COINS OF AGRIPPA II
STRUCK UNDER CLAUDIUS
MINT OF CAESAREA PANEAS
Border of dots both sides unless noted.
Axis is ↑ unless noted.

1259.   AE 23 mm.
    Obv: TI CLAVDIVS CAESAR AVG PM TR P IMP PP; laureate
       head of Claudius to l.
    Rev: ANTONIA BRITANNICVS OCTAVIA; Brittanicus flanked by
       Antonia, on l., and Octavia (the three children of Claudius), each
       holds a cornucopia.   1,500/4,000

1260.   AE 18 mm.
    Obv: TI CLAVDIVS CAESAR AVG PM TR IM PP; laureate head of
       Claudius to r.
    Rev: BRITANNICVS AVG; bare head of Brittanicus to r.
                                    750/2,000

1261.   AE 13 mm.
    Obv: BRITANNICVS AVG F; Bare head of Brittanicus to r.
    Rev: SC within wreath.   350/1,000

MINT OF CAESAREA MARITIMA

1262.   AE 26 mm.
    Obv: TI CLAVDIVS CAESAR AVG P M TR P IM PP; laureate head
       of Claudius to r.
    Rev: Rudder within wreath.   850/2,500

1263.   AE 23 mm.
    Obv: TI CLAVDIVS CAESAR AVG P M TR P IM PP; laureate head
       of Claudius to r.
    Rev: Inverted anchor within wreath.   300/1,000

1264.   AE 24 mm.
    Obv: ...KΛAY IOC...; laureate head of Claudius to r.;
    Rev: OB CS in wreath.   350/1,250

1265. AE 24 mm.
Obv: Laureate head of Claudius as 1264.
Rev: ΑΓΡΙΠΠΕΙΝΗΣ ΣΕΒΑΣΤΗΣ; *(of Agrippina Augusta)* veiled Agrippina II (mother of Nero), seated l., holds branch and cornucopia, crescent above head.

400/1,250

a. With countermark XF of Tenth Legion on obverse.

ERA OF CLAUDIUS
MINT OF TIBERIAS
YEAR 13, 53/4 CE

1266. AE 22 mm.
Obv: TIBE PIAC *(Tiberias)* within a wreath.
Rev: ΚΛΑΥΔΙΟΥ ΚΑΙCΑΡΟC *(of Claudius Caesar)*; L IΓ *(year 13)* in fields; palm branch upright.

300/900

1267. AE 18 mm, half-denomination.
Obv: TIBE PIAC within a wreath.
Rev: Palm branch upright as 1266.

250/650

1268. AE 14 mm, quarter-denomination.
Obv: TIBE PIAC within a wreath.
Rev: Palm branch upright as 1266.

200/500

STRUCK UNDER NERO
MINT OF CAESAREA PANEAS

1269 1270

1269. AE 18 mm.
Obv: AGRIPPIN AVG; Agrippina II (mother of Nero) seated l. holds branch and cornucopia.
Rev: OCTAVIA AVGVSTI; Veiled Octavia (wife of Nero) standing l., holds patera over flaming altar.

600/2,000

1270. AE 18 mm.

Obv: DIVA POPPAEA AVG; distyle temple, female figure seated l. within.

Rev: DIVA CLAVD NER F; round hexastyle temple, female figure stands l. within, holds cornucopia.   350/750

This is the only coin issued in the name of Claudia, Nero's daughter who died in infancy in 63 CE.

MINT OF CAESAREA MARITIMA

1271. AE 23 mm.

Obv: ΝΕΡΩΝΟΣ ΚΛΑΥΔΙΟΥ ΓΕΡΜΑΝΙΚΟΥ ΚΑΙΣΑΡΟΣ ΣΕ *(Nero Claudius Germanicus Caesar)*; laureate, slightly draped bust of Nero to r.

Rev: ΑΓΡΙΠΠΕΙΝΗΣ ΣΕΒΑΣΤΗΣ; veiled Agrippina II, seated l., holds branch and cornucopia, crescent above head.

                    500/1,500

a. With X or XF countermark of the Tenth Roman Legion on obverse.

1272

1272. AE 19 mm.

Obv: ΝΕΡΩΝΟΣ ΣΕΒΑΣΤΟΥ ΚΑΙΣΑΡΟΣ *(Nero Caesar Augustus)*; laureate, draped bust Nero to r.

Rev: ΑΓΡΙΠΠΕΙΝΗΣ ΣΕΒΑΣΤΗΣ; draped bust Agrippina II bust to l.   750/2,000

COINS OF AGRIPPA II AS KING
MINT OF CAESAREA PANEAS
STRUCK UNDER NERO

1273. AE 23 mm, full denomination.
Obv: ΝΕΡΩΝ ΚΑΙΣΑΡ ΣΕΒΑΣΤΟΥ *(of Nero Caesar Augustus)*; laureate bust of Nero to r., lituus in front of face.
Rev: ΕΠΙ ΒΑΣΙΛΕ ΑΓΡΙΠΠ ΝΕΡΩ ΝΙΕ *(in the time of King Agrippa, Neronias)*; within a circle and wreath.   200/550
This coin and the following two coins were issued to commemorate Agrippa's refounding of Caesarea Paneas as Neronias. It was once believed that the IE in the reverse legend referred to a date but this is not the case, instead it is the abbreviation for the name of the mint city Neronias.
1274. AE 18 mm, half-denomination.
Obv: Laureate bust of Nero as on 1273.
Rev: As 1273.   150/500

1275

1275. AE 14 mm, quarter-denomination.
Obv: Laureate bust of Nero as on 1273.
Rev: As 1273.   150/400

MINT OF SEPPHORIS (NERONIAS)
ERA OF NERO
YEAR 14 = 67/8 CE

1276. AE 24 mm.
Obv: ΕΠΙ ΟΥΕΣΠΑΣΙΑΝΟΥ ΕΙΡΗΝΟΠΟΛΙ ΝΕΡΩΝΙΑ ΣΕΡΠΦΩ *(in the time of Vespasian, in Irenopolis-Neronias-Sepphoris)*; two cornucopias crossed, caduceus between them.
Rev: ΛΔΙ ΝΕΡΩΝ ΚΛΑΥΔΙΟΥ ΚΑΙΣΑΡΟ C *(year 14 of Nero Claudius Caesar)* within circle and wreath.   300/1,000
This coin names Vespasian while he was still a general under Nero. It also refers to Sepphoris as "Neronias" in honor of the emperor, and as an "Irenopolis" or "City of Peace."

1276

1277. AE 20 mm.
Obv: ΕΠΙ ΟΥΕϹΠΑϹΙΑΝΟΥ ΕΙΡΗΝΟΠΟΛΙ ΝΕΡΩΝΙΑϹ ϹΕΠΦΩΡ; large SC.
Rev: Same as 1276.   500/1,750

Meshorer believed that the two coins above belonged in the Agrippa II series. Kushnir-Stein, on the other hand, believes they are city coins of Sepphoris. Since these would be the earliest coins of Sepphoris by quite some years, and no further coins were minted at Sepphoris until Trajan was emperor, I believe it was possible that Agrippa II was involved in the coinage.

ERAS BEGINNING 49 AND 54 CE
YEAR 11 WHICH IS ALSO YEAR 6, 60/1 CE

1278

1279

1278. AE 15 mm.
Obv: ΚΑΙϹΑΡΙΑ ΤΗ ΚΑΙ ΝΕΡΩΝΙΑΔΙ *(for Caesarea which is also Neronias)*; turreted bust of Tyche to r.
Rev: ΒΑϹ ΑΓΡ ΕΤΟΥϹ ΑΙ ΤΟΥ ΚΑΙ ⋉*(year 11 which is also year 6 of King Agrippa)*; double cornucopias crossed at base with winged caduceus arising between horns.   1,750/5,000

1279. AE 13 mm.
Obv: ΒΑϹΙΛΙΕΩϹ ΜΑΡΚΟΥ ΑΓΡΙΠΠΟΥ *(of King Marcus Agrippa)*; hand r., holding ears of barley and fruit.
Rev: ΕΤΟΥϹ ΑΙ ΤΟΥ *(year 11)* surrounding monogram ⋉ a combination of K for ΚΑΙ with ⋉*(year 6)*, all within diadem.
                                                                600/1,750

MINT OF TIBERIAS
ERA BEGINNING 54 CE
YEAR 15, 69/70 CE

1280. AE 18 mm
  Obv: ΒΑ ΑΓΡΙΠΑ ΝΙΚ ϹΕΒ *(King Agrippa, victory of Augustus);* ΕΤ ΙΕ
  (year 15) across fields; palm branch upright.
  Rev: ΤΙΒΕ ΡΙΑϹ within a wreath.   600/1,750
  *It has also been suggested that this coin might have been struck according to
  the era beginning in 60 CE, and thus dating to 74/75. In the first case, the coin
  would have been struck just after the Jewish War ended, and, in the second case,
  it would have been struck in the year after the absolute end of the war when
  Masada fell in 73 CE. In either case, the iconography, reflecting both the coins
  of Herod Antipas and the pre-royal issues of Agrippa II struck in Tiberias,
  suggests that this is a reference to the victory of Agrippa's Roman allies in the
  Jewish War.*

AGRIPPA II UNDER FLAVIAN RULE
MINT OF CAESAREA PANEAS
ERA BEGINNING 49 CE
YEAR 26, 74/5 CE

1281. AE medallion, 35 mm.
  Obv: ΑΥΤΟΚΡΑ • ΤΙΤΟϹ • ΚΑΙϹΑΡ • ΔΟΜΙΤΙΑΝΟϹ *(Emperor Titus Caesar Domitian);* confronted laureate busts of Titus, wearing
  paludamentum and cuirass decorated with gorgon head on l.,
  and Domitian, draped and with globe at point of neck on r.
  Rev: ΒΑϹΙΛΕΩϹ • ΑΓΡΙΠΠΑϹ • ΕΤΟΥϹ • ΚϹ • *(of King Agrippa
  year 26);* Pan walks l., playing pipes *(syrinx)* held in r. hand and
  pedum over l. shoulder, tree trunk on r.   UNIQUE
  *This coin, discovered late in 2009, is of great significance, since it estab-
  lishes the identification of the mint of Caesarea Paneas during the first year
  Flavian coinage was struck there. Previously only smaller module (c. 30 mm)
  coins, with simple busts of Titus and Domitian. were known (No. 1286). This
  coin seems to have been an inaugural medallion of Agrippa II's mint for Flavian coinage in Paneas. It is also noteworthy that Agrippa chose to honor the
  sons of the emperor on this issue.[165]*

1282

1282. AE 27 mm.

Obv: ΑΥΤΟΚΡΑ ΟΥΕΣΠΑΣΙ ΚΑΙΣΑΡ ΣΕΒΑΣΤΩ *(for Emperor Vespasian Caesar Augustus)*; laureate bust of Vespasian to r.

Rev: ΕΤΟΥ ΚΣ ΒΑ ΑΓΡΙ ΠΠΑ *(year 26, King Agrippa)* in fields; Tyche-Demeter stands l. wearing kalathos, holding grain ears in r. hand and cornucopia in l.   300/900

   a. Irregular, crude issue.

1283. AE 28 mm.

Obv: Bust of Vespasian as on 1282.

Rev: Tyche-Demeter as on 1282, but inscription all around instead of across fields.   350/900

1284a   1285c

1284. AE 27 mm.

Obv: ΑΥΤΟΚΡ ΤΙΤΟΣ ΚΑΙΣΑΡ ΣΕΒΑΣ *(Emperor Titus Caesar Augustus)*; laureate, draped and cuirassed bust of Titus to r.

Rev: ΕΤΟ ΚΣ ΒΑ ΑΓΡΙ ΠΠΑ *(year 15, King Agrippa)* across fields; Nike-Victory advances r., holds wreath in r. hand and palm branch over shoulder in l.   200/500

   a. Titus laureate, undraped, star in upper r. reverse field.

   b. Crescent in upper r. reverse field.

1285. AE 20 mm.

Obv: ΔΟΜΙΤ ΚΑΙCΑΡ *(Domitian Caesar)*; laureate bust of Domitian to r.

Rev: ET KS BACI ΑΓΡΙ ΠΠΑ *(year 26, King Agrippa)*; Nike-Victory stands r., l. foot on helmet, writes on shield which rests on her l. knee;   150/500

a. Star upper r. reverse field.

b. Crescent upper r. reverse field.

c. Countermarks of standing figure and head on obverse.

STRUCK YEAR 27, 75/7 CE

1286. AE 30 mm.

Obv: ΑΥΤΟΚΡΑ ΚΑΙCΑΡ ΤΙΤΟC ΚΑΙ ΔΟΜΙΤΙΑΝΟC *(Emperors Caesar Titus and Domitian)*; confronted laureate busts of Titus on l. and Domitian on r.

Rev: ΒΑCΙΛΕΩC ΑΓΡΙΠΠΑ ΕΤΟΥC ΚΖ; Pan walks l., playing pipes *(syrinx)* held in r. hand and holds *pedum* over l. shoulder, tree trunk on r., small crescent in upper l. field.   500/1,500

This coin copies the inaugural medallion struck in year 26 (No. 1279), but the Imperial portraits are less adorned, and it is struck upon a smaller flan.

1287. AE 34 mm, medallion.

Obv: ΑΥΤΟΚΡΑ ΟΥΕCΠΑCΙΑΝΩ ΚΑΙCΑΡΙ CΕΒΑCΤΩ *(for Emperor Vespasian Caesar Augustus)*; laureate, slightly draped bust of Vespasian to r.

Rev: ΒΑCΙΛΕΩC ΑΓΡΙΠΠΑ–ΕΤΟΥC ΚΖ *(of King Agrippa, year 27)*; Pan walks l., playing pipes (syrinx) held in r. hand and holds pedum over l. shoulder, tree trunk on r., small crescent in upper l. field.   1,500/5,000

a. A similar coin was struck on a smaller flan.

This is a second medallion struck at this mint. Agrippa probably recognized that a medallion honoring the emperor's sons without another medallion honoring Vespasian would have been impolitic.

1288. AE 30 mm.

Obv: ΑΥΤΟΚΡΑ ΟΥΕCΠΑCΙ ΚΑΙCΑΡ CΕΒΑCΤΩ *(for Emperor Vespasian Caesar Augustus)*; laureate bust of Vespasian to r.

Rev: ΕΤΟΥ ΚΖ ΒΑ ΑΓΡΙ ΠΠΑ *(year 27, King Agrippa)* across fields; Tyche-Demeter as on 1282, star in field l.   300/900

1288

1291

1289.   AE 25 mm.
   Obv: ΑΥΤΟΚΡ ΤΙΤΟC ΚΑΙCΑΡ CΕΒΑCΤΩ *(for Emperor Titus Caesar Augustus)*; laureate bust of Titus to r., draped and cuirassed.

   Rev: ΕΤΟΥ ΚΖ ΒΑ ΑΓΡΙΠΠΑ *(year 27, King Agrippa)* across fields; Nike-Victory advances as on 1284, star upper l. field.

   200/500

1290.   AE 20 mm.
   Obv: ΔΟΜΙΤΙΑΝ ΚΑΙCΑΡ *(Domitian Caesar)*; laureate bust of Domitian to r.
   Rev: ΕΤΟ ΚΖ ΒΑ ΑΓΡΙΠΠΑ *(year 27, King Agrippa)*; Nike-Victory with shield as on 1285, star in upper r.   150/500
   a. On reverse the first Α was left out and squeezed into the field.

1291.   AE 15 mm.
   Obv: ΔΟΜΙΤΙΑΝΟC ΚΑΙCΑΡ *(Domitian Caesar)*; laureate, draped, and cuirsassed bust of Domitian to r.
   Rev: ΑΓΡΙΠΠΑ ΕΤΟ ΚΖ *(King Agrippa, year 27)*; double cornucopias crossed at base, ΒΑ between them.   500/1,500

Year 29, 77/8 ce

1292.   AE 27 mm.
   Obv: ΑΥΤΟΚΡΑ ΟΥΕCΠΑCΙ ΚΑΙCΑΡΙ CΕΒΑCΤΩ *(for Emperor Vespasian Caesar Augustus)*; laureate bust of Vespasian to r.
   Rev: ΕΤΟΥ ΚΘ ΒΑ / ΑΓΡΙ ΠΠΑ *(year 29, King Agrippa)* across fields; Tyche-Demeter as on 1282.   500/1500

1292

1293a

1293. AE 25 mm.

Obv: ΑΥΤΟΚΡ ΤΙΤΩC ΚΑΙCΑΡ CΕΒΑCΤΩ *(for Emperor Titus Caesar Augustus)*; laureate, draped, and cuirassed bust of Titus to r.

Rev: ΕΤ ΚΘ ΒΑ ΑΓΡΙΠΠΑ *(year 29, King Agrippa)* across fields; Nike-Victory advances r. as on 1284.   200/500

a. Titus bust not draped.

1294. AE 21 mm.

Obv: ΔΟΜΙΤΙΑΝΟC ΚΑΙCΑΡ *(Domitian Caesar)*; laureate, draped and cuirassed bust Domitian to r.

Rev: ΕΤΟΥ ΚΘ ΒΑ ΑΓΡΙΠΠΑ *(year 29, King Agrippa)*; Nike-Victory with shield as on 1285.   150/400

YEAR 30, 78/9 CE

1295. AE 25 mm.

Obv: ΑΥΤΟΚΡ ΤΙΤΩ ΚΑΙCΑΡ CΕΒΑCΤΩ *(for Emperor Titus Caesar Augustus)*; laureate, draped bust of Titus to r.

Rev: ΕΤΟΥ Λ ΒΑ ΑΓΡΙΠΠΑ *(year 30, King Agrippa)* across fields; Tyche-Demeter as on 1282.   200/500

1296. AE 26 mm.

Obv: ΑΥΤΟΚΡΑ ΔΟΜΕΤ ΚΑΙCΑΡ ΓΕΡΜΑΝΙΚ *(Emperor Domitian Caesar Germanicus)*; laureate bust of Domitian to r.

Rev: ΕΤΟΥ Λ ΒΑ ΑΓΡΙΠΠ *(year 30, King Agrippa)* across fields; Tyche-Demeter as on 1282.   200/500

I have recorded an example of this coin in the Jerusalem market but was unable to obtain a photograph of it.

YEAR 34, 82/3 CE

1297

1298

1297.   AE 12 mm.
   Obv: BA AΓP *(King Agrippa)* across fields; turreted, veiled bust of
      Tyche to r.
   Rev: ET ΔΛ *(year 34)* across fields, cornucopia.   150/300

YEAR 35, 83/4 CE

1298.   AE 26 mm.
   Obv: AYTOKPA ΔOMITIA KAICAP A ΓEPMANI *(Emperor Domitian
      Caesar Germanicus)*; laureate bust Domitian to r.
   Rev: ETOY EΛ BA ΑΓPI ΠΠA *(year 35, King Agrippa)* across fields;
      Tyche-Demeter as on 1282.   300/900

1299.   AE 24 mm.
   Obv: Laureate bust of Domitian as on 1298.
   Rev: ETOY EΛ BA ΑΓPI ΠΠA *(year 35, King Agrippa)* across fields;
      Nike-Victory advances r. as on 1284.   200/600
   a. Reverse legend reads ETOY ΛE BA...

1300

1301

1300.   AE 15 mm.
   Obv: AYTO ΔOMIT *(Emperor Domitian)*; laureate bust of Domitian
      to r.
   Rev: BA ΑΓP ET EΛ *(King Agrippa, year 35)* within wreath. 150/400

CAESAREA MARITIMA
ERA BEGINNING 60 CE
YEAR 14, 73/4 CE

1301. AE 30 mm.
Obv: ΑΥΤΟΚΡΑ ΟΥΕϹΠΑϹΙ ΚΑΙϹΑΡΙ ϹΕΒΑϹΤΩ *(for Emperor Vespasian Caesar Augustus)*; laureate bust of Vespasian to r.
Rev: ΕΤΔΙ ΒΑ ΑΓΡΙΠΠΑ *(year 14, King Agrippa)* across fields; Tyche-Demeter stands l. wearing kalathos, holding grain ears in r. hand and cornucopia in l., star in top l. field.   300/900
  a. Smaller module and reverse inscription is ΛΙΔ ΒΑϹΙΛ ΑΓΡΙΠΟΥ *(year 14 of King Agrippa)*.

1302. AE 28 mm.
Obv: ΑΥΤΟΚΡ ΤΙΤΟϹ ΚΑΙϹΑΡ ϹΕΒΑϹ *(Emperor Titus Caesar Augustus)*; laureate, draped and cuirassed bust of Titus to r.
Rev: ΕΤΙΔ ΒΑ ΑΓΡΙ ΠΠΑ *(year 14 ,King Agrippa)* across fields; Nike-Victory advances r., holding wreath in r. hand and palm branch over shoulder in l.   300/900

1303. AE 26 mm.
Obv: ΑΥΤΟΚΡ ΤΙΤΟϹ ΚΑΙϹΑΡ ϹΕΒΑϹ *(Emperor Titus Caesar Augustus)*; laureate bust of Titus to r.
Rev: ΛΙΔ ΒΑϹ ΑΓΡΙΠΟΥ *(year 14 of King Agrippa)* across fields; Nike-Victory advances as on 1302.   250/800
  a. Irregular, crude issue.

1304.   AE 20 mm.
   Obv: ΔOMITIA KAICAP *(Domitian Caesar)*; laureate bust of Domitian to r.
   Rev: LIΔ BACI AΓ PIПOY across fields; Nike-Victory standing l., l. foot on helmet, writing on shield which rests on her l. knee.
                                                                      150/400
   a. Cut in half to use as change.

YEAR *15, 74/5* CE

1305.   AE 28 mm.
   Obv: Laureate bust of Vespasian as on 1301.
   Rev: ET IE BA AΓPI ΠΠA *(year 15, King Agrippa)* across fields; Tyche-Demeter as on 1301.   300/900

1306.   AE 20 mm.
   Obv: ΔOMITIA KAICAP *(Domitian Caesar)*; laureate bust Domitian to r.
   Rev: ETOY IE BACI AΓPIΠΠA *(year 15, King Agrippa)*; Nike-Victory stands r., l. foot on helmet, writing on shield which rests on her l. knee.   150/400
   a. On reverse legend is ETOY EI...

YEAR *18, 77/8* CE

1307

1307.   AE 25 mm.
   Obv: AYTOKPA OYECΠACI KAICAP CEBACTW *(for Emperor Vespasian Caesar Augustus)*; laureate bust of Vespasian to r.
   Rev: ETOY HI BA   AΓPI ΠΠA *(year 18, King Agrippa)* across fields; Tyche-Demeter as on 1301.   250/750

1308. AE 24 mm.
Obv: Laureate bust of Titus as 1303.
Rev: ET HI BA AΓP IΠΠA *(year 18, King Agrippa)* across fields; Nike-Victory advances r. as on 1302. 250/750

1309. AE 20 mm.
Obv: ΔΟΜΙΤΙΑΝΟC ΚΑΙCΑΡ *(Domitian Caesar)*; laureate bust Domitian to r.
Rev: ΕΤΟΥ ΗΙΒΑ ΑΓΡΙΠΠΑ *(year 18, King Agrippa)* Nike-Victory with shield as on 1306. 250/750

YEAR 19, 78/9 C.E.

1310. AE 26 mm.
Obv: ΑΥΤΟΚΡ ΤΙΤΟC ΚΑΙCΑΡ CΕΒΑCΤΟC *(Emperor Titus Caesar Augustus)*; laureate, draped, and cuirassed bust of Titus to r.
Rev: ΕΤΟΥ ΙΘ ΒΑ ΑΓΡΙ ΠΠΑ *(year 19, King Agrippa)* across fields; Tyche-Demeter as on 1301. 250/750

1311. AE 20 mm.
Obv: ΑΥΤΟΚ ΤΙΤΟC ΚΑΙC CΕΒΑCΤΟC *(Emperor Titus Caesar Augustus)*; laureate, draped, and cuirassed bust of Titus to r.
Rev: ΕΤΟ ΙΘ ΒΑΑΓΡ ΙΠΠΑ *(year 19, King Agrippa)* above galley with oars sailing l. 150/400
This coin and 1312 and 1313 commemorate the voyage of Agrippa and Berenice to Rome, where they hoped and expected that Titus would choose her as his wife.

1312. AE 16 mm.
Obv: ΔΟΜΙΤΙΑΝΟC ΚΑΙCΑΡ *(Domitian Caesar)*; laureate bust of Domitian to r.
Rev: ΕΤΟ ΙΘ ΒΑΑ ΓΡΙΠΠ *(year 19, King Agrippa)* above galley as on 1311. 150/400

1313.   AE 20 mm.
  Obv: Laureate bust of Domitian as on 1312.
  Rev: ΕΤΟΥ ΙΘ ΒΑ ΑΓΡΙΠ *(year 19, King Agrippa)*; Nike-Victory with
      shield as on 1306.   150/400

1314.   AE 12 mm.
  Obv: CEBACTH *(Augusta)*; Veiled head of Berenice, sister of Agrip-
      pa II, to r.
  Rev: ΛΙΘ ΒΑ *(year 19)* in fields, inverted anchor.   500/1500
  For discussion of the obverse portrait see p. 290–91.

YEAR 24, 83/4 CE

1315.   AE 22-24 mm.
  Obv: ΔΟΜΕΤ ΚΑΙCΑΡ ΓΕΡΜΑΝΙ *(Domitian Caesar Germanicus)*;
      laureate, draped, and cuirassed bust of Domitian to r.
  Rev: ΕΤΟ ΚΔ ΒΑ ΑΓΡΙ ΠΠΑ *(year 24, King Agrippa)* in fields; Nike-
      Victory advances as on 1302.   150/500

1316.   AE 20 mm.
  Obv: ΔΟΜΕΤ ΚΑΙCΑΡ ΓΕΡΜΑΝΙ; laureate bust of Domitian to r.
  Rev: ΕΤΟ ΚΔ ΒΑ Α ΓΡΙΠΠ within wreath.   150/500

1317.   AE 20 mm.
  Obv: ΔΟΜΕΤ ΚΑΙ ΓΕΡΜΑΝ; laureate bust of Domitian to r.
  Rev: ΕΤΟ ΚΔ ΒΑ / ΑΓΡΙ ΠΠΑ; Nike-Victory with shield as on
      1306.   150/500

YEAR 25, 84/5 CE

1318. AE 26 mm, axis ↓.

Obv: IMP CAES DIVI VESP F DOMITIAN AVG GER COS X; laureate bust of Domitian r.

Rev: MONETA ΕΠΙ ΒΑ ΑΓΡΙ AVGVST *(Money of Augustus, in the time of King Agrippa Augustus)*; ET KE *(year 25)* in fields, SC in exergue; draped Moneta stands l. holding scales in r. hand and cornucopia in l. 500/1,500

1319. AE 27 mm, axis ↓.

Obv: Laureate bust of Domitian as on 1318.

Rev: SALVTI ΕΠΙ ΒΑ ΑΓΡΙ AVGVST *(for the health of Augustus in the time of King Agrippa)*, ET KE *(year 25)* in fields, SC in exergue; square altar. 500/1,500

The above two coins as well as 1323 and 1324 were copied directly from Roman as coins of Domitian (see p. 309). They combine the original Latin legends with local Greek legends. Some theories suggest that these coins were minted in Rome, others suggest that the dies were made there or locally by Roman artisans and struck at Caesarea Maritima.

1320

1320. AE 16 mm.

Obv: ΔΟΜΕΤ ΚΑΙϹ ΓΕΡΜΑΝ *(Domitian Caesar Germanicus)*; laureate bust of Domitian r.

Rev: ET KE ΒΑϹ ΑΓΡ ΙΠ *(year 25, King Agrippa)* across fields; eight-branched palm tree with two bunches of dates. 150/400

1321. AE 19 mm.

Obv: ΔΟΜΙΤΙΑΝΟϹ ΚΑΙϹΑΡ *(Domitian Caesar)*; laureate bust of Domitian r.

Rev: Nike-Victory with shield as on 1306, date is EK *(year 25)*. 150/400

1322. AE 11 mm.
Obv: ΔOMET KAICAP ΓEPMANI *(Domitian Caesar Germanicus)*; laureate bust of Domitian to r.
Rev: ET KE BA AΓ *(year 25, King Agrippa)* across fields; cornucopia.   150/400

YEAR 26, 85/6 CE

1323

1323. AE 28 mm, axis ↓.
Obv: Laureate bust of Domitian as on 1318.
Rev: ET KS *(year 26)*; Moneta as on 1318.   350/900

1324. AE 26 mm, axis ↓.
Obv: Laureate bust of Domitian as on 1318.
Rev: ET KS; square altar as on 1319.   500/1,500

1325

1326

1325. AE 20 mm, axis ↓.
Obv: IM CA D VES F DOM AV GER COS XII; laureate bust of Domitian to r.
Rev: EΠI BA AΓPI *(in the time of King Agrippa)*; ET KS *(year 26)* in fields; SC *(by decree of the senate)* below double cornucopias crossed at base, winged caduceus between.   200/500

It is doubtful whether the Roman Senate actually approved these bronze coins (Nos. 1318, 1319, 1323, 1325, 1326), as they did with Roman issues, and as the SC (SENATVS CONSVLTO, by decree of the senate) indicates. Rather, these are likely copied from Roman prototypes and retained the conventional SC from bronze coins of this period. SC was also a common feature of Roman Syria provincial bronze coins struck at Antioch.

1326.   AE 20 mm, axis ↓.
   Obv: Laureate bust of Domitian as on 1325.
   Rev: ΕΡΙ ΒΑ ΑΓΡΙ *(in the time of King Agrippa)* around large SC *(by decree of the senate)*; ΕΤ ΚϚ *(year 26)* in exergue.   150/450

YEAR 29, 88/9 CE

1327.   AE 25 mm.
   Obv: Domitian r.; ΑΥΤΟΚΡΑ ΔΟΜΕΤ ΚΑΙCΑΡ ΓΕΡΜΑΝΙΚ *(Emperor Domitian Caesar Germanicus)*; laureate, draped, and cuirassed bust of Domitian to r.
   Rev: ΕΤΟΥ ΚΘ ΒΑ ΑΓΡΙ ΠΠΑ *(year 29, King Agrippa)* across fields; Tyche-Demeter as on 1301.   200/500

7.12. Two bronze *as* coins of Domitian; Agrippa II's Nos. 1318 and 1323 were copied from the coin on top (*RIC* II 756) and Agrippa II's Nos. 1319 and 1324 were copied from the coin below (*RIC* II 224).

7.13. Model of the Jerusalem Temple during the Second Temple Period at the scale model on display at The Israel Museum, Jerusalem. (Author photo.)

7.14. Reverse of aureus of Vespasian (No. 1584) with details showing weeping Jewess to l. of trophy and bearded Jew, hands tied behind his back, to r. (Photos: D. Sundman.)

CHAPTER EIGHT

THE ROMAN GOVERNORS OF JUDAEA

After Herod Archelaus was banished in 6 CE, Rome assigned a series of governors, called prefects (up to the time of Claudius) and procurators (thereafter), to govern Judaea directly. Josephus and Tacitus do not use the word prefects, and refer to these governors simply as procurators.[1]

The title prefect is known only from a stone discovered at Caesarea in 1961, now in the Israel Museum (a facsimile is on display at the site), inscribed with Pilate's name and title as "PRAEFECTVS IVDAEA." This is the only archaeological evidence for the existence of Pilate, even though he is known from historical accounts and the

...]S TIBERIVM
...PON]TIVS PILATVS
...PRAEF]ECTVS IVDA[EA]

8.1. Inscription mentions Pontius Pilate as well as his title "Prefect of Judaea," discovered on a stone in secondary use at the Roman theater at Caesarea Maritima. (Israel Museum.)

311

New Testament. Why don't we consider the coins struck under Pontius Pilate to be archaeological evidence? Simply this: the coins of Pontius Pilate, just like the coins of the other Roman governors of Judaea, never once mention their names. Instead, the only names used were those of emperors (or family members) at whose pleasure the prefects and procurators served. At this time, the province of Judaea (later including Galilee and Samaria) was linked to Syria, but had its own governor.

With the exception of the three years Agrippa I reigned as king (41–44 CE), the prefects and procurators governed until 66 CE, when the Jewish War erupted. A principal advantage of being governor was the power to levy taxes on behalf of Rome, and to retain a good portion of this wealth. Hence the seeds of the Jewish rebellion against Rome were firmly planted at the beginning of this era and fertilized by cruelty, greed, and oppressive taxation. For the most part the Roman governors minimized their contact with the Jews except when it involved enriching themselves. The policy of keeping their distance held true even for Tiberius Alexander, who was born a Jew, and Antonius Felix, who married a Jew, Drusilla, the daughter of Agrippa I.

The men appointed to these jobs between 6 and 41 CE governed Judaea and took a supervisory role over the Jerusalem Temple, including the power to appoint the high priest. Following Agrippa I's reign, the territory governed by these governors was expanded to include Samaria and Galilee. The right to appoint the high priest was transferred first to Agrippa I's brother Herod, king of Chalcis, and later to Agrippa I's son, Agrippa II.

The Roman governors of Judaea established their headquarters at Caesarea Maritima, Herod's magnificent harbor city. They traveled to Jerusalem only on special occasions, such as Jewish festivals, when they temporarily moved their seat of government in order to stay on top of the large influx of pilgrims to Jerusalem. Unlike the governors of Syria, the prefects and procurators of Judaea were not former senators or other aristocrats, but came from the social class known as equestrians or Roman knights. This group originally included members of the cavalry; membership was based upon personal wealth. Equestrians outnumbered Roman senators, but had fewer privileges. Antonius Felix, alone, was a freedman and not a member of this class.

Since only the names of members of the imperial household are used, the coins of the Roman governors must be attributed to individuals based on the dates of the coins, which correspond to the regnal years of the Roman emperors. For this reason, *Israel Numismatic Research*, the journal of the Israel Numismatic Society, has taken an editorial position on the appropriate way to attribute them. Alla Kushnir-Stein, a leading Israeli numismatist, writes that "if a coin is placed under a heading that includes…two basic components—the emperor's name and the year of his rule—it is easy to identify it immediately. Moreover, these components correspond to what one actually sees on a coin, with no speculative elements involved."[2]

Previous editions of this guide have referred to these coins in this way, but we have also added the generally accepted dates for each of the governors who may have ruled during each period. While this contains an element of speculation, it follows tradition. We continue to list the generally accepted dates, but call attention to some differing opinions.

Kushnir-Stein, who is also an expert in the translation and interpretation of the works of Josephus, points out that "Josephus gives few precise chronological indications about the periods of tenure of most of the governors involved, and the exact years of their comings and goings remain very unclear. For instance, the coin dated to 'year 5' of Nero (58/9 CE), often appearing under the name of Festus, has an equal, if not greater chance of having been struck under that official's predecessor, Antonius Felix.

"Another example is the issue under the emperor Augustus dated 'year 39.' If counted by a proper era—that of autumn 31 BCE—this issue belongs to 8/9 CE. Josephus tells us in a casual manner that there were three governors under Augustus—Coponius, Marcus Ambibulus, and Annius Rufus—and that the emperor died during the administration of Rufus. He further adds that Augustus' successor, Tiberius, dispatched Valerius Gratus to replace Rufus. We have no proper knowledge of when each of these governors replaced another, and most of the dates appearing in scholarly literature are no more than conjecture."

Kushnir-Stein further observes that "there seems to be no scholarly consensus even about the years of tenure of Pontius Pilate, which Josephus places in the later part of Tiberius' reign." Of course there are other clues about Pilate and some of the others in the New Testament, but they are equally difficult to date."[3]

With this in mind, we present the group as follows.

Governors of Judaea under Rome (Traditional Dating)
Augustus (27 bce–14 ce)
        Coponius (6–9 ce)
        Marcus Ambibulus (9–12 ce)
        *Annius Rufus (12–15 ce)
Tiberius (14–37 ce)
        Valerius Gratus (15–26 ce or possibly 15–17/18 ce)
        Pontius Pilate (26–36 ce or possibly 17/18–36 ce)
Caligula (37–41 ce)
        *Marullus (37–41 ce)
Claudius (41–54 ce)
        *Cuspius Fadus (44–46 ce)
        *Tiberius Alexander (46–48 ce)
        *Ventidius Cumanus (48–54 ce)
        Antonius Felix (52–54 ce)
Nero (54–58 ce)
        Antonius Felix (54–60 ce)
        Porcius Festus (60–62 ce)
        *Albinus (62–64 ce)
        *Gessius Florus (64–66 ce)
No known coins issued during these years

We do not know why coins were issued only during the rule of six of the fourteen prefects and procurators. Nor do we know why coins were struck irregularly, rather than every year. Meshorer suggests "it is possible that not all of them showed an interest in minting, and perhaps they inherited a market saturated with coins."[4] Perhaps, too, in some instances, coins from dated dies continued to be struck in subsequent years. Kanael writes that the mintage of Agrippa I's common *prutah* (No. 1244) was so great that the procurators who succeeded him did not need to strike coins for ten years.[5]

Governors before Agrippa I

Neither Josephus nor the other historians tell us much about the first three governors. With regard to **Coponius**, the first, Josephus reports that "the territory of Archelaus was now reduced to a province, and Coponius, a Roman of the equestrian order, was sent out as procurator, entrusted by Augustus with full powers, including the infliction of capital punishment."[6]

The Syrian governor Quirinus was sent to Judaea to accompany Coponius. Quirinus' task was to administer all of the property formerly owned by Herod Archelaus, and to undertake a census in order to determine taxation for Rome. A census was taken in every land that became a Roman province, but the Jews regarded it as a sign of servitude and protested vehemently. Eventually, the high priest intervened, the Jewish people were pacified, and the census was taken.

While Coponius was in office, the long-standing hatred and rivalry between the Jews and Samaritans was revived. Josephus reports that during a Passover celebration, "the priests were accustomed to throw open the gates of the Temple after midnight. This time, when the gates were first opened, some Samaritans, who had secretly entered Jerusalem, began to scatter human bones in the porticoes and throughout the Temple. As a result, the priests, although they had previously observed no such custom, excluded everyone from the Temple, in addition to taking other measures for the greater protection of the Temple."[7]

In spite of such disruptions, Coponius maintained a decent relationship with the Jews, and one of the gateways to the Temple Mount was called "the door of Coponius."

He was recalled to Rome in 9 CE, shortly after the Samarian incident, and **Marcus Ambibulus** was sent to succeed him.[8]

Following Marcus Ambibulus and **Annius Rufus**, Tiberius appointed **Valerius Gratus** as prefect of Judaea in 15 CE. Thus, he became the fourth prefect in fewer than ten years. Since the earlier prefects each had only a few years in Judaea, they had to act aggressively to acquire wealth.

Josephus tells us that "during the twenty-two years that he [Tiberius] was the emperor he sent altogether two men, Gratus and Pilate, his successor, to govern the Jewish people."[9]

Little is known about Gratus and his administration, even though it is believed his tenure lasted 11 years. He ousted High Priest Annas ben Seth, and appointed Ishmael ben Phabi I, Eleazar ben Ananias, and Josephus Caiphas. The Talmud suggests that motivation for the frequent changes was economic: "Because money was paid for the purpose of obtaining the position of high priest, [they] were changed every 12 months," and "Since they used to hire it [the office of high priest] out for money, their days were shortened."[10]

Kenneth Lönnqvist suggests that **Pontius Pilate** may have replaced Gratus as early as 17/18 CE and not in 26. Lönnqvist's thesis is based in part upon the metallurgy of the coins issued between 17/18 and 30/1 CE. These coins are made of a bronze alloy of tin and copper, eliminating lead, a previous ingredient.[11]

If this is the case, then three coins featuring a palm branch (Nos. 1338–40) may have been the first coins struck in Judaea under Pontius Pilate. Lönnqvist suggests that "It seems…that the palm branch is—as far as the Roman provincial coinage of Judaea is concerned—mostly

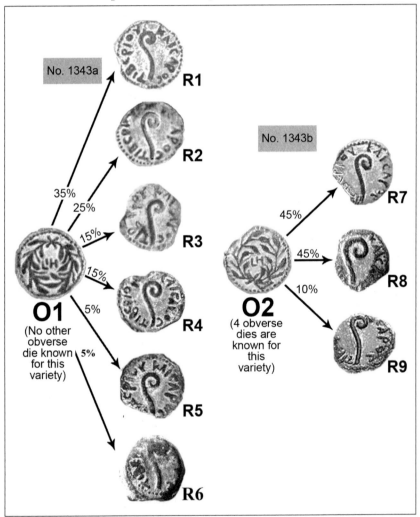

8.2. Connections show combination of obverse and reverse pairings for some coins dated to year 18 of Tiberius, 31/2 CE. (Graphic:Fontanille.)

or always connected with the arrival of a new Roman governor. Indirectly this seems to imply that the new coin type which was started to be struck in CE 17/18 may be connected in the same way, with the arrival of a new governor, prefect Pontius Pilate."[12]

Lönnqvist also points out that Pilate had a close relationship with Caiphas, the high priest who was chosen in around 17/18 CE and this may have been due to Pilate's arrival in Judaea earlier than previously believed. "It would also explain why Caiphas officiated throughout Pilate's term of office, until the 30s CE. Lowering the chronological limit to Pilate's term of office would not compromise the chronology of the events of the Gospels, but would, on the contrary, with regard to the numismatic and historical development, explain much better the events of the late 20s CE."[13]

The latest coins struck under Pilate's government are unique among those of the prefects and procurators, since they alone carry symbols that are specifically offensive to the Jews. Reasons for this are not clear, although it has been suggested that Pilate was a follower of the anti-Semitic usurper L. Aelius Sejanus in Rome, whose power peaked during 29–32 CE. Sejanus oversaw a mass expulsion of Jews from Rome beginning in 19 CE. Tiberius had Sejanus arrested for treason in 32 CE and executed, although his issues with the Jews did not play a big role in this.

Pilate's coins hold special interest because of his place in both Christian and Jewish history. Pilate is mentioned in all four of the Christian Gospels and Matthew tells that "when they had bound him [Jesus], they led him away, and delivered him to Pontius Pilate the governor."[14]

Pilate was the official responsible for the conviction of Jesus on the charge of sedition and the subsequent crucifixion. The power of capital punishment was a basic prerogative of the governors of Judaea.

Clues to the reasons why Pilate's coin motifs appeared to be antagonistic to Jews can also be found in the works of Philo and Josephus.

Philo describes Pilate's rule including "the bribery, the insults, the robberies, the outrages and wanton injuries, the executions without trial constantly repeated, the ceaseless and supremely grievous cruelty" adding, among other things, that Pilate did not "wish to do anything which would please his subjects."[15]

Josephus says that Pilate "took a bold step in subversion of the Jewish practices, by introducing into the city the busts of the emperor that were attached to the military standards, for our law forbids the making of images. It was for this reason that the previous procurators, when they entered the city, used standards that had no such ornaments. Pilate was the first to bring the images into Jerusalem and set them up, doing it without the knowledge of the people, for he entered in the night. But when the people discovered it, they went in a throng to Caesarea and for many days entreated him to take away the images."[16]

Pilate was eventually forced to remove the standards with portraits of the emperor and others, and also a series of inscribed golden shields that had been erected in Jerusalem.

The Jewish people seem to have had mixed feelings about Pilate who, Meshorer notes, seemed to "reveal a mixture of good will and creative rule...with continuous disputes, misunderstandings, and a lack of communication with the Jews."[17] If Pilate had really wanted to offend the Jews he would have portrayed the Roman emperor on his coins. Perhaps that was not within his mandate. But, he did use the images of two objects that were emblems of the Roman cult: the simpulum and the lituus.

The lituus is also known as an augur's wand. Florence Banks explains that "at the very time when he was trying to get along comfortably with the Jews, he had the effrontery to provide those devout people of Judaea for their daily use a coin bearing, in its augur's wand, a symbol of one of the very customs which the Children of Israel had been specifically taught to abominate. Ever since the days of Moses they had been warned repeatedly against divining or augury in any form."[18]

The simpulum, depicted on another Pilate coin, is a ladle with a high handle. It was used to make libations during pagan sacrifices and was a common symbol of the Roman priesthood.

It is a bit mysterious that the same coin that depicts the simpulum on the obverse has a reverse illustrating three ears of grain. This might indicate that Pilate's intentions were not so bad and it was his "ignorance rather than his unsympathetic nature which was the major cause of his difficulties,"[19] Meshorer notes. On the other hand, the outer two ears are shown as drooping. Was this a design element, or Pilate's proclamation of power over the Jewish inhabitants?

Pilate's term ended in 36 CE when he ordered the massacre of Samaritans on Mount Gerizim in Shechem (modern Nablus), where they had gathered for a religious ceremony. The Samaritan community convinced Vitellius, then Rome's legate in Syria, to order Pilate back to Rome for trial.

GOVERNORS AFTER AGRIPPA I

The governors who took power after Agrippa I's short reign (41–44 CE) were even worse than their predecessors. Neither Tiberius Julius Alexander nor Cumanus seem to have issued coins during their rule. But there was a bawdy incident that took place under Cumanus, during Passover in Jerusalem, that shows the way Roman soldiers treated the Jews. Cumanus sent a cohort of guards to prevent any disorders among the gathered crowd, and they stationed themselves on the roof of the portico of the Temple. Josephus reports that "thereupon one of the soldiers, raising his robe, stooped in an indecent attitude, so as to turn his backside to the Jews, and made a noise in keeping with his posture." The soldiers were brutal in the riot that ensued, and Josephus reports that more than 30,000 Jews were killed, not only by the soldiers but "trodden under foot and crushed to death by one another…and the feast was turned into mourning for the whole nation…"[20]

Antonius Felix was the final procurator sent to Judaea by Claudius and he remained after Nero became emperor. Felix married Drusilla, daughter of Agrippa I.

> *And after certain days, when Felix came with his wife Drusilla, who was a Jewess, he sent for Paul, and heard him concerning the faith in Christ* (ACTS 24:24).

Of Felix, the Roman historian Tacitus reports that he "played the tyrant with the spirit of a slave, plunging into all manner of cruelty and lust…"[21] This refers to Felix's lowly status as a freedman, the only procurator who was not an equestrian. Felix also oversaw the treacherous murder of Jonathan the high priest.[22]

Josephus reports that "when **Porcius Festus** was sent as successor to Felix by Nero, the principal of the Jewish inhabitants of Caesarea went up to Rome to accuse Felix; and he had certainly been brought to punishment…"[23]

8.3. Coin dated year 14 of Claudius, 54 CE, struck under A. Felix (No. 1348), copies design of **aureus** by Claudius (r.) struck 41–45 in the name of his father Nero Claudius Drusus.

Antonius Felix imprisoned Paul, but Porcius Festus sent him to Rome to be tried. Festus served as procurator under Nero, from 59 to 62 CE. According to traditional dating, he was the last governor of Judaea to issue coins during his reign, perhaps because of the confusion and strife leading up to the Jewish War, which began in 66 CE. The often violent Jewish Zealots, known as the Sicarii (literally, dagger-men), increased significantly in number during the rule of Festus, even though he tried in vain to crush them.

During Festus' tenure, Agrippa II (who did not rule Judaea, but received power from the emperor to control the Temple, its grounds, and to appoint high priests) added an additional level to the former Hasmonean palace. This allowed Agrippa, who was king, but not of a priestly family, to overlook the proceedings in the Temple court. To counter, the Jewish priests built a wall screening the Temple from Agrippa's palace.

At Agrippa's request, Festus ordered this wall demolished. However, a delegation headed by High Priest Ishmael ben Phabi traveled to Rome to petition the emperor to overrule Festus and allow the wall to stand. Nero's wife, Poppaea, interceded on behalf of the Jews and influenced her husband to support the high priest. It is not clear why Poppaea was sympathetic toward the Jews, but this is one of two instances in which she lobbied successfully on their behalf.

Festus died in 62, while still in office, and he was succeeded by **Albinus**.

Of Albinus, Josephus wrote, "Not only did he embezzle public moneys and rob a multitude of private citizens of their property and burden the whole people with imposts, but he released captive highwaymen for ransoms from their relatives.... Every villain gathered a band of his own, and Albinus towered among them like a robber-chief, using his adherents to plunder honest citizens. The victims remained silent; others, still exempt, flattered the wretch in order to secure immunity.

"...his successor, **Gessius Florus,** made him appear by comparison a paragon of virtue. [He] ostentatiously paraded his outrages upon the nation and, as though he had been sent as hangman of condemned criminals, abstained from no form of robbery or violence...he stripped whole cities, ruined entire populations...his avarice brought desolation upon all the cities, and caused many to desert their ancestral haunts and seek refuge in foreign provinces."[24]

Florus' abuses of the Jews mounted, antagonizing and punishing them until they could stand no more. The final insult came when Florus demanded 17 *talents* from the Temple treasury for government expenses, and no doubt his personal use. (In 1962, in *Jews, God, and History*, Max Dimont estimated 17 *talents* to be worth $350,000. Today, taking inflation into consideration, the figure would be many times that.) In their outrage, bands of sarcastic Jews took to the streets with signs begging pennies for "the poor, destitute Florus." This mockery enraged the procurator, who called upon his troops to sack the upper city; more than 600 Jews were killed.

His treachery was so great that Berenice, sister of Agrippa II, who was visiting Jerusalem at the time, went barefoot to Florus and implored mercy for her fellow Jews. But he insulted and ridiculed her and drove her away.[25]

To prevent Florus from plundering the Temple further, the Jews destroyed all the approaches and bridges to the holy site. Now, the Jews gathered around Agrippa II and begged him to denounce Florus to Nero. Agrippa demanded that first the people restore the broken connections to the Temple and pay the back taxes they owed to Rome. The Jews met both demands, but balked when Agrippa said they ought to honor Florus as the representative of Rome until he was replaced. Agrippa was pelted with stones and he quickly fled the city.

In their distaste for Florus and subsequent discontent with Rome, the Jews decided to cease the daily sacrifice for the emperor in the Temple, a tradition going back to the time of Augustus. This action was a declaration of war.[26]

With the exception of Pontius Pilate, the coins of the prefects and procurators do not carry symbols abhorrent to the Jews. They generally carry agricultural symbols, an amphora, or a goblet. One coin of Felix shows crossed shields and spears that were copied from Roman coins and "meant to express the might of his rule," according to Meshorer.[27]

IRREGULAR COINS

Irregular or crudely engraved and struck bronze coins were made during the reign of Herod I but they are difficult to assess since all of the coins of Herod I except for his dated series (in which irregulars do not occur) were so crudely engraved and manufactured. Under the Roman governors, however, the number and variations of struck irregular coins jumps tremendously. This can probably be attributed to the need for many more bronze coins in the increasingly Romanized economy of Judaea. During the early first century there were Jewish artisans, but few Jewish artists. The principal reason for this was the prohibition against graven images, so there was little demand for the fine arts of painting, sculpting, or engraving gems and dies. For each of the coin types issued in Judaea after the exile of Herod Archelaus in 6 CE, there exist several die types of fine, high style work, more dies exhibiting average work, and additional dies exhibiting crude work which also includes retrograde inscriptions, errors in inscription, and just peculiar-looking copies of the master designs (see pp. 39–42).

COUNTERMARKED COINS

Fr. A. Spijkerman published a countermarked coin of Valerius Gratus in 1963; it was the first noted example of a countermarked coin of a prefect or procurator of Judaea. In 1993, Lönnqvist published the most detailed study to date on these coins and reorted that there were "to our knowledge 20 countermarked coins of Valerius Gratus and Pontius Pilate."

The countermarks, which occur on Valerius Gratus' coins of the palm branch type (Nos. 1338–40) and both coin types of Pontius Pilate (Nos. 1341–43), consist of a palm branch within a circle. Sometimes the letters СП flank the palm branch. Lönnqvist identifies the first letter as a Greek *sigma*, which often appears in this lunate form on provincial coins and inscriptions. He cites evidence that it abbreviates the Greek word for "cohort"—a tactical military unit, which was a major element of a legion.

By examining the coins on which they were struck, Lönnqvist concludes that the countermarks appeared on the coins after 29/30 CE, but before 41 CE. He refers to the book of Acts:

> *Now there was a certain man at Caesarea named Cornelius, a centurion of what was called the Italian cohort...* (ACTS 10:1).

This cohort was comprised of Roman citizens and may be identified with the *Cohors II Italica*, known from inscriptions. Lönnqvist argues that this "had been the detachment which applied the countermarks on the coins of the Roman prefects of Judaea. The dating of this passage of the text of the Acts and the countermarks coincide well, the countermarks having been applied after 31/2 and before 41 CE, and the text of Acts being placed around 40. This new evidence from the countermarks of the Judaean provincial coinage lends strong support to the credibility of the New Testament on this point. Epigraphical material shows that this cohort had been transferred (back) to Syria by 69."[28]

Lönnqvist also cites a number of passages in the Book of Acts that discuss a certain Roman citizen cohort, or a part of it, that was stationed in the Antonia fortress in Jerusalem at around the time St. Paul was imprisoned there.

And while they were seeking to kill him, a report came up to the commander of the Roman cohort that all Jerusalem was in confusion (ACTS 21:31).

This unit was possibly a portion of the 1,000-man unit of the *Cohors II Italica* transferred to Judaea in 37 CE to escort Agrippa I to his new kingdom in Judaea, and then stationed in Caesarea Maritima. That unit was divided into three smaller units, which were garrisoned in Jerusalem, Caesarea, and possibly Masada. While there is no indication of where the countermarking operation was located, Lönnqvist suggests it was in Jerusalem, "which must have been the most important garrison of the cohort and where its role was to restore order after Pilate's rule."[29]

Even though these countermarked coins of the prefects and procurators are extremely rare today, Lönnqvist has identified at least 12 different countermark dies, thus indicating that the number of coins countermarked by the *Cohors II Italica* may have been significant.

COINS OF THE ROMAN GOVERNORS OF JUDAEA

All with border of dots on both sides.
Average weight before Agrippa I, 1.90g.
Axis is mostly vertical ↓ or ↑.

UNDER AUGUSTUS 27 BCE–14 CE, DATED TO HIS REGNAL YEARS.
BY COPONIUS 6–9 CE

1328	1329

1328.   AE *prutah.*
   Obv: KAICAPOC *(of Caesar)*; ear of grain curved to right.
   Rev: Eight-branched palm tree bearing two bunches of dates; LΛς
   (year 36 = 5/6 CE).   50/150
   a. Finely engraved dies.
   The ς sometimes looks like a Γ.

BY MARCUS AMBIBULUS 9–12 CE

1329.   AE *prutah.*
   Obv: KAICAPOC *(of Caesar)*; ear of grain curved to right.
   Rev: LΛΘ *(year 39 = 8/9 CE)* in fields; eight-branched palm tree bear-
   ing two bunches of dates.   35/125

1330.   AE *prutah.*
   Obv: KAICAPOC *(of Caesar)*; ear of grain curved to right.
   Rev: LM *(year 40 = 9/10 CE)* in fields; eight-branched palm tree bear-
   ing two bunches of dates.   50/150

1330	1331

1331. AE *prutah.*
   Obv: KAICAPOC (*of Caesar*); ear of grain curved to right.
   Rev: LMA (*year 41 = 10/11 CE*) in fields; eight-branched palm tree
      bearing two bunches of dates: 35/125
   a. Obverse is reverse brockage.

UNDER *TIBERIUS 14–37* CE, DATED TO HIS REGNAL YEARS.
BY *VALERIUS GRATUS 15–26* POSSIBLY *15–17/18* CE

1332   1333

1332. AE *prutah.*
   Obv: KAI CAP *(Caesar)* within wreath.
   Rev: TIB *(Tiberius)* LB (*year 2 = 15/16 CE*) between horns of crossed
      double cornucopias. 100/250
   a. Irregular, struck on a tiny flan.
   b. IOY ΛIA within wreath.

1333. AE *prutah*
   Obv: IOY ΛIA (*Julia*—Julia Livia, mother of Tiberius*)* within
      wreath.
   Rev: LB *(year 2 = 15/16 CE)* flank upright palm branch.
      100/300
   a. Irregular, crude.
   b. Irregular, crude, blundered obverse legend.
   c. Irregular, crude, obverse legend is retrograde.
   d. Irregular, KAI CAP retrograde within wreath.

1334. AE *prutah.*
   Obv: KAI CAP *(Caesar)* within wreath.
   Rev: TIBEPIOY *(of Tiberius)* above; LΓ *(year 3 = 16/17 CE)* in fields;
      crossed cornucopias, caduceus between. 75/200
   a. TIBEIPOY on reverse.

1335. AE *prutah*.
  Obv: IOY ΛIA *(Julia)* within wreath.
  Rev: LΓ *(year 3 = 16/17 CE)* flank three lilies in bloom.
                                                            150/200
  a. Irregular, small flan, obverse legend is retrograde.
  b. KAI CAP on obverse.

1336. AE *prutah*.
  Obv: IOY ΛIA *(Julia)* above vine leaf and small bunch of grapes.
  Rev: LΔ *(year 4 = 17/18 CE)* flanks narrow-necked amphora with
      scroll handles.   100/300
  a. Irregular, crude.

1337. AE *prutah*.
  Obv: TIBEPIOC *(Tiberius)* above vine leaf on tendril.
  Rev: KAICAP *(Caesar)* above, LΔ *(year 4 = 17/18 CE)* flanks kantharos
      with scroll handles.   150/350

1338. AE *prutah*.
  Obv: TIB KAI CAP *(Tib[erius] Caesar)* within wreath tied at base with
      an X.
  Rev: IOY ΛIA *(Julia)* and LΔ *(year 4 = 17/18 CE)* across fields palm
      branch curves to r.   50/150
  a. Irregular, both sides retrograde.

1339. AE *prutah*.
  Obv: TIB KAI CAP *(Tib[erius] Caesar)* within wreath tied at base with
      an X.
  Rev: IOY ΛIA *(Julia)* and LE *(year 5 = 18/19 CE)* across fields palm
      branch curves to r.   50/150

1338a   1339   1340

1340. AE *prutah.*

Obv: TIB KAI CAP *(Tib[erius] Caesar)* within wreath tied at base with an X.

Rev: IOY ΛIA *(Julia)* and LIΛ *(year 11= 24/25 CE)* across fields palm branch curves to r.   50/150

   a. Countermark of branch flanked by CΠ in oval on rev.

BY PONTIUS PILATE 26–36 CE POSSIBLY 17/18–36 CE

1341   1342   1342a

1341.   AE *prutah.*

Obv: TIBEPIOY KAICAPOC LIϛ *(of Tiberius Caesar, year 16 = 29/30 CE)*; libation ladle (simpulum).

Rev: IOYΛIA KAICAPOC *(Julia the Queen)*; three bound ears of grain, the outer two droop.   75/250

   a. Irregular, crude.

   b. Double struck both sides.

   c. Reverse is obverse brockage.

1342.   AE *prutah.*

Obv: LIZ *(year 17 = 30/31 CE)* within wreath.

Rev: TIBEPIOY KAICAPOC *(of Tiberius Caesar)*; lituus.

                                           75/250

   a. LIS (retrograde Z). This is possibly year 29.

   b. HZ (the L and the I carelessly engraved together appear as an H).

   c. Irregular, crude with blundered legends.

   d. Both sides fully retrograde.

   e. Double struck, lituus on both sides.

1343. AE *prutah*.
Obv: LIH *(year 18 = 31/32 CE)* within wreath.
Rev: TIBEPIOY KAICAPOC *(of Tiberius Caesar)*; lituus.   75/250
a. Wreath is upside down.
b. LH within wreath.
c. LHI within wreath.
d. Countermark of branch flanked by CΠ in oval on rev.

1344. AE *prutah*.
Obv: TIBEPIOY KAICAPOC LIϛ *(of Tiberius Caesar, year 16 = 29/30 CE)*; libation ladle (simpulum).
Rev: TIBEPIOY KAICAPOC *(of Tiberius Caesar)*; lituus.
     250/750
     This is a hybrid of types from 1341 and 1342.

1345. AE *prutah*.
Obv: IOYΛIA KAICAPOC *(Julia [mother] of Caesar)*; three bound ears of grain, the outer two droop.
Rev: TIBEPIOY KAICAPOC *(of Tiberius Caesar)*; lituus.
     250/750
     This is a hybrid of types from 1341 and 1342.

1346. AE *prutah*.
Obv: LIZ *(year 17 = 30/1 CE)* within wreath.
Rev: IOYΛIA KAICAPOC; three bound ears of grain, the outer two droop.   250/750
     This is a hybrid of types from 1341 and 1342.

UNDER CLAUDIUS 41–54 CE, DATED TO HIS REGNAL YEARS.
BY ANTONIUS FELIX 52–59/60 CE
Average weight after Agrippa I, 2.27g.

1347. AE *prutah.*

Obv: IOY ΛIA AΓ PIΠΠI NA *(Julia Agrippina—wife of Claudius)* within wreath tied at bottom with an X.

Rev: TI KΛAYΔIOC KAICAP ΓEPM *(Ti[berius] Claudius Caesar Germ[anicus])*; LIΔ *(year 14 = 54 CE)* beneath two crossed palm branches. 75/200

a. Irregular, crude.
b. Irregular with blundered legends, some retrograde.
c. Obverse is brockage of obverse, reverse is normal.
d. Irregular on odd-shaped flan which shows how large the coin on a fully rounded flan with all design and legend would be.
e. Reverse is obverse brockage.

1348. AE *prutah.*

Obv: NEPW KΛAY KAICAP *(Nero Clau[dius] Caesar—son of Claudius)*; two oblong shields and spears crossed.

Rev: BPIT *(Brit[annicus]—younger son of Claudius)* above; LIΔ KAI *(year 14 of Caesar = 54 CE)* in fields; six-branched palm tree bearing two bunches of dates. 75/200

a. Irregular, crude.
b. Irregular, crude.
c. Irregular, very crude, obverse legend is retrograde.
d. Reverse is obverse brockage.

1349   1350   1351

1349. AE *prutah*.
Obv: NEPW KΛAY KAICAP *(Nero Clau[dius] Caesar—son of Claudius)*; two oblong shields and spears crossed.
Rev: TI KΛAYΔIOC KAICAP ΓEPM *(Ti[berius] Claudius Caesar Germ[anicus])*; LIΔ **(year 14 = 54 CE)** beneath two crossed palm branches.   250/750
This is a hybrid of types from 1347 and 1348.

1350. AE *prutah*.
Obv: IOY ΛIA AΓ PIΠΠI NA *(Julia Agrippina—wife of Claudius)* within wreath tied at bottom with an X.
Rev: BPIT *(Brit[annicus]—younger son of Claudius)* above; LIΔ KAI *(year 14 of Caesar = 54 CE)* in fields; six-branched palm tree bearing two bunches of dates.   250/750
This is a hybrid of types from 1347 and 1348.

UNDER NERO 54–68 CE, DATED TO HIS REGNAL YEARS.
BY PORCIUS FESTUS 59/60–62 CE

1351. AE *prutah*.
Obv: NEP / WNO / C *(of Nero)* within wreath, bottom tied with X.
Rev: LE KAICAPOC *(year 5 = 58/59 CE, of Caesar)*; palm branch.
                    50/125

  a. Flan strips remain.
  b. Finely engraved dies.
  c. Irregular with blundered legends.
  d. Irregular with blundered legends.
  e. Irregular first N retrograde on obverse, fully retrograde reverse legend.
  f. Both Ns retrograde on obverse, reverse is brockage.
  g. Cut for change in ancient times.

CHAPTER NINE

THE JEWISH WAR

T he war of the Jews against Rome was not a local revolt but a full scale war. Josephus reports that it was "the greatest not only of the wars of our own time, but, so far as accounts have reached us, well nigh of all that ever broke out between cities or nations."[1] Ever since Archelaus was banished to Gaul in 6 CE, and the ensuing rule of the first Roman prefect, the Jews had been subjected to heavy Roman taxation, a real hardship for this predominantly poor, agrarian population.

Financial pressures were all the more intolerable since there was no longer a Jewish ruler of Judaea, but a series of Roman governors who heaped one abuse upon another. Complicating things further, the Jews were fragmented into several parties of various views and interests. The Jewish masses eked their livelihood from the land and could foresee little more than increasing poverty in the future. Most priests and landowners made up a rich, aristocratic class among the Jews in Jerusalem. Religion aside, they were similar to the Roman aristocrats. There was little recognition of the suffering by the majority of the Jews. A Jewish middle class, sandwiched between these two groups, consisted of small merchants, artisans, and some more affluent peasants. On one hand these Jews dearly wanted peace, yet they were proud, observant people and did not appreciate a Jewish aristocracy taking advantage of them.

Hence when the war with Rome erupted, the Jewish masses rebelled against the priests and princes of the Jews almost as much as against the Romans who, after all, had been masters of the rulers of Judaea since the first days of Herod I's reign.

During the summer of 66 CE, the procurator Florus conscripted 17 *talents* from the Temple treasury "making the requirements of the imperial service his pretext"[2] and this ignited an explosion against the Roman overlords. It's possible that this dispute might have been settled, since Agrippa II came to Jerusalem when he heard that many of his fellow Jews were killed while protesting Florus's treachery. Agrippa and his sister Berenice urged the Jews to comply with the wishes of Rome, which they might have been able to negotiate. Eloquently, and at length, Agrippa spoke mainly to the uncommitted majority, ignoring extremists whose minds he could not change. Some of the people said that their war was against Florus, not Rome. Agrippa had to explain that "your actions are already acts of war against Rome: you have not paid your tribute to Caesar, and you have cut down the porticoes communicating with Antonia. If you wish to clear yourselves of the charge of insurrection, re-establish the porticoes and pay the tax; for assuredly the fortress does not belong to Florus, and it is not Florus to whom your money will go."[3]

The Jews followed Agrippa's advice for a while, but he continued to urge submission to Florus, which could not be tolerated. Until this time Agrippa II had the middle class behind him, but when he and Berenice continued to push their positions as peace party advocates, they were forced to flee Jerusalem to escape the fury of the mob. Their departure dashed hopes of avoiding war, and placed Agrippa on the Roman side of the conflict. This allowed him to maintain his throne and influence in the area for a quarter of a century after the destruction of Jerusalem.

"Agrippa's blunder," writes Grayzel, "set the stage for the next step in the breach of relations with Rome. Until now the struggle had been against Florus; now a move was made against Rome itself."[4]

In the middle of the summer of 66, a group of *sicarii* (so-called "knife-men" named for the small blades they carried) commanded by a certain Menahem, attacked and massacred the Roman garrison at Masada. Now Masada became the first Jewish rebel stronghold; the desert fortress was the location of both the first and last major military action of the war.

Around this time in Jerusalem, one of the Temple priests, Eleazar, son of the former High Priest Ananias, convinced the Temple hierarchy to discontinue all sacrifices made for non-Jews. Thus the daily sacrifices on behalf of the Emperor no longer took place. "In effect, therefore, Eleazar's act meant a refusal of allegiance to Rome. The peace party and the aristocrats strongly objected to his action. But Eleazar, with the support of the younger priests and the revolutionaries refused to yield."[5] Josephus believed that more than any other act, this "laid the foundation for the war with the Romans."[6]

The high priests and religious leaders, whether Pharisee or Sadducee, maintained that Roman rule was not a threat to the Jewish religion, and most of them supported the peace party. Jewish fighting ability was diminished by the internal dissension between the peace party and the rebels, and later between the factions of rebels.

Recognizing the strength of the insurgents, the Jewish aristocrats asked Florus and Agrippa for military aid against their fellow Jews, and they complied. This small army captured all of Jerusalem except for the Temple area, where the zealots and *sicarii* maintained control. Fighting continued throughout Jerusalem and, Grayzel explains, "the significance of this fight lay in the fact that the masses of Jerusalem fought by the side of the revolutionaries, and that, as soon as they could, they burned the archives where records of debts...were kept [which helped win support of the poor]. They also burned down the palace of Agrippa and the homes of other aristocrats who had till then ruled the city. The aristocrats who did not flee were killed."[7]

The initial Jewish victories sent shock waves throughout the Roman Empire. As Agrippa II had predicted, Jews everywhere were murdered. In Caesarea, more than 20,000 Jews were massacred in a single bloody hour. In Damascus, 10,000 more were killed. And in Antioch, Alexandria and other cities, there was similar carnage.

The Romans knew that this rebellion had to be stamped out quickly, lest other local potentates get the wrong idea about the strength of the empire.

Late in 66, from their position in nearby Syria, Rome's Twelfth Legion under the leadership of the Roman governor of the province of Syria, Cestius Gallus, marched toward Jerusalem and aimed to quiet the embattled Jews. Even though the Jewish forces that met Gallus' army consisted of factions that continued to squabble among themselves, they united sufficiently to present a strong front and rout the Roman garrisons stationed in and around Jerusalem. "Rejoicing, [the Jews] returned to Jerusalem laden with booty...the unexpected had happened; a victory had been won against a Roman army. All the dreams of ultimate independence for Judaea were aroused,"[8] Grayzel writes.

Not only had Cestius Gallus and his troops been defeated, they were routed. The report from Josephus was that "they suffered heavily, without any retaliation upon their foes…in their utter helplessness the troops were reduced to groans and the wailings of despair, which were answered by the war-whoop of the Jews, with mingled shouts of exultation and fury. Cestius and his entire army were, indeed, within an ace of being captured."[9] The Romans fled that night under cover of darkness, but the Jews pursued them into the Beth Horon pass and cut the remnants of their force to ribbons. Jewish losses, according to Josephus, "had been quite inconsiderable; of the Romans and their allies they had slain five thousand three hundred infantry and four hundred and eighty of the cavalry."[10]

When word of Gallus' defeat reached Nero in Rome, he recognized the dangerous situation and called upon his most distinguished general, the aging Flavius Vespasianus, who had led Rome's armies to victory in Germany and Britain.

Vespasian arrived at Akko-Ptolemais in 67 along with the powerful Fifth and Tenth Legions, and soon was joined by his son Titus leading the Fifteenth Legion. Vespasian's first tactic was to encircle Galilee, where the Jewish forces were under the command of the general Joseph ben Matthias. Galilee fell within a few months, but before it did, Joseph surrendered to Vespasian and tried to convince his fellows to do the same. They did not. Meanwhile, Joseph befriended Vespasian and became a court follower and historian—known today by the name he took as freed slave of Vespasian's family—Flavius Josephus, the only Jewish historian of that time whose works survive today.

By the middle of 68, Vespasian's troops had succeeded in crushing the revolt throughout Palestine. Only Jerusalem and a few zealot fortresses such as Machaerus and Masada remained. Masada was ignored for the moment and Vespasian prepared to besiege Jerusalem. At about this time, Nero was murdered and civil war rocked Rome, which survived the tumultuous year of 68/9 CE, the year of the four emperors—Galba, Otho, Vitellius, and Vespasian. During this political upheaval the war was temporarily halted. The pause allowed Simon bar Giora, a charismatic Jewish-Idumaean rebel leader to regroup. His forces reconquered Hebron and parts of Idumaea, then entered Jerusalem and took over much of the city.

The Eastern legions proclaimed Vespasian emperor and within a year he successfully claimed the throne in Rome. Vespasian had, however, forgotten neither the Jews nor his desire to crush their uprising once and for all, and he sent his son Titus to finish the job. Three factions of Jews engaged in civil war within Jerusalem and provided the Romans with considerable help.

One faction of Jews was led by the firebrand Galilean John of Gischala, who entered the city at the end of 67 CE with the remnants of his army that had escaped the vengeance of Titus in the north. After some battles and intrigue, and the murder of a moderate leader and former High Priest Ananias, son of Ananias, John became the leader of the Zealots, who controlled the Temple and its environs. Josephus reports that some of John's Zealots put on women's clothes and perfume and went through the city with braided hair and painted eyes trying to attract men and then unexpectedly killing them for sport.[11] No wonder the people invited Simon bar Giora and his army into the city.

Simon bar Giora, another leader of rebel Jews, was joined by ordinary citizens in Jerusalem, where he laid siege to John and his forces at the Temple itself. At this time a priest named Eleazar ben Simon fell out with John and formed a third faction of armed Jews within the city. The civil war that ensued among Eleazar, John, and Simon was mutually suicidal and although each of them may have had a personal rationale, this was a war without achievement for the Jewish people. Tacitus reported that for the Jewish factions, "it was upon each other that they turned the weapons of battle, ambush, and fire, and great stocks of corn went up in flames."[12]

These were harsh days for the Jews, the situation was deteriorating rapidly and little hope was in sight. This led to an irrational growth of messianic hopes among the people, which was encouraged by the revolutionary leaders. Tacitus explains that "The majority were convinced that the ancient scriptures of their priests alluded to the present as the very time when the Orient would triumph and from Judaea would go forth men destined to rule the world."[13]

Both Tacitus and Josephus tell a similar story that reflects the superstitions running rife in Jerusalem at the time. Josephus says the tale "would, I imagine, have been deemed a fable, were it not for the narratives of eyewitnesses."[14] Tacitus' concise version says that, "In the sky appeared a vision of armies in conflict, of glittering armor. A sudden lightning flash from the clouds lit up the Temple. The doors of the holy place abruptly opened, a superhuman voice was heard to declare that the gods were leaving it, and in the same instant came the rushing tumult of their departure."[15]

Josephus reports that the fighting inside Jerusalem was so vicious that pious Jews had to climb over dead bodies to reach the Temple in order to offer sacrifices as usual. Eventually Eleazar's forces were diminished and those remaining were absorbed into the Zealots. Toward the end of the war, as Titus' troops were preparing to breach the walls, the scene inside Jerusalem was genuinely gruesome, but the Jews fought on. "They displayed an inflexible determination, women no less than men, and the thought that they might be compelled to leave their homes made them more afraid of living than of dying,"[16] Tacitus observes.

Titus' siege machines pounded the city and its walls with battering rams and huge stones. Even while Titus was at work on the outside of Jerusalem, his allies, famine and plague, struck down thousands of the besieged Jews. Slowly but surely, Titus' men and machines tore down the three walls of the city.

When the last wall fell, the survivors holed up in the Temple compound and continued to resist for six more days. It is said that Titus had ordered the Temple itself saved, but as his troops smelled the success that had so long eluded them, they burnt it to the ground and butchered its protectors. Even after this, however, isolated pockets of resistance flickered in the Temple area, and it was a month before all were wiped out.

Throughout the conflict, at least four ranking Jews stood with Titus: the apostate Tiberius Alexander of Alexandria, former procurator of Judaea, chief of staff; Agrippa II, commanded a large army of auxiliaries; Berenice, sister of Agrippa II, was the mistress of Titus and hoped to become his wife; and the turncoat historian, Josephus, who chronicled the campaign.

Upon Titus' victory, Josephus writes, a Roman officer "selected the tallest and most handsome of the youth and reserved them for the triumph; of the rest, those over 17 years of age he sent in chains to the works in Egypt, while multitudes were presented by Titus to the various provinces, to be destroyed in the theatres by the sword or by wild beasts; those under 17 were sold....The total number of prisoners taken throughout the entire war amounted to 97,000, and of those who perished during the siege, from first to last, to 1,100,000.[17] Of these the greater number were of Jewish blood, but not natives of the place; for, having assembled from every part of the country for the feast of unleavened bread, they found themselves suddenly enveloped in the war, with the result that this overcrowding produced first pestilence, and later the added and more rapid scourge of famine."[18]

Ironically, John and Simon were among the survivors. They approached Titus and asked him to allow them to go into the desert with their followers and their families, to resume their lives and way of worship. Titus was enraged by the vanquished leaders trying to dictate terms to him and ordered his army to enter Jerusalem and sack the city. John and Simon ended up being taken to Rome as captives and, after being paraded through Rome in the "Triumph," John was sentenced to life in prison and Simon was executed.

The golden showbread table, menorah, and other holy objects from the Temple were taken to Rome and put in the Temple of Peace.[19] They have long since disappeared, but we can see images of them today via the reliefs on the Arch of Titus that was built to commemorate his victory over the Jewish nation. That arch stands today not as a monument to its Roman builders, whose civilization has long since disappeared, but as a monument to the Jewish people who outlived their conquerors by many generations.

Actually, when the Jerusalem Temple was burnt, the Jewish revolt was not yet entirely crushed. After Titus sailed home to celebrate, Roman troops marched on Zealot fortresses at Herodium, just south of Jerusalem, and then went on to conquer the hilltop fortress at Machaerus

9.1. Relief on the Arch of Titus, Rome, depicts the Judaean triumph, in which the golden showbread table, menorah, and other holy objects were put on display. (Author photo.)

across the Jordan River, overlooking the Dead Sea. A band of Zealots held out at the mountain fortress Masada near the Dead Sea for a full three years.[20] Even when Masada succumbed, the Jewish people did not. Their faith depended more on tradition and laws than on sanctuary and sacrifices. Virtually at the moment of Rome's victory, Rabbi Johanan ben Zakkai, with Titus' blessing, was establishing a center of learning in the city of Jamina.

Smallwood observes that "Rabbi Johanan's escape, technically an act of treachery, was the Jews' spiritual salvation, when the Rabbinnic school which he founded took the place of the Sanhedrin as the supreme Jewish religious authority, and its president, the *Nasi* or patriarch, replaced the high priest as the Jews' leader and spokesman, both religious and political. But just as the high priests from 6 to 66 had been appointed by the procurators and then by client kings bound to support Roman interests, so the appointments of the Nasi after 70 were ratified by the Roman authorities, who could thus ensure that Jewish leadership remained in the hands of politically acceptable men."[21]

SILVER COINS OF THE JEWISH WAR

Precise manufacturing was a hallmark of the silver coins of the Jewish War. They were uniform in weight, purity, shape, and striking. Engraving of the dies was the best in the history of Judaea where, for the first time we can clearly see "a mint geared for large-scale production, not with the work of part-time amateur artisans," according to Roth.[22]

This consistency in the silver coins of the Jewish War is rather remarkable considering the ongoing civil war and changes in power within the Jewish community. The political situation was certainly "not consistent with the stable minting of coins by the rebels' government throughout the five years of the revolt,"[23] Rappaport notes. It is indeed remarkable that the changing situation among the Jews did not affect the striking of the silver coins, which reflected a "relatively settled condition and the confident atmosphere of the country at the time,"[24] according to Roth.

Neither Seleucids nor Romans had previously allowed the Jews to issue silver coins. Hence the autonomous series of *sheqels*, half-*sheqels*, and quarter-*sheqels* were designed not only as currency, but to make bold political statements—"an ostentatious demonstration of the recovery of independence,"[25] writes Roth, who argues that the minting of coins by an autonomous Jewish government "was a religious as well as a patriotic necessity."[26]

Rappaport suggests that the silver coinage of the Jewish War was "first and foremost minted to provide for the Temple's expenditures for provisions and maintenance and the pro-Roman Jewish aristocracy, both high priestly circles and rich noble laymen, by pretending to support the revolt, grasped onto the leadership of the rebellious movement in order to control the rebels, to weaken their hold on the people and to avoid a hopeless confrontation with Rome."[27]

Commodities and services required by the Temple included sacrificial animals, wine, incense, olive oil, wheat, and related products. Temple workers and craftsmen also needed to be paid, no matter how menial their jobs.

Thus the silver coins were needed for multiple reasons. Their importance was surely not taken for granted and there is every reason to believe that the symbols and slogans used on the coins were carefully selected.

The obverse of the *sheqels* depicts a chalice and the proto-Hebrew inscription "*Sheqel* of Israel," with the date in the same Hebrew letters above the chalice. The reverse shows a staff with three pomegranate buds and carries the inscription "Jerusalem the holy." Jewish *sheqels* weigh on average just less than 14 grams, (with a range of 11.8 to 14.8 grams) and the edges have been hammered (peened) uniformly, except on the specimens of the first year which are hammered, but in a somewhat cruder manner. This time-consuming manufacturing technique is unique to this series, and may have been undertaken to show the special nature of the coins, or even simply to thwart cheats who would shave or trim away the silver for their own gain.

Robert Deutsch, with Yehosua Drei's technical assistance, has shown that the *sheqel* and half-*sheqel* flans were hammered prior to striking.[28]

Average weight of the Jewish War half-*sheqels* is around 6.8 grams with a known range of 6 to 7.2 grams.

Scholarly controversies raged over these *sheqels* for hundreds of years. Once most scholars believed that the "thick Jewish *sheqels*," as they were called in the late 1800s and early 1900s, were issued under Simon Maccabee, who was at one time granted permission by Antiochus VII Sidetes, Seleucid king of Syria, to mint coins of his own for the land of Judaea.

By the mid-twentieth century, however, it became clear that Simon never actually issued coins since Antiochus revoked his grant. Archaeological and historical evidence have proven that the silver Jewish *sheqels* date from the Jewish War.

Striking of the Jewish War coins spanned the first five years of the war, until Jerusalem's destruction. Hence the *sheqels* were issued with five different dates, from year one to year five; the first year spanned May 66 (and possibly later) to March 67, the second, third, and fourth years spanned the months of April 67 to March 70 and the fifth year extended only from April to August of the year 70.

For his Ph.D. dissertation, Deutsch has documented more than 1,200 *sheqels* and half-*sheqels* of the Jewish War, and identified 515 different dies from which they were struck.[29] Goldstein and Fontanille previously reported on similar work, discussed below.

The other silver coins include quarter-*sheqels* (Nos. 1356, 1366) from the first and fourth years, which are excessively rare and struck from only one die set each. The fourth year quarter-*sheqels* are the only coins in this series that deviate from the standard design.

As one might expect, rarity of the various *sheqels* and half-*sheqels* is relative to the number of dies used in each year. For the *sheqels*, the coins of the second year make up around 50% of the known coins followed by year 3, around 25%, year 1, around 15%, year 4, around 6% and year 5 around 3%. The half-*sheqels* are split around 30% each for the first through third years with around 2% for the fourth year and only two known specimens for the fifth year.

These numbers and ratios make sense with one exception. According to the numbers of dies, the *sheqels* of the year 4 should be roughly comparable in number to those of the year 1. Instead, however, there are fewer than half as many year 4 *sheqels* as there are year 1 *sheqels*. The explanation for this phenomenon no doubt is due to dramatic deterioration of the situation within Jerusalem in the fourth year of the war. There was a possible shortage of silver as well as great turmoil, which must have resulted in less attention being paid to minting coins. It is also possible that some of these later coins remained in the mint where they were easily accessed by the Romans, who took and melted all coins that they found.

Goldstein and Fontanille also discovered that virtually none of the reverse dies are shared between years of production. In other words, even though more than 200 nearly identical reverse dies were used over five years of production, the reverses were each invariably used for only a single year. Thus, "each year's reverse dies apparently were discarded at the end of that year."[30] Among the rare exceptions is one reverse die that was used for both year 4 and year 5 half-*sheqels*.

While the obverse dies of the *sheqels* and half-*sheqels* are always dated, the reverses are virtually identical. Therefore, it is not clear why, in a time of duress, Jewish minters would go to the trouble to create new reverse dies for the *sheqels* and the half-*sheqels* every year, even though it was not necessary. Furthermore, the reverse dies outnumber the obverse dies by significant margins in each year, overall by a ratio of 5:1, according to Deutsch. This may have been due to mechanical issues, since the loose reverse dies may have deteriorated at a faster rate than the obverse dies. Technical evidence, however, leaves no doubt that perfectly good reverse *sheqel* dies were often discarded at the end of each minting year.

Sheqels	Obv. Dies	Rev. Dies
Year 1	10	27
Year 2	19	203
Year 3	20	96
Year 4	9	29
Year 5	5	10
Half-Sheqels	Obv. Dies	Rev. Dies
Year 1	5	12
Year 2	7	30
Year 3	6	23
Year 4	4	2
Year 5	1	1

9.2. Die tabulation for Jewish War *sheqels* and half-*sheqels,* after Deutsch 2009.

Until the beginning of the Jewish War the most common silver coins circulating in Judaea were the Tyre *sheqels* and half-*sheqels*. These coins are further discussed in Chapter 12, but it is not likely that these were silver coins of Herod I, as suggested by Meshorer.[31] On the other hand, it is possible that through the mid-first century the Tyre mint struck coins mainly for use by the Jews, "who used them for payment of all kinds to the Temple. Probably the Tyrian mint, as well as the money changers in Jerusalem, reaped a profit from the exchange of its coins. At the same time the Temple treasury got the purest silver coins on the market at the time. The Tyrian mint ceased to mint its *sheqels* before the revolt broke out and when the revolt began, the half-*sheqel* tax and other donations from the Diaspora to the Temple may have been reduced significantly. Concurrently the Temple authority combined its economic needs with popular national public opinion and minted—for its own use—coins,

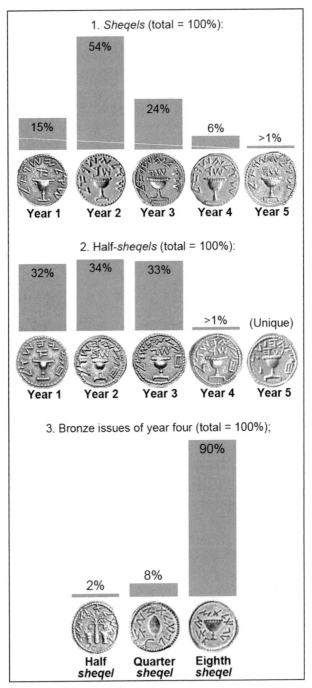

9.3. Frequency of Jewish War coins. (Graphic: Fontanille.)

with which it could acquire what was necessary for the continuation of the Temple's functioning."[32]

Silver stocks of the Jerusalem Temple were probably the source for the silver used to mint the silver *sheqels* and fractions. Since at one point in the war, Jerusalem was cut off from the Jewish Diaspora as well as areas of Judaea itself, the income to the Treasury was likely curtailed dramatically. However, there had been an accumulation of silver from previous contributions as well as the booty taken from Romans during Jewish successes early in the war.

Rappaport believes that the location of the mint of the silver coins was in the Temple area, and directed by Temple officials who were sympathetic to the aspirations of the Zealot party. "In any case the coins issued by the mint were intended primarily to meet the needs of the Temple and not mainly to supplant the Tyrian or any other coinage. At the same time the messages of these coins did not contradict the ideologies of any of the rebel parties and so could have been tolerated by all of them,"[33] he writes.

The legends and objects depicted on the *sheqels* are consistent with the ideology of the Zealots, who "did not have a charismatic or messianic leadership but a collective one. Their center and base was the holy mount and the Temple itself. They believed that Jerusalem was impregnable and that they had the right to use its resources because they were fighting for the Temple."[34]

Thus the *sheqels*, half-*sheqels*, and quarter-*sheqels* were adopted as significant currency in Judaea, "without regard to the political inclinations and aspirations of the various parties and groups."

BRONZE COINS OF THE JEWISH WAR

Bronze coins of the Jewish War differ from the silver coins in many respects, and there is an increasing body of research that points to a mint for bronze coins at a separate location and operated by a different political faction. The bronze coins, especially the *prutot*, were of very small value and were principally used as small change in the marketplace alongside other circulating coins.

Rappaport suggests that Simon bar Giora's party most likely minted the bronze coins. He observes that their slogans "represent a more radical ideology"[35] than the slogans on the silver coins. "Jerusalem the holy" proclaimed on the *sheqels* is less extreme than the "freedom of

Zion" slogan on the bronze coins dated to the second and third years, which is less radical than the "for the redemption (or salvation) of Zion" on the coins of the fourth year.

Furthermore, Rappaport points out, the bronze coins were dated only to the years 2, 3, and 4, which is consistent with Simon's activity. "In the first year of the revolt Simon was occupied with the stabilization of his party, moving from one place to another and chased by the

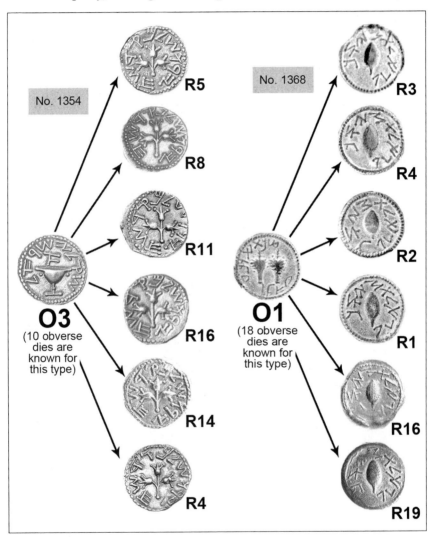

9.4. Connection chart showing how obverse and reverse dies could combine for year 1 silver *sheqels* (left) and year 4 bronze quarter-*sheqels*. (Graphic: Fontanille)

Hanan government. Only in years two and three was he able to initiate minting in bronze somewhere outside of Jerusalem. In year four Simon occupied the greater part of the city and became the most powerful and important leader. In year five the two camps, of Simon and of John and the Zealots, were united, and Jerusalem was besieged. Even the Temple minted few *sheqels* and bronze was not minted at all."[36]

Goldstein and Fontanille examined various aspects of the symbols and legends on the Jewish War coins and also suggest that the fourth year bronze coins were not struck by the same mint that issued the silver *sheqels*.[37] The year four bronzes vary from the *sheqels* in that they have a different symbolism, different legends, and a slightly different epigraphy for some letters. Rappaport argues that all of the bronze coins were issued at a mint under Simon bar Giora's rule, although he suggests that some technical differences between the earlier dated bronzes and the year four bronzes "may have been a result of bar Giora's moving the mint from its temporary location in his camp to a more stable and better equipped setting in Jerusalem... Also, it may be explained by Simon's elevation to the more important leader in Jerusalem and the subsequent Roman siege of the city. The upgrading of the message of his bronze coins from 'freedom' to 'salvation' may also be connected to the decision to mint heavier denominations."[38]

9.5. Irregular silver *sheqels* of the first, fourth, and fifth years with similar irregular engraving traits. (Fontanille.)

SIEGE COINS AND CIVIL WAR

As discussed, the Jewish War was fought during five calendar years, according to the Jewish calendar. The bronze coins of the fourth year coins date to 69/70 CE and comprise the first series of "siege coins" ever minted.

This group contains three different sizes of bronze coins, one inscribed with the denominations "half," "quarter," and one without a denomination, but which is clearly half of the quarter, or an eighth. It has been suggested that these were "fictitious" fractions of the Jewish silver *sheqels*, but because they were not actual fractions, the word *sheqel* itself was never mentioned on them.[39] These coins were struck by the Jews besieged in Jerusalem while the city was surrounded by the Roman army under Titus, not long before the destruction of Jerusalem itself.

"In every possible sense of the term these are true siege-pieces," according to E.T. Newell. "By the dates they bear they were struck in the city of Jerusalem itself when that city was being closely invested by Titus and his army; by the fictitious value inscribed on them they show that though of bronze, they were intended to pass as the half and quarter of a silver *sheqel*; and lastly by the legend *ligulat Zion* (redemption of Zion) they give us what must have been the daily prayer of the hard pressed and despairing Jews during the last few terrible months of their heroic revolt."[40]

Besieged by the Romans and fighting among themselves, the Jews in Jerusalem by the fourth year were in the midst of a terrible famine. Josephus relates that Jews terrorized Jews as they searched for food. "The recklessness of the insurgents kept pace with the famine... as corn [grain] was nowhere to be seen, they would rush in and search the houses, and then if they found any they belabored the inmates as having denied the possession of it; if they found none they tortured them for more carefully concealing it. The personal appearance of the wretches was an index whether they had it or not: those still in good condition were presumed to be well off for food, while those already emaciated were passed over, as it seemed senseless to kill persons so soon to die of starvation. Many clandestinely bartered their possessions for a single measure—of wheat, if they were rich, of barley, if they were poor; then shutting themselves up in the most remote recesses of their houses, some in the extremity of hunger devoured the grain un-ground, others so baked it as necessity and fear dictated. Nowhere was any table laid; they snatched the food half-cooked from the fire and tore it in pieces."[41]

Josephus tells of a famine so desperate that "necessity drove the victims to gnaw anything, and objects which even the filthiest of brute beasts would reject they condescended to collect and eat: thus in the end they abstained not from belts and shoes and stripped off and chewed the very leather of their bucklers."[42] In one gruesome tale, Josephus tells of a mother who ate the roasted body of her own child.[43] He concludes that "no other city ever endured such miseries, nor since the world began has there been a generation more prolific in crime."[44]

If it had not been for the strong will of John's and Simon's opposing factions, the simple, unaffiliated people of Jerusalem might have succumbed earlier. However, the rebels provided a strong backbone, possibly rooted in greed as well as devotion.

This is the background of the fourth and fifth years of the Jewish War, when the three bronze "siege coins" were issued. Newell suggests that the values "half" and "quarter" on the two larger pieces "show to what dire straits the once wealthy Temple treasury had been reduced by the war that it should have to thus substitute bronze for silver. As these coins are thus stamped with a purely fictitious value, they were evidently meant as a temporary expedient and, if the Jews had been successful, would probably have been redeemed for their face value at the end of the war. The fall of Jerusalem precluded this..."[45]

SLOGANS ON JEWISH WAR COINS

Precise wording in the legends and selection of the images on the coins of the Jewish War suggests that whatever else their faults might have been, the leaders involved had a clear understanding of how to use coins as a method of communication.

The first coins minted in the year 66 were the silver *sheqels* and half-*sheqels*, with the legends "Jerusalem [the] holy" and "Holy *sheqel*" or "half-*sheqel*." In these legends we see a parallel to the legend on the contemporary Tyrian silver coins which carried the legend "Of Tyre, the Holy and Inviolable." Even though the striking of these coins was revolutionary, their legends were rather generic, and likely to be embraced by all of the Jews.

The slogans on the lower value coins, clearly meant to be used in day-to-day transactions, differed significantly in tone. Huge numbers of bronze *prutot* were dated to the second and third years of the war, and each of them carried the words, "[for the] freedom of Zion," one of the earliest known records of a Zionistic slogan.[46]

That slogan represented a kind of rallying cry for the Jews. For years, the Romans had effectively used their coins to carry political messages; why shouldn't the Jews do the same? And so, in the days when there were no mass media and no internet, coins were used to communicate the Jewish message of hope for a free Jerusalem and a free people.

But after the initial Jewish victories, things began to go badly. By the middle of the year 68, Vespasian and his troops had crushed the revolt throughout the land. Only Jerusalem and the zealot fortresses of Machaerus, Herodium, and Masada remained in Jewish hands.

By the fourth year of the war, Jerusalem was under siege by Titus. Vespasian had ascended to the throne and the tide had turned against the Jews. At this time, the legends on the bronze Jewish coins were changed. No longer do we see the slogan, "freedom of Zion." It is replaced by the slogan, "for the redemption of Zion."

Roth agrees that the slogan change in the fourth year was "certainly not accidental [and] may well reflect the fresh political circumstances of this time, for Simon bar Giora had by now entered Jerusalem and established his supremacy there."[47] It is also possible that Simon relocated his mint to Jerusalem in this difficult time and that the change in language reflects the Jewish insurgents' realization that they would soon be defeated by the powerful Roman machine. Hence, the change in tone from the call for physical "freedom" from oppression versus "redemption" or "salvation," which has a more spiritual tone.

Goldstein and Fontanille add that "freedom does not necessarily imply confrontation and can conceivably be obtained by mutual consent, possibly as a result of negotiation, whereas redemption denotes salvation or a forced release from a status of war and oppression."[48]

Jerusalem was destroyed early in the war's fifth year. A new Jewish Diaspora grew throughout the ancient world. Refugees from Judaea bolstered Jewish communities already in exile in Rome, Alexandria, and other cities. Emotionally as well as practically, these Diaspora Jews of the first century CE looked toward the day that their Temple would be rebuilt and they would return to their holy Jerusalem.

SYMBOLISM OF THE FEAST OF TABERNACLES

This yearning was foreshadowed by the motifs used on the coins of the fourth year. The principal symbols on these coins reflect the Jewish holiday of Sukkot, also called the Feast of Booths or the Feast of Tabernacles. It was the most significant of three pilgrimage festivals (Passover, Shavout [Pentecost], Sukkot [Tabernacles]) during the days of the Second Temple. It was a popular holiday of harvest and thanksgiving with great festivity and rejoicing. Sukkot also plays a role in the New Testament, as background for one of Jesus' appearances in Jerusalem.

Now the Feast of Booths was at hand. His brothers therefore said to Him, 'Depart from here, and go into Judaea, that Your disciples also may behold Your works which You are doing' (JOHN 7:2–3).

The Book of Leviticus mentions some of the special observances of Sukkot:

...And ye shall take you on the first day the fruit of goodly trees, branches of palm-trees and boughs of thick trees, and willows of the brook, and ye shall rejoice before the Lord your God seven days....Ye shall dwell in booths seven days; all that are home-born in Israel shall dwell in booths; that your generations may know that I made the children of Israel to dwell in booths, when I brought them out of the land of Egypt... (LEVITICUS 23:39–43).

The types of vegetation referred to were named "the four species" by Rabbinnic authorities. The "fruit of goodly trees" is the citron, a lemon-like citrus fruit (*etrog* in Hebrew); the "boughs of thick trees" are myrtle twigs (*hadasim*); the palm branch is called *lulav*; and willows are called *aravot*. In the ancient world, there was a great deal of symbolism

9.6. Sukkot ritual items shown on Jewish War bronze coins, date palm with collection baskets, etrog, lulav bunch. (Graphic: Fontanille.)

linked to palm branches, not only by the Jews, but in the Greek and Roman worlds as well. Hence, Nike often holds a palm branch.

When the Jerusalem Temple was destroyed in 70 CE, Rabbi Johanan ben Zakkai ruled that wherever Jews celebrate the holiday of Sukkot, they should take "the four species" in their hand for seven days to commemorate the Temple. They were held while reciting certain prayers and psalms.

Even today, "the four species" are used by Jews throughout the world to celebrate Sukkot. The palm branch, two willow branches, and three myrtle twigs are wrapped together and held in a bunch in the right hand. This bunch became collectively known as a *lulav*, probably because the *lulav* is its largest component. The *etrog* is held in the left hand.

As a simple palm branch, we have already seen the *lulav* appear on coins of John Hyrcanus I, Alexander Jannaeus, Herod I, and Herod Antipas. Now, with the coins of the fourth year of the Jewish War, "the four species" as symbols of Sukkot and the pilgrimage to Jerusalem take center stage. The series of three bronze coins dated "year four" (Nos. 1367–69) each depicts variations of "the four species."

THE RITUAL CHALICE AND POMEGRANATE STAFF

The ritual chalice is also related to the Jewish holidays. Romanoff suggested it was related to the Omer, a sacrifice of first fruits mentioned in Leviticus:

> *When ye are come into the land which I give unto you, and shall reap the harvest thereof, then ye shall bring the sheaf of the first-fruits of your harvest unto the priest. And he shall wave the sheaf before the Lord, to be accepted for you...* (LEVITICUS 23:9–11).

Earlier descriptions of this cup suggested it was related to drinking wine, but Romanoff argues that this is not a drinking chalice. "It is doubtful whether or not the vessel was a drinking cup. The dotted [beaded] border would make drinking almost impossible. The cup, '*kos*', in the Temple was used for sacrificial blood; while the drinking of wine in the Temple was forbidden, and...the Jewish coins do not contain any symbol of blood sacrifices." Romanoff continues by explaining that "The 'chalice', or 'cup', rather signifies the golden vessel that contained the Omer and was used on the second day of Passover when a measure of barley, a tenth of an ephah, equal to one and a half pints of fine flour, was offered to the Temple as the first-fruits of the field. The waving of this vessel in different directions during the offering corresponded to the waving of the lulav."[49]

On the other hand, Goldstein and Fontanille observe that an omer cup is not described in any ancient sources, and believe it is equally likely that this is a generic Temple chalice, and perhaps even a "chalice of salvation." In either case we note that this chalice with a beaded rim is the only design that exists on both the silver and the bronze coins of the Jewish War.

Pomegranates as used on earlier Judaean coins are discussed on pp. 178–80. The pomegranate buds on the sheqels have often been described as hanging on a sprig or branch. Deutsch, however, asserts that this symmetrical object with a clear round base (or handle) more likely represents "a man-made staff...such an artifact matches a sacred object, a staff used by the high priests in the Temple and explains its appearance on the silver coins. Therefore the staff is likely to represent the minting authority, which is the high priesthood or the Temple as an institution."[50] (See Chapter 6 note 76.)

DATE PALM TREE

According to Rabbinic tradition, the "honey" listed among the seven species that bless the land of Israel was the honey from dates (DEUTERONOMY 8:8).

The impressive bronze half-*sheqel* of the fourth year of the Jewish War against Rome depicts a date palm, together with baskets for gathering its first fruit for sacrifice.

The first appearance of the date palm tree (as opposed to a *lulav* or palm branch) occurs on the first coin of Herod Antipas and later appears on coins of the Roman prefects of Judaea. Even though the palm tree had been used on coins of other cities, especially Tyre, it became a symbol commonly associated with ancient Judaea, especially in the eyes of the Romans and others who visited, but did not live there.

Significantly, a large number of the Judaea Capta coins struck by the Roman emperors Vitellius, Vespasian, Titus, and Domitian to commemorate their victory over Judaea in 70 CE depict the palm tree, using the tree to symbolize ancient Judaea itself. At this point it becomes obvious that, to Rome at least, the date palm tree was the single symbol that was directly associated with the land of the Jews.

The most extensive use of the palm tree on ancient Jewish coinage occurs during the Bar Kokhba Revolt. They are especially interesting since in almost every instance, even on the irregular coins, the palm tree is shown with seven branches. (This is also true of the bronze half-*sheqel* of the Jewish War.) It is tempting to make a connection with the seven-branched menorah that once stood in the Jerusalem Temple. Since Rabbinnic teachings forbade depiction of the Temple implements themselves (specifically the menorah and the showbread table), it is possible that the seven-branched palm tree reflected the menorah.

Oddly, Romanoff does not mention the menorah-palm tree connection at all. Here is what he says about the palm tree: "The palm, a fruit-bearing tree, growing near water, had already in biblical times been synonymous with height and abundance. The sight of such a tree meant the presence of water, an ever-ready meal, and rest in its shade. This tree became the symbol of Judaea where palm trees grow in greater number than in any other part of Palestine. It also represented Judaea the productive, Judaea the blessed, and the palm motif figured prominently on the walls, doors and pillars of the Tabernacle and the Temple....The palm tree has thus a double meaning, the symbol of Judaea and the symbol of abundance and plenty. As symbols have the tendency of ever spreading, the palm, in time, became the symbol of Palestine. The palm tree symbolizing Judaea is illustrated on the Judaea Capta coins. The palm tree has also become an emblem of (modern) Israel."[51]

9.7. Jewish War bronze half-*sheqel* (No. 1367), year 4, and pilgrim's ring with similar palm tree and basket motif from the same period. Such rings were probably purchased by pilgrims who traveled to Jerusalem for holidays such as the Feast of Tabernacles.

AMPHORA AND VINE LEAF

The amphora and vine leaf designs were used initially on a coin of Valerius Gratus. But, if one studies that coin (No. 1336) and compares it to the *prutot* of the Jewish War, one can see that the vessels are different. Both the procurator coins and the Jewish War coins depict a vessel on one side and a vine leaf on the other side. Kadman and Meshorer, among others, conclude that this supports the supposition that this amphora was probably used for wine libations.

Meshorer notes that coins of the Roman governors were widely circulated right up until the Jewish War. "Although the procurators attempted to mint coins depicting designs which would not offend the local populace, the symbol of the amphora reminded the Jews of the Roman libations of wine poured out before idols."[52]

On the other hand, Meshorer suggests that the Jewish War bronze coins represent the antithesis of the Roman motifs. He writes that the amphoras "on the Jewish issues may symbolize the sacred libations of wine made in the Temple. The vessels depicted on the coins of the revolt are not copies of the Roman amphoras; they are Jewish and of a different style than the classical Greco-Roman models represented on the coinage of Valerius Gratus."[53]

Romanoff adds that "From mishnaic sources we learn that only two liquids, water and wine, usually required covers."[54] (Actually, containers with milk also needed to be covered.) This requirement is of interest since the amphora shown on the 'year three' coin is clearly covered.

They used to fill a golden flagon holding three logs with water from Siloam. When they reached the Water Gate, they blew on the shofar a sustained, a quavering and another sustained blast. The priest whose turn of duty it was went up the Altar-Ramp and turned to the right where were two silver bowls…. They had each a hole like a narrow snout, one wide and the other narrow so that both bowls emptied themselves together…. The bowl to the west was for water and that to the east was for wine…. As was the rite on a weekday so was the rite on a Sabbath save that on the eve of the Sabbath they used to fill with water from Siloam a golden jar that had not been hallowed, and put it in a special chamber. If it was upset or uncovered, they refilled it from the laver, for wine or water which has been uncovered is invalid for the Altar (MISHNAH, SUKKAH 4, 9–10).

"Here we have our vessels," E.W. Klimowsky writes. "The big golden flagon holding three logs was that with a lid and also the one without it, which is on the coins of the First Jewish War." He adds that in describing the "natural size of the golden amphora, the Mishnah reports that the contents were three logs of water taken from Siloam. This would be about one and a half pints…[thus] the size of the golden amphora was not considerable."[55]

THE UNDATED PRUTAH

In the third edition of this book, we discussed an undated *prutah* (No. 1357) that had been previously published by Deutsch as a unique coin, attributed to the first year of the Jewish War.[56] In the fourth edition I cited a second example that was overstruck on a coin dated to the second year. Evidence suggested that the undated coin was actually struck in the fourth year—since it was struck upon a coin of the second year it must have come later.

Even though conclusions regarding overstrike were confirmed by other numismatists, there was a different scenario I neglected to consider. That is, simply, that the dies from a trial strike late in the first year remained in the mint after the manufacturing of the second year coins began and the overstrike occurred early in the second year.

The two known examples of this coin are from different die sets, and this suggests the evolution of the beginning of a bronze coin mint that later struck huge quantities of year 2 and 3 *prutot*.

Deutsch observed that the obverse inscription, "Jerusalem [the] Holy" was identical to the inscription on the Year 1 *sheqels* (omitting the article "the"). This is the only instance of identical legends on the bronze and silver coins of the Jewish War and suggests that the legends and designs for this coin were derivative of the first coins struck by the Temple mint. The later *sheqels* are inscribed "Jerusalem the Holy."

On Deutsch's first discovered (and still the most complete) specimen, the only visible inscription on the reverse consists of the final three Hebrew letters of the word "(Is)rael," and on the second (overstruck) specimen we can read two additional letters, a "yod" and a "shin," thus completing the word Israel. Deutsch suggests that a possible full legend for the reverse is "freedom of Israel." We posit that the reverse inscription might have carried a date, such as "Year one of Israel."

Another possibility is that since these undated coins were at least somewhat reflective of the first year *sheqels*, a missing element in the inscriptions is the denomination. All of the silver coins of the Jewish War state their denominations—*sheqel*, half-*sheqel*, and quarter or quarter-*sheqel*. It is therefore possible that the missing initial word on the reverse was the name of this small denomination, such as "*prutah* of Israel."

Perhaps at some future date a more complete specimen of this coin will be discovered and resolve the mystery. Until then it seems likely that this is a prototype for the massive issue of *prutot* during the second and third years of the Jewish War.

TEMPLE TRIBUTE AND OTHER JEWISH RITUALS

According to the Mishnah and other sources, the Temple tribute was payable only in Tyrian coinage, and this included the annual half *sheqel* that every Israelite had to pay to the Temple.

> *The five* selas *due for the [firstborn] son should be paid in Tyrian coinage the thirty due for the slave [that was gored by an ox] and the fifty due from the violator and the seducer, and the hundred due from him that hath brought up an evil name, are all to be paid according to the value of the* sheqels *of the sanctuary, in Tyrian coinage. Aught that is to be redeemed may be redeemed with silver or its value, save only the* sheqel-dues (MISHNAH, BEKHOROTH 8:7)

Since the Mishnah was not codified until the third century CE, well after the Jewish War, one might infer that even during the Jewish War the payment made to the sanctuary should be in the coinage of Tyre.

Still, there is a widespread belief that the Jewish War half-*sheqels* were issued specifically to fill the need for contributions to the Temple. Goldstein and Fontanille suggest that the quantity of the half-*sheqels* was more tightly controlled than that of the *sheqels* and, furthermore, "since the half-*sheqels* were needed in the Temple by the beginning of each year, they were slated for the earliest production. They were struck before the *sheqels*, allowing the required quota of half-*sheqels* to be minted in years with regular production."[57]

There is further discussion and a description of the use and origins of Tyrian *sheqels* in Chapter 12.

COINS OF THE JEWISH WAR
YEAR ONE, MAY 66 (OR LATER) – MARCH 67 CE
All with border of dots on both sides unless noted.
Average weight Jewish War *sheqels*, 13.8g, 6.8 g (half).
Average weight of the Jewish War *prutah*, 2.51 g.

1352

Ϝ ↳Ϝⴹ𐤔⅃ ↳ᛟϺ
שקל ישראל א
ⴹϺⴹ ᛎ⅁ ↳Ϻⵝⴹ⅃
ירושלם קדשה

1352. AR *sheqel*.
  Obv: ↳ϜⴹϺⴹ ↳ᛟϺ (*sheqel of Israel*); Ϝ (*[year] 1*) above ritual chalice
    with smooth, wide rim, pellet on either side, the base has pearled
    ends, circle of dots all around chalice and also outer legend.
  Rev: ⴹϺⴹ ᛎ⅃Ϻⵝⴹⴹ (*Jerusalem [the] holy*); stem with three pome-
    granates, pearl at base, circle of dots all around pomegranates
    and also around outer legend.   RRR

One specimen sold for $242,000 in Bromberg I.

This is a prototype for the first year sheqel *and is, therefore, the first coin
type of the Jewish War. Two specimens are known to exist, one in the Israel
Museum and the second in a private collection.*

In the late 1970s, an Arab dealer in Jerusalem offered me a group of six
sheqels. *Three were year two, two were year three, and the sixth was one of
these two coins. The price asked for the six coins was $6,000. The dealer was
well known for often dealing in forged coins. I rejected the deal, but instead
offered $4,000 for the five* sheqels, *not including the sixth. At the time, this
type had not been published. While it looked authentic to me, I was not certain
enough to overcome my doubts, and $2,000 for a questionable coin was a lot
of money. It was to my chagrin that in 1991 the Bromberg specimen sold at
auction for $242,000.*

1353. AR *sheqel*.
  Obv: ↳ϜⴹϺⴹ ↳ᛟϺ (*sheqel of Israel*); Ϝ (*[year] 1]*) above wide-rim ritual
    chalice with wide, smooth rim, pellet on either side, flat base with
    pearled ends.
  Rev: ⴹϺⴹᛟ ᛎ⅃Ϻⵝⴹⴹ (*Jerusalem [the] holy*); staff with three pome-
    granate buds, round base.   5,500/7,000

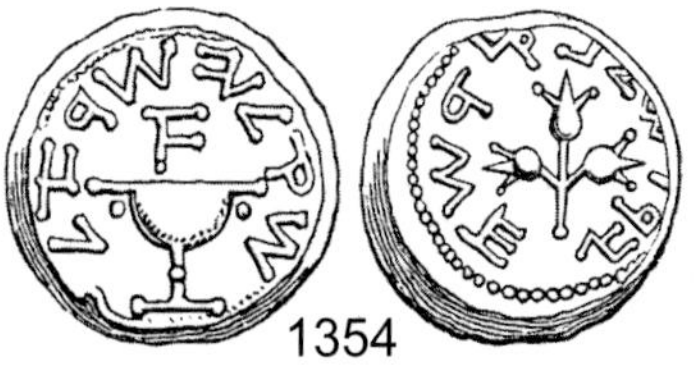

1354

1354. AR *sheqel.*

Obv: 𐤔𐤒𐤋 𐤉𐤔𐤓𐤀𐤋 *(sheqel of Israel)*; 𐤀 *([year] 1])* above ritual chalice with wide, smooth rim, pellet on either side, flat base with pearled ends.

Rev: 𐤉𐤓𐤅𐤔𐤋𐤌 𐤄𐤒𐤃𐤔𐤄 *(Jerusalem [the] holy)*; staff with three pomegranate buds, round base. 4,000/6,000

a. Reverse die is a bit crude.

1355

𐤇𐤑𐤉 𐤄𐤔𐤒𐤋
חצי השקל

1355. AR half-*sheqel.*

Obv: 𐤇𐤑𐤉 𐤄𐤔𐤒𐤋 *(half of a sheqel)*; 𐤀 *([year] 1)* above ritual chalice with smooth rim, pellet on either side, flat base with pearled ends

Rev: Pomegranate staff as on 1354. 4,500/8,500

a. Variety with large chalice.

1356

𐤓𐤁𐤏 𐤄𐤔𐤒𐤋
רבע השקל

1356. AR quarter-*sheqel.*

Obv: 𐤓𐤁𐤏 𐤄𐤔𐤒𐤋 *(quarter of a sheqel)*; 𐤀 *([year] 1)* above ritual chalice as on 1355.

Rev: Pomegranate staff as on 1354. RRR

(One specimen sold for $253,000 in Bromberg I.)

1357

1357. AE *prutah*.
  Obv: ℈WᑫᕹℲ ℽℓWℾᑫ℞ *(Jerusalem [the] holy)*; amphora with fluted
    body, broad rim and two handles.
  Rev: ∟Ⅎᑫ ... *(... [Is]rael)*; vine leaf on small branch.   RRR
  a. Overstruck specimen
    There are two known examples, see discussion on p. 354.

YEAR TWO, APRIL **67** – MARCH **68** CE

1358

𝔍W ∟ℲᑫWℶ ∟ᕹW

שקל ישראל שב

℈WℾᑫᕹℲ ℽℶℓWℾᑫ℞

ירושלים הקדושה

1358. AR *sheqel*.
  Obv: ∟ℲᑫWℶ ∟ᕹW *(sheqel of Israel)*; 𝔍W *(year 2)* above ritual chalice
    with pearled rim, the base is raised by projections on ends.
  Rev: ℈WℾᑫᕹℲ ℽℶℓWℾᑫ℞ *(Jerusalem the holy)*; staff with three pome-
    granate buds, round base.   3,000/5,000

1359

∟ᕹW℈ ℶᔦ𐤁

חצי השקל

1359. AR half-*sheqel*.
  Obv: Ritual chalice with pearled rim, the base is raised by projec-
    tions on ends, above chalice date 𝔍W *(year 2)*; ∟ᕹW℈ ℶᔦ𐤁 *(half of
    a sheqel)*.
  Rev: Pomegranate staff as on 1355.   4,000/7,500

1360

1360a

שֲZXw XZw
שנת שתים

Y YZk X[Y]9 B
חר]ו[ת ציון

1360. AE *prutah*.

  Obv: שֲZXW XZW *(year two)*; amphora with broad rim and two handles.

  Rev: ЗtZ X9A *(the freedom of Zion)*; vine leaf on small branch with tendril.   50/150

  a. Reverse inscription is ЗtZ Xt9A.

  b. Irregular issue.

  c. Irregular issue, retrograde both sides.

  d. Double struck both sides.

  Large numbers of irregular issues occur in many forms from the crudely engraved to those with completely retrograde inscriptions.

YEAR THREE, APRIL 68 – MAY 69 CE

1361

1362

٦W
שג

1361. AR *sheqel*.

  Obv: LF9WZ LPW *(sheqel of Israel)*; ٦W *(year 3)* above ritual chalice with pearled rim, the base is raised by projections on ends.

  Rev: ЗWt9PЗ שֲZ∠Wt9Z *(Jerusalem the holy)*; staff with three pomegranate buds, round base.   3,500/5,500

1362. AR half-*sheqel*.

  Obv: LPWЗ ZA *(half of a sheqel)*; ٦W *(year 3)* above ritual chalice with pearled rim, the base is raised by projections on ends.

  Rev: Pomegranate staff as on 1361.   4,000/7,500

1363. AE *prutah.*

Obv: ᗯ⅄ᒪᗯ ×ℶᗯ *(year three)*; amphora with broad rim, two handles, and conical lid decorated with tiny globes hanging around edge.

Rev: ℶ⅂⅄ᒿ↑ ×⅄ᑫᗺ *(the freedom of Zion)*; vine leaf on small branch.

75/200

a. With long flan strips.

b. Reverse inscription is ℶ⅂⅄ᒿ↑ ×ᑫᗺ.

Less common than the second year issue; the ratio is estimated to be be roughly 1 to 8, a significantly reduced production. Irregular issues of the third year are very rare.

Year Four, April 69 – March 70 ce

1364. AR *sheqel.*

Obv: ᒪᖴᑫᗯℶ ᒪᖴᗯ *(sheqel of Israel)*; ᑫᗯ *(year 4)* above ritual chalice with pearled rim, the base is raised by projections on ends.

Rev: ℥ᗯ↑ᑫᕒℲ ⅄ℶ⅂ᗯ↑ᑫℶ *(Jerusalem the holy)*; staff with three pomegranate buds, round base.

25,000/35,000

a. Irregular variety exists from a single die set.

We see here for the first time since the first year coins some poorly engraved (irregular) dies, possibly reflecting fewer available artisans due to the stressful condition of the Jewish government near the end of the Jewish War.

1365. AR half-*sheqel.*

Obv: 𐤇𐤑𐤉 𐤄𐤔𐤒𐤋 *(half of a sheqel)*; 𐤔𐤃 *(year 4)* above ritual chalice with pearled rim, the base is raised by projections on ends.

Rev: Pomegranate staff as on 1364. 100,000/200,000

1366

𐤃 𐤓𐤁𐤏 𐤄𐤔𐤒𐤋

ד רבע השקל

1366. AR quarter-*sheqel.*

Obv: 𐤓𐤁𐤏 𐤄𐤔𐤒𐤋 *(quarter of a sheqel)*; three palm branches tied together at their stalks.

Rev: 𐤃 *(4)* surrounded by a wreath of palm branches, tied in X at bottom. RRR

For many years the single example of this coin existed in the collection of the British Museum, London. G.F. Hill the legendary Keeper of the Coins, wrote in his catalog of this collection that it was "unique but of not absolutely undoubted authenticity, which was acquired with the Hamburger collection...I am distinctly inclined...to accept the coin as antique; but I include it in the catalog with some reserve."[58]

Hill's instinct has proven to be correct. After the year 2000, two additional examples of this coin, from the same dies, surfaced in the market. I had previously examined the coin in the British Museum, and I was fortunate to personally examine one of the recent finds microscopically and to study the other one in photographs taken before, during, and after cleaning of the original thick crust of oxidation and encrustation. Thus there are three known examples of this coin; the location of the two recent finds is not known at this writing.

Hill made another interesting observation unrelated to authenticity. He pointed out that unlike the other coins of the Jewish War, this coin shows the distinct influence of the procurator coins in that there is an X at the bottom of the wreath and the obverse of three palm branches "recall the three barley-ears on the procurator coins of year 17/18 CE *of Tiberius (No. 1341)."*[59] *We note that three ears of grain also adorn the prutah of Agrippa I. Why this change of types took place, we simply do not understand at this time.*

ל‎גאלת ציון

שנת ארבע חצי

1367. AE half, 26mm, average 15.5 g, range 12.3 to 17.7 g.

Obv: ⨯⅃W *(year four, half)*; two lulav bunches flank an etrog (citron).

Rev: *(to the redemption of Zion)*; Seven-branched palm tree with two bunches of dates, flanked by baskets of dates.

4,000/12,500

a. Cut in half to make smaller unit of money.

שנת ארבע רביע

1368. AE quarter, 22mm, average 8.9 g, range 5.55 to 10.62 g.

Obv: ⨯⅃W *(year four–quarter)*; two lulav bunches.

Rev: *(to the redemption of Zion)*; etrog.   1,500/4,000

1369b

1369. AE eighth, AE 20mm, 5.5 g, range 4 to 9.7 g.

Obv: ⨯⅃W *(year four)*; lulav bunch flanked by an etrog on either side.

Rev: *(to the redemption of Zion)*; chalice with pearled rim.   200/550

a. Irregular, crude lettering.

b. Irregular, retrograde reverse.

c. Irregular, retrograde both sides.

YEAR FIVE, APRIL – AUGUST, *70 CE*

1370

ℲW
שה

1370a

1370.   AR *sheqel*
   Obv: ⱶℲꟻWⱶ ⱶꟼW *(sheqel of Israel)*; ℲW *(year 5)* above ritual chalice
   with pearled rim, the base is raised by projections on ends.
   Rev: ℲWⱵꟼℲ ꟿⱶⱶWⱵꟻⱶ *(Jerusalem the holy)*; staff with three pomegranate buds, round base.   50,000/125,000
   a. Irregular issue.
   *The widely discussed irregular example of this coin was struck from a
single pair of dies. In the mid-1980s, thirteen Year 5 sheqels, all struck from
the same die set, and all heavily cleaned, were found in the vault of Baldwin's
a legendary London coin dealer. At the beginning of the twentieth century, an
unknown person had marked the group as forgeries. However, the dies matched
the previously-thought-to-be unique specimen in the British Museum collection
(BM p. 271, 20), which had been acquired in 1887. Upon examination of the
BM specimen, one observes that its reverse is covered by a thick layer of silver
chloride. This type of corrosion is formed during a long period underground.
This, plus the circumstances of acquisition of the BM specimen, not only seems
to establish its authenticity, but also eliminates the possibility that the additional group of coins from the same dies were manufactured from it. Scanning
electron microscopic studies of the entire group further established their authenticity (INJ 9, 1986–7, pl. 9,10). Optical microscopic examination of the coins
shows specific manufacturing attributes that would not have been known to
forgers of the nineteenth century, or even today.*

1371.   AR half-*sheqel*.
   Obv: ⱶꟼWℲ ⱶⱵꟿ *(half of a sheqel)*; ℲW *(year 5)* above ritual chalice
   with pearled rim, the base is raised by projections on ends.
   Rev: Pomegranate staff as on 1370.   RRR
   *This limited issue was struck with a single obverse die combined with a
reverse die of the year 4.*

Mint of Gamla, 66–67 ce

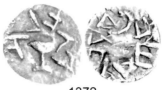

1372

1372. AE 20–22 mm.

  Obv: Crude paleo-Hebrew or Aramaic, see below, crude ritual chalice.

  Rev: Crude paleo-Hebrew or Aramaic, see below.   RRR

  a. Reverse struck from a different die.

  (One specimen sold for $7,425 in Bromberg II.[60])

  Seven examples of this coin, inspired by the silver sheqels of Jerusalem, were discovered in excavations at Gamla in the central Golan Heights, a few examples, between two and four, are in private collections. All were struck from the same obverse die and two reverse dies.[61] Gamla was described by Josephus as a town and stronghold of Jews during this period, and he reported that Romans led by Vespasian and Titus conquered Gamla on October 20, 67 ce.

  The crudeness of the paleo-Hebrew and Aramaic inscription makes it diffi-cult to read. Meshorer first read the inscriptions לגאלת (for the redemption of) *(obv.) and* [דשה]ירשלם הק (ho[ly]) Jerusalem) *(rev.).[62] Farhi later read the obverse as* ב גמלא (Gamla [year] 2).[63] *Most recently Sahuri read the coin as Aramaic with obverse* א תרחל *(retrograde)* (to the freedom) *and the reverse* ...יהוד חבר ש (y[ear] the Jewish People). *He reads the coin in its entirety "Year one to the Freedom of the Jewish People."[64]*

  "The benefits of this modest coin surpass its local significance, [it] is possi-bly the only item that offers us a glimpse into the ideology that guided a provin-cial rebel authority far from the provisional government in Jerusalem (which would probably have disapproved of its minting if asked)."[65]

  The Aramaic name Gamla originates from the shape of the hill, which resembles the back of a camel. Around the early first century ce, Gamla occu-pied around 36 acres and had a population of 3,000 to 5,000.[66] Archaeological remains suggest that the town's principal economy was olive and grain cultiva-tion, olive oil, and livestock. Josephus and archaeological evidence suggest that most or all of Gamla's population was Jewish.

CHAPTER TEN

BAR KOKHBA REVOLT

There shall step forth a star out of Jacob, and a scepter shall rise out of Israel (NUMBERS 24:17).

Simon bar Kosiba, President over Israel, to Yehonathan and Masaba-la, peace. [My order is] that you search and seize the wheat which is in the possession of Hanun (BAR KOKHBA'S LETTERS, THE WOODEN LETTER).

After the Jews were expelled from Jerusalem by Titus and his troops and the warriors of Machaerus and Masada finally fell, a new Diaspora grew throughout the ancient world. A wave of refugees from the Holy Land bolstered Jewish communities already in exile. Emotionally as well as practically, the Diaspora Jews of this time looked toward the day that the Temple would be rebuilt and they would return to their holy Jerusalem.

These feelings simmered for decades, until just more than forty years after the fall of the Second Temple, when they boiled over. From 115 to 117 CE, the Jews, especially those living in the Diaspora, began a series of revolts that may have reached the Jews remaining in the ancient land of Judaea. These revolts became known as the War of Quietus, since the revolt in Mesopotamia was crushed by the Roman general L. Quietus, who later was made governor over the area of ancient Judaea.

By 132 CE, a new Jewish revolt arose, but this time it was fought again in Judaea, where the fervent followers of the faith went "underground" both figuratively and literally and began to torment the Romans once again. The spiritual leader of this revolt was Rabbi Akiba and the military leader was Simon ben Kosiba, also known as Simon bar Kokhba. (The word *ben* in Hebrew means son of, and has the same meaning as *bar* in Aramaic.)

Akiba recognized Bar Kokhba as the Messiah. But not all of his colleagues agreed. Rabbi Johanan ben Tortha told Akiba: "Grass will grow in your cheeks and He (the Messiah) will still not have come."[1]

The Bar Kokhba Revolt arose due to a combination of factors. According to the *Historia Augusta*, Hadrian made circumcision a crime punishable by death.[2] Cassius Dio does not mention such a law, but blames the revolt upon Hadrian's rebuilding of Jerusalem as Aelia Capitolina. Either or both may have been significant factors, but there is no doubting that only 60 years after the end of the Jewish War, there were many Jews who remained preoccupied with regaining Jerusalem and rebuilding the Temple and its cult. Bar Kokhba, bolstered by Rabbi Akiba's endorsement, had the messianic aura.

Although Bar Kokhba was the leader of a relatively small army, legends say that he was a great warrior. Once when he went into battle, he implored his Lord to "Neither help us nor discourage us!"[3] And when his enemies hit him with their missiles, "He would catch the missiles from the enemy's catapults on one of his knees and hurl them back, killing many of the foe."[4]

Saint Jerome wrote that Bar Kokhba gave the impression that he was spewing out flames by "fanning a lighted blade of straw in his mouth with puffs of breath."[5]

Bar Kokhba and his followers were a true underground army. Roman historian Cassius Dio notes that they "occupied the advantageous positions in the country and strengthened them with mines and walls, so that they would have places of refuge when hard pressed and could

10.1. Hadrian's bronze coin depicts a classic Roman foundation scene in which the veiled emperor symbolically plows (around the city) a cow and a bull, imperial standard behind, the Latin legend is COL[ONIA] AEL[IA] KAPIT[OLINA] COND[ITA], "The Colony of Aelia Capitolina, the foundation." Hadrian's bust is shown on obverse. *cf.* Meshorer (Aelia) 2.

communicate with one another unobserved underground; and they pierced these subterranean passages from above at intervals to let in air and light."[6]

When Hadrian sent his general Julius Severus to Judaea, he began slowly to smother the flames Bar Kokhba had ignited. Dio reports that, "Very few of [the Jews] in fact survived. Fifty of their most important outposts and nine hundred and eighty-five of their most famous villages were razed to the ground. Five hundred and eighty thousand men were slain in the various raids and battles, and the number of those that perished by famine, disease and fire was past finding out."[7]

Dio doesn't report in the same detail about Roman difficulties. He notes, however, that, "Many Romans...perished in this war." Just how many can be seen by his next sentence: "Therefore Hadrian in writing to the senate did not employ the opening phrase commonly affected by the emperors, 'If you and your children are in health, it is well; I and the legions are in health.'"[8]

Thus, at great expense to Rome, another flicker of freedom was extinguished for Jews. Bar Kokhba's coins mark an end to the minting of Jewish coins in antiquity.

Bar Kokhba never captured Jerusalem, a fact underlined by coin finds: of more than 50,000 coins found in archaeological excavations there, only two were Bar Kokhba coins.[9] Probably these were pocket souvenirs of Jews or Roman soldiers, similar to other single Bar Kokhba coins found in places as diverse as Spain and England. Most Bar Kokhba hoards and single finds have been found in the general area of Hebron, between the hills and the west coast of the Dead Sea, and this is considered to be the focal point of the war.[10] Distribution of known find spots for Bar Kokhba coins, and how these find spots might help to define the territory under Bar Kokhba's control, is a topic of extensive study. Numismatic material found after 2000 in controlled excavations shows that the Bar Kokhba coins circulated further west and north of Jerusalem, and rebel activities also took place there.[11]

David Amit and Gabriela Bijovsky of the Israel Antiquities Authority point out that the question of the territory where Bar Kokhba was active has been a key issue between the minimalists, who believe the revolt took place only in Judaea, and others who believe that the territory of the revolt should be expanded farther to the north.

During the last decade archaeological evidence has increased dramatically and it "includes the remains of settlements, hiding complexes, pottery and numismatic evidence, and enable[s] us today to determine that the area of the revolt included the region of Judaea from the northern Negev in the south to the area of Modein-Lod in the north" and specifically "the northern limits of the Lod foothills,"[12] Amit and Bijovsky report.

Like his predecessors in the Jewish War as well as his Roman foes, Bar Kokhba understood the political impact that coins could have. Thus coins were struck with slogans designed to keep the spark of hope kindled among his people: "Year one of the redemption of Israel," "Year two of the freedom of Israel," "For the freedom of Jerusalem," and a simple, hopeful, "Jerusalem." Bar Kokhba's first name, "Simon," also appeared on the coins, and he sometimes styled himself "Prince of Israel." Another somewhat mysterious name, "Eleazar the Priest," also appears on both bronze and silver coins.

Mildenberg, author of the standard work on coins of the Bar Kokhba Revolt, wrote a seminal 1949 article on "The Eleazar Coins of the Bar Kokhba Rebellion," which reminds us of the vintage of most knowledge about this topic.

At that relatively recent time, neither Mildenberg nor anyone else knew even the identity of the issuing authority of the Bar Kokhba coins. Mildenberg writes: "Bar Kokhba himself may well have given the order for the coinage, but we cannot justifiably assume that he desired to put his own first name on the coins, particularly as there is not the slightest indication that his name was actually Simon. Whatever claims this man, whose deeds have thrilled later ages, may have made even in those years, he would surely not have described himself as *Nasi* (Hebrew for 'President'), since this was the title of a house of scribes who succeeded each other in the presidency of the Sanhedrin." Mildenberg further added in a footnote that "it seems improbable that 'Simon' of the coins can be identified with Bar Kokhba and Bar Kokhba regarded as the authority for the coinage."

How dramatically knowledge can change quickly after relevant archaeological discoveries!

As the late Israeli archaeologist Yigael Yadin has written, "When all the fragmentary tales and traces of Bar Kokhba were assembled they amounted to no more than the lineaments of a ghost. He figured in Jewish folklore more as a myth than a man of flesh and blood, as impersonal as a Hercules or a King Arthur. It was centuries of persecution of the Jews and their yearning for national rehabilitation that turned Bar Kokhba into a people's hero—an elusive figure they clung to because he had demonstrated, and was the last to demonstrate, that the Jews could fight to win spiritual and political independence."[13]

In the 1950s, along with a team of archaeologists, Yadin discovered a group of coins, objects, and papyrus documents in Judaean desert caves near the Dead Sea. These documents were the famous Bar Kokhba letters. In his book about the discovery, Yadin recalls the emotion of his initial report:

"There has grown up a custom for the President of Israel to invite archaeologists to his home from time to time to report on their discoveries. To one of these meetings in 1960 were invited all the leaders of an expedition of four teams searching caves in the Judaean Desert. It was to be attended by the Prime Minister, then Mr. David Ben-Gurion, Cabinet ministers, Members of the Knesset, and distinguished writers and other guests. I had led one of the four teams and I set out for the President's home with my secret in my brief case.

"A screen had been erected at [President] Ben Zvi's house, and when my turn came to report, I projected on to the screen through a film slide the colored photograph of part of a document and read out aloud the first line of writing upon it: 'Shimeon Bar Kosiba, President over Israel'. And turning to our Head of State, I said, 'Your Excellency, I am honored to be able to tell you that we have discovered fifteen dispatches written or dictated by the last President of ancient Israel 1800 years ago.'"[14]

Until Yadin and his colleagues translated the name on these documents, there was no proof that Bar Kokhba's first name was Simon *except for the coins*. Indeed, as Mildenberg's work showed, some doubted that it was his name at all. In fact, the Bar Kokhba letters also show that the man's name was actually Bar Kosiba. Yadin noted, "His name was written KSBA, without the vowels, as is the custom in Aramaic and Hebrew. It was only from one of the Greek letters that we learned that his name was pronounced Kosiba."[15]

The name Bar Kokhba is one of the versions that came to us through the literature. It probably related to the leader's messianic aspirations. Bar Kokhba means "son of a star" and most believe that it is a reference to Rabbi Akiba's recitation of scripture in support of Bar Kokhba as Messiah: "There shall go forth a star out of Jacob" (NUMBERS 24:17).

On the other hand, most Jewish sources refer to him as Bar (or Ben) Koziba, which can be translated as "son of a liar" or "deceiver." Perhaps this reference evolved after his failed mission to overcome

Hadrian's forces. Note, however, that his actual name as shown in his own letters is closer to the Bar Koziba than the Bar Kokhba, so maybe it was simply a misinterpretation.

The Bar Kokhba letters also shed some light on the money of this period of Jewish history. One of the documents is a lease transaction. After dealing with the particulars, it says that the parties will each "pay half of the money less sixteen *dinars*, which are four *sela'im* only..." This is interesting. The money is referred to in its "foreign currency" value, that is, *dinars* (*denarii* or *drachms*) as well as its value in "Jewish currency" of the day, *sela'im* (*tetradrachms*). Four *dinars* equal one *tetradrachm*, therefore the actual name used for the large silver Bar Kokhba coins at the time was *sela*. In another of the documents, it is written that "Eleazar receives for the lease twelve silver *zuzim* which are 'three *sela'im*.'"[16] Thus the Jewish name for the *drachm-denarius* during Bar Kokhba's time was *zuz*.

Unfortunately, the Eleazar named in the lease document was almost certainly not the same Eleazar on the Bar Kokhba coins. There are several individuals named Eleazar mentioned in the Bar Kokhba letters. But it does not seem that any of them are important enough to correspond to "Eleazar the Priest." Perhaps some day additional documents will come to light to clarify this mystery, just as the Bar Kokhba letters clarified the mystery of Bar Kokhba's real first and last name.

WHO WAS ELEAZAR THE PRIEST?

Who was this enigmatic Eleazar the Priest?

The bronze and silver coins with the name *Eleazar* were struck primarily in the first year of the war. Hybrid *Eleazar* coins, combining first year dies with later ones, were struck sparingly in both the second and third years of the war.

This frequency (more accurately, this later *infrequency*) seems to support a classic idea that Eleazar the Priest was in fact Rabbi Eleazar of Modein, who was said to have been Bar Kokhba's uncle. However, the Romans conspired with a Samaritan (Cuthean) to make it appear as if Eleazar wanted to surrender to Hadrian's army. The plot was successful because Bar Kokhba went to him, "flew into a rage, kicked him with his foot and killed him."[17]

Schürer notes that, "Since in late Rabbinnical documents the R. Eleazar of Modein, who is also known from the other sources, is described as the uncle of Bar Cosiba, some have ventured to conjecture that this man is the same as the one named Eleazar the priest on the coins. But there is nothing to indicate that Eleazar of Modein was a priest."[18] In fact, the Talmud quotes "R. Eleazar of Modein."[19] Meshorer notes that Modein was "the residence of priestly families, and [Eleazar] was thus a priest."[20]

Mildenberg, however, argues that, "If 'Eleazar the Priest' and Eleazar of Modein were one and the same man, then the tradition of kinship between the priest and the prince of the Bar Kokhba coins would allow only one interpretation: the mother of the rebel leader and Eleazar of Modein were brother and sister. Were Simon's father, Kosiba, and Eleazar of Modein brothers, then Simon would have been a priest, too. If this had, in fact, been the case, both he and his contemporaries as well as later Jewish tradition would certainly have proclaimed the priesthood of Simon loudly, and not concealed it."[21] Mildenberg concludes that the identity of 'Eleazar the Priest' remains nothing but conjecture.

On the contrary, it seems probable that Eleazar the Priest was indeed Rabbi Eleazar of Modein. Such a connection would have meant that Bar Kokhba himself was of a priestly family. Why, then, did he not proclaim his own priestly blood in order to further cement his position as leader? Certainly, Bar Kokhba would have wanted to suggest himself as high priest if that had been possible. But, in ancient Judaism, the high priests were required to be without major bodily blemish. Rabbinnic literature relates that Bar Kokhba wanted only the bravest, strongest men in his army. To test each of young man, he would cut off a part of his little finger. Eventually, the Sages sent him a message asking, "How long will you continue to make the men of Israel blemished?"[22]

Bar Kokhba replied, "How else shall they be tested?"

The Sages replied: "Let anyone who cannot uproot a cedar from Lebanon be refused enrollment in your army."[23]

Bar Kokhba then agreed to the change in his military testing procedures. But, if the leader himself initially insisted that his men prove their mettle by having a part of their little fingers cut off, is it not safe to assume that he had undergone the same test? Thus blemished in body, the messianic warrior could not claim the high priesthood even if it had been available to him.

Mint and Methods

The mints of Bar Kokhba were unlike other mints in the ancient world. *All* of the coins struck under the Jewish leader were overstruck on contemporary coins circulating in Judaea at the time. While the phenomenon of overstriking coins in ancient times is not unique, it is especially interesting in this case since, as Meshorer notes, it enabled Bar Kokhba to make both political and religious statements. "Not only did he deface the portraits of the despised emperors by this technique, he was also able to depict Jewish symbols and nationalistic inscriptions."[24]

Most of the silver *tetradrachms* (or *sela*, pl. *sela'im*) were struck upon *tetradrachms* of Antioch or similar coins and weigh around 14 grams (Mildenberg recorded specimens ranging from 11.4 to 15.4 grams). The silver *zuz* (pl. *zuzim*) was struck upon local *drachms*, including Nabataean *drachms*, or Roman *denarii* and weigh around 3.3 grams (recorded range is 2.1 to 3.7 grams). The bronze coins had much greater weight variances since they were struck upon coins from Ashqelon, Gaza, Caesarea, or other local cities. Occasionally, a Bar Kokhba coin was struck upon a Ptolemaic bronze coin which had remained in circulation for hundreds of years before being re-validated by the Jewish rebels.

In addition to silver coins, the Bar Kokhba mints struck large, medium, and small bronze coins. They were struck upon all kinds of coins in circulation, so it is difficult to determine their exact value. Meshorer observes that, "The difference in weight between coins that are ostensibly of the same denomination can reach 200%."[25]

The Talmud explains: "For it was taught: The *prutah* which the Sages mentioned is an eighth of an Italian *issar*. Thus one *denar* = six silver *ma'ahs*; one *ma'ah* = two *pundion*; one *pundion* = two *issars*; one *issar* = two *musmis*; one *musmis* = two *kuntrunk*; one *kuntrunk* = two *prutahs*. Hence the *prutah* is an eighth of an Italian *issar*."[26]

Based on this, Meshorer suggest that the large Bar Kokhba coins are equal to one *ma'ah* (*sestertius*), the medium coins equal one *pundion* (*dupondius*), and the small coins equal one *issar* (*as*). There may be a fourth bronze denomination equal to a *semis*, but because of the overstriking on such a wide variety of coins this is not fully understood.[27]

The Bar Kokhba Revolt was a time of severe economic and political stress for the Jewish fighters struggling to reestablish a nation where one had not existed for more than 60 years. He "neither controlled an already established mint, nor possessed a city large enough to support a new one."[28] Avoiding the expensive, messy operations of smelting bronze alloy and casting flans allowed the rebels to quickly begin minting coins with political statements of strength and sovereignty. Bar Kokhba's coins boosted the morale of his followers.

Foreign coins were prepared by hammering in metal "pans" (for silver coins) or both hammering and filing (for the bronze) to remove traces of the hated alien symbols. However, traces of the original coin can almost always be seen on the silver coins, and file marks are not uncommon on the bronze coins. Rarely, an imperial portrait or a few letters from the original coin remain on bronzes.

Bar Kokhba's coins were struck in silver and bronze in several denominations. But the most interesting distinction among them may be between the "regular" issues and the "irregular" issues. Barag aptly pointed out that contrary to Mildenberg's suggestion, there were certainly two Bar Kokhba mints, one of which manufactured the "regular" and another mint that issued the "irregular" coinage. Not a single die link exists between "regular" and "irregular" Bar Kokhba issues, further bolstering this theory. Barag hastens to add that the terminology of "regular" and "irregular" coins can be confusing since:

"From the Roman point of view, both were irregular rebel mints. For the Bar Kokhba administration the 'irregular' mint was a second, subsidiary, mint operating not at the central mint but at a different location, and there is no reason to assume that it was considered to be irregular. The occasional reference to these coins as 'irregular' does not carry much weight—in the eyes of the Greeks and Romans all Jewish coinage was no doubt considered 'irregular coinage.'"[29]

Barag suggests that Herodium was a likely location for the central mint of Bar Kokhba. Since 2002 significant excavations have been carried out at Herodium by Ehud Netzer. Herod's personal tomb and an elegant small amphitheater with an astonishing, beautifully decorated royal box are among the most remarkable discoveries.[30] As of this writing, these excavations have not been fully published; however, I have visited and explored the site and the recent excavations. Other than a large number of Bar Kokhba coins from an earlier excavation,[31] no coin manufacturing artifacts have yet been discovered at this site.

Barag adds that the second mint of the "irregular" issues might have been set up in the area north or north-west of Jerusalem.

Shortly after Mildenberg's book was published, he described a unique *didrachm* (half-*sela*) of Bar Kokhba, which depicted a distyle Temple (as opposed to the tetrastyle Temple on the larger silver denomination) with the showbread table shown lengthwise inside.[32] (See below for further discussions of the showbread table.) Barag notes that this coin is similar in style to the "irregular" issues and, in fact, is the only coin of this denomination issued during the Bar Kokhba war thus this *didrachm* is a unique innovation, probably from the second mint, which otherwise simply copied other Bar Kokhba silver and bronze coins of all denominations. Since Mildenberg published this coin a second example, acquired in 1921–22 by Samuel Rafaeli, was found in the collection of the Israel Antiquities Authority.[33]

Even though the second mint produced a generally cruder version of Bar Kokhba coins, it nevertheless supplied official money to the population where it operated and disseminated the same messages as the central mint. Proof of this aspect is that the hoards of Bar Kokhba coins contain both "regular" and "irregular" issues, which circulated together.

Bar Kokhba Test Strike

The die types of Bar Kokhba War coins have been well-published by Mildenberg and supplemented by Kaufman.[34] Since the Bar Kokhba mint overstruck circulating coins, there are a number of odd results. These include coins depicting motifs from both the Bar Kokhba strike and the previous coin, coins struck upon unusually large or small host coins, *drachms* (*zuzim*) struck upon *fourreé* (silver plated) *drachms* or *denarii*, and at least one *tetradrachm* (*sela*) struck upon a bronze flan for unknown reasons. (See below for the story of one fascinating overstrike.)

Nothing in the published Bar Kokhba corpus, however, hinted at this unusual object brought to my attention by a private collector.

10.2. Bar Kokhba test strike.

Bar Kokhba, 132–135 ce, struck in the third year 134/135 ce.
Obv. Ancient Hebrew inscription in two lines "SIMON" within a wreath, medallion at top, and all within a border of dots.

Rev. Ancient Hebrew inscription around, beginning lower left "To the Freedom of Jerusalem" around upright palm branch with tip curled slightly to left, all within a border of dots.

Bronze rectangle, 6.46 g, 21.9 x 16.4 mm, the thickest part is 3.3 mm, the thinnest is 2.6 mm near the center of the longest dimension. Axis is 12 o'clock. The obverse is slightly convex and reverse slightly concave. All edges show evidence of having been chopped from a larger piece of flat bronze before striking.

Same dies as Mildenberg 205, no. 65, (O–14, R–37).[35]

Microscopic examination with 5x to 35x magnification reveals a hard, compact encrustation of earth on the obverse and the edges. This condition is consistent with similar encrustations seen on many Bar Kokhba coins. The reverse of the coin had been cleaned manually prior to our inspection; microscopic study reveals that the person who cleaned the coin was somewhat crude in his efforts and not only scratched some of the immediate patina of the coin, but "cleaned" the second letter in such a way that it appears to have a strange shape (although it does not).

This small bronze rectangle was struck from a well-documented pair of dies from the Bar Kokhba mint. In other die pairings this obverse die is also coupled with reverse dies dated to the second year of the Bar Kokhba Revolt. Thus we can safely establish the first use of this die set early in the third year, after the year 2 dies were no longer used. There is so little deterioration in this obverse die that this may represent the first instance in which it was paired with an undated reverse die.

Because this die set can be placed at or near the beginning of the undated *zuzim* of Bar Kokhba, it is likely a test strike. It may have been created to establish that the new undated die would "strike" well when paired with a die from the previous year, thus sparing the need for a fresh die to be put into use immediately. Mildenberg shows that this obverse die was eventually used to strike hundreds, if not thousands of undated coins as well as a number dated to the second year.[36]

Most known ancient test pieces were struck upon lead flans, and they are frequently (but not exclusively) uniface. One should then ask why this test piece was struck on a bronze fragment. The logical reason is that the Bar Kokhba mint did not include a smelting and flan manufacturing operation. Therefore, unlike other "full-service mints," the Bar Kokhba mint had no reason to store raw metal such as lead, which would have been used to make bronze alloy.

Given the nature of the Bar Kokhba style of minting, it is curious that a piece of "scrap" bronze would be used instead of a bronze "blank" that had been prepared for re-striking a bronze coin. But, since the bronze coins retained a fiduciary value higher than their value as bronze, the use of scrap has some logic.

OVERSTRIKE WITH A STORY

As mentioned above, minting upon previous coins often creates interesting situations. In this case, a Bar Kokhba *denarius* was struck upon one of the Judaea Capta *denarii* of Vespasian, and the legend IVDAEA from the previous coin remains quite clear!

This coin (No. 1432) was one of the many Judaea Capta coins struck at Roman mints to commemorate the Flavian defeat of the Jews in 70 CE that found their way back to the homeland of the Jews. It eventually fell into the hands of the fervent followers of Bar Kokhba in around 133/34 CE, and was restruck with their own designs and legends.

At least one coin had come full circle in its existence. Novels could (and have) been written covering less time, and have told stories less convincingly than does this coin. It commemorated the defeat of the Jews, and was part of a series of coins that humiliated them. It was later resurrected during Bar Kokhba's nationalistic revolt, and when it was overstruck, helped humiliate Hadrian's armies, which finally overcame Bar Kokhba's rebels, but not without difficulty.

All of the story is in the coin, since the legend IVDAEA can be seen clearly as the undertype on the reverse of the coin, which also depicts two ceremonial trumpets and the legend "For the freedom of Jerusalem." On the obverse of the coin the full outline of Vespasian's portrait along with a few letters of the Latin legend can be seen with the bunch of grapes and portions of "Simon."

Was it random that this coin of Vespasian, struck in 71 CE, was restruck more than 60 years later? It's an interesting question. It means that this coin had been in circulation for at least 60 years. Bar Kokhba coins were struck upon imperial and provincial coins from Nero to Nerva.[37] Mildenberg concludes that this indicates that most of the restruck coins were not captured directly from Roman legions in the area, but were instead "gifts, contributions, taxes, rent or war loans from the Jewish population," thus "returning the heavily circulated, by and large pre-Hadrianic money to the Jewish peasants whence it had come, but in a new and specifically Jewish guise."[38]

Imagine that a Jew had obtained this Judaea Capta coin from circulation and had held it, possibly as a souvenir. When the time came, under Bar Kokhba, he or she gladly turned it in to be restruck by a "sovereign" Jewish nation—or at least rebels who sought to form one.

TEMPLE AND OTHER SYMBOLS

Although issued in a period of severe economic and political stress, the Bar Kokhba coins are the most beautiful and diverse series of ancient Jewish coins. Notable designs include an image of the Temple with an unusual object within it, sacred vessels and musical instruments used within the Temple, and agricultural objects such as the etrog and lulav, palm tree, branch, grapes, and vine leaves.

Meshorer summarizes various proposals as to the identification of the tetrastyle structure, and concludes that it is "a schematic geometric shape representing the Temple to all who viewed it, but not the actual building." In fact, given historic descriptions of the Jerusalem Temple, it may be a lot less "schematic" than Meshorer suggests. The Temple facade is shown on Bar Kokhba coins in several variations.

Isadore Goldstein has done extensive studies of the Jerusalem Temple and made remarkable observations about the depiction. First, he notes, that the wavy line (Nos. 1413, 1414) and the cross or star (Nos. 1387, 1388, 1411, 1412) above the Temple are not fanciful, but have a real meaning. The Mishnah says that "a golden vine was positioned over the entrance to the sanctuary and hung over the beams" (MIDOT 3:8). Goldstein points out that only the vine was initially hung, and the golden grapes were added as donations from the people. Thus he suggests that the schematic view shown on the coins was a look at the sanctuary, a view that could be seen from the Temple courtyard.

Goldstein points to another portion of Mishnah (YOMA 3.10), that says, "Helena set a golden candelabra over the door of the Sanctuary." This refers to a gift from Helena, queen of Abiabene, a converted Jew who visited Jerusalem and was buried there around 56 CE. Goldstein cites other Rabbinnic literature that says that this candelabrum sparkled with rays and reflected light that could be seen from many places in Jerusalem. Thus, he concludes, "there are many renditions

10.3. Reconstructed view of the Jerusalem Temple looking toward the entrance to the sanctuary. This image shows both the golden vine, which appears on some Bar Kokhba *sela`im* as a wavy line, and the twinkling golden chandelier donated by Helena, queen of Abiabene, depicted as a cross or star on some Bar Kokhba *sela`im*. The twelve steps are also represented on the *sela`im*, shown as a kind of horizontal ladder below the Temple. (Graphic: Fontanille.)

of the star form, but they all represent the artist's interpretation of the chandelier or of its twinkling."[39]

Dan Barag suggests that the object between the central pair of columns is the showbread table.[40] Previously, Romanoff suggested it might be the Ark of the Covenant.[41] Reifenberg suggested an Ark of the Torah with scolls.[42] Meshorer passed and observed "scholars have reached no consensus" about either the object or the exact nature of the structure that stands within. Meshorer mentions Barag's suggestion that it could be the showbread table, but does not further discuss it.

The Babylonian Talmud states that while a man could not make a house or a porch copied from the Temple or "a table after the design of the table [in the Temple] or a candelabrum after the design of the candelabrum. He may, however, make one with five, six, or eight [branches] but with seven he may not make it even though it be of other metals" (AVODAH ZARAH: 43, 1).

Thus Meshorer suggests that the Temple is depicted, but possibly not accurately because of the prohibition. On the other hand, Mattatayah Antigonus had no problem replicating both the showbread table and the menorah on one of his coins, even though the Temple was still standing and these equally holy implements were still in daily use. In that instance Meshorer observes that, "The menorah and the showbread table on the coins [of Antigonus] were a sort of proclamation or call to the people to protect...their lives, the nation's sacred objects lest they fall into the hands of a man of Idumaean origin who was supported by the Romans,"[43] namely Herod I.

It is not clear why Meshorer felt that this was something that Mattatayah Antigonus might have done, but Bar Kokhba, in a similar political situation *vis à vis* the Romans, would not dare do. After all, by the time of the Bar Kokhba Revolt it had been more than sixty years since the Temple and all of its implements had been destroyed or taken as booty by the Romans. Thus few living people had seen the Temple or its holy objects and most had only heard about them. Because of this it seems that Barag's suggestion ought to be given more attention.

Barag cites the design within the distyle shrine on the obverse of the Bar Kokhba half-*sela* (or *didrachm*, No. 1415). He suggests that "The table depicted on the *didrachm* can...refer only to the showbread table. This representation also affords us with an entirely new insight into the problem of the object on the *tetradrachms*. A comparison between the two shows that these are two views of the same table depicted on the *didrachm* lengthwise and on the *tetradrachms* from its narrow side."

Barag finds a parallel to an engraved plaster fragment that Avigad discovered in the Jewish Quarter of the Old City of Jerusalem (see page 208 for illustration).[44] This fragment "depicts the showbread table with raised sides which are rectangular rather than convex—the shape envisaged on the Bar Kokhba *tetradrachms*."[45] Avigad dates the fragment to the period of Herod I.

The raised sides of the object within the tetrastyle Temple, according to Barag, were intended to secure the "two sets of six loaves of bread placed on the table from toppling and falling down."[46] He also notes that "there was no Ark of the Covenant in the Second Temple and one may doubt whether a Bar Kokhba coin would proclaim the reintroduction of the Ark which was not included in any of the previous restorations of the Temple because of the loss of the tablets."

Mildenberg suggests that the object "resembles a chest with a semi-circular lid, seen from one of the small sides," and sees a parallel between it and the Ark of the Covenant. While the Ark is used in synagogues world-wide today to hold the Torah scrolls, Barag finds the theory of the Torah chest unlikely. "It is possible, although by no

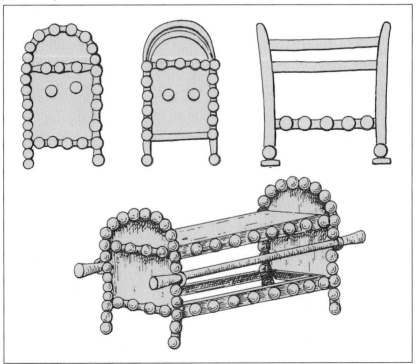

10.4. Possible reconstruction of the showbread table based upon images on the Bar Kokhba large silver sela`m. (Courtesy Dan Barag.)

means certain, that the Torah chests of that time may have looked similar to the piece of furniture on the latter coins. Scrolls of the Torah were certainly kept in the Temple and read from during the rituals but there is no reference where and how they were kept and there is certainly no mention of a Torah chest in the Temple."

"But carrying more weight is the fact that Bar Kokhba and his followers' aim was to rebuild the Temple and revive its cult and ritual, the essence of which cannot be expressed by placing in the center of the Temple an object which would turn it into a synagogue." Barag further observes that the showbread motif fits "well with the other Temple vessels and musical instruments represented on Bar Kokhba's coins, which were to be used if the Temple rituals were to have been revived."[47]

Goldstein's study suggests that this part of the representation of the Temple may not be an object at all, but is simply the entrance, showing a generic object within. He also observes that the horizontal ladder-like object is not a balustrade or fence as some have suggested but represent the twelve steps leading up to the Temple that were described by both Josephus and in the Mishnah. "Not one of the dies recorded by Mildenberg depicts more than twelve steps,"[48] Goldstein explains.

Trumpets and several styles of lyres or harps are also depicted on Bar Kokhba's coins. The trumpets recall an inscription discovered on a stone from the Jerusalem Temple, now in the Israel Museum, that declares in Hebrew "To the place of the trumpeting…"

The harp, which has a sound box shaped like a skin bag (*nevel* in Hebrew, *chelys* in Greek), and the narrower lyre, with a chest-like sound box (*kinor* in Hebrew, *kithara* in Greek), have been associated with the Jewish religion since ancient times.

Praise him with lyre and harp. (PSALM 150:3)

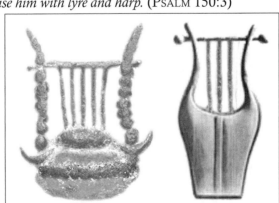

10.5. From coin images a lyre (l.) and a harp.

Hanan Eshel explains: "The considerable difference between the weight of bronze coins with a harp issued in the first and second year of the revolt created confusion as coins with the same design were of different weights. This may have led to a change in the design from a harp to a lyre in the undated/third-year issues of the revolt."[49]

Other objects depicted on the Bar Kokhba coins include the palm tree, by now a clear symbol of Judaea, as well as objects related to Sukkot, the Feast of Tabernacles, some of which were also used on the coinage of the Jewish War.

The *lulav* bunch, which contains palm, myrtle, and willow, along-side the *etrog* are shown on the *tetradrachms* and the lulav bunch alone on the *didrachm*. Other coins depict only a branch, the most prominent part of the lulav bunch.

Grape clusters and vines already appeared on a coin of Herod I and his son Archelaus (Nos. 1187 and 1196), and a vine leaf was used on Jewish War *prutot*. Grape bunches are a common motif in Jewish art in the first and second centuries and seem to be related not only to the agricultural bounty of the land and related celebrations such as Sukkot, but also to use of "the fruit of the vine" in Jewish ritual from ancient times. Barag writes that the use of these motifs on coins "manifests the hope for the resumption of another essential part of the cult, the pilgrimage on the three festivals demonstrated by the symbols of Sukkot."[50]

The jug appearing on the Bar Kokhba *zuzim* may also be related to celebrations of Sukkot, according to Adler, who believes it represents "the golden flagon used in the water libation ceremony performed on the Temple altar during the Feast of Tabernacles. The branch appearing to the side of this flagon, previously identified as a palm frond, should be recognized instead as a willow-branch, symbolizing the willow-branch ceremony that took place at the Temple altar in conjunction with the water libation ceremony...the numismatic evidence provided by the Bar Kokhba *denarii* is the only evidence of the willow-branch ritual outside of Rabbinnic literature."[51]

In ancient times, the willow branch ritual was carried out daily in the Jerusalem Temple, according to the Talmud: "There was a place below Jerusalem called Motsa. They went down to there, and collected young willow branches, and then came and set them upright along the sides of the altar, with their tops bent over the top of the altar. They then sounded a prolonged [trumpet] blast, a quavering note, and a prolonged blast."[52]

Story of the Split "Abu Jara"

Bronze and silver coins chopped in half for use as small change are a well-known phenomenon in the ancient Levant.[53] Some Bar Kokhba coins were cut in this way during the time they circulated.[54]

It has also been suggested that the Bar Kokhba coins are cut because after the war they were invalidated. However, the number of cut Bar Kokhba coins is so small as compared to the number of intact coins, that this reason does not seem to be a phenomenon that was related to invalidation.

Some years ago a friend phoned from the Old City of Jerusalem to say that one of the villagers from Beitar, near Bethlehem, had brought him half of an "Abu Jara," a large bronze struck by Bar Kokhba during the first and second years of the revolt (Nos. 1375, 1376, 1404, 1405). The Arabic nickname *Abu Jara*, literally, "father of the jar," refers to the size of the coin and the large amphora [jar] it depicts.

On my next visit to Jerusalem I went to pick up the half-coin and to my surprise learned that the same villager found the other half of the *same coin*, about 600 yards away.

This may be the only example of an ancient cut coin, in which both halves of the same coin have been recovered. Logically, the distance between the two parts of a cut coin is a function of the time the parts circulated—more time, farther apart. Since these halves were found so close together, we can guess that the cutting of this coin took place very near the end of the Bar Kokhba War.

Dating the coin in this way leads to a second theory. The modern Arab village of Beitar is in the immediate vicinity of the ancient town of Beitar, the village where Bar Kokhba's men fought their last battle against Hadrian's troops in 135 CE. We know from the Talmud that after the revolt, the coins struck by Simon no longer had any value. Thus, it's possible that this coin was cut in half by two Bar Kokhba

10.6. The split Abu Jara, type as No. 1376.

followers—maybe soldiers who fought together—and one half kept by each as a souvenir. Perhaps two Roman soldiers did the same.

Cassius Dio reports that by the end of the Bar Kokhba Revolt, "nearly the whole of Judaea was made desolate, a result of which the people had forewarning before the war. For the tomb of Solomon, which the Jews regard as an object of veneration, fell to pieces of itself and collapsed, and many wolves and hyenas rushed howling into their cities."[55]

COINS OF BAR KOKHBA
YEAR ONE, 132/133 CE

שֵׁנָת אַחַת
לגאלת ישראל

1373

1373. AR *sela*.

Obv: רושלם *(Jerusalem)* on three sides of facade of the Jerusalem Temple, showbread table (?) seen from end in center of entrance.

Rev: שנת אחת לגאלת ישראל *(year one of the redemption of Israel)*; *lulav* with *etrog* at left.   30,000/75,000

a. Irregular issue of 1373.

אלעזר הכוהן

1374

1374. AR *zuz*.

Obv: אלעזר הכהן *(Eleazar the priest)*; jug with handle, willow branch at r.

Rev: שנת אחת לגאלת ישראל *(year one of the redemption of Israel)*; bunch of grapes with branch and small leaf.   15,000/35,000

1375

יֶר֔
שׁ֔לֵ

ירו
שלם

1375.   AE large bronze, 32 mm.
Obv: שׁלֵ יֶר֔ (*Jerusalem*) within a wreath.
Rev: ישׂראל גׂאלת תׁחׁ שׁנת (*year one of the redemption of Israel*); amphora with two handles.   7,000/20,000

1376

שׁמעׂן נׁשׁיא
ישׂראל

שמעון נשיא
ישראל

1376.   AE large bronze, 31 mm.
Obv: ישׂראל נׁשׁיא שׁמעׂן (*Simon, Prince of Israel*) within a wreath.
Rev: ישׂראל גׂאלת תׁחׁ שׁנת (*year one of the redemption of Israel*); amphora with two handles.   6,000/15,000

1377

1377. AE middle bronze, 24 mm.

    Obv: ⌐ꞰꟼꟿⱲꞀ ꞁꟿⱲꞀ ꞁꝒoꟿⱲ *(Simon Prince of Israel)*; palm branch
    within a wreath.

    Rev: ⌐ꞰꟼꟿⱲꞀ ✕⌐Ʞꞁꞁ ✕ꞌꟼ ✕ꞀⱲ *(year one of the redemption of Is-*
    rael); wide lyre *(nevel* or *chelys)* of 6 (sometimes 4 or 5) strings.

                                            500/1,500

    a. Irregular issue of 1377.

1378   1379

1378. AE middle bronze, 27 mm.

    Obv: ⌐ꞰꟼꟿⱲꞀ ꞁꟿⱲꞀ ꞁꝒoꟿⱲ *(Simon Prince of Israel)* across fields;
    seven-branched palm tree with two bunches of dates.

    Rev: ⌐ꞰꟼꟿⱲꞀ ✕⌐Ʞꞁꞁ ✕ꞌꟼ ✕ꞀⱲ *(year one of the redemption of Is-*
    rael); vine leaf on tendril.   550/1,250

    a. A different style of epigraphy.

    b. Irregular issue of 1378.

1379. AE middle bronze, 25 mm.

    Obv: oꟿⱲ *(Sma*—abbreviating Simon*)* across fields; seven-branched
    palm tree with two bunches of dates.

    Rev: ⌐ꞰꟼꟿⱲꞀ ✕⌐Ʞꞁꞁ ✕ꞌꟼ ✕ꞀⱲ *(year one of the redemption of Is-*
    rael); vine leaf on tendril.   550/1,250

    a. Irregular issue of 1379.

1380

a   b   c

1380. AE small bronze, 18 mm.

Obv: ꭎꜱꜱ꜠ꜱ ꜱꭏꭏꭏꭏ *(Eleazar the priest)* across fields; seven-branched palm tree with two bunches of dates.

Rev: ꭏꭏꜱꭏꭏ ꭏꭏꭏꭏꭏ ꭏꭏꭏ ꭏꭏꭏ *(year one of the redemption of Israel)*; bunch of grapes with branch and small leaf.   250/500

a. Obverse retrograde inscription.

b. Obverse retrograde variation.

c. Obverse inscription variation.

d. Irregular issue of 1380.

1381

1381. AE small bronze, 21 mm.

Obv: ꭏꭏꭏꭏꭏ *(Jerusalem)*; seven-branched palm tree with two bunches of dates.

Rev: ꭏꭏꭏꭏꭏ ꭏꭏꭏꭏꭏ ꭏꭏꭏ ꭏꭏꭏ *(year one of the redemption of Israel)*; bunch of grapes with branch and small leaf.   1,500/3,000

a. Galley in rectangular countermark on obverse.

b. Irregular issue of 1381.

HYBRID COINS DATED WITH BOTH YEAR ONE AND YEAR TWO

1382. AR *zuz*.

Obv: ⌷⌷⌷ ⌷⌷⌷ ⌷⌷⌷ ⌷⌷⌷ *(Year one of the redemption of Israel)*; bunch of grapes with branch and small leaf.

Rev: ⌷⌷⌷ ⌷⌷⌷ ⌷⌷ *(year two of the freedom of Israel)*; palm branch.

4,500/10,000

1383. AR *zuz*.

Obv: ⌷⌷⌷ ⌷⌷⌷ ⌷⌷⌷ ⌷⌷⌷ *(Year one of the redemption of Israel)*; bunch of grapes with branch and small leaf.

Rev: ⌷⌷⌷ ⌷⌷⌷ ⌷⌷ *(year two of the freedom of Israel)*; wide lyre (*nevel* or *chelys*) with three strings, four dots on sound box.

5,000/12,000

1384. AR *zuz*.

Obv: ⌷ ⌷⌷ *(Sma—abbreviating Simon)*, the letters in a triangle, in a wreath of thin branches wrapped around eight almonds, medallion at top, tendrils at bottom.

Rev: ⌷⌷⌷⌷ ⌷⌷⌷⌷ *(Eleazar the priest)*; fluted jug, handle on l., willow branch on r.

3,000/5,000

While this coin is not dated, the only other use of the Eleazar name on a zuz is combined with a die of the first year. Thus, this must be a hybrid issue of the first and second year rather than a coin of the third year, where other undated issues are assigned.

The abbreviation "Sm'" can also be read "Shma." It has been proposed that there is a dual meaning in this use of the first three letters of Bar Kokhba's first name; first, a simple abbreviation, and second, as the first word of the prayer, the Shema, which is believed was one of Bar Kokhba's rallying cries.

COINS DATED YEAR TWO, 133/34 CE

1385. AR *sela*.
   Obv: ꝘᒪW➤ꝘꝚ (Jerusalem) on three sides of facade of Jerusalem Temple, showbread table (?) seen from end in center of entrance.
   Rev: ᒪꝦꝘꟿꝚ Ꝙᕒᒪ ꟊꟿ (*year two of the freedom of Israel*); *lulav* with *etrog* at l.   8,500/17,500
   This type of sela *was struck with an obverse die type of the first year, thus it is also a hybrid. We place it here because it is clearly dated in the reverse die to the second year.*

1386. AR *sela*.
   Obv: ꝘᒪW ➤ꝘꝚ (Jerusalem) on three sides divided by + above facade of Jerusalem Temple, showbread table (?) seen from end in center of entrance.
   Rev: ᒪꝦꝘꟿꝚ Ꝙᕒᒪ ꟊꟿ (*year two of the freedom of Israel*); lulav with etrog at l.   8,500/17,500
   a. Irregular issue of 1386.

Ꝙ ᕒᒪ ꟊꟿ
ᒪ ꝦꝘꟿ Ꝛ

שב לחר
ישראל

1387. AR *sela*.
   Obv: ꝘᒪW ➤ꝘꝚ (Jerusalem) on two sides; + above facade of Jerusalem Temple, showbread table (?) seen from end in center of entrance.
   Rev: ᒪꝦꝘꟿꝚ Ꝙᕒᒪ ꟊꟿ (*year two of the freedom of Israel*); lulav with etrog at l.   5,500/10,000
   a. Same as 1387 with variations; Ꝧ instead of Ꝛ on obverse and W instead of ꟿ in reverse legends.

1388. AR *sela*.

Obv: ꓒꓤꝋꓬꟽ *(Simon)* on two sides; star above facade of the Jerusalem Temple, showbread table (?) seen from end in center.

Rev: ｌꟻꝯꟽꓷ ꝯꝷ ꓩW *(year two of the freedom of Israel)*; lulav with etrog at l. 3,000/8,000

a. Irregular issue of 1388.

1389. AR *zuz*.

Obv: ꝋ ꟽꟽ *(Sm'—abbreviating Simon)*, the letters in a triangle, in a wreath of thin branches wrapped around eight almonds, medallion at top, tendrils at bottom.

Rev: ｌꟻꝯꟽꓷ ꝯꝷ ꓩW *(year two of the freedom of Israel)*; wide lyre (*nevel* or *chelys*) with three strings, four dots on sound box.

1,500/3,000

1390. AR *zuz*.

Obv: Paleo-Hebrew as on 1389.

Rev: ｌꟻꝯꟽꓷ ꝯꝷ ꓩW *(year two of the freedom of Israel)*; palm branch. 500/850

1391. AR *zuz*.

Obv: Paleo-Hebrew as on 1389.

Rev: ｌꟻꝯꟽꓷ ꝯꝷ ꓩW *(year two of the freedom of Israel)*; fluted jug, handle on l., willow branch on r. 500/850

1392.   AR *zuz*.
Obv: Paleo-Hebrew as on 1389.
Rev: Lᖴ૧ШⱵ ૧ᕆL ⥾W *(year two of the freedom of Israel)*; two trum-
pets upright.   600/900

1393.   AR *zuz*.
Obv: ⥾ɣ०४Ш *(Simon)* bunch of grapes in three lobes hanging from
branch, which has a leaf to the left and a tendril to the right.
Rev: Lᖴ૧ШⱵ ૧ᕆL ⥾W *(year two of the freedom of Israel)*; wide lyre
(*nevel* or *chelys*) with three strings, four dots on crescent-shaped
sound box.   1,500/3,000

In this series, sometimes the obverse may use the letter vav *in either* ⋏ *or*
Ⱶ *form.*

1394

1395

1394.   AR *zuz*.
Obv: Bunch of grapes as on 1393.
Rev: Lᖴ૧ШⱵ ૧ᕆL ⥾Ш *(year two of the freedom of Israel)*; fluted jug,
handle on l., willow branch on r.   2,500/5,000

1395.   AR *zuz*.
Obv: Bunch of grapes as on 1393.
Rev: Lᖴ૧ШⱵ ૧ᕆL ⥾W *(year two of the freedom of Israel)*; fluted jug,
handle on l., willow branch on r.   500/850

1396.   AR *zuz*.
Obv: Bunch of grapes as on 1393.
Rev: Lᖴ૧ШⱵ ૧ᕆL ⥾W *(year two of the freedom of Israel)*; elongated
lyre (*kinor* or *kithara*) with three strings.   500/850

1397

1397. AR zuz.

Obv: חנועש *(Simon)*, the letters form a square with one in the center, within a wreath of thin branches wrapped around eight almonds, medallion at top, tendrils at bottom.

Rev: לארשי ארח של *(year two of the freedom of Israel)*; elongated lyre *(kinor* or *kithara)* with three strings.   RRR

1398. AR zuz.

Obv: Paleo-Hebrew as on 1397.

Rev: לארשי ארח שש *(year two of the freedom of Israel)*; Palm branch.   RRR

1399. AR zuz.

Obv: Paleo-Hebrew as on 1397.

Rev: לארשי ארח של *(year two of the freedom of Israel)*; fluted jug, handle on l., willow branch on r.   RRR

The obverse die used in coins 1397–99 was used on only a very few coins. It may have been a trial die whose use was never extended further.

1400. AR zuz.

Obv: Paleo-Hebrew as on 1397 but letters are arranged ןועמש *(Simon).*

Rev: לארשי ארח של *(year two of the freedom of Israel)*; palm branch.   RRR

1401. AR zuz.

Obv: ןועמש *(Simon)*, five letters in two lines, within a wreath of thin branches wrapped around eight almonds, medallion at top, tendrils at bottom.

Rev: לארשי ארח של *(year two of the freedom of Israel)*; palm branch.   500/850

1402.   AR *zuz*.
Obv: Paleo-Hebrew as 1401.
Rev: ⌐ℲꟼШꓭ ꟼθᒷ ꓲW *(year two of the freedom of Israel)*; two trumpets upright, dot between.   600/900

1403.   AR *zuz*.
Obv: Paleo-Hebrew as 1401.
Rev: ⌐ℲꟼШꓭ ꟼθᒷ ꓲW *(year two of the freedom of Israel)*; elongated lyre (*kinor* or *kithara*) with three strings.   500/850

1404.   AE large bronze, 32 mm.
Obv: ШⵎШ ⊁ꟼꓲ *(Jerusalem)* within a wreath.
Rev: ⌐ℲꟼШꓭ ꟼθᒷ ꓲW *(year two of the freedom of Israel)*; amphora with two handles.   7,000/20,000

1405.   AE large bronze, 35 mm.
Obv: ꓓ⊼ꝋ ШⵎШ *(Simon)* within a wreath.
Rev: ⌐ℲꟼШꓭ ꟼθᒷ ꓲW *(year two of the freedom of Israel)*; amphora with two handles.   10,000/25,000
The photographed example is double struck on the obverse.

1406

1407

1406. AE middle bronze, 20 mm.

Obv: שמעון נשיא ישראל *(Simon Prince of Israel)*; palm branch within a wreath.

Rev: שב לחר ישראל *(year two of the freedom of Israel); wide lyre (nevel or chelys)* of four or five strings. 850/2,000

1407. AE middle bronze, 23 mm.

Obv: לחרות ירושלם *(for the freedom of Jerusalem)*; palm branch within a wreath.

Rev: שב לחר ישראל *(year two of the freedom of Israel)*; wide lyre (*nevel* or *chelys*) of four or five strings. 850/2,000

1408

1408a

1408. AE middle bronze, 25 mm.

Obv: שמע *(Sma—abbreviating Simon)* across fields; seven-branched palm tree with two bunches of dates.

Rev: שב לחר ישראל *(year two of the freedom of Israel)*; vine leaf on tendril. 150/350

a. Many variations of this type, Simon in 5 letters on obverse.

1409. AE small bronze, 20 mm.

Obv: אלעזר הכהן *(Eleazar the priest)* across fields; seven-branched palm tree with two bunches of dates.

Rev: שב לחר ישראל *(year two of the freedom of Israel)*; bunch of grapes with branch and small leaf. 2,000/4,500

1410

1410. AE small bronze, 23 mm.
Obv: ЫLШ⋗Яᒷ (*Jerusalem*); seven-branched palm tree with two bunches of dates.
Rev: ᒷ∓ЯШᒷ Яᗺᒷ ᒷW (*year two of the freedom of Israel*); bunch of grapes with branch and small leaf. 300/650

UNDATED COINS ATTRIBUTED TO YEAR THREE, *134/135* CE

1411

1411a

1411. AR *sela*.
Obv: ᒷ⋎○ЫШ (*Simon*) on two sides; star above facade of the Jerusalem Temple, showbread table (?) seen from end in center of entrance.
Rev: ЫLШ⋏Яᒷ Х⋏Яᗺᒷ (*for the freedom of Jerusalem*); *lulav* with *etrog* at l. 2,000/5,000
a. Irregular variety of 1411.

1412. AR *sela*.
Obv: ᒷ⋎○ЫШ (*Simon*) on two sides; star above facade of the Jerusalem Temple, showbread table (?) seen from end in center of entrance.
Rev: ЫLШ⋏Яᒷ Х⋏Яᗺᒷ (*for the freedom of Jerusalem*); *lulav*, no *etrog*. 2,250/6,000

1413. AR *sela.*
Obv: ᒻᐪ◊ᎩᏔ *(Simon)* on two sides; wavy line above facade of the Jerusalem Temple, showbread table (?) seen from end in center of entrance.
Rev: ᎩᒪᏔᐱᎬᒻ ᙭ᐱᏃᗉᒪ *(for the freedom of Jerusalem)*; *lulav* with *etrog* at l. 3,000/8,500
a. Variety with reverse in a different style.

1414. AR *sela.*
Obv: ᒻᐪ◊ᎩᏔ *(Simon)* on two sides; wavy line of four semi-circles connected by horizontal lines above facade of the Jerusalem Temple, showbread table (?) seen from end in center of entrance.
Rev: ᎩᒪᏔᐱᎬᒻ ᙭ᐱᏃᗉᒪ *(for the freedom of Jerusalem)*; *lulav* with *etrog* at l. 3,500/9,500

1415. AR half-*sela.*
Obv: ᒻᐪ◊ᎩᏔ *(Simon)* on sides of distyle facade representing the Jerusalem Temple, showbread table (?) seen from side in center of entrance.
Rev: ᎩᒪᏔᐱᎬᒻ ᙭ᐱᏃᗉᒪ *(for the freedom of Jerusalem)*; *lulav*, no *etrog.*
RRR
It is not known whether the building depicted here was meant to also be a schematic image of the Jerusalem Temple, as Meshorer suggested, or if the building simply received two columns instead of four because it was half the denomination. Barag suggests that this type was struck at Bar Kokhba's second mint, responsible for the irregular coins, and this explains the somewhat unusual epigraphy.[56]

1416. AR *zuz.*
Obv: ᒻᒣ◊ᎩᏔ *(Simon)* within a wreath of thin branches wrapped around eight almonds, medallion at top, tendrils at bottom.
Rev: ᎩᒪᏔᐱᎬᒻ ᙭ᐱᏃᗉᒪ *(for the freedom of Jerusalem)*; palm branch.
350/750

1416   1418

1417. AR *zuz.*

    Obv: Paleo-Hebrew as on 1416.

    Rev: 𐤉𐤋𐤅𐤔𐤀𐤓𐤉 𐤕𐤀𐤓𐤇𐤋 *(for the freedom of Jerusalem)*; trumpets upright, dot between.   350/750

1418. AR *zuz.*

    Obv: Paleo-Hebrew as on 1416.

    Rev: 𐤉𐤋𐤅𐤔𐤀𐤓𐤉 𐤕𐤀𐤓𐤇𐤋 *(for the freedom of Jerusalem)*; fluted jug, handle on l., willow branch on r.   350/750

1419. AR *zuz.*

    Obv: Paleo-Hebrew as on 1416.

    Rev: 𐤉𐤋𐤅𐤔𐤀𐤓𐤉 𐤕𐤀𐤓𐤇𐤋 *(for the freedom of Jerusalem)*; elongated lyre (*kinor* or *kithara*) with three strings.   350/750

1420. AR *zuz.*

    Obv: 𐤔𐤌𐤏𐤅𐤍➤ *(Simon, in this case, actually Simna, since letters are rearranged)* within a wreath of thin branches wrapped around eight almonds, medallion at top, tendrils at bottom, there are a pair of dots, one inside and one outside, between each section.

    Rev: 𐤉𐤋𐤅𐤔𐤀𐤓𐤉 𐤕𐤀𐤓𐤇𐤋 *(for the freedom of Jerusalem)*; palm branch.   350/750

1421. AR *zuz.*

    Obv: Paleo-Hebrew as on 1420.

    Rev: 𐤉𐤋𐤅𐤔𐤀𐤓𐤉 𐤕𐤀𐤓𐤇𐤋 *(for the freedom of Jerusalem)*; two trumpets upright, dot between.   400/800

1422. AR *zuz.*

    Obv: Paleo-Hebrew as on 1420.

    Rev: 𐤉𐤋𐤅𐤔𐤀𐤓𐤉 𐤕𐤀𐤓𐤇𐤋 *(for the freedom of Jerusalem)*; fluted jug, handle on l., willow branch on r.   350/750

1423.   AR *zuz*.
    Obv: Paleo-Hebrew as on 1420.
    Rev: ꓨلШᴀꟼꓞ ×ᴀꟼᗺL *(for the freedom of Jerusalem)*; fluted jug, handle on l., no willow branch.   350/750

1424.   AR *zuz*.
    Obv: Paleo-Hebrew as on 1420.
    Rev: ꓨلШᴀꟼꓞ ×ᴀꟼᗺL *(for the freedom of Jerusalem)*; elongated lyre (*kinor* or *kithara*) with three strings.   350/750

1425.   AR *zuz*.
    Obv: ꓕꓩOꓯꓨШ *(Simon, see 1420)* within a wreath of thin branches wrapped around eight almonds, medallion at top, tendrils at bottom; there are a pair of dots, one inside and one outside, between each section.
    Rev: ꓨلШᴀꟼꓞ ×ᴀꟼᗺL *(for the freedom of Jerusalem)*; palm branch.
                                    350/750

1426.   AR *zuz*.
    Obv: Paleo-Hebrew as on 1425.
    Rev: ꓨلШᴀꟼꓞ ×ᴀꟼᗺL *(for the freedom of Jerusalem)*; two trumpets upright, dot between.   400/800

1427.   AR *zuz*.
    Obv: Paleo-Hebrew as on 1425.
    Rev: ꓨلШᴀꟼꓞ ×ᴀꟼᗺL *(for the freedom of Jerusalem)*; fluted jug, handle on l., willow branch on r.   350/750

1428. AR *zuz.*
Obv: Paleo-Hebrew as on 1425.
Rev: 𐤋𐤇𐤓𐤅𐤕 𐤉𐤓𐤅𐤔𐤋𐤌 *(for the freedom of Jerusalem)*; fluted jug, handle on l., no willow branch. 350/750

1429

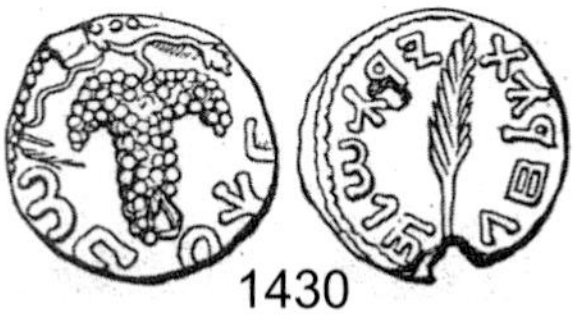
1430

1429. AR *zuz.*
Obv: Paleo-Hebrew as on 1425.
Rev: 𐤋𐤇𐤓𐤅𐤕 𐤉𐤓𐤅𐤔𐤋𐤌 *(for the freedom of Jerusalem)*; elongated lyre (*kinor* or *kithara*) with three strings. 350/750

1430. AR *zuz.*
Obv: 𐤔𐤌𐤏𐤅𐤍 *(Simon)*; bunch of grapes in three lobes hanging from branch, which has a tendril to the left and a leaf to the right.
Rev: 𐤋𐤇𐤓𐤅𐤕 𐤉𐤓𐤅𐤔𐤋𐤌 *(for the freedom of Jerusalem)*; palm branch. 350/750

a. Irregular variety of 1430.

1431

1431a

1431. AR *zuz.*
Obv: Bunch of grapes as on 1430.
Rev: 𐤋𐤇𐤓𐤅𐤕 𐤉𐤓𐤅𐤔𐤋𐤌 *(for the freedom of Jerusalem)*; two trumpets upright, dot between. 350/750

Drawing 1431a shows a denarius *of Trajan similar to a* drachm *struck in Bostra. This type was overstruck by many Bar Kokhba* zuz *coins and drawing 1431 shows an example of this phenomenon.*

1432.   AR *zuz.*

Same as 1431 but struck on a Vespasian Judaea Capta *denarius* with IVDAEA legend, which is clear on this example.

RRR

a.   Another example this is No. 1392 struck upon IVDAEA type.

This could take place with any zuz. *There are three known examples with the* IVDAEA *remaining clear.*

1433.   AR *zuz.*

Obv: Bunch of grapes as on 1430.

Rev: 𐤉𐤋𐤔𐤀𐤓𐤂 𐤗𐤀𐤒𐤀𐤋 (for the freedom of Jerusalem); fluted jug, handle on l., willow branch on r.   350/750

1434.   AR *zuz.*

Obv: Bunch of grapes as on 1430.

Rev: 𐤉𐤋𐤔𐤀𐤓𐤂 𐤗𐤀𐤒𐤀𐤋 *(for the freedom of Jerusalem)*; fluted jug, handle on l., no willow branch.   350/750

1435. AR *zuz.*

Obv: Bunch of grapes as on 1430.

Rev: 𐤋𐤉𐤋𐤔𐤀𐤓𐤂 𐤗𐤀𐤒𐤀𐤋 *(for the freedom of Jerusalem)*; elongated lyre (*kinor* or *kithara*) with three strings.   350/750

a.   *Fourrée* example.[57]

b.   Reverse with regular design plus obverse brockage.

c.   Same as 1435 but cut to invalidate or make change.

There has been some support for the idea that Bar Kokhba coins were cut to invalidate them after the war. However, since such a miniscule percentage of both bronze and silver coins have been cut, it seems far more likely they were simply cut to make change.

1436. AE middle bronze, 22 mm.

Obv: ᘓᒪᘺᗯᐱᔭᒷ ᙭ᐱᔭᘓᒪ *(for the freedom of Jerusalem)*; palm branch within a wreath.

Rev: ᒚᐱᐤᘓᗯ *(Simon)*; elongated lyre *(kinor* or *kithara)* with three strings.

350/500

a. Some examples of this coin were struck from "clashed dies" and show several incuse letters from the reverse on the right side of the obverse.

1437. AE middle bronze, 27 mm.

Obv: ᒚᐱᐤᘓᗯ *(Simon)*; seven-branched palm tree with two bunches of dates.

Rev: ᘓᒪᘺᗯᐱᔭᒷ ᙭ᐱᔭᘓᒪ *(for the freedom of Jerusalem)*; vine leaf on tendril.

150/300

a. Irregular variety of 1437.

1438. AE small bronze, 19 mm.

Obv: ᒚᔭᐱᒚᔭ ᔭᘘᐤᒪᖴ *(Eleazar the priest)* across fields; seven-branched palm tree with two bunches of dates.

Rev: ᒪᘺᐱᔭᒷ ᙭ᐱᔭᘓᒪ *(for the freedom of Jerusalem)*; bunch of grapes with branch and small leaf.

750/1,750

1439. AE small bronze, 18 mm.

Obv: ᘓᒪᘺᗱᔭᒷ *(Jerusalem)* across fields; seven-branched palm tree with two bunches of dates.

Rev: ᒪᘺᐱᔭᒷ ᙭ᐱᔭᘓᒪ *(for the freedom of Jerusalem)*; bunch of grapes with branch and small leaf.

150/250

a. Irregular variety of 1439.

1440.   AE small bronze, 20 mm.

Obv: ꓘꓥ꒦ꕐꓤ *(Simon)*; across fields; seven-branched palm tree with two bunches of dates.

Rev: ꒦ꒊꕐꓤꓱ ꘉꕐꓤꓱꓶ *(for the freedom of Jerusalem)*; bunch of grapes with branch and small leaf.   150/250

  a. Regular style, but size and weight of a *prutah*.
  b. Irregular variety of 1440.
  c. Irregular variety of 1440 struck on *prutah* flan.

10.7. This inscription, on display at the Colosseum in Rome, records restoration during the reigns of Theodosius II and Valentinian III, who reigned from 425-455 CE, perhaps to repair damages from an earthquake in 443. However, this inscription was cut upon a piece of marble that contained an earlier inscription. The original inscription probably stood above one of the entrances. The "ghost" inscription, has been recreated from a series of small holes in the marble, and stated that the Colosseum was built with "booty" probably taken from the Jerusalem Temple in 70/71 CE (see p. 413). This event is also commemorated on the Arch of Titus, located nearby at the entrance to the Roman Forum. (Author photo.)

CHAPTER ELEVEN

JUDAEA AND ROME

ROMAN REPUBLICAN JEWISH REFERENCE COINS

*A*ristobulus was not able to make resistance, but was deserted in
his first onset, and was driven to Jerusalem: he also had been
taken at first by force, if Scaurus, the Roman general, had not
come and seasonably interposed himself and raised the siege. (JOSE-
PHUS, WARS, 1, VI: 2)

ROMAN REPUBLIC. M. AEMILIUS SCAURUS AND PUB. PLAUTIUS HYPSAEUS, 58 BCE

1441

1441.   AR *denarius*.
  Obv: M SCAVR AED CVR above, EX S C in fields, REX ARETAS
    below; King Aretas kneels r. with palm branch in l. hand, along-
    side camel.
  Rev: P HVPSAEVS AED CVR above, CAPTVM on r., C HVPSAE
    COS PREIVE in exergue; Jupiter drives *quadriga* l. and hurls
    thunderbolt, scorpion below horses.   150/550

1442.   AR *denarius.*
  Obv: M. SCAVR above and AED CVR in exergue on obv.
  Rev: Jupiter drives *quadriga* as on 1441, no scorpion.

150/550

When M. Aemilius was governor of Syria, this type was struck to commemorate the defeat of Aretas III by Pompey's general Marcus Scaurus. Aretas was a supporter and ally of John Hyrcanus II in his battles against his brother, Aristobulus II. Aretas was required to surrender and pay a 300 talent fine to Pompey. Pub. Plautius was curule aedile with M. Aemilius in 58 BCE. This coin is one of the earliest examples of a Roman moneyer memorializing an event from his own history on coinage.

A. PLAUTIUS, C. *54* BCE

1443

1443.   AR *denarius.*
  Obv: A.PLAVTIVS AED CVR S C.; turreted head of Cybele r.
  Rev: BACCHIVS IVDAEVS; bearded male figure kneels r. with
      palm branch in l. hand, alongside camel.   200/600

Except for the inscription, this coin is of the same reverse type as the previous coin's obverse. The "Bacchius the Jew" referred to on this coin is an enigma of Jewish numismatics. The most popular opinion is that the coin represents Aristobulus II, ally of Aretas III, mentioned on the previous coin, and commemorates Aristobulus' unsuccessful insurrection.

JUDAEA CAPTA COIN OF C. SOSIUS

While the first in the well-known Judaea Capta series of coins was struck under Vitellius (see below), a distinct prototype was struck in 36 BCE by C. Sosius under Mark Antony. Sosius, a Roman general and governor of Syria, conquered Jerusalem in 37 BCE, while supporting Herod the Great in his battle against Mattatayah Antigonus.

Sosius' Jerusalem victory coin depicts figures of both a mourning Judaea and a naked male (probably generic, but possibly representing M. Antigonus) with his hands tied behind him.

Antigonus had been re-installed as King of the Jews by the Parthians in 40 BCE. In the same year, the Roman Senate and Octavian (Augustus) named Herod king of Judaea. To gain his "rightful" place, Herod marched against Antigonus. Mark Antony appointed Sosius governor of Syria and ordered him to support Herod. Sosius sent two legions and personally followed with the remainder of his army, which joined Herod and began a siege of Jerusalem. The city was taken in 37 BCE and Sosius ordered his soldiers to pillage. After a horrendous massacre of Jewish occupants, Herod himself managed to restrain the soldiers from further destroying his new capital by promising to reward them appropriately from his own funds. Antigonus surrendered to Sosius, who insulted him and derided him by calling him "Antigone." Finally, Sosius "dedicated a golden crown to God and departed from Jerusalem, taking Antigonus in chains to Antony,"[1] according to Josephus. In 37 BCE, Antony was wintering in Antioch.

It is not clear why these coins were struck in Zacynthus, but the attribution seems probable. Antony had a fleet stationed in Zacynthus in 39 BCE, and Sosius himself commanded the left wing of Antony's fleet at Actium. The authors of RPC also note that the provenance of these coins confirm Zacynthus as the location of their production.[2]

COIN OF C. SOSIUS, ZACYNTHUS, ACHAEA, 36 BCE

1444

1444. AE 19 mm.
  Obv: Mark Antony's head to r., ZA behind.
  Rev: C SOSIVS IMP; trophy between Jewess, head in hands, seated on l., and naked Jewish captive, looking back, seated on r, both to r. RRR

JUDAEA CAPTA

Thy men shall fall by the sword, And thy mighty in the war. And her gates shall lament and mourn; And utterly bereft she shall sit upon the ground. (ISAIAH 3:25, 26)

So fell Jerusalem in the second year of Vespasian's reign, on the 8th September, captured five times before and now for the second time laid utterly waste. . . . There was no one left for the soldiers to kill or plunder. (JOSEPHUS, THE JEWISH WAR, 21, 22)

Two thousand years ago when the Near East erupted in violent warfare, there was no internet or cable news network to inform the world of events. The Roman emperors could not depend on radios, magazines, or newspapers. On the other hand, they used one method of communication with extraordinary skill—coins.

One does not usually equate coins with communications. Nevertheless, in ancient times, coins were a genuine method of mass communications.[3]

Hart discusses three methods of official commentary on the ongoing events taking place in Rome, "whereby men might be instructed how they ought to think of this or that transaction, or this or that notable public figure..." These are public occasions such as triumphs, public buildings such as arches or other monuments, and coins.

Unlike the first two categories, coins represented a program of outreach, since triumphs and public buildings were in one place and the coins could travel across the world as quickly as a person, and carry the news as well.

This medium was the ultimate political use of coins, which allowed the authorities to "not only indicate how you should think of passing public events, they could also to a great...extent determine upon which passing public events out of an always wide choice your attention should be fixed."[4]

M.P. Charlesworth observed that the Romans used this method of communication with great skill. "Coins passed through the hands of the highest and lowest, into the coffers of the rich and under the country farmer's hearthstone, might be stored in imperial Rome itself or in some hut along the mountains of Lusitania, and upon these coins were placed words and symbols that could be understood by the simplest. This use of coinage with its legends and pictures, gave emperors, and the city mints that echoed Roman policy, a most potent instrument in the ancient world for fashioning opinions and influencing men's views..."[5]

Michael Grant writes that Roman coins, "served a propaganda purpose far greater than has any other national coinage before or since. This was the means which the Roman government, lacking modern media of publicity, used to insinuate into every house in the empire each changing nuance of imperial achievement and policy. Their unremitting use of this means is evidence enough...that in the course of their vast circulation these coins were studied with an attentiveness that is quite alien to our practices."

Even Vespasian's second son, Domitian, issued a series of coins echoing his family's victory, struck in Caesarea Maritima, although he had nothing to do with the campaigns against the Jews. And during his brief reign, Vitellius, who preceded Vespasian, mounted his own public relations campaign with some Judaea Capta issues designed to capitalize on Vespasian's success.

VITELLIUS BEGINS THE SERIES

It is generally, but incorrectly, believed that the first Judaea Capta coins commemorating the Roman defeat of the Jews in 70 CE were struck by Vespasian. Experts have always acknowledged that during his short reign Vitellius struck several Judaea Capta issues.

The Roman campaign against the Jews began in 66 CE and was led by the distinguished general Vespasian, and concluded by his son Titus after Vespasian was proclaimed emperor. This war began while Nero was emperor. When Nero committed suicide on June 9, 68 CE, he was succeeded by Galba, governor of Spain. Galba was assassinated on January 15, 69 CE, after a reign of only seven months. Galba was followed by Otho, but Otho's reign lasted only three months because the Roman legions in Upper Germany had proclaimed Vitellius emperor on January 2, 69 CE. Otho committed suicide on April 17. Sadly for Rome, Vitellius was an obnoxious glutton who was held in contempt by the Roman Senate. He was assassinated and his body dragged through the streets of Rome and thrown into the Tiber.

Vespasian was proclaimed emperor at Alexandria on July 1, and other legions declared for him and invaded Italy on his behalf shortly thereafter.

Thus, there were four emperors involved in the Jewish War before Vespasian—Nero, Galba, Otho, and Vitellius. Nero was probably in no position to issue coins because it was so early in the war that the outcome was not clear. Galba and Otho had such short and tumultuous reigns that they probably had no time to consider the issue.

Vitellius, on the other hand, apparently knew Vespasian, his chief rival for the throne, was approaching victory. In an effort to consolidate and spread word of his power, Vitellius issued the first Judaea Capta coins. The basic types are two bronzes:

1. Bronze (brass) *sestertius*, reverse showing Victory, naked to waist, standing r., l. foot set on helmet, inscribing OB CIVES SERV in three lines on round shield attached to palm tree. VICTORIA AVGVSTI, S C (No. 1462).

2. Bronze *as*, reverse showing Victory, draped, stepping l. and placing a shield on a trophy, beneath which is a captive seated l. on a globe. VICTOR AVGVSTI, S C (No. 1463).

Both of these reverse types were later struck under Vespasian, and the *sestertius* reverse was also struck under Titus. Neither coin when struck under the Flavians was ever thought to be anything other than a Judaea Capta issue.

Mattingly misses a point when he talks about the *sestertius* mentioned above: "A favourite Victory theme—Victory inscribing a shield OB CIVES SERV: the idea that the safety of Rome is bound up with the Victory of Vitellius is aptly conveyed."[6] Mattingly does not mention that the Victory is associated with a palm tree, a clear reference to victory over Judaea.

In describing the *as*, however, he notes that, "For the motif of Victory erecting a trophy, compare types of Vespasian, showing Victory inscribing shield. The captive seated below reminds one of the Jewish captives on Vespasian's Judaea Capta types."[7]

Hart sheds additional light on these coins: "Her [Victory's] first appearance with a palm tree is not with Vespasian, but with Vitellius of evil memory. We may accordingly submit that the Vitellius types are already celebrating, and are the true numismatic beginning of the celebration of the Jewish defeat in the First Revolt. The fact that this type and modifications of it are used by Vespasian and Titus for this purpose, and that a variant of the same design appears on the cuirass of the Sabratha statue, are best explained by supposing that it was for this very purpose that the type had first been used in the time of Vitellius," Hart writes. "This case is much strengthened by the fact that the very same reverse sestertius dies for this type were used by both Vitellius and Vespasian."[8]

Hart further notes evidence from Tacitus that the "back of the war was broken" early in 68 CE. "There is therefore time for Vitellius also to anticipate the final victory. The palm-tree firmly connects his Victoria type with Judaea."

Here, a surprising coin enters this discussion: a *fourrée denarius* of Vitellius with a clear, classic Judaea reverse (No. 1461). It shows beyond a doubt that Vitellius did issue Judaea Capta coins. Some may argue that this coin is a *fourrée*, and thus a contemporary (ancient) forgery, not a mint issue. This may be the case, but if it was a contemporary forgery, it would have been made during the reign of Vitellius. Because Vitellius was so thoroughly disliked, it is hardly thinkable that a forgery of a Vitellius coin would have been created after Vespasian ascended to the throne. Therefore, as a forgery, it must have been copied after a coin type that was already known at the time. Since during Vitellius's reign Vespasian had not yet issued any coins, this *fourrée* must have been copied from a coin of Vitellius.

THE FLAVIAN DYNASTY

The Judaea Capta series was the broadest and most diverse series of coins commemorating a Roman victory issued to that time. Vespasian and his sons intended for their victory over the Jews to be the "talk of the empire." Universal attention was their desire, observes H. St. J. Hart: "All the world must know and meditate upon the destruction of that rebellious and warlike nation, the Jews, and that a long and difficult war, with disturbing possibilities of complications throughout the empire is over."[9]

No doubt, Vespasian and his sons also looked at the victory as a stabilizing factor. It came, after all, just after Vespasian became emperor, at the end of the alarming year of four emperors. Such a victory was the stuff of which a new dynasty was made, and Vespasian was successful in establishing it. What better way to let the world know of his strength, wisdom, and good judgement than to proclaim his greatest victory publicly—even, perhaps, to make it sound more grandiose than it was.

Vespasian could proclaim his victory in a triumphal celebration, and by building a victory arch or two. But, these were stationary items or single events — the people had to come to observe them. What was really needed was a form of mass communication to spread the word widely and often. The perfect vehicle for this need was the coin of the realm, since coins were handled and examined many thousands of times each day throughout the empire.

Flavius Vespasianus was born in 9 CE, the son of a tax collector and knight. After serving as a legionary commander in the invasion of Britain (43–44 CE), as consul and governor of Africa, and accompanying Nero to Greece in 66 CE, Vespasian was sent to Judaea. The Jews had already dealt some severe blows to Rome, but by June of the year 68 CE Vespasian had claimed victory over all of Judaea except Jerusalem and a few minor fortresses, including Masada.

When Nero died, Rome was plunged into confusion, and three emperors followed in rapid succession. In July 69, Vespasian's eastern legions proclaimed him emperor. Shortly thereafter, he returned to Rome and sent his son Titus to finish his chores in Judaea. On June 23, 79, Vespasian died an apparently natural death.

Titus Flavius Vespasianus succeeded his father on the throne immediately upon his death. Titus had been entrusted with full command of the Jewish war after mid-69, when his father was required to focus his attention on the rebellion against Vitellius. Titus was victorious in Judaea late in 70, when the Temple and much of Jerusalem was burned.[10]

David Vagi narrates that "because of the suspicion aroused by the extreme loyalty of his soldiers, Titus sailed at once for Italy, arriving early in 71. Upon reaching Rome he surprised his father (who was not expecting him) saying 'Here I am father, here I am!' Together Titus and his father celebrated the Judaean Triumph, with young Domitian at their side."[11]

Titus was in love with the Jewish princess Julia Berenice, sister of Agrippa II. They lived together in Rome for a while, but he soon sent her away. She returned when he became emperor, but he rejected her again. It is said that Titus was in love with Berenice, but couldn't risk the wrath he would incur by marrying an eastern princess, the memory of Cleopatra was still on the minds of Roman senators.

Titus died at age 42, on September 13, 81 CE, from unknown causes. He was succeeded by his younger brother **Titus Flavius Domitianus**.

DEFINING THE SERIES

Roman coins of the Judaea Capta series were issued in gold, silver, and bronze of various denominations. Bronze coins were also issued locally in ancient Israel, struck in Caesarea, with the Greek legend ΙΟΥΔΑΙΑΣ ΕΑΛΩΚΥΙΑΣ (sometimes written ΕΑΛΩΚΥΙΑΣ).

The Roman Judaea Capta coins carry legends such as IVDAEA CAPTA, IVDAEA DEVICTA, DE IVDAEVS, and simply IVDAEA. A number of VICTORIA AVGVSTI types carry images that belong to this series. Some of the coins have no legend at all; the scene depicted tells the entire story.

The connection between a coin's design and the Jewish War can be in the images (types), the legend, or more tentatively the date of issue. Sometimes all three factors are involved. Often scholars who have written in this field make their best educated guess based upon information ranging from gut instinct and up on the scholarly ladder.

Creation of the Judaea Capta coinage seems to have been a multilayered program intended to focus and influence public opinion. The coins can be set into different categories.

- Coins that carry specific legends together with specific types.
- Coins that carry specific legends and types.
- Coins that depict specific types: emperor and captive(s); Victory and captive; Victory with palm tree, captives, palm tree, trophy, or triumphal parade.
- Coins that have some similarities to the above types, and were struck in relevant years. This group includes the bronze *asses* and *dupondii* with the legends VICTORIA AVGVSTI and VICTORIA NAVALIS.

The Judaea Capta theme is featured on coins from the beginning of Vespasian's reign until 73 CE. But almost no Judaea Capta coins were struck again until 77/8 when they may have commemorated the tenth anniversary of the outbreak of the Jewish War. When Vespasian died and Titus became emperor, the Roman mints once again produced a number of the Judaea Capta issues.

The Flavian coinage comprised an ongoing public relations campaign designed to immediately and dramatically portray the new Flavian dynasty as formidable. Images on the coins portray the physical dominance of Rome, the emperor, and the legions as well as the humiliation of the defeated enemy.

Coins with victory legends such as VICTORIA AVGVSTI and VICTORIA NAVALIS and generic victory motifs without captives, a palm tree, or other specific reference to Judaea are secondary extensions of the original campaign; leading their audience to a broader impression of glory and victory than a single campaign. It is not clear that every victory-themed Flavian coin was related to the Jewish War victory, and we have omitted them from this catalog.[12] On the other hand, there are sufficient clues to indicate those coins that are surely linked to the Judaea Capta series.

The single coin listed here that does not carry the precise imagery described above is the *sestertius* (Nos. 1518, 1524, 1530, 1535), illustrating a scene described by Josephus, in which the mounted Titus battles a fallen enemy on foot.[13]

One of the standard symbols used in conjunction with the Judaea Capta motifs is the trophy, which requires some explanation to readers familiar with modern trophies. The Roman trophy of this period is also referred to as a field trophy of arms as opposed to the marble trophies in the forms of monuments that were built as public monuments. The trophies depicted on coins were generally created on the battlefield, where victorious soldiers decorate a tree trunk or a spear thrust into the ground with arms of the vanquished including the helmet, cuirass, crossed swords, and shield.

COLOSSEUM TYPE LINKED TO JUDAEA

No previous reference has suggested that the legendary Flavian colosseum *sestertii* should be considered part of the Judaea Capta series. Late in 2007, Arturo Russo of the firm *Numismatica Ars Classica* in London and Zurich, showed me a colosseum *sestertius* he described as possibly depicting a palm tree with Vespasian standing on its left and a captive to the right in a tableau of sculptures, and directly below it was a victory *quadriga* facing front.[14] These standard Judaea Capta motifs are on the highest point of relief on the obverse of these coins, and on the vast majority of specimens either one or both scenes are worn or obscured because the coins were frequently weakly struck or worn.[15]

The colosseum coins of Titus (and those in his memory by Domitian) are certainly an extension of the Judaea Capta series because:

- Iconography on the coins links directly to known Judaea Capta types.
- The colosseum *sestertii* were struck in 80/1 CE, the tenth anniversary of the destruction of Jerusalem and the Jewish Temple.
- Titus's depiction, on the reverse (!), of the coin shows him surrounded by military booty.
- The colosseum was financed by booty from the Jewish War and this was recognized at the time it was built and dedicated.

In 1995, Prof. Géza Alföldy of the University of Heidelberg published a remarkable reading of a "ghost" inscription behind a later marble inscription.[16] The inscription was on a stone that had been discovered in secondary use in the Colosseum in 1913. The later inscription, quite easily legible, refers to repairs to the building that took place around 444 CE. Even the first scholars who studied this stone noted a series of small holes that were drilled to fasten metal letters to the marble for an earlier inscription.

Using established techniques, Alföldy reconstructs the earlier inscription as follows:

I[MP(ERATOR)] T(ITVS) CAES(AR) VESPASI[ANVS AVG(VSTVS)] / AMPHITHEATRV[M NOVVM?] / [EX] MANVB(I)S (vacat) [FIERI IVSSIT (?)]

The Emperor Titus Caesar Vespasian Augustus ordered the new amphitheater to be made from the (proceeds from the sale of the) booty.

There is also evidence that the letter T for Titus was squeezed into the inscription in antiquity. This addition is possible since Vespasian first dedicated the Colosseum in 75 CE when only the first three stories had been completed, and it was re-dedicated by Titus in 80/1 CE, when he may have modified the original inscription to include reference to his name.

Louis Feldman points out that Alföldy's reconstruction is hypothetical, but has already been endorsed by other key scholars in the field. Feldman notes that none of the ancient sources mentions how the Colosseum was financed. But apparently these inscriptions appeared in abbreviated form at the minor doorways. If this follows a standard pattern in Roman buildings, there may have been a larger and more complete version of the same inscription at the main entrance.[17]

When Vespasian became emperor, Rome had just been through civil war and the year of four emperors. Suetonius points out that Rome was literally bankrupt, and Vespasian himself "declared at his accession that 40 billion gold pieces were needed to put the country on its feet again."[18] This huge deficit was the largest sum of money ever mentioned in antiquity, Feldman says. He further suggests that Judaea was the only logical conquered area under Vespasian that could have yielded substantial booty although Vespasian had earlier commanded troops in Germany and Britain.[19]

Josephus describes the Temple as opulent "covered on all sides with massive plates of gold." He says that the golden altar and golden menorah alone weighed at least two *talents* and, further, that huge amounts of treasures were found in the Temple's vaults. "The spoils in general were borne in promiscuous heaps; but conspicuous above all stood out those captured in the Temple at Jerusalem,"[20] Josephus writes. The *Letter of Aristeas*, as paraphrased by Josephus, describes the Temple as extravagant and sumptuous beyond any precedent, in which no expense had been spared. The lavishness of the booty of Judaea was also depicted on the Arch of Titus.

It was probably in CE 75 that Vespasian dedicated the first three levels of the Colosseum, but he died before it was completed. It is not even clear if it was completely finished in time for its dedication by Titus in 80/81, on the tenth anniversary of the destruction of Jerusalem. Elkins says that many Roman buildings were shown on coins as completed before they actually were.

"The reverse of Titus' *sestertii* depicts the emperor as a triumphant ruler surrounded by the spoils of war, with which the construction of the Colosseum was funded," according to Elkins.[21]

Elkins has also argued convincingly that the Colosseum *sestertii* are different from most other Roman bronze coins because they are smaller than most *sestertii* of the period and, more significantly, carry no imperial portrait on the obverse.[22] Elkins also says that the image of the Colosseum on a coin represents the first appearance of any entertainment venue on a Roman coin. A spectacular aerial view is shown, which allows us to see both the interior of the Amphitheater as well as its facade. Inside it we see a clear representation of the imperial box.[23]

The Colosseum is flanked on the coins by the *Meta Sudans* (a fountain) and the porticus of the Baths of Titus, which in some coins appear on the left and right and in others on the right and left. While some have suggested this perspective represents two different views of the building, it is more likely artistic license, since the imperial box could not be seen from both the south and the north but can be clearly seen on both varieties. Elkins' research suggests that the imperial box was on the northern side of the building, so our view of the entrance facade is probably from the south.[24]

Elkins believes these *sestertii* were initially issued as largess "for distribution by the emperor at games in the Colosseum."[25]

"If all Titus's (Colosseum) *sestertii* were struck before July 80, they could have been distributed during the inaugural games; if, as I have suggested, they were struck both in CE 80 and 81, they could have been distributed piecemeal throughout the first couple years of the Colosseum's use. Domitian's small issue of Colosseum *sestertii* would have been distributed at the games held in honour of his deceased and divine brother." It is also possible, Elkins says, that Titus might have ordered one Colosseum piece to be given "to every spectator at the inaugural games."[26]

Perhaps the most convincing argument of all linking the Colosseum *sestertii* to the Judaean issues is the construction of the building as portrayed on some of the coins (Nos. 1594, 1599).[27] The facade had four tiers of arches; the lowest tier has four empty arches, the second tier has six arches all containing figures, large sculptures, the center of which depicts a *quadriga* to front; the third tier has seven arches and the center arch contains a palm tree flanked by two figures, probably the emperor or Nike and a Jewish captive.

The fact that the Judaea tableau along with the victory *quadriga* sit in the exact focal point of the facade of this impressive building convincingly identifies the building, as well as the coin commemorating it, as a fixture in the Judaea Capta series.

DOMITIAN'S JUDAEA CAPTA

It was long believed that the coins of Domitian struck at Caesarea Maritima were the last of the Judaea Capta series.[28] In the 1960s, scholars began a shift and in 1962 Weisbrem wrote that "No coin of Domitian bears a legend referring to such a victory [over the Jews], such as occurs on the coins of Vespasian and Titus. Domitian took no part in the war between Rome and Judaea and furthermore, as Titus' rival, tried to belittle his accomplishments. It is, therefore, most unlikely that

Domitian would issue coins in commemoration of Titus' victory in Judaea."[29]

In 1983, Ian Carradice published an article in the *INJ* which seems to have codified the revised theory: "The coins issued by the Roman administrators of the province of Judaea during the reign of Domitian used to be classified a continuation of the early Flavian Judaea Capta series, but now it is generally recognized that they are a separate series whose types do not refer to the Flavian victories in Judaea."

The authors of *Roman Provincial Coinage* state that these coins of Domitian "are now accepted as a separate series. They are strongly 'Imperial' in character, with the emperor's portrait, Latin inscriptions and some designs clearly borrowed from the coinage of Rome."

I do not accept the reinterpretation.[30] It is true that Domitian, the second son of Vespasian, did not play a part in the Jewish War. On the other hand, we find no evidence that he made any effort to distance himself from this major victory belonging to his father and his brother—in fact the Judaean Victory was the source and the legend of the Flavian dynasty.

The ancient sources state that Domitian was envious and competitive with his brother Titus. Those who argue against the Domitian coins being part of the Judaea Capta series suggest that he would never boast of a victory that was mainly associated with his brother and father.

Historians, however, do not say that Domitian spurned association with the family victory in Judaea. Josephus writes that in Titus's triumphal parade in Rome there appeared ". . . a large group carrying images of Victory, all fashioned of ivory and gold. Behind them Vespasian drove first, with Titus behind him, while Domitian rode alongside in magnificent apparel and mounted on a horse that was itself a sight worth seeing."[31] Surely then, Domitian had no embarrassment in being associated with this victory.

Suetonius reports that upon Vespasian's death, Domitian claimed that "his father's will must have been tampered with, since it originally assigned him a half-share in the Empire. He never once stopped plotting, secretly or openly, against his brother. When Titus fell suddenly and dangerously ill, Domitian told the attendants to presume his death by leaving the sick-bed before he had actually breathed his last; and afterwards granted him no recognition at all, beyond approving his deification. In fact, he often slighted Titus's memory by the use of ambiguous terms in speeches and edicts"[32]

In spite of this (possibly true) tale, however, it was during the reign of Domitian that the Arch of Titus was built in Rome. This arch specifically commemorated his brother's victory in the Jewish War, but in general it is a monument to Flavian domination and victory in the Jewish War, thus indirectly a monument to Domitian himself, the last reigning Flavian emperor.

Let us first consider the coin struck in the name of Domitian by Agrippa II, great friend of the Flavians. Qedar first explained this coin (No. 1280), struck by Agrippa in year 15 of his era beginning in 54 CE, or 69/70 CE. This coin seems to be Agrippa II's own Judaea Capta coin commemorating the victory of his Flavian allies over his own Jewish nation.

Another series of Agrippa II's coins began in the year 14 of his era of 60 CE, and was struck at Caesarea Maritima (see p. 282 for a full discussion of the eras of Agrippa II). Among these year 14 coins are several types that are repeated under Agrippa II. One of them deserves closer examination: the coin with Nike standing left and writing on a shield resting on her knee (No. 1304). Similar coins were struck in at least eight additional years by Agrippa II, although after the first issue the direction of Nike moves from left to right. The year 14, when the first of these types was struck, corresponds to the years 73/4 CE. Since Domitian did not issue his first GERMANIA CAPTA coin until 85 CE there would seem to be no connection at all.[33]

The prototype for these coins of Agrippa II may have been the VICTORIA AVGVSTI *sestertius*, first struck by Vitellius, and later repeated by both Vespasian and Titus, from Rome and other European mints.

Agrippa adopted the design without the date palm tree, which had already become a symbol of ancient Israel. Interestingly, all examples of this coin type struck under Agrippa II carry the obverse portrait of Domitian. Furthermore, it is relevant that in the long series of coins struck in ancient Judaea by Agrippa II, the coins with Domitian's portrait are more common than those coins with portraits of Vespasian or Titus.

An almost identical coin struck was struck under Domitian at the mint of Pella and dated to 82/3 CE.

Is this a coincidence? If so, how can we then further explain another Domitian coin of Pella struck in 82/3, this one depicting a date palm tree. Agrippa II struck a similar coin with Domitian's head and palm tree in year 25 (84/5 CE).

Meshorer cites Eusebius, who "relates that after the destruction of Jerusalem, some Jewish-Christian inhabitants fled to Pella, and perhaps it is they who inspired the issue of coins commemorating Rome's victory over Jerusalem." Thus while Meshorer rules out the Domitian coins of Caesarea as commemorating Rome's victory over Jerusalem, he inconsistently suggests that Pella's coins of Domitian commemorated this victory.[34]

With this background, we focus on the coins of Domitian struck at Caesarea Maritima in following the coins with portraits of Vespasian and Titus.

Carradice has broken these coins into three groups based on obverse legends and portrait styles. The first group (Nos. 1450–53) is dated to 81/2 CE and contains the rarest examples, the foundation coin and emperor in military dress, Victory with wreath, and rudder. These coins were struck before Domitian's Roman mint issued any coins related to Germany.

The second group (Nos. 1454–57), dated after 83 CE, displays the Minerva and Victory series. Domitian claimed Minerva's special protection, and her worship reached its highest popularity under him. Minerva was very closely associated with Athena and Nike, the goddess who bestows victories.

The final group (Nos. 1458–60), dated to 92/3 CE, depicts the palm tree, Nike/Victory, and trophy.

From the third group, ironically the latest, the smallest coin seems to be patterned after a Vespasian *aureus* of DE IVDAEA (No. 1472).

Certainly the palm tree is also connected to the earlier palm tree motifs of Pella and Agrippa, as well as other palm tree coins linked to Judaea.

Now let us look at some of the comparative evidence, and ask: Why should Domitian play such a prominent role on various "Victory" type coins struck in ancient Israel, if it was not intended as a continuing message to the local populace?

It seems logical that local officials, perhaps even Agrippa II, were declaring the message to the populace that what applied to the father and the first son also held true for the second son. While the local coinage follows Domitian's Roman series and does not mention Judaea specifically, how could the interests of Domitian have been hurt by the self-glorification and positive propaganda that came from association with the victory in the Jewish War? Domitian's claim was closer than most—Vespasian and Titus were his father and brother.

The Talmud contains a legal status called *chazaka*, essentially that the *status quo* is always assumed unless compelling factors mitigate against it.[35] It would seem that, similarly, Domitian invoked the status quo, and followed Vespasian and Titus by striking a series of coins depicting Victory-style reverses in mints very near the not-yet-forgotton battlegrounds of the Jewish War. It must be assumed that the people of Judaea interpreted these images as nothing less than a continuation of the Judaea Capta coinage.

It appears then that the Judaea Capta motifs had not disappeared from the local coinage with the death of the two actual victors. Some coins with the Victory motif issued under Domitian—minted before this emperor's successes in Germany—seem logically to relate to the Roman victory in the Jewish War. On other coins of the same emperor, types previously associated with the Jewish War were repeated. These latter types were deliberately open to interpretation, but their association with the Jewish War, both in the minds of the issuing authorities and of the local population, appears more than likely.[36]

THE JUDAEA CAPTA COINS
MINT OF CAESAREA MARITIMA

VESPASIAN

1445. AE 20 mm
  Obv: ΑΥΤΟΚΡ ΟΥ ΕΣΠΑΣΙΑΝΟΥ *(of Emperor Vespasian)*; laureate head of Vespasian to r.
  Rev: ΙΟΥΔΑΙΑΣ ΕΑΛWΚΥΑΣ *(Judaea captured)*; Nike stands r. with l. foot on helmet; she writes with r. hand on shield hanging from palm tree.   500/1,500

TITUS

1446. AE 20 mm.
Obv: ΑΥΤΟΚΡ ΤΙΤ ΟΣ ΚΑΙΣΑΡ *(of Emperor Titus Caesar)*; laureate head of Titus to r.
Rev: ΙΟΥΔΑΙΑΣ ΕΑΛWΚΥΑΣ; Nike stands r. with l. foot on helmet; she writes ΑΥΤ Τ ΚΑΙC with r. hand on shield hanging from palm tree. 125/300
  a. Head and standing figure in two rectangular countermarks obv.

1447. AE 20 mm.
Obv: ΑΥΤΟΚΡ ΤΙΤ ΟΣ ΚΑΙΣΑΡ; laureate head of Titus to r.
Rev: ΙΟΥΔΑΙΑΣ ΕΑΛΩΚΥΑΣ; Nike stands r., writing on shield supported by her knee, palm tree at r. 125/300

1448. AE 20 mm.
Obv: ΑΥΤΟΚΡ ΤΙΤ ΟΣ ΚΑΙΣΑΡ; laureate head of Titus to r.
Rev: ΙΟΥΔΑΙΑΣ ΕΑΛΩΚΥΙΑΣ; Nike stands r. with l. foot on helmet; she writes with r. hand on shield on her knee (no palm tree!). 150/400

1449

1449. AE 24–25 mm.
Obv: ΑΥΤΟΚΡ ΤΙΤ ΟΣ ΚΑΙΣΑΡ; laureate head of Titus to r.
Rev: ΙΟΥΔΑΙΑΣ ΕΑΛΩΚΥΙΑΣ; (sometimes different forms of C, Σ and Ω, W) trophy, Judaea sits mourning l. below l., her hands tied, shield to r. of trophy. 150/400
  a. Rectangular countermark with head to r. on obverse.

DOMITIAN
STRUCK 81/2 CE

1450. AE 30 mm
Obv: IMP DOMITIANVS CAESAR DIVI F AVG; laureate head of of Domitian to r.
Rev: DIVOS VESPASIANVS above and below; founder plows with ox and cow to r. 500/1,350

1451. AE 24–26 mm.
  Obv: IMP DOMITIANVS CAESAR DIVI F AVG; laureate head of
    Domitian to r.
  Rev: DIVOS T AVG; Titus in military dress stands and faces front
    holding spear in r. hand and *parazonium* in l.   500/1,250

1452. AE 22–24 mm.
  Obv: IMP DOMITIANVS CAESAR DIVI F AVG; laureate head of
    Domitian to r.
  Rev: VICTORIA AVG; Nike in long gown advances l. holding wreath
    in r. hand.   350/850

1453. AE 13-15 mm.
  Obv: IMP DOMITIANVS CAESAR DIVI F AVG; laureate head of
    Domitian to r.
  Rev: Rudder.   350/850

STRUCK 83 (?) CE

1454. AE 26–28 mm.
  Obv: IMP DOMITIAN CAES AVG GERMANICVS; laureate head
    of Domitian to r.
  Rev: Minerva stands r. on galley with shield in l. hand and spear in
    r.; on l. is a trophy, on r. a palm branch.   150/400

1455

1455. AE 23 mm.
  Obv: DOMITIANVS CAES AVG GERMANICVS; laureate head of
    Domitian to l.
  Rev: Minerva in flowing gown advances l. holding trophy in r. hand
    and shield and spear in l.   150/350

1456. AE 16–18 mm.
Obv: IMP DOMITIANVS CAESAR GERMANICVS; laureate head of Domitian to r.
Rev: Nike in flowing gown advances l., holding wreath in r. hand and trophy in l.   125/350

1457. AE 13–15 mm
Obv: IMP DOMITIANVS; laureate head of of Domitian to l.
Rev: CAES AVG GERMANICVS; winged caduceus.   25/350

STRUCK 92/93 CE

1458. AE 26–28 mm
Obv: IMP CAES DOMIT AVG GERM PM TR P XI; radiate head of Domitian to r.
Rev: IMP XXI COS XVI CENS P P P; seven-branched palm tree with two bunches of dates.   250/600
a. Rectangular countermark with Tyche l. and oval countermark with bust r. on obverse.

1459. AE 23–24 mm.
Obv: IMP CAES DOMIT AVG GERM TR P XII; laureate head of Domitian to r.
Rev: IMP XXIII COS XVI CENS P P P; Victory in flowing gown advances l., holding wreath in r. hand and small trophy in l.
                                                        200/450
a. Rectangular countermark with bust r. on obverse.

1460

1460. AE 18–20mm.
Obv: IMP DOMIT AVG GERM; laureate head of Domitian to r.
Rev: VICTOR AVG; trophy.   200/500

MINT OF ROME
VITELLIUS, 69 CE, COMMEMORATING VICTORY OVER THE JEWS

1461. AR *(fourrée) denarius.*
   Obv: A VITELLIVS GERMAN IMP TR P; laureate head, Vitellius to r.
   Rev: IVDAEA in exergue; mourning Jewess sits to r. of trophy, facing r. **UNIQUE**

1462. AE *sestertius.*
   Obv: A VITELLIVS GERM IMP AVG PM TR P; laureate head of Vitellius to r.
   Rev: VICTORIA AVGVSTI; S C in fields; palm tree, mourning Jewess sits on r. to r., behind tree; Victory stands with l. foot on helmet, inscribing OB CIVES SER (or variant) on shield set on tree. **3,000/8,500**
   a. S C in exergue.

1463. AE *as.*
   Obv: A VITELLIVS GERM IMP AVG PM TR P; laureate head of Vitellius to r.
   Rev: Draped Victory steps l. and places shield on trophy, captive sits beneath upon globe; around VICTOR AVGVSTI; S C in exergue. **1,500/3,500**

MINT OF ROME
VESPASIAN, 69–79 CE, COMMEMORATING VICTORY OVER THE JEWS
GOLD AUREI
UNDATED, C. 21 DECEMBER 69–EARLY 70 CE

1464. AU *aureus.*
   Obv: IMP CAESAR VESPASIANVS AVG; laureate head of Vespasian to r.
   Rev: IVDAEA in exergue; mourning Jewess sits to r. to r. of trophy, head resting on hand. **15,000/50,000**

1465   1466

1465. AU *aureus.*
Obv: IMP CAESAR VESPASIANVS AVG; laureate head of Vespasian to r.
Rev: IVDAEA in exergue; on r. mourning Jewess sits of palm tree, to
r., hands bound behind her back.   20,000/65,000

MINT OF ROME
72–73 CE

1466. AU *aureus.*
Obv: IMP CAES VESP AVG PM COS IIII; laureate head of Vespasian to r.
Rev: Palm tree; on l. Vespasian stands r. in military dress facing r., l.
foot on helmet, holding spear in r. hand and *parazonium* in l.; on
r. mourning Jewess sits to r.   20,000/65,000

1467. AU *aureus.*
Obv: IMP CAES VESP AVG PM COS IIII; laureate head of Vespa-
sian to r.
Rev: Vespasian stands in triumphal *quadriga* to r., holds branch in r.
hand and scepter in l.   20,000/60,000
Aureus and denarius are considered forgeries when IMP *is in exergue.*

1468. AU *aureus.*
Obv: T CAES IMP VESP PON TR POT; laureate head of Titus to
r.
Rev: Palm tree; on l. Titus stands r. in military dress facing r., l. foot
on helmet, holding spear in r. hand and *parazonium* in l.; on r.
mourning Jewess sits to r.   20,000/65,000

1469. AU *aureus.*
Obv: T CAES IMP VESP PON TR POT; laureate head of Titus to
r.
Rev: Titus stands in triumphal *quadriga* to r., holds branch in r. hand
and scepter in l.   20,000/60,000

79 CE

1470. AU *aureus.*
  Obv: IMP CAESAR VESPASIANVS AVG; laureate head of Vespasian to r.
  Rev: TR POT X COS VIII; draped Victory advancing l. erecting a trophy; beneath it sits weeping Jewish captive to l.   12,500/45,000

1471. AU *aureus.*
  Obv: T CAESAR IMP VESPASIANVS; laureate head of Titus to r.
  Rev: TR POT VIII COS VII; male Jewish captive kneels r., hands bound behind; above is trophy made of helmet, cuirass, crossed swords, and shield.   12,500/40,000

MINT OF LYON
UNDATED, C. **71** CE

1472

1474

1472. AU *aureus.*
  Obv: IMP CAESAR VESPASIANVS AVG TR P; laureate head of Vespasian to r.
  Rev: DE IVDAEIS; trophy.   20,000/65,000
  a. *Fourrée* silver denarius as 1472.

1473. AU *aureus.*
  Obv: IMP CAESAR VESPASIANVS AVG TR P; laureate head of Vespasian to r.
  Rev: IVDAEA in exergue; on r. mourning Jewess sits of palm tree, to r., hands bound behind her back.   20,000/65,000

1474. AU *aureus.*
  Obv: IMP CAESAR VESPASIANVS AVG TR P; laureate head of Vespasian to r.
  Rev: IVDAEA DEVICTA; Jewess stands on l. of palm tree facing l., hands bound in front.   20,000/65,000

1475. AU *aureus*.
  Obv: IMP CAESAR VESPASIANVS AVG TR P; laureate head of
  Vespasian to r.
  Rev: TRIVMP AVG; Emperor stands in triumphal *quadriga* with
  horses pacing r., he holds palm branch and eagle-tipped scepter; behind stands Victory crowning him accompanied by trum-
  peter; in front of the horses is a soldier escorting a captive.

35,000/125,000

1476. AU *aureus*.
  Obv: IMP CAES VESPAS AVG PM TR P IIII P P COS IIII; laureate
  head of Vespasian to r.
  Rev: DE IVDAEIS; trophy.   20,000/65,000

MINT OF SPAIN (TARRACO ?)
UNDATED, C. LATE 69–70 CE

1477. AU *aureus*.
  Obv: IMP•CAESAR•VESPASIANVS•AVG; laureate head of Vespa-
  sian to r. (dots not always present).
  Rev: IVDAEA in exergue; mourning Jewess sits on r. to r. of trophy.

20,000/65,000

MINT IN JUDAEA[37]
70 CE

1478. AU *aureus*.
  Obv: IMP T CAESAR VESPASIANVS; laureate head of Vespasian
  with aegis to r.
  Rev: IVDAEA DEVICTA (outward from top l.); Victory stands r., l.
  foot on helmet, inscribes IMP T CAES on shield hanging on palm
  tree.   RRR
  a. IVDAEA DEVICTA (from low r.), inscribes VICT AVG on shield.

MINT OF ROME
SILVER DENARII
UNDATED, C. 21 DECEMBER 69–EARLY 70 CE

1479. AR *denarius*.
Obv: IMP CAESAR VESPASIANVS AVG; laureate head of Vespasian to r.
Rev: IVDAEA in exergue; mourning Jewess sits on r. to r. of trophy, head resting on hand.   500/1,750

1480. AR *denarius*.
Obv: IMP CAESAR VESPASIANVS AVG; laureate head of Vespasian to r.
Rev: IVDAEA in exergue; on r. mourning Jewess sits of palm tree, to r., hands bound behind her back.   600/2,000

71 CE

1481. AR *denarius*.
Obv: IMP CAES VESP AVG P M; laureate head of Vespasian to r.
Rev: Vespasian stands in triumphal *quadriga* to r., holds branch in r. hand and scepter in l.   750/2,500

72–73 CE

1482. AR *denarius*.
Obv: T CAES IMP VESP PON TR POT; laureate head of Titus to r.
Rev: Palm tree; on l. Titus stands r. in military dress facing r., l. foot on helmet, holding spear in r. hand and *parazonium* in l.; on r. mourning Jewess sits to r.   750/2,500

1483. AR *denarius*.
Obv: T CAES IMP VESP PON TR POT; laureate head of Titus to r.
Rev: Titus stands in triumphal *quadriga* to r., holds branch in r. hand and scepter in l.   750/2,500

74 CE

1484. AR *denarius.*
  Obv: IMP CAESAR in exergue; Titus stands in triumphal *quadriga* to
    r., holds branch in r. hand and scepter in l.
  Rev: IMP VESP across fields; Victory stands r. on prow holding
    branch and wreath.   1,000/3,000
  a. T CAESAR in exergue on obverse.
  Copies a denarius *struck by Octavian at the time of the Battle of Actium
  (BMCRE 4343, RSC 115), however, it appears that Vespasian's mint selected
  this design because of its similarities to earlier issues commemorating the vic-
  tory in Judaea. It may have been struck only a few months after the holdouts at
  Masada were defeated by Titus.*

79 CE

1485. AR *denarius.*
  Obv: IMP CAESAR VESPASIANVS AVG (outward); laureate head
    of Vespasian to r.
  Rev: TR POT X COS VIIII; draped Victory advancing l. erecting a
    trophy; beneath it sits weeping Jewish captive l.   400/1,250
  a. Laureate head of Vespasian l.

1486. AR *denarius.*
  Obv: T CAESAR IMP VESPASIANVS (outward); laureate head of
    Titus to r.
  Rev: TR POT VIII COS VII; male Jewish captive kneels r., hands
    bound behind, trophy above.   350/1,000

MINT OF LYON
UNDATED, C. 71 CE

1487. AR *denarius.*
  Obv: IMP CAESAR VESPASIANVS AVG TR P; laureate head of
    Vespasian to r.
  Rev: IVDAEA in exergue; on r. mourning Jewess sits of palm tree, to
    r., her hands bound behind her back.   750/2,750

1488.   AR *denarius.*
Obv: IMP CAESAR VESPASIANVS AVG TR P; laureate head of Vespasian to r.
Rev: IVDAEA DEVICTA; palm tree; on l. Jewess stands facing l.

                                                        500/1,750

MINT OF SPAIN (TARRACO ?)
UNDATED, C. LATE 69–70 CE

1489.   AR *denarius.*
Obv: .IMP•CAESAR•VESPASIANVS•AVG; laureate head of Vespasian to r. (dots not always present).
Rev: IVDAEA in exergue; mourning Jewess sits on r. to r. of trophy.

                                                           750/2,750

MINT OF ANTIOCH
72–73 CE

1490.   AR *denarius.*
Obv: IMP CAES VESP AVG COS IIII; laureate head of Vespasian to r.
Rev: Palm tree; on l. Vespasian stands r. in military dress facing r., l. foot on helmet, holding spear in r. hand and *parazonium* in l.; on r. mourning Jewess sits to r.   750/2,500

1491.   AR *denarius.*
Obv: IMP CAES VESP AVG COS IIII; laureate head of Vespsian r.
Rev: Vespasian stands in triumphal *quadriga* to r., holds branch in r. hand and scepter in l.   750/2,500

1492.   AR *denarius.*
Obv: T CAES IMP VESP PON TR POT; laureate head of Titus r.
Rev: Palm tree; on l. Titus stands r. in military dress facing r., l. foot on helmet, holding spear in r. hand and *parazonium* in l., on r. mourning Jewess sits to r.   750/2,500

1493.   AR *denarius.*
Obv: T CAES IMP VESP PON TR POT; laureate head Titus to r.
Rev: Titus stands in triumphal *quadriga* to r., holds branch in r. hand and scepter in l.   750/2,500

MINT OF ROME
SESTERTII
70 CE

1494.   AE *sestertius.*
   Obv: IMP CAES AVG VESPAS COS II TR POT; laureate head of
   Vespasian to r., draped, globe below.
   Rev: S C in fields; palm tree; Victory on l. stands r. and inscribes
   shield on tree VIC AVG; mourning Jewess sits on r. to r.
                                                              500/3,500

1495.   AE *sestertius.*
   Obv: IMP CAES AVG VESPAS COS II TR POT; laureate head of
   Vespasian to r.
   Rev: IVDAEA CAPTA; S C in fields; palm tree; male captive on l.,
   stands l. looking back; mourning Jewess sits on r. to r. on cuirass,
   arms around both figures.   750/6,500

1496.   AE *sestertius.*
   Obv: IMP CAESAR VESPASIANVS AVG P M TR P; laureate head
   of Vespasian to r.
   Rev: VICTORIA AVGVSTI; S C in fields; palm tree; Victory on l.
   stands r., l. foot on helmet, and inscribes shield on tree OB CIV
   SERV (or variation).   550/3,500
   a. Laureate head to l.

1497

1497.   AE *sestertius.*
   Obv: IMP CAESAR VESPASIANVS AVG P M T P P P COS III;
   laureate head of Vespasian to r.
   Rev: DEVICTA IVDAEA; S C in fields; palm tree; Victory on l.,
   stands r. and inscribes SPQR on shield on tree; on r. mourning
   Jewess sits on r. to r.   2,000/8,500

a. Laureate bust to r. with drapery on l. shoulder.
b. Rev. S C in exergue.

1498. AE *sestertius.*
Obv: IMP CAESAR VESPASIANVS AVG P M T P P P COS III;
laureate head of Vespasian to r.
Rev: IVDAEA CAPTA; S C in exergue; palm tree; male captive on l.,
stands r.; mourning Jewess sits on r. to r. on cuirass, arms around
both figures.   750/6,500

1499. AE *sestertius.*
Obv: IMP CAESAR VESPASIANVS AVG P M T P P P COS III;
laureate head of Vespasian to r.
Rev: VICTORIA AVGVSTI; S C in fields; palm tree; Victory on l.
stands r., l. foot on helmet, and inscribes shield on tree OB CIV
SERV (or variation).   500/5,500
a. Laureate bust of Vespasian to r., draped.
b. Obv. legend starts high r.
c. As 1499a, but laureate bust of Vespasian to r., draped.

71 CE

1500. AE *sestertius.*
Obv: IMP CAE[S] VESPASIAN AVG PM TR P P P COS III; laureate head of Vespasian to r.
Rev: IVDAEA CAPTA; S C in exergue; palm tree; male captive on l.,
stands facing r., on r. mourning Jewess sits to r. on cuirass, arms
around both figures.   750/5,500
a. Laureate head of Vespasian l.
b. IVDEA CAPTA S C is reverse legend.
c. CAPTA IVDAEA S C is reverse legend.

1501. AE *sestertius.*
Obv: IMP CAE[S] VESPASIAN AVG PM TR P P P COS III; laureate head of Vespasian to r.
Rev: IVDAEA CAPTA; S C in exergue; palm tree; male captive on
l., looking back, on r. mourning Jewess sits to r. on cuirass, arms
around both figures.   750/6,500
a. S C in fields.

1500   1502

1502.   AE *sestertius*.
Obv: IMP CAE[S] VESPASIAN AVG PM TR P P P COS III; laureate head of Vespasian to r.
Rev: IVDAEA CAPTA; S C in exergue; palm tree; mourning Jewess sits on l., to l. on cuirass; male captive stands on r. facing l., arms around both figures.   750/5,500

1503.   AE *sestertius*.
Obv: IMP CAE[S] VESPASIAN AVG PM TR P P P COS III; laureate head of Vespasian to r.
Rev: IVDAEA CAPTA; S C in exergue; palm tree; mourning Jewess sits on l., to l. on cuirass; male captive on r. faces r., looking back, arms around both figures.   750/6,500

1504.   AE *sestertius*.
Obv: IMP CAE[S] VESPASIAN AVG PM TR P P P COS III; laureate head of Vespasian to r.
Rev: IVDAEA CAPTA; S C in exergue; palm tree; mourning Jewess sits (sometimes on cuirass) r. on r.; to l. of palm Vespasian stands r. in military dress with spear and *parazonium*, l. foot on helmet.   750/5,500

a.   IVDEA CAPTA S C.
b.   Laureate head of Vespasian to l.
c.   One obverse die of this type reads COS II, probably an engraver's error.

1505.   AE *sestertius.*
Obv: IMP CAE[S] VESPASIAN AVG PM TR P P P COS III; laureate head of Vespasian to r.
Rev: VICTORIA AVG; S C in fields; Victory stands to l. of palm tree facing r., l. foot on helmet, inscribing OB CIV SER (or variant) on shield on tree.   500/5,500
a. Laureate head of Vespasian l.

1506.   AE *sestertius.*
Obv: IMP CAE[S] VESPASIAN AVG PM TR P P P COS III; laureate head of Vespasian to l.
Rev: VICTORIA AVG; S C in fields; palm tree; mourning Jewess sits on r. to r.; behind tree Victory stands with l. foot on helmet, inscribing OB CIV SER (or variant) on shield set on tree.
                                                       650/5,000

1507.   AE *sestertius.*
Obv: IMP CAE[S] VESPASIAN AVG PM TR P P P COS III; laureate head of Vespasian to r.
Rev: VICTORIA AVGVSTI; S C in exergue; Victory stands to l. of palm tree facing r., l. foot on helmet, inscribing OB CIV SER (or variant) on shield.   550/4,500
a. S C in fields.
b. Laureate head of Vespasian to l.
c. AVGVSTI VICTORIA S C.
d. AVGVSTI VICTORIA S C and laureate head of Vespasian l.

1508.   AE *sestertius.*
Obv: IMP CAE[S] VESPASIAN AVG PM TR P P P COS III; laureate head of Vespasian to r.
Rev: VICTORIA AVGVSTI; S C in exergue; palm tree; mourning Jewess sits on r. to r.; Victory stands on l. to r., with l. foot on helmet, inscribing OB CIV SER (or variant) on shield set on tree.
                                                       500/3,500
a. Laureate bust of Vespasian to r. drapery on l. shoulder.
b. Laureate head of Vespasian to l.
c. S C in fields.
d. Mourning Jewess sits to l. of palm facing toward Victory, S C in exergue.
e. As 1508d, laureate head of Vespasian to l.

1509.   AE *sestertius*.
> Obv: IMP CAES VESPAS AVG P M TR P P P COS III; laureate head of Vespasian to r.
> Rev: IVDAEA CAPTA; S C in exergue; palm tree; male captive on l., stands facing r.; mourning Jewess sits on r. to r., cuirass, arms around both figures.   750/5,500
> a. Similar but on this reverse die alone, behind standing Jew, is shown a helmet hanging upon a spear.

1510.   AE *sestertius*.
> Obv: IMP CAES VESPAS AVG P M TR P P P COS III; laureate head of Vespasian to r.
> Rev: IVDAEA CAPTA; S C in exergue; palm tree; male captive on l., looking back; mourning Jewess sits on r. to r. on cuirass.   750/6,500

1511.   AE *sestertius*.
> Obv: IMP CAES VESPAS AVG P M TR P P P COS III; laureate head of Vespasian to r.
> Rev: IVDAEA CAPTA; S C in exergue; palm tree; mourning Jewess sits to r., on r.; to l. of palm Vespasian stands r. in military dress with spear and *parazonium*, l. foot on helmet.   750/6,500

1512.   AE *sestertius*.
> Obv: IMP CAES VESPAS AVG P M TR P P P COS III; laureate head of Vespasian to r.
> Rev: IVDAEA CAPTA; S C in exergue; palm tree; male captive on r. stands l., hands tied; to l. of palm Vespasian stands r. in military dress with spear and *parazonium*, l. foot on helmet.   750/6,500

1513

1513. AE *sestertius*.
Obv: IMP CAES VESPAS AVG P M TR P P P COS III; laureate head of Vespasian to r.
Rev: S C in exergue; Vespasian stands l., r. foot on prow, holding Victory and vertical spear; before him Jew kneels r., holding out hands and Jewess advances r. with extended right arm holding branch, palm tree on far l.   1,250/10,000

1514. AE *sestertius*.
Obv: IMP CAES VESPAS AVG P M TR P P P COS III; laureate head of Vespasian to r.
Rev: VICTORIA AVGVSTI; S C in exergue; Victory stands to l. of palm tree facing r., l. foot on helmet, inscribing OB CIV SER (or variant) on shield.   500/4,000

1515. AE *sestertius*.
Obv: IMP CAES VESPAS AVG P M TR P P P COS III; laureate head of Vespasian to r.
Rev: VICTORIA AVGVSTI; S C in exergue; palm tree; mourning Jewess sits on r. to r.; behind tree Victory stands with l. foot on helmet, inscribing OB CIV SER (or variant) on shield set on tree.   500/4,000

72–73 CE

1516. AE *sestertius*.
Obv: IMP CAES VESPAS AVG P M TR P P P COS IIII; laureate head of Vespasian to r.
Rev: IVDAEA CAPTA; S C in exergue; palm tree; male captive on l., stands facing r.; mourning Jewess sits on r. to r. on cuirass, arms around.   750/6,500

1517. AE *sestertius*.
Obv: IMP CAES VESPAS AVG P M TR P P P COS IIII; laureate head of Vespasian to r.
Rev: IVDAEA CAPTA; S C in exergue; palm tree; male captive on r. stands l., hands tied; to l. of palm Vespasian stands r. in military dress with spear and *parazonium*, l. foot on helmet.
                                                 750/6,500

1518. AE *sestertius*.
Obv: IMP CAES VESPAS AVG P M TR P P P COS IIII; laureate head of Vespasian to r.
Rev: S C in exergue; Titus in military dress, cloak flies behind him, his horse rearing as he attacks prostrate Jew, who lies left, armed with sword and shield.   550/5,000
See note at No. 1524.

1519. AE *sestertius*.
Obv: IMP CAES VESPAS AVG P M TR P P P COS IIII; laureate head of Vespasian to r.
Rev: S C in exergue; Vespasian stands l., r. foot on prow, holding Victory and vertical spear; before him Jew kneels right, holding out hands and Jewess advances r. with extended right arm holding branch, palm tree on far l.   1,250/10,000

1520. AE *sestertius*.
Obv: IMP CAES VESPAS AVG P M TR P P P COS IIII; laureate head of Vespasian to r.
Rev: S C in exergue; Vespasian stands in triumphal *quadriga* to r., holds branch in r. hand and scepter in l., on side of cart is Victory to r. holding wreath.   750/6,500

1521. AE *sestertius*.
Obv: IMP CAES VESPAS AVG P M TR P P P COS IIII; laureate head of Vespasian to r.
Rev: VICTORIA AVGVSTI; S C in fields; Victory stands to l. of palm tree facing r., l. foot on helmet, inscribing VIC AVG on shield.   500/4,000

1522. AE *sestertius*.
Obv: T CAES VESPAS IMP PON TR POT COS II; laureate head of Titus to r.
Rev: VICTORIA AVGVSTI; S C in fields; Victory stands to l. of palm tree facing r., l. foot on helmet, inscribing VIC AVG on shield.   550/4,500

1523. AE *sestertius*.

Obv: T CAES VESPASIAN IMP PON TR POT COS II; laureate head of Titus to r.

Rev: IVDAEA CAPTA; S C in exergue; palm tree; mourning Jewess sits on r. to r.; to l. of palm Vespasian stands r. in military dress with spear and *parazonium*, l. foot on helmet.   750/6,500

1524. AE *sestertius*.

Obv: T CAES VESPASIAN IMP PON TR POT COS II; laureate head of Titus to r.

Rev: S C in exergue; Titus in military dress, cloak flies behind him, his horse rearing as he attacks prostrate Jew, who lies left, armed with sword and shield.   550/5,000

a. S C in fields.

It seems probable (even though Mattingly describes the horse as "prancing," no equestrian would describe this pose as anything other than "rearing") that the reverse motif on this coin, as well as Nos. 1518, 1530, 1535, 1539 refers to the following passage in Josephus (WARS V: 2). Certainly Titus would have wanted to perpetuate this tale:

"So long as he rode straight along the high road leading direct to the wall, no one appeared outside the gates; but when he diverged from the route and led his troop of horse in an oblique line towards the tower Psephinus, the Jews suddenly dashed out in immense numbers at a spot called 'the Women's towers,' through the gate facing Helena's monuments, broke through the cavalry, and placing themselves in front of those who were still galloping along the road, prevented them from joining their comrades who had left it, thus cutting off Titus with a handful of men. For him to proceed was impossible, because the ground outside the ramparts was all cut up by trenches for gardening purposes and intersected by cross walls and numerous fences; while to rejoin his own men was, he saw, impracticable owing to the intervening masses of the enemy and the retirement of his comrades on the highway, most of whom, unaware of the prince's peril and believing that he too had turned simultaneously, were in full

retreat. Perceiving that his safety depended solely on his personal prowess, he turned his horse's head and shouting to his companions to follow dashed into the enemy's midst, struggling to cut his way through to his own party. Then, more than ever, might the reflection arise that the hazards of war and the perils of princes are under God's care; for, of all that hail of arrows discharged at Titus, who wore neither helmet nor cuirass—for he had gone forward, as I said not to fight, but to reconnoiter—not one touched his person, but, as if his assailants purposely missed their mark, all whizzed harmless by. He, meanwhile, with his sword constantly dispersing those on his flank and prostrating multitudes who withstood him to the face, rode his horse over the fallen foes. At Caesar's intrepidity the Jews shouted and cheered each other on against him, but wherever he turned his horse there was flight and a general stampede. His comrades in danger closed up to him, riddled in rear and flank; for each man's one hope of escape lay in pushing through with Titus before he was cut off. Two, in fact, further behind, thus fell: one with his horse and was surrounded and speared, the other who dismounted was killed and his steed led off to the city; with the remainder Titus safely reached the camp. The Jews thus successful in their first onset were elated with inconsiderate hopes, and this transient turn of fortune afforded them high confidence as to the future."

1525. AE *sestertius*.
Obv: T CAES VESPASIAN IMP PON TR POT COS II; laureate head of Titus to r.
Rev: S C in exergue; Titus stands in triumphal *quadriga* to r., holds branch in r. hand and scepter in l., on side of cart is Victory to r. holding wreath.   750/6,500

1526. AE *sestertius*.
Obv: T CAES VESPASIAN IMP PON TR POT COS II; laureate head of Titus to r.
Rev: VICTORIA AVGVSTI; S C in fields; Victory stands to l. of palm tree facing r., l. foot on helmet, inscribing VIC AVG on shield.   500/4,500

1527. AE *sestertius*.
Obv: T CAESAR VESPASIAN IMP PON TR POT COS II; laureate head of Titus to r.
Rev: IVDAEA CAPTA; S C in exergue; palm tree; mourning Jew stands on r., facing l.; on l. of palm Vespasian stands r. in military dress with spear and *parazonium*, l. foot on helmet.   750/6,500

1528. AE *sestertius*.
Obv: T CAESAR VESPASIAN IMP PON TR POT COS II; laureate head of Titus to r.
Rev: S C in exergue; Titus stands in triumphal *quadriga* to r., holds branch in r. hand and scepter in l., on side of cart is Victory to r. holding wreath. 750/6,500

1529. AE *sestertius*.
Obv: T CAESAR VESPASIAN IMP PON TR POT COS II; laureate head of Titus to r.
Rev: VICTORIA AVGVSTI; S C in exergue; Victory stands to l. of palm tree facing r., l. foot on helmet, inscribing VIC AVG on shield. 500/4,500
a. S C in fields.

1530. AE *sestertius*.
Obv: T CAESAR VESPASIAN IMP III PON TR POT II COS II; laureate head of Titus to r.
Rev: S C in exergue; Titus in military dress, cloak flies behind him, his horse rearing as he attacks prostrate Jew, who lies left, armed with sword and shield. 550/5,000
See note at 1524.

1531. AE *sestertius*.
Obv: T CAESAR VESPASIAN IMP III PON TR POT II COS II; laureate head of Titus to r.
Rev: S C in exergue; Titus stands in triumphal *quadriga* to r., holds branch in r. hand and scepter in l., on side of cart is Victory to r. holding wreath. 750/6,500
a. Laureate bust of Titus to r., wearing cuirass and aegis; on side of cart is figure of Titus, standing, putting hand on head of Jewish captive who kneels toward him.

1532. AE *sestertius*.
Obv: T CAESAR VESPASIAN IMP III PON TR POT II COS II; laureate bust Titus to r.
Rev: VICTORIA AVGVSTI; S C in exergue; Victory stands to l. of palm tree facing r., l. foot on helmet, inscribing VIC AVG on shield. 500/4,500

1533. AE *sestertius*.

Obv: T CAESAR VESPASIAN IMP III PON TR POT II COS II;
laureate bust Titus to r. wearing cuirass and aegis.

Rev: S C in exergue; Titus stands l. r. foot on prow, holding Victory
on globe and vertical spear; before him Jew kneels right, holding
out hands and Jewess advances r. with extended right arm holding branch, palm tree on far l.   1,250/10,000

1534. AE *sestertius*.

Obv: T CAESAR VESPASIAN IMP IIII PON TR POT II COS II;
laureate head of Titus to r.

Rev: IVDAEA CAPTA; S C in exergue; palm tree; mourning Jewess
sits on r. to r.; to l. of palm Titus stands r. in military dress with
spear and *parazonium*, l. foot on helmet.   750/6,500

1535. AE *sestertius*.

Obv: T CAESAR VESPASIAN IMP IIII PON TR POT II COS II;
laureate head of Titus to r.

Rev: S C in exergue; Titus in military dress, cloak flies behind him,
his horse rearing as he attacks prostrate Jew, who lies l., armed
with sword and shield.   550/5,000
See note at 1524.

1536. AE *sestertius*.

Obv: T CAESAR VESPASIAN IMP IIII PON TR POT II COS II;
laureate head of Titus to r.

Rev: S C in exergue; Titus stands in triumphal *quadriga* to r., holds
branch in r. hand and scepter in l., on side of cart is Victory to r.
holding wreath.   750/6,500

1537. AE *sestertius*.

Obv: T CAESAR VESPASIAN IMP IIII PON TR POT II COS II;
laureate head of Titus to r.

Rev: S C in exergue; Vespasian stands l. r. foot on prow, holding
Victory on globe and vertical spear; before him Jew kneels right,
holding out hands and Jewess advances r. with extended right
arm holding branch, palm tree on far l.   1,250/10,000

1538. AE *sestertius*.
Obv: T CAESAR VESPASIAN IMP IIII PON TR POT III COS II;
laureate head of Titus to r.
Rev: IVDAEA CAPTA; S C in exergue; palm tree; mourning Jew
stands on r., facing l.; on l. of palm Titus stands r. in military dress
with spear and *parazonium*, l. foot on helmet.   750/6,500

1539. AE *sestertius*.
Obv: T CAESAR VESPASIAN IMP IIII PON TR POT III COS II;
laureate head of Titus to r.
Rev: S C in exergue; Titus in military dress, cloak flies behind him,
his horse rearing as he attacks prostrate Jew, who lies l., armed
with sword and shield.   550/5,000
See note at No. 1524.

1540. AE *sestertius*.
Obv: T CAESAR VESPASIAN IMP IIII PON TR POT III COS II;
laureate head of Titus to r.
Rev: VICTORIA AVGVSTI; S C in exergue; Victory stands to l. of
palm tree facing r., l. foot on helmet, inscribing shield on tree.
                                                           550/5,000
a. VICTORIA AVGVSTA.

1541. AE sestertius.
Obv: IMP CAES VESP AVG P M T P P P COS IIII CENS; laureate
head of Vespasian to r.
Rev: S C in exergue; Vespasian stands in triumphal *quadriga* to r.,
holds branch in r. hand and scepter in l., on side of cart is Victory
to r. holding wreath.   750/6,500

1542. AE *sestertius*.
Obv: T CAES VESP IMP PON TR POT COS II CENS; laureate
head of Titus to r.
Rev: S C in exergue; Titus stands in triumphal *quadriga* to r., holds
branch in r. hand and scepter in l., on side of cart is Victory to r.
holding wreath.   750/6,500

MINT OF LYON
SESTERTII
71 CE

1543. AE *sestertius*.
Obv: IMP CAES VESPASIAN AVG PM TR P P P COS III; laureate head of Vespasian to r., globe below r. sometimes missing.
Rev: IVDAEA CAPTA; S C in exergue; palm tree; mourning Jewess sits on r. to r.; to l. of palm Vespasian stands r. in military dress with spear and *parazonium*, l. foot on helmet.   750/6,500
a. Laureate head of Vespasian l.

72 CE

1544. AE *sestertius*.
Obv: IMP CAES VESPASIAN AVG P M TR P P P COS IIII; laureate head of Vespasian to r., globe below r. sometimes missing.
Rev: IVDAEA CAPTA; S C in exergue; palm tree; mourning Jewess sits on r. to r.; to l. of palm Vespasian stands r. in military dress with spear and *parazonium*, l. foot on helmet.   750/6,500

77–78 CE

1545. AE *sestertius*.
Obv: IMP CAES VESPASIAN AVG PM TR P P P COS VIII; laureate head of Vespasian to r., globe below r. sometimes missing.
Rev: IVDAEA CAPTA; S C in exergue; palm tree; mourning Jewess sits on r. to r.; to l. of palm Vespasian stands r. in military dress with spear and *parazonium*, l. foot on helmet.   750/6,500

1546. AE *sestertius*.
Obv: IMP CAES VESPASIAN AVG PM TR P P P COS VIII; laureate head of Vespasian to r., globe below r. sometimes missing.
Rev: IVDAEA CAPTA; S C in exergue; palm tree; male captive on l., stands facing r.; on r. mourning Jewess sits to r. on cuirass, arms around.   750/6,500

1547. AE *sestertius*.
Obv: T CAES IMP AVG F PON TR P COS VI CENSOR; laureate head of Titus to r., globe below r. sometimes missing.

Rev: IVDAEA CAPTA; S C in exergue; palm tree; male captive on l., stands facing; mourning Jewess sits on r. to r. on cuirass, arms around both figures. 750/6,500

1548. AE *sestertius.*

Obv: T CAES IMP AVG F PON TR P COS VI CENSOR; laureate head of Titus to r., globe below r. sometimes missing.

Rev: IVDAEA CAPTA; S C in exergue; palm tree; male captive on l., looking back; mourning Jewess sits on r. to r., cuirass, arms around both figures. 750/6,500

MINT OF ROME

DUPONDII AND ASES

71 CE

1549. AE *dupondius.*

Obv: IMP CAESAR VESPASIANVS AVG P M TR P; laureate head of Vespasian to r., with globe.

Rev: IVD CAPT in exergue; S C in fields; mourning Jewess, hands bound behind back, sits r. on r. of palm tree. 500/3,500

1550. AE *dupondius* or *as.*

Obv: IMP CAESAR VESPASIANVS AVG P M TR P; laureate head of Vespasian to r., with aegis.

Rev: VICTORIA AVG; S C in exergue; draped Victory strides l. places shield with both hands on trophy l.; at foot of trophy is mourning Jewess seated l. 350/1,750

1551. AE *as.*

Obv: IMP CAESAR VESPASIANVS AVG COS III; laureate head of Vespasian to l.

Rev: IVDAEA CAPTA; S C in exergue; palm tree, mourning Jewess seated on r. to r. on cuirass, surrounded by arms. 650/4,500

1552. AE *dupondius.*

Obv: IMP CAES VESPASIAN AVG COS III; radiate head Vespasian to r.

Rev: IVDAEA CAPTA; S C in exergue; palm tree, mourning Jewess seated on r. to r. on cuirass, surrounded by arms. 650/4,500

1553.   AE *dupondius.*
Obv: IMP CAES VESPASIAN AVG COS III; radiate head of Vespasian to r.
Rev: VICTORIA AVG; S C in fields; draped Victory strides l. places shield with both hands on trophy l.; at foot of trophy is mourning Jewess seated l.   350/1,750

1554a

1554.   AE *as.*
Obv: IMP CAES VESPASIAN AVG COS III; laureate head of Vespasian to r.
Rev: IVDAEA CAPTA; S C in exergue; palm tree, mourning Jewess seated on r. to r. on cuirass, head on her hand, two shields on r.   650/4,500
a. Jewess surrounded by arms.
b. IVDEA CAPTA S C.
c. Laureate head of Vespasian to l.
d. IVDEA CAPTA; S C in fields; Jewess on l. to l.

1555.   AE *as.*
Obv: IMP CAES VESPASIAN AVG COS III; laureate head of Vespasian to r.
Rev: IVDEA CAPTA; S C in exergue; trophy, mourning Jewess sits on cuirass on r. to r., hands bound behind back, surrounded by arms.   650/4,000

1556.   AE *as.*
Obv: IMP CAES VESPASIAN AVG COS III; laureate head of Vespasian to r.
Rev: VICTORIA AVG; S C in exergue; draped Victory strides l. places shield with both hands on trophy, at foot of trophy is mourning Jewess seated l.   350/1,750
a. Laureate head of Vespasian to l.
b. VICTOR AVGVSTI S C.

1557. AE *as.*

Obv: IMP CAES VESPASIAN AVG COS III; laureate head of Vespasian to r.

Rev: VICTORIA AVG; S C in exergue; Draped Victory stands r. places shield with both hands on trophy, at foot of trophy is mourning Jewess seated r. 350/1,750

72 *CE*

1558. AE *as.*

Obv: T CAES VESPASIAN IMP PON TR POT COS II; laureate head of Vespasian to r.

Rev: IVDAEA CAPTA; S C in exergue; palm tree, mourning Jewess seated on r. to r. on cuirass. 650/4,000

1559. AE *as.*

Obv: CAESAR AVG F DOMITIANVS COS DES II; laureate head of Domitian to r.

Rev: S C in exergue; Vespasian stands in triumphal *quadriga* to r., holds branch in r. hand and scepter in l. 650/4,000

a. CAESAR AVG F DOMITIANVS COS II is obverse legend.

73 *CE*

1560. AE *as.*

Obv: T CAES VESP IMP PON TR POT COS II CENS; laureate head of Titus to r.

Rev: IVDAEA CAPTA; S C in exergue; palm tree, mourning Jewess seated on r. to r. on cuirass. 650/4,000

MINT OF LYON
77–78 *CE*

1561. AE *as.*

Obv: IMP CAES VESPASIAN AVG COS VIII; laureate head of Vespasian to r.

Rev: IVDAEA CAPTA; S C in exergue; palm tree, mourning Jewess seated on r. to r., arms around on l. of tree. 650/4,000

1562

1562. AE *as.*
  Obv: T CAES IMP AVG F TR P COS VI CENSOR; laureate head of Titus to r.
  Rev: IVDAEA CAPTA; S C in exergue; palm tree, mourning Jewess seated on r. to r., arms to l. of tree.   550/3,500
  a. Arms to l. of tree and r. of Jewess.

MINT OF SPAIN (TARRACO?)
70 CE

1563. AE *as.*
  Obv: IMP•CAESAR•VESPASIANVS•AVG; laureate head of Vespasian to r. (Sometimes without dots in legend).
  Rev: IVDAEA in exergue; S C in fields; mourning Jewess sits on r. to r. of trophy.   650/4,000

MINT OF ROME
SMALL BRONZE DENOMINATIONS
71 CE

1564. AE *quadrans.*
  Obv: IMP CAES VESPASIAN AVG; palm tree.
  Rev: PON M TR P P P COS III; S C in fields; vexillum.
          150/550
  a. IMP VESPASIAN AVG.

1565. AE *quadrans.*
  Obv: IMP CAES VESPASIAN AVG; palm tree.
  Rev: PON M TR P P P COS III; S C in fields; priestly implements.
          100/400
  a. IMP VESPASIAN AVG.

1566. AE *quadrans*.
Obv: IMP CAES VESPASIAN AVG; trophy.
Rev: PON M TR P P P COS III; S C in fields; vexillum.

100/400

1567. AE *quadrans*.
Obv: IMP CAES VESPASIAN AVG; trophy.
Rev: PON M TR P P P COS III; S C in fields; crossed spears with
shield.   100/400

1568. AE *quadrans*.
Obv: IMP VESPASIAN AVG; palm tree.
Rev: P M TR P P P COS III; S C in fields; caduceus.

250/750

1569. AE *quadrans*.
Obv: IMP VESPASIAN AVG; palm tree.
Rev: P M TR P P P COS III; S C in fields; vexillum.

150/550

a. IMP CAES VES AVG.

1570. AE *quadrans*.
Obv: IMP VESPASIAN AVG; trophy.
Rev: P M TR P P P COS III; S C in fields; vexillum.

100/400

72–73 CE

1571. AE *quadrans*.
Obv: IMP VESPASIAN AVG; palm tree.
Rev: P M TR P P P COS IIII; S C in fields; vexillum.

200/650

a. P M T P P P COS IIII.

1572. AE *quadrans*.
Obv: IMP VESPASIAN AVG; trophy.
Rev: P M TR P P P COS IIII; S C in fields; vexillum.

100/400

MINT OF ASIA MINOR (EPHESUS?)
NON-STANDARD ROMAN DENOMINATIONS
77–78 CE

1573. AE medium denomination, 24-25 mm.
Obv: T CAESAR IMPER PONT; laureate head of Titus to r.
Rev: TR POT COS VI CENSOR; S C in exergue; Titus (or the
Genius of the Roman People) wearing toga (possibly naked to
waist), stands front holding scepter, his r. hand upon trophy at l.;
Jewish captive, hands bound, sits l. below, looking back. RRR

1574. AE small denomination, 18-20.
Obv: T CAESAR IMPEP (sic) PONT; laureate head of Titus to r.
Rev: S C in fields; palm tree; mourning Jewess seated on r. to r. on
cuirass, arms to l. 350/1,500
a. T CAESAR IMP PONT.

PROVINCIAL MINT: KOINON OF BITHYNIA

1575. AE 25-27 mm *as*. M. Maecius Rufus, proconsul of Bithynia
under Vespasian.
Obv: ΑΥΤΟΚΡΑ ΤΙΤΟΣ ΚΑΙΣΑΡ ΣΕΒΑΣ ΥΙΟΣ *(Emperor Titus Caesar, son of Augustus)*; laureate head of Titus to r.
Rev: ΕΠΙ Μ ΜΑΙΚΙΟΥ ΡΟΥΦΟΥ ΑΝΘΥΠΑΤΟΥ *(in the proconsulship
of M. Maecus Rufus)*; palm tree, on l. cuirass, two spears, and helmet; on r. two spears and shield. 650/3,500
*This provincial Roman coin as well as No. 1575, attributed to the Koinon
of Bithynia, are clearly related to the Jewish War. RPC notes that this coin has
"...a significance beyond Bithynia: the palm tree with obverse of Titus is a clear
allusion to Titus' participation in the defeat of Judaea...."[38]*

1576. AE 25-27 mm *as*. M. Salvidenus Asprenas, proconsul of
Bithynia under Vespasian.
Obv: ΑΥΤΟΚΡΑ ΤΙΤΟΣ ΚΑΙΣΑΡ ΣΕΒΑΣ ΥΙΟΣ *(Emperor Titus Caesar, son of Augustus)*; laureate head of Titus to r.
Rev: ΕΠΙ Μ ΣΑΛΟΥΙΔΗΝΟΥ ΑΣΠΡΗΝΑ ΑΝΘΥΠΑΤΟΥ *(in the proconsulship of M. Saluidenus Asprenas)*; palm tree, on l. cuirass, two
spears, and helmet; on r. two spears and shield. 650/3,500
a. Obverse countermark ΜΗΤΒ.

MINT OF ROME

TITUS, 79–81 CE, COMMEMORATING VICTORY OVER THE JEWS

GOLD AUREI

79 CE

1577. AU *aureus.*
  Obv: IMP T CAESAR VESPASIANVS AVG; laureate head of Titus
  to r.
  Rev: TR POT VII COS VII; male Jewish captive kneels r., hands
  bound behind, trophy above.   10,000/35,000

1578. AU *aureus.*
  Obv: IMP TITVS CAES VESPASIAN AVG P M (outward); laureate
  head of Titus to r.
  Rev: TR P VIIII IMP XIIII COS VII; male Jewish captive kneels r.,
  hands bound behind, trophy above.   10,000/35,000
  a. TR P VIIII IMP XIIII COS VII P P.
  b. TR P VIIII IMP XV COS VII P P.

80 CE

1579. AU *aureus.*
  Obv: IMP TITVS CAES VESPASIAN AVG P M; laureate head of
  Titus to r.
  Rev: TR P IX IMP XV COS VIII P P; trophy flanked by seated
  captives, hands tied behind backs, female on l., male on r.
                                                12,500/40,000
  a. Laureate head of Titus to l.

80–81 CE, VESPASIAN DEIFIED

1580. AU *aureus.*
  Obv: DIVVS AVGVSTVS VESPASIANVS (outward); laureate head
  of Vespasian to r.
  Rev: EX S C in exergue; *quadriga* l., with temple upon or behind
  cart, flanked by two wreath-bearing Victories.   12,500/40,000

1581. AU *aureus*.

Obv: DIVVS AVGVSTVS VESPASIANVS (outward); laureate head of Vespasian to r.

Rev: EX S C across fields; draped Victory strides l. with both hands placing shield on a trophy; mourning Jewess sits l. below.

10,000/35,000

MINT OF ROME
SILVER DENARII
79 CE

1582. AR *denarius*.

Obv: IMP T CAESAR VESPASIANVS AVG; laureate head of Titus r.

Rev: TR POT VII COS VII; male Jewish captive kneels r., hands bound behind, trophy above. 350/1,250

1583. AR *denarius*.

Obv: IMP TITVS CAES VESPASIAN AVG P M (outward); laureate head of Titus to r.

Rev: TR P VIIII IMP XIIII COS VII P P; male Jewish captive kneels r., hands bound behind, trophy above. 350/1,250

  a. Laureate head of Titus l.

  b. TR P VIIII IMP XV COS VII P P.

  c. As 1583b, but laureate head of Titus l.

1584. AR *denarius*.

Obv: IMP TITVS CAES VESPASIAN AVG P M; laureate head of Titus to r.

Rev: TR P IX IMP XV COS VIII P P; trophy flanked by seated captives, hands tied behind backs, female on l, male on r.

350/1,250

  a. Laureate head of Titus to l.

  b. Similar but male on l., woman on r.

  c. As 1584b, but laureate head of Titus l.

1585. AR *denarius*.
  Obv: DIVVS AVGVSTVS VESPASIANVS (outward); laureate head
    of Vespasian to r.
  Rev: EX S C in exergue; *quadriga* l., with temple upon or behind cart,
    flanked by two wreath-bearing Victories.   350/1,250
  a. DIVVS VESPASIANVS AVGVSTVS; *quadriga* to r.

1586. AR *denarius*.
  Obv: DIVVS AVGVSTVS VESPASIANVS (outward); laureate head
    of Vespasian to r.
  Rev: EX S C across fields; draped Victory strides l. with both hands
    placing shield on a trophy; mourning Jewess sits l. below.
                                                    300/1,000

1587. AR *denarius*.
  Obv: IMP TITVS CAES VESPASIAN AVG P M (outward); laureate
    head of Titus to l.
  Rev: EX S C across fields; draped Victory strides l. with both hands
    placing shield on a trophy; mourning Jewess sits l. below.
                                                    350/1,250

MINT OF ROME
SESTERTII
79 CE

1588. AE *sestertius*.
  Obv: IMP TITVS CAES VESPASIAN AVG P M (outward); laureate
    head of Titus to r.
  Rev: IVDAEA CAPTA; S C in exergue; palm tree, male captive on
    l., stands facing r., mourning Jewess sits on r. to r. on arms.
                                                    750/6,500

80 CE

1589. AE *sestertius*.
  Obv: IMP T CAES VESPASIAN AVG P M TR P P P COS VIII;
    laureate head of Titus to r.
  Rev: IVDAEA CAPTA; S C in exergue; palm tree; male captive on l.,
    stands facing r.; mourning Jewess sits on r. to r. on cuirass, arms
    around both figures.   750/6,500

1590.   AE *sestertius.*

Obv: IMP T CAES VESPASIAN AVG P M TR P P P COS VIII (outward); laureate head of Titus to r.

Rev: S C in exergue; Titus stands in triumphal *quadriga* to r., holds
branch in r. hand and scepter in l., on side of cart is Victory to r.
holding wreath.   750/6,500

80–81 CE

1591.   AE *sestertius.*

Obv: IMP T CAES VESP AVG P M TR P P P COS VIII; laureate
head of Titus to r.

Rev: IVD CAP across fields; S C in exergue; palm tree; mourning
Jewess sits on r. to r. on pile of arms; on l. of tree mourning Jew
with hands bound stands l., arms on ground.   850/7,500

a. Laureate head of Titus to l.
b. S C in fields.
c. Laureate head of Titus to l.; S C in fields.
d. IVDAEA CAPTA around, S C in exergue.

1591

1592.   AE *sestertius.*

Obv: IMP T CAES VESP AVG P M TR P P P COS VIII; laureate
head of Titus to l.

Rev: IVD CAP across fields; S C in exergue; palm tree; on l. mourning Jewess sits to l. on pile of arms; on r. of tree mourning Jew
with hands bound stands r. looks back over shoulder, arms on
ground.   750/7,000

1593. AE *sestertius*.

Obv: IMP T CAES VESP AVG P M TR P P P COS VIII; laureate head of Titus to r.

Rev: IVD CAP across fields; S C in exergue; palm tree; on l. mourning Jewess sits to l. on pile of arms; on r. of tree mourning Jew with hands bound stands r., arms on ground.   850/7,500

a. Laureate head Titus l.

b. S C in fields.

c. Laureate head Titus l.; S C in fields.

1594. AE *sestertius*.

Obv: Flavian amphitheater (Colosseum) seen from ¾ aerial view showing both facade as well as inside of building, the *Meta Sudans* on l. and building with portico on r. The facade of the building shows four tiers, the lowest tier with five empty arches; the second tier with six arches, each arch contains a statue and in the central arch is a facing Victory *quadriga*, the third tier with seven arches containing statues and in the central arch is a palm tree flanked by a standing emperor (or Nike) on left and a Jew or Jewess on right; the fourth tier has seven compartments filled with globes and squares. The interior shows rows of seats and boxes, and, notably the royal box in the center of the crowd.

Rev: IMP T CAES VESP AVG P M TR P P P COS VIII; S C in fields; Titus seated left on curule chair holding branch and scroll; arms (and booty?) scattered.   35,000/85,000

a. *Meta Sudans* on r. and building with portico on l.

b. As 1593a but S C in obverse fields, absent on reverse.

Not all obverse dies depict identical statues in building facade.

1595. AE *sestertius*.

Obv: DIVVS AVGVSTVS VESPASIAN PATER PAT (outward); laureate head of Vespasian to r.

Rev: IVDAEA CAPTA; S C in exergue; palm tree; male captive on l., stands facing r., on r. mourning Jewess sits to r. on cuirass, head in hand, arms surround both figures.   750/6,500

EASTERN MINT (THRACE ?)
80–81 CE

1596. AE *sestertius*.
> Obv: IMP T CAES DIVI VESP F AVG P M TR P P P COS VIII; laureate head of Titus to r.
> Rev: IVD CAP across fields; S C in fields; palm tree; on l. mourning Jewess sits to l. on pile of arms; on r. of tree mourning Jew with hands bound stands r., arms on ground.   850/7,500
> a. Mourning Jew stands on r. of tree, looks back over shoulder.
> b. IVDAEA CAPTA around, S C in exergue; mourning Jew stands l. on l. looking back, Jewess sits r. on r., arms on ground.

1597. AE *sestertius*.
> Obv: IMP T CAES DIVI VESP F AVG P M TR P P P COS VIII; laureate head of Titus to r.
> Rev: IVDAEA CAPTA; S C in exergue; palm tree; on r. mourning Jewess sits to r. on cuirass; to l. of palm Titus stands r. in military dress with spear and *parazonium*, l. foot on helmet.
> 750/6,500

EASTERN MINT (THRACE?)
AE SEMIS

1598a

1598. AE *semis*.
> Obv: IMP T CAESAR DIVI VESPAS F AVG; laureate head of Titus to r.
> Rev: IVD CAP and S C across fields; palm tree; mourning Jewess sits on l. to l., yoke to r. of tree.   550/1,750
> a. IMP T CAESAR DIVI VESPASI AVG.

Mint of Rome
Domitian, 81–96 ce, Commemorating Victory Over the Jews
81–82 after death of Titus

1599. AE *sestertius.*
  Obv: Flavian amphitheater (Colosseum) seen from ¾ aerial view
    showing both facade as well as inside of building, the *Meta Sudans*
    on l. and building with portico on r. The facade of the building
    shows four tiers, the lowest tier with five empty arches; the second
    tier with six arches, each arch contains a statue and in the central
    arch is a facing Victory *quadriga*, the third tier with seven arches
    containing statues and in the central arch is a palm tree flanked
    by a standing emperor (or Nike) on left and a Jew or Jewess on
    right; the fourth tier has seven compartments filled with globes
    and squares. The interior shows rows of seats and boxes, and,
    notably the royal box in the center of the crowd.
  Rev: DIVO AVG T DIVI VESP F VESPASIAN; S C in exergue; Ti-
    tus seated left on curule chair holding branch and scroll; arms
    (and booty?) scattered.   35,000/85,000
  Not all obverse dies depict identical statues in building facade.

Unknown Mint

1600. AR (*fourrée*) *denarius.*
  Obv: IMP CAES DOMIT AVG GERM PM TR P XIII; laureate bust
    Domitian r.
  Rev: IVDAEA in exergue; mourning Jewess sits of trophy on r. to r.
                                                    UNIQUE

RESTORED COINS OF TRAJAN

"Restored" coins are re-issues of previous coins whose designs were no longer in use, together with the name and titles of the emperor and the word RESTITVIT (or REST). These commemorative types were first issued under the Flavians, but the most significant series was struck under Trajan. In 107 Trajan recalled large numbers of worn coins. "The withdrawal of masses of familiar money from circulation suggested that some permanent memorial of the old coin should be associated with the mint of Trajan." Thus, "Roman history, from its earliest times, is envisiged as a harmonius whole," according to Mattingly.[39]

This strategy was a clever way for Trajan to connect his own reign with the glorious monuments and victories of his predecessors. In this way, Trajan may have been the first emperor to recognize coins, a product of the Sacra Moneta, as a way of recalling history.

VESPASIAN RESTORED

1601. AU *aureus*.
   Obv: IMP CAESAR VESPASIANVS AVG COS VIIII, laureate head
     of Vespasian to r.
   Rev: IMP CAES TRAIAN AVG GER DAC P P REST; male
     Jewish captive kneels l., hands bound behind, trophy above.
                                      25,000/8,5000
   a. Captive kneels r.

TITUS RESTORED

1602. AU *aureus*.
   Obv: IMP TITVS CAES VESPASIAN AVG P M; laureate head of of
     Titus to r.
   Rev: IMP CAES TRAIAN AVG GER DAC P P REST; Trophy.
                                        25,000/85,000
   a. Laureate head of of Titus to l.

Nerva's Fisci Ivdaici, 96–98 ce

Domitian was a cruel and vindictive man who continued to collect the Jewish Tax his father had imposed upon all Jews in the Roman Empire. The tax was two *drachms*, half a *sheqel*, since Vespasian had reasoned that the Jews could enrich his coffers instead of offering the tribute they had voluntarily paid to their own Temple, as prescribed in Exodus 30:13.

Domitian ordered his tax collectors to work with a vengeance never imagined by his father and brother. Collectors often employed severe insult and abuse (*calumnia*). To collect the tax from a Jew, they first of all had to determine whether the man was indeed a Jew. The fastest way of doing this was to see if he had been circumcised. Thus, the unscrupulous tax collectors frequently demanded humiliating exposure of the genitals, usually in public places or official meetings, but also at family gatherings or other times when embarrassment would be caused.

According to the Roman historian Seutonius: "More than any other, the *Fiscus Iudaicus* was administered very severely; and to it were brought, or reported, those who either had lived the life of a Jew unprofessed, or concealing their origin, had not paid the tax imposed upon the people. I remember that it was of interest to me during my youth when a ninety-year-old man was brought before the procurator and a very crowded court to see whether he was circumcised."[40]

When Domitian was assassinated on September 18, 96 ce, Nerva succeeded him. Nerva instituted an extensive series of popular changes, one of which was the abolition of the insulting method of collecting the Jewish tax. The tax itself was not revoked, only the degrading method of collecting it. To proclaim his benevolence, Nerva ordered a coin to be issued.

The Jewish tax apparently remained in effect until the reign of Julian the Apostate, 361–363 ce. In a letter to the Jews, he says: "In the past your liability to new taxes and the constraint to give to the treasury numberless quantities of gold made the yoke of servitude especially oppressive. With my own eyes I have seen a part of this misery; a larger one I have perceived by finding the rolls kept to be used against you. I have reduced these rolls to ashes."[41]

Alternate Theory for Nerva's Fisci Iudaici

When interpreting the meaning of Nerva's *sestertius* we must, above all, bear in mind that it is a Roman coin, not a Jewish coin. It represents the Roman viewpoint, exclusively. On the best spirited of occasions Romans could celebrate provincials (for example, Hadrian's travel series), but political correctness was not in Rome's dialogue, and she was never apologetic toward provincial subjects.

Despite his alleged gentleness, Nerva was emperor by way of a coup against Domitian, who was sorely missed by the legions. Nerva's life was in constant danger and he went to great effort to placate the army. Thus, he would not have offended the legions by apologizing to a conquered people—especially one that in recent memory had revolted at great cost to the Roman army, and to Roman pride.

Instead, we must find a more direct explanation for this type. In all likelihood it celebrates Vespasian's requirement of 71/2 CE that the annual *didrachm* Temple Tax, the *Fiscus Iudaicus*, be paid to Rome rather than to the Jewish Temple. This tax was extended to every Jew, male and female, from the age of three, and even to slaves of Jewish households. The proceeds were earmarked for the rebuilding of the Temple of Jupiter Optimus Maximus Capitolinus in Rome, which had been destroyed in the last days of the Roman Civil War of 68–69.

Thus, FISCI IVDIACI CALVMNIA SVBLATA ("the insult of the Jewish Tax has been removed") would refer to Vespasian's removal of the insult that prior to 71/2 the Jewish Temple Tax had been collected by Jews for their own use. After all, Romans considered themselves the only legitimate taxing authority within the empire, and the only rightful beneficiary of tax revenues.

In summary, the idea that this coin represents a Roman apology, or a Roman acknowledgement of its own callous behavior, must be abandoned. Those are modern notions that we cannot retroactively apply to the Romans. Had Nerva been a Jew, and this *sestertius* a Jewish coin, we would be right to consider otherwise, but Nerva was very much an old fashioned, noble Roman who would not have used the instrument of Roman coinage to make an apology to a conquered people.

(Alternate theory by David Vagi.)

MINT OF ROME
NERVA, 96–98 CE

1603

1603.   AE *sestertius*.
  Obv: IMP NERVA CAES AVG P M TR P COS II P P; laureate head
    of Nerva to r.
  Rev: FISCI IVDAICI CALVMNIA SVBLATA *(the insult of the Jew-
    ish Tax has been removed)*; S C in fields; large palm tree with two
    bunches of dates. Struck 96 CE.   1,250/8,500
  a. IMP NERVA CAES AVG P M TR P COS II DESIGN III P P is
    obverse legend. Struck 96 CE.
  b. IMP NERVA CAES AVG P M TR P COS III P P is obverse leg-
    end. Struck 97 CE.
  c. IMP NERVA CAES AVG P M TR P COS IIII P P is obverse leg-
    end. Struck 98 CE.

HADRIAN AND JUDAEA, 117–138 CE

Hadrian traveled across his entire empire during his reign. In 130 CE he traveled from Arabia to Egypt by way of Judaea. On these journeys the emperor secured his borders and established necessary government offices. Hadrian had coins issued to commemorate his visits to various provinces, including Egypt, Macedonia, and Spain, as well as Judaea. It is not known whether these coins were issued to commemorate Hadrian's victory over Bar Kokhba, or prior to the outbreak of hostilities.

HADRIAN'S JUDAEA COINS, STRUCK AT ROME

1604a   1605

1604.   AE *sestertius*.
    Obv: HADRIANVS AVG COS III P P; laureate head of Hadrian r.
    Rev: ADVENTVI AVG IVDAEAE; S C in exergue; Hadrian, togate, stands r., raising r. hand, facing Judaea, who holds object (cup?) in l. hand, a bull alongside the altar, child stands l. in front of Judaea holding palm, a second child stands l. behind her also holding a palm.   2,000/12,500
   a.   Bare draped bust of Hadrian r.
   b.   Similar reverse with a third child in front of Judaea, no bull.
   c.   Obverse as 1603a, reverse with third child.
   d.   On reverse children stand on either side of altar.
   e.   Obverse as 1603a, children stand on either side of altar.

1605.   AE *sestertius*.
    Obv: HADRIANVS AVG COS III P P. bare head of Hadrian r.
    Rev: IVDAEA in exergue; S C in fields; Hadrian, togate, stands r. raising r. hand, facing Judaea, who holds a patera over altar, a sacrificial bull stand beside it, two children stand in the center hold palm branches and greet Hadrian, a third child stands behind Judaea.   6,000/17,500

1606.   AE *as.*
  Obv: HADRIANVS AVG COS III P P. bare bust of Hadrian r.
  Rev: ADVENTVI AVG IVDAEAE; S C in exergue; Hadrian, togate,
    stands r., raising r. hand, facing Judaea, who holds object (cup?)
    in l. hand, bull alongside altar, child stands l. in front of Judaea
    holding palm, a second child stands l. behind her also holding a
    palm.   3,500/12,500

COUNTERMARKS OF THE ROMAN LEGIONS

Apparently five Roman legions and one Roman cohort (a principal
part of a legion) played important roles in the military activity in ancient Israel, mostly during the Jewish War and the Bar Kokhba War,
but also at the time of the New Testament (as previously discussed
regarding countermarks on the coins of the prefects and procurators).

There has been much discussion about why people countermarked
coins in ancient times. Both civil and military countermarking took
place, and the countermarks of the Roman Legions apply to the latter.
In his comprehensive book *Greek Imperial Countermarks*, Christopher
Howgego says, "Countermarking took place in military contexts in
many parts of the Roman Empire."

He observes that, "Legionary countermarks are usually found on
worn coins. It is likely that their primary purpose was to make such
coins acceptable to the troops as pay or change. Since each group of legionary countermarks (in the East at least) is found on one size of coin
only, they may have guaranteed a specific value also. The evidence
of finds does not suggest that the countermarks turned the coins into
tokens for use by the legions only. The countermarks could be applied
either at a legion's permanent camp or on campaign, and probably by
detachments as well as legions. A study of the brick stamps of the *Legio X Fretensis* (by Dan Barag of Hebrew University) shows the iconographic tradition to which the countermarks belonged."[42]

It is possible that the countermarking of coins was necessary
for the legionary soldiers more as a psychological tool than a fiscal
one. After being drilled and "psyched" into hating their enemies, the
legionnaires may have been unable to adapt to local coinage without
it being stamped with their own insignias. Of course the very visible
circulation of countermarked coins could also have a devastating

psychological effect on the people living in the territory occupied by the legionary force.

The Roman forces active in ancient Israel were the *Cohors II Italica* and the *Legiones V Macedonica* (also known as the *V Scythica*), *VI Ferrata*, *X Fretensis*, *XII Fulminata*, and *XV Apollinaris*. The countermarks of the Second Cohort were discussed in Chapter 6 (pp. 322–323). Josephus mentions the five legions—V, VI, X, XII, XV—by numbers only, without their names. For the most part we have been able to fill in the legionary names from contemporary numismatic and epigraphic evidence that is available.

LEGIO V MACEDONICA (ALSO KNOWN AS LEGIO V SCYTHICA)

Not much is known about the origins of the Fifth Legion, usually called Macedonica. The earliest records are reports by Strabo of settlement of its veterans at Berytus by Agrippa in 15 BCE. The legion may have fought at Philippi or perhaps it simply garrisoned in Macedonia before moving into Moesia.

Josephus mentions the Fifth Legion's activity in Judaea during the Jewish War. Nero appointed Vespasian to lead Roman troops to crush the Jewish Revolt. He gathered his forces at Antioch near the end of 66 CE and marched with two legions to Akko-Ptolemais, where he met Titus, who had been in Alexandria. When Titus reached Akko-Ptolemais, Josephus reports, "...there finding his father, together with the two legions, the Fifth and the Tenth, which were the most eminent legions of all, he joined them to that Fifteenth legion which he had brought ..."[43]

The Fifth and the Tenth Legions with the Fifteenth, fought together at Jotapata, which the Romans conquered in June/July 67 after a 48 day siege. Before Jotapata fell, Sextus Cerealis Vettulenus, commander of the Fifth, took a force of 600 cavalry and 3,000 infantry to Mt. Gerizim where they massacred more than 11,000 rebellious Samaritans. Next, Vespasian besieged Gamla with the Fifth, Tenth, and Fifteenth. During the siege the Fifth suffered major losses. After the fall of Gamla, in October of 67, Vespasian led the Fifth and Tenth to winter quarters in Caesarea. In the spring of 68, Vespasian moved the Fifth to Nicopolis-Emmaus, where it apparently stayed until the siege of Jerusalem in 70.

Advancing against Jerusalem, the legions built siege ramps "after seventeen days of continuous toil." One ramp, "facing the Antonia was thrown up by the Fifth Legion across the pool called Struthion...." The Fifth besieged the Antonia and took it in a surprise attack in July of 70. In 71 CE, the Fifth Legion moved from Alexandria to Moesia.

The Fifth Legion has generally been identified as *Macedonica* because of three inscribed tombstones of its soldiers found at Nicopolis-Emmaus late in the 19th century. But Barag and Qedar presented four coins countermarked by the Fifth Legion in Judaea during the Jewish War. Surprisingly, however, the inscription on the coins, LVS, points to the name *Legio V Scythica*. They write, "The countermark LVS belongs ...to the *Legio V Scythica* and was punched on bronze coins at Caesarea between the late summer of 68 CE and the legion's departure for Alexandria with Titus late in 70 CE or early in 71 CE, en route back to its quarters at Oescus in Moesia. How can the discrepancy be resolved between the countermarks of the *Legio V Scythica* and other evidence that the Vth Legion, fighting in Judaea during the Jewish War, was the *Legio V Macedonica*?"[44]

Barag and Qedar explain that the three soldiers of the Fifth, whose tombstones have been found "were soldiers in active service, and not veterans, and were buried at Emmaus between the spring of 68 CE and summer of 70 CE."

They further explain that, "In the summer of 68 CE, or somewhat later, bronze coins were countermarked at Caesarea for use in the camp of the Vth legion at Emmaus as *L(egio) V S(cythia)*. A possible solution for this apparent discrepancy may be found in the history of the legion before the Jewish War. The *Legio V Macedonica* had its quarters, with the *Legio IIII Scythica*, in the part of Macedonia that was eventually transferred to Moesia. In 33/4 CE, the former legion is mentioned, together with the latter, in an inscription set up during the construction of a road in Moesia Inferior, and during the principate of Claudius, it is referred to, together with *Legio IIII Scythica*, in an inscription of its legatus L. Martius Macer."[45]

Barag and Qedar also refer to a fragmentary inscription from Peltvinum, a city of the Vestinians on the Via Claudia Nova, Italy, which reads "LEG• V• Scythica• IN • AR...." They suggest that the last two letters may be completed to read AR(menia), since the Fifth fought in the Armenian war under Corbulo's command.

"The fragment from Peltvinum and the countermark from Caesarea constitute the only evidence that the *Legio V Macedonica* was referred to as the *Legio V Scythica* in 62 CE (or earlier) and in 68–70 CE, respectively. The parallel and contemporary use of the name Macedonica on the epitaphs at Emmaus and Scythica on the countermark used at Caesarea is difficult to explain. Was the name Scythica an official name, introduced after the name Macedonica was in use and prevailed? The inscription fragment from Peltvinum and the countermark from the Jewish War show that the occasional inconsistency in the names of legions continued to the end of the Julio-Claudian period," according to Barag and Qedar.[46]

LEGIO VI FERRATA

The Sixth Roman Legion, known as the "iron legion" (*ferrata*) was probably one of Mark Antony's original legions at the battle of Philippi in 42 BCE, but at the time had not yet acquired its nickname.

The Sixth Legion was stationed in northern Syria as early at 4 BCE and by 19 CE it had moved to Laodicea, south of Antioch. Early in the second part of the first century, the Sixth took part in the successful Armenian campaign. When Cestius Gallus, governor of Syria, advanced on Jerusalem at the beginning of the Jewish War, his principal force was the Twelfth Legion, but a detachment of the Sixth Legion and its legate accompanied them.

The Twelfth Legion was badly defeated while retreating from Jerusalem and the legate of the Sixth Legion was killed. Thereafter, the Sixth Legion was moved to Italy to take part in the battle for the throne against Vitellius before it was moved back to Syria.

Josephus reports Titus' advance on the city that led to the destruction of Jerusalem this way: "He led the three legions which under his father had previously laid Judaea waste (V, X, and XV), and the Twelfth, which under Cestius had once been defeated. This legion, generally renowned for its valor and now remembering what it had suffered, advanced the more eagerly to seek revenge. Of these he ordered the Fifth to join him via the Emmaus route, and the Tenth to ascend by way of Jericho, while he himself set out with the others, being further attended by the greatly increased contingents from the allied kings and a considerable body of auxiliaries from Syria. The four legions from which Vespasian had selected men to go with Mucianus to Italy were brought up to strength with the troops supplied by Titus; he had with him two thousand picked men from the armies in Alexandria and three thousand guards from the Euphrates."[47]

After the Jewish War, the Sixth Legion was moved to Samosata on the Euphrates. Later, in 106 CE, the Sixth Legion was sent by Trajan to convert Nabataea from a client kingdom into the Roman Province of Arabia. Once this mission was accomplished, the Sixth Legion was stationed at Bostra. Later, the Sixth Legion helped build the major Roman highway connecting Damascus with the Gulf of Aqaba in the south and in 115, the Sixth joined other Roman forces for Trajan's campaign in Parthia.

The Sixth Legion countermark most frequently seen is LVIF, which occurs on heavily worn coins of about 20 mm in diameter. The VI countermark is also known.

LEGIO X FRETENSIS

The Tenth Legion probably acquired its name, *Fretensis*, from the *Fretum Siculum*, the straits where the legion fought successfully in the Sicilian War against Sextus Pompey. From at least 6 CE, the troops of the Tenth Legion were stationed in northern Syria at Cyrrhus north of Antioch. In 18 CE at the Tenth Legion's camp, Tacitus reports on a confrontation between Germanicus and Piso. Thereafter, Germanicus suddenly died, likely from poisoning, and possibly on the orders of the jealous Tiberius. Piso, who was accused of the deed, took his own life in Rome rather than stand trial.

Still stationed in northern Syria, the Tenth took part in Corbulo's successful Armenian campaign of 57–58 CE. From there, the legion was moved to Cilicia in southeastern Turkey, but was moved back to Syria in 63 CE.

The Tenth Legion, then commanded by Marcus Ulpius Traianus (father of the future Emperor Trajan), formed part of the forces that Vespasian led to Akko and against other northern portions of ancient Israel in his campaign of 66 CE. The legion participated in the sieges and capture of Tarichaeae and Gamla and advanced on Jerusalem via the Jordan River valley, taking Jericho and destroying Qumran. The Tenth also made up a part of the force that destroyed Jerusalem under Titus in 70 CE. During the siege, it was stationed on the Mount of Olives overlooking the city. Three years later, the same unit besieged and destroyed the zealot fortress of Masada.

The Tenth Legion soon became the official, permanent unit of the Roman Province of Judaea. After the Bar Kokhba War, the province was renamed Syria-Palestina and the legion was garrisoned in Aelia Capitolina (formerly Jerusalem). The Tenth remained in Jerusalem until Diocletian, at the end of the third century, moved south to the port of Eilat to help safeguard the sea access to the East from the developing power of the Arabs.

Some years ago, archaeologists discovered an extensive Tenth Legion camp at the Ramat Rachel Kibbutz on the outskirts of Jerusalem. In the early 1990s, another major Tenth Legion site, perhaps its headquarters, was discovered during the excavation of a parking lot next to Jerusalem's National Auditorium. The archaeologists did their work, and today a good part of that site, including a portion of the Tenth Legion's pottery kiln to manufacture ceramic tiles and water conduit pipes, is preserved and on display in the downstairs section of the National Auditorium.

Insignias of the Tenth Legion were the boar, the galley, the dolphin, and Neptune as well as various abbreviations of its name (LX, XF, LEX, LXF, XFR). These abbreviations can be found on ceramic tiles produced by the Tenth Legion in the aforementioned kiln-factory. A stone lamp post near the Jaffa Gate in Jerusalem's Old City bears a Latin inscription referring to the Tenth Legion as LEXFR. Many coins are countermarked with the Tenth Legion's various insignias, among them city coins, especially from Sebaste, Ashqelon, and Sidon, and some local Judaea Capta issues.

Barag concludes that the coins countermarked by the Tenth Legion date from about 68 to 96 CE, or possibly 132 CE at the latest.[48]

LEGIO XII FULMINATA

The Twelfth Legion was one of the legions of Augustus. It possibly existed at the time of Julius Caesar, and may have been in Mark Antony's army in the East. The Twelfth was in North Africa in 30 BCE and in Syria in 14 and 23 CE. The legion was also part of the army in 62 CE during the Roman campaign and defeat in Armenia.

By 66 CE, the Twelfth Legion, "renowned for its valor," according to Josephus, had returned to Syria and Cestius Gallus moved it into Judaea to capture Jerusalem. However, Gallus and the Twelfth, with a detachment from the Sixth, turned back from Jerusalem and were soundly defeated by an army of Jews between Jerusalem and Antipatris.

The Twelfth Legion was one of the legions that helped capture and destroy Jerusalem in 70 CE. But the legion did not participate in the sieges of Machaerus and Masada because it was transferred back to Syria and stationed at Miletus on the Euphrates, since Titus wished to send the Twelfth away as quickly as possible on account of its ignominious defeat at the beginning of the First Revolt.

Joining other legions, the Twelfth was also part of Trajan's army that defeated the Parthians and may have accompanied Trajan as far as the Persian Gulf.

Countermarks of the Twelfth Legion occur most frequently on the coins of Antioch with the large S C reverse design.

LEGIO XV APOLLINARIS

Augustus formed the Fifteenth Legion while he was still known as Octavian, and was named after his protecting god, Apollo.

After the death of Augustus, while stationed in Carnuntum just east of Vienna, Austria, the Fifteenth Legion joined the Ninth (*Hispana*) and the Eighth (*Augusta*) in a rebellion for more pay and shorter service. Tacitus reports that Drusus was finally able to extinguish this rebellion with the help of a lunar eclipse and some heavy storms.

The Fifteenth was part of Corbulo's successful Armenian campaign in 63 CE and was shortly thereafter moved to Egypt where it ended a local rebellion of Jews in Alexandria, who had attacked the Greek population after an incident in the local amphitheater. Josephus reports that when Tiberius Alexander, the apostate Jew who was prefect of Egypt, "realized that nothing less than a major calamity would quell the rebels, he let loose among them the two Roman legions [*XV Apollinaris* and *XXII Deioteriana*] stationed in the city, together with two thousand soldiers who happened to have come from Libya, to complete the ruin of the Jews. He gave them leave not merely to kill them but to plunder their property and burn down their houses."[49]

Once Vespasian was ordered by Nero to crush the Jewish revolt in Judaea, Titus was dispatched to Alexandria to bring the Fifteenth Legion to Ptolemais to join the Fifth and Tenth. The Fifteenth Legion took part in battles for Gamara near Ptolemais and then the siege of Jotapata in Galilee, in which Josephus himself commanded the defending Jewish army. Titus and a small detachment of the Fifteenth made a surprise night time assault on Jotapata after a 48-day siege, and took the defenders by surprise. The city was captured and Josephus surrendered, thus ending his career as a Jewish patriot and beginning one as the most important contemporaneous historian of Jewish history during the Flavian dynasty.

Next, the Fifteenth was sent to Nysa-Scythopolis to reorganize itself, while the other two legions were sent to Caesarea. In September, Vespasian united all three legions at Nysa and attacked Tarichaeae on the Sea of Galilee. The Jews who were defending their city climbed aboard their boats, but Vespasian had his troops construct rafts from which the legions fought a sustained sea battle resulting in an important victory for the Romans. Many believe that Vespasian's VICTORIA NAVALIS coins were struck to commemorate this bloody battle.

In late September, the legions attacked Gamla, in the Golan near the Sea of Galilee. It was a tenacious battle and when Gamla's wall was finally breached, the Fifteenth poured into the city. The Jews, however, stood on the rooftops and pelted the soldiers with missiles. The Fifteenth fought its way up the heights of the city in a bitter battle, and Vespasian himself was nearly killed or captured. Ultimately, Gamla was destroyed and the legions marched to Jerusalem. Today, the ruins at Gamla are preserved along with many of the Roman siege missiles used in that battle.

At Jerusalem, the Fifteenth built an important siege tower, but the Jews destroyed the tower and the Fifteenth rebuilt it. This time they used the tower and its battering ram to accomplish the first Roman breach of Jerusalem's walls.

Once Jerusalem was destroyed, the Fifteenth was moved to Caesarea, then to Egypt, then back to Carnuntum. In 115 CE, the Fifteenth was moved back to the Middle East permanently, where it was stationed at Satala in northeastern Turkey.

Countermarks of the Fifteenth Legion are hard to find, and the coin published here (No. 1617) is the first example ever published of a Fifteenth Legion countermark struck on a coin of the Jewish War, although other LXV countermarks are known to occur on coins of Neapolis and Arados.

COINS WITH LEGIONARY COUNTERMARKS

1607.   AE 22 mm coin of Nero from Caesarea, Samaria.
Very worn
Obv: LVS and KAI in rectangular countermarks.   250/750
a. Coin type as above , obv. rectangular countermark is LVS (the S
is retrograde); rev. bust in oval countermark

1608.   AE 25 mm worn bronze probably Nos. 1145–47.
LVIF and a bust in rectangular countermarks.   200/500

1609   1615

1609.   AE 25 mm worn bronze probably Domitian from Caesarea,
Samaria.
Obv: Rectangular countermark, L.X.F. above boar advancing r. and
dolphin in same countermark and just below boar.; second rectangular countermark of a galley to r.; rev. bust in oval countermark.   250/750
a. Another example, without galley countermark; on reverse, bust r.
in rectangular countermark, struck upon a 20–22 mm coin, probably No. 1446–47 types.

1610.   AE 13–14 mm coin of Ashqelon, Judaea.
Obv: Head of Tyche with turreted crown r.. Countermark L•X with-
in incuse rectangle.
Rev: Galley r.   125/300

1611.   AE 13–14 mm coin of Ashqelon, Judaea.
Obv: Head of Tyche with turreted crown r. Countermark XF with
within incuse rectangle.
Rev: Galley r. inscription obliterated.   200/350

1612.   AE 20–22 mm worn, probably Nos. 1145–47.
Obv: Galley in a rectangular countermark.
Rev: Bust in an oval countermark.   200/350

1613.   AE 22–23 mm. Coin of Sebaste under Domitian.
Rev: LXF in rectangular countermark, second countermark of head
      in oval, possibly Trajan.   200/500
   a. Similar, but only LXF countermark on obverse.

1614.   AE 22 mm coin of Nero, Caesarea, Samaria, as No. 1607.
XF countermark in rectangular countermark.   200/400
   a. XF countermark on a 22 mm coin of Dora, Phoenicia.
   b. XF countermark on a Roman *as* of Vespasian.

1615.   Various 22–28 mm bronzes of Antioch and Commagene.
XF in rectangular countermark on coin of Tiberius from Commagene.   150/350

1616.   AE 28 mm. worn coin probably of Antioch.
Obv: Five contermarks, two are XII, one is a thunderbolt, one is a
      bust l., and one that may be a standing figure.   200/350
   a. XIIF countermark on a 26 mm coin of Hadrian struck in Cae-
      sarea in Cappadocia

1617.   AE 19 mm. Coin of Jewish War, fourth year (No. 1369).
XV in rectangular countermark.   UNIQUE
   *At first glance the countermark appears to read XVI. However, careful ex-
amination shows that what looks like an "I" is really the side of the rectangle
enclosing the countermark. Furthermore, countermarks of a Sixteenth Legion
are not known to exist.*

CHAPTER TWELVE

NEW TESTAMENT COINS

COINS OF JESUS AND HIS WORLD

Coins of his time can help us to better reconstruct the world in which Jesus lived as well as the man himself. First one must consider two important variables, namely the time and place that Jesus was born.

Volumes could be (and have been) written about these topics. British historian Michael Grant writes in his book *JESUS: An Historian's View of the Gospels* that, "The belief that he was born in CE 1 came into existence in the sixth century CE when a monk from South Russia living in Italy, Dionysius Exiguus, made a mathematical miscalculation. His birth-date should be reassigned to 6 or 5 or 4 BCE, though some prefer 11 or 7."[1]

About the place of Jesus's birth, Grant says, "There is also a notorious difficulty about determining Jesus' birthplace. For whereas Matthew and Luke name it as Bethlehem, which the Christian world has accepted, the Gospel of John takes a different view...(that) Jesus came from Galilee. The same Gospel also indicates that his place of origin in that country was Nazareth. Mark seems to imply agreement..."[2]

As mentioned earlier, struck coins were invented in Western Asia Minor late in seventh century BCE, and they were introduced in the ancient Near East early in the fifth century BCE. However, coins did not replace the previous economic systems of barter and weighed metal overnight. It was an evolutionary process.[3] By the first century CE, coins were widely used in parallel with the older systems.[4]

Jesus was well aware of the importance of money, whether coins or other forms of currency. During his life, bronze coins of various denominations were manufactured in the Galilee, Judaea, and Samaria, and various silver coins also circulated in these areas even though none were manufactured there. (Gold coins were also used, but they represented large sums of money, and were used mainly in commercial transactions and especially for war expenses.) Bronze coins were widely used, but silver coins were less common, and were used in larger transactions as well as in paying the annual Temple dues. Since Jesus traveled widely in these lands, he was familiar with the use of money in both large and small transactions.

Rev. Rogers points out that Jesus often drew lessons from the "common use and existence of money. For [God] it is part of human life and human intercourse and therefore it is the concern of God. For the numismatist his study accordingly acquires an importance and a sanction, which dignify it as nothing else can."[5]

"It is only natural," Rogers writes, "that many, beyond the somewhat narrow circle of numismatists, should want to know as accurately as possible what this money is; should want to possess it, should want at least to have it so described as to be able to visualize it for themselves."

Rogers' discussion remains true in spite of nearly a century of additional research: "Unhappily there is very little trustworthy account of New Testament monies. Wholesale criticism may seem impertinent, but it does remain true that many first rate commentaries of the Bible, and Dictionaries of the Bible, are woefully misinformed in their account of New Testament money."[6]

THE POOR WIDOW'S MITES

We know very little about the poor widow's mites, made famous by the story in Mark 12:41–44.

And Jesus sat over against the treasury, and beheld how the people cast money into the treasury: and many that were rich cast in much. And there came a certain poor widow, and she threw in two mites (λεπτόν), which make a farthing (κοδράντης). And he called unto him his disciples, and saith unto them, Verily I say unto you, That this poor widow hath cast more in, than all they which have cast into the treasury: For all they did cast in of their abundance; but she of her want did cast in all that she had…

The story is repeated more succinctly in Luke 21:1–4:

And he looked up and saw the rich men casting their gifts into the treasury. And he saw also a certain poor widow casting in thither two mites. And he said...

The term "mite" first appears in the books of Mark and Luke in the initial publication of *Tyndale's New Testament*, published in 1525, where it was probably intended as a shortened version of the word "minute" and not as the name of a denomination. As Fr. Spijkerman has noted, the word *lepton* "implies very small coins...even we may say...the smallest coin being in circulation in Palestine at the time concerned."[7]

It is not surprising that scholars who did early translations of the Bible to English had a tendency to "reinterpret the ancient coin denominations of the Greek, Latin, and Hebrew scriptural sources in terms of contemporary sixteenth- and seventeenth-century English money,"[8] according to Oliver Hoover, who discusses this in detail and points out that neither the original Greek text of the New Testament nor the Latin Vulgate Bible, mention the "mite." Instead the Greek or Latin words refer to either *lepta* or *minuta,* respectively.

The word "mite" was most widely spread in the King James version of the Bible, printed in 1611, after translation efforts by 47 scholars that lasted nearly seven years. "Not only would this translation become one of the most popular English versions of the Bible ever published, but the artistry of its language ensured that it would also become one of the greatest single influences on the development of English literature well into the twentieth century," Hoover explains.

The translators wished their work to "speak like itself, as in the language of Canaan, that it may be understood even of the very vulgar." For this reason, the King James Bible and some earlier English translations are of "some interest to numismatists, given their tendency to reinterpret the ancient coin denominations of the Greek, Latin, and Hebrew scriptural sources in terms of contemporary sixteenth and seventeenth-century English money. Thus, in a small way, the King James Version serves as a document for the circulating coinage of early modern Great Britain," Hoover writes.

However, there was no *mite* coin known in British coinage of this period. "In fact, the *mite* (meaning "small cut piece" in Old Dutch) was only created as a circulating coin of Flanders in the fourteenth century.

Initially, the *mite* was a small billon coin...but by the sixteenth century it had become copper," he notes.

One might guess, therefore, that this denomination was imported and used in Britain at the time, but "there is little evidence to support this possibility," Hoover says. Even though the Dutch mite did not circulate in Britain, and no British *mites* existed, the *mite* was mentioned in sixteenth-century arithmetic books as a fraction of a *farthing*, varying from one-third to one-sixteenth.

It seems quite "likely that the mite has entered into the King James Version...as a result of a translational quandary created by the original..." Hoover says.

In these early versions, Mark gives the value of two *lepta* as a *kodrantes* or *quadrans*. But Hoover pinpoints the crunch: while "any Latin grammarian would have known that a *quadrans* was a bronze coin worth one-fourth of a Roman *as*, making its English translation as *farthing* (one-fourth of a *penny*) almost unavoidable. Unfortunately, in the English coinage system there were no denominations smaller than a *farthing*, creating the problem of how to deal with Mark's *lepta / minuta*."

Thus there was no British parallel for any coin smaller than a *farthing,* and there is a good chance that the arithmetic term *mite* was now brought into play. Hoover also speculates, however, that possibly

12.1. Fourteen various dies and strikes of the many styles of small *prutot* of Jannaeus (No. 1153) or successors, which have come to be known as *mites*.

William Tyndale's pre-King James translation might "have been a little influenced by the contemporary Flemish monetary system when he chose his words. After all, Tyndale is known to have had good Flemish connections, and he composed and printed his translation of the New Testament while in the nearby German cities of Hamburg, Cologne, and Worms. In 1534, Antwerp became his home and a base for shipping his contraband translations into Tudor England, until he was finally arrested and executed for heresy in 1536. Thus, Tyndale is likely to have been conversant with the Flemish currency system, in which there were twenty-four *mites* to the *penning*."

It is logical that people who are interested in the stories of the Bible would want to know more about these coins and exactly which coins could be associated with the stories.

Madden, in 1864, wrote that "The *mite*...was the smallest coin current in Palestine in the time of our Lord."

In 1914, Rogers wrote that "it is natural to conclude that the coins being cast into the treasury were strictly Jewish coins....the choice of strictly Jewish copper is accordingly limited to the coins of the Hasmonean or the Herodian families....and with some degree of certainty it may be said that the popular coins for this purpose were the small copper of Alexander Jannaeus and his successors..."

Whatever its origin, the poor widow's *mite* has become one of the most frequently referenced and most popular ancient biblical coin.

Here are two things we know about the widow's *mite* story, as related by both Mark and Luke:

- It is certainly a story about charity and goodwill, rather than a story about money. The poor woman gave all she had to the treasury of the Jewish Temple in Jerusalem, while, relatively speaking, many rich people gave little of themselves.
- The amount of money the widow threw into the Temple treasury was two coins of the smallest size in existence in Jerusalem at that time. There is no doubt that the small *prutah* (Nos. 1152, 1153) or half-*prutah* (Nos. 1134, 1138, 1147, 1185–87) coins of the Hasmonean kings and Herod the Great, fit that description. The most common coin among them, easily by a factor of more than 1000 to 1, is the small *prutah* of Jannaeus and possibly his successors.

The massive issue of these tiny bronze pieces in this poor land filled a market need. These coins first struck around 78 BCE under Jannaeus, and may have continued through the reign of his wife and successor Salome Alexandra.

During the first century, the *sheqel* was made up of 256 *prutot*. Consider that there are 100 *cents* to the *dollar*, hence this amount was very small change indeed. In those days one pomegranate cost only a *prutah* and, after all, pomegranates grew wild and could be plucked off trees in many areas (as they can today in Israel) for free.

Even though these coins were struck in the first century BCE, *prutot* continued to circulate well into the first century when Jesus lived, but also through the fourth century as well. This has been shown by archaeological excavations in Israel.[9] When I worked as numismatist at the Joint Sepphoris excavation in 1985, we found the small *prutot* of Jannaeus in the same areas as fourth-century Roman bronze coins. These were useful pieces of small change, at a time and place that small change was not easy to find[10] (note that many late Roman and Byzantine small bronze coins that were chopped in halves and quarters to accommodate the market need[11]).

Another aspect of the story of the poor widow's mite remains relevant today. Many people of great means contribute little to charitable causes, while less wealthy individuals contribute a great deal relative to their ability. This is a topic fit for everyone to ponder.

SHEQELS OF TYRE

The *sheqels* and half-*sheqels* of Tyre (also called *tetradrachms* and *didrachms*) were first issued as autonomous silver coins of the city after it was freed from Seleucid domination in 126/5 BCE. They were patterned after the Seleucid coins with an eagle on the reverse, but the inscription no longer included the name of a king, and was replaced with the name and titles of the city: "of Tyre the holy and city of refuge." Tyre's chief god, Herakles-Melqart, took the place of the king's bust. A date, according to Tyre's era, beginning in 126/5 BCE appears along with various monograms of uncertain meaning.

Tyrian *sheqels* and half-*sheqels* were prescribed as the coins of choice for payments to the Jerusalem Temple, including the half-*sheqel* tribute that every Jewish male over the age of twenty was obliged to pay (EXODUS 30:11–16; MISHNAH SHEKALIM 2,4), individual contributions and vows, as well as the redemption-price of the first-born, and the purchase of sacrificial offerings.

The coins of Tyre were so commonly used in Judaea in the first century that the Tosefta, another compilation of oral law from the time of the Mishnah, says that "Silver, wherever mentioned in the Pentateuch, is Tyrian silver. What is Tyrian silver? It is a Jerusalemite" (TOSEFTA KETUBBOT 13,20).[12]

A frequently asked question is why the Jews felt comfortable using Tyre coinage that depicted the graven image of a pagan god to make their annual payment to the Temple. The reason for this is, as the Mishnah makes clear, that valid money is not subject to being unclean, and is only susceptible to uncleanliness when it is used for another purpose such as jewelry or a weight (KELIM 12,7). Since a viable coin cannot be defiled, the only relevance is its value and purity, not its design.

Brooks Levy, a leading scholar of Tyre *sheqels*, has examined the question of when the Jerusalem Temple tax began: "It is agreed that the passage in Exodus is a late feature of the book, and in any case the tax there was not to be annual, but levied on the occasion of a national census. Not until the time of Nehemiah, that is, in the later fifth century, is it first described as a yearly levy. There, the sum to be given is not a half but a third-*sheqel*, which may reflect the currency system of the Persian Empire, in whose domain the newly built temple then lay (NEHEMIAH 10:32). But many scholars believe that the regular collection of an annual tax dates only from the time of the Maccabees—from the late second or even the late first century BCE. It has been argued that only then was there a large and stable enough Judaean state to make such an effort possible."[13]

However, Levy suggests that the collection of the annual tax began earlier rather than later: "It seems clear that it wasn't the inhabitants of Judaea but Diaspora Jews who were the main contributors, and some Diaspora communities—certainly those of Babylonia and Egypt— went back very far. Josephus and Philo attest to the importance of the evidently well-established tax-bearing embassies that came from these areas in their day, the first century CE."[14]

Tyre, as a mother city to a widespread group of colonies, also received annual offerings. This method of tribute was certainly visible to the Jews as well as the Samaritans, Tyre's closer neighbors. Levy cites two inscriptions from the island of Delos[15] as well as a passage in Josephus,[16] which indicate that "Samaritan diasporas in Egypt and on Delos were sending offerings to Jerusalem's rival temple on Mt. Gerizim possibly as far back as the early second century BCE. The

Delian inscriptions speak of the Samaritan offerings as *aparkhai* –
literally 'first fruits,' but in fact money is doubtless meant."

As a parallel, Levy points out that the Jewish-Egyptian historian
Philo specifically refers to the Jewish half-*sheqel* offerings as *aparkhai*.
He also refers to the distant Jewish communities as "colonies," *apoikiai*,
although these communities were not political colonies as they were in
the case of Tyre. Levy believes that "this could reflect a Tyrian model –
for both Samaritan and Jewish practice. An early beginning of annual
offerings would explain why Tyre's autonomous coinage so closely
imitates the Seleucid issues that immediately preceded it. These, like
the Tyrians, are commonly found in Judaea, and could have served for
the Temple tax, as the only silver currency readily available to Jews."

Once Rome took over the area that contained Jerusalem, there was
quite a different aspect to the Jewish Temple tax, Levy suggests. This
was Rome's attempt to block the export of funds to Jerusalem from
Jewish inhabitants of the outlying Greek communities in the Roman
Empire. Levy cites seven documents, one in Cicero (*Pro Flacco*), and six
in Josephus (*Ant.* XVI: 172–3) concerning this topic. In Cicero's day,
Rome apparently halted exports from Italy. But later, according to the
documents Josephus offers us, Roman officials, responding to Jewish
complaints, ordered the Greek communities of Asia Minor to allow
the export of these moneys, thus respecting the ancestral customs of
the Jews.[17]

Why did official Rome change its mind on this matter? Levy attributes this to "an abiding Roman respect for alien religious customs,
especially when provably ancient. But it was an equally high Roman
priority to reward active loyalty. In Rome's Civil Wars, Jewish troops
in the East helped Caesar against Pompey. Later Herod the Great, after
the defeat of Mark Antony, switched his support to Augustus, and received the latter's trust and friendship until almost the end of Herod's
long reign."

Indeed, Levy notes, "Augustus's own final pronouncement on the
subject even defines those who take such money from its collection
point in synagogues as temple robbers, an accusation that carried very
heavy penalties. This general picture is confirmed by Philo (*De specialibus legibus* 1,77), who attests that it was Augustus who authorized Jews
everywhere to send their *aparkhai* to Jerusalem."[18]

The Romans changed their tune once again after the destruction
of the Temple in 70 CE, when Josephus reports that Titus reproached
the defeated Jews: "We permitted you to exact tribute for God and to

collect offerings, without either admonishing or hindering those who brought them—only that you might grow richer at our expense and make preparations with our own wealth to attack us."[19]

From this background Levy draws two interesting conclusions. First, Rome sanctioned the annual half-*sheqel* tax for the Jerusalem Temple, and also potentially much greater free-will offerings, "making the privilege a much more generous one than most modern scholars have supposed. In fact the permissions recorded in Josephus's documents never use the word 'tax'... but only the broader term 'sacred money.' "

Her second conclusion, farther reaching for the Jewish community in the ancient world, is that Titus referred to this sacred money as "our wealth," and this shows that ultimately Rome controlled the money supply. Indeed after the Jewish War the half-*sheqel* Jewish tax was continued, but now it was paid to Rome.

The minting place of the Tyre *sheqels* has been a subject of discussion since Meshorer's revolutionary concept, published in 1982, that Herod the Great and the authorities at the Jerusalem Temple feared a cessation of minting in Tyre, and transferred this issue to a mint in Jerusalem in around 19/18 BCE. At this time, Meshorer observed, the letters KAP, shortened to KP after the first few years, appeared on virtually all of the Tyre *sheqels*, where various initials or monograms had appeared on earlier coins. He suggested the letters KP abbreviated *Kratos Romaion* (power of the Romans).

One of Meshorer's principal arguments was based on the decline in style of Tyre *sheqels* of the later type. He believed this degradation was due to the lack of skill of Jewish mintmasters, not to mention their disinterest in the pagan designs that they treated with disdain. He referred to them as barbaric and clunky, and suggested their smaller, thicker shape hinted they were direct predecessors to the thick *sheqels* struck by the Jews during the Jewish War.[20]

Levy, on the other hand, offers evidence that these stylistically crude coins, often difficult to read, were not struck at the end of the series, but earlier.[21] She also believes that "it is unlikely that the Roman government would have countenanced the permanent transfer of a prestigious allied city's coinage to the capital of Herod's Judaea. Within the coin series itself there is no sign of a stylistic break at the proposed moment of transfer, nor of consistent and gradual later deterioration. Since it seems that users of the *sheqel* became increasingly limited to those who paid the Temple tax, a concentration of find-spots in Judaea should not surprise us; but in fact, the largest single find of *sheqels*—the Usfiye hoard of over 4,000 pieces, closing in 53/4 CE—was buried much closer to Tyre than Jerusalem. Finally, the *sheqel* of Israel differs in fabric from its predecessors at least as much as it resembles it."[22]

The Usfiye hoard was named after the Druze village in which it was found, around five miles southeast of Haifa. The coins in the hoard ranged from 38 BCE to 54 CE and in addition to the Tyre *sheqels* and half-*sheqels* there were 157 Augustan and three Tiberian *denarii*. Much of the group found its way into the markets, but the Israel Antiquities Authority has the largest component, around 700 coins, along with records of much of the rest of the group.

In 1963, at a Jerusalem symposium convened to celebrate the discovery of the Usfiye hoard, Israeli numismatist Gerhard Cohn observed that some 15 percent of the Tyre *sheqels* and half-*sheqels* were of the crude and difficult to date variety. "We don't know what to make of these. Normally, at the end of a certain period there is a deterioration," Cohn said. Leo Kadman (who died during the opening ceremony of this symposium) and later Meshorer agreed with this chronology, placing the "crude" pieces after the hoard's dated issues.

Yet Cohn made another relevant observation—that the Usfiye hoard contained no datable coins from the years 23 through 29 CE. Levy focuses on this issue and notes that "there were (with one exception) no Tyrians between 20/21 and 34/35 in the Jerusalem hoards reported by Ariel. The excavations at Gamla, in an otherwise quite full year-by-year representation of later Tyrians…lack issues from 21 through 34." Other smaller hoards confirm these observations. Thus Levy concludes that either the Tyrian mint was producing very little and very poor work from 21 through 33, or wasn't working at all.[23]

This suggests that Kadman's, Cohn's, and later Meshorer's ideas about the late issue of all the crude Tyre *sheqels* can no longer be taken for granted. It must be decided where such pieces belong: in the 20s, at the end of the series, or both. Levy thinks it probable that close comparison of undatable pieces with datable will show that many of the former actually belong in the 20s. These observations of the chronology, especially that the "crude" pieces did not appear at the end of the series, weigh in favor of the production of these coins having remained at Tyre throughout the series.

Levy notes that thought must be given to the techniques by which such pieces were produced. Some examples seem to come from more or less brutally reworked authentic dies—or possibly from crudely touched-up dies made by molding from earlier coins. On some it seems that recutting was chiefly, though not exclusively, applied to the reverses. This bias suggests that the aim of recutting was not so much legibility as sharpness in the "legible" areas that would allow the coins to be assessed at full value.

Levy observes, "the ancient term used to describe a sharp coin was a tactile one that might also be used, say, for the feel of a cat's tongue: *asper* in Latin, *aspros* in Greek. The few known applications of this term to coinage are clustered between about 50 and 150 CE [for example] in a text associated with Nero, who was said to demand his tax money in sharp coin, *nummus asper* (Suetonius, *Nero*, 44: 2.)" In the Talmud the rabbis suggest that if a person redeems a worn *tetradrachm* in change for *prutot*, he must estimate the coin at its worn (intrinsic) value, but if he uses the coin to pay the Second Temple Tithe he can give the coin the value as if it is unworn.[24] This shows there was significant attention paid to worn silver coins. Even though the late Tyre *sheqels* were crude, if they were not worn and were made of good silver they may have been acceptable for the Temple tax where a Roman *denarius* or a *tetradrachm* of Roman Antioch would not. If so, that is, another sign of how seriously the Mosaic prescription was taken.

The definition of "good silver" is a key point here for fineness, not degree of wear alone, now determined the value of a coin. It is well known that Ptolemaic and Seleucid coinage, as well as Roman Imperial coinage from Augustus's day on, became increasingly debased. Thus it is highly significant, Levy says, that as other civic issues of the region petered out or grew baser, Tyre alone annually struck silver over 90 percent fine until the outbreak of the Jewish War. "When Josephus tells us that the Tyrian *tetradrachm* of his day is worth four Attic *drachmas* (*BJ* 2: 592), he is referring not to its weight (well below traditional Attic) but to the amount of silver it contains. It is significant that the only other coin of which he says this is the legendary 'holy *sheqel*' of Exodus 30 (*Ant.* 3: 195)."[25] This passage confirms Mishnaic statements that only Tyrian silver could be used for the Temple tax.

Discussion of the Tyre *sheqels* and half-*sheqels* of various styles will continue for many years to come. Still to be explained is the enigmatic KP monogram. Whether the "late series" of the *sheqels* and half-*sheqels* of Tyre were actually minted in Tyre or Jerusalem becomes slightly less relevant when one recognizes that the coins in this series struck after about 20 BCE were almost certainly issued, at least in part, to help the Jews satisfy their needs to pay dues to the Jerusalem Temple in appropriate coinage.

In fact, among the various monograms and control marks, there are a number that can be translated to the letters HPΔ from coins struck in the years 27, 25, 20, 19, and 17 BCE. The letters HΣ are used in the years 19 and 18 BCE, and a symbol that may represent the Phoenician H (*het*) is used from 14 to 11 BCE. Levy says, "None of these marks appear anywhere else in the series. All could stand for the name Herod (*Herodes*)."[26]

The minting of the Tyre *sheqels* was halted with the onset of the Jewish War in 65/66 CE, although there are occasional reports of coins that are said to be dated as late as 69/70. Since many of the later Tyre *sheqels* are extremely crude and difficult to decipher, any dates after the beginning of the Jewish War are problematic.

THE 30 PIECES OF SILVER

> *Then one of the 12, called Judas Iscariot, went unto the chief priests, and said unto them, What will ye give me, and I will deliver him unto you? And they covenanted with him for 30 pieces of silver* (MATTHEW 26:14–15).

It is logical to assume that the "30 pieces of silver" paid to Judas were Tyre *sheqels*, since these coins were the most commonly used and accepted large silver coins at the time.

Michael Grant concludes that payment was made to Judas for his deed, even if the amount may not have been exactly 30 pieces of silver: "Although the report that his fee was 30 pieces of silver is dubious because, like so much else in this part of the Gospels, it is an echo of the scriptures, it is probable enough that Judas was paid for what he did."

Here are some mentions of the same sum in earlier books of the Bible:

> *If the ox gore a bondman or a bondwoman, he shall give unto their master thirty sheqels of silver, and the ox shall be stoned* (EXODUS 21:32).

> *And I said unto them: "If ye think good, give me my hire; and if not, forbear." So they weighed for my hire thirty pieces of silver. And the*

Lord said unto me: "Cast it into the treasury, the goodly price that I was prized at of them." And I took the thirty pieces of silver and cast them into the treasury, in the house of the Lord (Zechariah 11:12, 13).

Requirements to use Tyre *sheqels* and half-*sheqels* in the Jerusalem Temple indirectly led to Jesus's disgust at the money changers in the Temple court. When Jewish pilgrims came to Jerusalem from around the ancient world they carried money of their own nations, and had to make a currency exchange.

The money changers set up in an area close to the Temple. In calling out for business—their form of advertising—these merchants often shouted their exchange rates. Jesus found this commercialism crass and offensive so near the Temple, so he threw over the tables of these merchants.

The Coin in the Fish's Mouth

As a practicing and observant Jew, Jesus was aware of his annual obligation to the Temple. This tax is nicely illustrated in the parable of the coin in the fish's mouth.

Each year, Jewish officials requested the annual Temple contribution at the beginning of the month of Adar, preceding Passover. On the fifteenth day of Adar, tables of the money-changers (discussed on pages 20–24) were set up throughout the country to receive these contributions. After ten days, the money changers ceased their local collections and resumed operations at the Jerusalem Temple.[27]

Virtually all Jews, including those who had expressed reservations about the current state of the Temple, also sent their contributions. Matthew 17:24–27 tells how Jesus and his disciples were solicited and gave their contribution to the collectors of the Temple tribute:

And when they had come to Capernaum, those who collected the two-*drachm* tax came to Peter and said, "Does your teacher not pay the two-*drachm* tax?" He said, "Yes." And when he came into the house, Jesus spoke to him first, saying, "What do you think, Simon? From whom do the kings of the earth collect customs or poll-tax, from their sons or from strangers?" And upon his saying, "From strangers," Jesus said to him, "Consequently the sons are exempt. But, lest we give them offense, go to the sea, and throw in a hook, and take the first fish that comes up; and when you open its mouth you will find a *stater*.[28] Take that and give it to them for you and Me."

It seems clear from Matthew's report that the coin in the fish's mouth was a *sheqel* of Tyre since it was supposed to pay the annual half-*sheqel* Temple tribute for both Jesus and for Peter the fisherman, although the *kolbon* (pp. 20–24) is not mentioned.

SHEQELS OF TYRE

All with border of dots on both sides.
Tyre *sheqel* weight standard 14 g.
Era begins 126/125 BCE.
Axis is ↑.

1618

EARLY STYLE

1618.   AR *sheqel*.
   Obv: Laureate head of Melqart r., wears lion skin knotted around neck.
   Rev: ΤΥΡΟΥ ΙΕΡΑΣ ΚΑΙ ΑΣΥΛΟΥ *(of Tyre the holy and inviolable)* Eagle standing l. with r. foot on prow of ship, palm branch over r. shoulder, date and club are in field to l., a Phoenician letter between eagle's legs, in right field are letters or monogram. The dates range from 126/5 BCE to 20/19 BCE. (Drawing ΘΙ =19 = 108/7 BCE, photo LK = year 20 = 107/106 BCE.)   450/850
   a. ΖΝ = 57 = 69/68 BCE.

1619.   AR half-*sheqel*.
   Obv: Melqart as on 1618.
   Rev: Eagle as on 1618, date EM = 45 = 82/81 BCE.   350/750
   a. ΑΝ = 51 = 76/75 BCE.

KP ISSUES

1620

1620. AR *sheqel.*
Obv: Melqart as on 1618, but of a generally cruder fabric and style.
Rev: Eagle as on 1618, but of a generally cruder style, plus the Greek
  letters KP to the right of the eagle. The dates range from 19/18
  BCE to 65/66 CE, and possibly a few years later. (Drawing PKH =
  2/3 CE, photo PM = 140 = 14/15 CE.)   350/750
  a.   PΛϚ = 146 = 20/21 CE.
  b.   PΞH = 168 = 42/43 CE.

1621. AR half-*sheqel.*
Obv: Same as 1620.
Rev: Same as 1620. date PKΓ = 123 = 4/3 BCE.   350/750
  a. PΛB = 132 = 6/7 CE.

THE TRIBUTE PENNY

> *Is it lawful to give tribute to Caesar, or not? Shall we give, or shall
> we not give? But He, knowing their hypocrisy, said unto them, Why
> tempt ye me? Bring me a penny, that I may see it. And they brought it.
> And He saith unto them, Whose is this image and superscription? And
> they said unto Him, Caesar's. And Jesus, answering, said unto them,
> Render to Caesar the things that are Caesar's and to God the things
> that are God's (MARK 12:14–17).*

In this story Jesus was probably referring to a coin that was not local—
a silver coin with an image of Caesar, either Augustus or Tiberius.
Most numismatists suggests it was a *drachm* or *denarius*, the former a
Greek and the latter a Roman denomination. In either case these represent one-quarter of a *tetradrachm* or *sheqel*. Augustus reigned from 27
to 14 BCE. Tiberius reigned from 14 to 37 CE.

Thus at the death of Augustus in 14 BCE, Jesus was a young man of about 18. This means that during most of his ministry, Tiberius was the emperor, while Augustus was the emperor of Jesus' childhood.

The PONTIF MAXIM *denarius* represents more than 98 percent of the known *denarii* struck under Tiberius. The other two reverse types are quite rare and were used on coins by Tiberius for the first two years of his reign. After that, he employed only one type until his death in 37 CE. This most common type carries a portrait of the emperor on the obverse, along with the inscription TI CAESAR DIVI AVG F AVGVSTVS (Tiberius, Caesar Augustus, Son of the Divine Augustus), hence his "image and superscription." The reverse of these coins shows a seated female figure, with the inscription PONTIF MAXIM, or high priest, another of the emperor's titles and later a title of the Bishop of Rome.

Neither the Augustus nor the Tiberius *denarii* are common in excavations or in the markets of Israel, and there is no reason to believe they were common in ancient times. They show up from time to time, but not in any sizeable quantities. (The provincial *tetradrachms* of Augustus and Tiberius, also posited as possible options, don't show up too often either.)

With information available to them, scholars of biblical coins of the nineteenth century, such as the Reverends Rogers and Madden, both tentatively identified the Tiberius *denarius* as the most likely to have been the "Tribute penny." This choice was always done with plenty of caveats. Throughout the twentieth and into the twenty-first century, this remains the generally repeated wisdom.

We do not know more and probably never will. For those who want to show off a coin that was similar to the "Tribute penny" of Mark, either an Augustus or Tiberius *denarius* or a provincial *drachm* would qualify.

In the 1611 edition of the King James Bible, the word for *denarius* was translated to the Anglo-Saxon Britsh *penny*, the standard silver denomination of the time. The British have used the initial "d" (referring to *denarius*) as an abbreviation for *penny* or *pence* for hundreds of years.

The Greek equivalent to the silver *denarius* was the *drachm*, which was the same size and value in the Roman period. *Drachms* are also found in markets and excavations in the area of ancient Judaea and the Galilee. Here are some other references to the *denarius/drachm* denomination.

- Matthew 18:28. "But the same servant went out, and found one of his fellow servants, which owed him a hundred *pence*: and he laid hands on him, and took him by the throat saying, Pay me that thou owest."
- Matthew 20:2, 9, 10, 13. This is the parable of the laborers in the vineyard: "And when he had agreed with the laborers for a *penny* a day, he sent them into his vineyard."
- Mark 6:37. "He answered and said unto them, Give ye them to eat. And they say unto him, Shall we go and buy two hundred *penny*worth of bread, and give them to eat?"
- Mark 14:4–5. Judas asks about the value of the alabaster box of spikenard which the woman broke over Jesus's feet at Bethany: "Why was this waste of the ointment made? For it might have been sold for more than three hundred *pence*. . . ." (See also John 12:5.)
- Luke 7:41. Jesus puts the parable question to Simon: "There was a certain creditor which had two debtors: the one owed five hundred *pence*, and the other fifty. And when they had nothing to pay, he frankly forgave them both. Tell me therefore, which of them will love him most?"
- Luke 10:35. In the parable of the good Samaritan: "He took out two *pence*, and gave them to the host, and said unto him, Take care of him; and whatsoever thou spendest more, when I come again, I will repay thee."
- Luke 15:8–9. This is the parable of the woman sweeping her house for the lost piece of silver.
- Revelations 6:6. "A measure of wheat for a *penny*, and three measures of barley for a *penny*; and see thou hurt not the oil and the wine."

THE TRIBUTE PENNY

1622

1622. AR *denarius*.
   Obv: TI CAESAR DIVI AVG F AVGVSTVS; laureate bust of Tiberius r.
   Rev: PONTIF MAXIM; female figure (Livia?) sits on a plain chair r., she holds olive branch in her l. hand and long scepter in her r.

600/1,500

FARTHING

The *farthing* is another denomination mentioned in the King James version; of course, it was a common English denomination in the seventeenth century. The Greek words translated as *farthing* were *assarion* (MATTHEW 10:29; LUKE 12:6) and *kodrantes* (MATTHEW 5:26; MARK 12:42). This denomination may have been a *quadrans*, although some have suggested it was equivalent to the Roman *as*. Bronze coins of these denominations struck at Antioch were in abundance, and commonly circulated in the Holy Land.

- Matthew 5:26. "Till thou has paid the uttermost *farthing*."

- Matthew 10:29. "Are not two sparrows sold for a *farthing*?"

- Luke 12:6. "Are not five sparrows sold for two *farthings*?"

THE TRAVELS OF PAUL OF TARSUS

The apostle Paul was most responsible for helping to create a world-wide Church. He was a native of Tarsus, a Roman town with an established Jewish community. Paul was a traditional Jew, a follower of the famous Rabbi Gamaliel. His given name was Saul. In his early life, Saul joined in the persecution of the Jewish-Christians. In fact, he received letters from the high priest to introduce him to the synagogues of various groups in Damascus, so he could visit them and preach his basic form of Judaism.

Saul set out for Damascus, on the road to which he experienced the revelation that revolutionized Christianity. Now called Paul, the former persecutor of Jewish-Christians traveled far and wide preaching the Gospel of Jesus and encouraging conversion. Paul also widely disseminated a change in Christianity. Until that time, it was a basic concept that the only true believers in Jesus Christ were individuals who were Jews in the first place. Even Jesus espoused this:

These twelve Jesus sent out, charging them, 'Go nowhere among the Gentiles, and enter no town of the Samaritans, but go rather to the lost sheep of the house of Israel' (MATTHEW 10:5–6).

Paul, however, stressed the concept that a Gentile did not need to become a Jew in order to follow Jesus, leading to the famous agreement of Jerusalem, which eventually led to the complete break between the Christian Church and the Jewish Temple.

It is said that Paul was probably a dealer in woven goods and this activity explains the wide scope of his travels and missionary activities. Below, we list the places visited by Paul during his four major journeys. Most of these cities issued coins in ancient times, and collectors are often fond of assembling sets of coins from the cities of Paul's four journeys.

Paul's First Journey (ACTS 13:1–14:28)
Antioch, Seleucis-Pierea
Salamis, Cyprus
Paphos, Cyprus
Perga, Pamphylia
Antioch, Pisidia
Iconium, Lycaonia
Lycaonia
Lystra, Lycaonia
Derbe, Lycaonia

Paul's Second Journey (ACTS 15:36–18:22)
Antioch, Syria
Tarsus, Cilicia
Derbe, Lycaonia

Lystra, Lycaonia
Iconium, Lycaonia
Antioch, Pisidia
Troas
Neapolis, Macedonia
Philippi, Macedonia
Thessalonica, Macedonia
Beroea, Macedonia
Athens, Attica
Corinth, Corinthia
Ephesus, Ionia
Paphos, Cyprus
Caesarea, Samaria
Jerusalem, Judaea

Paul's Third Journey (Acts 18:23–21:16)
Antioch, Seleucis-Pierea
Iconium, Lycaonia
Ephesus, Ionia
Thessalonica, Macedonia
Corinth, Corinthia
Philippi, Macedonia
Miletus, Ionia
Rhodes
Paphos, Cyprus
Tyre, Phoenicia
Ptolemais, Phoenicia
Caesarea, Samaria
Jerusalem, Judaea

Paul's Voyage to Rome (Acts 15:36–18:22)
Caesarea, Samaria
Sidon, Phoenicia
Myra, Lycia
Crete
Malta
Syracuse, Sicily
Rhegium, Bruttium
Puteoli, Italy
Rome, Italy

SEVEN CHURCHES OF ASIA MINOR

The book of Revelation is named for John of Patmos' vision of Jesus, and his resulting commission to write about what he saw and heard. John received his vision on the tiny Aegean island of Patmos, where he found himself "on account of the word of God and the testimony of Jesus." This phrase probably means that John had been exiled because he was a Christian. Exile was one of Rome's most lenient punishments, used especially for notable or wealthy people. John sees the revelation on the "Lord's day."

At first, John hears a loud voice behind him; it commands him to write his visions in a book addressed to the seven churches of Asia Minor. The cities of the seven churches represent an interesting and historic series for collectors, and readers who wish to pursue these coins should refer to *Roman Provincial Coinage*, which offers a complete listing of the types.

Write in a book what you see, and send it to the seven churches: to Ephesus and to Smyrna and to Pergamum and to Thyatira and to Sardis and to Philadelphia and to Laodicea (REVELATIONS 1:11).

In response to the voice, John turns around and sees seven golden lamp stands. These lamps are reminiscent of the seven-branched menorah that stood in the Jerusalem Temple. In the midst of the lamp stands, John saw "one like a son of man" who had hair like white wool, eyes like flames, feet burnished like polished bronze, and a voice like the sound of rushing waters. He held seven stars in his right hand, a sharp sword came from his mouth, his face shown like the sun in full strength.

John collapses, paralyzed by fear. But, the figure urges John not to be afraid and identifies himself as Jesus. Each of the seven letters to the churches is introduced by a different visual or verbal attribute from John's vision of the description of Jesus.

Each of the seven letters is really a prophetic message conveyed by Jesus through John. However, the specific reason these seven churches were chosen is not known. There were certainly other important Christian churches in Asia Minor at this time. It is very possible that Paul established many, or even all, of these churches, although many of the seven cities are not specifically listed in any of his three journeys or his journey to Rome. After Jerusalem fell to Rome in 70 CE, this area both became one of the most important geographic centers of Christianity. There were already many Jews in Asia Minor in the Hellenistic period. Ironically, the earlier Seleucids liked to hire them and settle them there as mercenaries. Perhaps these seven churches were singled out because of specific problems or opportunities. Each one of them was within 100 miles of Ephesus in the Roman province of Asia, and they may have been part of a preaching circuit for itinerant Christian teachers and prophets.

Seven Churches of Asia Minor
Ephesus, Ionia
Smyrna, Ionia
Pergamum, Mysia
Thyatira, Lydia
Sardis, Lydia
Philadelphia, Lydia
Laodicia, Phrygia

12.2. Remains of the Roman Library of Celsus at Ephesus, Ionia, now Turkey. Ephesus and the Ephesians are mentioned more than 20 times in the New Testament. Ephesus was perhaps the most important city in Asia Minor. John's letter commends the Church of Ephesus for persevering amidst persecution by the Romans and for ostracizing evil men and false apostles. (Author photo.)

ENDNOTES

Chapter One: Collecting Biblical Coins

1. Madden 1864: iii.
2. Rogers 1914: 6–7.
3. Banks 1955: 1.
4. Sperber 2007: 435–436.
5. Danby 1933: 53, note 1.
6. I. (Zev) Goldstein, personal communication 2008–09.
7. Baba Metziah, 25b.
8. *Ibid*.
9. Art Scroll translation Talmud Baba Metzia, 25b, notes.
10. Dayan 1978: 111.
11. Abu Ali told me this story at least twice, each time in Arabic (he spoke little English, I speak little Arabic), through both Ya'akov Meshorer and Shraga Qedar, who acted as interpreters. However, when I wrote about this in a magazine after Abu Ali's death, my friend the Jerusalem attorney and numismatist Arnold Spaer wrote to say that he had been the attorney for Abu Ali for many years, and Abu Ali was absolutely not one of the finders of the Dead Sea Scrolls. After receiving Mr. Spaer's letter, I double checked with Qedar, since Meshorer had died, and he confirmed that he translated this story to me from Abu Ali himself, and said that he had also told this story at other times. I do not know why Mr. Spaer denied this on behalf of the deceased Abu Ali, but I include the story here because, as Moshe Dayan has noted (*ibid*. 1978), Abu Ali was not one to tell tall tales.
12. D.T. Ariel, personal communciation.
13. Mildenberg 1984.
14. www.menorahcoinproject.org
15. Barag 2000–02b: 153–156.
16. C. Lorber, personal communications 2009.
17. Meshorer 2001: 80.
18. Mildenberg 1984: 22.

19. According to Y. Meshorer (various personal communications 1976–2004), Israeli numismatists have used the word *perutah* (by Israelis who emigrated from Europe) or *prutah* (by native Israelis) since at least the late 1950s. Klimowsky (1963: 68–69) was the first to explain the term in this context.
20. *E.g.*, Mishnah Kiddushin, 1:1.
21. Houghton *et al.* II, Vol. II: 41.
22. Sperber 1974: 104.
23. In context (Mark 12:42) *lepton* seems to be a coin rather than a denomination, which is the usage modern students have applied to the term. Although the word is used in the New Testament, it is never mentioned in the Talmud. The term *lepton* is further discussed in Burnett *et al. RPC* I: 31.
24. Kindler 1967: 186.
25. Klimowsky 1963: 68–69.
26. Hendin 2010.
27. Meshorer (2001: 30) was specifically discussing the Jannaeus anchor/star-in-diadem coin (*TJC*–K, *GBC*–469). From our data, however, it is clear that the same range existed for every issue that we have studied.
28. Meshorer (2001: 71) states that "The decisive factors in determining the denominations in a series of coins are their relative weights and designs that appear on them." Here he refers specifically to the four coins in the Herodian dated series. While the weights of these denominations certainly overlap, one may be absolutely certain which coin is being dealt with because the motifs are quite different.
29. Flan strips were cast in chalkstone molds (Meshorer 2001: 50). The space for each flan was drilled, but the controls for measuring the exact depth of the drilling were not accurate and some coins are more than double the thickness of others, with a resultant increase in weight.
30. As Lorber suggests (2009, personal communication), the lack of weight control for bronze coins is one of our major clues that they were fiduciary currency.
31. Hill 1914: xcv.
32. If indeed no coins were issued in Judaea between the death of Jannaeus and the rule of Mattatayah Antigonus (40–37 BCE), there would have been a gap of 36 years without coins being struck by Jewish rulers, which seems like a very long period.
33. Bijovsky 2002: 202.
34. Seaford notes (2004: 145), "The result is the paradox that even coinage of unadulterated silver (let alone bronze) may tend to become in effect fiduciary coinage: although the silver contributes to confidence, it is not envisaged as a commodity. And so whereas we frequently hear of metal artefacts being melted down to make coins, we do not hear of Greek coins being melted down by Greeks to create bullion or artefacts."

35. Van Alfen 2009.
36. Hendin (2007–8) for a discussion of these matters regarding Hasmonean coinage.
37. Mørkholm *et al.* 1991: 6.
38. *Ibid.*
39. I Maccabees 16: 6 for the grant, discussed further in *RPC* I, *TJC*, and *GBC*.
40. Baba Metziah 55: 1, which states that it is forbidden to steal even an amount less than a *prutah*, but if one does steal less than a *prutah* he cannot be subpoenaed to court. At the same time, he must answer to God even for such a tiny transgression.
41. Meshorer: 2001: 176. Judaean coins of various types have been discovered in excavations as distant as Antioch, Dura Europos, Athens, and Cyprus.
42. Baba Metziah 44b.
43. Baba Metziah 46a.
44. Since the Herodian coinage, like the Hasmonean coinage before it, was both fiduciary and intended for local circulation, this is credible. An earlier, possibly relevant parallel from a fourth century BCE inscription from Olbia proclaims that only Olbian coinage may be used within the polis and sets exchange rates for various foreign coinages (Dittenberger 1915: 218).
45. C. Lorber, personal communications, 2009.
46. Meshorer 2001: 33.
47. Seaford 2004: 144.
48. Sperber 1974.

Chapter Two: Balance Weights to Coinage

1. Today we think of cattle as cows. But the classic definition of cattle also, included all domestic quadrupeds, including sheep, goats, horses, mules, asses, and swine.
2. Petruso 1981: 44.
3. Qedar 2001: 23.
4. Powell 1992: 899.
5. Scott 1959: 32.
6. Petruso 1992: 18.
7. Heltzer 1996: 33.
8. Parise 1989: 27.
9. Powell 1979: 88.
10. Scott 1959: 32–33.
11. Kokhavi: 1969: 40.
12. Biran & Gophna 1970: 151–169.
13. Qedar 2001: 23.

14. Powell 1992: 906.
15. *Ibid.*
16. Meshorer 1978: 31.
17. *cf.* Gittin & Golani 2001: 43, Gitler & Tal 2006: 11, Van Alfen 2005: 21.
18. Powell 1979: 8.
19. Yeivin 1990: 43–57.
20. Avi Yonah 1975: 374.
21. Dever 2001: 50.
22. Meshorer 1961: 185.
23. Stern 1982: 215.
24. *Ibid.*
25. Mays 1988: 574.
26. Kletter 2001: 8.
27. Dayton 1974: 44.
28. Hafford 2005: 367.
29. Dayton 1974: 43.
30. Pulak 1996: 17.
31. Powell 1979: 83.
32. Leemans 1950: 14.
33. Pulak 1996: 281.
34. Hafford 2005: 347.
35. Kletter 1998: 49, 51.
36. *Ibid.*: 101.
37. Meshorer 1978: 131–33.
38. Kletter 1998: 37.
39. *Ibid.*: 119.
40. Scott 1985: 198.
41. Kletter 1998: 127.
42. *Ibid.*: 101.
43. Hendin 2007a.

CHAPTER THREE: PERSIAN PERIOD: PHILISTIA

1. Hill 1914: lxxxiii.
2. Gitler & Tal 2002: 35.
3. Mildenberg 1992: 33–40.
4. Gitler & Tal 2002: 9.
5. *Ibid.*
6. *Ibid.*
7. Mildenberg 1992: 36.
8. *Ibid.*: 39.
9. Tal 2007: 17–28.
10. Hendin 2007a: 91, and pp. 184–189 for photos and descriptions of a similar, extensive group of bronze weights, many with Phoenician letters.

11. Tal, 2007: 25
12. Nevo 2001: 31.
13. Stern 1982: 217.
14. Tal 2007: 25.
15. Tal 2007: 26.
16. Friedman, T. *NY Times*, 1987.
17. Rappaport 1970: 75–76.
18. Gitler and Tal 2006: 130.
19. Gitler and Tal 2009: 21–38.
20. Gitler *et al.* 2007: 47.
21. Tal, 2007: 18–19.
22. Gitler & Tal 2006: 312–313.
23. Meshorer and Qedar 1991: 67.
24. Gitler and Tal 2006: 312.
25. *Ibid.*: 172.

Chapter Four: The Persian Period: Samaria and Judah

1. Meshorer & Qedar 1999: 19.
2. Meshorer and Qedar 1991: 9.
3. Miller & Hayes 1986: 336–338.
4. Meshorer & Qedar 1991: 1.
5. *Ibid.*: 11.
6. Shen 2004: 248–260.
7. Quoted in Johnson 1987: 85.
8. Roth 1954: 58–59.
9. Barag 1966 : 6–12.
10. Gitler and Tal 2006: 11, regarding double darics; single daric, personal communication with Y. Meshorer.
11. Meshorer 1982 I: 31–33.
12. Ronen, 2007, published an additional 20 previously unrecorded Samaritan coins.
13. Meshorer & Qedar 1991: 65.
14. *Ibid.*: 9–10 & 1999: 15.
15. *Ibid.*: 20.
16. *Ibid.*: 25.
17. *Ibid.*: 31.
18. Meshorer & Qedar 1999: 34.
19. *Ibid.*: 21.
20. *Ibid.*: 22.
21. *Ibid.*: 23.
22. Spaer 1986–87: pl. 2:1–2.
23. Meshorer & Qedar 1999: 23–24.
24. Josephus Ant. XI: 302.

25. Meshorer & Qedar 1999: 28.
26. Sukenik 1934: 178–182.
27. Mildenberg 1979: 183–196.
28. *Ibid.*
29. Meshorer 1982: 13.
30. Spaer 1977: 200–203.
31. Barag 1993, in which he makes this same suggestion.
32. Meshorer 1982 I: 115.4 and Meshorer 2001: 197.6.
33. Meshorer 1967, 116.
34. Mildenberg 1994–99: 15–16.
35. Meshorer 2001: 8.
36. *Ibid.*: 13.
37. Ronen 1998: 122–123.
38. *Ibid.*
39. *Ibid*: 124.
40. Hendin 2007a: 80–86 for a further discussion.
41. Ronen 2003–06: 29 says the exception that proves this rule is a single known example of a base-metal Yehud coin with no traces of silver plating at all, so it may indeed have even been a trial strike.
42. Hoover 2007a: 155.
43. Ronen 2003–06: 30.
44. Gitler & Lorber 2006: 1–41.
45. Ronen 1998: 124.
46. Ariel 2002 and Gitler/Lorber 2006: 6.
47. Tal: 2007: 26.
48. Gitler & Lorber 2008: 61–82.
49. Fontanille & Lorber 2008.
50. Gitler & Lorber 2008: 70–73.
51. Porter *et al.* 2004.
52. Hendin 2007a: 144.
53. Gitler & Lorber 2006: 16–18.
54. Barag 1994–1999b: 29.
55. *Ibid.*: 37.
56. Gerson 2001: 119.
57. *Ibid.*
58. Barag 1986–87: 20.
59. Fontanille, 2008.
60. Hendin 2007b: 42 ff.
61. This person is not the governor of Judaea in the late fifth century BCE, named Bagohi, whose name is mentioned in the Elephantine papyri.
62. Barag 1993: 264.
63. Gitler & Tal 2002: 230.
64. Gerson 2001: 100.
65. Ronen 2010: 39–45.
66. Josephus *Against Apion* I: 186–187 (22).

Chapter Five: Macedonian, Ptolemaic, & Seleucid Coins

1. Josephus *Ant.*, XI: 321.
2. *Ibid.*, XI: 328.
3. *Ibid.*, XI: 329–339.
4. Yoma 69a.
5. Primary source of this story is the Letter of Aristeas translated and reported in Josephus, *Ant.* XII: 55–60.
6. Barag 1994–99: 27–38.
7. Josephus *Against Apion* II: 48.
8. Josephus *Ant.* XII: 130–131.
9. Barag 1994–1999: 37.
10. Josephus *Ant.* XII: 140.
11. II Maccabees 4: 9–10.
12. II Maccabees 4: 15–16.
13. I Maccabees 1: 15.
14. Josephus *Ant.* XII: 385.
15. I Maccabees 37–40.
16. II Maccabees 6: 1–2.
17. Hoover 2007b: 77–88.
18. Barag 2000–2002a: 59–77.
19. SC II, I: 546–547.

Chapter Six: Hasmonean Coins

1. Many of Jerusalem's citizens "placed no value on their hereditary dignities, but cared above everything for Hellenic honors." (II Maccabees 4: 15–16). The High Priest Jason had built a Greek-style athletic stadium in the Tyropoeon Valley, a stone's throw from the Temple. There was no law against Jewish youths participating in the games. However, all athletes who participated in the games were required to be naked. This was abhorrent to the religious Jews, and the problems became more severe when a number of Jewish athletes had surgical operations that "made themselves uncircumcised" (I Maccabees 1: 15) in order to save embarrassment during competitions. On the other hand, these Hellenized Jews must not have been a very large number, since in order to coerce the Jews to his way of thinking, "Day after day [Antiochus IV] tortured distinguished citizens and publicly flaunted the spectacle of a captured city, until his criminal excesses provoked the victims to reprisals." (Josephus: BJ I: 35).
2. "Hasmonean," is another name for the family of Judah Maccabee, used in Josephus (*Ant.* 12: 263), the Mishnah (Middoth 1:6), and the Talmud (Shabbath. 21b), but is never mentioned in the Book of Maccabees.

Josephus says the name derives from the great-grandfather of the patriarch Mattathiyah of Modiin, Asamonaios.

3. Zeitlin I. 1988: Chapter 2. It is at least possible that the Essene movement and many of the Dead Sea Scrolls are related to the belief that the Hasmoneans had unlawfully usurped the position of high priest from the Sadducees.

4. Nadich, J. 1983: 66 ff. for a complete discussion of this story and other tales, especially p.80, n. 9.

5. Reifenberg, 1947: 11.

6. Hoover 2003: 33.

7. Houghton et al. 2002 and Houghton et al. 2008. In 221 pages of photographs of Seleucid coins one finds only eight coins with neither human nor animal images. Except for this Jerusalem issue all of the others are either scarce or very rare.

8. *Ibid.* nos. 831–834. The establishment of the mint of Antiochus VII at Jerusalem followed his siege (c. 134–132 BCE) and the surrender of Hyrcanus I.

9. Further, this *prutah*-sized coin has a beveled edge as do the subsequent Hasmonean issues of the Jerusalem mint. While A. Kushnir-Stein: 2000–2002: 78–83 discusses the coins with the beveled edges, she does not mention this specific issue, although by following her argument, one can conclude, that this particular type was issued from Jerusalem.

10. Hoover 2003: 29.

11. Madden 1864: 37–51; Hill 1914: 184–187; Reifenberg 1947. Madden attributed both silver *sheqels* and bronze coins to Simon. Hill and Reifenberg, who expressed doubt even about the bronze coins, nevertheless attributed them to Simon.

12. Sellers 1933: 89–90. Simon's fortress was excavated at Beth Zur, and not a single one of the bronze coins now known to be from the Jewish War was found there, whereas large numbers of Seleucid coins from the second half of the second century BCE were unearthed. In contrast, the excavations at Masada yielded 106 bronze coins from "Year Four" in contexts of the Jewish War. Meshorer 1989a: 73, 79, 118f, nos. 3492–3594.

13. Kindler 1974. This book represents a consensus version of the general views held at this time, including that of Meshorer.

14. Hendin 1996: 66–77. This was the first published report of the empirical proof that had long been sought, although the theory was previously posited in an important article by Barag and Qedar 1980: 8–21.

15. D. Barag, personal communications and quoted in Hendin 1996: 66–67.

16. Qedar, personal communications.

17. Barag & Qedar 1980.

18. Magen 1986: 91–101 (Hebrew) and 1990: 70–96 with discussion on coins pp. 74f, 87, 90 (Hebrew).

19. Meshorer, personal communications 1988–90.

20. Adler 1976: 419.
21. Stein 1943: 19–21.
22. Madden 1864: 57.
23. Barag and Qedar 1980: 18.
24. Hoover 1994: 41–57.
25. Barag and Qedar 1980: 18.
26. Josephus, *BJ* XXI: 273, 269.
27. Hoover 1994: 49.
28. Barag 2007, personal communication.
29. Eshel E. *et al.* 1992: 199–229.
30. McLean 1982: 158.
31. Avigad 1975.
32. Hendin & Shachar 2009: 87–96.
33. Shachar 2004: 5–33.
34. Hendin & Shachar 2009: 94.
35. Krupp 2007–8: 57–75.
36. Kindler 1991: 16–18.
37. Meshorer, personal communications.
38. Kanael 1963: 44.
39. Naveh, 1987: 119.
40. Meshorer 1982: 51.
41. Meshorer 2001: 40.
42. VanderKam & Flint 2002: 151.
43. Meshorer 2001: 40.
44. Meshorer 1967: 48.
45. Barkay *et al.* 2003: 162–171. The cave at Ketef Hinnom was excavated by archaeologist Gaby Barkay and the scroll was later identified by Ya'akov Meshorer, then chief curator of Archaeology at The Israel Museum, Jerusalem.
46. Meshorer 1967: 49.
47. Meshorer 2001: 41.
48. Kiddushin 66, 1.
49. Josephus: *Ant.* XIII, 408.
50. Newell 1937.
51. Madden 1864; Reifenberg 1947; Romanof 1971; Kindler 1974; Kanael 1950, 1963; Barag and Qedar 1980; Meshorer 1982, 2001.
52. Kindler 1974: 10.
53. Meshorer 1982 I: 61.
54. Romanoff, 1971: 9.
55. Kanael 1963: 43.
56. While these coins were apparently struck under authority of the Persian sovereign, via his satraps, the fact that Hebrew, Aramaic, and Samarian inscriptions occur on many of them indicates that the local authorities were certainly involved in their design and issue.

57. Roth 2007.
58. Meshorer 1982 I: 57–59 discusses the silver coins in circulation during the Hasmonean period. The principal coin was the *sheqel* of Tyre, although Seleucid, Ptolemaic, and rarely Roman Republican coins were used as well. In a conversation regarding this phenomenon, Dan Barag explained that even though all of these coins carried graven images of heathen gods or rulers, the Jews seemed to accept them as a part of the way the world worked. While the Jews used these coins, they were not coins of the Jews. It is known that the annual half-*sheqel* tribute for each Jewish male for the Jerusalem Temple, was payable only in Tyrian silver. Each Tyre silver coin of this time carried a portrait of the Phoenician god Melqart. We also have noted in Chapter 12 that coins are not subject to the regular rules of uncleanliness, according to the Talmud.
59. An apparent severe, local shortage of small change for use in markets of this economically deprived territory left a window for Hyrcanus to issue small denomination bronze coins that would see heavy use for years to come.
60. Meshorer 2001: 64.
61. Meshorer 1981 I: 64 citing Talmud, Yoma, 72, 2.
62. Kanael 1963: 44.
63. Kanael 1963: 44, 34.
64. English pl. cornucopias. Latin pl. *cornucopiae*.
65. Meshorer 1976: 282.
66. Barag & Qedar 1980: 17.
67. Romanoff 1944: 26.
68. Meshorer 1982 I: 67.
69. This may be yet another reference to the lily of Jerusalem that appears on the Jerusalem issue of Antiochus VII, struck under Hyrcanus I.
70. Meshorer 1976: 285.
71. Romanoff 1944: 44.
72. Hendin 1979: 1.
73. As listed in Deuteronomy 8: 8 they are wheat, barley, figs, pomegranates, olives, honey (from dates), and grape vines.
74. M. Brody, personal communications.
75. Romanoff 1944: 52, note 239 with a number of citations from ancient sources.
76. The ivory pomegranate inscribed "[Belonging] to the Temple of [Yahweh] h, consecrated to the priests" in paleo-Hebrew script was purchased by The Israel Museum in the 1980s. In 2005 a committee of the Israel Antiquities Authority and the Israel Museum found the pomegranate to be ancient, but the inscription to be a modern addition. However, in 2008, Prof. Yitzhak Roman, former academic director of Hebrew University's scanning electron microscope (SEM) examined the pomegranate under

SEM and concluded that the inscription was genuine and original to the pomegranate.

77. Klimowsky 1974: 34.
78. The lily (*shoshan* in Hebrew) as a Jewish symbol is discussed extensively by Romanoff 1944: 45–51. Meshorer 2001: 8–10, 34–35, further discusses this flower as a specific symbol of Jerusalem and its Temple.
79. Romanoff 1944: 50.
80. Hoover 2003: 29–39.
81. Meshorer 1982 I: 60.
82. Graetz 1927: Vol II, 1.
83. Josephus *BJ* I: 57–60.
84. Josephus *Ant*. XIII: 262–266.
85. Josephus *BJ* I, II: 8.
86. Graetz Vol. II p. 36.
87. Josephus *BJ* I: 77–84.
87a. Hendin 2010a.
87b. *Ibid*.
88. Madden 1864: 66, 4.
89. Reifenberg 1947: 41, 14.
90. Kanael 1963: 34.
91. *Ibid*.
92. *Ibid*.
93. de Saulcy 1871: 243ff, mentioning a specimen from Jerusalem in his own collection.
94. Meshorer 1967: 56.
95. Kindler 1974: 14.
96. Naveh 1968: 20–26.
97. I have examined at least portions of three true hoards of these lead pieces, two contained at least 50 pieces, and one may have been smaller. All three groups may have originated in Jordan and each group could be seen to be a true hoard by their uniform patination, albeit slightly different in each situation. These hoards suggest that the lead pieces were indeed tokens and as such were at some point collected and maintained separately from circulating coinage.
98. Hendin 1994–99: 13.
98a. Hendin 2010a.
99. Meshorer 2001: 39.
100. Barag in press.
101. Bijovsky, personal communication.
102. Josephus *BJ* I: 269–270.
103. Josephus *BJ* I: 272.
104. Bachmann 1972–73: 82–90.
105. Meshorer 2001: 220, type 38.

106. No single coin of this type with anywhere near complete inscriptions in either Greek or Hebrew has ever been found. Fontanille has created composite photos showing that the obverse die for the showbread table is far larger than the die for the menorah side.

107. Meshorer 2001: 55 citing Avodah. Zarah 40: 1.

108. The symbols on Hasmonean coinage reflect the attitude in the public domains to figurative art. In private life, matters were, at times, different. The monumental tomb of Jason, about 1.8 km. west of Hasmonean Jerusalem (in the modern quarter of Rehavia) displays different attitudes to figurative art. The tomb dates from the period of Hyrcanus I to early in the reign of Herod I. On the western wall of its portico is a painting of a naval battle with warriors on three ships and on its northern wall a painting of a reclining stag. Into the plaster of the eastern wall are scratched five seven-branched menorahs in a space of 0.70 x 0.61 m. For this tomb see Rahmani 1967; Avigad 1967; P. Benoit 1967. The tomb belonged, apparently, to an estate of a wealthy priestly family. A forthcoming study by Barag, "The Tomb of Jason Reconsidered" was submitted for the I.L. Levin Festschrift in a forthcoming issue of the Harvard Theological Review. This note courtesy D. Barag.

109. Meshorer 1982 I: 94.

110. Rahmani 1967: 61–100.

111. Barag, personal communication 2008.

112. *CNG* 78, Lot: 931.14 May 2008.

113. Barag, personal communication 2008.

114. Barag, personal communication 2008.

115. Barag 1988–89: 40–48.

116. DeSaulcy 1871.

117. Barag 1988–89: 47–48

118. *Ibid.*

CHAPTER SEVER: HERODIAN COINS

1. Strabo. *Geog.* 16.2.34.

2. Richardson 1996: 55.

3. Sifre Zuta, cited by Richardson 1996: 55.

4. Richardson 1996: 55.

5. Josephus *Ant.* XIV: 13.

6. Josephus *Ant.* XIV: 158. However, many scholars point to probable calculation errors and suggest that Herod was probably closer to age 25 at this time as discussed in Netzer 2006: 5.

7. Josephus *Ant.* XIV: 160.

8. *Ibid.* XIV: 161.

9. *Ibid.* XIV: 173–174.

10. Josephus *BJ* I: 244.

11. *Ibid.* I: 270.
12. *Ibid* I: 272.
13. Macrobius, *Saturnalia* 2.4.11.
14. Netzer 2006: 243.
15. Netzer, 2009 personal communications.
16. Broshi 2001: 188–89.
17. Josephus *BJ* I: 427.
18. *Ibid.* I: 417–425.
19. *Ibid.* I: 428.
20. Josephus *Ant.* XVI: 156–157.
21. Richardson 1996: 215.
22. Josephus *Ant.* XVII: 25.
23. *Ibid.* XVI: 27–60.
24. *Ibid.* XVI: 63.
25. Persius, translated in Walsh 1882: 480.
26. Grant 1977: 71.
27. Tabor 2006: 66.
28. Josephus *BJ* I: 650.
29. *Ibid.* I: 660.
30. Matthew 2: 1.
31. Grant 1977: 71.
32. Levy, B. personal communications.
33. Meshorer 2001: 168.
34. Ariel 2006: 62.
35. Harl 1996: 56.
36. Josephus *Ant.* XV: 368–271.
37. Josephus *BJ* I: 415.
38. Ariel 2006: 74.
39. Josephus *Ant.* XV: 423.
40. Josephus *BJ* I: 356; *Ant.* XIV: 486.
41. Ariel 2006: 76.
42. Ariel & Fontanille forthcoming.
43. Ariel 2000–02.
44. Hendin 1990–91: 32–33.
45. Meshorer 2001: 66.
46. Avigad 1980: 70.
47. Mishnah Shekalim, 15b.
48. Romanoff 1971: 19.
49. K'rithoth 5b.
50. Meshorer 1979: 158–161.
51. Kanael 1963: 290.
52. J.P. Fontanille, personal communications.
53. Price 1979: 358.

54. Price 1968 points out that coins were issued not only at times of economic need, but often because of need for sovereigns to generate a profit. Certainly, with his wide range of expensive building projects, Herod needed to generate funds wherever he could.

55. Ariel 2006: 118 calls our attention to another, albeit less likely possibility. He cites a series of four bronze denominations struck at Aigion, which Kroll was able to correlate with *obols*. The denominations were 1 *hemiobol* – 1/3 *obol* – ¼ *obol* – 1/6 *obol*; use of the name "*obol*" is not necessarily relevant, but the ratios 1– 2/3 – ½ – 1/3 may suggest a "similar distant ancestor in common," according to Ariel.

56. Meshorer 2001: 62.

57. *Ibid.*: 62–63.

58. Ariel 2000-02: 121–122.

59. *Ibid.*: 119.

60. *Ibid.*: 118.

61. *Ibid.*: 118.

62. *Ibid.*: 109.

63. *Ibid.*: 122.

64. Ariel 2002.

65. G. Bijovsky, personal communication.

66. Josephus *BJ* II: 10–15.

67. Josephus *Ant.* XVII: 224–228. After their father's death, Archelaus and Antipas sailed to Rome hoping to win favor from Augustus. Antipas had been "encouraged by [his mother] Salome's promises to believe that he would rule, and considered that he would be taking over the government with greater right than Archelaus because he had been designated as king in Herod's earlier will, which he held to be more binding than the one written later."

68. Josephus *Ant.* XVII: 317–320.

69. Josephus *BJ* II: 3.

70. Josephus *Ant.*, XVIII: 27–28.

71. Stern, M. 1975: 132.

72. Mark 6: 22–25.

73. Josephus *BJ* II: 181–183.

74. Ariel 2000–2002: 109. Ariel's "Conjectural absolute chronology of Herod's undated coins" places the anchor/double cornucopia type as Herod's very last issue. He also suggests that this type is "copied exactly on coins of his son Archelaus," (pp. 109), which is certainly of chronological significance suggesting that these were among the first issues of Archelaus. Consistency in style and production of these coins points to them being issued at the same mint.

75. Avi Yonah 1950: 168.

76. Meshorer 2001: 81.

77. Meshorer 1982: 35.

78. Hendin 2003–06: 56–61.
79. It is, of course, possible that more specimens of this coin will be discovered. However, considering that until now the coin is unique, one must recognize its great rarity and at least consider the possibility that it was a trial coinage and not a full issue.
80. Kushnir-Stein 2000–02. This article contains relevant discussions of the manufacture and style of this type of coinage in ancient Judaea during this period.
81. Individual grains of wheat or barley may appear scattered around the cornucopias on some of the Hasmonean issues.
82. Hill 1910: 240–264. The bronze and silver coins of Tyre circulated widely throughout ancient Israel at this time.
83. Meshorer 2001: 226–228. This form of the word tetrarch corresponds with the coins issued by Antipas at Tiberias in year 43 (39/40 CE).
84. Ariel 2002.
85. Archelaus' coins are undated. However, thanks to Ariel's chronology we can surmise that the anchor/double cornucopias coins came first, followed by the similar anchor/wreath series. In both cases, the names are in the nominative form.
86. The two most prominent proponents are: Hoehner 1972: 105 and Kokkinos 1998: 226, note 78.
87. Kushnir-Stein 1999: 195 had already forcefully argued against this possibility in her review of Kokkinos's book. "In fact, neither 'dropping' nor 'adopting' [the so-called 'dynastic' name of Herod] follow from numismatic evidence, since no documentation exists on the exclusive official use of the names Archelaus and Antipas beforehand. What we do know is that at least two other sons of the king bore the name Herodes, and there it was certainly not a 'dynastic title' but simply a part of their cognomia."
88. Meshorer 2001: 228, coins 97 and 98.
89. *Ibid.*: 233, 127–128. The earliest coins attributed to Sepphoris until now were those with the name of Vespasian when he was still a general. These coins are dated to year 14 = 67/68 CE.
90. Ariel 2003: 116.
91. One evening during the 1985 season of the Joint Sepphoris Excavation (Meyers-Netzer-Meyers), the author presented a talk on ancient Jewish numismatics to the staff and volunteers. One of the topics discussed was the minting of the Jewish *prutot*, and the author drew a model of the typical flan mold on the blackboard. The very next morning one of the volunteers called the author to her excavation grid and showed a small piece of chalkstone with shallow holes drilled into it. There was no doubt that this was a piece of a casting mold for flans of beveled-edge *prutah* coins. Unfortunately the small stone piece has been lost or misplaced and there is no photographic record.

92. E.M. Meyers, personal communication 12/17/03. Also see Meyers 2002: 110–120 and Meyers 1999: 127–140.

93. I feel comfortable with the attribution of this coin, but nevertheless present here a far less-likely scenario. Upon first discovering this coin, my impression was that it was a coin of Herod Antipas, based mainly on the "tetrarch" inscription. However, because of the style of its manufacture, I considered other possibilities. None of the coin types of Herod Antipas struck at Tiberias were struck in the style of a Jewish *prutah*, that is, upon a cast flan with beveled edges, and chopped from a strip. This led me, on technical grounds, to consider the possibility that this was a coin of Herod I, struck in his fourth year as tetrarch, approximately 37/36 BCE.

I re-evaluated this idea on reading Donald Ariel's 2002 article regarding the chronology of the coins of Herod I, in which he notes specifically the apparent chronology and form of the letter "omega" in the later coins of Herod I and the earlier coins of Archelaus.

From an historical perspective, it is also not likely that this is a coin of Herod I. Josephus (*BJ* 243–244) puts Herod's appointment as tetrarch by Antony after the latter's meeting with Cleopatra, *i.e.* toward the end of 41 BCE. Kushnir-Stein notes that the appointment of Herod and his brother Phasael as tetrarchs "can mean one of two things: they were given the title, but remained subordinate to Hyrcanus II or they were made independent rulers with their own territories over which Hyrcanus II had no jurisdiction. The last possibility seems very remote. Antony had seemingly no reasons to punish Hyrcanus, and Josephus does not say anything about Hyrcanus ceasing to be the head of the Jewish state. If neither Herod nor his brother were made genuinely independent rulers, they would not have been in a position to mint their own coins."

Finally, I note that if the Δ on the obverse refers to the "fourth year" by this time Herod would have already became king, and had issued royal coinage dated to his third year as tetrarch.

94. Meshorer 2001: 84.

95. Stern, M. 1975: 135.

96. Josephus *Ant.* XVIII: 107.

97. Strickert 2002.

98. *Ibid.* XVIII: 28.

99. Schwartz 1990: 40.

100. Josephus *BJ* I: 555.

101. Schwartz 1990: 171–172.

102. Josephus *BJ* II: 218–219.

103. Josephus *Ant.* XIX: 330–333.

104. Deuteronomy 17:15.

105. Sotah 41a.

106. Acts 12:1–19.

107. Josephus *Ant.* XIX 338.

108. *Ibid.*: 339.
109. *Ibid.*: 341–342.
110. Schwartz 1990: 175.
111. Josephus *Ant.* 346–361.
112. Acts 12: 19–23.
113. Meshorer, personal communications as cited in previous editions.
114. Lönnqvist 1997: 429–440 suggests that Agrippa II was a full client of Rome and even though he was Jewish, represented Roman interests in the area. Lönnqvist suggests that "the Emperor granted him the permission for striking the coins in gratitude of his loyalty to Rome and for participating in the Jewish War." Lönnqvist also asserts that this issue was struck over a period of many years, first because of the large number of coins in existence, and second because a huge number of dies (hundreds of pairs or more) were used. Certainly Agrippa II issued many larger denomination coins throughout his reign. Lönnqvist also supports his theory with the spelling of ΑΓΡΙΠΑ, with only one letter Π. All other coins of Agrippa I spell his name ΑΓΡΙΠΠΑ. However, there are coins of Agrippa II in which his name is spelled ΑΓΡΙΠΑ (Nos. 1303, 1304). In other words, both Agrippa I and Agrippa II spell their names both ways on their coins.
115. Epstein *et al.* 2010.
116. Kovacs 2008: 337–350.
117. Josephus *Ant.* XXI: 5.
118. *Ibid. Ant.* XX: 158.
119. Josephus *BJ* VII: 226.
119a.Kovacs, personal communications 2010.
120. Meshorer 1982 II: 171.
121. Gittin 56:1.
122. Josephus *Ant.* XIX: 362.
123. *Ibid.* XX: 9.
124. Madden 1864.
125. Kanael 1963: 53.
126. Barag 1978: 14–23.
127. Meshorer 2001: 102–114.
128. Kushnir-Stein 2002.
129. *Ibid.*
130. Schwartz 1990: 48.
131.Qedar *INJ* 1986-87: 29–35.
132. Meshorer *et al.* forthcoming: 252, cites Kushnir-Stein.
133. Kushnir-Stein 2002: 127–128, observes in a note that "It would not be entirely surprising if the mention of the era of 49 in Josephus turns out to be correct. The Jewish historian was the commander of the rebel forces in Galilee in 66/67, and since a significant part of the territory under his control belonged to Agrippa's kingdom, he is bound to have come

across various documents and decisions dated by the regnal years of this king."

134. *Ibid.*: 129.
135. *Ibid.*: 130.
136. Burnett *et al.* 1999, *RPC* II, I: 309.
137. Meshorer 2001: 103.
138. Josephus *The Life*, 38.
139. Meshorer 2001: 105.
140. *Ibid.*: 104-5.
141. *Ibid.*: 104.
141. Josephus *BJ* III: 30.
142. *Ibid.*: 14.
143. Meshorer 1982 II: 76.
144. Hendin 2007c: 123–130.
145. Meshorer 1982: 76.
146. Barag, personal communications.
147. Josephus *BJ* II: 399–402.
148. Hendin 2007c: 123–130 where the matter of these references to the Roman victory over the Jews, and the coins commemorating it, are discussed.
149. Gabba 30, cited in Schwartz 1990: 32, note 101.
150. *Jewish Encyclopedia Online*, "Other Jews Honored." http://www.jewish-encyclopedia.com/view.jsp?artid=2083&letter=A&search=#6361
151. Schürer 1890: 2, 195–196.
152. Acts 26: 30–32.
153. Josephus *BJ* II: 310–314.
154. *Ibid.*: 341.
155. Smallwood 1981: 386.
156. Tacitus, *Histories* II, 2.
157. *Ibid.* II, 81.
158. Cassius Dio LXV, 15, 4.
159. Smallwood 1981: 387.
160. Malteil-Gerstenfeld 1980: 6.
161. Smallwood 1981: 388.
162. Suetonius, *Titus*, 7.
163. Ariel 2003.
164. Hendin 2003–06.
165. Meshorer 1982 II: 91.
166. Hendin 2009: 57–62.

CHAPTER EIGHT: THE ROMAN GOVERNORS OF JUDAEA

1.   Josephus, *BJ* II: 117–118.
2.   Kushnir-Stein 2007: 3.

3. *Ibid.*: 4.
4. Meshorer 2001: 168.
5. Kanael 1963.
6. Josephus *BJ* II: 117–118.
7. Josephus *Ant.* XVIII: 30.
8. *Ibid.* XVIII: 31.
9. *Ibid.* XVIII: 177.
10. Sifri Numbers 131
11. Lönnqvist 2002: 466–469. His theory revolves around his historic reconstruction in which Pilate was involved in building an aqueduct at this time. "It seems feasible that Pilate's mint officials may have put aside the lead reserved for the provincial coinage and passed it on by the governor's orders to the aqueduct engineers."
12. *Ibid.*: 467–468, note 28.
13. *Ibid.* 468.
14. Matthew 27: 2.
15. Philo, *Embassy to Gaius:* 299–303.
16. Josephus *Ant.* XVIII: 59.
17. Meshorer 1982 II: 179.
18. Banks 1955: 97.
19. Meshorer 1982 II: 179.
20. Josephus *BJ* II: 227.
21. Tacitus *Histories* V: 10.
22. Josephus *Ant.* XX: 163.
23. *Ibid.* XX: 182.
24. Josephus *BJ* II: 277–279.
25. *Ibid.* II: 313–314.
26. *Ibid.* II: 409.
27. Meshorer 2002: 174.
28. Lönnqvist 1992–93: 63.
29. *Ibid.*: 66

CHAPTER 9: THE JEWISH WAR

1. Josephus *BJ* I: 1.
2. *Ibid.* II: 293–294.
3. *Ibid.* II: 403–405.
4. Grayzel 1948: 161.
5. *Ibid.*
6. Josephus *BJ* II: 409.
7. Grayzel 1948: 162.
8. *Ibid.*: 163.
9. Josephus *BJ* II: 543–550.
10. Josephus *BJ* II: 555.

11. *Ibid. BJ* IV: 560–563

12. Tacitus *Histories* 5: 12.

13. *Ibid.*: 13.

14. Josephus *BJ* VI: 297–298.

15. Tacitus *Histories* 5:13.

16. *Ibid.*

17. U. Rappaport, among others, points out that this number must be a great exaggeration. "It is simply an incredible number in antiquity considering the means for supplying provisions. Assembling 1,000,000 people in one place (with the exception of Rome and Alexandria) would mean starving them to death. Also the estimated number of Jews in Israel at that time was about one to two million and most of the people survived the revolt. Tacitus (*Histories* V: 13) mentioned 600,000 assembled in Jerusalem when Titus arrived there, but this also is an exaggerated number, he may have been influenced by the Exodus story" (personal communication of 6/1/09).

18. Josephus *BJ* VI: 420–422.

19. *Ibid.* VII: 148–152.

20. It is a matter of great interest that three *sheqels* dated to the fifth year were found in the excavations at Masada. From this we can deduce that some Jews escaped from Jerusalem to Masada near the end of the war.

21. Smallwood 1981: 349.

22. Roth 1962: 40.

23. Rappaport 2007: 103.

24. Roth 1962: 39.

25. *Ibid.*: 34.

26. *Ibid.*: 33.

27. Rappaport 2007: 104.

28. Deutsch 2009, English summary.

29. *Ibid.*

30. Goldstein & Fontanille 2006: 17–19.

31. Meshorer 2001: 72–78.

32. Rappaport 2007: 107.

33. *Ibid.*: 109.

34. *Ibid.*: 109.

35. *Ibid.*: 111.

36. *Ibid.*: 112.

37. Goldstein & Fontanille 2006: 23.

38. Rappaport 2007: 113–114.

39. Meshorer 1975: 101, 84. A parallel exists in contemporary Nabataean coinage with a bronze coin inscribed "half silver."

40. Newell 1913: 544.

41. Josephus *BJ* V: 424–428.

42. *Ibid.* VI :196–197.

43. *Ibid.* VI: 206–213.
44. *Ibid.* V: 445–446.
45. Newell 1913: 545.
46. The modern word Zionism, according to the *Encyclopedia Judaica*, "first appeared at the end of the 19th century, denoting the movement whose goal was the return of the Jewish people to *Eretz Israel*." But, the word Zion itself is ancient, referring most often to the city of Jerusalem or the people of Judaea. Some two thousand years ago there was a Zionism very similar to the "modern" Zionism. Nowhere is this more clearly shown than on the Zionist slogans of the coins minted during the Jewish wars of the first and second centuries CE.
47. Roth 1962: 43.
48. Goldstein & Fontanille 2006: 21.
49. Romanoff 1944: 22–23.
50. Deutsch 2009, English summary.
51. *Ibid.*: 16–17.
52. Meshorer 1982 II: 112.
53. *Ibid.*
54. Romanoff 1944: 31.
55. Klimowsky 1974: 80.
56. Deutsch 1992–93: 71–72.
57. Goldstein & Fontanille 2006..
58. Hill 1914: cii–ciii.
59. *Ibid.*: cii.
60. It would be misleading, however, not to note that at this auction, a well-known Israeli dealer let it be known that he was bidding on this coin on behalf of the Israel Museum. While a few bidders who were unaware of the situation placed bids, most dealers and collectors in attendance declined further bids in favor of allowing the museum to purchase it at an unrealistically low price relative to its importance and rarity. We also note that the proceeds of the sale of the Bromberg collection were donated directly to the numismatic department of the Israel Museum, so there was no harm done to the seller in this situation.
61. For extensive, interesting discussion on these coins see Syon 1993–94 and 2007, and Farhi 2003–2006.
62. Meshorer 2001: 244.
63. Farhi 2003-06: 69-76.
64. Sahuri. 2010
64. Arbel 2007: 273
65. Gihon 1987, Syon & Yavor 2001

Chapter Ten: The Bar Kokhba Revolt

1. Midrash Rabbah Lamentations 2.2, 4.
2. See Rabello 1995 for a legal discussion and Magie 1979: 1, 42–45 *Scriptores historiae Augustae: Hadrian* 14.2 for historical reference.
3. Midrash Rabbah Lamentations 2.2–4.
4. *Ibid.*
5. Hritzu 1965: 202.
6. Cassius Dio, *Roman History* 69.12.3.
7. *Ibid.*: 12.1–14.3.
8. *Ibid.*
9. Meshorer 1982 II: 134. Knowledge of the second coin is anecdotal from an expert in Jerusalem.
10. Barag 1980: 30–33.
11. Bijovsky 2004: 248–251.
12. Amit and Bijovsky 2007: 133–36.
13. Yadin 1971: 27.
14. *Ibid.*: 15.
15. *Ibid.*: 124.
16. *Ibid.*: 176.
17. Midrash Rabbah Lamentations 2, 2–4.
18. Schürer 1890, Division 1, Vol. 2: 299.
19. Midrash Rabbah Lamentations 2, 2–4.
20. Meshorer 2001: 142.
21. Mildenberg 1984: 29–30.
22. Midrash Rabbah Lamentations 2.2–4.
23. Midrash Rabbah Lamentations 2.2–4. (y Ta'anit 4: 8/28; Ekha Rabba 2: 4; Ekha Rabba, ed. Buber, p. 101.)
24. Meshorer 1982 II: 135.
25. Meshorer 2001: 139. The author has made personal observations of differences higher than 300%.
26. Kiddushin 12a.
27. Meshorer 2001: 122–23, 155.
28. Meshorer 1982 II: 135.
29. Barag 2000-02: 153–156.
30. Haaretz.com Sat., February 14, 2009. For information about the tomb itself. The royal box and amphitheatre were not formally announced as of this writing, but have been seen by the author.
31. Spijkerman 1972.
32. Mildenberg 1984–5: 32–36. Mildenberg describes the object within the Temple as "a low chest on two feet. The chest itself, which entirely lacks three-dimensionality, was meant to be without lid, as the upper border is rendered by a single concave line and not by the convex double line which is the way the chest on the tetradrachms is depicted."

33. Barag 1986: 222. Further discussion of Bar Kokhba's second mint can be found in Kindler 1984:172–179 (Hebrew) in which he describes a mobile mint of Bar Kokhba found at Horbat 'Eged in the Jerusalem Shefla.
34. Kaufman 2000–02, 2007–08.
35. Hendin 2006: 111–116.
36. Mildenberg 1984: 203–216, nos. 61–84.
37. *Ibid*. 1984: 87.
38. *Ibid*.
39. Goldstein 2010; and personal communications.
40. Barag 1986: 217–222.
41. Romanoff 1944: 40.
42. Reifenberg 1947: 30–32.
42. Avodah Zarah: 43, 1.
43. Meshorer 2001: 56–57.
44. Avigad 1980:147–149.
45. Barag 1986: 220–221.
46. *Ibid.*: 219.
47. *Ibid.*: 221.
48. Goldstein 2010.
49. Eshel 2007–08: 126.
50. Barag 1986: 221.
51. Adler 2007–08: 135.
52. M Sukkah 4: 5, 6.
53. Leonard 1993.
54. Examples published in Mildenberg, Meshorer. Barag also called our attention to a significant number of examples in a private collection in Jerusalem. In Meshorer 2001, he shows (348, 306) a similar Abu Jara, and Leo Mildenberg depicts one in his classic book on coins of the Bar Kokhba War ("N"). (Middle- and small-sized bronze Bar Kokhba coins were also cut for small change, and in Hendin 2001, no. 734a we show a Bar Kokhba silver coin cut in ancient times.
55. Cassius Dio, *Roman History* 69: 12.1–14.3.
56. Barag 2000–02.
57. Hendin 1980.

CHAPTER ELEVEN: JUDAEA AND ROME

1. Josephus. *Ant.* XIV: 488.
2. RPC I, I: 263.
3. Hart 1952 remains the best on this subject.
4. *Ibid.*: 175.
5. Charlesworth 1937: 8.
6. Mattingly 1965: ccxxv.
7. *Ibid.*: ccxxvii.

8. Hart 1952: 191.
9. *Ibid.*
10. Avigad 1980: 127. Avigad discusses his team's emotional discovery in 1970 when they found in excavations in Jerusalem a house that had clearly been burnt during this destruction. "For the first time in the history of excavations in the city, vivid and clear archaeological evidence of the burning of the city had come to light....Something amazing occurred in the hearts of all who witnessed the progress of excavations here. The burning of the Temple and the destruction of Jerusalem—fateful events in the history of the Jewish People—suddenly took on a new and horrible significance. Persons who had previously regarded this catastrophe as stirring but abstract and remote, having occurred two millennia ago, were so visibly moved by the sight that they occasionally would beg permission to take a fistful of soil or a bit of charred wood...." This site, known today as the Burnt House of Kathros, has been restored as a museum in the Jewish Quarter in the Old City of Jerusalem, and a visit there must not be missed.
11. Vagi 1999: 213.
12. Although I do not rule these coins out as being related to the victory over Judaea, those responsible for the coinage were not shy about very specific depictions of objects, and scenes related to Judaea, so I am including only types specific to the conflict.
13. Also issued with an obverse portrait of Vespasian, the proud father, who left his son in charge of finishing the victory in Judaea.
14. *Numismatica Ars Classica*, Auction 51, 5 March, 2009, lot 234.
15. Although the relief on these coins may not seem unusual at first glance, the lowest point of the coin is inside the colosseum and the highest point is the center of the facade of the building. This is quite a differential even for a large Roman bronze, and results in the frequent flat strikes and heavy wear at the highest point.
16. Alföldy 1995: 195–226.
17. Feldman 2001.
18. Suetonius 1957 (tr.): 283.
19. Feldman 2001.
20. Josephus *BJ* VII: 148.
21. Elkins 2006: 215.
22. *Ibid.*: 218. "Even the imperial depiction on the reverse is unusual in showing a seated figure rather than a bust."
23. *Ibid.*: 218.
24. Elkins 2004: 153.
25. Elkins 2006: 219.
26. *Ibid.*
27. Although it is not clear that every die is identical in these respects.

28. Madden 1864 and Reifenberg 1947 were among the early scholars who described these coins in this way.
29. Weisbrem 1962.
30. Hendin 2007c.
31. Josephus *Ant.* VII: 152
32. Suetonius 1957 (trans.): 296–297.
33. Jones 1993: 144–49. Domitian's greatest Germanic battles were against the Chatti, a 'war' that was 'solved' by diplomacy only in the mid-80s, and the tribe later sided with Saturninus during his rebellion in 89. RPC II: xiii notes that Domitian did not issue his first GERMANIA CAPTA coin until 85 CE and the title GERMANICVS first appears on Roman issues only in July or August 83 CE. Carradice 1982–83 shows that on the Judaean issues, GERMANICVS was not used prior to 84 CE.
34. Meshorer 2001: 192–193.
35. Malamed 2005: 172.
36. Hendin 2007c: 129.
37. Carradice & Buttrey 2007: 46. "This group of *aurei* has a distinctive style, with elongated portraits, outward facing legends and heavily pelleted borders, which can be linked to a group of Syrian *tetradrachms* (RPC II, 1963-9). Stylistic links with the provincial 'Judaea Capta' coinage and other evidence points to a Judaean origin for these coins."
38. RPC II: 97.
39. Mattingly 1966b: lxxxix–xc.
40. Suetonius *Domitian*: 12.
41 Julian 1923 (trans.): Letter 51, Epistle 25.
42 Howgego 1985: 16.
43. Josephus *BJ* III: 65–66.
44. Barag and Qedar 1994–99.
45. *Ibid.*
46. *Ibid.*
47. Josephus *BJ* V: 41–43.
48. Barag 1967.
49. Josephus *BJ* II: 494.

CHAPTER TWELVE: NEW TESTAMENT COINS

1. Grant 1977: 71.
2. *Ibid.*: 72.
3. Barter continues to be a common method for financial transactions in the world today; for discussion see Hendin 2007a: 23–29.
4. Duncan-Jones 1994: 3.
5. Rogers 1914: 67.
6. *Ibid.*: 68.
7. Spijkerman 1956: 297.

8. Hoover 2006: 13.
9. For some of the available excavation data related to this topic, see Ariel 2002: 281–305; and Bijovsky 2000: 155–189.
10. Hasmonean coins circulated in ancient Palestine even through the fifth century CE, so there is every reason to believe it was well used during the lifetime of Jesus. *cf.* Bijovsky 2000–2002: 202.
11. Leonard 1993: 363–370.
12 In recent excavations by Shukrun and Reich in the main drainage channel of Jerusalem from the Second Temple, a Tyre half-*sheqel* dated 22 CE was discovered. The coin and its use in ancient times is discussed at http://www.antiquities.org.il/article_Item_eng.asp?sec_id=25&subj_id=240&id=1353&module_id=#as.
13. Levy 2005: 5.
14. Josephus, *Ant.* 18: 312–13; Philo, *De specialibus legibus* 1: 76–8, and *Legatio ad Gaium*, 311.
15. *Bulletin de correspondance hellenique* 1982.
16. Josephus *Ant.* XIII: 62–73.
17. Levy 2005: 5–6.
18. *Ibid.*: 8.
19. Josephus *BJ* VI: 335.
20. Meshorer 1982 II: 9.
21. Levy 2005a: 885–89.
22. *Ibid.*: 885. For a more complete discussion of Meshorer's arguments, see Levy 1993: 267–74.
23. Levy 2005a: 887.
24. Baba Metzia 59b.
25. Levy 2005: 18–19.
26. Cited in Ariel 2006: 102–3.
27. Moed, Shekalim, 1.3.
28. *Stater* is a Greek silver coin denomination that in general pre-dates the *sheqel* or *tetradrachm*, however, in many areas of the Greek world the words may have been used interchangeably.

BIBLIOGRAPHY

Adler, A.
1976   Notes on the Beginning of Ancient Jewish Coinage. *Judaica Post* 4, 6: 416–420.

Adler, Y.
2007–08 Temple Willow-Branch Ritual Depicted on Bar Kokhba Denarius. *Israel Numismatic Journal* 16: 131–135.

Alföldy, G.
1995   Eine Bauinschrift aus dem Colosseum. *Zeitschrift für Papyrologie und Epigraphik*, 109: 195–226.

Amit, D. and Bijovsky, G.
2007   A Numismatic Update on the Northwestern Border of the Territory Controlled by Bar Kokhba Rebels. *Israel Numismatic Research* 2: 133–136.

Applebaum, S.
1976   *Prolegomena to the Study of the Second Jewish Revolt (A.D. 132–135).* Oxford, British Archaeological Reports (Supp. Series 7).

Arbel, Y.
2007   The Gamla Coin: A New Perspective on the Circumstances and Date of its Minting. In *Milk and Honey, Essays on Ancient Israel and the Bible In Appreciation of the Judaic Studies Program at the University of California,* D. Miano and S. Malena eds. Winona Lake: Eisenbrauns: 257–275.

Ariel, D.T.

2000–2
> The Jerusalem Mint of Herod the Great: A Relative Chronology. *Israel Numismatic Journal* 14: 99–124.

2002   The Coins from the Surveys and Excavations of Caves in the Northern Judaean Desert. *Atiqot* 41 (2): 281–304.

2003   Flan Molds from the Temple Mount Excavations. In E. Mazar: *The Temple Mount Excavations in Jerusalem 1968–1978 Directed by Benjamin Mazar. Final Report. Volume II. The Byzantine and Early Islamic Periods* (Qedem monograph series 43). Jerusalem: 115–119.

2006   *A Numismatic Approach to the Reign of Herod the Great.* Unpublished Ph.D. dissertation under the supervision of Alla Kushnir-Stein, Tel Aviv University.

— and Fontanille J.P.

Forthcoming. *The Coins of Herod.* Accepted for the Ancient Judaism and Early Christianity monograph series. Leiden: E.J. Brill.

Avigad, N.

1967   Aramaic Inscriptions in the Tomb of Jason. *Israel Exploration Journal* 17, 2: 101–111.

1975   A Bulla of Jonathan the High Priest. *Israel Exploration Journal* 25, 1: 8–12.

1980   *Discovering Jerusalem.* Nashville: Thomas Nelson.

Avi-Yonah, M.

1950   The Foundation of Tiberias. *Israel Exploration Journal* 1: 168.

1975   (ed.) *Encyclopedia of Archaeological Excavations in the Holy Land*, Vols. 1–4. New Jersey: Prentice-Hill.

Bachmann, H-G.

1972–73 The Metrological Composition of the Hasmonean Coins. *Museum Ha'aretz*, 15–16: 82–90.

Banks, F.A.

1955   *Coins of Bible Days.* New York: Macmillan 1955.

Barag, D.

1966   The Effects of the Tennes Rebellion on Palestine. *Bulletin of the American Schools of Oriental Research* 183: 6–12.

1967   The Countermarks of the Legio Decima Fretensis. In *Proceedings of the International Numismatic Convention* (Jerusalem, 26–31 December, 1963): 9–11, 117–25. Jerusalem: Schocken.

1967a   Brick-Stamp Impressions of the Legio X Fretensis. *Bonner Jahrbücher* 167: 244–267.

1978   The Palestinian 'Judaea Capta' Coins of Vespasian and Titus and the Era on the Coins of Agrippa II Minted Under the Flavians. *Numismatic Chronicle*: 14–23.

1980   A Note on the Geographical Distribution of Bar Kokhba Coins. *Israel Numismatic Journal* 4: 30–33.

1986   New Evidence for the Identification of the Showbread Table on Coins of the Bar Kokhba War. *Proceedings of the 10ʰ International Congress of Numismatics, London:* 217–222.

1986–7   A Silver Coin of Yohanan the High Priest and the Coinage of Judea in the Fourth Century B.C. *Israel Numismatic Journal* 9: 4.

1988–9   The Islamic Candlestick Coins of Jerusalem. *Israel Numismatic Journal* 10: 40.

1992–3   New Evidence on the Foreign Policy of John Hyrcanus I. *Israel Numismatic Journal* 12: 1–13.

1993   Bagoas and the Coinage of Judea. *Proceedings of the XIth International Numismatic Congress, Brussels, September 8ʰ–13ʰ 1991,* Louvain-la-Neuve: 261–265.

1994–9   The Coinage of Yehud and the Ptolemies. *Israel Numismatic Journal* 13: 27–38.

2000–2a   Mint of Antiochus IV in Jerusalem. *Israel Numismatic Journal* 14: 59–77.

2000–2b   The Two Mints of the Bar Kokhba War. *Israel Numismatic Journal* 14: 153–156.

In Press   Alexander Jannaeus Priest and King. Volume in Honor of Hanan Eshel. To appear in the *Supplement Series* of the *Journal for the Study of Judaism in the Persian, Hellenistic and Roman Period* (JSJS). Leiden: E.J. Brill.

— and Qedar.
1980   The Beginning of Hasmonean Coinage. *Israel Numismatic Journal* 4: 8–21.

1994–9   A Countermark of the *Legio Quinta Scythica* from the Jewish War. *Israel Numismatic Journal* 13: 66–70.

Barkay, G. *et al.*
2003   The Challenges of Ketef Hinnom: Using Advanced Technologies to Recover the Earliest Biblical Texts and their Context. *Near Eastern Archaeology* 66, 4: 162–171.

Bartlett, John.
1973   The First and Second Books of The Maccabees; *The Cambridge Bible Commentary.* Cambridge: Cambridge University Press.

Bellinger, Alfred R.
1940   *The Syrian Tetradrachms of Caracalla and Macrinus.* New York:
        American Numismatic Society:

Benoit, P.
1967   L'Inscription grecque du tombeau de Jason. *Israel Exploration
        Journal* 17, 2: 112f.

Bijovsky, G.
2000   The Coins from Horbat Zalit. *'Atiqot* 39: 155–189.
2000–2 The Currency of the Fifth Century CE in Palestine : Some
        Reflections in Light of the Numismatic Evidence. *Israel Numismatic
        Journal* 14: 196–210.
2004   The Coins from Khirbet Badd 'Isa—Qiryat Sefer. Isolated Coins
        and Two Hoards Dated to the Bar Kokhba Revolt. In Y. Magen,
        D.T. Ariel, G. Bijovsky, Y, Tzionit, and O. Sirkis. *The Land of
        Benjamin* (Judea-Samaria Publications 3). Jerusalem: 243–300.

Biran, A. and Gophna, R.
1970   An Iron Age Burial Cave at Tel Halif. *Israel Exploration Journal* 20:
        151–169.

Brauer, G.
1970   *Judaea Weeping.* New York: Crowell.

Burnett, A., Amandry M., and Ripolles, P.
1992   *Roman Provincial Coinage*, Vol. I, Parts I and II. London: British
        Museum Press.
1998   *Roman Provincial Coinage*, Supp. I. London: British Museum Press.

Burnett, A., Amandry, M., and Carradice, I.
1999   *Roman Provincial Coinage*, Vol. II, Parts I and II. London: British
        Museum Press.

Broshi, M.
2001   *Bread, Wine, Walls and Scrolls.* London: Sheffield Academic Press.

Carradice, I.
1982–3 Coinage in Judaea in the Flavian Period, AD 70–96. *Israel
        Numismatic Journal* 6–7: 14–21.

—and Buttrey, T.
2007   *The Roman Imperial Coinage,* Volume II, Part 1, Second Fully
        Revised Edition. London: Spink.

Charlesworth, M.P.
1937   The Virtues of a Roman Emperor: Propaganda and the Creation of Belief. Raleigh Lecture on History. British Academy.

Cohen, H.
1880–90 *Médailles Impériales*, I–VIII, 2nd ed., Paris.

Crawford, M.
1974   *Roman Republican Coinage*. Vols. 1 and 2. New York: Cambridge University Press.

Danby, H.
1933   *The Mishnah, Translated from the Hebrew with Introduction and Brief Explanatory Notes*. Oxford: Oxford University Press.

Dayton, J.
1974   Money in the Near East Before Coinage. *Berytus* 23: 41–52.

Deutsch, R.
1986–7 A Portrait Coin of Agrippa II Reconsidered. *Israel Numismatic Journal* 9: 36–37 .
1992–3 A Unique Prutah from the First Year of the Jewish War Against Rome. *Israel Numismatic Journal* 12: 71–72.
2009   *The Jewish Coinage During the First Revolt Against Rome, 66–73 CE*. Unpublished PhD dissertation submitted to the Senate of Tel Aviv University.

Dever, W.
2001   The Silver Trail: Response to the Papers of Ephriam Stern and Seymour Gitin. In *Hacksilber to Coinage: New Insights into the Monetary History of the Near and Greece*. New York: American Numismatic Society: 49–52.

Dio Cassius
1925   *Roman History Books 61–70* (Loeb Classical Library 176). Trans. Earnest Cary. London-Cambridge.

Dittenberger, W,
1915.   *Sylloge Inscriptionum Graecorum*, 3rd edition, Leipzig.

Duncan-Jones, R.
1994.   *Money and Government in the Roman Empire*. Cambridge: Cambridge University Press.

Dayan, M.
1978.   *Living with the Bible*. New York: William Morrow.

Elkins, N.
2004   Locating the Imperial Box in the Flavian Amphitheater: the
        Numismatic Evidence. *The Numismatic Chronicle*, 164: 147–157.
2006   The Flavian Colosseum Sestertii: Currency or Largess? *The
        Numismatic Chronicle*, 166: 211–221.

Encyclopedia Judaica
1971–2   Jerusalem.

Epstein, M.S., Hendin, D.B., Yu, L.L, and Bower, N.W.
2010   Chemical Attribution of Corroded Coins Using X-ray Fluorescence
        and Lead Isotope Ratios: A Case Study from First Century Judaea.
        Applied Spectroscopy 64.

Eshel E., Eshel H., and Yardeni A.
1992   A Qumran Composition Containing Part of Ps. 154 and a Prayer
        for the Welfare of King Jonathan and His Kingdom. *Israel
        Exploration Journal* 42: 199–229.

Eshel, H.
2007–8 On Harps and Lyres: A Note on the Bronze Coinage of the Bar
        Kokhba Administration. *Israel Numismatic Journal* 16: 118–130.

Farhi, Y.
2003–06 The Bronze Coins Minted at Gamla Reconsidered. *Israel
        Numismatic Journal* 15: 59–67.

Feldman, L.H.
2001   Financing the Colosseum. *Biblical Archaeology Review* 27: 22 f.

Fontanille, J.P.
2008   Extreme Deterioration and Damage on *Yehud* Coin Dies. *Israel
        Numismatic Research* 3:29–43.

—and Gosline, F.
2001   *The Coins of Pontius Pilate*. Warren Center, Pa.: Shangra La.

—and Lorber, C.
2008   Silver Yehud Coins with Greek or Pseudo-Greek Inscriptions.
        Israel Numismatic Research 3: 51–64.

Friedman, T.
1987   When Dogs Become an Archeologist's Best Find. *The New York Times*, August 14, 1987.

Gerson, S.
2001   Fractional Coins of Judea and Samaria in the Fourth Century BCE. *Near Eastern Archaeology* 64, 3: 106–121.

Gihon, M.
1987   The Golan and the Battle for Gamla. *Ariel* 50-51: 79.

Gitin, S. and Golani, A.
2001   The Tel Miqne-Ekron Silver Hoards: The Assyrian and Phoenician Connections. In *Hacksilber to Coinage: New Insights into the Monetary History of the Near East and Greece*. New York: American Numismatic Society: 27–48.

Gitler, H. and Lorber, C.
2006   A New Chronology for the Ptolemaic Coins of Judah. *American Journal of Numismatics*, 2nd ser Vol. 18: 1–41.
2008   A New Chronology for the Yehizkiyah coins of Judah. *Schweizerische Numismatische Rundschau* 87: 61–82.

Gitler, H. and Tal, O.
2006   *The Coinage of Philistia of the Fifth and Fourth Centuries BC: A Study of the Earliest Coins of Palestine*. Milano: Ennerre/New York: Amphora.
2009   More Evidnce on the Collective Mint of Philistia. *Israel Numismatic Research* 4:21–38.

Gitler, H., Tal. O., and Van Alfen, P.
2007   Silver Dome-shaped Coins from Persian-Period Southern Palestine. *Israel Numismatic Research* 2: 47–62.

Goldstein, I.
2010   Bar Kokhba Sela—The Design Schemes. *The Celator* 24, 4.

Goldstein, I. and Fontanille, J.P.
2006   A New Study of the Coins of the First Jewish Revolt Against Rome, 66–70 CE. *American Numismatic Assn. Journal* 1, 2: 9–32.

Goodenough, E.R.
1953–68 *Jewish Symbols in the Graeco-Roman Periods*, Vols. 1–12. New York: Pantheon.

Graetz, H.
1927   *History of the Jews*, Vols. 1–6. New York: G. Dobsevage.

Grant, M.
1971   *Herod the Great*. New York: American Heritage Press.
1973   *The Jews in the Roman World*. New York: Scribner's.
1974   *The Army of the Caesars*. New York: Scribner's.
1977   *Jesus: An Historian's Review of the Gospels*. New York: Scribner's.

Grayzel, S.
1948   *A History of the Jews*. Philadelphia: Jewish Publication Society.

Hafford, W.B.
2005   Mesopotamian Mesuration Balance Pan Weights from Nippur.
       Journal of the Economic and Social History of the Orient, 48, 3: 345–387.

Harl, K.W.
1996   *Coinage in the Roman Economy, 300 BC to AD 700*. Baltimore: Johns
       Hopkins University Press.

Hart, H.St.J.
1952   Judaea and Rome: the Official Commentary. *Journal of Theological
       Studies*: 172–198.

Hebrew-Greek Key Study Bible
1990   *New American Standard Bible*. Chattanooga: AMG Publishers.

Heltzer, M.
1996   The 'Unification' of Weights and Measure Systems in Foreign
       Trade in the Eastern Mediterranean (1500–700 BCE). *Michmanim* 9:
       31–38.

Hendin, D.
1976   *Guide to Ancient Jewish Coins*. New York: Attic Books.
1979   A New Way to Look at the Thick Silver Shekels. *The Numismatic
       Review* II, 2: 1–2.
1980   Plated Coins of Bar Kokhba. *Israel Numismatic Journal* 4: 34–37.
1981   Clashed Die Errors in Bar Kokhba Coins. *Israel Numismatic Journal*
       5: 44–45.
1987   *Guide to Biblical Coins 2nd Edition*. New York: Amphora.
1990–1 New Discovery on a Coin of Herod I. *Israel Numismatic Journal* 11:
       32.
1994–99 Four New Jewish Lead Coins or Tokens. *Israel Numismatic Journal*
       13: 63–65.

1996   *Guide to Biblical Coins 3rd Edition.* New York: Amphora.

2001   *Guide to Biblical Coins 4th Edition.* New York: Amphora.

2003–06 A New Coin Type of Herod Antipas. *Israel Numismatic Journal* 15: 56–61.

2005   *Not Kosher, Forgeries of Ancient Jewish and Biblical Coins.* New York: Amphora

2006   A Bronze Test Strike from the Bar Kokhba Revolt. *Israel Numismatic Research* 1: 111–116.

2007a *Ancient Scale Weights and Pre-Coinage Currency of the Near East.* Nyack: Amphora.

2007b Further Discussions on an Interesting Yehud Type. *The Celator* 21, 10: 42 f.

2007c Echoes of 'Judaea Capta': The Nature of Domitian's Coinage of Judea and Vicinity. *Israel Numismatic Research* 2: 123–130.

2007–8 Numismatic Expressions of Hasmonean Sovereignty. *Israel Numismatic Journal* 16: 76–91.

2007–8a A Rare Judaea Capta Type of Asia Minor. *Israel Numismatic Journal* 16: 109–111.

2009   A New Medallion of Agrippa II. *Israel Numismatic Research* 4: 57–61.

2010   The Metrology of Judaean Small Bronze Coins. *American Journal of Numismatics* Second Series 21: 105–121.

2010a Hasmonean Coin Chronologies: Two Notes. *Israel Numismatic Journal* 17: in press.

—and Shachar

2008   The Identity of YNTN on Hasmonean Overstruck Coins and the Chronology of the Alexander Jannaeus Types. *Israel Numismatic Research* 3: 87–94.

Hill, G. F.

1910   *Catalogue of the Greek Coins of Phoenicia.* London: British Museum.

1914   *Catalogue of the Greek Coins of Palestine (Galilee, Samaria, and Judaea).* London: British Museum.

1922   *Catalog of the Greek Coins of Arabia, Mesopotamia, and Persia.* London: British Museum.

Hoehner, H.W.

1972   *Herod Antipas.* Cambridge: Cambridge University Press.

Holy Scriptures
1917, 1945 *Holy Scriptures according to the Masoretic Text*. Philadelphia: The
    Jewish Publication Society of America.

Hoover, O.
1994   Striking a Pose: Seleucid Types and Machtpolitik on the Coins of
        John Hyrcanus I. *The Picus* 3: 40–57.
2003   The Seleucid Coinage of John Hyrcanus I: The Transformation of
        a Dynastic Symbol in Hellenistic Judaea. *American Journal of
        Numismatics*, Second Series 15: 29–39.
2006   The Authorized Version: Money and Meaning in the King James
        Bible." *American Numismatic Society Magazine*, 5, 2.
2007a   *Coins of the Seleucid Empire from the Collection of Arthur
        Houghton, Part II*. Ancient Coins in North American
        Collections, New York: American Numismatic Society.
2007b   Seleucid Coinage of Demetrias by the Sea. *Israel Numismatic
        Research* 2: 77–88.

Houghton, A.
1983   *Coins of the Seleucid Empire from the Collection of Arthur Houghton*,
        Ancient Coins in North American Collections. New York:
        American Numismatic Society.

— and Spaer, A.
1998   *The Arnold Spaer Collection of Seleucid Coins*, SNG Israel. London: I.
        Vecchi.

— and Lorber, C.
2002.   *Seleucid Coins, a Comprehensive Catalog*, Part I, Vols I & II. New York:
        American Numismatic Society and Classical Numismatic Group.

— and Lorber, C., and Hoover, O.
2008.   *Seleucid Coins, A Comprehensive Catalog*, Part II, Vols. I & II. New
        York: American Numismatic Society and Classical Numismatic
        Group.

Howgego, C.J.
1985   *Greek Imperial Countermarks*. London: Royal Numismatic Society,
        1985.

Hritzu, J.N. (trans.)
1965   'The Apology Against the Books of Rufinus' in *Saint Jerome;
        Dogmatic and Polemical Works. In The Fathers of the Church*,
        Vol. 53, Washington DC: 202.

Israel Numismatic Society.
1954   *Recent Studies and Discoveries on Ancient Jewish and Syrian Coins.*
        Jerusalem: Israel Numismatic Society.
1958   *The Dating and Meaning of Ancient Jewish Coins and Symbols.*
        Jerusalem: Israel Numismatic Society.
1967   *Patterns of Monetary Development in Phoenicia and Palestine in
        Antiquity.* Proceedings of the International Numismatic
        Convention, Jerusalem, 27–31 December 1963. Jerusalem:
        Schocken.

Jeselsohn, D.
1974   A New Coin Type with Hebrew Inscription. *Israel Exploration
        Journal* 24: 77– 78.

Johnson, P.
1987   *A History of the Jews.* New York: Harper & Row.

Jones, A.H.M.
1938   *The Herods of Judaea.* Oxford: Clarendon Press.

Jones, B. (trans. and commentary)
1993   *Suetonius: The Emperor Domitian.* London-New York: Bristol
        Classical Press.

—and Milns, R. (trans. and commentary)
2003   *Suetonius: The Flavian Emperors.* London: Bristol Classical Press.

Josephus
        Ant.: Josephus *Jewish Antiquities* (Loeb Classical Library 242, 326,
        365, 410, 433, 489 and 490). Transl. H.St.J. Thackeray (Books
        I–III), H.St.J. Thackeray and R. Marcus (Books IV–VI), H.St.J.
        Thackeray and R. Marcus (Books V–VIII), R. Marcus (Books IX–
        XIII), R. Marcus and A. Wikgren (Books XIV–XVII) and L.H.
        Feldman (Books XVIII–XX). London-New York 1930–1965.

        BJ: Josephus *The Jewish War* (Loeb Classical Library 203, 303, and
        487). Transl. H.St.J. Thackeray. London-New York 1927–1928
        (bound in three volumes in 1997).

        Vita: Josephus *Josephus in Nine Volumes.* I. *The Life. Against Apion*
        (Loeb Classical Library 186). Transl. H.St.J. Thackeray. London-
        New York 1926. pp. 2–159.

        see also Thackeray, and Whiston entries.

Julian, Emperor, The Works of
1923   Wilmer Cave Wright (edit. and trans.). Loeb Classical Library, Vol.
         III. Letter 51 (Epistle 25)

Kadman, L.
1960   *The Coins of the Jewish War.* (Corpus Nummorum
         Palaestinensium 3). Jerusalem: Schocken.
1961   *The Coins of Akko Ptolemais.* (Corpus Nummorum Palaestinensium
         4). Jerusalem: Schocken.

Kanael, B.
1950-1 The Beginning of Maccabean Coinage. *Israel Exploration Journal* 1:
         170–75.
1952   The Greek Letters and Monograms on the Coins of Jehohanan the
         High Priest. *Israel Exploration Journal* 11: 190–194.
1963   Ancient Jewish Coins and their Historical Importance. *Biblical
         Archaeology* 26: 38ff.

Kaufman, J.C.
1995   *Unrecorded Hasmonean Coins from the J.Ch. Kaufman Collection.*
         Jerusalem: Israel Numismatic Society.
2000–2 Additions to Leo Mildenberg's Corpus of The Coinage of the Bar
         Kokhba War. *Israel Numismatic Journal* 14: 129–152.
2004   *Unrecorded Hasmonean Coins from the J. Ch. Kaufman Collection, Part II.*
         Jerusalem: Israel Numismatic Society.
2007–08 Additions to the Corpus of Leo Mildenberg's Coinage of the Bar
         Kokhba War. *Israel Numismatic Journal* 16: 136–139.

Kindler, A.
1967   The Monetary Pattern and Function of the Jewish Coins.
         Proceedings of the International Numismatic Convention 1963.
         Jerusalem: Schocken: 180–203.
1974   *Coins of the Land of Israel.* Jerusalem: Ketter.
1984   Mobile Mint of Bar Kokhba. In *The Bar Kokhba Revolt, New
         Approaches*, A. Oppenheimber, U. Rappaport, eds. Yad Ben-Zvi:
         Jerusalem: 172–79.

King James Version of The Holy Bible.
         New York: American Bible Society.

Kletter, R.
1998   *Economic Keystones: The Weight System of the Kingdom of Judah.*
         Sheffield: Sheffield Academic Press.

2001 Weights and Weighing in Eretz Israel in Antiquity. In *Measuring and Weighing in Ancient Times*, Haifa: Reuben and Edith Hecht Museum.

Klimowsky, E.W.
1963 Danka and *prutah*: the *prutah*. *Israel Numismatic Journal* 1, 4: 68–69.
1974 *On Ancient Palestinian and Other Coins, Their Symbolism and Metrology.* Tel Aviv: Israel Numismatic Society.

Kokhavi, M.
1969 *Quadmoniot II*, 2: 40 (Hebrew).

Kokkinos, N.
1998 *The Herodian Dynasty. Origins, Role in Society and Eclipse.* Sheffield: Sheffield Academic Press.

Kovacs, F. L.
2008 Tigranes IV, V, and VI: New Attributions. *American Journal of Numismatics* 20: 337–350.

Kushnir-Stein, A.
1999 Review of Kokkinos, N. *The Herodian Dynasty. Scripta Classica Israelica* 18: 195.
2002 The Coinage of Agrippa II. *Scripta Classica Israelica* 21:123–131.
2000–2 Some Observations on Palestinian Coins with a Beveled Edge. *Israel Numismatic Journal* 14: 78–83.

Krupp, M.
2007–8 A Metallurgical Examination of Hasmonean Coins. *Israel Numismatic Journal* 16: 57–75.

Leemans, W.F.
1950 *The Old-Babylonian Merchant; His Business and His Social Position*, Vol. 3 Studia et Documenta ad Iura Orientis Antiqua Perinentia. Leiden: E.J. Brill.

Leonard, R.
1993 Cut Bronze Coins in the Ancient Near East. *International Congress of Numismatics (11th, 1991, Brussels) Actes.* Louvain-la-Neuve, 1993: 1, 363–370.

Levy, B.
1993 Tyrian *Sheqels* and the First Jewish War. Proceedings of the 11th International Numismatic Congress (Brussels 1991): 267–274.

2005 Holy Sheqels and the Currency of Jerusalem's Temple Tax. Third Leo Mildenberg lecture at Harvard University, April 15, 2005 (unpublished).

2005a Later Tyrian *Sheqels*: Dating the 'Crude' Issues, Reading the Controls. In: *XIII Congreso Internacional de Numismatica*.1: 885–890.

Lönnqvist, K.
1992–3 New Vistas on the Countermarked Coins of the Roman Prefects of Judaea. *Israel Numismatic Journal* 12: 56–60.
1997 A Re-Attribution of the King Herod Agrippa I 'Year 6' Issue. *Liber Annus* 47: 429–440.
2002 Pontius Pilate—Aqueduct Builder?—Recent Findings and New Suggestions. *Klio* 82: 459–475.

Maccabees, First and Second Books
1973 Commentary by John R. Bartlett. Cambridge: Cambridge University Press.

Madden, F. W.
1864 *History of Jewish Coinage and of Money in the Old and New Testament*. London: Quaritch.
1881 *The Coins of the Jews*. London: Quaritch.
1903 *The Coins of the Jews*. London: Quartich.

Magen, Y.
1986 A Fortified Town of the Hellenistic Period on Mount Gerizim. *Qadmoniot* 19, 1986: 91–101 (Hebrew) and *Qadmoniot* 23, 1990: 70–96 with discussion on coins pp. 74f, 87, 90 (Hebrew).

Magie, D. (trans.)
1979. Scriptores Historiae Augustae: Hadrian 14.2, in *The Scriptores Historiae Augustae*, 3 vols. 1:42–45. Cambridge: Harvard University Press.

McLean, M.
1982 *The Use and Development of Palaeo-Hebrew in the Hellenistic and Roman Periods*. Unpublished Ph.D. Dissertation, Harvard University.

Malamed, E.Z.
2005 *Aramaic/Hebrew/English Dictionary of the Babylonian Talmud*. Jerusalem.

Maltiel-Gerstenfeld, J.
1980   A Portrait Coin of Berenice Sister of Agrippa II? *Israel Numismatic Journal* 4: 25–26.
1982   *260 Years of Ancient Jewish Coins*. Tel Aviv: Kol.
1987   *New Catalog of Ancient Jewish Coins*. Tel Aviv: Minerva.

Mattingly, H.
1965   *Coins of the Roman Empire in the British Museum*, Vol. I. London: British Museum.
1966a *Coins of the Roman Empire in the British Museum*, Vol. II. London: British Museum.
1966b *Coins of the Roman Empire in the British Museum*, Vol. III. London: British Museum.

Mattingly, H., and Sydenham, E.
1968   *The Roman Imperial Coinage*, Vol. II. London: Spink and Son.

Matsson, G.O.
1999   *The Gods, Goddesses, and Heroes of the Ancient Coins of Bible Lands*. Stockholm: Mälartyrckeriet AB.

Mays, J.L., general editor.
1988   *Harper's Bible Commentary*. San Francisco: Harper & Row.

Meshorer, Y.
1961   An Attic Archaic Coin from Jerusalem. *Atiqot* 3 (English Series): 185.
1966   A New Type of YHD Coin. *Israel Exploration Journal*, 16: 217-219.
1967   *Jewish Coins of the Second Temple Period*. Tel Aviv: Am Hassefer and Masada Publishers.
1970   *Production of Coins in the Ancient World*. Jerusalem: Israel Museum.
1974   *Coins of the Ancient World*. Minneapolis: Lerner.
1975   *Nabataean Coins*. QEDEM 3, Monographs of the Institute of Archaeology, Jerusalem, Hebrew University.
1976   The Double Cornucopiae as a Jewish Symbol. *Judaica Post* 4: 282–286.
1978   Early Means of Payment and the First Coinage. *Ariel* 45–46: 127–143.
1979   On the Nature of the Symbols on the Coins of Herod the Great. *Festschrift Reuben R. Hecht*, Jerusalem: 158–161.
1982   *Ancient Jewish Coinage* I and II. New York: Amphora.
1983   *Coins Reveal*. New York: The Jewish Museum.
1985   *City Coins of Eretz-Israel and the Decapolis*. Jerusalem: Israel Museum.

1989a   The Coins of Masada. In *Masada, I, The Yigael Yadin Excavations 1963–1966: Final Reports*, Jerusalem.

1989b   *The Coinage of Aelia Capitolina.* Jerusalem: Israel Museum.

1990–1   Ancient Jewish Coinage Addendum I. *Israel Numismatic Journal* 11: 1.

1997   *A Treasury of Jewish Coins* (Hebrew). Jerusalem: Yad Itzhak Ben-Zvi Press.

2001   *A Treasury of Jewish Coins (English).* Jerusalem and New York: Amphora.

—and Qedar, S.

1991   *The Coinage of Samaria in the Fourth Century* BCE. Jerusalem: Numismatic Fine Arts International, Inc., 1991.

1999   *Samarian Coinage.* Jerusalem: The Israel Numismatic Society.

—*et.al.*

Forthcoming   *The Abraham Sofaer Collection at the American Numismatic Society.* New York.

Meyers, C, *et al.*

2000   *Women in Scripture.* New York: Houghton Mifflin.

Meyers, E.M.

1999   Sepphoris on the Eve of the Great Revolt (65–67 CE): Archaeology and Josephus. In *Galilee Through the Centuries: Confluence of Cultures*, ed. E.M. Meyers, Winona Lake: Eisenbrauns: 127–140.

2002   Sepphoris City of Peace. In *The First Jewish Revolt: Archaeology, History, and Ideology*, A.M.Berlin and J.A. Overman, eds. Routledge: London and NY, 2002: 110–120.

Meyshan, J.

1968   *Essays in Jewish Numismatics.* Jerusalem: Israel Numismatic Society.

Mildenberg, L.

1949   The Eleazar Coins of the Bar Kokhba Rebellion. *Historica Judaica* 11: 77–108.

1979   Yehud: A Preliminary Study of the Provincial Coinage of Judaea. In *Essays in Honor of Margaret Thompson*, Wettern: 183–196.

1984   *The Coinage of the Bar Kokhba War.* Salzburg: Verlag Sauerlander.

1984–5   A Bar Kokhba *Didrachm. Israel Numismatic Journal* 8: 32–36.

1990–1   Notes on the Coin Issues of Mazday. *Israel Numismatic Journal* 11: 9–23.

1992   The Philisto-Arabian Coins—A Preview. Preliminary Studies of the
        Local Coinage in the Fifth Persian Satrapy. Part 3, *Studia Phoenicia*
        9, Numismatique et Historie Économique Phéniciennes et
        Puniques, Louvain-la-Neuve, pp. 33–40.

Miller, M. and Hayes, J.H.
1986   *A History of Ancient Israel and Judah*. Philadelphia: Westminster
        Press.

Mindlin, V. & G. Cornfeld.
1962   *The Epic of the Maccabees*. New York: Macmillan.

Mørkholm, O.
1981   Some Coins of Ptolemy V from Palestine. Israel Numsimatic
        Journal: 5-11.

—Grierson, P., Westermark, U.
1991   *Early Hellenistic coinage: From the Accession of Alexander to the*
        Peace of Apamea (336–188 B.C.). Cambridge: Cambridge
        University Press.

Nadich, J.
1983   *Jewish Legends of the Second Commonwealth*. Philadelphia:
        Jewish   Publication Society.

Naveh, J.
1968   Dated Coins of Alexander Jannaeus. *Israel Exploration Journal*,
        18: 20f.
1987   *Early History of the Alphabet*. Jerusalem: The Magnes Press.

Nevo, Y.
2001   Ottoman Weight Units and the Transition to the Metric
        System in Eretz Israel. In *Measuring and Weighing in Ancient*
        Times, Haifa: Reuben and Edith Hecht Museum: 31–34.

Newell, E.T.
1913   The Oldest Known "Siege-Pieces." *Numismatist* 26: 543.
1937   *Royal Greek Portrait Coins*. Racine, Wisconsin: Whitman.

Nercessian, Y.T.
1995   *Armenian Coins and their Values*. Los Angeles: Armenian
        Numismatic Society.

Netzer, E.
2006   *The Architecture of Herod the Great Builder*. Grand Rapids, Baker
         Academic.

Neusner, J.
1970   *A Life of Yohanan Ben Zakkai Ca. 1–80 CE*. Leiden: EJ Brill.

Numismatica Ars Classica
2009   *Auction 51*, 5 March: lot 234.

Parise, N.F.
1989   The Mina of Ugarit, the Mina of Karkemish, the Mina of Khatti.
         In: C. Zaccagnini (ed.) *Production and Consumption in the Ancient Near
         East*, Budapest: 333: 41.

Parker, H.M.D.
1928   *The Roman Legions*. New York: Dorset Press, 1992 (reprint).

Perlman, Moshe.
1973   *The Maccabees*. New York: Macmillan 1973.

Petroso, K.M.
1981   Early Weights and Weighing in Egypt and the Indus Valley.
         Bulletin of the Museum of Fine Arts, Boston 79: 144.
1992   *Ayia Irini: The Balance Weights* (Keos VII, Results of the Excavations
         Carried out by the University of Cincinnati under the Auspices of
         the American School of Classical Studies at Athens) Mainz: Von
         Zabern Verlag.

Porter, R.F., Christensen, S., and Schiermacker-Hansen, P.
2004   *Field Guide to Birds of the Middle East*. Princeton: Princeton
         University Press.

Powell, M.A.
1979   Ancient Mesopotamian Weight Metrology: Methods, Problems
         and Perspectives. In M.A. Powell *et.al.* (eds.). *Studies in Honor of J.B.
         Jones*, Kevelaer: 71–201.
1992   Weights and Measures. *Anchor Bible Dictionary*, 6: 898–908, David
         N. Freedman (ed.) New York: Doubleday.

Price, M.J.
1968   Early Greek Bronze Coinage. Kraay C. M. & Jenkins G. K.,
         Essays in Greek Coinage presented to Stanley Robinson: 90–104.
         Oxford: Clarendon Press.

1975   *Coins and the Bible.* London: V.C. Vecchi & Sons.
1979   The Function of Early Greek Bronze Coinage. *Instituto Italiano di Numismatica Annali, Supplemento al. v. 25*: 351–358.
1991   *The Coinage in the Name of Alexander the Great and Philip Arrhidaeus.* I & II. Zurich/London.

—and Trell, B.
1977   *Coins and Their Cities.* Detroit: Wayne State University Press.

Pulak, C.
1987   *A Late Bronze Age Shipwreck at Uluburun: Preliminary Analysis (1984–1985 Excavation Campaigns).* Unpublished MA Thesis Texas A & M University.

Qedar, S.
1986–7 Two Lead Weights of Herod Antipas and Agrippa II and the Early History of Tiberias." *Israel Numismatic Journal* 9: 29–35.

2001   Weights of Eretz Israel in the Roman-Byzantine Period. In *Measuring and Weighing in Ancient Times.* Haifa: Reuben and Edith Hecht Museum: 23–27.

—and Hendin, D.
1996   *Ancient Weights of the Holy Land.* Unpublished manuscript.

Rabello, A. M.
1995   The Ban on Circumcision as a Cause of Bar Kokhba's Rebellion. *Israel Law Review* 29: 176–214.

Rahmani, L. Y.
1971   Silver Coins of the Fourth Century BC from Tel Gamma. *Israel Exploration Journal* 21: 158f.
1967   Jason's Tomb. *Israel Exploration Journal* 17, 2: 61–100.

Rappaport, U.
1970   Gaza and Ascalon in the Persian and Hellenistic Periods in Relation to their Coins. *Israel Exploration Journal* 20: 75–80.
2007   Who Minted the Jewish War's Coins? *Israel Numismatic Research* 2: 103–116.

Reifenberg, A.
1947   *Ancient Jewish Coins.* Jerusalem.

Richardson, P.
1996   *Herod: King of the Jews and Friend of the Romans*. Columbia:
        University of South Carolina Press.

Rogers, E. A.
1914   *Handy Guide to Jewish Coins*. London: Spink & Son.

Romanoff, P.
1944   *Jewish Symbols on Ancient Jewish Coins*. 1971 reprint. New York:
        American Israel Numismatic Assn.

Ronen, Y.
1996   The Enigma of the Shekel Weights of the Judean Kingdom.
        Biblical Archaeologist 59, 2: 122–25.
1998   The Weight Standards of the Judean Coinage in the Late Persian
        and Early Ptolemaic Period." *Near Eastern Archaeology* 61, 2: 122–26.
2003–6 Some Observations on the Coinage of Yehud. *Israel Numismatic
        Journal* 15: 28–31.
2007   Twenty Unrecorded Samarian Coins. *Israel Numismatic Research* 2:
        29–34.
2010   On the Chronology of the *Yehud* Falcon Coins. *Israel
        Numismatic Research* 4: 39–45.

Roth, C.
1954   *History of the Jews*. (Reprint 1961) New York: Schocken.

1962   Historical Implications of the Jewish Coinage of the First Revolt.
        Israel Exploration Journal 12,1: 33–46.
2007   Art. *Encyclopaedia Judaica*, 2nd edition Vol. 2: 491–494.

de Saulcy, L.F. J. C.
1871   Catalogue raisonné de monnaies judaiques recueillies à Jérusalem
        en Novembre. *Numismatic Chronicle* 11: 235–255.
1874   *Numismatique de la Terre Sainte, description des monnaies autonomes et
        imperiales de la Palestine et de L'Arabie Petree*. Paris: J. Rothschild.

Schalit, A. (ed.)
1972   *The Hellenestic Age: World History of the Jewish People* Vol. 6. New
        Brunswick: Rutgers University Press.

Schürer, E.
1890   *The History of the Jewish People in the Age of Jesus Christ* (175 BC–AD
        135). Edinburgh: T & T Clark.

1987   *The History of the Jewish People in the Age of Jesus Christ* (175 BC–AD 135). Revised and edited by G. Vermes and F. Millar: Edinburgh: T & T Clark.

Schwartz, D.R.
1990   *Agrippa I, The Last King of Judaea.* Tübingen, J.C.B. Mohr.
Scott, R.B.Y.
1959   Weights and Measures of the Bible. *Biblical Archaeologist* 22: 22–40.

Seaford, R.
2004   *Money and the Early Greek Mind: Homer, Philosophy, Tragedy.* Cambridge: Cambridge University Press.

Sellers, O.R.
1933   *The Citadel of Beth Zur.* Philadelphia: Westminster Press.

Shachar, I.
2004   The Historical and Numismatic Significance of Alexander Jannaeus' Later Coinage as Found in Archaeological Excavations. *Palestine Exploration Quarterly* 136: 5–33.

Shen S., *et.al.*
2004   Reconstruction of Patrilineages and Matrilineages of Samaritans and Other Israeli Populations From Y-Chromosome and Mitochondrial DNA Sequence Variation. *Human Mutation* 24: 248–260.

Smallwood, M.
1981   *The Jews Under Roman Rule From Pompey to Diocletian: A Study in Political Relations.* Leiden, E.J. Brill.

The Soncino Talmud
1995   CD ROM. Davka Corp.

Spaer, A.
1977   Some More 'Yehud' Coins. *Israel Exploration Journal* 27, 4: 200–203.
1986-7 Jaddua the High Priest? *Israel Numismatic Journal* 9: 1–3.

Sperber, D.
1974   *Roman Palestine 200–400 Money & Prices.* Ramat Gan: Bar Ilan University Press.
2007   Money Changers. In *Encyclopedia Judaica*, eds. Michael Berenbaum and Fred Skolnik. Vol. 14. 2nd ed. Detroit: Macmillan Reference USA: 435–436.

Spijkerman, A.
1956   Coins Mentioned in the New Testament. *Liber Annus*: 279–98.
1972.   *Herodion, Catalogo Delle Monete*. Jerusalem: Franciscan Printing
        Press.

Stein, H.J.
1943   Hitherto Unexplained Symbols on the Coins of John Hyrcanus.
        Numismatic Review Sept.: 19–21.

Stern, E.
1982   *Material Culture of the Land of the Bible in the Persian Period 538–
        332 BC.* Jerusalem: Israel Exploration Society.

Stern, M.
1975   The Herodian Dynasty and the Province of Judea at the End of
        the Period of the Second Temple. In *World History of Jewish People
        VII, The Herodian Period*, M. Avi Yonah, ed. New Brunswick:
        Rutgers University Press.

Strickert, F.
2002   The First Woman to be Portrayed on a Jewish Coin: Julia Sebaste.
        *Journal for the Study of Judaism in the Persian, Hellenistic, and Roman
        Periods* XXXIII, 1: 65–91. Leiden: E.J. Brill.

Suetonius
1957   *The Twelve Caesars.* Translated by Robert Graves. Baltimore, Penguin
        Books.
1993   *The Emperor Domitian.* Translated by B. Jones. London–New York:
        Bristol Classical Press.
2002   *The Flavian Emperors.* Translated by B. Jones and R. Milns. London:
        Bristol Classical Press.

Sukenik, E. L.
1934   Paralipomena Palestinensia. *Journal of the Palestine Oriental Society*
        14: 178–184.
1935   More About the Oldest Coins of Judaea. *Journal of the Palestine
        Oriental Society*, 15: 341–343.

Superior Galleries
1991–2 The Abraham Bromberg Collection of Jewish Coins Part I (1991)
        and Part II (1992). Beverly Hills: Superior Galleries.

Svornos, J.N.
1904   Ta Nomismata tou Kratous ton Ptolemaion(Ptolemaic Coinage).
        Athens.

Sydenham, E.A.
1952   *The Coinage of the Roman Republic*. London: Spink and Son.

Syon, D.
1992–3 Coins from Gamla—Interim Report. *Israel Numismatic Journal*
        12: 34–55.
2007   Yet Again on the Bronze Coins Minted at Gamla. *Israel
        Numismatic Research* 2: 117–122.

2001
—and Yavor, Z. Gamla Old and New. *Qadmoniot* 121: 2-33.

Tabor, J.
2006   *The Jesus Dynasty*. New York: Simon & Schuster.

Tacitus.
1964   *The Histories*. Translated by Kenneth Wellesley. Baltimore: Penguin
        Books.

Tal, O.
2007   Coin Denominations and Weight Standards in Fourth Century BCE
        Palestine. *Israel Numismatic Research* 2: 17–28.

Thackeray, H. St. J.
1928   *Works of Josephus*. Oxford: Loeb Editions.

Troxell, H.A.
1983   Arsinoe's Non Era. *American Numismatic Society. Museum Notes*
        28:.35-70.

Vagi, David.
1999   *Coinage and History of the Roman Empire*, Vols. 1 and 2.
        Sydney: Coin World.

Van Alfen, P.
2005   Herodotus' 'Aryandic' Silver and Bullion Use in Persian-Period
        Egypt. *American Journal of Numismatics* 16–17: 7–46.
2009   Personal communications regarding works in progress.

VanderKamm, J.C. and Flint, P.
2002   *The Meaning of the Dead Sea Scrolls*. San Francisco: Harper.

Walsh, R.
1882   *Works of the British Poets*. XLIV. Satires 5: 480. London: Bradford.
Weisbrem, M.
1962   Do the Coins of Domitian Minted in Palestine Belong to the
         'Judaea Capta' Series? *Israel Numismatic Bulletin* I: 6–7.

Whiston, William.
1899   *The Complete Works of Flavius Josephus*. Chicago: Thompson &
         Thomas.

Yadin, Y.
1971   *Bar-Kokhba*, New York: Random House.

Yeivin, Z.
1990   Notes of the Weight System at Alalakh VII. *Or.* 48, 1979: 472–475.

Zeitlin, I.
1988   *Jesus and the Judaism of His Time,* Cambridge: Basil Blackwell.

GBC 5	GBC 4	GBC 2	TJC	AJC	OTHER
1001	—	—	—	—	G&T II,1D
1002	—	—	—	—	G&T II,2D
1003	—	—	—	—	G&T II,9O
1004	—	—	—	—	G&T III,1T
1005	—	—	—	—	G&T III,20D
1006	—	—	—	—	G&T III,18D
1007	—	—	—	—	G&T III,11O
1008	—	—	—	—	G&T V, 5T
1009	—	—	—	—	G&T V,18T
1010	—	—	—	—	G&T VI,16D
1011	421	—	—	—	G&T V,25D
1012	422v	—	—	—	G&T VI,2D
1013	423v	—	—	—	G&T VI,7O
1014	424	—	—	—	G&T V,21O
1015	425	—	—	—	G&T V,10O
1016	—	—	—	—	G&T XV,1T
1017	—	—	—	—	G&T XIV,35D
1018	435	—	—	—	G&T,XVII,1D
1019	—	—	—	—	G&T XVIII,6D
1020	—	—	—	—	G&T XVIII,8D
1021	—	—	—	—	G&T XIX,20D
1022	—	—	—	—	G&T XIX,21O
1023	—	—	—	—	G&T XII, 13O
1024	—	—	—	—	G&T XIV,22O
1025	—	—	—	—	Gitler *et. al.* 2007: 54-56
1026	—	—	—	—	Gitler *et. al.* 2007: 54-56
1027	446	—	—	—	*Sam.* 13
1028	—	—	—	—	*Sam.* 16
1029	—	—	—	—	*Sam.* 28
1030	445	—	—	—	*Sam.* 38
1031	431	—	—	—	*Sam.* 39
1032	—	—	—	—	*Sam.* 41
1033	—	—	—	—	*Sam.* 52
1034	—	—	—	—	*Sam.* 61
1035	—	—	—	—	*Sam.* 77
1036	—	—	—	—	*Sam.* 80
1037	—	—	—	—	*Sam.* 87

GBC 5	GBC 4	GBC 2	TJC	AJC	OTHER
1038	—	—	—	—	*Sam.* 90
1039	—	—	—	—	*Sam.* 96
1040	—	—	—	—	*Sam.* 129
1041	—	—	—	—	*Sam.* 130
1042	—	—	—	—	*Sam.* 141
1043	—	—	—	—	*Sam.* 159
1044	—	—	—	—	*Sam.* 216
1045	434	4	1	1	*BMC* 181, 29
1046	—	—	—	—	Gitler in press
1047	436	—	—	—	Sofaer 1
1048	—	—	—	—	G & T XI.3D
1049	—	—	—	—	G & T XI.3O
1050	426v	1a	6a	2	
1051	—	—	5	3	
1052	—	—	10	—	
1053	—	—	10A	5	
1054	—	—	11	—	
1055	—	—	12	2a	
1056	—	—	13	—	
1057	426v	2	6	4	
1058	—	—	—	—	Gerson 2003-06: 32-34
1059	427	1	15	8	
1060	—	1a	16	—	
1060a	429v	—	16b	9a	
1060b	—	—	—	—	
1060c	—	—	16e	9b	
1060d	—	—	—	—	
1060e	—	—	16f	—	
1061	428	—	18	—	Deutsch 1994-9: 6, 1
1062	—	—	19	—	Deutsch 1990-1: 5, 5
1063	—	—	—	—	Deutsch 1990-1: 5, 4
1064	—	—	26	—	
1065	433	3a	24	12	
1066	—	—	25	13	
1067	—	—	—	—	Gitler & Lorber 2008: 77-78
1068	—	—	25a	12a	

GBC 5	GBC 4	GBC 2	TJC	AJC	OTHER
1069	430	3	22	10	
1070	—	—	22e	—	Fontanille & Lorber 2008: 45-50
1071	432	—	20	—	Barag 1986-87: Pl. 1, 1-3
1072	—	—	21	10	
1073	—	5	14	11	Deutsch 1990-91: 5. 3
1074	—	—	28	—	
1075	440	—	27	17sa	
1076	—	—	—	—	Barag 1994-99 pl. 4, 11-12
1077	—	—	30	—	
1078	437	—	29	14	
1079	—	—	—	—	Gitler & Lorber 2006: 7,5
1080	—	—	—	—	Deutsch 1994-9: 26, 2
1081	439	—	33	15	
1082	439	5a	34		
1083	—	—	35	—	Deutsch 1994-99: 26.3
1084	438a	—	31	184,1	
1085	438b	—	31a	184,2	Deutsch 1994-99: 26.5
1086	—	—	—	—	Deutsch 1994-99: 26.4
1087	438	5	32	16	
1088	—	—	—	—	Unpublished
1089	400	—	—	—	Price 1991: 3277
1090	401	—	—	—	Price 1991: 3283
1091	402	—	—	—	Price 1991: 3255
1092	403	—	—	—	cf. Price 1991: 3253
1093	404	—	—	—	Svornos 778
1094	404a	—	—	—	Svornos 790
1095	404a	—	—	—	Troxell 1983: 52, 36
1096	407	—	—	—	Mørkholm 1981: 8, 1-9
1097	408	—	—	—	Svoronos 821в
1098	409	—	—	—	Svoronos 817
1099	410	—	—	—	Svoronos 799
1100	—	—	—	—	Svoronos cf. 794
1101	411	—	—	—	BMC 54, 77
1102	412	—	—	—	Mørkholm 1981: 8, 1-4
1103	—	—	—	—	SC I,1096

GBC 5	GBC 4	GBC 2	TJC	AJC	OTHER
1104	—	—	—	—	*SC* II,1476
1105	413	—	—	—	*SC* II,1484.2
1106	—	—	—	—	*SC* II,1478.1
1107	—	—	—	—	*SC* II,1479
1108	—	—	—	—	*SC* II, 1581
1109	—	—	—	—	*SC* II,1678
1110	—	—	—	—	*SC* II,1679
1111	—	—	—	—	*SC* II,2046
1112	—	—	—	—	*SC* II,2116
1113	—	—	—	—	*SC* II,2271
1114	—	—	—	—	*SC* II,2336
1115	—	—	—	—	*SC* II,2390.5
1116	—	—	—	—	Kadman 1961 cf. 11-14
1117	416	—	—	—	*SC* II,1495
1118	—	—	—	—	*SC* II, 2026
1119	—	—	—	—	*SC* II,2048
1120	—	—	—	—	*SC* II,2122
1121	—	—	—	—	*SC* II,2276.1
1122	417	—	—	—	*SC* II,2339.3
1123	—	—	—	—	*SC* II,2395
1124	—	—	—	—	Hoover 2007: 80, 2a
1125	—	—	—	—	*SC* II,1852
1126	—	—	—	—	*SC* II,1975
1127	418	—	—	—	*SC* II,2028 (as Marisa)
1128	—	—	—	—	*SC* II,2125
1129	—	—	—	—	Barag *2000-2a:* Pl. 11-12
1130	—	—	—	—	*SC* II,2394
1131	451	6	p. 30	I, 160: 1-3	
1132	454	22	A	M	
1133	455-56	23	B	N	
1134	458	25	C	O	
1135	453	21	D	P	
1136	462	29	H	R	
1137	459-60	26,27	I	S	
1138	461	28	J	T	

GBC 5	GBC 4	GBC 2	TJC	AJC	OTHER
1139	464	30	E	L	
1140	463	30	G	Q	
1141	—	20	F	K	
1142	466	33	V	Jc	
1143	465	32	U	Ja-b	
1144	474	15	Q	F	
1145	473	14	P	E	
1146	475	16	R	G	
1147	468	8	O	B	
1148	467	7	N	A	
1149	478	17	T	I	
1150	469	10	K	Ca	
1151	470	11	K 17	Cb	
1152	471	12	L	Cd	
1153	472	13	L 5	Ce	
1154	477	—	L 17	Cf1	
1155	476	9	M	D	
1156	477	—	—	—	Hendin 1994-9: pl.8,3
1157	—	—	—	—	Hendin 1994-9: pl.8,4
1158	—	—	—	—	Hendin 1994-9: pl.8,6
1159	479	18	S	H	
1160	479A		S 39	Hc3	
1161	480	19	S 42-4	Hd	
1162	481	34	36	U	
1163	482	35	37	V	
1164	483	36	40	Y	
1165	—	—	39	X	
1166	—	37	38a,b	W 1-3	
1167	484	—	38c	W 4	
1168	485	38	41	Z	
1169	486	39	44	1	*RPC* I, 4901
1170	487	40	45	2	*RPC* I, 4902
1171	488	41	46	3	*RPC* I, 4903
1172	489	42	47	4	*RPC* I, 4904
1173	498	51	60	18	
1174	499	52	61,63	19	
1175	—	—	62	—	

GBC 5	GBC 4	GBC 2	TJC	AJC	OTHER
1176	—	—	64	21	
1177	—	—	61c	—	
1178	490	43	48	7	*RPC* I, 4905
1178a	490a		49	8	
1179	491	44	50	9	*RPC* I, 4906
1180	—	—	51	10	
1181	—	—	52	11	
1182	—	—	53	12	
1183	492	45	54	13	
1184	493, 494	—	54a	—	
1185	495	48	55	14	*RPC* I, 4907
1186	496	49	56	15	
1187	497	—	58	16	
1188	500	54	59	17	*RPC* I, 4910
1189	—	—	59n	17l	
1190	501	56	66	23	*RPC* I, 4909
1191	502	57	65	22	*RPC* I, 4908
1192	508	58	67	1b	*RPC* I, 4912
1193	507	59	69c	2b	*RPC* I, 4913
1194	503	61	70	3	*RPC* I, 4914
1195	504	62	71	4	*RPC* I, 4915
1196	505	63	73	6	*RPC* I, 4917
1197	506	60	72	5	*RPC* I, 4916
1198	—	—	—	—	Hendin 2003-06: 56-61
1199	509	64	75	1	*RPC* I, 4918
1200	510	65	76	2	*RPC* I, 4919
1201	511	—	77	3	*RPC* I, 4920
1202	—	—	78	4	*RPC* I, 4921
1203	512	—	79	5	*RPC* I, 4922
1204	513	—	80	6	*RPC* I, 4923
1205	514	—	81	7	*RPC* I, 4924
1206	515	—	82	8	*RPC* I, 4925
1207	516	66a	83	9	*RPC* I, 4926
1208	517	66	84	10	*RPC* I, 4927
1209	518	—	85	11	*RPC* I, 4928
1210	519	67	86	12	*RPC* I, 4929

GBC 5	GBC 4	GBC 2	TJC	AJC	OTHER
1211	520	—	87	13	*RPC* I, 4930
1212	521	—	88	14	*RPC* I, 4931
1213	522	—	89	15	*RPC* I, 4932
1214	523	—	90	16	*RPC* I, 4933
1215	524	68	91	17	*RPC* I, 4934
1216	525	68a	92	18	*RPC* I, 4935
1217	526	—	93	19	*RPC* I, 4936
1218	527	—	94	—	*RPC* I, 4937
1219	528	70a	95	1	*RPC* I, 4938
1220	529	—	96	2	*RPC* I, 4939
1221	531	71	97	3	*RPC* I, 4941
1221a	531a	—	97b	3b	*RPC* I, 4940
1222	532	—	98	4	
1223	533	—	99	5	*RPC* I, 4942
1224	534	72a	101	7	*RPC* I, 4943
1225	535	—	102	8	*RPC* I, 4944
1226	536	—	103	9	*RPC* I, 4945
1227	—	—	—	—	unpublished
1228	537	—	104, 105	10, 10a	*RPC* I, 4947, 4946
1229	530	70	100	6	*RPC* I, 4951
1230	538	—	106	11	*RPC* I, 4948
1231	540	71b	107	278,1	*RPC* I, 4949
1232	541	71a	108	12	*RPC* I, 4950
1233	542	72	109	14	*RPC* I, 4952
1234	543	—	110	—	*RPC* I, 4949
1235	544	—	111	13	*RPC* I, 4953
1236	545	—	112	—	*RPC* I, 4973
1237	546	73	113	1	*RPC* I, 4974
1238	547	—	114	—	*RPC* I, 4975
1239	548	—	115	—	*RPC* I, 4980
1240	549	74	116	2	*RPC* I, 4976
1241	550	—	117	3	*RPC* I, 4977
1242	551	—	118	7	*RPC* I, 4978
1243	552	79	119	4	*RPC* I, 4979
1244	553	75	120	11	*RPC* I, 4981
1245	544	76	121	8	*RPC* I, 4983
1246	555	76b	122	6	*RPC* I, 4985

GBC 5	GBC 4	GBC 2	TJC	AJC	Other
1247	556	81	123	—	*RPC* I, 4987
1248	557	76a	124	5a	*RPC* I, 4982
1249	558	—	125	10	—
1250	559	—	126	9	*RPC* I, 4986
1251	560	—	361	—	*RPC* I, 4977
1252	561	77	362	1	*RPC* I, 4978
1253	562	—	363	2	*RPC* I, 4979
1254	563	—	364	3	*RPC* I, 4980
1255	564	78	365	5	*RPC* I, 3840
1256	565	—	366	4	*RPC* I, 3839
1257	—	—	—	—	Sofaer 171
1258	566	—	367	6	
1259	567	—	350	—	*RPC* I, 4842
1260	568	—	351	—	*RPC* I, 4843
1261	569	—	352	—	*RPC* I, 4844
1262	570	—	355	—	*RPC* I, 4847
1263	571	—	356	—	*RPC* I, 4848
1264	572	—	357	—	*RPC* I, 4858
1265	573	—	358	—	*RPC* I, 4859
1266	574	—	347	S. III, 5	*RPC* I, 4851
1267	575	—	348	S. III, 6	*RPC* I, 4852
1268	576	—	349	S. III, 7	*RPC* I, 4853
1269	577	—	353	—	*RPC* I, 4845
1270	578	—	354	—	RPC I, 4846
1271	579	—	359	—	*RPC* I, 4860
1272	580	—	360	—	RPC I, 4861
1273	581	—	129	1	*RPC* I, 4988
1274	582	80	130	2	RPC I, 4989
1275	583	—	131	3	*RPC* I, 4990
1276	586	—	127	8	*RPC* I, 4849
1277	587	—	128	9	*RPC* I, 4850
1278	584	82	132	5	*RPC* I, 4991
1279	585	83	133	6	*RPC* I, 4992
1280	588	—	134	—	*RPC* II 2242
1281	—	—	—	—	Hendin 2009: 57-61
1282	610	—	158	30	*RPC* II, 2274
1283	611	—	159	31	

GBC 5	GBC 4	GBC 2	TJC	AJC	Other
1284	—	—	160	32	*RPC* II, 2276
1284a	612	—	160A	32	*RPC* II, 2277
1285	617	—	165	37a	*RPC* II, 2279
1286	621	—	168	41	*RPC* II, 2284
1287	618	—	167	39	*RPC* II, 2282
1288	619	84	166	38	*RPC* II, 2283
1289	620	—	169	—	*RPC* II, 2285
1290	622	93	170	42	*RPC* II, 2286
1291	623	94	171	43	*RPC* II, 2287
1292	624	—	172	44	*RPC* II, 2288
1293	625	—	173	45	*RPC* II, 2290
1294	627	—	175	48	*RPC* II, 2292
1295	628	—	176	49	*RPC* II, 2293
1296	629	—	177 (?)	50	noted in market
1297	630	97	178	52	*RPC* II, 2295
1298	631	—	179	53	*RPC* II, 2296
1299	632	—	180	54	*RPC* II, 2297
1300	634	99	182	56	*RPC* II, 1299
1301	589a	—	—	8	*RPC* II, 2244
1302	590	—	137	9	*RPC* II, 2246
1303	591	—	138	10	*RPC* II, 2248
1304	592	87	139	11	*RPC* II, 2250
1305	593	—	140	12	*RPC* II, 2252
1306	594	—	141	13	*RPC* II, 2253
1307	595	—	142	14	*RPC* II, 2254
1308	596	—	143	15	*RPC* II, 2255
1309	—	—	144	16	
1310	597	85	145	17	*RPC* II 2257
1311	598	—	146	18	*RPC* II, 2258
1312	599	88	148	20	*RPC* II, 2260
1313	600	—	147	19	*RPC* II, 2259
1314	601	88a	149	21	*RPC* II, 2261
1315	602	89	150	22	*RPC* II,,2262
1316	603	90	151	23	*RPC* II, 2263
1317	604	—	152	24	*RPC* II 2264
1318	605	—	153	25	*RPC* II, 2265
1319	606	—	154	26	*RPC* II, 2266

GBC 5	GBC 4	GBC 2	TJC	AJC	OTHER
1320	607	91	156	28	*RPC* II, 2267
1321	608	—	155	—	ADD I 27/28
1322	609	92	157	29	*RPC* II, 2268
1323	613	—	161	33	*RPC* II, 2269
1324	614	—	162	34	*RPC* II, 2270
1325	615	96	163	35	*RPC* II, 2271
1326	616	95	164	36	*RPC* II, 2272
1327	624	—	174	47	*RPC* II, 2289
1328	635	100	311	1	*RPC* I, 4954
1329	636	101	313	3	*RPC* I, 4955
1330	637	102	314	4	*RPC* I, 4956
1331	638	103	315	5	*RPC* I, 4957
1332	639	104	316	6	*RPC* I, 4958
1333	640	105	317	8	*RPC* I, 4959
1334	641	106	320	10	*RPC* I, 4960
1335	642	107	321	12	*RPC* I, 4961
1336	643	108	326	16	*RPC* I, 4953
1337	644	109	325	15	*RPC* I, 4952
1338	645	110	327	17	*RPC* I, 4964
1339	646	111	328	18	*RPC* I, 4965
1340	647	112	329	19	*RPC* I, 4966
1341	648	113	331	21	*RPC* I, 4967
1342	649	114	333	23	*RPC* I, 4968
1343	650	115	334	24	*RPC* I, 4969
1344	—	—	337	26	
1345	—	—	339	28	
1346	—	—	338	27	
1347	651	116	342	32	*RPC* I, 4970
1348	652	117	340	29	*RPC* I, 4971
1349	—	—	343	—	
1350	—	—	344	—	
1351	653	118	345	35	*RPC* I, 4972
1352	654	—	183	1	
1353	655	—	184	2	
1354	655a	119	187	3	
1355	656	120	188	6	
1356	657	120a	186	7	

GBC 5	GBC 4	GBC 2	TJC	AJC	OTHER
1357	658	—	192	—	Deutsch 1992-3: 71-72
1358	659	121	193	8	
1359	660	122	195	10	
1360	661	123	196	12	
1361	662	124	202	18	
1362	663	125	203	19	
1363	664	126	204	20	
1364	665	127	207	23	
1365	666	128	209	25	
1366	667	—	210	26	
1367	668	129	211	27	
1368	669	130	213	29	
1369	670	131	214	30	
1370	671	132	215	31	
1370a	671a	—	215a	31a	
1371	672	—	216	—	
1372	673	—	217	32	
1373	674	133	218	1	Mild 1-5
1374	675	—	219	2	Mild 1-2
1375	676	135	221	4	Mild 12-18
1376	677	136	220b	3	Mild 1-11
1377	680	139	223	6	Mild 20-26
1377a	680a	—	223h	6h	Mild 161
1378	678	137	222	5	Mild 34, 38-46
1378a	—	—	222e	5d	Mild 35-37
1378b	678a	137a	222d	5c	Mild 162
1379	679	138	257	40	Mild 47
1379a	679a	—	258	—	Mild 164-68
1380	681	140	224	7	Mild 47-150
1381	682	141	227	10	Mild 151
1382	683	142	237	20	Mild 10
1383	684	143	236	19	Mild 9
1384	685	144	235	17	Mild 3-8
1385	686	145	229	12	Mild 6-9
1386	687	—	230	12a	Mild 10-12
1387	688	144	230a	13a	Mild 13-26

GBC 5	GBC 4	GBC 2	TJC	AJC	Other
1388	689	146	233	16a	Mild 27-45
1389	690	151	238	21	Mild 12-13
1390	691	149	245	28	Mild 17, 29
1391	692	148	250	33	Mild 16,21,22,28,30-36
1392	693	147	243	26	Mild 18,19,20,23-26
1393	694	153	240	23	Mild 43, 44
1394	695	154	248	31	Mild 38,40-42,48-50
1395	696	155	253	36a	Mild 37
1396	697	152	242	25	Mild 47
1397	—	—	239	22	Mild 53
1398	—	—	246a	—	Mild 52
1399	700	—	252	35	Mild 54
1400	—	—	246a	29a	Mild 55
1401	701	—	246	29	Mild 59, 60
1402	—	—	244	27	Mild 56
1403	703	150	241a	24	Mild 57, 58
1404	704	156	255	38	Mild 18
1405	705	157	256	39	Mild 19
1406	707	158	263	46	Mild 28
1407	706	159	296	50	Mild 29, 30
1408	708	160	260a	43	Mild 48-93
1409	709	—	265	48	Mild 152
1410	710	161	266	49	Mild 153, 154
1411	711	162	267	51	Mild 46-49,51-57,59,60,62-87
1411a	711a	—	268	52	Mild 101-104
1412	712	—	270	54	Mild 50, 58, 61
1413	713,713a	163	269	53	Mild 89-96
1414	—	—	—	—	Mild 88
1415	714	—	271	—	Mild —
1416	715	—	279c	62b	Mild 61-66
1417	716	165	276b	59b	Mild 67, 68
1418	717	—	283b	66b	Mild 72-83
1419	718	—	272	55	Mild 69-71, 84
1420	719	166	279a	62a	Mild 92
1421	720	—	276a	59a	Mild 90
1422	721	—	283a	66a	Mild 85-87,89,104-107,109-111

GBC 5	GBC 4	GBC 2	TJC	AJC	Other
1423	722	—	284a	67a	Mild 88, 108
1424	723	167	272a	55a	Mild 94-101
1425	724	—	279	62	Mild 115, 122, 136
1426	725	—	276	59	Mild 123-125, 129
1427	726	164	283	66	Mild 113,116,121,126 133-5,138
1428	727	164a	284	67	Mild 128, 132
1429	728	—	272c	55c	Mild 112,114,117- 20,127,130,137,139-40
1430	729	169	281	64	Mild 145-51,168-71,190
1431	730	171	277	60	Mild 152-54,162,166- 7,187,198-200
1432	731	—	—	—	Mild —
1433	732	170	285	68	Mild 156-8,161,163, 189-92, 194-5,197
1434	733	—	286	69	Mild 155, 164, 188
1435	734	172	274	57a	Mild 159-60,172-86, 193,196,201-20
1436	735	174	297	77	Mild 31-33
1437	736	173	291	74	Mild 94-146
1438	737	175	300	79	Mild 155
1439	738	176	301	80	Mild 156, 157
1440	739	177	302b	81a	Mild 158-60
1441	740	—	—	—	Syd. 913
1442	—	178	—	—	Syd. 912
1443	741	179	—	—	Syd. 932
1444	741a	—	—	—	*RPC* I,1291
1445	742	180	380	1	*RPC* II, 2310
1446	743	181	381	2	*RPC* II, 2311
1447	744	182	382	3	*RPC* II, 2312
1448	—	—	383	4	
1449	745	183	384	5	*RPC* II, 2313
1450	—	—	386	1	*RPC* II, 2300
1451	753	191	387	2	*RPC* II, 2301
1452	752	190	388	3	*RPC* II, 2302
1453	754	—	389	4	*RPC* II, 2303
1454	748	187	391	6	*RPC* II, 2304
1455	749	188	392	7	*RPC* II, 2305
1456	750	186	393	8	*RPC* II, 2306

GBC 5	GBC 4	GBC 2	TJC	AJC	OTHER
1457	—	—	—	—	*RPC* II, 2025
1458	746	184	394	9	
1459	747	185	395	10	
1460	751	189	390	5	
1461	755	—	—	—	
1462	756	—	—	—	*BMC* 61
1463	757	—	—	—	
1464	758	197	—	—	*RIC* 1
1465	760	189	—	—	*RIC* 3
1466	762	206	—	—	*RIC* 363
1467	764	—	—	—	*RIC* 364
1468	—	—	—	—	*RIC* 368
1469	—	—	—	—	*RIC* 370
1470	766	—	—	—	*RIC* 1067
1471	—	—	—	—	*RIC* 1075
1472	—	—	—	—	*RIC* 1115
1473	—	—	—	—	*RIC* 1117
1474	—	—	—	—	*RIC* 1119
1475	768	—	—	—	*RIC* 1127
1476	769	—	—	—	*RIC* 1179
1477	—	198	—	—	*RIC* 1315
1478	—	—	—	—	*RIC* 1535
1478a	—	—	—	—	*RIC* 1536
1479	759	—	—	—	*RIC* 2
1480	761	199	—	—	*RIC* 4
1481	—	—	—	—	*RIC* 49
1482	—	206	—	—	*RIC* 369
1483	289	214	—	—	*RIC* 371
1484	—	—	—	—	*RIC* 688
1484a	—	—	—	—	*RIC* 697
1485	767	211	—	—	*RIC* 1068
1485a	—	—	—	—	*RIC* 1069
1486	—	213	—	—	*RIC* 1076
1487	—	—	—	—	*RIC* 1118
1488	770	200	—	—	*RIC* 1120
1489	—	—	—	—	*RIC* 1316
1490	—	—	—	—	*RIC* 1558

GBC 5	GBC 4	GBC 2	TJC	AJC	Other
1491	—	—	—	—	*RIC* 1559
1492	—	—	—	—	*RIC* 1562
1493	—	—	—	—	*RIC* 1563
1494	—	—	—	—	*RIC* 14
1495	—	—	—	—	*RIC* 51
1496	—	—	—	—	*RIC* 57
1496a	—	—	—	—	*RIC* 58
1497	776	—	—	—	*RIC* 68
1497a	—	—	—	—	*RIC* 69
1497b	—	—	—	—	
1498	—	—	—	—	*RIC* 81
1499	—	—	—	—	*RIC* 127
1499a	—	—	—	—	*RIC* 128
1499b	—	—	—	—	*RIC* 129
1499c	—	—	—	—	*RIC* 130
1500	—	201	—	—	*RIC* 159
1500a	—	—	—	—	*RIC* 160
1500b	—	—	—	—	*RIC* 161
1500c	—	—	—	—	*RIC* 162
1501	—	—	—	—	*RIC* 163
1501a	—	—	—	—	*RIC* 164
1502	774	202	—	—	*RIC* 165
1503	—	—	—	—	*RIC* 166
1504	—	203	—	—	*RIC* 167
1504a	—	—	—	—	*RIC* 168
1504b	—	—	—	—	*RIC* 169
1504c	—	—	—	—	error? Cos II
1505	—	—	—	—	*RIC* 213
1505a	—	—	—	—	*RIC* 214
1506	—	—	—	—	*RIC* 215
1507	—	—	—	—	*RIC* 216
1507a	—	—	—	—	*RIC* 217
1507b	—	—	—	—	*RIC* 218
1507c	—	—	—	—	*RIC* 219
1507d	—	—	—	—	*RIC* 220
1508	—	—	—	—	*RIC* 221
1508a	—	—	—	—	*RIC* 222

GBC 5	GBC 4	GBC 2	TJC	AJC	Other
1508b	—	—	—	—	*RIC* 223
1508c	—	—	—	—	*RIC* 224
1508d	—	—	—	—	*RIC* 225
1508e	—	—	—	—	*RIC* 336
1509	—	—	—	—	*RIC* 233
1510	—	—	—	—	*RIC* 234
1511	—	—	—	—	*RIC* 235
1512	—	—	—	—	*RIC* 236
1513	—	—	—	—	*RIC* 249
1514	—	—	—	—	*RIC* 255
1515	—	—	—	—	*RIC* 256
1516	—	—	—	—	*RIC* 375
1517	—	209	—	—	*RIC* 376
1518	—	—	—	—	*RIC* 386
1519	—	—	—	—	*RIC* 387
1520	—	—	—	—	*RIC* 388
1521	—	—	—	—	*RIC* 389
1522	—	216a	—	—	*RIC* 412
1523	—	—	—	—	*RIC* 422
1524	—	—	—	—	*RIC* 429
1524a	—	—	—	—	*RIC* 430
1525	790	214a	—	—	*RIC* 431
1526	793	—	—	—	*RIC* 433
1527	—	—	—	—	*RIC* 457
1528	—	—	—	—	*RIC* 462
1529	—	—	—	—	*RIC* 463
1529a	—	—	—	—	*RIC* 464
1530	—	—	—	—	*RIC* 474
1531	—	—	—	—	*RIC* 475
1531a	—	—	—	—	*RIC* 476
1532	—	—	—	—	RIC 479a Supp.
1533	791	—	—	—	*RIC* 477
1534	—	—	—	—	*RIC* 495
1535	—	—	—	—	*RIC* 497
1536	—	—	—	—	*RIC* 498
1537	—	—	—	—	*RIC* 499
1538	—	—	—	—	*RIC* 562

GBC 5	GBC 4	GBC 2	TJC	AJC	OTHER
1539	791a	—	—	—	*RIC* 564
1540	—	—	—	—	*RIC* 565
1540a	—	—	—	—	*RIC* 566
1541	—	—	—	—	*RIC* 577
1542	—	—	—	—	*RIC* 611
1543	775	203	—	—	*RIC* 1134
1543a	—	—	—	—	unpublished
1544	773	208	—	—	*RIC* 1181
1545	—	—	—	—	*RIC* 1204
1546	—	—	—	—	*RIC* 1205
1547	—	—	—	—	*RIC* 1245
1548	—	—	—	—	*RIC* 1246
1549	—	—	—	—	*RIC* 59
1550	—	—	—	—	*RIC* 65
1551	—	—	—	—	*RIC* 134
1552	—	—	—	—	*RIC* 271
1553	—	—	—	—	*RIC* 283
1554	—	—	—	—	*RIC* 303
1554a	—	—	—	—	*RIC* 304
1554b	—	—	—	—	*RIC* 305
1554c	—	—	—	—	*RIC* 306
1554d	—	—	—	—	*RIC* 307
1555	—	—	—	—	*RIC* 308
1556	—	—	—	—	*RIC* 328
1556a	—	—	—	—	*RIC* 329
1556b	783	—	—	—	*RIC* 332
1557	—	—	—	—	*RIC* 300
1558	—	—	—	—	*RIC* 445
1559	—	—	—	—	*RIC* 490
1559a	—	—	—	—	*RIC* 673
1560	794	217	—	—	*RIC* 626
1561	781	—	—	—	*RIC* 1233
1562	—	—	—	—	*RIC* 1268
1563	—	—	—	—	*RIC* 1332
1564	—	—	—	—	*RIC* 340
1564a	—	—	—	—	*RIC* 341
1565	—	—	—	—	*RIC* 342

GBC 5	GBC 4	GBC 2	TJC	AJC	OTHER
1565a	—	—	—	—	*RIC* 343
1566	—	—	—	—	*RIC* 344
1567	—	—	—	—	*RIC* 345
1568	—	—	—	—	*RIC* 350
1569	—	—	—	—	*RIC* 351
1569a	—	—	—	—	*RIC* 352
1570	—	—	—	—	*RIC* 353
1571	784	—	—	—	*RIC* 408
1571a	—	—	—	—	*RIC* 409
1572	—	—	—	—	*RIC* 410
1573	—	—	—	—	*RIC* 1514
1574	—	—	—	—	*RIC* 1515
1574a	795a	—	—	—	
1575	794a	—	—	—	*RIC* 604
1576	—	—	—	—	*RIC* 612
1577	—	—	—	—	*RIC* 1
1578	—	—	—	—	*RIC* 11
1578a	—	—	—	—	*RIC* 29
1578b	785	—	—	—	*RIC* 48
1579	—	—	—	—	*RIC* 100
1579a	—	—	—	—	*RIC* 101
1580	—	—	—	—	*RIC* 360
1581	—	—	—	—	*RIC* 363
1582	—	—	—	—	*RIC* 12
1583	—	—	—	—	*RIC* 30
1583a	—	—	—	—	*RIC* 31
1583b	—	—	—	—	*RIC* 49
1583c	—	—	—	—	*RIC* 50
1584	788	215	—	—	*RIC* 102
1584a	—	—	—	—	*RIC* 103
1584b	—	—	—	—	*RIC* 104
1584c	—	—	—	—	*RIC* 105
1585	789a	—	—	—	*RIC* 361
1585a	—	—	—	—	*RIC* 362
1586	772a	212	—	—	*RIC* 364
1587	—	—	—	—	*RIC* 368
1588	—	—	—	—	*RIC* 57

GBC 5	GBC 4	GBC 2	TJC	AJC	OTHER
1589	—	—	—	—	*RIC* 133
1590	—	—	—	—	*RIC* 135a Supp.
1591	—	—	—	—	*RIC* 145
1591a	—	—	—	—	*RIC* 146
1591b	—	—	—	—	*RIC* 147
1591c	—	—	—	—	*RIC* 148
1591d	—	—	—	—	NAC 40,331
1592	792	216	—	—	*RIC* 149
1593	—	—	—	—	*RIC* 150
1594	—	—	—	—	*RIC* 184
1594a	—	—	—	—	*RIC* 185
1594b	—	—	—	—	*RIC* 186
1595	—	—	—	—	*RIC* 369
1596	—	—	—	—	*RIC* 500
1596a	—	—	—	—	
1596b	—	—	—	—	ex. Hendin coll.
1597	—	—	—	—	*RIC* 502
1598	—	—	—	—	*RIC* 504
1598a	795	—	—	—	Helios I, 447
1599	—	—	—	—	*RIC* 131
1600	796	—	—	—	Abramowitz 12/8/93, 135
1601	—	—	—	—	826
1601a	—	—	—	—	827
1602	—	—	—	—	*RIC* (old) II, 831
1602a	—	—	—	—	*RIC* (old) II, 832
1603	—	—	—	—	*BMCRE* 88
1603a	—	—	—	—	*BMCRE* 98
1603b	797	219	—	—	*BMCRE* 105
1603c	—	—	—	—	
1604	798	—	—	—	*RIC* 890 obv c
1604a	—	220	—	—	*RIC* 890 obv f
1604b	—	—	—	—	*RIC* 893
1604c	—	—	—	—	*RIC* 893 obv f
1604d	—	—	—	—	*RIC* 894 obv c
1604e	—	—	—	—	*RIC* 894 obv f
1605	799	221	—	—	*RIC* 853

GBC 5	GBC 4	GBC 2	TJC	AJC	OTHER
1606	800	—	—	—	*RIC* 891
1607	800a	—	—	—	
1608	801	—	—	—	
1609	802	192	—	—	
1610	803	193	—	—	
1611	804	194v	—	—	
1612	805	195	—	—	
1613	806a	—	—	—	
1614	—	196	—	—	
1615	—	—	—	—	
1616	807a	—	—	—	
1617	807b	—	—	—	
1618	917	305	—	—	see *BMC & RPC*
1619	918	306	—	—	see *BMC & RPC*
1620	919	307	—	—	see *BMC & RPC*
1621	920	308	—	—	see *BMC & RPC*
1622	916	304	—	—	*BMCRE* 34

Note about Concordance:

Abbreviations are listed on page 580.

Please note that *GBC* 5 numbers are intended to be coin TYPES and not necessarily specific dies. Thus there may be multiple matches in, for example, Mildenberg.

AJC I and II and Mildenberg are not numbered consecutively but according to section entries. In *AJC*, each ruler starts numbering anew. In the case of Mildenberg large silver, small silver, and bronze have their own numbering. To save space in this concordance chart, we have listed *AJC* and Mildenberg numbers, which should be read with common sense regarding the location of the numbers. In case of possible confusion, more specific numbers have been provided.

Regarding other multiple volume references, the reader should apply common sense and if the reference is to *RIC* and the coin is one of Hadrian, it is obviously in the volume containing the coins of Hadrian.

APPENDIX A. ALPHABETS AND NUMERIC EQUIVALENTS

GREEK

LETTER	FORM	NUM.
ALPHA	A	1
BETA	B	2
GAMMA	Γ	3
DELTA	Δ	4
EPSILON	E	5
DIGAMMA	ς	6
ZETA	Z	7
ETA	H	8
THETA	Θ	9
IOTA	I	10
KAPPA	K	20
LAMDA	Λ	30
MU	M	40
NU	N	50
XI	Ξ	60
OMICRON	O	70
PI	Π	80
RHO	P	100
SIGMA	Σ	200
TAU	T	300
UPSILON	Y	400
PHI	Φ	500
CHI	X	600
PSI	Ψ	700
OMEGA	Ω	800

HEBREW

LETTER	FORM	COIN FORM	NUM.
ALEPH	א	𐤀	1
BET	ב	𐤁	2
GIMMEL	ג	𐤂	3
DALET	ד	𐤃	4
HE	ה	𐤄	5
VAV	ו	𐤅	6
ZAYIN	ז	𐤆	7
CHET	ח	𐤇	8
TET	ט	NONE	9
YOD	י	𐤉	10
KAPH	כך	𐤊	20
LAMED	ל	𐤋	30
MEM	מם	𐤌	40
NUN	נן	𐤍	50
SAMEKH	ס	NONE	60
AYIN	ע	𐤏	70
PE	פף	NONE	80
TSADIK	צ	𐤑	90
KOPH	ק	𐤒	100
RESH	ר	𐤓	200
SHIN	ש	𐤔	300
TAV	ת	𐤕	400

Appendix B. Metrological Chart for Jewish Bronze Coins

Name	Sample Size	Avg. Wt.	Range
Antiochus VII	162	2.47 +/- .03	1.62–3.41
Yehohanan	599	1.92 +/- .01	1.12–3.06
Yehonatan	520	1.81 +/- .02	0.96–3.57
Yonatan	432	2.00 +/- .02	0.85–3.27
Jannaeus H-467/78	344	2.15 +/- .02	1.04–3.50
Jannaeus H-469	523	1.71 +/- .03	0.64–3.85
Jannaeus H-471	200	1.20 +/- .02	0.61–1.79
Jannaeus 476	196	4.10 +/-.07	2.36–7.96
Jannaeus H-472	1251	0.81 +/-0.01	0.20–1.70
M. Antigonus H-481	171	14 +/- .09	11.67–17.64
M. Antigonus H-482	1066	7.19 +/- .07	4.47–8.79
M. Antigonus H483	144	1.68 +/- .02	1.18–2.34
Herod H-486	354	6.93 +/- .07	2.75–11.46
Herod H-487	130	4.45 +/-.07	2.91–6.52
Herod H-488	76	3.12 +/- .08	1.7–5.34
Herod H 489	73	2.50 +/- .05	1.55–3.62
Herod H-490	194	2.94 +/- .05	1.30–4.6
Herod H-491	153	1.48 +/- 0.3	0.78–2.6
Herod H-499	298	0.94 +/- .01	0.49–1.78
Herod H-500	480	1.42 +/- .01	0.81–2.11
Herod H-501	278	0.86 +/- .01	0.41–1.42
Archelaus H-508	76	1.16 +/- .03	0.59–1.99
Archelaus H-507	64	1.28 +/- .04	0.83–2.52
Archelaus H-506	391	1.19 +/- .01	0.44–2.1
Archelaus H-505	317	2.06 +/- .02	0.70–3.37
Procur pre Agr. I	759	1.90 +/- .01	0.83–2.85
Agrippa I H-553	428	2.33 +/- .02	1.13–3.40
Procur post Agr.I	476	2.27 +/- .02	1.15–3.66
Jewish War H-461/4	1257	2.51 +/- .02	0.93–4.24

Calculations according to standard formulas, using the Maths Calculator at http://www.easycalculation.com/statistics/standard-deviation.php.

The average standard deviation is calculated by dividing the standard deviation by the square root of the number of specimens in a particular sample.

APPENDIX C: INDEX OF LATIN LEGENDS

A VITELLIVS GERM IMP AVG P M TR P, 1462–63
A VITELLIVS GERMAN IMP TR P, 1461
A.PLAVTIVS AED CVR S C, 1443
ADVENTVI AVG IVDAEAE; S C, 1604, 1606
AED CVR, 1442
AVGVSTI VICTORIA S C, 1507c, d
BACCHIVS IVDAEVS, 1443
C HVPSAE COS PREIVE, 1441
C SOSIVS IMP, 1444
CAES AVG GERMANICVS, 1457
CAESAR AVG F DOMITIANVS COS DES II, 1570
CAESAR AVG F DOMITIANVS COS II, 1559a
CAPTA IVDAEA S C, 1500c
CAPTVM, 1441
DE IVDAEIS, 1472, 1476
DEVICTA IVDAEA S C, 1497
DIVO AVG T DIVI VESP F VESPASIAN S C, 1599
DIVOS T AVG, 1451
DIVOS VESPASIANVS, 1450
DIVVS AVGVSTVS VESPASIAN PATER PAT, 1595
DIVVS AVGVSTVS VESPASIANVS, 1580–81,1585, 1586
DIVVS VESPASIANVS AVGVSTVS, 1585a
DOMITIANVS CAES AVG GERMANICVS, 1455
EX S C, 1441, 1580–81, 1585, 1586a, 1587
FISCI IVDAICI CALVMNIA SVBLATA S C, 1603
HADRIANVS AVG COS III P P, 1604–06
IMP CAE[S] VESPASIAN AVG P M TR P P P COS III, 1500–08
IMP CAES AVG VESPAS COS II TR POT, 1494–95
IMP CAES DIVI VESP F DOMITIAN AVG GER COS X, 1318–
    19, 1323–24
IMP CAES DOMIT AVG GERM P M TR P XI, 1458
IMP CAES DOMIT AVG GERM P M TR P XIII, 1600
IMP CAES DOMIT AVG GERM TR P XII, 1459
IMP CAES TRAIAN AVG GER DAC P P REST, 1601–02
IMP CAES VES AVG, 1569a
IMP CAES VESP AVG COS IIII, 1490–91
IMP CAES VESP AVG P M COS IIII, 1466–67
IMP CAES VESP AVG P M T P P P COS IIII CENS, 1541
IMP CAES VESP AVG P M, 1481
IMP CAES VESPAS AVG P M TR P IIII P P COS IIII, 1476

IMP CAES VESPAS AVG P M TR P P P COS III, 1509–15
IMP CAES VESPAS AVG P M TR P P P COS IIII, 1516–21
IMP CAES VESPASIAN AVG COS III, 1552–55, 1557, 1568
IMP CAES VESPASIAN AVG COS VIII, 1561
IMP CAES VESPASIAN AVG P M TR P P P COS III, 1543
IMP CAES VESPASIAN AVG P M TR P P P COS IIII, 1544
IMP CAES VESPASIAN AVG P M TR P P P COS VIII, 1545–46
IMP CAES VESPASIAN AVG, 1564–67
IMP CAESAR VESPASIANVS AVG COS III, 1551
IMP CAESAR VESPASIANVS AVG COS VIIII, 1601
IMP CAESAR VESPASIANVS AVG P M T P P P COS III, 1497–99
IMP CAESAR VESPASIANVS AVG P M TR P, 1496, 1549, 1550
IMP CAESAR VESPASIANVS AVG TR P, 1472–75, 1487–88
IMP CAESAR VESPASIANVS AVG, 1464–65, 1470, 1479, 1480, 1485
IMP CAESAR, 1484
IMP DOMIT AVG GERM, 1460
IMP DOMITIAN CAES AVG GERMANICVS, 1454
IMP DOMITIANVS CAESAR DIVI F AVG, 1450–53
IMP DOMITIANVS CAESAR GERMANICVS, 1456
IMP DOMITIANVS, 1457
IMP NERVA CAES AVG P M TR P COS II DESIGN III P P, 1603a
IMP NERVA CAES AVG P M TR P COS II P P, 1603
IMP NERVA CAES AVG P M TR P COS III P P, 1603b
IMP NERVA CAES AVG P M TR P COS IIII P P, 1603c
IMP T CAES DIVI VESP F AVG P M TR P P P COS VIII, 1596–97
IMP T CAES VESP AVG P M TR P P P COS VIII S C, 1594
IMP T CAES VESP AVG P M TR P P P COS VIII, 1591–93
IMP T CAES VESPASIAN AVG P M TR P P P COS VIII, 1589–90
IMP T CAESAR DIVI VESPAS F AVG, 1598
IMP T CAESAR DIVI VESPASI AVG, 1598a
IMP T CAESAR VESPASIANVS AVG, 1577, 1582
IMP T CAESAR VESPASIANVS, 1478
IMP TITVS CAES VESPASIAN AVG P M, 1578–79, 1583–84, 1587–88, 1602
IMP VESP, 1484
IMP VESPASIAN AVG, 1564a, 1565a, 1568–72

IMP XXI COS XVI CENS P P P, 1458

IMP XXIII COS XVI CENS P P P, 1459

IMP•CAESAR•VESPASIANVS•AVG, 1477, 1489, 1563

IVD CAP S C, 1591–93, 1596, 1598

IVD CAPT S C, 1549

IVDAEA CAPTA S C, 1495, 1498, 1500–04, 1509–12, 1516–17,
 1523, 1527, 1534, 1538, 1543–48, 1551–52, 1554, 1560–62,
 1569, 1588–89, 1591d, 1595, 1596b, 1597

IVDAEA DEVICTA, 1474, 1478, 1488

IVDAEA S C, 1563

IVDAEA, 1461, 1464–65, 1473, 1477, 1479, 1480, 1487, 1489,
 1600, 1605

IVDEA CAPTA S C, 1500b, 1504a, 1554b, 1554d, 1556

M SCAVR AED CVR, 1441–42

MONETA ΕΠΙ ΒΑ ΑΓΡΙ AVGVST, 1318, 1323

P HVPSAEVS AED CVR, 1441

P M T P P P COS IIII, 1571a

P M TR P P P COS III S C, 1568–70

P M TR P P P COS IIII S C, 1571–72

PON M TR P P P COS III S C, 1564–67

PONTIF MAXIM, 1622

REX ARETAS, 1441

S C, 1494, 1513, 1518–20, 1524–25, 1528, 1530–31, 1533,
 1535–37, 1539, 1541–42, 1570, 1574, 1590, 1594b

SALVTI ΕΠΙ ΒΑ ΑΓΡΙ AVGVST, 1319, 1324

T CAES IMP AVG F PON TR P COS VI CENSOR, 1547–48

T CAES IMP AVG F TR P COS VI CENSOR, 1562

T CAES IMP VESP PON TR POT, 1468–69, 1482–83, 1492–
 93

T CAES VESP IMP PON TR POT COS II CENS, 1542, 1560

T CAES VESPAS IMP PON TR POT COS II, 1522

T CAES VESPASIAN IMP PON TR POT COS II, 1523–26,
 1529

T CAESAR IMP PONT, 1574a

T CAESAR IMP VESPASIANVS, 1471, 1486

T CAESAR IMPEP PONT, 1574

T CAESAR IMPER PONT, 1573

T CAESAR VESPASIAN IMP III PON TR POT II COS II, 1530–
 40

T CAESAR VESPASIAN IMP PON TR POT COS II, 1527–29

T CAESAR, 1484a

TI CAESAR DIVI AVG F AVGVSTVS TI CAESAR DIVI AVG F
 AVGVSTVS, 1622
TR P IX IMP XV COS VIII P P, 1579, 1584
TR P VIIII IMP XIIII COS VII P P, 1578a, 1583
TR P VIIII IMP XIIII COS VII, 1578
TR P VIIII IMP XV COS VII P P, 1578b, 1583b
TR POT COS VI CENSOR S C, 1573
TR POT VII COS VII, 1577, 1582, 1471, 1486
TR POT X COS VIII, 1470
TR POT X COS VIIII, 1485
TRIVMP AVG, 1475
VICTOR AVG, 1460
VICTOR AVGVSTI S C, 1463, 1567b
VICTORIA AVGVSTI S C, 1521, 1523, 1526
VICTORIA AVG S C, 1505–06, 1550, 1553, 1567–68
VICTORIA AVG, 1452
VICTORIA AVGVSTA, 1540a
VICTORIA AVGVSTI S C, 1462, 1496, 1499, 1507–08, 1514–
 15, 1529, 1532, 1540
ZA, 1444

ABBREVIATIONS

AE	bronze or any copper alloy
Ant.	*Antiquities of the Jews* by Flavius Josephus
AR	silver
AU	gold
BJ	*Bellicum Judaicum* (*The Jewish War* by Flavius Josephus)
BMC	*British Museum Catalog of Greek Coins* (Hill 1910, 1914)
BMCRE	*British Museum Catalog of Coins of the Roman Empire* (Mattingly 1965, 1966)
cm	centemeters
g	grams
G & T	Gitler and Tal 2006 (*The Coinage pf Philistia of theFifth and Fourth Centuries BC*)
GBC	*Guide to Biblical Coins* (Hendin 2001)
l.	left
M	Mildenberg 1984 (*The Coinage of the Bar Kokhba War*)
MCP	Menorah Coin Project (www.menorahcoinproject.org)
mm	millimeters
Obv.	obverse
Pb	lead
r.	right
Rev.	reverse
RIC	*Roman Imperial Coinage* (Burnett et. al. 1992, 1999)
RPC	*Roman Provincial Coinage* (Carradice & Buttrey 2007 & Mattingly & Sydenham 1968)
RRR	extremely rare
Sam.	*Samarian Coinage* (Meshorer & Qedar 1999)
SC	*Seleucid Coinage* (Houghton *et. al.* 2002, 2008)
Sofaer	*The Abraham Sofaer Collection at the American Numismatic Society* (Meshorer *et. al.* forthcoming).
TJC	*A Treasury of Jewish Coins* (Meshorer 2001)
v	variety (when occurring after a catalog number)

PLATE 1

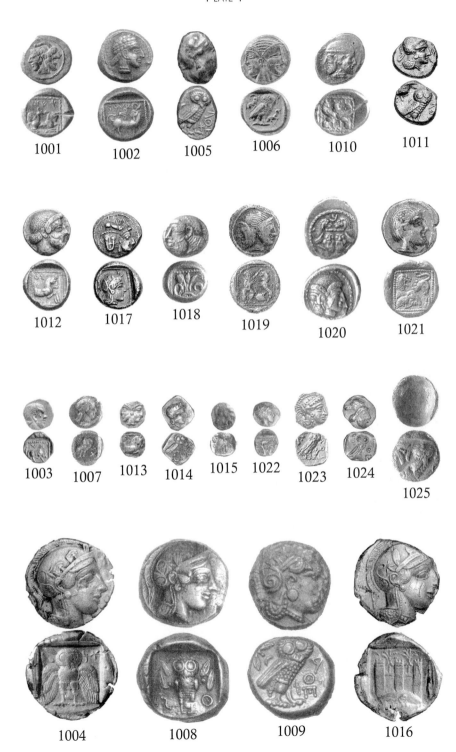

1001 1002 1005 1006 1010 1011

1012 1017 1018 1019 1020 1021

1003 1007 1013 1014 1015 1022 1023 1024 1025

1004 1008 1009 1016

PLATE 2

1001
2x

1002
2x

1005
2x

1006
2x

1010
2x

1011
2x

1012
2x

1017
2x

1018
2x

1019
2x

Plate 3

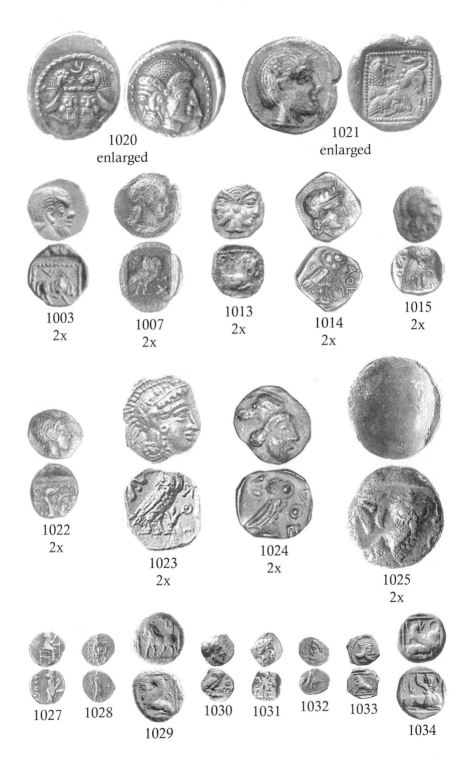

1020
enlarged

1021
enlarged

1003
2x

1007
2x

1013
2x

1014
2x

1015
2x

1022
2x

1023
2x

1024
2x

1025
2x

1027

1028

1029

1030

1031

1032

1033

1034

PLATE 4

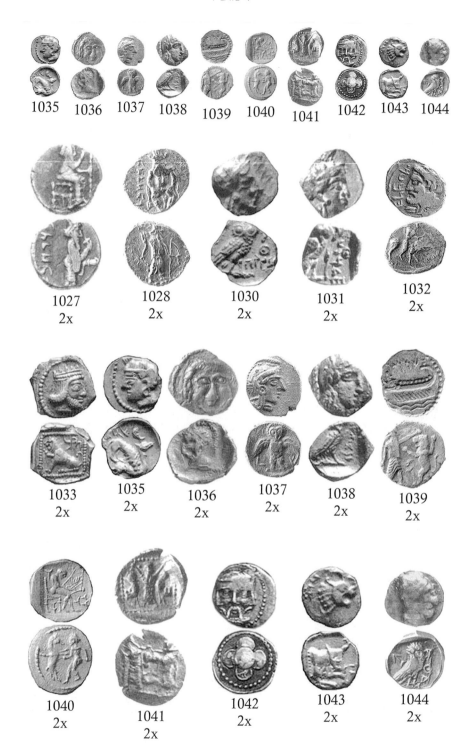

1035 1036 1037 1038 1039 1040 1041 1042 1043 1044

1027
2x

1028
2x

1030
2x

1031
2x

1032
2x

1033
2x

1035
2x

1036
2x

1037
2x

1038
2x

1039
2x

1040
2x

1041
2x

1042
2x

1043
2x

1044
2x

Plate 5

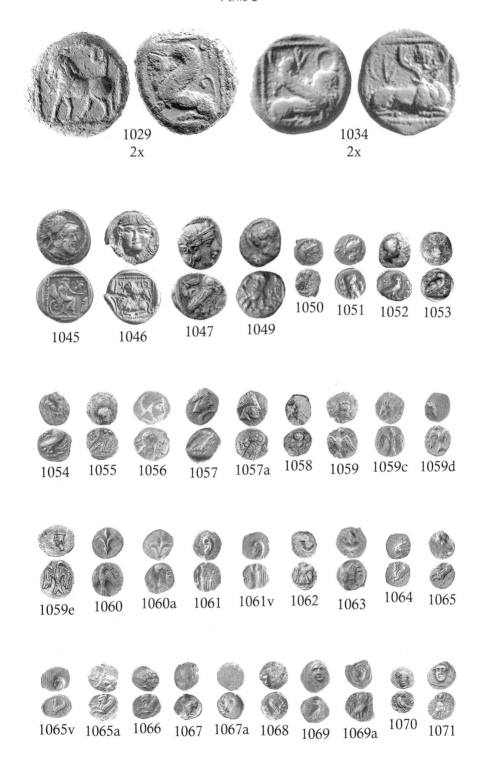

1029
2x

1034
2x

1045   1046   1047   1049   1050   1051   1052   1053

1054   1055   1056   1057   1057a   1058   1059   1059c   1059d

1059e   1060   1060a   1061   1061v   1062   1063   1064   1065

1065v   1065a   1066   1067   1067a   1068   1069   1069a   1070   1071

PLATE 6

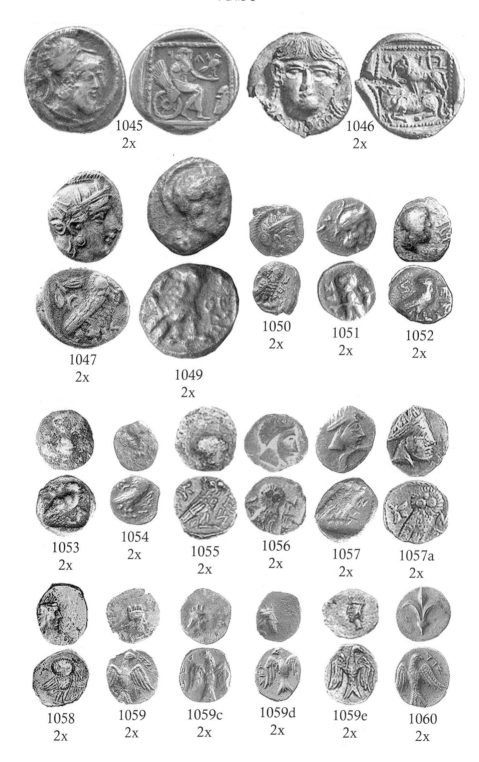

1045
2x

1046
2x

1047
2x

1049
2x

1050
2x

1051
2x

1052
2x

1053
2x

1054
2x

1055
2x

1056
2x

1057
2x

1057a
2x

1058
2x

1059
2x

1059c
2x

1059d
2x

1059e
2x

1060
2x

PLATE 7

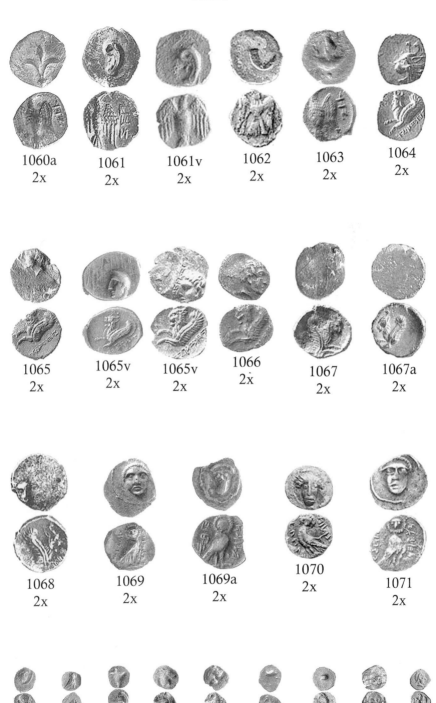

1060a
2x

1061
2x

1061v
2x

1062
2x

1063
2x

1064
2x

1065
2x

1065v
2x

1065v
2x

1066
2x

1067
2x

1067a
2x

1068
2x

1069
2x

1069a
2x

1070
2x

1071
2x

1072

1073

1074

1075

1075a

1075b

1075c

1076

1077

PLATE 8

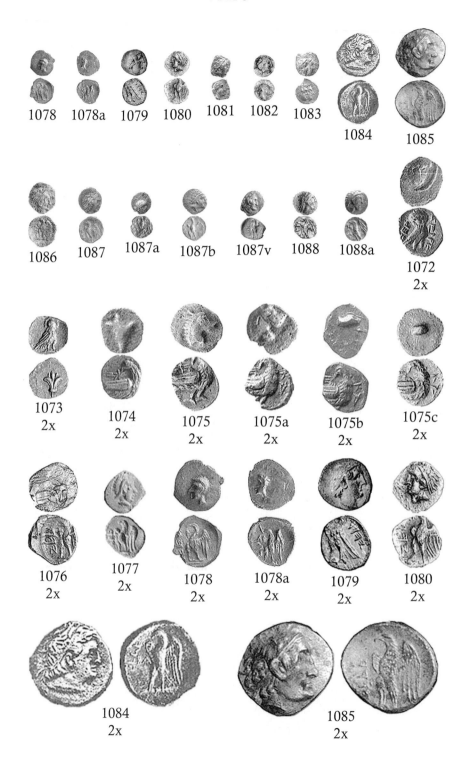

1078   1078a   1079   1080   1081   1082   1083

1084   1085

1086   1087   1087a   1087b   1087v   1088   1088a

1072
2x

1073
2x

1074
2x

1075
2x

1075a
2x

1075b
2x

1075c
2x

1076
2x

1077
2x

1078
2x

1078a
2x

1079
2x

1080
2x

1084
2x

1085
2x

PLATE 9

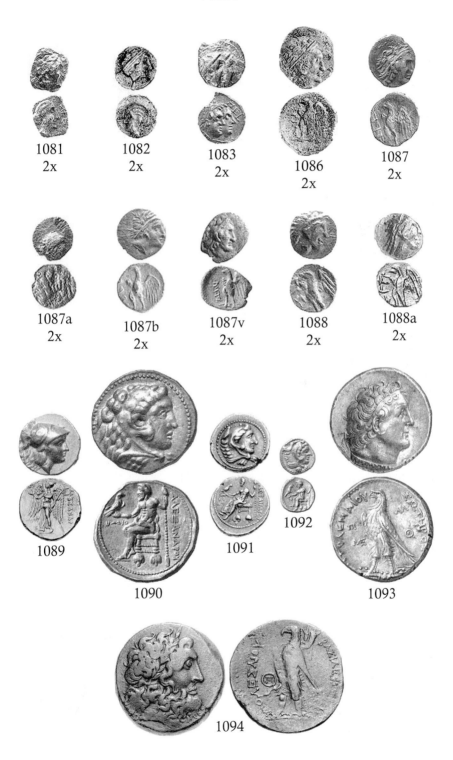

1081
2x

1082
2x

1083
2x

1086
2x

1087
2x

1087a
2x

1087b
2x

1087v
2x

1088
2x

1088a
2x

1089

1090

1091

1092

1093

1094

PLATE 10

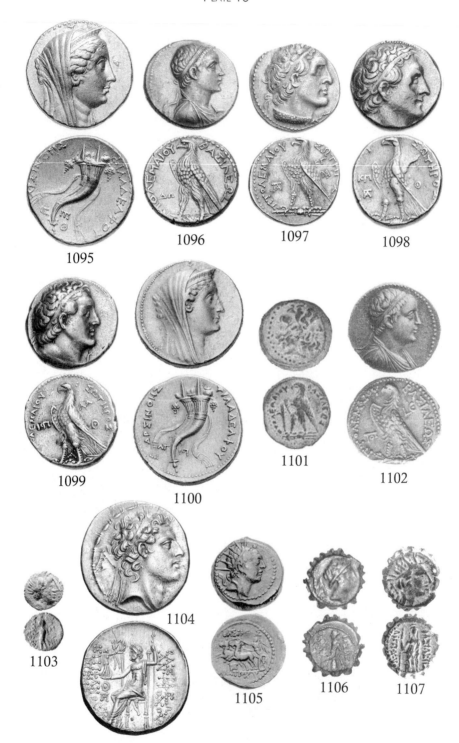

1095

1096

1097

1098

1099

1100

1101

1102

1103

1104

1105

1106

1107

PLATE 11

1108

1109

1110

1111

1112

1113

1114

1115

1116

1117

1118

1119

1120

PLATE 12

1121

1122

1123

1124

1125

1126

1127

1128

1129

1130

1130
2x

1131

1131a

1131b

1131c

1132

PLATE 13

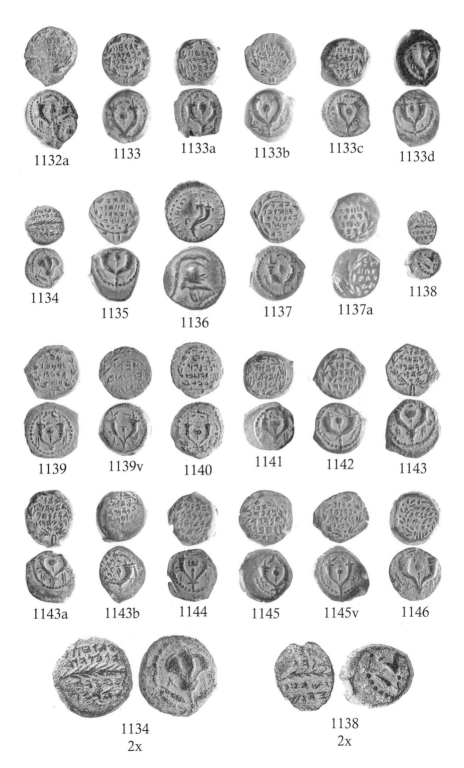

1132a   1133   1133a   1133b   1133c   1133d

1134   1135   1136   1137   1137a   1138

1139   1139v   1140   1141   1142   1143

1143a   1143b   1144   1145   1145v   1146

1134
2x

1138
2x

PLATE 14

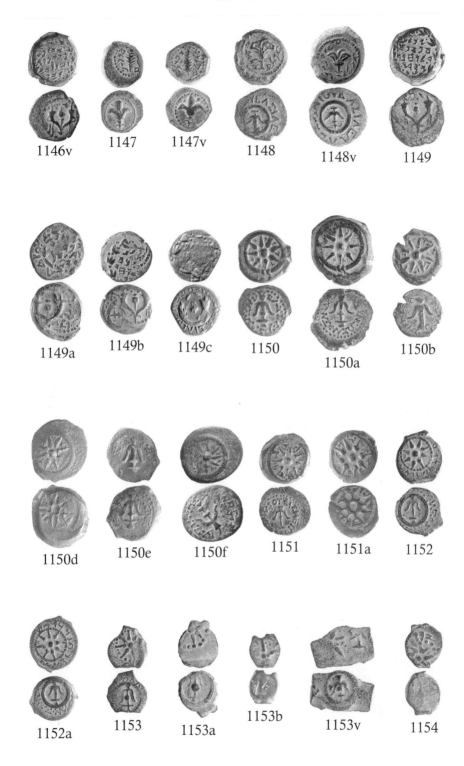

1146v   1147   1147v   1148   1148v   1149

1149a   1149b   1149c   1150   1150a   1150b

1150d   1150e   1150f   1151   1151a   1152

1152a   1153   1153a   1153b   1153v   1154

PLATE 15

1155 1155a 1155b 1156 1157 1158 1159

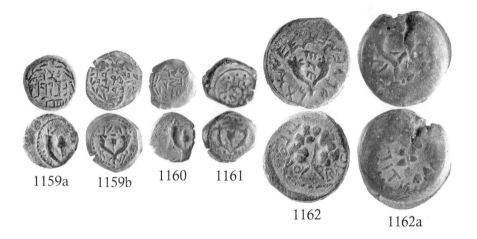

1159a 1159b 1160 1161 1162 1162a

1162b 1163 1163a 1163b 1163c

PLATE 16

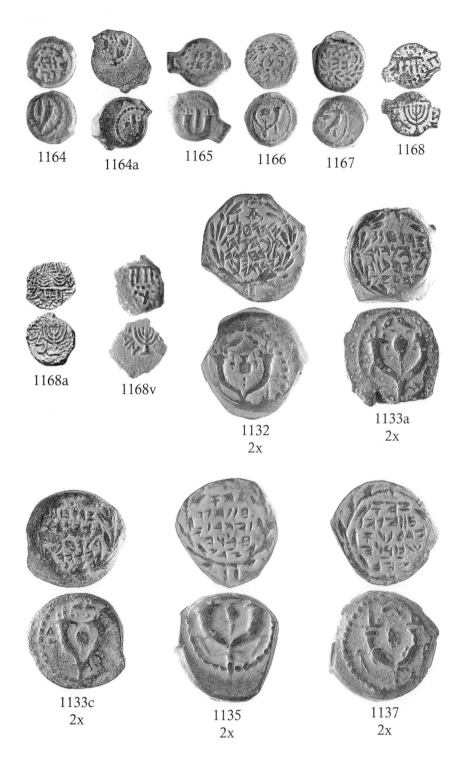

1164

1164a

1165

1166

1167

1168

1168a

1168v

1132
2x

1133a
2x

1133c
2x

1135
2x

1137
2x

PLATE 17

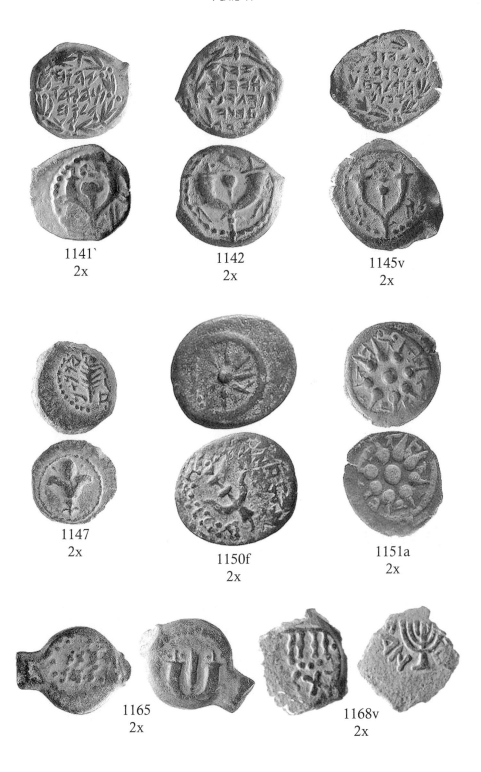

1141`
2x

1142
2x

1145v
2x

1147
2x

1150f
2x

1151a
2x

1165
2x

1168v
2x

PLATE 18

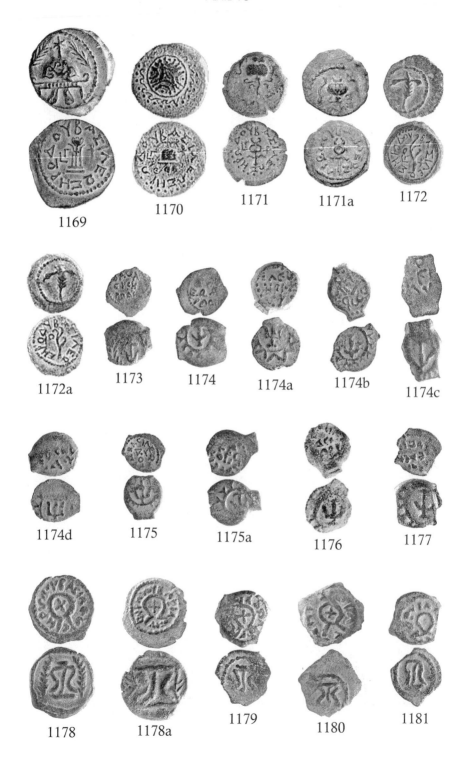

1169

1170

1171

1171a

1172

1172a

1173

1174

1174a

1174b

1174c

1174d

1175

1175a

1176

1177

1178

1178a

1179

1180

1181

PLATE 19

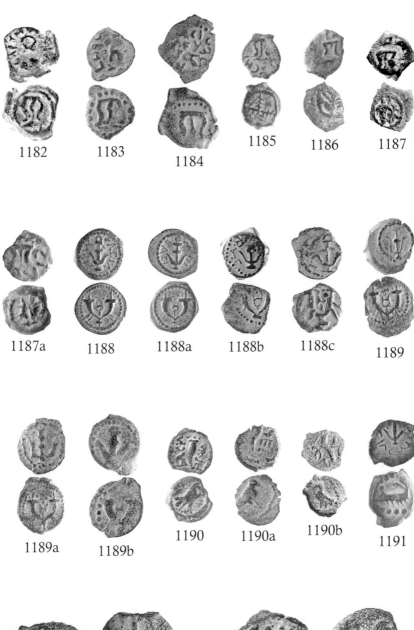

1182   1183   1185   1186   1187

1184

1187a   1188   1188a   1188b   1188c

1189

1189a   1189b   1190   1190a   1190b

1191

1175
2x

1190
2x

PLATE 20

1192   1193   1194   1194a   1195   1195a

1196   1196a   1196b   1196c   1197   1197a

1198   1199   1200   1201   1202

PLATE 21

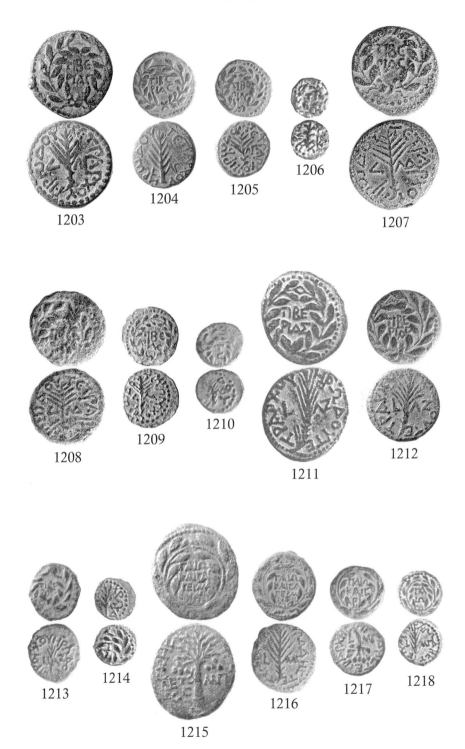

1203

1204

1205

1206

1207

1208

1209

1210

1211

1212

1213

1214

1215

1216

1217

1218

PLATE 22

1219

1220

1221

1221a

1222

1223b

1224

1225

1226

1227

1229

1229a

1231

1233

1232

1235

PLATE 23

1236 1237 1238 1239 1240

1241 1242 1243 1244 1244a 1244b

1245 1246 1247 1248

Plate 24

1249a

1251

1252

1253

1254

1255

1257

1257a

1258

1259

1260

1261

1262

PLATE 25

1263   1264   1265a   1266

1267   1268   1269   1270   1271

1272   1273   1274   1275

PLATE 26

1276

1277

1278

1279

1280

1281

1282

1282a

1283

1284

1284a

1285c

PLATE 27

1286

1287

1287a

1288

1289

1290

1290a

1291

1292

1293

PLATE 28

1294   1295   1298

1297

1299   1299a   1301

1300

1301a   1302   1303   1303a

PLATE 29

1304

1304a

1305

1306

1306a

1307

1308

1309

1310

1311

1312

1313

1314

PLATE 30

1315

1316

1317

1319

1320

1322

1323

1325

1326

1328

1328a

1329

1330

1331

1311a

PLATE 31

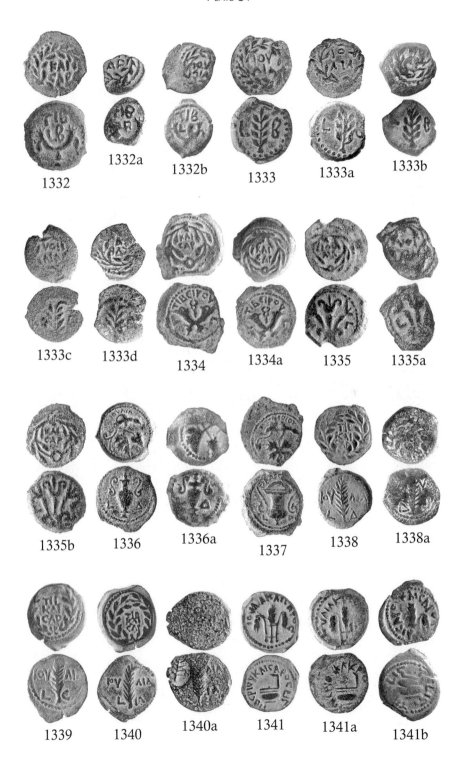

1332

1332a

1332b

1333

1333a

1333b

1333c

1333d

1334

1334a

1335

1335a

1335b

1336

1336a

1337

1338

1338a

1339

1340

1340a

1341

1341a

1341b

PLATE 32

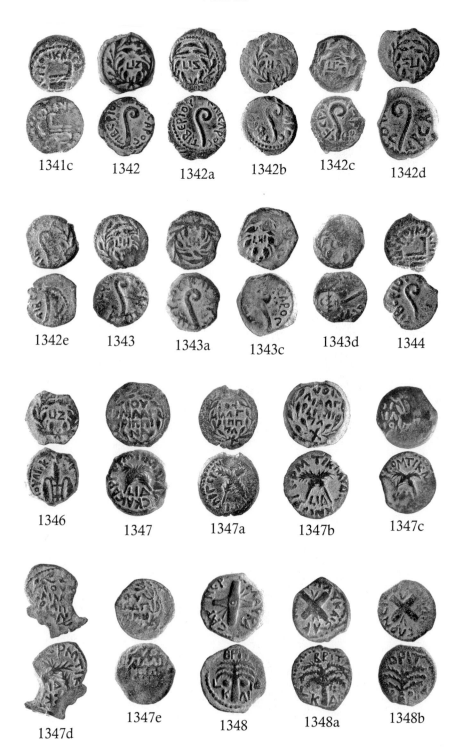

1341c 1342 1342a 1342b 1342c 1342d

1342e 1343 1343a 1343c 1343d 1344

1346 1347 1347a 1347b 1347c

1347d 1347e 1348 1348a 1348b

PLATE 33

1348c 1348d 1349 1351 1351a

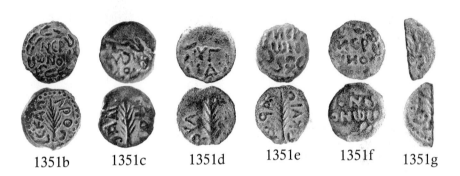

1351b 1351c 1351d 1351e 1351f 1351g

1352 1353 1354 1355

PLATE 34

1355a

1356

1357

1357a

1358

1359

1360

1360a

1360b

1360c

1360d

1361

1362

1363

1363a

PLATE 35

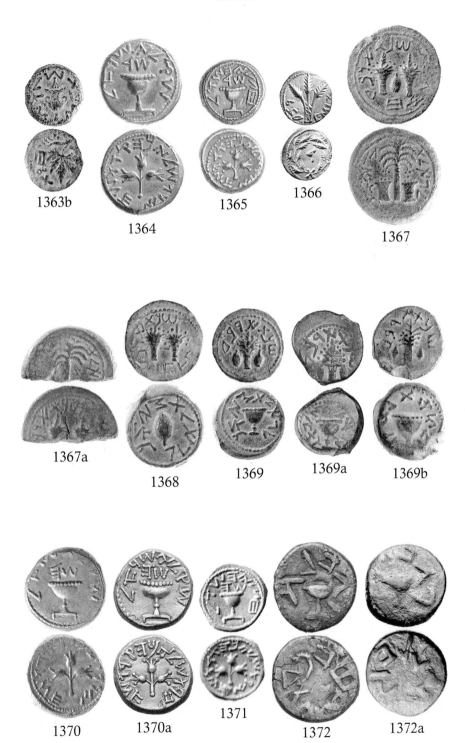

1363b

1364

1365

1366

1367

1367a

1368

1369

1369a

1369b

1370

1370a

1371

1372

1372a

PLATE 36

1373

1373a

1374

1375

1376

1377

1377a

1378

1378a

1378b

1379

1379a

PLATE 37

1380   1380a   1380c   1381a   1382

1383   1384   1385   1386

1387   1387a   1388   1389

PLATE 38

1390

1391

1392

1393

1394

1396

1397

1399

1400

1401

1403

1404

1405

1406

PLATE 39

1407

1408

1408a

1409

1410

1411

1411a

1412

1413

1413a

1414

1415

PLATE 40

1416   1417   1418   1419   1422

1423   1424   1425   1426   1427

1428   1429   1430   1430a   1431

1432   1432a   1433   1434   1435

PLATE 41

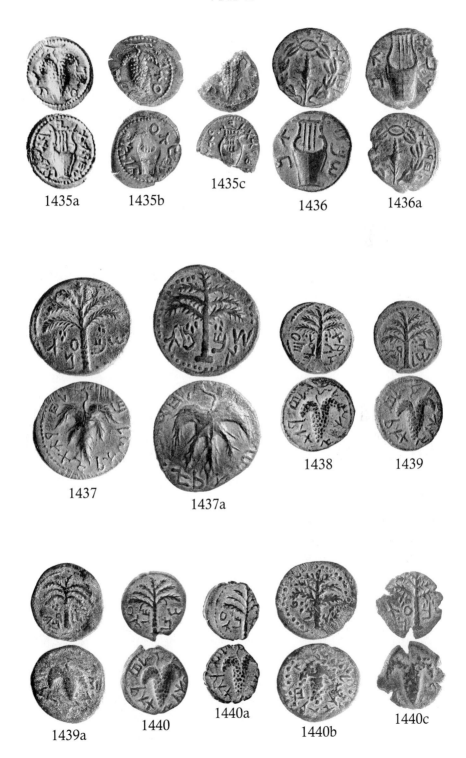

1435a   1435b   1435c   1436   1436a

1437   1437a   1438   1439

1439a   1440   1440a   1440b   1440c

PLATE 42

1441   1442   1443   1444   1445

1446   1446a   1447   1449

1449a   1451   1452   1453   1457

PLATE 43

1454

1455

1456

1458

1458a

1459

1459a

1460

1461

1462

1462a

PLATE 44

1463

1464

1465

1466

1467

1468

1472a

1475

1476

1477

1478a

1479

1480

1482

1483

PLATE 45

1484a 1485a 1486 1487

1488 1490 1491 1492 1493

1497 1500 1500c

PLATE 46

1501

1502

1504

1506

1507b

1507d

1508a

PLATE 47

1508d

1509a

1517

1522

1525

1527

1531a

PLATE 48

1532

1533

1535

1537

1540

1541

1542

PLATE 49

1543a

1547

1552

1553

1554b

1554d

1555

Plate 50

1560

1561

1562

1564

1566

1567

1571

1573

1574

1574a

1575

PLATE 51

1576a

1577 1578b 1579a 1580

1582 1583 1583a 1583c 1584

1584a 1586

1590

PLATE 52

1591a
1592
1593a

1594
1594a
1596

PLATE 53

1596a

1596b

1597

1598

1602

1603

1603c

PLATE 54

1604

1604a

1604c

1605

1606

1607

1607a

1608

1609

PLATE 55

1609a 1610 1611 1612 1613

1613a 1614 1614a 1614b

1615 1616 1616a 1617

PLATE 56

1618   1618a   1619   1619a

1620   1620a   1620b

1621   1621a   1621b   1622

ABOUT THE AUTHOR

David Hendin is a leading authority on Biblical and ancient Judaean coins and artifacts. His original research has been published frequently in scholarly journals and he is the author of hundreds of original articles on these topics for *The Celator* and other magazines.

Hendin has pursued his four-decade interest in coins and archaeology of the Middle East alongside his successful careers as an award-winning medical journalist, publishing executive, and literary agent for clients who have included cartoonists Charles M. Schulz (creator of Peanuts®) and Lincoln Peirce (creator of Big Nate®) as well as authors such as Judith Martin (Miss Manners®), mystery writer Elaine Viets, and Alan M. Dershowitz.

He is the author of five editions of *Guide to Biblical Coins* as well as *Collecting Coins, Ancient Scale Weights,* and *Not Kosher (Forgeries of Ancient Jewish and Biblical Coins).* He is also the author of the national bestseller *Death as a Fact of Life* and eight other nonfiction books which have been translated into six languages.

His work has earned more than a dozen literary awards, ranging from the Numismatic Literary Guild's "Best Magazine Column" to the Medical Journalism Award of the American Medical Association.

Hendin has lectured on Judaean and Biblical coins in Italy, England, and Israel as well as at seminars of the American Numismatic Society, the American Numismatic Association, and many colleges and other organizations. In 1985 and 1986 he was chief numismatist of the Joint Sepphoris Project under the auspices of Duke University and Hebrew University. As chairman of the numismatic committee of the Jewish Museum in New York, Hendin prepared and acquired coins for the exhibit *Coins Reveal,* with Ya'akov Meshorer. He edited and published *A Treasury of Jewish Coins* and *Ancient Jewish Coinage* I & II by Ya'akov Meshorer.

Hendin is a life fellow of the American Numismatic Society and has been listed in *Who's Who in America* since 1974.

OTHER BOOKS FOR YOUR REFERENCE LIBRARY

ANCIENT SCALE WEIGHTS and Pre-Coinage Currency of the Near East
By David Hendin

More than 450 ancient weights and pieces of pre-coinage currency, 6 x 9 inch, 240-page hardcover with all objects illustrated.
$65.00 plus shipping.

NOT KOSHER: Forgeries of Ancient Jewish and Biblical Coins
By David Hendin

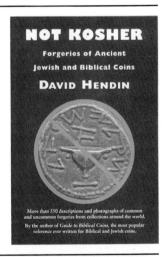

More than 550 long-neglected forgeries of this series of coins are photographed and discussed, along with diagnostic methods for detecting coins that are "Not Kosher." 6 x 9 inch, 224-page hardcover with all coins photographed.
$50.00 plus shipping.

A Treasury of Jewish Coins
By Ya'akov Meshorer.

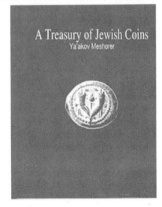

Winner of Israel's Ben Zvi Award. 8 1/2 x 11 inch, 356-page hardcover, 80 pages of photographic plates, drawings and illustrations.
$95.00 plus shipping

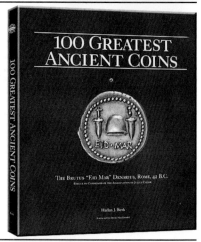